Ways to Writing

LINDA C. STANLEY
DAVID SHIMKIN
ALLEN H. LANNER

Queensborough Community College
City University of New York

Ways to Writing

Purpose, Task, and Process

SECOND EDITION

MACMILLAN PUBLISHING COMPANY

NEW YORK

Macmillan Publishing Company
866 Third Avenue, New York, New York 10022

Library of Congress Cataloging-in-Publication Data
Stanley, Linda
  Ways to writing.
  Includes index.
  1. English language—Rhetoric. 2. Exposition
(Rhetoric) I. Shimkin, David. II. Lanner, Allen H.
III. Title.
PE1408.S684   1987   808'.042   87-11105
ISBN 0-02-415540-3

Printing: 1 2 3 4 5 6 7   Year: 8 9 0 1 2 3 4

ACKNOWLEDGMENTS

*The authors would like to thank the following authors and publishers for their
permission to reprint various selections in this book (listed in approximate order
of quotation):*
Journal entries by Margaret Ryan, from *Ariadne's Thread: A Collection of Contemporary Women's Journals,* edited by Lyn Lifshin. Copyright © 1982 by
  Lyn Lifshin. Reprinted by permission of Harper & Row, Publishers, Inc.
Journal entries by Susan Kinnicutt, from *Ariadne's Thread: A Collection of Contemporary Women's Journals,* edited by Lyn Lifshin. Copyright © 1982 by
  Lyn Lifshin. Reprinted by permission of Harper & Row, Publishers, Inc.
Journal entries from The Introduction to *Letters Home: Correspondence 1950–
  1963* by Sylvia Plath, selected and edited with commentary by Aurelia
  Schober Plath. Copyright © 1975 by Aurelia Schober Plath. Reprinted by
  permission of Harper & Row, Publishers, Inc.
''50,000 on Beach Strangely Calm as Rocket Streaks Out of Sight'' by Gay
  Talese. *The New York Times,* 1 Feb. 1962. Copyright © 1962, 1979, 1983
  by The New York Times Company. Reprinted by permission.

ISBN 0-02-415540-3

From "The Angry Winter" by Loren Eiseley, in *The Unexpected Universe*. Copyright © 1969 by Loren Eiseley. Reprinted by permission of Harcourt Brace Jovanovich, Inc.

From *I Know Why the Caged Bird Sings*, by Maya Angelou. Copyright © 1969 by Maya Angelou. Reprinted by permission of Random House, Inc.

"My Lack of Gumption" from *Growing Up* by Russell Baker. Copyright © 1982 by Contemporary Books, Inc. Reprinted by permission of the publisher.

"Still the Same" by Patrick Fenton. Reprinted by permission of the author.

From "Encouraging Honest Inquiry in Student Writing" by David V. Harrington, in *College Composition and Communication*, Vol. XXX, No. 2 (May 1979). Reprinted by permission of the National Council of Teachers of English.

From *To Jerusalem and Back* by Saul Bellow. Copyright © 1976 by Saul Bellow. Reprinted by permission of Viking Penguin, Inc.

"The Iowa State Fair" by Paul Engle. Reprinted by permission of the author.

From *Hunger of Memory: The Education of Richard Rodriguez* by Richard Rodriguez. Copyright © 1982 by Richard Rodriguez. Reprinted by permission of David R. Godine, Publisher, Inc.

From *The Death and Life of Great American Cities* by Jane Jacobs. Copyright © 1961 by Jane Jacobs. Reprinted by permission of Random House, Inc.

From *Calcutta* by Geoffrey Moorhouse. Published by Weidenfeld & Nicolson Ltd., 1971. Reprinted by permission of A.P. Watt Ltd., literary agent.

"What Effect Is TV Having on the Evolution of English?" by Edwin Newman. *The New York Times*, 14 Sept. 1986. Copyright © 1986 by The New York Times Company. Reprinted by permission.

"Supermarket Erotica" by Carol Thurston and Barbara Doscher, from the April 1982 issue of *The Progressive*. Copyright © 1982 by The Progressive, Inc. Reprinted by permission of the publisher.

"The Fizz Bizz: Tiny Bubbles" by Bernice Kanner, from *New York* Magazine, 16 Jan. 1984. Copyright © 1986 by News America Publishing, Inc. Reprinted by permission of *New York* Magazine.

Reprinted from *Ever Since Darwin: Reflections in Natural History,* by Stephen Jay Gould, by permission of W. W. Norton & Company, Inc. Copyright © 1973, 1974, 1975, 1976, 1977 by The American Museum of Natural History.

From *The Dragons of Eden: Speculations on the Evolution of Human Intelligence,* by Carl Sagan (New York: Random House, 1977). Copyright © by Carl Sagan. Reprinted by permission of the author.

From *The American Political Tradition and the Men Who Made It* by Richard Hofstadter. Copyright © 1948, © 1973 by Alfred A. Knopf, Inc. Reprinted by permission of the publisher.

Specified excerpt from *The Magic Years* by Selma H. Fraiberg. Copyright © 1959 by Selma H. Fraiberg. Reprinted by permission of Charles Scribner's Sons.

"It's Failure, Not Success" from *Close to Home* by Ellen Goodman. Copyright © 1979 by The Washington Post Company. Reprinted by permission of Simon & Schuster, Inc.

From *The Lives of a Cell* by Lewis Thomas. Copyright © 1971 by the Massachusetts Medical Society. Originally published in the *New England Journal of Medicine*. Reprinted by permission of Viking Penguin, Inc.

Preface

It has been gratifying to see the success of the first edition of *Ways to Writing*. The text has been received and used with an enthusiasm that confirms our original premise in writing it: Students may best understand the writing process when it is presented through a series of integrated activities that take them through each stage of the process. In this second edition, the premise and hence the essential character and structure of *Ways to Writing* have not changed. The book continues to offer a coherent, unified sequence of specific writing assignments intended to show students how their decisions as to purpose, invention, audience, arrangement, revision, and style are crucial to the effectiveness of their writing. The changes that we have made, in response to extensive feedback from students and reviewers, are intended to improve upon and refine both individual assignments and the sequence as a whole. We believe that in making them we have strengthened the book dramatically. The most important of them are as follows:

1. Chapter 1 has been thoroughly revised to give more emphasis to the journal as a semester-long project. Different ways of starting, keeping, and thinking about a journal have been given prominence, and a wealth of student and professional examples has been added.
2. Chapter 6 has also been thoroughly revised to clarify for students the act of explanation and its role in their movement from the more personal, expressive and exploratory writing of the earlier chapters to the more public, expository writing of the later ones. Discussions of exemplification, generalization, and public voice lead to an assignment in which students are asked to draw conclusions about the significance of a theme they have traced in one or another aspect of the media.
3. Chapter 9 on writing about literature has been replaced with an entirely new chapter on critical thinking. Students are invited to use critical thinking skills in order to synthesize disparate arguments made in professional

essays on a controversial issue and then develop their own theory about
the issue.

4. New professional models have been added to every chapter of the text,
   so that now at least two appear in each chapter. In some chapters, both
   professional essays are new, as are many of the student essays.

5. The easy-reference Handbook of common grammatical and mechanical
   problems, included at the end of the book, has been expanded with more
   examples and new summary exercises.

We have made other changes to clarify concepts or facilitate the use of different parts of the book. Those familiar with the first edition will, we hope,
find that the major change is simply that *Ways to Writing* is now more effective
in initiating students to the process of writing college-level essays. For those
who are using the text for the first time, a few more comments about its rationale and organization may be helpful.

In their effort to write more effectively, our students have taught us the
urgency of starting with what the writer already knows. They remind us that
even very good writers do not use personal experience or expressiveness merely
as a springboard to writing about something outside themselves, namely the
world of ideas or abstractions, but that their work is in the fullest sense "expressive" of their own voice and vision. Thus, in Chapters 1–3 we emphasize
the value of the journal, of free writing, of a first-person perspective on things,
ideas, and institutions. Because we want our students to become more conscious of themselves as writers writing, we guide them first to what they can
express or explain with the power that comes from having experienced the
subject directly.

With increased ability to write about their perceptions, students can do better with the complex demands of expository writing. In Chapters 4–6 we ask
them to examine and explore their environment and values by gathering, analyzing, and interpreting information. In Chapters 7–9 we introduce them to
library research, methods of argumentation, and critical thinking.

The central focus of our book is the task that sets each writing assignment
in motion. We lead the student writer through a series of prewriting activities
that culminate in the preparation of an essay. To this end, we have placed the
task for each chapter after the prewriting sections, which suggest ways of generating ideas for completing a task as well as of analyzing audience considerations. The sections following the presentation of the task guide the writer through
the various stages of writing the essay. They encourage students to apply what
they have learned in the prewriting sections to the task at hand, and they
suggest patterns of arrangement, present professional essays based on a similar
task, and offer the rough draft of a student essay in fulfillment of the task.

Concluding each chapter is a "Focus" section stressing matters of style and structure; a "Rewriting" section suggesting different approaches to revising, along with a revised version of the student essay in the chapter; and "Becoming Aware of Yourself as a Writer," a series of questions on the chapter's writing process that encourage students to become more conscious of what they do when they write.

We have found many advantages for the student in this task-centered approach. First, the student benefits from a "hands-on" approach that provides concrete, specific assistance for an actual writing assignment. Second, the task itself enables the student to draw from a broad range of experiences and, through a sequence of self-designed strategies, to arrive at a conclusion that follows naturally from the student's own cognitive processes. Third, and probably most important for the student writer, each task builds on the skill and awareness acquired in completing the previous tasks. Beginning with expressive writing, the writer is encouraged to move beyond narrative writing to tasks requiring more complex analytic and critical thought. In fact, it was our desire to help students to make this transition that drew us to this cumulative, task-centered method.

We believe our task-centered approach will also be of practical advantage to the instructor, who can relate the writing strategies to the actual assignment at hand. The many rhetorical exercises and examples of readings should also help the instructor focus on the problems that often arise in discussions of "good" and "bad" writing. The task format yields even greater benefits, we believe, in assignments that require the student to absorb, evaluate, and synthesize reading material—assignments such as the research paper or the essay exam. Here the student is guided through the difficult stages of writing such essays, from formulating the shaping idea to revising the rough draft.

The authors feel that both student and teacher will benefit from the unity of design and purpose that we have created in each chapter. Of course, no approach to teaching writing can or should presume to be prescriptive or definitive in its methods, and we encourage the users of this text to choose what they think useful and to modify what they think does not respond expressly to the needs of their own students. The "Generating Ideas" and "Audience" sections are not bound to the process of writing on a particular task and can be used in other chapters or in class activities devised by the instructor. An instructor can quite easily restructure some of the tasks to suit a particular expressive or expository demand. Although the chapters cover most of the customary writing assignments undertaken in college writing classes, an instructor need not use every chapter, for each individual chapter provides the student with parallel purposive activities. One of our intentions has been to encourage instructors to modify or augment our tasks and activities with their own.

Ways to Writing offers instructor and student concrete direction through the process of writing but without the reductive "by-the-numbers" approach of many basic writing texts or the exhaustive minutiae of the all-encompassing rhetoric. By engaging student writers in activities that are both interesting and immediately useful, we hope to give them ways to gauge their own progress in expressing themselves effectively and to direct their vision beyond the classroom to the world that they have already experienced and observed.

We have also prepared an instructor's manual that introduces the pedagogy of the text, offers suggestions for approaching the tasks, includes a twelve-week and fifteen-week syllabus, and lists sources for the instructor who seeks more information on both traditional and current approaches to the teaching of writing.

The authors wish to express their admiration for, and indebtedness to, James Moffett's *A Student-Centered Language Arts Curriculum: K–13*. We have drawn from Moffett's work the central role of the task in the formulation of a writing consciousness, as well as his important contribution to the study of how and why students write, and of the interplay between "concrete" and "abstract" as the basis for the development of sound thinking and writing. We are also most obviously indebted to James Kinneavy for his analysis of the different underlying purposes in writing; expressive, referential, and persuasive.

The authors wish to thank the many students who over the seven-year gestation period of this book have good humoredly submitted themselves to the trials and errors that we have put them through while developing both approach and materials in their classrooms. We wish to thank particularly the students whose work—both in rough and more polished stages—we have used as models for each task: Carolyn Bunkley, Italo Ferrari, Liliana Gonzalez, Janice Gordon, Kathy Greene, Lisa Halpin, Hennessy Levine, Virginia McLaughlin, Marc Pressman, Patricia Sadhoff, Anastasia Schneider, and Alyce Zimerman.

We are indebted to those reviewers who gave us valuable suggestions and comments throughout the process of writing this text: Robert Becker, Queensborough Community College; Robert M. Esch, University of Texas at El Paso; Gwendolyn Gong, Texas A & M University; Elaine Good, Queensborough Community College; Barbara Griffin, Catonsville Community College; Juliet Kincaid, Johnson Community College; Elaine Levy, Queensborough Community College; Lewis Myers, Hunter College; Arlyne Samuels, Queensborough Community College; John C. Schafer, Humboldt State University; Tyrone Teekah, Queensborough Community College; and Barbara Witenko, Queensborough Community College.

At Macmillan we thank Eben Ludlow, Executive Editor for the College Division, for his intelligent guidance and patience; Wendy Polhemus-Annibell, our production editor, for seeing the manuscript through production; Kathleen Keller, marketing manager, for her thorough approach to marketing; and Holly Reid McLaughlin and Alma Orenstein, book designers.

L. C. S.
D. S.
A. H. L.

To The Student

By now you must have arrived at some definite view of yourself as a writer. After many years of writing in one school or another, you probably have concluded that you are either a "good" or a "bad" writer. Those words are written with quotation marks around them for a specific reason: They really have no meaning. Or at least no meaning that can be of any usefulness in evaluating yourself as a writer. The words *good* and *bad* imply some kind of absolute standard of judgment—perhaps the grade you received on a high-school essay exam or a report on gerbils you prepared in the third grade. But they just won't do for an evaluation of writing once you become aware of all the complexities involved in any act of written expression. This textbook attempts to take those complexities and arrange them into a coherent pattern so that they can be studied and perhaps even mastered.

But writing, as you know, is not plane geometry or biology or accounting. When you write, you don't necessarily begin at the beginning. You write because you have something to communicate, and often only after you have already begun to write do your thought processes go to work to determine the form that your writing will take. Our textbook is based on the assumption that you will write more effectively if you clarify your purpose in writing and if you are aware of how the ways you develop ideas, as well as what your audience expects, can give direction and weight to your writing. We have arranged the text in a way that we feel will increase your skill in these elements of communication.

The central focus of each chapter in *Ways to Writing* is a specific writing task. In the earlier chapters, the tasks are more personal: You may be asked to evaluate something you have learned about yourself by keeping a journal, or something you have learned about your attitude toward a place by visiting and studying that place. In the latter chapters of the book, the tasks become more analytic, and you will be asked, for example, to explain why an idea that you hold is sensible or to argue why a position that you take is valid. In completing each task, you will be invited to employ a different way of developing ideas, and you will be asked to write for a different kind of audience. To guide you through these tasks, we have arranged our text so that the completion of a writing assignment is supported on one side by general prewriting activities and on the other by prewriting, writing, and rewriting activities directed specifically to the completion of the task at hand.

Beginning each chapter is a ''Purpose'' section that provides a brief explanation of the writing aim for that chapter. Following this is a section called ''Generating Ideas'' that offers ways for you to get started writing. Some ways are traditional; others are relatively new. Some require no deliberation; others demand logical concentration. You will find that you can apply these procedures in writing to the tasks in other chapters. They form a kind of cumulative reserve to draw on when you need to develop ideas for an essay.

Another important consideration before you begin writing is, naturally enough, your audience. You don't usually write in a vacuum: you write to and for others. Thus you need to know who your readers are, how to interest them, what kind of stance you need to take toward them. Clarity is important, but more than that is required to move an audience, to make it see what you want it to see. Through discussion and exercises, we hope to make you more conscious of the crucial role that an audience plays in determining the shape of your writing.

After announcing the task in each chapter, we guide you through the writing of an essay, showing you how to use the prewriting techniques, stressing the importance of a shaping idea, suggesting ways to arrange your discussion, directing you to the structural and stylistic characteristics of effective writing. As you will notice in your own writing, revision is an indispensable follow-up to any writing effort. By studying the rough drafts of other students, as well as peer evaluations of their work, you will become more aware of the contribution that these activities can make to your own writing.

Finally, we ask you some questions to encourage you to think about your own writing process, to become aware of the tentative, provisional nature of all writing as the unfolding of a mind. Clearly, this is not the same thing as counting the errors in each of your papers and then trying to find the mathematical formula for determining a grade. If we succeed in conveying to you some of the satisfaction you can derive from expressing yourself effectively to others through the act of writing, we will have accomplished our purpose in preparing this text.

Contents

2   Writing About an Incident   49

3 Writing About a Stage in Your Life

PART **II**

Exploration

4 Writing About a Place   133

5 Writing a Case   172

PART **III**

Explanation

6 Writing About the Media   215

7   Writing About Research   258

PART IV

Persuasion

8 Writing Persuasively   313

9   Writing About an Issue   364

Handbook

Grammar   425

Punctuation   458

Mechanics   475

Rhetorical Contents

PURPOSE

Expressive—Chapters 1–3
   From Journal to Essay—Chapter 1
   Narration—Chapter 2
   Narration and Exposition—Chapter 3
Expository—Chapters 4–7
   Exploration—Chapters 4–5
   Explanation—Chapters 6–7
Persuasive—Chapters 8–9

GENERATING IDEAS

The Journal—Chapter 1
The Journalist's Questions—Chapter 2
Free Writing—Chapter 3
The Explorer's Questions—Chapter 4
The Classical Questions—Chapters 5–8
Induction—Chapters 7, 8
Deduction—Chapter 8
Critical Thinking—Chapter 9

AUDIENCE ANALYSIS

Private Voice—Chapter 1
Frame of Reference—Chapter 2
Selecting a Voice—Chapter 3
Depth of Information—Chapter 4
Writing for Publication—Chapter 5
Public Voice—Chapter 6

Ways to Writing

PART I

Self-Expression

INTRODUCTION

Imagine yourself describing an incident to a close friend, a member of your family, or a schoolmate. Everything about you—your voice, your facial expressions, your body movements, even your dress—establishes a unique physical presence that gives force to your story. Like a musical instrument, your voice rises and falls, emphasizing key words at moments of high drama or anxiety. Every gesture of your hands, every arching of your eyebrows reveals to the other person the unity of your voice and being.

Now imagine yourself wishing to transform this spoken narrative into a written account. Immediately your hand freezes, your brain numbs, and your eyes gaze fixedly at pen and paper. What was so easy and spontaneous an act of language now becomes weighted with the difficulty of premeditation, the self-consciousness of beginnings.

Ironically, our membership in a literate culture further inhibits our powers of self-expression, because we so often experience events through the language of others, for example, the press, government, business, and artistic communities. How, we might ask, can we then develop in our writing an honest expression of our own? If we write on a sports event, must we see it only through the television language of the "thrill of victory and the agony of defeat"? If we already have a cultural overlay of meaning to apply to experience, we do not express the world as *we* have seen and experienced it.

We hope to provide a context for writing in Part I that will encourage you to develop your own voice and perceptions, your individual sense of yourself. By reporting the world as you see and experience it directly, you will engage in what is fundamentally an act of self-expression, even as you begin to learn how to adjust your voice so that it is appropriate to your subject and understandable to your audience.

In Chapter 1, you can begin to experiment with self-expression in the privacy of a journal. As a journal writer, you do not need to worry if a reader will understand you or not. You are writing for yourself alone, and so you are free to examine in any way you choose your feelings and thoughts about yourself and your world, and about writing as well.

Chapters 2 and 3 introduce you to the challenge of self-expression as a way of writing for someone other than yourself. In Chapter 2, your task is to write about the details of an incident so that a reader can experience the incident as you did. In Chapter 3, the task is to write about an experience that occurred over a longer period of time, such as a stage in your life, so that you may have to compress and combine a number of incidents to convey the overall equality of the experience.

We suggest that you try starting with the journal not only because of the opportunity it provides to express yourself openly, without feeling inhibited by rules or the expectations of others, but also because of the source it may turn out to be of ideas for many of the writing assignments that follow. Thus, once we have introduced you to journal writing in Chapter 1, we will continue to suggest that you keep up your journal and make use of it in each of the subsequent chapters in the book.

1
Writing About Yourself

If you wish to set down your day-to-day experiences and observations and responses to life as directly, completely, and honestly as possible, you may seek a form of writing that is flexible enough so that you do not have to be overly concerned with the effect on others of what you write or how you write it. For many writers, this form has been the journal.

A journal is a record, often kept daily, of one's life, a kind of personal account book. In the privacy of your journal, you can write about your conflicts and pleasures with family, friends, and associates without worrying about offending or embarrassing anyone. You can try out your responses to events, people, and things without worrying about the critical eye of a teacher or the difficulty of writing without error. You can open up and express yourself without fear of being poorly understood or harshly judged by anyone other than yourself. In short, you can discover your own uniquely personal voice.

To some students, the keeping of a journal or notebook seems a useless indulgence, a waste of time that has little to do with the next required theme or the grade that will be given to it. But this view is as impractical as it is misguided. Most writers are in constant search of new material, or of old material seen from a new perspective. How much easier it is to draw from a full well than to try to reclaim a few drops from the bottom. Thus many writers fill their journals or notebooks with materials as diverse as they can find.

3

Sometimes, you may focus in your journal on your inner life: your private feelings, thoughts, memories, dreams. Sometimes, you may focus on your experiences in and perceptions of the world outside yourself, writing narratives of your day, details of your observations, or ideas, questions, and notes about the things you learn from listening to or reading someone else's words. Your journal may serve you as a diary, but it should be more than that as well. It should be a place in which you can collect and develop your thoughts as a student and a writer, serving possibly as a notebook, for example, in which you record details of a lecture or a reading assignment in school and then write down your reactions.

It was customary for writers in the past to keep a personal notebook of their reading and observations by collecting sayings, quotations, philosophical reflections, lines from favorite poems, and formulas for success, anything that struck their interest. Such a collection was called a *commonplace book,* not only for its ordinary, everyday usefulness but also for its ability to supply fresh material for the common places, or topics, of writing. One modern compiler of a commonplace book, W. H. Auden, called it "a map of my planet." Like every map, it marks out boundaries, it locates the topics of deepest interest to a writer, and at the same time, it offers the possibility of new topics to explore.

The journal acts for many writers as a means of testing the self in its confrontations with the world. In your journal entries, you can express your confusion and disillusionment, your whimsicality and curiosity toward all the eccentric shapes of daily experience. Often, writing in your journal about an experience you have had can reveal to you something about yourself or your perceptions that you might not have realized as clearly before.

In this chapter, we ask you to keep a daily journal as a means of both learning about yourself and collecting material that you might use in writing a formal essay.

GENERATING IDEAS: THE JOURNAL

Starting a Journal

In starting a journal, you are making a kind of contract with yourself. You agree to record your observations and reactions over an extended period of time and expect in return a writer's bounty: some usable glimpses of yourself or others that you can work into a finished essay, or perhaps some developing pattern of feeling or thought that reveals you in the act of resolving some personal conflict or perceiving a subject in a new way. Although you receive no guarantee that your entries will be more interesting, less common, or even less boring than your daily routine or your usual thoughts may seem to you, what is surprising is how often the bright hue of fresh observation emerges from the uniform gray of the workaday world.

But how do you start? What do you write about first? The answer, of course, is whatever you want. Still, it may be helpful to take a look at how others have gotten started.

Often in starting journals, writers focus first on themselves *as writers,* on how they feel about keeping a journal or about writing in general. Here are early entries from the journals of four students:

Feb. 4

10:00 P.M.--You know, I've always wanted to keep a diary but always put it off. Sometimes you just have more things to say than others. I think it could be interesting to read something you've written a long time ago. Surprisingly enough, you might even find that certain values and attitudes have changed about yourself. Diaries are good for letting out your feelings. Writing them down, knowing no one will ever read them, is a good release. Diaries trace a person's emotional development.

Feb. 5, 1985

The teacher says to write and practically all the kids cringe about it. "Oh no, we have to write!" Writing--I love to write! Sometimes writing is the only way I can express something or get some understanding. The words just flow faster than I can get them on the paper, there's so much to write about. . . . The most wonderful thing about writing is that you can write anything, absolutely anything, and the paper doesn't talk back--

Moving along--to me, this journal is no hassle. In fact it will probably help. . . . I will just write how I feel when I feel it, and then I'll try to make sense of what it is I wrote later on.

2/9/85

When I first started thinking about writing this journal, I said to myself "I don't know what to write," and I still don't know what to write. When I think of writing I usually think that some important conclusion has to be reached. If not, then it is a waste. I am usually very opinionated and always have some important topic which I discuss with family and friends. But when it came down to writing this journal my mind kept going blank. I haven't had much time this first week to really get adjusted and get into the swing of academic life again. . . . At this point though, I'm thankful to have time to reflect, and to set new goals for the weeks ahead.

2/12

8:25 P.M.--Today is Lincoln's Birthday, so I stayed home all day. Since I had homework and quite a lot of reading to do, I decided to stay in the house. It was a good day to study because my son was in school, so I really got quite a lot accomplished. . . . Right now I am downstairs with my son in the living room. He is watching T.V., and I am busy writing in my Journal. Writing a Journal is a new experience for me. Sometimes it is difficult to find things to write about. I guess that as time goes on it gets easier. . . . It's like anything else, when one does something for the first time, it takes time to get used to it.

It is not only students who approach the task of starting a journal this way. Here are entries from the journals of two professional writers, Susan Kinnicutt and Sylvia Plath, each of whom is puzzling over the purpose of their keeping a journal:

January 1, 1978. Vermont

This diary looked so inviting when I first bought it, just like all the enticing "Blue Horse" notebooks I hoarded in Carolina. And then left unfilled though I sniffed them a lot. The smell of books and paper used to be so wonderful. But this isn't big enough, for one thing; I feel limited by the short page. And it doesn't open up, bend nicely, invite me to write, like the first hole of a good golf course should invite you to play. It looks official, though, it *demands* I mention the day. If I used my old Blue Horse, I probably wouldn't start at all.

But "journal" sounds so formal, so egocentric. (Who cares?) It's supposed to warm you up for writing; maybe there'll be bits and pieces of possible stories. That thought is depressing. I never seem to get to write all the stories I want to. Life interferes, always, and I haven't solved that problem.

And I feel as if someone were looking over my shoulder. What is this book for? What I did? What happened? What I think and *feel*? What I did is on the engagement calendar, not much usually, small events and sometimes outlandish. More important, *who* is this book for? Posterity? What a sickly sweet *Ladies' Home Journal* picture I could paint of myself, but what a finicky, mouth-tightening chore that would be. I guess what I'll do is run on and if I use this book up on July 6, go out and buy another and keep going. I hope, reading back, I can remember happy times, learn from sad—or skip the whole day if it's desperate.

—Susan Kinnicutt

November 13, 1949

As of today I have decided to keep a diary again—just a place where I can write my thoughts and opinions when I have a moment. Somehow I have to keep and hold the rapture of being seventeen. Every day is so precious I feel infinitely sad at the thought of all this time melting farther and farther away from me as I grow older. *Now, now is the perfect time of my life.*

In reflecting back upon these last sixteen years, I can see tragedies and happiness, all relative—all unimportant now—fit only to smile upon a bit mistily.

I still do not know myself. Perhaps I never will. But I feel free—unbound by responsibility, I still can come up to my own private room, with my drawings hanging on the walls . . . and pictures pinned up over my bureau. It is a room suited to me—tailored, uncluttered and peaceful. . . . I love the quiet lines of the furniture, the two bookcases filled with poetry books and fairy tales saved from childhood.

At the present moment I am very happy, sitting at my desk, looking out at the bare trees around the house across the street. . . . Always I want to be an observer. I want to be affected by life deeply, but never so blinded that I cannot see my share of existence in a wry, humorous light and mock myself as I mock others.

I am afraid of getting older. I am afraid of getting married. Spare me from cooking three meals a day—spare me from the relentless cage of routine and rote. I want to be free—free to know people and their backgrounds—free to move to different parts of the world, so I may learn that there are other morals and standards besides my own.

—Sylvia Plath

In the second entry, Plath goes on to introduce herself. The pages of her journal become, in this sense, a kind of mirror in which she can see who she is. For many students, this is the first purpose a journal serves also. In the following entry, a student starts her journal by introducing herself:

6/10/86 (Home)

Since it is the first page in my journal, I would like to introduce myself to the reader. You, probably, already guessed that my native language is not English. My first introduction to English started seven years ago, and if somebody would have told me that some day I will speak and even write in English, I would have been very sceptical. All my life, I have been dreaming about going to college, getting a degree, but my life had its own surprises for me, like getting married, having children, and finally coming to the USA. Of course, these excuses are very old and common, but nevertheless, they are legitimate.

There are less direct ways to introduce yourself in your journal. You might simply record the events of a day, as the following writer did:

6/9/86

9:15 P.M.--After class this evening I was thinking about writing-- what was I going to write about? I was going to discuss the way my day began--that would be easy enough.

My first week of no longer working full-time and a day when I could sleep late and what happens? The phone rings at 7:50 A.M. My girl- friend calls from Florida. Her brother is dying and she's very upset and there is nothing that I can say to make her feel better. He's 29 and he's dying. He's got AIDS and there's not a damn thing that anybody can do for him. There's nothing I can do for her and that hurts be- cause I love her. I can't lie to her and say that everything is going to be OK. So we cry together. That's all I <u>can</u> do.

Now mind you that was the way my day began. I got a letter from Abe (my guy) and that made me happy. Then I went to class and that made me happy (sort of). Then the Mets were losing 1-0 to the Phillies in the 3rd or 4th inning and I wasn't very happy. Then I turned the game off because I had writing that I <u>had</u> to do.

First though I saw my brother's new motorcycle and he was happy so that made me happy (doesn't take much, does it!). Then I started to read those essays that we had been assigned. The "Autobiography" was interesting, but then I got to "Shooting an Elephant" and I found my- self getting very upset. I think I understand the meaning of the story-- you know, doing something not because you want to but feel you have to due to the pressure from others. That's not what got to me. It was the actual shooting that made me sad. All I could think of was this poor animal suffering and dying slowly, frightened and alone. How very sad (my dog died alone in a hospital). It's kind of silly mentioning that now, but it just crossed my mind.

I guess the beginning of my day and the end were very similar--my girlfriend's brother and a silly elephant both dying and dying slowly. I've had enough.

Note how this writer includes her thoughts about a reading assignment and how these then lead her to a perception about herself.

Or, you might get started by simply describing a scene you observed or another person, as the writers of the following two entries did:

October 18, 1979. Napa Valley

Today I watched trucks pull orange gondolas filled with dark purple grapes along the road outside my office window. The workers were hurrying to get in the last of the Zinfandel. It is six in the evening now. A steady gray rain is falling. There are patterns of wet leaves on the lawn. Something is very emotional about this moment. Tears are squeezing out of the corners of my eyes. I am not sad. Perhaps I am feeling the seasons changing, my children growing, the skin at my elbows wrinkling.

—Eleanor Coppola

Mon., 2/10

That's what it was, it was time with Brian. He was a brand-new sponge soaking up a big-new world and I was old and broken-down. Eventually, I was not broken-down at all. Eventually, I was a human being again, and an uncle. A GOOD UNCLE. We spent a lot of good hours together. . . . I made a million silly noises for Brian. When he learned to crawl, I crawled with him. When he ran, I chased him. I fed him, burped him, changed him (AND HE CHANGED ME).

Before I met Brian, I hadn't had any experience raising a kid. I'd seen 'em before but never so much as changed a diaper. Wasn't looking forward to such stuff, smelly and all that. Feeding an infant--HOLDING an infant is a thrill at first. "Oh, he's so tiny." "Look at those teeny little fingernails." "Can you believe those eyes?" Brian was fun to watch. Even when he was just sleeping he was fun to watch. It was so funny to watch him try to turn over, from his back to his chest. Looked like a bug, a fat bug. It was funny to watch Brian trying to pick the flowers off the wallpaper. He thought he was looking at solid objects and he was trying to pick them off the wall.

He took his socks off. He took his diapers off, wet or dry, and threw them out of the crib. By winter, he was strong enough to remove anything from the crib; clothes, toys, bottles, food--no not food. He only drank from the bottle. But when food came along a little later, he flung that out too.

Each of these writers, Eleanor Coppola in the first case and a student who had suffered a disabling injury in the second, offers a subtle insight into the self, by writing about the world outside the self. So does the writer who expressed her feelings about her psychology teacher in the next entry:

Tues., Feb. 11

I cannot tolerate that Psych instructor. She is totally obnoxious. How can they have a woman with no children teach a child psychology course? And she's so adamant about everything! "Never, never discipline your children!" "Always, always speak to a child at his physical level!" "Believe me 'people'--it works!" Balony!--imagine poor Aunt Jeanine talking to 7 kids at their level--she'd be crawling around all day! I told John about her--figured I'd get his professional opinion--he agreed--she doesn't know what she's talking about!

I have enough pressure as a single parent. I second guess myself enough, without some idiot with no kids and no idea of what she's talking about telling me that you don't discipline a child--"you guide them." I wonder how she thinks you can "guide" a child in a temper tantrum. I'm sure her answer would be that she'd never let it get as far as a temper tantrum. Idiot!

Commenting, like this student, on something that you have learned or listened to or read is another good way of getting started on your journal. You might take down a remark of a television personality, for example, or copy a quotation from a magazine article. Then write a few sentences in which you apply these comments to an experience you have had recently or to an idea that you have been thinking about.

Of course, you don't have to start by *consciously* writing about anything at all. Another way of starting is to do some free writing, which is also an effective way of getting in touch with your most honest feelings and thoughts. Free writing is based on the belief that writers need to free themselves from the image of the perfectly formed and finished writing product in order to let the free play of language emerge in all its roughness, incoherence, and occasional imaginative sparkle. In free writing, you simply let the pen move as spontaneously and automatically as possible without the intervention of rational thought and order, without pause, and without lifting pen from paper. The result may be something like this:

May 1st 1986

    8:30 A.M.--Good morning it's May Day to some people Mayday is the time to dance around the maypole an ancient ritual in the communist countries or is it more broad than that it's the workers holiday May 1st was the day I moved back to the Bronx after having lived in Manhattan for four years May 1st same year a friend of mine moved to America to some people May 1st is their birthday to a pilot "mayday" means an emergency but I don't think that's related to May 1st one thing that May 1st is to all people is Spring no that's not true south of the equator May is like our November

How long could this have taken to write? Perhaps no more than a minute. Remember, our language-making power never stops working, not even during sleep. In fact, in a way, free writing resembles the flow of language in dreams. There is no "correct" order of events in dreams, and rules of grammar and sentence structure are irrelevant. Try to tap this flow of verbal energy and put it to work for you. Free writing, for timed intervals, is a practical means of "priming the pump." It helps a writer to overcome that initial fear of beginning, and it is another way of discovering what is going on within your mind. We will work more with free writing in Chapter 3.

Keeping a Journal

Begin now to keep a journal. Your instructor may have a preference, but otherwise use a notebook or the blank diaries available in bookstores or stationery departments. Perhaps you will want to discuss with your instructor just how to set the journal up, the type and range of subject matter that seem appropriate to include, and what role overall the journal will play in the course. Here are notes that one student took in her composition class about these things:

Class Notes: 9/18/85

    10 A.M.--We will be writing to show that we understand what we read and then convey that information to others. Daily journal--will be graded. 2 sides, 8 1/2 x 11:

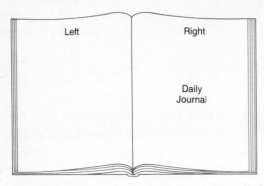

Right side
5 days a week
date entries
time entries
15 minutes a day
write what you want (free write)

Grammar doesn't matter--punctuation, etc. Only interested in words. Talking about yourself, your thoughts and inhibitions.

Left side: Write about the reading you do. Also, take class notes on left side. For each essay you read, write 5 minutes about your reactions. First "free write" about the essay--write questions about the essay--comments about the essay.

This is actually the first entry in the student's journal. It suggests a number of basic guidelines that are worth following. Starting each entry with a notation of the date, the time, and even the place that you are writing is a good idea. The regularity with which you write in your journal is important, and you may want to settle with your instructor on a set number of times that you will write each week. Also, you need not worry about grammar, punctuation, spelling, organization, or even necessarily about making much sense. Writing freely and honestly, no matter what your subject, may be the best way to make keeping a journal a productive experience.

Finally, note that another good way to get started writing in your journal is to use it as a notebook in class or when you read. Then, like the student who wrote about her psychology teacher, add your own comments and questions about what you are learning. This suggests, in fact, one further guideline you may decide to follow: read back over your entries, at periodic intervals, and write your thoughts and feelings about what you find there. Some writers even leave blank pages in their journal, so that when they do go back and read previous entries, they have the open space to write their comments and reactions in.

Using Your Journal as a Source of Ideas for Writing an Essay

Our reactions to people and events seldom occur in isolation. Usually, we can trace a thought or feeling through a series of journal entries and discover that seemingly random observations actually have a shape, an order, a logic. In other words, your private journal may reveal a pattern of ideas or emotions connected to one subject. This pattern can become the basis for a public piece of writing, a formal essay. As you continue to write in your journal, you may find yourself noting over a period of time sufficient ideas on enough different topics for all the formal writing you must do, whether the subject is personal experience or, more objectively, thoughts about the world you live in.

SOME PRACTICE IN USING YOUR JOURNAL

The following exercises suggest topics and/or ask you to experiment with your journal as a method for discovering ideas that can give content and form to an essay:

1. Suggested Topics

    a. Reserve the same time each day for several days for writing in your journal. Note the difference in your attitude from day to day. What has caused you to have these differing feelings? Can you trace your feelings to a specific incident that occurred that day? Does any pattern of response emerge as you reread your entries for the preceding days?

    b. Write a number of entries, preferably on successive days, that record your activities with, and feelings toward, one person. What do these comments reveal about the nature of your relationship to this person? Can you notice a change in this relationship or recognize a phrase that you are going through with this person?

    c. Forever, it seems humankind has been afflicted by, and sometimes consumed by, boredom. In the Middle Ages, monks feared the onset of midday, the "demon of noontide," when life seemed particularly empty and joyless. Is there any time of day when you feel the regular approach of the demon boredom? Select this time to record your response in your journal, preferably over a period of several days. Explain how you attempted to slay the demon. In addition, become an observer of others' boredom, writing down what you see of boredom in its public forms, namely, in shopping centers, in the student lounge, at airline terminals, or on mass transportation.

    d. Over a period of time, note your reactions to a particular public personality: a television performer, a newspaper columnist, or an author. What do your reactions tell you about yourself? What do they tell you about the subject you have been studying?

    e. Has a public issue, local or national or even international, captured your attention? As it develops in the press, record your reactions and interpretations. How does the issue affect you personally? What contributions might you make to general opinion about the subject?

2. Experiments With Your Journal Entries

a. After you have written entries for a week or longer, write a commentary on one of your previous entries in which you related your feelings about an emotional confrontation with another person. Do you see this encounter in the same way you did when you experienced it? If you see it differently, how would you have changed your original response? How do you explain your change of attitude? What implications could your thoughts about this encounter have for the next time you have a similar experience?

b. Rewrite a previous journal entry so that it ends in a way that you find more satisfying or pleasing to your view of yourself. What kinds of changes did you make? Would another reader be able to see through your deception?

c. Are there any previous entries that now appear to you false or inaccurate, either because you failed to observe carefully or because you willfully distorted the "facts"? Rewrite, this time giving a more reliable account and adding an explanation of the inaccuracies, along with a summary of the differences in the two versions.

d. Reread the entries in your journal that relate different encounters that you have had with others during a period of at least a week, in school, at work, or at home. Is there any pattern to these encounters? For example, was there a kind of forced casualness with other students, an unexpected tenseness at home, or a pleasing sense of friendship at work? What do these various encounters say about you and your social relations? Is there anything inconsistent in your different responses to other people?

e. In preparing your entries, seek for some evidence of the serendipitous, that is, an unexpected yet fortunate occurrence. For example, a fellow student you thought to be aloof and unfriendly surprisingly turns out to be quite helpful and concerned in explaining a mathematics problem. Can the writer always recognize these fortunate circumstances when they occur? What might prevent the writer from seeing them?

f. After you write an entry about an experience, write another in which you see yourself as a writer would see you going through the same experience. Change the narrative point of view (the voice telling the story) from the personal "I" to the impersonal "he" or "she." What differences are there in the two versions? What possible advantages are there in this change?

ADDRESSING YOUR AUDIENCE: PRIVATE VOICE

Your Private Voice

Writing in a journal is like talking to yourself. Because there is no one around, you can say what you want to without worrying about whether anyone is listening to you, judging your sincerity, or evaluating your skill as a writer.

You can test out your thoughts and feelings, as well as your ability to express them openly and directly. You can listen to your most private and personal voice.

This is not necessarily easy to do. For one thing, you may not wish to hear your private voice, the honest and original expression of yourself; there may be feelings you wish to hide from, to keep out of your own conscious awareness. Keeping a journal can be a way of tapping those feelings, but only if you allow it to.

Even if you are quite uninhibited about revealing your feelings, you may find that the language you use to convey them has a false note to it, is not unique or original enough, does not really sound like you. When we write, we often imitate one or another public voice that seems to us to command wide attention, or we adopt the voice of a close associate or a friend or a parent, or we rely on trite, clichéd expressions because they come readily to mind.

You may feel, for example, that it is a good idea to draw your ideas and language from the world of advertising, television, or popular journalism, for these media provide us with a stock of ready-made expressions and current attitudes. But in a way, allowing your voice to be an echo of someone else's is like wearing someone else's name on your clothes, applying to yourself a kind of designer's label of the mind. And this process may actually make you even more inhibited about expressing your most original ideas and observations.

For example, think of how often you, as a student, are tempted to imitate a teacher in order to make a good impression. In yielding to this temptation, you may feel uncomfortable, even guilty, about pretending to be someone that you're not. Feeling this way, you may reveal even less about yourself and hide your thoughts even more, rather than express them in an inauthentic way.

Consider the student who wrote the following note:

Dear Professor Ames,

Due to circumstances beyond my control, the paper on <u>Hamlet</u> was not submitted. I shall complete said paper and submit it as soon as possible prior to the final date of failure previously determined by the departmental authorities.

The student begins by sounding like a television announcer, then goes on to employ a pretentious, abstract style of phrasing that is perhaps meant to echo the academic language of the classroom. The effect is phony, unnatural, and unconvincing.

Nor would this student make a much better case if he or she tried to convey a false sense of familiarity that actually says little:

Dear Professor Ames,

    I'm sorry I can't hand in my paper on <u>Hamlet</u> today. I've been having a rough time lately. But I'm getting myself together now, so I definitely should have the paper done by next week, OK?

Again the writing is unconvincing because it hides more than it tells. Phrases like "getting myself together" are so trite and commonplace that we use them most often as a way of avoiding telling what we really feel.
    But what if the student wrote the following:

Dear Professor Ames,

    I'm sorry that I don't have my paper on <u>Hamlet</u> for you today. I had a biology test yesterday and now I've got a math test today, and I'd fallen behind in my studying for both. So I didn't get the paper done. Would you still accept it if I write it tonight and get it to you first thing tomorrow?

Might this note have more success? Whether or not it would depends, of course, on the sort of person and teacher Professor Ames is. But at least the student sounds more forthright.
    This might not always be the best strategy to take when you write. If you honestly feel that *Hamlet* is a rotten play and Professor Ames is a rotten teacher for making you write a paper on it, you probably would be wise to exercise a certain diplomacy and edit these feelings out of your note. Sometimes you will have thoughts and feelings that you rightly choose to keep to yourself. Often you will want to adjust your voice to the expectations and values of your audience (a subject we take up in Chapter 2 and examine in most of the audience sections thereafter). But you do want to develop a firm sense of your own most direct and original voice, because even when you edit this voice, it will remain the foundation of all the writing that you do.

Discovering Your Own Voice

Other than simply trying to write about your observations and experiences as freely and honestly as possible, what can you do to write in the voice that is most uniquely an expression of yourself?

Ken Macrorie, in his book *Telling Writing*, speaks of truthfulness in writing as a way to achieve this kind of personal authenticity. By *truthfulness* he does not mean simply the avoidance of lies and dishonesty; rather, he means the willingness to figure out what we really do want to say and to find a way of saying it. This approach recognizes, first, that we do not often know what we think unless we write about it and, second, that in order to express exactly what we think we need to find the words and the examples that will best convey it. We do not, in other words, think and then write. A process is involved in which thinking and writing are intertwined. This process is an arduous one; the right words do not always flow easily from the pen of even the greatest writer.

What you write about is less a problem than how you approach the subject. Taking an approach that allows you to learn something new from writing about the subject and to see the subject in a new, perhaps even contradictory, light will help you locate the truth.

Looking for unexpected perceptions that contrast with the perceptions of others or even with perceptions you have previously held yourself is, in fact, an excellent way of discovering something new, fresh, and original to say about a subject. If you feel there really is something rotten about a play that everyone tells you is a great classic, this feeling may be worth exploring in a paper. Perhaps the personality of one of the characters is offensive to you, and by writing about it, you may discover something new and vital about the character and about yourself as well. Macrorie suggests that the writer would be wise always to look for unexpected or opposing perceptions. Consider the positive aspects of a subject that strikes you as negative and vice versa. You thus treat a subject in all of its complexity and give yourself the opportunity to reveal the complexity of your own character.

Finding the words and phrases that reveal rather than mask this complexity is a challenge. By trying to be as concise and, at the same time, as detailed as possible in your choice of words, you can at least avoid sounding overly imitative of others.

On the one hand, you do not want to waste words. A phrase may convey more than a sentence or even a paragraph. Try not to use more words than you need to make your point. Why write, "When a black cat crosses my path, I am a superstitious enough person to believe that it is apt to be prophetic of misfortune," when you can write, "When a black cat crosses my path, I fear it will bring me bad luck"? Why be long-winded when you can be direct and to the point?

But truthfulness in writing is not just bare-bones economy. Although empty phrases should be pared from your writing, details that convey the uniqueness of your observations and experiences should be included. Work to find the specific nouns and the active verbs, adjectives, and adverbs that will bring your thoughts and feelings to life. Why write, "I felt very uptight," when you can write, "My stomach was doing triple somersaults, and every time I swallowed,

I felt like a wad of cotton had been stuffed down my throat." Try to make your ideas more specific, more concrete, by offering detailed examples of what you mean. Try to re-create the feel of your experiences by telling the reader how they were like or unlike comparable experiences.

How Others Hear You

The test of how truthful you have been will be the response of the reader. Have you expressed yourself clearly, colorfully, and concisely enough so that your reader believes in your experiences, trusts your feelings, and understands and respects your thoughts? Have you given the reader a good sense of who you are and what you are all about?

Once you are writing for an audience* and not just for yourself, you may feel reticent about expressing yourself openly and honestly. If your subject itself is very private, you may decide not to write about it for a particular audience or not to write about it at all. But when this is not the case, the chances are that your reader will draw you along the path to honesty by his or her interest in your subject, rather than putting up roadblocks that will inhibit you.

For example, a student wrote the following entry in her journal:

Sat., Sept. 25

12:00 noon--I just got out to lunch. The most terrible thing has just happened to me! I just got mugged. The two creeps that mugged me caught me off guard. I mean who would expect two clean-cut American kids to mug you on 86th St. and 3rd Avenue? I'm really shocked to hell! I think I've never been so afraid of New York City in all the 19 years that I've lived here.

The student followed this with a brief entry the next day saying that she had been robbed of her self-confidence as well as her money. In another entry two days after that, she wrote, "I am beginning to get over my feelings of bitterness about the mugging—my roommate's been quite a lot of help."

How honestly does she probe her feelings about being mugged? To what degree is her private voice hidden here behind pat phrases like "shocked to hell"? To what degree does she express the complexity of her feelings and especially the reality of her fear?

---

*We use *reader* and *audience* interchangeably here to mean either a group of readers or an individual. Each task in the book will specify whether your audience is to be a group or a particular individual.

She decided to write more about the mugging, in order to see if she could convey her experience vividly enough so that a reader might feel what she did, and submitted the following paragraphs to other members of the class:

Just two hours ago I got mugged. The two muggers were pushy, and for the first time in my life, I was actually afraid. I was so angry, not just at the muggers but at New York in general.

Before this incident occurred, I was very confident about living in New York. I mean, for nineteen years, I lived in the Bronx and never had any problems whatsoever. I guess one can say that all the years in New York gave me some kind of instinct for distinguishing the good from the bad. It turned out to be wrong, at least in my case. I never thought that the two "gentlemen" that approached me would turn out to be two of the "bad" guys. I always pictured the "bad" guy as a shabbily dressed, dirty-looking being. However, my stereotyping cost me 150 bucks!

If I had been a lot wiser about who I allowed to come near me (whether shabbily dressed or not), this would never have happened to me. I should have applied caution to everything and everyone. I should never trust anyone right off. My problem was that I applied caution in only one area (bad neighborhoods and shabby-looking people), instead of all neighborhoods and all people.

I guess it's not fair to blame all of New York; however, for a while there, I was really upset and I still carry a lot of the bitterness around with me. I blame the city because it disappoints me to see and feel that I could be harmed in a place and an area in which I've been brought up and have grown accustomed to. It really hurts to feel afraid suddenly when you've never known that feeling before; and it's really awful to have to think that two people can make you fear a whole city.

When her classmates read her story, they felt that her concise style and use of slang conveyed her anger and disappointment well. But they did not feel that her fear came through fully, even though she refers to it repeatedly. To be as convincing as possible, she may need to convey her fear more thoroughly. How might she accomplish this?

Her classmates suggested that she describe her attackers and the mugging incident itself in detail. They felt that a more concrete narrative of what actually happened might capture more of her feelings and attitudes and might allow a reader to get to know her more fully. Here, in response, is what the student added between the second and third paragraphs:

I was on my way out to lunch from work when the two creeps caught me off guard. I mean, who would expect two clean-cut American types to mug you on 86th St. and 3rd Avenue. Maybe that made it worse. They were nice-looking guys.

One minute they were walking past me; then before I knew what was happening, the big one reached out and grabbed my arm hard. His hand was so big, it filled all the way around my arm muscle. I must've looked shocked, 'cause all of a sudden he laughed in my face. He didn't have his two front teeth. For some reason, I keep remembering that.

The next thing I knew they'd pushed me against the wall of a building. I'm not sure I ever felt it when the other one tore my bag from off my shoulder. The next thing I knew, they were gone.

I was so shocked for a while I just stood there looking at the people walking by. It was like nobody even noticed. Then I got the shakes. I mean the shakes! I shook so hard, I thought I'd cry. I think I've never been so afraid of New York City in all of the nineteen years that I've lived here. Those two muggers have robbed me of more than just my money: they robbed me of my self-confidence.

In this case, the student's consciousness of her audience may have helped her to convey her experience more honestly and originally than she might otherwise have, in a voice that more thoroughly captured the range of her emotions. At first, you may feel intimidated by the recognition that you really do have an audience. But after writing several papers for a variety of readers, you should begin to sense how you can express your individuality to others in language that has the feel of a real person behind it.

SOME PRACTICE WITH VOICE

1. In the student's notes to Professor Ames above, how does the choice of words affect the overall tone of the language? For example, how do the words *de-*

partmental authorities function in the first note? What words create a vague, ambiguous feeling in the second note? What words clear up this ambiguity in the third note?

2. What can you conclude about the intentions and the character of the voices in the following quotations?

    a. I have resolved on an enterprise which has no precedent, and which, once complete, will have no imitator. My purpose is to display to my kind a portrait in every way true to nature, and the man I shall portray will be myself. . . . I am like no one in the whole world. I may be no better, but at least I am different.

                —**Jean-Jacques Rousseau,** *Confessions*

    b. When in the course of human events, it becomes necessary for one people to dissolve the political band which have connected them with another, . . . a decent respect to the opinions of mankind requires that they should declare the causes which impel them to the separation.

                —**Thomas Jefferson,** *"Declaration of Independence"*

    c. Psychopathology: Aimed at understanding obsessions and phobias, including the fear of being suddenly captured and stuffed with crabmeat, reluctance to return a volleyball serve, and the inability to say the word "mackinaw" in the presence of women. The compulsion to seek out the company of beavers is analyzed.

                —**Woody Allen,** *"Spring Bulletin"*

    d. It is a truth universally acknowledged, that a single man in possession of a good fortune must be in want of a wife.

                —**Jane Austen,** *Pride and Prejudice*

3. Select a popular newspaper or magazine with a distinctive voice. Write an entry in your journal on some commonplace event for that day, but try to narrate it in the voice of the magazine.

4. Write a brief advertisement for an expensive perfume, but use the voice you would expect to hear in a beer commercial. What kind of voice is usually used for these products? What are some words that would most likely appear in these commercials to create a distinctive voice?

5. Select sentences from your journal that don't really sound the way you think you sound, that distort or mask your most private voice. How do you account

for this writing? Rewrite the sentences so that they seem to be more "truthful." What changes did you make?

6. Collect examples of newspaper and magazine advertisements that take on a voice that you find to be manipulative, deceitful, or dishonest. What kind of language do these voices use? What kinds of audiences are addressed by these advertisements?

7. Working against the most individual self-expression is the tendency of student writers to rely on clichés—secondhand thoughts and feelings. For example, a reference at the beginning of the chapter to the "thrill of victory and the agony of defeat" suggests the abundance of clichés in the language of sports. Make a list of the sports clichés that you know. Collect clichés characteristic of other special-interest groups. What phrases can one substitute for the easily recognized expressions on your lists?

8. Change the following expressions into phrases that establish a more concrete voice in their description of objects or events:

   Example
   Fantastically beautiful autumn woodland
   An October forest of red- and golden-leafed oak and maple trees

   a. Wonderful beach of sun worshipers

   b. Exciting marathon runners passing by

   c. Laughing students hanging out on campus

   d. Municipal hospital admissions room filled with people

9. Restore the common expressions disguised by an inflated voice in these sentences.

   Example
   A rapidly accelerating glacial deposit accumulates zero spongy vegetation.
   A rolling stone gathers no moss.

   a. A military consortium peregrinates on its internal digestive organ.

   b. A feathered biped retained manually is cost-effectively superior to pairs inhabiting low-lying vegetation.

   c. Avoid enumerating domestic fowl prior to their postovum existence.

   d. Contemporaneously with the feline's exodus is experienced the diminutive rodent's ludic spontaneity.

TASK: WRITING A JOURNAL OR AN ESSAY BASED ON YOUR JOURNAL

The primary task in this chapter is to keep up your journal. If you have tried some of the exercises at the end of the sections on generating ideas and addressing your audience, you already have used your journal to write about yourself in a number of different ways, narrating your experiences, perhaps, or recording your sense impressions, or revealing your thoughts and feelings, or experimenting with your voice. You may have written entries about other things as well, other people, events in the news, classroom lectures, or reading assignments. As you continue to do so, begin to look for the subjects that you keep coming back to and the feelings that you keep focusing on, for the patterns of thought and interest that appear. We would like you to begin writing about these patterns, too. Doing so should help you grow more conscious of and comfortable with your private voice.

A second and optional task in this chapter is to write an expressive essay on a series of connected entries and what they reveal about you. The revelation may surprise you in some way: perhaps the entries confirm something that you already knew but that you did not realize you would focus on so much when you began keeping your journal; perhaps the entries indicate something new about you of which you were unaware.

Some classes may try the essay assignment now. Others may postpone it until a later point in the term, perhaps until they have had more time to develop their journals at length. But whichever of the two tasks you take up, try as you write to record and listen to your private voice as directly as you can.

In the next section of this chapter, ''Writing the Journal,'' we discuss how patterns of thought and feeling can emerge in a journal, the role that developing your private voice plays in helping you to trace and understand these patterns, and how you might formulate a general statement about an emerging pattern, a statement that could point you to the subject of a possible essay.

WRITING THE JOURNAL

Tracing a Pattern in Your Journal

When you read over your journal, you probably will begin to notice that certain concerns come up again and again, or certain moods recur, or certain ideas get examined, reexamined, and reexamined again. Maybe you enjoy a particular kind of music, and so you write about it regularly in your journal. Maybe you have been feeling down lately, and this is reflected in the way you perceive and write about your daily experiences. Maybe you are intrigued by what you are learning in a particular class, and so you repeatedly devote space in your journal to raising questions and formulating opinions about that subject.

The patterns that weave through your journal may be obvious or subtle. But even the most obvious will hold subtleties of meaning. It is one thing to note that you are an avid sports fan. It is quite another to puzzle out what this means about you, what a pattern of references to sports in your journal reveals about you as a unique individual.

Look, for example, at the following series of entries, written by a poet named Margaret Ryan during her pregnancy. There is an obvious pattern here in terms of subject; the writer was, naturally, preoccupied with being pregnant. But what are the more subtle patterns of thought and feeling? What kind of complexities of personality emerge? What might the writer conclude about herself and about her attitude toward being pregnant, after reading over these entries?

October 3

Odd, I haven't written since I learned I am pregnant. I've been withholding my mind from it, trying not to think about it, not to intellectualize it to death. Life does not all happen above the neck but happens in the belly, the breasts. Morning sickness since the third or fourth week—awful heaving, nausea; still, knowing I am not sick is a comfort. Breasts tender as bruises, swollen, my nipples darken, little nightfalls. Stretch marks. I fear the deformity of my body and the almost physical need I have to write.

My family is excited about the baby. Mother is prouder of this than of anything I have ever done—degrees, honors, publications, jobs. Timmy, who has two children of his own, is more excited than when Mary told him she was pregnant. "My baby sister is going to be a mother," he keeps saying. "My baby sister." Eileen, who has three children, is all unalloyed joy. But my other sister, Anne, who has no children, who has had her uterus removed because of cancer, is frankly envious. When she recovers enough to be civil, she asks me if I'm frightened, if I think I'm well enough.

The women in my husband's family have stopped asking me about my work. Though I am producing my first videotape, they talk to me only of my pregnancy. How much weight have I gained? Do I still throw up in the morning?

October 31

In Atlanta to attend a sporting goods meeting I produced. The baby is my carry-on luggage, the size of my crooked thumb. It is lonely at night in my hotel, but I go to sleep thinking of the baby traveling with me, and I am comforted.

November 6

The cleaning woman is thrilled that I am pregnant. She tells me stories: about her daughter's breech birth, and how she was in labor for three days before finally having a Caesarean. About the birth of her own fourth child, who was coming before the doctor got there, and how the nurse tried to hold the child in with a towel, pressing against its head, and about the child's neck breaking.

November 8

I am working on a tedious project with a sweet but tedious old man. He wants me to come in at 7 A.M. to view football footage for his presentation. I don't want to, so I tell him I am three months pregnant and don't feel so well in the mornings. He tells me his daughter has just given birth to his first grandchild, and that he has carefully monitored her pregnancy. He tells me I must be careful. He becomes sweet and tractable—apparently it's no longer necessary for me to view footage at all, much less at 7 A.M.

Another man I work with accuses me of wanting to have things both ways, of unfair tactics. He says, how can you be a feminist yet use your pregnancy to get special treatment, to make your clients behave? I tell him that in baseball, anyone who doesn't steal a base when the chance arises is considered a fool.

November 23

Thanksgiving. My mother-in-law gives me a pat on the rump and says, Look at the little pregnant lady. You're carrying behind. It's going to be a girl. I feel like a head of cattle. It angers and humiliates me to be treated like this. I tell my mother about it later on the phone, and she says, It'll get worse. Wait until the baby's born. It will have Steven's nose, her hair, his sister's eyes. You'll feel as if you had nothing to do with it. This news does not thrill me, but it does comfort me to know that my mother also went through it, and that she understands.

December 14

Christmas approaching, and the anniversary of my father's death. Nineteen years this year. I still wear the wool shirt I inherited from him when he died. Though I am 4½ months pregnant, it still fits. Odd, how many of my clothes still fit—bras, slips, sweaters—though finally my jeans won't zip. It's as if I always bought everything a few sizes too large, as if I were still that fat unhappy eighth grader who wore a size 16 dark-brown tent. I look forward to getting my figure back—I miss being slim. My face seems more beautiful now—perhaps as a consolation for my lack of shape below. Round, Steven says, asked to describe my shape. And I am round, a pear. (I used to think of souls as pear-shaped when I was in first grade, white and pear-shaped, and black spots indicated sins.)

January 7

I am in the sixth month of my first pregnancy, and I feel like running away. I feel as if I've not made good use of my (relative) freedom while I've had it, and that sometime in early May, it's all going to disappear. I feel panicky and desperate. But what would running away solve? What does it ever solve? I would still be carrying this child with me, and perhaps more important, I would still be carrying this paralyzed will. I would lack as much freedom in Paris as I do here—perhaps I would even be less free there, because my tongue would be tied. Here, at least, I can voice my distress, and am at least sometimes understood.

January 9

Last night I dreamt of loving and wanting to marry a very wealthy man. Apparently, the only difficulty was the fact that I was pregnant by another man. My pregnancy is interfering with my happiness, the union of myselves? Perhaps. But really, only if I let it. It is too late now to reconsider this child—and I think that if I could, I would probably choose to have it anyway. But it is certainly not too late to make myself happy, to take care of myself.

January 10

Carole has invited me to participate in a writers' conference at her college in Georgia, to read my poems, give workshops, talk about writing for money. The conference is in April—my ninth month. I said, Let me think about it, let me ask my doctor, not wanting to say no. This is the chance I've been waiting for, hoping for, for years. This morning I asked my doctor. He said, Going won't make anything happen, but if I were you, I wouldn't take the chance. I've spent the day feeling sorry for myself, talking to Sally, who thinks I shouldn't let anything stop me, and Steven, who definitely feels I shouldn't go. Already the child is impeding my career. But who can I blame? Not the child; not my husband; not the fates. I decided to have this baby, and like a responsible adult I now must live with the decision. I took a long walk by the river this afternoon, a continuity. And I realize that this child I carry, my health and safety, are more important to me than anything else. I spoke to Carole this evening, and told her I couldn't make it, to try me again next year.

—**Margaret Ryan**

Try rereading your journal now, with an eye to those entries that seem to form a pattern, an obvious pattern of subject, or some more subtle pattern of emotions, perhaps, or ideas. Once you begin to trace a pattern, you can look for other entries that fit into it or have a bearing on it in some way, that offer explanations about it, for example, or that even seem to contradict it. If you are going to write the essay in this chapter, try to look for a series of entries that surprise you, that teach you something new about yourself, or that reveal you to be more interested in or absorbed by something than you would have guessed you were.

It is possible, of course, that a pattern will fail to emerge clearly in your journal. In this case you might use one of the exercises in "Some Practice in Using Your Journal" (pp. 13–14) to develop a topic. Or, you would work with a single entry, completing the story of an event or experience, for example, and speculating about the causes that led you to write about it in your journal in the first place.

Developing Your Private Voice

In the entries about her pregnancy, Margaret Ryan expresses various and at times contradictory feelings, uncertainty, comfort, fear, humor, reluctance, vanity, acceptance. She does not fill the old stereotype of the mother-to-be, blushing with pride and happiness in anticipation of the new arrival. Her private voice is a rich and complex one, revealing a good deal about who she is and what she is experiencing.

Where would you say is she most truthful and open about her feelings? Are there any entries in which she seems to modify her private voice, out of shyness or in deference to what others might think? Does it seem, overall, that she expresses a firm and individualized sense of herself in her journal?

As you write in your journal, try like Ms. Ryan to aim for the sort of truthfulness that arises out of unexpected or opposing perceptions, concrete words and details, and short narrative examples. Try to avoid the pitfalls to which the best intentioned writer can succumb: substituting other voices for your own, feeling intimidated by your audience, or relying on vague, overused words and omitting vivid detail. Strive for a voice that is your own, that is unaffected by what you have heard or what you think others want to hear.

If you are writing the essay for Chapter 1, we suggest that you use the private voice of your journal in it, in order to offer a complete and characteristic expression of yourself. Write for an audience of readers who are sympathetic to and interested in your self-revelation, because they too are involved in self-discovery.

Finding a Shaping Idea

Margaret Ryan does not offer any overall assessment of what her journal entries reveal. But she might. In the contradictions of feeling that her private voice expresses, for example, she might find a key to the shape or structure that the pattern of her entries unfolds. Perhaps, they tell us something about the ironies of modern motherhood. Perhaps they tell us about the ambiguities involved in pregnancy for an individualistic woman in any age.

Is there a sentence in Ms. Ryan's journal or one you could formulate yourself that captures, for you, the essential meaning of what she has written? Selecting or creating such a sentence about one or another pattern in your journal is a way of discovering what we will call a *shaping idea*. If you intend to write the essay for this chapter, you will need to formulate such a shaping idea, one that can crystallize for you the main point of your essay. (See "Focus: Shaping A Subject," pp. 37–41.)

Now, take a look at the following two series of entries, one from the journals of the nineteenth-century American essayist Ralph Waldo Emerson, the other from the journal of a student. What kinds of patterns do you find tie the entries together in each case? How thoroughly does each writer seem to reveal his or her private voice? What sort of shaping idea might you formulate about the significance of each set of entries? Consider how, in each case, your answer to this last question accords with the main point of the essay that follows and that was in part structured out of the writer's entries.

From the Journals of Ralph Waldo Emerson

April 18, 1824

Myself.—. . . I am beginning my professional studies. In a month I shall be legally a man. And I deliberately dedicate my time, my talents, and my hopes to the Church. . . .

I cannot dissemble that my abilities are below my ambition. . . . I have, or had, a strong imagination, and consequently a keen relish for the beauties of poetry. The exercise which the practice of composition gives to this faculty is the cause of my immoderate fondness for writing, which has swelled these pages to a voluminous extent. My reasoning faculty is proportionably weak. . . .

But in Divinity I hope to thrive. I inherit from my sire a formality of manner and speech, but I derive from him, or his patriotic parent, a passionate love for the strains of eloquence.

September 27, 1830

Self-Reliance.—. . . Every man has his own voice, manner, eloquence, and, just as much, his own sort of love and grief and imagination and action. Let him scorn to imitate any being, let him scorn to be a secondary man, let him fully trust his own share of God's goodness, that, correctly used, it will lead him on to perfection which has no type yet in the universe, save only in the Divine Mind.

April 20, 1834

Awake, arm of the Lord! Awake, thou Godlike that sleepest! Dear God that sleepest in man, I have served my apprenticeship of bows and blushes, of fears and references, of excessive admiration.

The whole secret of the teacher's force lies in the conviction that men are convertible. And they are. They want awakening. Get the soul out of bed, out of her deep habitual sleep, out into God's universe, to a perception of its beauty, and hearing of its call, and your vulgar man, your prosy, selfish sensualist awakes, a god, and is conscious of force to shake the world.

March 14, 1837

Edward Taylor came last night and gave us in the old church a Lecture on Temperance. A wonderful man; I had almost said, a perfect orator. The utter want and loss of all method, the ridicule of all method, the bright chaos come again of his bewildering oratory, certainly bereaves it of power,—but what splendor! what sweetness! what richness! what depth! what cheer! How he conciliates, how he humanizes! how he exhilarates and ennobles!

May 7, 1837

. . . I cannot hear the young men whose theological instruction is exclusively owed to Cambridge and to public institution, without feeling how much happier was my star, which rained on me influences of ancestral religion. The depth of the religious sentiment which I knew in my Aunt Mary, imbuing all her genius and derived to her from such hoarded family traditions, from so many godly lives and godly deaths of sainted kindred at Concord, Malden, York, was itself a culture, an education. I heard with awe her tales of the pale stranger who, at the time her grandfather lay on his death-bed, tapped at the window and asked to come in. The dying man said, "Open the door"; but the timid family did not; immediately he breathed his last, and they said one to another, "It was the Angel of Death."

May 21, 1837

I see a good in such emphatic and universal calamity as the times bring, that they dissatisfy me with society. . . . Society has played out its last stake; it is check-mated. Young men have no hope. Adults stand like day-laborers idle in the streets. None calleth us to labor. The old wear no crown of warm life on their gray hairs. The present generation is bankrupt of principles and hope, as of property. I see man is not what man should be. He is the treadle of a wheel. He is a tassel at the apron-string of society. He is a money-chest. He is the servant of his belly. This is the causal bankruptcy, this the cruel oppression, that the ideal should serve the actual; that the head should serve the feet.

October 20, 1837

Wild man attracts.—As the contemporaries of Columbus hungered to see the wild man, so undoubtedly we should have the liveliest interest in a wild man, but men in society do not interest us because they are tame. We know all they will do, and man is like man as one steamboat is like another. Tame men are inexpressibly tedious.

November 7?, 1837

"Miracles have ceased." Have they indeed? When? They had not ceased this afternoon when I walked into the wood and got into bright, miraculous sunshine, in shelter from the roaring wind. Who sees a pine-cone, or the turpentine exuding from the tree, or a leaf, the unit of vegetation, fall from its bough, as if it said, "the year is finished," or hears in the quiet, piny glen the titmouse chirping his cheerful note, or walks along the lofty promontorylike ridges which, like natural causeways, traverse the morass, or gazes upward at the rushing clouds, or downward at a moss or a stone and says to himself, "Miracles have ceased"?

November 3, 1838

I should not dare to tell all my story. A great deal of it I do not yet understand. How much of it is incomplete. In my strait and decorous way of living, native to my family and to my country, and more strictly proper to me, is nothing extravagant or flowing. I content myself with moderate, languid actions, and never transgress the staidness of village manners. Herein I consult the poorness of my powers. . . . I see very well the beauty of sincerity, and tend that way, but if I should obey the impulse so far as to say to my fashionable acquaintance, "you are a coxcomb,—I dislike your manners—I pray you avoid my sight,"—I should not serve him nor me, and still less the truth; I should act quite unworthy of the truth, for I could not carry out the declaration with a sustained, even-minded frankness and love, which alone could save such a speech from rant and absurdity.

We must tend ever to the good life.

September 14, 1839

I lament that I find in me no enthusiasm, no resources for the instruction and guidance of the people, when they shall discover that their present guides are blind. . . . I hate preaching, whether in pulpits or in teachers' meetings. Preaching is a pledge, and I wish to say what I think and feel today, with the proviso that tomorrow perhaps I shall contradict it all. Freedom boundless I wish. I will not pledge myself not to drink wine, not to drink ink, not to lie, and not to commit adultery, lest I hanker tomorrow to do these things by reason of my having tied my hands. Besides, man is so poor he cannot afford to part with any advantages, or bereave himself of the functions even of one hair. I do not like to speak to the Peace Society, if so I am to restrain me in so extreme a privilege as the use of the sword and bullet. For the peace of the man who has forsworn the use of the bullet seems to me not quite peace, but a canting impotence; but with knife and pistol in my hands, if I, from greater bravery and honor, cast them aside, then I know the glory of peace.

October 18, 1839

For the five last years I have read each winter a new course of lectures in Boston, and each was my creed and confession of faith. Each told all I thought of the past, the present and the future. Once more I must renew my work. . . . What shall be the substance of my shrift? Adam in the garden, I am to new name all the beasts in the field and all the gods in the sky. I am to invite men drenched in Time to recover themselves and come out of time, and taste their native immortal air. . . . I am to celebrate the spiritual powers in their infinite contrast to the mechanical powers and the mechanical philosophy of this time.

April 7?, 1840

In all my lectures, I have taught one doctrine, namely, the infinitude of the private man.

October 7, 1840

I have been writing with some pains Essays on various matters as a sort of apology to my country for my apparent idleness. But the poor work has looked poorer daily, as I strove to end it. My genius seemed to quit me in such a mechanical work, a seeming wise—a cold exhibition of dead thoughts. When I write a letter to anyone whom I love, I have no lack of words or thoughts. I am wiser than myself and read my paper with the pleasure of one who receives a letter, but what I write to fill up the gaps of a chapter is hard and cold, is grammar and logic; there is no magic in it.

January 1, 1841

I begin the year by sending my little book of Essays to the press. What remains to be done to its imperfect chapters I will seek to do justly. I see no reason why we may not write with as much grandeur of spirit as we can serve or suffer. Let the page be filled with the character, not with the skill of the writer.

From "Self-Reliance"

. . . To believe your own thought, to believe that what is true for you in your private heart is true for all men,—that is genius. Speak your latent conviction, and it shall be the universal sense; for the inmost in due time becomes the outmost, and our first thought is rendered back to us by the trumpets of the Last Judgment. Familiar as the voice of the mind is to each, the highest merit we ascribe to Moses, Plato and Milton is that they set at naught books and traditions, and spoke not what men, but what *they* thought. A man should learn to detect and watch that gleam of light which flashes across his mind from within, more than the lustre of the firmament of bards and sages. Yet he dismisses without notice his thought, because it is his. In every work of genius we recognize our own rejected thoughts; they come back to us with a certain alienated majesty. Great works of art have no more affecting lesson for us than this. They teach us to abide by our spontaneous impression with good-humored inflexibility then most when the whole cry of voices is on the other side. Else tomorrow a stranger will say with masterly good sense precisely what we have thought and felt all the time, and we shall be forced to take with shame our own opinion from another.

There is a time in every man's education when he arrives at the conviction that envy is ignorance; that imitation is suicide; that he must take himself for better for worse as his portion; that though the wide universe is full of good, no kernel of nourishing corn can come to him but through his toil bestowed on that plot of ground which is given to him to till. The power which resides in him is new in nature, and none but he knows what that is which he can do, nor does he know until he has tried. . . .

Trust thyself: every heart vibrates to that iron string. Accept the place the divine providence has found for you, the society of your contemporaries, the connection of events. Great men have always done so, and confided themselves childlike to the genius of their age, betraying their perception that the absolutely trustworthy was seated at their heart, working through their hands, predominating in all their being. And we are now men, and must accept in the highest mind the same transcendent destiny; and not minors and invalids in a protected corner, not cowards fleeing before a revolution, but guides, redeemers and benefactors, obeying the Almighty effort and advancing on Chaos and the Dark.

What pretty oracles nature yields us on this text in the face and behavior of children, babes, and even brutes! . . . Infancy conforms to nobody; all conform to it; so that one babe commonly makes four or five out of the adults who prattle and play to it. So God has armed youth and puberty and manhood no less with its own piquancy and charm, and made it enviable and gracious and its claims not to be put by, if it will stand by itself. Do not think the youth has no force, because he cannot speak to you and me. Hark! in the next room his voice is sufficiently clear and emphatic. It seems he knows how to speak to his contemporaries. Bashful or bold then, he will know how to make us seniors very unnecessary.

The nonchalance of boys who are sure of a dinner, and would disdain as much as a lord to do or say aught to conciliate one, is the healthy attitude of human nature. A boy is in the parlor what the pit is in the playhouse; independent, irresponsible, looking out from his corner on such people and facts as pass by, he tries and sentences them on their merits, in the swift, summary way of boys, as good, bad, interesting, silly, eloquent, troublesome. He cumbers himself never about consequences, about interests; he gives an independent, genuine verdict. You must court him; he does not court you. But the man is as it were clapped into jail by his consciousness. . . .

These are the voices which we hear in solitude, but they grow faint and inaudible as we enter into the world. Society everywhere is in conspiracy against the manhood of every one of its members. Society is a joint stock company, in which the members agree, for the better securing of his bread to each shareholder, to surrender the liberty and culture of the eater. The virtue in most request is conformity. Self-reliance is its aversion. It loves not realities and creators, but names and customs.

Whoso would be a man, must be a nonconformist. He who would gather immortal palms must not be hindered by the name of goodness, but must explore if it be goodness. Nothing is at last sacred but the integrity of your own mind. Absolve you to yourself, and you shall have the suffrage of the world. I remember an answer which when quite young I was prompted to make to a valued adviser who was wont to importune me with the dear old doctrines of the church. On my saying, "What have I to do with the sacredness of traditions, if I live wholly from within?" my friend suggested,—"But these impulses may be from below, not from above." I replied, "They do not seem to me to be such; but if I am the Devil's child, I will live then from the Devil." No law can be sacred to me but that of my nature. Good and bad are but names very readily transferable to that or this; the only right is what is after my constitution; the only wrong what is against it. A man is to carry himself in the presence of all opposition as if every thing were titular and ephemeral but he. I am ashamed to think how easily we capitulate to badges and names, to large societies and dead institutions. Every decent and well-spoken individual affects and sways me more than is right. I ought to go upright and vital, and speak the rude truth in all ways. . . .

What I must do is all that concerns me, not what the people think. This rule, equally arduous in actual and in intellectual life, may serve for the whole distinction between greatness and meanness. It is the harder because you will always find those who think they know what is your duty better than you know it. It is easy in the world to live after the world's opinion; it is easy in solitude to live after our own; but the great man is he who in the midst of the crowd keeps with perfect sweetness the independence of solitude. . . .

FROM THE JOURNAL OF LISA H.

9-25-85 Wednesday

Tonight I called Heidi and asked her when the hell she was gonna call me. She said her grandfather from Florida was over and she didn't get a chance!

I am really torn about what to do about it. She said some really unfair things to me and I really wanna tell her off, but the day we had

the fight it was a Sunday and I went to Church and all three readings
were about forgiving and turning the other cheek. . . .

   If I let it go and I don't tell her how I feel, I will never be friends
with her again. I'll always be thinking about the things I want to say
to her. I want to do the right thing--the Christian thing, but I don't
think our relationship could be the same. Believe it or not, I'm very
religious. I have my own set of moral standards, but basically I'm a
good Catholic.

9/28/85

   After a terrible day, I went home, took a nap and then Joe and Mike
picked me up. We drove to a bar called Buttles, which had no admission price, but it did have a dance floor. The bartender there was such
a gentleman--he lit my cigarette and he had a nice name--Evan. Joe got
me ticked because his manners were especially bad tonight. Or maybe
because Evan's were so nice. Anyway, it was downhill from there. We
went to a diner and I was OK. Then Joe and Mike wanted to smoke a
joint, but Mike said he won't drive if he smokes, so that would mean
Joe, who already had three drinks and now is gonna get high, is gonna
drive 'cause I can't! I GOT SO TICKED! I told them forget it--smoke
some other night when we don't have a half-hour drive home, but Joe
said to be quiet and stop worrying, and all I could picture was the 3 of
us wrapped around some ____ pole. So I started screaming, "Let me
out," and Joe said "I'm getting sick of this, Lisa!" That was it. I shut
up. Silence all the way home. Mike dropped me off at Joe's and I
screamed and cried and carried on about every fear and paranoia I
have in the world. I guess I went too far. I went overboard. But Joe
took it all too lightly, like everything else. I left his home feeling a million miles away from him. Premenstrual Syndrome perhaps. I don't
know. All I know is that I feel terrible, sad, depressed, angry, and stupid. Mike must think I'm a jerk, and Joe must think I'm a head case.
And I think I need a good listener. Or a good shrink!

9/29/85 Sunday

   P.M.--I decided to call Heidi. I said everything I wanted to say now
for a week, and I think she understood, and it's resolved. I told her to

call me, but either way I don't care 'cause at least I got everything off my chest.

Tuesday 10/1/85

Today in Speech class this guy Mike told a story about his friend's sister, who he witnessed trying to commit suicide. It was really a sad story. I think Mike is a sweet guy. I wonder what he's really like. I'd like to be his friend. I still haven't spoken to Heidi yet. I refuse to call her. It's up to her now.

I sent out my monthly NORAID check. I help support the families of IRA members who are in jail or are dead. It makes me feel like I'm doing something good for the oppressed there in N. Ireland. My father said that for my graduation, he's gonna give me a trip to London, but I may change it to go to Belfast or Dublin to see it first hand. I won't see Joe until Thursday. Damn! Tomorrow I have to work!

12/26/85

Isn't it terrible that when I have the opportunity to do whatever I like, I have nothing to do? Isn't it terrible that I want to read my book but can't because I want to write also, and the two can't be done at the same time?

Life is terrible.

Isn't it terrible that I can say life is terrible when there are people who have terrible lives out there compared to mine? Isn't it terrible that people have terrible lives? Isn't it terrible that I can call my life terrible, when at least I have a life? Why do people waste their lives?

Tonight was, well, terrible.

Isn't it terrible that the English language feels the need to have a word like terrible? That people feel terrible so often that they need a word to express this feeling?

Tonight was terrible.

Tonight I was supposed to go see Rickey play.

I can't sleep--it's 3:17 A.M. and I am still _____ awake.

I really don't feel like writing all of this.

I waited all day for tonight. I talked to Vickie about five times today and she couldn't tell me what time she'd be out of work. I should've realized at some time today that there was the possibility she wouldn't be able to make it to see Rick tonight. So I lied to myself, which was terribly stupid because I ended up just as upset as I did hours later. I'm not explaining well. I'm at a terrible loss for words.

It's terribly late--I must go on.

So at 7:30 I took a shower. I planned my clothes, carefully, changing three times. I finally looked good. I did my hair. I looked nice. I decided to wait on doing my make-up till Vickie called and told me she was home and ready.

8:00 passed. Vickie is still at work.

9:00, she is still at work. I start to think maybe she won't make it tonight.

She calls at 10:00. She's home. I sigh with relief. Rickey goes on at 11:00. We have an hour to get to Manhattan. But she tells me she can't go. She worked so late, her mom says she can't go out. I beg her to talk to her mother again. Tell her I have been ready since 8:00 and she has to let you go. I can't go alone! Please--It's so important to me!

I think it's terrible that friends let other friends down. I think it's terrible that I am ready to go--hopes high because she told me she was going 2 weeks now--2 weeks of planning, 2, not one. I think it's terrible that Vickie has disappointed me. That she is not assertive enough to tell her boss that she has plans and <u>has</u> to leave at 7:00 as usual.

I think it's terrible that Rickey is going to be disappointed in me. I feel guilty about all the times I said I'd meet him and didn't show through my own fault. Now it's Vickie's fault. I am so terribly angry and disappointed in her.

She calls me back--her mom won't let her go. I cry, I scream and throw my shoes. I hung up on Vickie for the first time in our 7-year friendship. Our first real fight. A terrible one.

Rickey doesn't call to see where I am. Probably thinks it's just another one of my "no shows" for no good reason.

I have cried wolf one too many times with him.

Perhaps he'll never call again.

The writer of these entries put together the following rough draft in the process of writing the essay for Chapter 1:

I COME LAST

When I looked over a series of journal entries, I found that I worry about everyone else's troubles as if they were mine. I worry so much, I often end up feeling miserable about my own life. When I finally devote time to my own problems, they are usually huge or they seem minute compared to the worries of my friends.

For instance, the first full day of classes, I met my friend Dave, who I haven't seen all summer. He started telling me that he was having doubts about marrying his girlfriend, but that during the summer he had convinced her to move in and now he felt he had no choice. He had also told her that he was planning on giving her an engagement ring for Christmas, but after living with her for 2 months, he wasn't as sure as he was before that they are right for each other. This made me feel terrible, because I could see in his eyes how trapped he feels, and then I started wondering about my own relationship. I tried to think of ways Dave could explain to his girlfriend how he felt without hurting her feelings, but that seemed impossible and I got really upset that I couldn't help.

Then there was the night that my boyfriend Joe and I went out to a new club. We were drinking and dancing, and then we sat down and Joe looked pale and said he needed air fast! After we took a walk around the block, we went back to the club, and he said he felt better, but I didn't. I couldn't enjoy myself anymore because I kept asking Joe how he felt, and I kept worrying that he had caught some sort of bug. My night was ruined even though Joe felt much better.

The next incident occurred when the newspaper Newsday ran a three-day special report on Northern Ireland. My parents are originally from Derry, Northern Ireland, and I feel a sort of attachment to the people there. I felt so lousy after three days of reading about religious persecution, British fighting with Irish, the IRA bombing a hotel in London, Protestants fighting with Catholics, I wanted to hop on a plane and take the whole damn country with me to America where no one has to suffer racial and religious persecution. I guess I really do take people's problems to heart, but when it comes to my own, I leave them until they're huge.

I had a fight with my best friend of four years on September 1st, and when I finally decided to try and work on it, it was September 29th, and so much had happened we found it hard to feel comfortable enough and attached enough to even argue, never mind try and work the fight out. I tried to explain to her that I had a lot of things I was trying to work out for other people, and she said that when I was ready to play "Dear Abby" for myself, she'd talk.

Now that I realize that my helping others has hampered my powers to help myself, I will think twice before I say "Yes" to the question, "I have a problem. Will you help me?"

In the section on "Rewriting" (see pp. 42–47), we will look at the response to this draft of other students in the writer's class and then at how the writer revised her essay.

Now, if you plan to do the essay assignment in this chapter, you should get ready to write your rough draft.

First, like a professional writer, choose an appropriate time and place to write. Set aside a specific place for writing: a quiet area of your home that has a table or desk, a special part of your dorm room, or the least distracting desk in your local or school library. Also set aside a block of two to three hours, possibly the same time each day, when you do not have to worry about other responsibilities. This kind of regularity—call it discipline, if you wish—can help you to create a mood for writing. Now, all you need are the tools of the trade: lots of paper, pencils, pens, and/or a typewriter or word processor.

Once you have written through to the end of your first draft, stop writing and take a long break—twenty-four hours, if time permits.

FOCUS: SHAPING A SUBJECT

When we begin to write we may think of ourselves as engines that need to be ignited by some mysterious spark before all our potential creative energy can be utilized. The time that elapses between our exploring a subject and our writing a first draft is often spent in confused mental conflict. During this time, we submit our topic to stern questioning. We turn it over and examine it from various angles. We try to establish its limits, even though we know that each thing we experience seems to overlap with and cast light on something else. We begin to carve from the stone of our subject a self-contained whole, a main idea that will give form or structure to our many thoughts by fusing them into a pattern of significance.

As part of this chapter's task, we asked you to review your journal as a source of ideas about yourself. If you were to write an essay about what you learned by doing this, like the student who wrote "I Come Last," you would need to formulate a main point around which to organize your ideas. We suggested that you look for a pattern of thought or feeling in your journal entries, then produce a single statement expressing what this pattern is and what significance it holds. Doing this, you are employing one possible strategy for developing a main or shaping idea.

Each of the sections on "Writing the Essay" that follow in this book suggests other possible strategies for developing shaping ideas. Right now, we would like you to think a bit more about just what qualities a good shaping idea should have.

Another student who decided to write on something he learned by keeping a journal began by jotting down a page of notes, shown on p. 39. Working with these notes, he produced a draft of a paper in which he made these points:

1. It was hard to start, and at first he grasped for subjects to write about.
2. Once he began to write about his new identity as a student, he felt more comfortable with the journal.
3. At first he wrote more about inanimate objects and their role in his life than he did about people.
4. He wrote about peanut butter, zip codes, and batteries.
5. While much of what he wrote might bore someone else, it was interesting to him because it was a part of his life.
6. He wrote about his niece and then about his nephew.
7. The entry about his nephew seemed to him to be "serious writing," and it became the basis for his first paper.
8. The more he wrote about people, the more he noticed "more verbs than nouns, more adverbs than adjectives," in his writing.
9. This reflected a shift "from writing about seeing things and knowing things to writing about doing things and thinking about things."
10. He now feels more confident of his ability to write.

Which of these points or which combination of them might make for a good shaping idea? Which might serve best as a main point or *thesis*, as some writers call it?

The student is focusing on how he gained more confidence as a writer, as the difference between his first and last point makes clear. Point 5 suggests he is uncertain about the value to others of his writing, when he writes about inanimate objects. Point 7 contrasts with this, in suggesting that when he wrote about his nephew, he felt others might be interested. Perhaps his shaping idea could come from point 9, which offers evidence of his growing confidence and implies a possible reason for it.

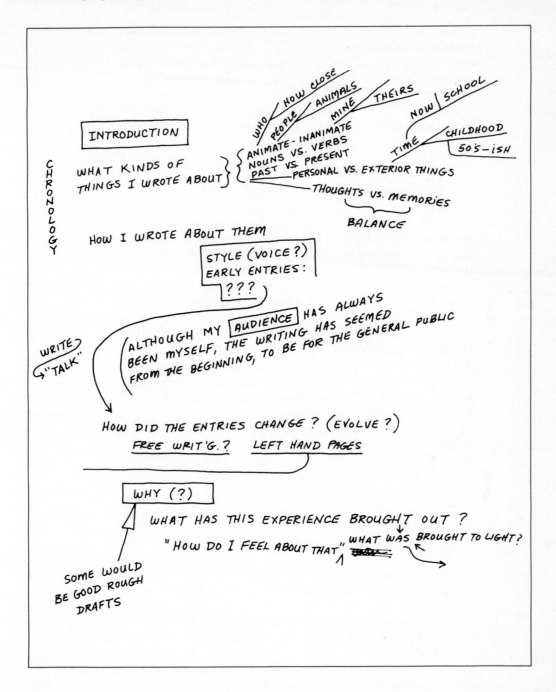

In noting the relationships between one point and another, a writer forms a more exact view of his or her subject and may come to the shaping idea of an essay. In the case of the above example, in fact, the student worked up to a final draft which he began with the following introduction:

In three short months, I progressed from being a letter writer to being a student who was learning how to write an essay. I was the same person, living the same life. But I had begun to acquire the tools of a writer. My journal has been one of those tools.

The idea shaping his paper was the exploration of how one tool, the journal, helped him develop other tools, such as "a better ability to reflect upon my thoughts and my life," and how having such tools made him more confident as a student writing essays that might be of interest to others as well as himself.

The shaping idea, then, is a statement defining the subject matter and expressing what the author wants us to understand about that subject. It also sets the writer's tone, letting a reader know something about how the subject will be treated, whether seriously or comically, for example, logically or emotionally, with an eye to explain or an eye to persuade.

Once you determine your shaping idea for a paper (note that you may need to write a number of drafts before you settle on a shaping idea), you will want to state this idea in a single declarative sentence (not a phrase, not a question) that contains both your subject and the main point that you are making about it. Your statement of your shaping idea should be precise, unambiguous, and grammatically correct. We advise that, as an apprentice writer, you place this statement in the first paragraph or two of your essay (although, as you will see, many skilled writers state the shaping idea elsewhere in the essay). By writing your main thought in one sentence and placing it at the beginning of your essay, you will be better able to keep focused during additional drafting stages, and you also will give your reader a clear sense of the purpose of your essay at the outset.

The first paragraph or two in a final draft should do more than simply note the writer's shaping idea. In the introduction to a paper, a writer has the chance to use his or her imagination to attract the interest of an audience and lead them to read on. In the section on "Rewriting" that comes next, examine the final draft of the student essay "I Come Last." Note how the writer has revised both the introduction and the conclusion of her rough draft. How has she improved these important parts of her paper in revision? How thoroughly does her revised introduction do all that a good introduction should, state the shaping idea, set the tone or mood of the essay, and create an imaginative hook for the reader?

SOME PRACTICE WITH SHAPING YOUR SUBJECT

1. From the following ideas, select the one that you think will create a sharply focused and organized essay and explain why you think so:

   a. Major league baseball is boring.

   b. Fast food is dangerous to your health.

   c. I don't like science fiction movies.

   d. My high-school biology teacher's persistent encouragement helped me to overcome my learning disabilities.

2. From the following related statements, form a clear shaping idea that will explain what they refer to:

   a. The neighborhood bars have been turned into "eating boutiques."

   b. Old, established small businesses have been driven out by high rents.

   c. Young executives and trendy singles have displaced the original ethnic mix of immigrant families.

   d. Tenements and row houses area being replaced by luxury high-rise condominiums.

   e. Schools and playgrounds are in need of restoration and expansion.

   f. Traditional political alignments are being revised.

3. Expand the following subjects to form shaping ideas. For example, "teenage alcoholism" to "Teenage alcoholism can be reduced if the drinking age is raised to twenty-one":

   a. Nuclear energy plants . . .

   b. The decline of the American automobile industry . . .

   c. Television soap operas . . .

   d. The nursing profession . . .

4. Select a topic that you are studying in another course. From your class notes or journal entries, write down several ideas that you have on this subject and begin to develop them into a shaping idea. For example, in business you are studying the Federal Reserve Board and its role in controlling the money supply. You might write down some of its duties and then formulate a statement that would work these ideas into a shaping idea ready to be developed into an essay.

REWRITING

Obtaining Feedback on Your Rough Draft

If you are working on the essay in this chapter, after you have written your rough draft and have taken a break, you can resume the writing process by revising what you have written. Of course, you may already have made changes as you were writing the first draft, and in fact, your copy may look much worked-over already. However, looking again at what you have written after a rest period will help you to read your paper as your audience will read it: more-or-less objectively.

In a sense, another self will take over, a self that may have been looking over your shoulder as you wrote the rough draft, keeping track of what you were doing, evaluating how each part fits in with the whole, noting problems and possible solutions, criticizing, and encouraging. This other self needs to be given full permission to comment at this point, because it has a distance that you didn't have while immersed in writing the essay.

Your teacher may also wish to play the role of the "other self" at this point and to comment on your first try. And a third source of feedback is your peers. Your instructor may ask a group of your classmates to react to your paper, or if not, you may select a group yourself to do this job. Do not be afraid to show your work to your classmates. You can assume that most students have passed through similar periods of self-discovery and will be sympathetic to you.

Regardless of who provides the feedback—you, your instructor, your peers, or any combination—your paper should receive an evaluation that answers the following four questions of the "Audience Response Guide."

———— AUDIENCE RESPONSE GUIDE ————

1. What do you think the writer wanted to say in this paper? What is his or her purpose in writing? What does he or she want the paper to mean?
2. How does the paper affect the reader for whom it was intended?
3. How effective has the writer been in conveying his or her purpose and meaning? What are the strengths of the paper? What are the weaknesses?
4. How should the paper be revised to better fulfill its purpose and meaning?

The following is a peer evaluation of the rough draft of the student essay "I Come Last" (pp. 36–37) in response to the four questions above:

1. The writer's opening paragraph makes her thesis clear. A review of her journals leads her to believe that she takes on other people's troubles to an excessive degree. She does this instead of worrying about her own problems and helping herself.

2. The essay was interesting, because she expressed herself honestly. She sounded annoyed, upset, and frustrated in each example that she gave. The conclusion was unclear, however. Although she said she was going to think twice about helping others, she seems to mean she wants to stop helping people altogether.

3. She conveyed her meaning well, because she gave concrete examples of how she felt she puts other people's problems first. The examples were her strong point. One weakness was that the part about the fight with her friend wasn't developed enough, considering that it is a main theme.

4. Add more detail, especially about how listening to other people's problems affects her. Give more emphasis to the fight with her girlfriend and clarify what she means in the conclusion.

Here is a revised draft of "I Come Last." In what ways has the writer responded to the group's suggestions, as well as to her own sense of how the paper should be improved?

I COME LAST

After reviewing a series of journal entries, I found that I often worry about other people's problems as if they were mine. I found that I devote so much time to other's troubles, I end up neglecting my own until they are huge, or until I realize that my problems are minute compared to many other people's. It seems to me that my friends, their friends, casual acquaintances, and even total strangers have always sought me out to play their "Dear Abby."

One example was the night I went to a dance club with my boyfriend Joe and his friend Mike. After we were drinking and dancing, the place got really hot. My boyfriend said he felt dizzy and needed air, so he and I took a walk around the block. When we went back inside, he said he felt better, but I just couldn't enjoy myself in between asking him how he felt every five minutes. I even started to feel some of his symptoms! The night was ruined even though Joe was perfectly healthy. I, on the other hand, was extremely uptight.

What one must realize is that the problems I worry about don't have to be the problems of someone as close to me as my boyfriend Joe. It can be people as far away as Northern Ireland. My family originally came from Derry, one of the six states making up the war-torn Northern Ireland. The Newsday, a Long Island paper, ran a three-day special about the problems going on there. I guess because of my ancestry, I feel a tie with the people there, and after reading for three days about British fighting with the Irish, Protestants fighting with Catholics, Brits bombing innocent civilian towns, IRA members bombing hotels in London, and people being unable to fly a flag in their own homeland, I wanted to fly there and take the entire continent home with me so they could live in America, where neither would be persecuted. The knot in my stomach seems like it will never go away, probably because the problems there will never go away.

Need more examples? Well, I now know that John is gay, Francesca has cheated on her boyfriend 4 times just this summer alone, Ellen had to have a tumor removed from her ovary, Mitch is having an affair with a woman 8 years his senior, Marybeth is going on the pill, and Vicki just found out that the guy she is dating has a criminal record. And that was just last week. If I charged a fee to hear this stuff, I'd be living in a condominium in the Bahamas by now. It all seems to pile up on me, and my own problems seem to end up on a back burner until they explode in my face.

Probably the best example of this is in my working through a problem I was having with my best friend of 4 years, Heidi. She and I had a small argument on September 1, and when I finally called her to talk it out (on September 29!), she was less than eager to try to work it out. She said that she knew exactly what my problem was, a common case of Lisa trying to please everybody and having nothing left for herself. We eventually got around to talking about the original fight, and it was resolved in just a few minutes, leaving Heidi with plenty of time to tell me all about her father's cancer.

When we started this assignment, I thought it really wouldn't help me, since I already keep a daily diary and since I am "gifted" with the power to write songs, but I found that this self-discovery theme was very helpful. I will definitely think twice about saying yes to the question, "I've got this problem. Will you help me?" Or maybe I'll start saving for that condo in the Bahamas.

One change that the writer made was to eliminate her second paragraph, with the example about Dave, then add a new paragraph, after the part about Northern Ireland, with brief examples and a concluding sentence about what happens to her own problems as a result of her "Dear Abby" reputation. Perhaps this gives an added emphasis to the importance of her last example about Heidi. What other changes have been made? What do you think, for example, of the way she revised her introductory paragraph? Does her revised conclusion clarify what she wants to say at the end?

In this and subsequent chapters, once you have feedback from your other self, your instructor, or your peers, you can revise your rough draft.

Revising

Revising affects the content and organization of your essay. The revising that your other self, your instructor, or your peer group suggests you do will no doubt be one or more of six activities: cutting, adding, rearranging, substituting, distributing, or consolidating. The writer of "I Come Last," for example, decided both to cut material out of her rough draft and to add new material in her final draft. Such revisions affect the meaning of the essay, some to a greater extent than others.

Each of these activities will receive a full discussion in a subsequent chapter, but in case when revising you wish to move ahead, we list the pages for each discussion:

Cutting, the following section

Adding, pp. 86–87

Rearranging, pp. 127–128

Substituting, pp. 169–170

Distributing, p. 210

Consolidating, pp. 255–256

Additional sections on revising in Chapters 7–9 focus on revision techniques for scientific (pp. 306–310) and persuasive writing (pp. 362–363), and techniques to sharpen critical thinking (pp. 420–421).

Cutting.   When you write for yourself in your journal, you can be wordy or vague or irrelevant if it suits you. But when you write for others, for an audience, it is helpful to be concise, detailed, and to the point. Cutting or deleting words and phrases from a rough draft that are redundant, for example, that are needlessly repetitious, should make the writing more readable. Why write "in this day and age" when you can simply write "today"? Why begin a sentence with the phrase, "Personally, in my opinion," when you can give your opinion directly?

You may decide while revising a paper to cut out whole passages that you originally included less because they contributed to the point of the paper than because you simply liked what you said or sounded like in them. Might this be the case, for example, with the second paragraph, the one about Dave, in the rough draft of "I Come Last"?

The student writer of "I Come Last" did more than cut out that paragraph when she revised her essay. She added sentences that explain and develop her main point at the end of her first, second, and fourth paragraphs; she substituted shorter, more direct phrasing for the lengthy, poorly focused sentences in the first draft's paragraph about Heidi; and she clarified her conclusion. In each case, she worked to communicate in a more straightforward manner with her reader, to reveal herself and her thoughts as directly as possible.

When you revise, try to cut out vague, overused, and imitative words or phrases, as well as material that does not really help your reader understand the point you want to make, material that leaves your reader asking, "Why did the writer include this?" Such cutting can be as important to the success of your work as adding, substituting, or any of the other revisions you might choose to make.

The Final Product

Presentation.   After a day, reread your revised essay for mechanical errors such as spelling, grammar, punctuation, and capitalization. (Refer to the Handbook on pages 424–492 if you are uncertain about how to correct a mechanical error.)

Neatness is the key at this final stage. Write neatly on good-quality lined paper, such as that from a loose-leaf notebook or a pad of lined paper. Do not write on spiral notebook paper.

Write on one side of the page, leaving two inches at the top of the first page for the title. Number the pages after page 1 in the upper-right-hand corner.

If you type your paper, choose a good-quality bond paper. Leave margins of one inch on all four sides. Type double-spaced on one side of the paper, again leaving room at the top of page 1 for your title and numbering the pages from page 2 on.

Your Title.   A title fulfills two functions: it attracts your readers' attention and gives them some indication of your subject, although often the meaning of a title is not clear until the essay is read. And titles are fun to write; you can be as creative as you like.

In choosing a title, consider your shaping idea as the best source of the meaning of your title. Then, once the meaning has been established, use your creativity to devise a word or a phrase that conveys that meaning in an interesting way.

Proofreading.   By now, you might expect that your work is over. Not quite. One final step is necessary. You must now proofread.

Proofreading is reading your final copy to check for mistakes, omissions, and typos that might have occurred in the transcription from the revised essay to the final copy that will be submitted to your instructor. This process is a tedious one and should be undertaken at a time when you are alert and calm. It is advisable, if time permits, to proofread some time after typing your essay; it is also advisable to proofread the draft at least three times. Make your corrections neatly and clearly.

1. Read slowly what is on the page, not what you think is on the page. Correct mistakes as you see them: spelling, punctuation, and so on.
2. Read again, out loud. Sometimes you will hear mistakes that you cannot see.
3. Read your essay backward from end to beginning, sentence by sentence. This procedure will relieve you of analyzing the content and will help you to focus on words and punctuation.
4. Skim from right to left and top to bottom, looking for misspellings and other errors.

BECOMING AWARE OF YOURSELF AS A WRITER

Make use of your journal to record your thoughts and feelings about the task in Chapter 1. As you write in your journal, consider the following questions:

1. What effect does writing a journal entry have on you? What value have you found in the process?

2. Do you think that a writer's journals should be read by others? How would you feel if others read your journals? How would the presence of others affect what you write?

3. What kinds of subjects make keeping a journal useful to you?

4. Which are your most interesting journal entries? Why do you think so?

5. What connection can you make between keeping a journal and writing an essay?

6. How successful were you in hearing and conveying your private voice? What methods contributed to your success? What effect did writing for an audience have on your attempts to be honest and authentic?

7. If you wrote the optional essay, in what ways did your shaping idea affect what you said and how you said it? In what ways was your shaping idea effective or ineffective? What did it make your audience feel or do? Was this result intended by you?

2

Writing About
an Incident

PURPOSE

Recording your private voice is one way you can learn how to express yourself more clearly and understandably as a writer. But it is not the only way, nor is it sufficient by itself. For one thing, your audience will probably never share your attitudes and perspectives completely. There will always be a gap between you and even your most sympathetic reader. Adjusting your voice to bridge this gap can be as important as discovering what your most honest and authentic voice is.

This chapter will begin to introduce you to the different kinds of adjustments that a writer may make in his or her voice for different audiences. We will ask you in your writing for this chapter to order a series of impressions, a group of details about an important event in your life, so that a reader other than yourself can experience them in much the same way that you did.

If your reader is to understand an event you have experienced, you need to convey the facts of that experience, investigating them with the same sort of thoroughness that a journalist employs to report a news event. You also need to record your impressions, reactions, and interpretations vividly, concretely, and intelligibly enough so that your reader can see the event as you did and can share your responses with you.

In order to help your reader not only understand the event but see it from your point of view, you will want to consider your reader's point of view as well as your own, particularly as you try to determine what selection and arrangement of details will convey the essence of your experience of the event most effectively. But first you want to collect as many details as possible, to gather the facts. As one way of getting started, consider how, as an essayist, you can use the tools that a professional reporter uses when she or he investigates the facts of a newsworthy incident.

GENERATING IDEAS: THE JOURNALIST'S QUESTIONS

The news reporter often gets started on a story by asking six questions about whatever incident he or she is covering. The six questions are introduced by the following words:

who	*when*
what	*how*
where	*why*

If you examine the following article, which was taken from *The New York Times* of February 21, 1962, you will notice how the answers to the journalist's questions are integrated into it.

50,000 on Beach Strangely Calm as Rocket Streaks Out of Sight

"He's in the Hands of the Lord Now," Woman Says—Hilarity Erupts at Word of Recovery—900 Pound Cake Is Cut

By Gay Talese
Special to the New York Times

COCOA BEACH, Feb. 20—At 9:47 A.M. today the rocket rose slowly over the beach like a high infield fly, but moments later it was streaking out of sight, leaving a thin, white and fluffy vapor trail.

Fifty thousand spectators stood along the beach watching the climbing Atlas carrying Lieut. Col. John H. Glenn Jr. into orbit. Some cheered, some clapped. An elderly woman said solemnly: "He's in the hands of the Lord now." Most remained silent.

They watched the sky until there was nothing left to see except pelicans and sea gulls, and until the rocket's vapor trail had lost its shape and become a floating, upside-down question mark.

Then they slumped on the beach to hear the rest by radio, or returned to homes, motels or taverns to watch on television, as millions were doing around the country.

Not until 3:01 P.M., when the astronaut had gone thrice around the earth and had been safely retrieved from the Atlantic by the destroyer Noa, did the hilarity begin. Faces lost their looks of concern.

Cheers Go Up

A 900-pound cake, the size and shape of the Mercury capsule, was sliced. And a huge movie-type marquee along the main road lighted up to say: "Our Prayers Were Answered."

There were cheers around poolsides when it was reported that President Kennedy would come here Friday to honor Colonel Glenn. By twilight, Cocoa Beach's jazz bands and cash registers were swinging and ringing in merry syncopation.

"Oh, he done it, buddy, he done it, so let's have a drink," John Godbee of Deland called to the crowd around him at the Vanguard Bar.

"I said 'go, go, go,' and seeing it go gave me a glorious feeling," John Pellegrino, the Vanguard's bass player, said.

"It was just undescribable," said Mrs. Thomas J. Knight of Baltimore, relaxing on the beach.

"Undescribable is right," Mrs. Howard Balliet of Orlando agreed with a nod.

Though the countdown was halted a few times, there was an undefinable feeling of optimism. People seemed to sense that this was finally the big day, that after ten postponements the orbital shot would leave the launching pad.

At 9:23, radios in cars, on people's shoulders and in their pockets could be heard everywhere saying, "T minus 22, and counting . . . T minus 20 minutes, and counting . . . T minus 17 minutes . . . T minus 13 minutes."

Now there was a vast quiet along the beach. People stood on sand dunes, motel porches, trucks and trailers, all with eyes fixed on the missile gantries, towering like a mirage eight miles north over the waves.

"Rosemary!" screamed a mother, almost hysterically, grabbing her fleeing child. "Get over here."

"T minus 3 minutes," went the radio. "T minus 30 seconds . . . 20 seconds . . . 10 seconds . . . 5 . . . 4 . . . 3 . . . 2 . . . ."

"Lift off!" somebody yelled.

"Look, it's up!"

"Go, baby, go!" a man cried, clenching his fist.

But the great majority watched silently as the missile moved slowly skyward. There was a red flame behind it as it began to climb. Then it was just a blazing speck, rising higher and higher, with only the vapor trail marking the ascent for those without binoculars.

Pensiveness Noted

The lack of delirium, the pensiveness of the thousands who stared toward the sky were hard to interpret. The flights of Comdr. Alan B. Shepard and Capt. Virgil

I. Grissom here had brought rousing demonstrations. Each had evoked cheers usually heard after a game-winning world series home run.

Perhaps the crowd was quieter because it had been let down by the postponements, or maybe it thought there was no cause for cheering until Colonel Glenn was safely returned.

There was noticeable excitement at 2:30 P.M. when somebody at the Holiday Inn's television set shouted, "He's coming down, he's on his way down!"

Nine-year-old Michael von Fremd of Bethesda, Md., jumped up and down.

"I knew things would go right today," said Mrs. Marion Fega of Los Angeles.

A few hours later, the happy trailer caravans began to leave the beach, where some had been entrenched more than a week. The drivers shook hands and promised to write.

"Today was the highlight of my life," said Ernest Perkins, gunning his motor and heading back to Toledo.

We can reconstruct the six questions asked by the writer of this article, as well as the answers:

1. Who (or what) was involved in the incident? (Fifty thousand spectators and Lieut. Col. John H. Glenn Jr.)
2. What was the incident? (The lift-off of the Atlas rocket carrying Glenn into orbit; the journalist examines the reaction of the spectators.)
3. Where did the incident occur? (Cocoa Beach, Florida.)
4. When did the incident occur (February 20, 1962, at 9:47 A.M.)
5. How did the incident occur? (The rocket rose slowly, then streaked out of sight; the spectators watched silently, for the most part, with looks of concern.)
6. Why did the incident occur? (The journalist speculates that the crowd might have been quiet because they had been let down by postponements or because they thought that there was no cause to cheer until Glenn had returned safely.)

Notice how the six questions generate additional questions, which contribute more details to the report:

1. Who were some of the spectators, by name and age?
2. What were the spectators doing during the liftoff? What did they do and say afterward?
3. Where did the spectators come from? Where did they go after the liftoff?
4. When did the crowd leave the beach?
5. How did the crowd's reaction compare to the reaction of the spectators at previous space shots? How did the crowd's reaction change after Glenn had landed?

Using the Journalist's Questions in Writing an Essay

The journalist's questions can be used for writing essays as well as newspaper or magazine articles. The responses of the essayist, however, may differ in form and substance from those of the journalist. Whereas the journalist usually writes under the pressure of a deadline, the essayist often has more time for contemplation and hence the opportunity to find longer and more fully developed answers to the six questions. Also, whereas a journalist is expected to record the facts as objectively as possible, an essayist is free to offer the most subjective insights into and interpretations of the facts.

The following questions are among those that an essayist may generate from the six basic ones:

Who   What must the reader know about the person or persons involved in order to understand what happened? What objective details must be included: age, appearance, social status, economic status, family relationships? What subjective elements about the person(s) should be supplied: background, philosophy, values, emotions?

What   What led up to the event? In what order did the stages of the event occur? Were there any foreshadowings of what was to come? What effect(s) did the event have, both immediate and long-range? What details must be included to convey the drama of the event to someone who was not there?

Where   How many locations are involved? How much description of the location(s) does the reader require? What details will convey the scene?

When   What time of day, what week, what year did the event occur? Of what significance was the date, the time of day, the weather?

How   In what way did the incident happen? How involved a description of the process is necessary? What details are required?

Why   Is the cause known for sure? Was there more than one cause? Was one person or thing more responsible than others? Can immediate causes be distinguished from distant ones? If there was no known cause, what interpretation can you bring to bear on the event? What general conclusions can be drawn?

Another major distinction between the essayist's responses and those of the journalist is the style in which they are written. The journalist tends to use a spare style, one stripped of those elements that personalize the essayist's work. Whereas the journalist tries consistently to sound direct, straightforward, and factual, the essayist may play more freely with such elements as tone of voice (see Chapter 1, pp. 14–22, and this chapter, p. 67); complex and varied sentence structuring (see Chapter 5, pp. 197–206, and Chapter 6, pp. 242–249); and comparisons such as metaphors, similes, and analogies (see this chapter, p. 64; Chapter 6, pp. 242–249; and Chapter 8, pp. 351–352; and Chapter 9, pp. 412–416).

Whereas the journalist, then, is usually concerned simply with reporting an event, the essayist may utilize fuller, more subjective responses and stylistic embellishments to dramatize the event, inviting the reader to participate in it vicariously. Put another way, whereas the journalist usually *tells* what happened, the essayist often *shows* what happened.

Finally, although in this chapter's task we will ask you to use the journalist's questions to report on an incident, you can also use these questions to develop ideas and information about many different topics. For example, if you were asked in an economics course to write an essay on a topic such as inflation, you might use the journalist's questions to develop information about what inflation is, who it affects and how, when and why it occurs, and so forth. Furthermore, although you may use all six questions in writing the narrative task for this chapter, other topics may require that you emphasize or focus on answers to only one or two of the questions. We encourage you, then, to use this method of generating ideas, along with others that we will introduce you to in later chapters, not only to complete the task at hand but also to develop ideas and information for other assignments in this and other courses.

SOME PRACTICE WITH THE JOURNALIST'S QUESTIONS

1. Read a newspaper article (preferably one that reports an event—a happening) and identify the answers to the journalist's six questions.

    a. Who?

    b. What?

    c. Where?

    d. When?

    e. How?

    f. Why?

2. a. Use the journalist's questions in order to gather information about an incident that you observed as an outsider rather than as a participant. Choose an incident that is limited in time and space, a distinct piece of action.

    b. Either with your class or on your own, analyze the details that you have gathered: How concrete, how specific, are they? Which aspect of the incident did you gather the most information about: The who? The what? The where? The when? The why? Or the how? Are there any questions that you have left unanswered? Did you describe actions and objects only, or did you also describe thoughts and feelings?

3. Reread the article by Gay Talese and then analyze the reporter's impressions. Was his information about the thoughts and feelings of the spectators factual? To what degree did Talese include his own subjective thoughts and feelings in the article?

4. Using the journalist's questions, develop an account of a historical event. The event may have occurred in the recent past, such as the explosion of the space shuttle Challenger, or in a distant time, such as the trial and sentencing of Socrates.

5. Using the journalist's questions, generate information that you might use in writing an account of your views on a topic that you are now studying in a class other than your English class.

ADDRESSING YOUR AUDIENCE: FRAME OF REFERENCE

Because the purpose of most writing, with the exception of the personal journal, is to communicate something to another person, you may find that you can write more effectively when you know, as well as you can, with whom you are communicating. Your audience—the people you write for—can affect both what you write about and the way in which you write about it. Just as you have attitudes toward your subject, so will your audience, and unless you consider your potential readers' attitudes as well as your own, you may be unable to keep your readers' attention; you might even offend them.

For example, pretend that you are going to write an essay entitled "The Facts of Life." Your audience is a class of first-graders and their mothers. What sort of essay would you write? What material would you include? What material would you exclude? What sort of tone would you adopt?

Now, change your audience. Pretend that you are writing the essay for a class of teenagers. Obviously, such an audience would be bored by the essay that you wrote for the class of first-graders. How might you write so as to capture the interest of the teenage students?

Your reader's attitudes should not necessarily affect the authenticity or truthfulness of your voice. But they may suggest adjustments in how you convey the truth of your subject. What these adjustments are and how they can be made is the subject of the "audience" section in Chapter 3 and of subsequent "audience" sections (see also in this chapter, pp. 63–65).

When you write, you are engaging in an activity that might be graphically portrayed as a triangle:

You are involved in both your own attitude and your reader's attitude toward the subject matter. These attitudes we will call *points of view*. In order to better understand each point of view, you will want to take into account what we will call the *frame of reference* both of yourself and of your reader.

The Writer's Frame of Reference

Whenever you write, you are discovering how you feel about your subject. How you feel and hence what you write are a reflection of who you are. You have a particular set of ideas and values because of where and how you have lived, whom you have known, what you have gone through, and what reading you have done. You come to your subject with a preconceived view of the world, and this view of the world, in turn, colors the way you perceive the subject: your *frame of reference* is your view of the world, which, in turn, determines your way of perceiving the subject, your *point of view.*

The way in which one's frame of reference influences one's point of view toward a subject can be illustrated by the following examples: If you are writing about space travel and are a socially concerned person, you might feel that tax dollars could be better spent on social programs. On the other hand, if you are a science major, you might support the point of view that space travel will contribute significantly to our expanding knowledge of the universe. Finally, if you are a science fiction fan, you might see space travel as providing an infinite range of exciting adventures. Your frame of reference will affect your view of your subject and hence how you write about it.

Or what if the topic is single parenthood? If you were a thirty-five-year-old divorced mother of three, had a very good job in a social service agency that was funding your education, loved your children, and were too busy to marry again at the moment, your point of view might be that under favorable economic and emotional conditions, single parenthood is a viable option. On the other hand, if you were raised by one parent who worked a double shift to support the family and had no time or energy left over for personal contact with family members, you might feel that single parenthood is a burden to the parent and inadequate for the children.

The following ten questions will help you to determine your own frame of reference:

1. How old are you?
2. Of what ethnic background are you? What economic or social class are you in?
3. Do you have a job or career? If so, what do you do? If not, what are your career plans?
4. Where were you born? Where do you live now?
5. What is your religious affiliation, if any?
6. Are you a member of a political party? If so, which one?
7. What roles do you play in your family?
8. What significant events have occurred in your life?
9. What are your hobbies or other leisure activities?
10. What are your goals for your life?

SOME PRACTICE WITH YOUR FRAME OF REFERENCE

How would your frame of reference, based on your answers to the preceding questions, affect your point of view on the following topics?

1. Single parenthood.

2. Chemical waste disposal.

3. Nuclear energy.

4. Nursing homes for the elderly.

5. The popularity of new religions.

SOME PRACTICE WITH YOUR POINT OF VIEW

1. a. Based on the details that you gathered by using the journalist's six questions (exercise 2a. on p. 54), write a one-paragraph description of the incident. Keep yourself completely outside the action. Just write what your sense impressions registered, what you saw and heard.

   b. Rewrite the paragraph, this time including your personal reactions, how you felt as an observer, and what thoughts went through your head.

   c. Rewrite the paragraph again, this time pretending that you were one of those involved in the incident.

d. Either with your class or on your own, analyze the point of view of each paragraph. Why did you choose to write about certain details in the first paragraph? How did your frame of reference affect your point of view in Paragraph 2 as opposed to Paragraph 1? How did your attitude toward the incident change in the third paragraph, when you imagined yourself in the shoes of one of the participants?

2. In the following paragraphs, part of an incident is described. Complete the narrative from the point when the performers begin to play:

> The performers entered forty minutes late, buttoning their shirts and adjusting the slings on their instruments as they moved to center stage. They bowed nervously, turned awkwardly to one another, then got ready to play.
>
> The audience had restrained itself for the first thirty minutes but grew noticeably restless in the last few minutes before the performers appeared. Several people were throwing empty cans and boxes toward the stage. Others were standing, directing their boos and cries to the absent performers.
>
> Several security police, hired for the occasion, paced the hall nervously, fearing an outburst of violence from the impatient crowd.

a. What does the ending that you have created reveal about your point of view toward the incident?

b. How might you have changed the ending you wrote if you were attempting to see the incident from the point of view of one of the performers, or of a member of the audience, or of a security police officer?

The Reader's Frame of Reference

Just as you have your frame of reference or set of attitudes, values, and beliefs, so do your readers. And your readers' frame of reference is probably different from yours. One way you can try to make sure that your essay communicates to them, that it has some meaning for them, is to set about purposefully to understand the frame of reference of your readers.

Knowing your readers' frame of reference, and hence their point of view on a subject about which you are writing, may result in many adjustments—some fine, some major—during the course of writing your paper. One student, about to write an essay for her classmates on her recently acquired ethnic pride in being a Lithuanian, came to realize that few of her readers had any notion of what this meant. She had to alter her expressive purpose by providing some exposition on what it meant to be Lithuanian. Because the class did understand what it meant to become aware of one's ethnic identity, the writer could use this frame of reference to build on, and she gained some new understanding of her experiences by learning how others had responded to theirs. Perhaps she learned more about her subject and its relation to her life by having to see it as others would. She was able to gain a certain distance from her subject, to see it from the perspective of others, and finally to see where she could meet her readers on a common ground. These are essential advantages in knowing your audience's point of view. They send you back to your writing with a sharpness and a clarity of purpose that you might not have gained otherwise.

Of course, even when you don't think about it consciously, you are making assumptions about your readers whenever you write. Take a look at the three descriptions of an incident that you wrote (Exercise 1, p. 57). What sort of unconscious assumptions did you make about your audience in each? Did you assume that they knew anything that, in reality, they might not? What details might you have explained more fully, so that someone who did not witness the incident could follow your description? Did the style and vocabulary of your descriptions suggest that you had a particular sort of reader in mind? Were you appealing more, for example, to your teacher or to your classmates?

SOME PRACTICE WITH A READER'S FRAME OF REFERENCE

1. a. Choose a classmate and construct his or her general frame of reference by asking the ten frame-of-reference questions (see p. 57).

   b. Using the information you gather, construct a brief biography of your classmate. If the responses to the frame-of-reference questions are not sufficient to construct a narrative, reinterview your subject in order to obtain fuller information. If necessary, prepare additional questions to ask.

2. What can you find out about the frame of reference of someone to whom you would feel uncomfortable asking some of the ten frame-of-reference questions, about a teacher, for example, to whom it might be tactless to ask questions about age, or economic background, or religious affiliation? Choose a course you are taking and phrase a set of questions you could ask the instructor about his or her knowledge of, attitude toward, and feelings about a topic discussed in the course. Which of the ten frame-of-reference questions might you also ask? How much can you learn about another's frame of reference this way?

SOME PRACTICE WITH A READER'S POINT OF VIEW

1. From the answers that you received when you interviewed your classmate, attempt to determine your classmate's attitude toward the five topics listed in ''Some Practice With Your Frame of Reference'' on page 57. If the answers are

not helpful, perhaps they were not specific enough. How might you reformulate your questions to elicit the information you need?

2. Each of the following passages offers a different impression of the same incident. Describe the point of view of the speaker in each case. What point of view might each take toward an incident that you observed recently. In each case, how would it compare with the point of view that you took?

   a. This crazed maniac walked into the college cafeteria, picked up a boiling-hot plate of soup, and dropped it over the head of this gorgeous, innocent blond. Everyone was simply mortified by this sickie's routine. He should get twenty years.

   b. You should have seen the hysterical performance in the college caf yesterday. This clown poured some red stuff on his girlfriend's goofy bleached head and broke the whole place up. They should do their act on the stage--they were a riot.

   c. A riot call placed from the Holbrook College Cafeteria was responded to immediately by Patrolman Hodges, who found Jack Jenkins, the alleged perpetrator, with an empty plastic dish standing next to the plaintiff, Betty Lou Jones, a student at the college. Several witnesses were questioned. An investigation is under way.

   d. If you want some idea of today's college student, you should see what goes on in the cafeteria. Two students, I am told, acted in the kind of barbaric manner suggested in the movie Animal House. What can you expect with the kind of music they play over the loudspeakers there?

Making Inferences About Your Reader

We regularly make inferences about other people, assumptions about what they are like or how they will react to us. We base these inferences on our observations of their appearance, conversation, and other aspects of their behavior. For example, you may decide that you want to make friends with one person but not with another, because of the first impression each makes on you. Based on what is undoubtedly partial evidence, you infer that one will be worth having as a friend yet the other will not.

As a writer, the inferences you make about your potential readers will help you adjust what and how you write so that others will understand and appreciate you better. Inference, in fact, may be the only way that you can easily and quickly determine vital information concerning the frame of reference and point of view of a large group of potential readers. With most groups, you can go a long way in inferring the answers to the ten frame-of-reference questions. You will, of course, have to generalize about the group and not record data about individual members. The general frame of reference of a group would include the following information:

1. Age.
2. Ethnic background, education, and economic and social class.
3. Occupation (or career plans).
4. Place of habitation.
5. Religious affiliation.
6. Political affiliation.
7. Family structure.
8. Significant experiences (shared by the group).
9. Leisure interest and activities.
10. Goals.

SOME PRACTICE WITH INFERENCE

1. Using your class that has the largest enrollment this semester, infer the class's frame of reference. Then determine the point of view of the majority of the students on the following topics:

   a. Teacher–student relationships.

   b. Coed dormitories.

   c. The student newspaper.

   d. Abortion.

   On what basis have you inferred the group's attitude in each case?

2. A certain student in your English class has freely voiced her opinions that children should be strictly disciplined, that marijuana use should remain illegal, and that juvenile offenders should be prosecuted as adults. Therefore it would be reasonable, if you were writing to her, to infer that she believes that society needs strict discipline. What do you think her point of view would be on the following issues? Formulate one or more statements on each topic that you think would represent her point of view:

   a. Alimony.

   b. A worker's right to strike.

   c. The draft.

   d. Children's rights.

TASK: WRITING ABOUT AN INCIDENT

To begin the task for this chapter, search your memory for an incident that you observed or were involved in that abruptly changed your mood or your thoughts, that suddenly caused you to reassess your feelings toward or attitudes about something, and that thus in some way affected your life. This may be an event that impressed you when you were younger, or it may be a more recent event. Try to focus on an incident that occurred over the course of a few hours or a few days, but not beyond a week; then record the incident in detail, clarifying for the reader the important aspects of the experience, as well as what you think its significance was for you.

We suggest that you devote special attention to specific details in order to make your account of the incident vivid and authentic. The journalist's questions can help you to recall such details. Also, you will want to pay attention to the arrangement of your details, so that you can offer your readers a clear sense of the chronology of the incident, of the order in which the events of your story unfolded.

Your peers are the most likely audience for this essay. They may have experienced an incident similar to yours and therefore are likely to prove both interested and sympathetic readers. But even though you will be writing to an audience whose frame of reference is similar to your own, you cannot expect the group as a whole to understand all of your perceptions and feelings automatically. Subtle differences in point of view will have to be bridged, as they always must be, even between the closest of friends.

In the remaining sections of this chapter, we will discuss how to use the journalist's questions to generate ideas about your subject, how to build bridges between you and your readers, how to arrange the details of your incident, how to move into your rough draft, and how to revise your essay.

WRITING THE ESSAY

Using the Journalist's Questions

Once you have decided on an incident to write about, begin recalling and recording as much specific and related information as possible about your subject. Earlier in the chapter, you were introduced to the journalist's method of search and discovery, and you can use this method to discover relevant and telling details about the event that you have chosen as the subject of your essay. Apply the six questions of the news reporter to the event.

After you have generated information from the six basic questions, see if further questions arise, those subquestions that it is the luxury of the essayist to answer (see p. 53). Answer these as well. Do not worry if you seem to have a lot of information; when you begin to arrange your essay, you will probably discard some of it. If, however, you find that you lack specifics, that is cause for worry; you might need to go out and gather more information from other sources, such as relatives, friends, diaries, journals, photographs, and your own memories.

Your own journal can be helpful here. It can be used, for example, as a reporter's notebook in which you gather details of incidents that you observe during the next few days and that seem like potentially good subjects for your essay. Or, you can use the journal like a diary to probe your memory for incidents from the past worth writing about. In either case, if you collect details in your journal, you then can go back and read over them in order to assess your thoughts and feelings about how an incident affected you.

Determining Your Audience's Frame of Reference

As indicated in the description of the task (p. 62), you are writing this essay to be read by your peers—probably the members of your freshman composition class.

An earlier section of this chapter discussed the importance of discovering the frame of reference of your audience. Now try using either direct questioning or inference (see pp. 58–61) to determine the frame of reference of your peers and hence how their point of view toward the incident that you are writing about might differ from yours. An incident that you found shocking, for example, they may feel more blasé about. Consider a student who wrote about the upsetting effect of finding her car vandalized on the city street outside her own house. She needed to find ways to bridge the gap between her point of view and that of an audience of her fellow students, most of whom, on the one hand, had not been similarly victimized and, on the other hand, were used to hearing about such acts of random violence both in the news and from their neighbors and acquaintances. For these reasons, they felt less shocked reading about the incident than the victim herself felt experiencing it firsthand. She had to look at the incident from their perspective as well as her own, in order to begin finding ways to help them understand and appreciate her response.

Bridging the Gap Between Your Audience's Point of View and Your Own

Evaluating the point of view of your audience may lead you to explain things that you might have assumed were clear enough, had you not considered your reader(s). We will look into this subject at greater length in the "audience" sections of subsequent chapters. What we would like you to consider right now is how your knowledge of your audience's point of view may help you, when you are writing expressively, to show rather than simply to tell what your experiences, thoughts, and feelings are, to be, in Ken Macrorie's term, as "truthful as possible" (see Chapter 1, pp. 16–20).

For one thing, taking your audience and their perspective into account might lead you to describe details of an experience you are narrating that you otherwise might not have thought to describe. For example, it would be simple enough to *tell* your audience that an incident occurred on a romantic night. But if you want to *show* the audience how romantic the night was, you need to describe details that not only you but your readers will feel made the night romantic. The fact that it was the night of your senior prom might not touch a romantic chord in older readers, who probably are too far removed from their high-school days to share a senior's thrill over prom night. For such an audience, other details would have to be emphasized, perhaps the soft summer breeze and the clear, star-filled sky, to help them feel the romance of the evening.

Another way that you might use your knowledge of your audience to help them enter into an experience that you have had is to employ dialogue in your narration of the experience. Re-creating in your narrative the details of a dialogue that occurred between you and someone whose point of view reflects thoughts and feelings that your audience might have should help your audience experience the incident more vividly.

Taking the point of view of your audience into account might also lead you to create analogies so that your readers can relate to your thoughts and feelings in terms of thoughts and feelings more familiar to them, and so that they can share your thoughts and feelings rather than simply being told about them. For example, what if you are a long-distance runner, and you want to show your readers—in this case your fellow students, many of whom are not athletes—what it felt like the first time you won a race? You might compare your feelings about winning to the sort of feelings many students have after a marathon study session that results in their scoring well on an exam.

Finally, your choice of words will be influenced by your knowledge of your audience. If you want to bridge the distance between your readers and you, if you want them to see as you saw and feel as you felt, you must be careful to employ language that they will understand and appreciate. Your peers may be drawn into your narrative if you employ the latest slang, but older readers may simply be put off. For some readers, you will use a more formal, sophisticated vocabulary; for others, a plainer, simpler one. Your analysis of your audience should help you to make adjustments not only in what you write but also in how you write it.

Answering the following questions of the "Audience Analysis Guide" will help you prepare to write for your audience:

─────── **AUDIENCE ANALYSIS GUIDE** ───────

1. Who is my audience?
2. What is the frame of reference of this audience?
3. What point of view is my audience likely to have on my subject?
4. How do my own frame of reference and point of view differ from those of my audience?
5. How can I bridge any gap that exists between my audience's point of view and my own?

Arranging Your Essay: Narration

Once you have discovered, through the journalist's questions, something to say about your subject and have formulated your answers to the "Audience Analysis Guide" you are faced with the problem of selecting and arranging the material in the order that best serves your purpose. You will want to formulate a shaping idea that indicates what significance the incident had for you. Then, in telling your story, you can select from the details that you have gathered those that are the most relevant and memorable and omit those that are unimportant and unnecessary. The next step is to arrange your material in such a way that you clearly convey the event to your readers, emphasizing its most important aspects and what it means to you.

Duration. How do you decide on a particular order or arrangement of ideas for this chapter's essay? You are being asked to write about an event that took place in the past. You are being asked to elaborate on the journalist's question "What happened?" You can answer this question in several ways, depending on the purpose that you have in mind. First, you might decide to write a straightforward, chronological narrative that describes the event just as it occurred in time: an A-to-Z arrangement, with A as the beginning of the event and Z as the end. In the following selection, "The Angry Winter," Loren Eiseley used an A-to-Z arrangement, taking us through a series of steps in an incident that began when he laid a fossil bone on the floor of his study.

The Angry Winter
Loren Eiseley

As to what happened next, it is possible to maintain that the hand of heaven was involved, and also possible to say that when men are desperate no one can stand up to them.   —XENOPHON

A time comes when creatures whose destinies have crossed somewhere in the remote past are forced to appraise each other as though they were total strangers. I had been huddled beside the fire one winter night, with the wind prowling outside and shaking the windows. The big shepherd dog on the hearth before me occasionally glanced up affectionately, sighed, and slept. I was working, actually, amidst the debris of a far greater winter. On my desk lay the lance points of ice age hunters and the heavy leg bone of a fossil bison. No remnants of flesh attached to these relics. The deed lay more than ten thousand years remote. It was represented here by naked flint and by bone so mineralized it rang when struck. As I worked on in my little circle of light, I absently laid the bone beside me on the floor. The hour had crept toward midnight. A grating noise, a heavy rasping of big teeth diverted me. I looked down.

The dog had risen. That rock-hard fragment of a vanished beast was in his jaws and he was mouthing it with a fierce intensity I had never seen exhibited by him before.

"Wolf," I exclaimed, and stretched out my hand. The dog backed up but did not yield. A low and steady rumbling began to rise in his chest, something out of a long-gone midnight. There was nothing in that bone to taste, but ancient shapes were moving in his mind and determining his utterance. Only fools gave up bones. He was warning me.

"Wolf," I chided again.

As I advanced, his teeth showed and his mouth wrinkled to strike. The rumbling rose to a direct snarl. His flat head swayed low and wickedly as a reptile's above the floor. I was the most loved object in his universe, but the past was fully alive in him now. Its shadows were whispering in his mind. I knew he was not bluffing. If I made another step he would strike.

Yet his eyes were strained and desperate. "Do not," something pleaded in the back of them, some affectionate thing that had followed at my heel all the days of his mortal life, "do not force me. I am what I am and cannot be otherwise because of the shadows. Do not reach out. You are a man, and my very god. I love you, but do not put out your hand. It is midnight. We are in another time, in the snow."

"The *other* time," the steady rumbling continued while I paused, "the other time in the snow, the big, the final, the terrible snow, when the shape of this thing I hold spelled life. I will not give it up. I cannot. The shadows will not permit me. Do not put out your hand."

I stood silent, looking into his eyes, and heard his whisper through. Slowly I drew back in understanding. The snarl diminished, ceased. As I retreated, the bone slumped to the floor. He placed a paw upon it, warningly.

And were there no shadows in my own mind, I wondered. Had I not for a moment, in the grip of that savage utterance, been about to respond, to hurl myself upon him over an invisible haunch ten thousand years removed? Even to me the shadows had whispered—to me, the scholar in his study.

"Wolf," I said, but this time, holding a familiar leash. I spoke from the door indifferently. "A walk in the snow." Instantly from his eyes that other visitant receded. The bone was left lying. He came eagerly to my side, accepting the leash and taking it in his mouth as always.

A blizzard was raging when we went out, but he paid no heed. On his thick fur the driving snow was soon clinging heavily. He frolicked a little—though usually he was a grave dog—making up to me for something still receding in his mind. I felt the snowflakes fall upon my face, and stood thinking of another time, and another time still, until I was moving from midnight to midnight under *ever more remote and vaster snows.* Wolf came to my side with a little whimper. It was he who was civilized now. "Come back to the fire," he nudged gently, "or you will be lost." Automatically I took the leash he offered. He led me safely home and into the house.

"We have been very far away," I told him solemnly. "I think there is something in us that we had both better try to forget." Sprawled on the rug, Wolf made no response except to thump his tail feebly out of courtesy. Already he was mostly asleep and dreaming. By the movement of his feet I could see he was running far upon some errand in which I played no part.

Softly I picked up his bone—our bone, rather—and replaced it high on a shelf in my cabinet. As I snapped off the light the white glow from the window seemed to augment itself and shine with a deep, glacial blue. As far as I could see, nothing moved in the long aisles of my neighbor's woods. There was no visible track, and certainly no sound from the living. The snow continued to fall steadily, but the wind, and the shadows it had brought, had vanished.

Eiseley narrated the incident in a step-by-step fashion. He omitted few steps between the beginning and the end, perhaps because the incident took a relatively short time. Are there moments in the incident that you would like to know more about? To what degree did Eiseley record objective facts? To what degree is the focus of his essay more on his subjective insights into and interpretations of the facts?

The longer the incident about which you are writing, of course, the more decisions you must make about which steps should be omitted from your narrative, which should be given only passing attention, and which should be emphasized with detail. Both your own point of view and that of your audience should be taken into consideration when you determine what parts of your narrative to emphasize or deemphasize.

What is Eiseley's shaping idea? Where does it occur in the essay?

What is Eiseley's point of view in his narrative? Is he serious, reasonable, scientific? What does he express about himself? How would you compare his voice to that of Gay Talese in his article about spectators who witnessed John Glenn's space shot? How do you account for any differences? What sort of assumptions did Eiseley seem to make about his audience's frame of reference and point of view?

Details.   As we have suggested, in writing your narrative it will help you to keep in mind that your readers want to become a part of what happened; they want to see and hear what you did. This is one reason for you to include memorable and relevant details conveyed in vivid language, including details of dialogue. Further, analogy might be used to help your readers share your thoughts and feelings about the incident.

Every detail included should contribute to what you want your readers to know and feel about the event. These details should elaborate the who, where, when, and how of your incident. The why and what may be answered through more direct statement. At the same time, irrelevant details should be omitted.

Reread the essay by Loren Eiseley, paying close attention to how the author used details to retell an event.

Now answer the following questions:

1. What role do the following details play in the essay?
   • winter
   • wind
   • fire and light
   • midnight
   • snow
   • shadows
2. The author mentioned in the first paragraph that the dog "glanced up affectionately." What role does this detail play in the story? Why did he add that the dog was big?
3. What details did Eiseley include to convey the dog's metamorphosis into a fierce beast? What further details dramatize the ambivalence that the dog feels about his new ferocity?

In the next selection, Maya Angelou does not begin to narrate her incident until the fifteenth paragraph. What does she write about first, and why? How does her long introduction help to bridge the gap between her point of view and that of her readers? What assumptions does she make about her readers' frame of reference and point of view? How has her own point of view changed since that time in her childhood when she experienced the incident?

Momma's Private Victory

Maya Angelou

"Momma's Private Victory" (editor's title) is the fifth chapter of Angelou's book *I Know Why the Caged Bird Sings.* Since their early childhood, she and her brother, who was a year older, had lived with their grandmother ("Momma" of the narrative), who operated a store in the front room of her home in the black section of their small Arkansas town.

"Thou shall not be dirty" and "Thou shall not be impudent" were the two commandments of Grandmother Henderson upon which hung our total salvation.

Each night in the bitterest winter we were forced to wash faces, arms, necks, legs and feet before going to bed. She used to add, with a smirk that unprofane people can't control when venturing into profanity, "and wash as far as possible, then wash possible."

We would go to the well and wash in the ice-cold, clear water, grease our legs with the equally cold stiff Vaseline, then tiptoe into the house. We wiped the dust from our toes and settled down for schoolwork, cornbread, clabbered milk, prayers and bed, always in that order. Momma was famous for pulling the quilts off after we had fallen asleep to examine our feet. If they weren't clean enough for her, she took the switch (she kept one behind the bedroom door for emergencies) and woke up the offender with a few aptly placed burning reminders.

The area around the well at night was dark and slick, and boys told about how snakes love water, so that anyone who had to draw water at night and then stand there alone and wash knew that moccasins and rattlers, puff adders and boa constrictors were winding their way to the well and would arrive just as the person washing got soap in her eyes. But Momma convinced us that not only was cleanliness next to Godliness, dirtiness was the inventor of misery.

The impudent child was detested by God and a shame to its parents and could bring destruction to its house and line. All adults had to be addressed as Mister, Missus, Miss, Auntie, Cousin, Unk, Uncle, Buhbah, Sister, Brother and a thousand other appellations indicating familial relationship and the lowliness of the addressor.

Everyone I knew respected these customary laws, except for the powhitetrash children.

Some families of powhitetrash lived on Momma's farm land behind the school. Sometimes a gaggle of them came to the Store, filling the whole room, chasing out the air and even changing the well-known scents. The children crawled over the shelves and into the potato and onion bins, twanging all the time in their sharp voices like cigar-box guitars. They took liberties in my Store that I would never dare. Since Momma told us that the less you say to white-folks (or even powhitetrash) the better, Bailey and I would stand, solemn, quiet, in the displaced air. But if one of the playful apparitions got close to us, I pinched it. Partly out of angry frustration and partly because I didn't believe in its flesh reality.

They called my uncle by his first name and ordered him around the Store. He, to my crying shame, obeyed them in his limping dip-straight-dip fashion.

My grandmother, too, followed their orders, except that she didn't seem to be servile because she anticipated their needs.

"Here's sugar, Miz Potter, and here's baking powder. You didn't buy soda last month, you'll probably be needing some."

Momma always directed her statements to the adults, but sometimes, Oh painful sometimes, the grimy, snotty-nosed girls would answer her.

"Naw, Annie . . ."—to Momma? Who owned the land they lived on? Who forgot more than they would ever learn? If there was any justice in the world, God should strike them dumb at once!—"Just give us some extra sody crackers, and some more mackerel."

At least they never looked in her face, or I never caught them doing so. Nobody with a smidgen of training, not even the worst roustabout, would look right in a grown person's face. It meant the person was trying to take the words out before they were formed. The dirty little children didn't do that, but they threw their orders around the Store like lashes from a cat-o'-nine-tails.

When I was around ten years old, those scruffy children caused me the most painful and confusing experience I had ever had with my grandmother.

One summer morning, after I had swept the dirt yard of leaves, spearmint-gum wrappers and Vienna-sausage labels, I raked the yellow-red dirt, and made half-moons carefully, so that the design stood out clearly and mask-like. I put the rake behind the Store and came through the back of the house to find Grandmother on the front porch in her big, wide white apron. The apron was so stiff by virtue of the starch that it could have stood alone. Momma was admiring the yard, so I joined her. It truly looked like a flat redhead that had been raked with a big-toothed comb. Momma didn't say anything but I knew she liked it. She looked over toward the school principal's house and to the right at Mr. McElroy's. She was hoping one of those community pillars would see the design before the day's business wiped it out. Then she looked upward to the school. My head had swung with hers, so at just about the same time we saw a troop of the powhitetrash kids marching over the hill and down by the side of the school.

I looked to Momma for direction. She did an excellent job of sagging from her waist down, but from the waist up she seemed to be pulling for the top of the oak tree across the road. Then she began to moan a hymn. Maybe not to moan, but the tune was so slow and the meter so strange that she could have been moaning. She didn't look at me again. When the children reached halfway down the hill, halfway to the Store, she said without turning, "Sister, go on inside."

I wanted to beg her, "Momma, don't wait for them. Come on inside with me. If they come in the Store, you go to the bedroom and let me wait on them. They only frighten me if you're around. Alone I know how to handle them." But of course I couldn't say anything, so I went in and stood behind the screen door.

Before the girls got to the porch I heard their laughter crackling and popping like pine logs in a cooking stove. I suppose my lifelong paranoia was born in those cold, molasses-slow minutes. They came finally to stand on the ground in front of Momma. At first they pretended seriousness. Then one of them wrapped her right arm in the crook of her left, pushed out her mouth and started to hum. I realized that she was aping my grandmother. Another said, "Naw, Helen, you ain't standing like her. This here's it." Then she lifted her chest, folded her arms and mocked that strange carriage that was Annie Henderson. Another laughed, "Naw, you can't do it. Your mouth ain't pooched out enough. It's like this."

I thought about the rifle behind the door, but I knew I'd never be able to hold it straight, and the .410, our sawed-off shotgun, which stayed loaded and was fired every New Year's night, was locked in the trunk and Uncle Willie had the key on his chain. Through the fly-specked screen-door, I could see that the arms of Momma's apron jiggled from the vibrations of her humming. But her knees seemed to have locked as if they would never bend again.

She sang on. No louder than before, but no softer either. No slower or faster.

The dirt of the girls' cotton dresses continued on their legs, feet, arms and faces to make them all of a piece. Their greasy uncolored hair hung down, uncombed, with a grim finality. I knelt to see them better, to remember them for all time. The tears that had slipped down my dress left unsurprising dark spots, and made the front yard blurry and even more unreal. The world had taken a deep breath and was having doubts about continuing to revolve.

The girls had tired of mocking Momma and turned to other means of agitation.

One crossed her eyes, stuck her thumbs in both sides of her mouth and said, "Look here, Annie." Grandmother hummed on and the apron strings trembled. I wanted to throw a handful of black pepper in their faces, to throw lye on them, to scream that they were dirty, scummy peckerwoods, but I knew I was as clearly imprisoned behind the scene as the actors outside were confined to the roles.

One of the smaller girls did a kind of puppet dance while her fellow clowns laughed at her. But the tall one, who was almost a woman, said something very quietly, which I couldn't hear. They all moved backward from the porch, still watching Momma. For an awful second I thought they were going to throw a rock at Momma, who seemed (except for the apron strings) to have turned into stone herself. But the big girl turned her back, bent down and put her hands flat on the ground—she didn't pick up anything. She simply shifted her weight and did a hand stand.

Her dirty bare feet and long legs went straight for the sky. Her dress fell down around her shoulders, and she had on no drawers. The slick pubic hair made a brown triangle where her legs came together. She hung in the vacuum of that lifeless morning for only a few seconds, then wavered and tumbled. The other girls clapped her on the back and slapped her hands.

Momma changed her song to "Bread of Heaven, bread of Heaven, feed me till I want no more."

I found that I was praying too. How long could Momma hold out? What new indignity would they think of to subject her to? Would I be able to stay out of it? What would Momma really like me to do?

Then they were moving out of the yard, on their way to town. They bobbed their heads and shook their slack behinds and turned, one at a time:

" 'Bye, Annie."

" 'Bye, Annie."

" 'Bye, Annie."

Momma never turned her head or unfolded her arms, but she stopped singing and said, " 'Bye, Miz Helen, 'bye, Miz Ruth, 'bye, Miz Eloise."

I burst. A firecracker July-the-Fourth burst. How could Momma call them Miz? The mean nasty things. Why couldn't she have come inside the sweet, cool store when we saw them breasting the hill? What did she prove? And then if they were dirty, mean and impudent, why did Momma have to call them Miz?

She stood another whole song through and then opened the screen door to look down on me crying in rage. She looked until I looked up. Her face was a brown moon that shone on me. She was beautiful. Something had happened out there, which I couldn't completely understand, but I could see that she was happy. Then she bent down and touched me as mothers of the church "lay hands on the sick and afflicted" and I quieted.

"Go wash your face, Sister." And she went behind the candy counter and hummed, "Glory, glory, hallelujah, when I lay my burden down."

I threw the well water on my face and used the weekday handkerchief to blow my nose. Whatever the contest had been out front, I knew Momma had won.

I took the rake back to the front yard. The smudged footprints were easy to erase. I worked for a long time on my new design and laid the rake behind the wash pot. When I came back to the Store, I took Momma's hand and we both walked outside to look at the pattern.

It was a large heart with lots of hearts growing smaller inside, and piercing from the outside rim to the smallest heart was an arrow. Momma said, "Sister, that's right pretty." Then she turned back to the Store and resumed, "Glory, glory, hallelujah, when I lay my burden down."

Like Eiseley, Angelou relies on details of scene, action, and dialogue to re-create the incident for her readers. Which details stand out most vividly for you as a reader? What effect does the incident have on you? What effect did it have on Angelou?

Now look at the rough draft of a student's essay on an incident in which she was involved. Note that, like Eiseley, the student begins her narrative immediately and arranges the details of it in fairly strict chronological order. Might she have improved the draft by delaying the start of her narrative and including, as Angelou did, an introduction with background material?

THE INCIDENT
(WORKING TITLE)

The beautiful, sunny day gave no hint as to what had happened. It was Monday, March 31, 1986, at 1 PM, and Gregory (my son, aged 6 years and one day) and I were leaving the house to pick up Aunt Barbara and cousin Lee. The spring vacation had started the Friday before, and the unusually temperate weather afforded us the opportunity to spend time outdoors. We were supposed to be at Barbara's house at 1:15, and then we would go out for lunch together and afterwards, to a park. There was no way I could have anticipated the occurrence that was to completely ruin our day.

Greg and I were approaching the car when I noticed the broken glass. I warned him to be careful and started to put the key in the door. That was when I noticed that the fragments and shards had come from my car's sideview mirror. My first thought was that someone had "accidentally' broken the mirror with a rock, ball, or similar projectile. I was just about to usher Greg into the car (my first stop being the service station, to inquire about a replacement mirror), when I noticed the additional damage. The windshield wipers were not merely snapped off, but forcibly ripped from the hood; the antenna was completely broken off, and it lay in the gutter. Even the small plaques, announcing the name of the car, were pulled off. (The molding had torn off years before.) Then I noticed the four flat tires.

Why would anybody do this? It's not as if anyone could possibly be jealous that I own this car. It's a 1972 Ford Maverick--it runs, but the body is half rusted away, and it sounds like a centennial Fourth of July celebration. Nobody could have profited financially from the destruction. What was the purpose? And why my car?

These questions ran through my mind; but rather than analyze the situation, I just felt an overwhelming anger. I also felt helpless and frightened that I wouldn't have the money needed to fix the car. (It's our only car, and we use it for work, school, shopping, the doctor, etc.) So I did the only thing I could. I cried in frustration. Then I started ringing the doorbells of almost every neighbor on our block. Nobody had heard or seen anything.

So I called the police. The first precinct I called couldn't respond, because although I live in Flushing and the 109th is in Flushing, my area is covered by a precinct located in Bayside. Finally I reached the 111th Precinct and relayed my story. They said they'd send a patrol car. Then I called my husband, Marty, at work. I wept and complained into the phone, and I asked if he could come home early, as I was very upset. (He agreed.) At about 1:30, I remembered about Barbara and Lee. Since they were waiting outside at home, it took about 15 rings for Barbara to answer the telephone. I told her about my car having been vandalized and, obviously, cancelled our plans for the afternoon. She asked if there was anything that she could do, and I told her that I'd call back later if we needed a ride anywhere. Luckily, Greg was busy with my upstairs neighbor's kids for the last half hour or so, leaving me free to make phone calls.

Coincidentally, my friend Julie stopped over a few minutes later, and we commiserated. Her car had been stolen, damaged, and recovered twice in the last 4 months! She gave me the opportunity to vent some of my anger and verbalize all the things I wanted to do to whomever had attacked my car.

Just as Julie was leaving, at 2:30, the police arrived. The two officers and I walked over to the car. One was especially grim-faced, and they both looked like they'd rather be anywhere else. Their attitudes reflected boredom, but they asked me a few questions, nonetheless. They wanted to know if anybody held a grudge against me, or if I had cut someone off recently while driving. Then they asked if either my husband or myself were teachers, having noticed my college parking sticker. The friendlier of the two patrolmen, a tall, slim, good-looking man of about forty-five, said that it was very common for students to do things like this to a teacher that had failed them, etc. I said that neither of us were teachers, and I had no idea who could have done this. The other officer, shorter and stockier, was writing up a report. He said that he felt the act of violence had been deliberately aimed at us. He didn't feel it was a prank (it was, indeed, one day before April Fool's Day) acted out by fun-loving, healthy teenagers. He thought that the damage was too extensive and, also, that it was unusual for such an old, beat-up car to be the random victim of this type of act.

Marty appeared at this moment and asked the police to see if they could get any fingerprints off the car. They made a call on their radio and said that the print team would come over later that day. (They did, but the effort proved fruitless.)

Before 3, the police left, and Marty and I went inside. I called the Mobil Auto Club, and they sent someone over to inflate the tires. We had already determined that they didn't appear to be slashed. Then Marty drove the car to a nearby service station.

All in all, the car was "patched up" for $100, which I put on my Sunoco credit card. I had the Maverick back by the next afternoon. But for the next 2 weeks, I woke up every night at about 3 A.M. and stared out the window, to see if my car had been vandalized again. The police had indicated that deliberate attacks are usually repeated, and I was as paranoid as I could possibly be. I felt scared and terribly violated. I also worried that this type of violence could extend to myself or my family.

I'm happy to say that there has been no repeat performance. However, although almost four months have passed since the incident, I still approach my car a little warily every morning. I don't understand senseless violence, and I don't think I ever will.

How effective is this student's use of details? Are there any details that need to be more fully developed? Are there any that seem overemphasized? How well does the writer show rather than tell about the incident as well as the effect that it had on her? How well does she bridge the gap between her readers' point of view and her own?

Like the student who wrote this essay, you may want to follow a strict chronological order from A to Z in arranging the details of your narrative. Or, like Angelou, you may decide to offer background information first, to help the reader see the incident from your point of view. The latter tactic also may help to heighten the drama of the narration. So might the use of a flashback technique, in which you begin at the end, perhaps with the overall effect of the incident on you, or in the middle, and then flash back to earlier events. Thus, you may go from Z to A or from M to A to Z.

Arranging the Details of Your Essay.   Try the following procedure in organizing your essay: make a list of the stages in your incident, arranging them in the order that you think is most effective: A to Z, Z to A to Z, or M to A to Z; asterisk those aspects of the incident that you think are the most important; cross out those aspects that do not contribute much to what you wish to convey about your incident; beside each stage, jot down those details that you feel are necessary to convey the importance of each stage and the overall significance of the event.

Writing the Rough Draft

All of the preceding sections in "Writing the Essay" have prepared you to write your essay on an incident. It is now time to write it.

In Chapter 1, we suggested that different people go about writing in different ways. Just how you go about writing your rough draft, just what process you employ in getting the words down on paper, is a personal matter. Perhaps you are beginning to find that the words come more easily to you if you write freely at first, without stopping to edit your sentence structure or the arrangement of your details. Perhaps you do better if you focus on one paragraph at a time, working each paragraph into as final a shape as you can before moving on to the next.

Perhaps you will want to start your rough draft by writing down your shaping idea and then reviewing the list of concrete details that you put together by answering the journalist's questions. By now, you may also have decided on a rough pattern of arrangement, both details and arrangement chosen with the audience's point of view in mind. Now place yourself in your chosen spot for writing and begin.

Once you start, keep on going. Refer to your notes on details, audience, and arrangement as often as you need to. Bear in mind the need for chronological sequencing and specific details. Write through to the end in one sitting.

FOCUS: TRANSITIONS

Transitions are words and phrases that establish connections between words, sentences, and paragraphs. Through the use of transitions, the writer emphasizes the coherence of the essay for the reader. The most common form of transition is the conjunction. Conjunctions form such connections between thoughts as addition *(and)*, contrast *(but)*, comparison *(as)*, causation *(for)*, choice *(or)*, process *(after)*, and chronology *(before)*. Transitional phrases can also be employed to make the same connections, for example, "in addition," "on the other hand," "as well as," "as a result," and "after a while."

A second means of creating transitions between thoughts is to refer to the shaping idea throughout the essay by repeating the key words that you have used to express it (or synonyms or pronouns clearly referring to it). The repetition of key words assures the reader of the unity of the paper and of its development of one main point.

In Passage 1, following, most of the transitions have been omitted. After reading the first passage, read Passage 2. Does the writing in the second version seem much clearer with the transitions (underlined) restored?

Passage 1
I think I was in the first press bus. I can't be sure. Pete Lisagor of the *The Chicago Daily News* says he was in the bus. He describes things that went on aboard it that didn't happen on the bus I went in. I think I was in the bus.

Confusion is the way it was in Dallas in the early afternoon of Nov. 22. No one knew what happened, or how, or where, much less why. Bits and pieces fell together. A reasonably coherent version of the story was possible. I know no reporter who was there who has a clear and orderly picture of the afternoon; it is a matter of bits and pieces thrown hastily into something like a whole.

Passage 2
I think I was in the first press bus. But I can't be sure. Pete Lisagor of *The Chicago Daily News* says he knows he was in the first press bus and he describes things that went on aboard it that didn't happen on the bus I was in. But I still think I was in the first press bus.

I cite that minor confusion as an example of the way it was in Dallas in the early afternoon of Nov. 22. At first no one knew what happened, or how, or where, much less why. Gradually, bits and pieces began to fall together, and within two hours a reasonably coherent version of the story began to be possible. Even now, however, I know no reporter who has a clear and orderly picture of that surrealistic afternoon; it is still a matter of bits and pieces thrown hastily into something like a whole.

—**Tom Wicker,** *Times Talk,* 1963

In analyzing Tom Wicker's use of transitions in Passage 2, you might notice first that he used words like *but, and, or,* and *however* to form very specific connections (addition, choice, and contrast) between his words, phrases, sentences, and even paragraphs.

Second, as Wicker was narrating the events on the day of the assassination of John F. Kennedy, he used many conjunctive words and phrases that indicate chronology, thus clarifying the sequence of events: "at first," "gradually," "within two hours," "even now," and "still."

Finally, he inserted key words in every sentence. This repetition of key words builds bridges by establishing that his sentences and paragraphs cluster around his shaping idea, the confusion surrounding the president's assassination. This shaping idea is conveyed through the use of the key word *bus* in the first paragraph and the use of the word *confusion* and its synonyms *bits and pieces* and *surrealistic afternoon* in the second. Even the demonstrative adjective *that* is used several times to refer to the confusion of that afternoon. (The demonstrative adjectives *this, that, these,* and *those* also act as transitions.)

As a further example, notice the use of transitional words and phrases in the following paragraph:

William Wolcott died and went to heaven. Or so it — *Shaping key idea*
seemed. Before being wheeled to the operating table, — *Conjunction indicating*
he had been reminded that the surgical procedure would   *beginning of*
entail a certain risk. The operation was a success but just   *chronology*
as the anesthesia was wearing off, his heart went into   *Conjunction*
fibrillation and he died. It seemed to him that he had   *establishing a*
somehow left his body and was able to look down upon   *contrast of ideas*
it, withered and pathetic, lying on a hard and unforgiv-   *Repetition of key idea*
ing surface. He was only a little sad, regarded his body
one last time—from a great height, it seemed—and con-   *Conjunctions and other*
tinued a kind of upward journey. While his surroundings   *words that establish*
had been suffused by a strange permeating darkness, he   *chronology*
realized that things were now getting brighter—looking
up, you might say. And then he was being illuminated
from a distance, flooded with light. He entered a kind of
radiant kingdom and there, just ahead of him, he could
make out in silhouette, magnificently lit from behind, a   *Repetition of key idea*
great godlike figure whom he was now effortlessly ap-
proaching. Wolcott strained to make out His face . . .
And then awoke. In the hospital operating room, where — *Conjunction of*
the defibrillation machine had been rushed to him, he   *chronology*
had been resuscitated at the last possible moment. Ac-   *Conjunctive word*
tually, his heart had stopped and, by some definitions of   *indicating contrast*
this poorly understood process, he had died. Wolcott
was certain that he *had* died, that he had been vouch-   *Repetition of key idea*
safed a glimpse of life after death and a confirmation of
Judaeo-Christian theology.

—**Carl Sagan,** "The Amniotic Universe," *Atlantic,* April 1974

SOME PRACTICE WITH TRANSITIONS

1. Underline the transitional words in each of the following paragraphs. Indicate whether each word (or phrase) underlined is a conjunction or a key word. Be specific about what type of relationship each conjunctive word and phrase has formed (causal, contrast, and so on).

> In the cinders at the station boys sit smoking steadily in darkened cars, their arms bent out the windows, white shirts glowing behind the glass. Nine o'clock is the best time. They sit in a line facing the highway—two or three or four of them—idling their engines. As you walk by a machine may growl at you or a pair of headlights flare up briefly. In a moment one will pull out, spinning cinders behind it, to stalk impatiently up and down the dark streets or roar half a mile into the country before returning to its place in line and pulling up.
>
> —*The Single Voice: An Anthology of Contemporary Fiction*, ed. Jerome Charyn

> Thus was born the original Women's Rights Movement, which became known as the Women's Suffrage Movement because the single great issue, of course, was legal political recognition. But it was never meant to begin and end with the vote, just as the abolitionist movement was never meant to begin and end with the vote. Somehow, though, that awful and passionate struggle for suffrage seemed to exhaust both the blacks and the women, especially the women, for when the vote finally came at the end of the Civil War, it was handed to black males—but not to women; the women had to go on fighting for 60 bitterly long years for suffrage. And then both blacks and women lay back panting, unable to catch their breath for generation upon generation.
>
> —**Vivian Gornick**, "The Next Great Moment in History is Theirs," *Village Voice*, Nov. 27, 1969

2. Combine the sentences below into one paragraph. Using transitional words and phrases, build bridges between the sentences, creating a paragraph unified in meaning.

   a. The most traumatic change now under way in American higher education is the shift from a seller's to a buyer's market.

   b. Many colleges now use promotional tactics that are downright dishonest.

   c. The most popular come-on is the so-called no-need scholarship, designed to lure academically able students.

   d. Promotional brochures are beginning to look like cigarette ads.

   e. One woman's college produced a brochure showing a girl with long blond hair lying in a field of flowers. "Especially for women,''' reads the caption, "because women are creative, intelligent and beautiful, resourceful and sweet and generally different from men."

f. Entrepreneurs don't pussyfoot around with such indirect approaches. If freshmen are what you want, then that's what they deliver—a $250 at head and up.

g. Serious problems are becoming apparent in the headlong rush to embrace the latest marketing strategies of the corporate world.

3. Insert transitional words and phrases in the following student essay:

THE HALLOWEEN PARTY

My friend decided to have a Halloween party on the Saturday before Halloween. I was invited. I had to decide on what costume I would wear. I went to Rubie's Costume Rental and picked out a Minnie Mouse costume.

I was especially excited about this party. Everyone would be wearing costumes. Costume parties always seem to be lively. The disguises are usually amusing, funny, scary, or creative, making the party interesting. It can be fun to be surrounded by imaginative figures. Each person's identity is disguised, and it's easy to play practical jokes on each other. My costume disguised me from head to toe. No one would know my real identity.

Saturday night came. I got dressed in my costume and headed over to the party. The house was full of people in their Halloween costumes. My friends could not recognize me under my mask. I had to identify myself to each one of them.

I noticed someone wearing a Mickey Mouse costume. He was taking pictures of some of the people at the party. He noticed me in my Minnie Mouse costume and motioned for me to come over. He handed his camera to someone wearing a Peter Pan costume so that Peter Pan could take a picture of Mickey and me together. After all, Mickey and Minnie Mouse are a pair. He thanked me for being in the photograph with him. I left the picture-taking scene to find my friends. I wondered who it was wearing the Mickey Mouse costume. He'd said only two words to me. I hadn't recognized his voice.

I saw an old friend of mine who happened to look really cute in a Little Bo-Peep outfit. I went over to talk to her for a while. We decided to look for more of our friends. We found them on the dance floor and joined them. Mickey Mouse happened to be dancing away on the dance floor. He spotted me, came over, and we danced together. Everybody was working up a good sweat. I got tired after dancing to a couple of songs. I went to get something to drink.

The movie Halloween was being played on a VCR in the TV room. I decided to watch it. By the time the movie was over, it had got rather late. I started to clean up the house while my friend broke up the party. I happened to turn around and catch Mickey Mouse without his mask on. He was saying goodnight to some people. To my surprise, I found that the man under the Mickey Mouse mask was my ex-boy-friend--the same ex-boyfriend that I usually feel so uncomfortable around and try to avoid.

Our relationship had been a good one until he had to move to Flor-ida with his family. The day he left for Florida was a sad one. We wrote each other letters twice a week. We called each other on the phone at least once a week. After the first month, our communications grew less frequent.

Four months had passed. I had received only two short letters from him. Then I got a call from him. He told me that he would be moving back to New York within the next few months. I was extremely happy to think that I would be with him again. I counted the days until he moved back to New York.

After he had moved back here, I realized that our relationship had changed. He treated me as a friend instead of as a girlfriend. I realized that we no longer had a romantic relationship. I felt foolish. I decided to avoid him whenever possible.

My experience with him at the Halloween party made me realize that there is no need for me to feel foolish or uncomfortable with him. The masks we wore helped me to relate to him as a person rather than as an ex-boyfriend. Feeling foolish was no longer an excuse for me to avoid him. It is okay to feel for him as a friend. I looked back at our relationship and was able to accept the change that had taken place.

Ending my relationship with him as a girlfriend did not end my relationship with him as a friend. I had not been a friend to him because of fear that rejection of me as a girlfriend had affected his attitude toward me as a person. It did not mean rejection of friendship. I now want a friendly relationship, like the one we had the night of the party.

Images, impressions, fears, perceptions, and feelings toward others affect our relationships. We may see only one side of a situation or a person. The outside world can be very misleading about the real inside world that we live in and know. When we are disguised, our fears and anxieties, perceptions and worries, are put aside. We can be ourselves and learn to see another side of the world we live in or of the people we know. If we look closely enough, we can see ourselves.

REWRITING

Obtaining Feedback on Your Rough Draft

After you have written your rough draft, take a break for a period of time. This period should be long enough for you to be able to return to your essay refreshed. Once you have rested, your "other" self can emerge, the self that can see your essay objectively and make any necessary revisions.

You may also want to obtain peer feedback at this point. Because your peers are your audience for this essay, the responses of your classmates should be particularly useful in determining how well you have written for your readers.

Regardless of who provides the feedback—you, your instructor, your peers, or any combination—your paper should receive an evaluation that answers the four questions of the "Audience Response Guide."

——— AUDIENCE RESPONSE GUIDE ———

1. What do you think the writer wanted to say in this paper? What is her or his purpose in writing? What does she or he want the paper to mean?

2. How does the paper affect the reader for whom it was intended?

3. How effective has the writer been in conveying her or his purpose and meaning? What are the strengths of the paper? What are the weaknesses?

4. How should the paper be revised to better fulfill its purpose and meaning?

Following is a peer evaluation of the rough draft of the student essay on an incident (pp. 72–74). Compare your own evaluation of the draft to that of the peer group by answering the four questions of the "Audience Response Guide" yourself before reading their answers.

1. The writer wanted to indicate the effect that an act of senseless violence had on her. Her purpose is to give a step-by-step account of the incident and describe her reactions, the fear and frustration she felt as a result.

2. She involves the reader in the incident and its aftermath. The reader knows what she felt when she saw the condition her car was in and appreciates her reactions because such acts of violence can happen to anyone.

3. The writer uses the reporter's questions well. The paper's strength is in its use of details in describing the damage to the car and in giving a chronological account of what she did about it. But there are two weaknesses: Some of the details, such as the information about the police precincts, seem irrelevant. Also, the writer could do more to explain the significance of the incident both to her personally and in general.

4. Decide what the most crucial details are and cut out those that distract readers from the story. Stand back from the event, analyze it a bit, and draw some conclusions about such senseless violence and how we respond to it. This will help the reader share in the incident more fully.

A revised version of that student essay, now titled "A Victim of Strangers?" follows. How were the group's suggestions incorporated? What changes did the writer make herself? Is her expanded conclusion an improvement? How successfully does she create transitions within and between the last five paragraphs? Are there any other additions that she might have made? How, for example, might the addition of some dialogue have improved this final draft?

A VICTIM OF STRANGERS?

The beautiful sunny day gave no hint about what had happened. On Monday, March 31st, 1986, at 1:00 P.M., Gregory (my son, aged 6 years and 1 day) and I were leaving the house to pick up Aunt Barbara and cousin Lee. Spring vacation had started the Friday before, and the unusually temperate weather gave us the opportunity to spend time outdoors. We were supposed to be at Barbara's house at 1:15, then go out for lunch together, and afterwards, go to a park. In no way could I have anticipated what was to ruin our day completely.

As Greg and I approached the car, I noticed the broken glass. I warned him to be careful and started to put the key into the door. When I noticed that the fragments and shards had come from my car's sideview mirror, my first thought was that someone had "accidentally" broken the mirror with a rock, ball, or some other projectile. I was just about to usher Greg into the car, my first stop being the service station to inquire about a replacement mirror, when I noticed the additional damage. The windshield wipers were not merely snapped off, but forcibly ripped from the hood; the antenna was lying in the gutter. Even the small plaques, announcing the name of the car, had been pulled off. (The molding had torn off years before.) Then I noticed the four flat tires.

Why would anybody do this? It's not as if anyone could possibly be jealous of my owning the car. It's a 1972 Ford Maverick--it runs, but the body is half-rusted away, and it sounds like a centennial Fourth of July celebration. Nobody could have profited financially from the destruction. What was the purpose? Why my car?

The questions ran through my mind, but rather than analyze the situation, I just felt an overwhelming anger. I also felt helpless and frightened that I wouldn't have the money needed to fix the car. (It's our only car, and we use it for work, school, shopping, the doctor, etc.) So I did the only thing I could. I cried. Then I started ringing the doorbells of almost every neighbor on our block. To my frustration, nobody had heard or seen anything. So I went inside and called the police, who said that a patrol car would respond as soon as possible. Then I called my husband, Marty, at work, to whom I wept and complained, and I asked if he could come home early, as I was very upset. Finally, I called Barbara to tell her about my car having been vandalized and cancelled our plans for the afternoon. She asked if there was anything that she could do, and I told her that I'd call back later if we needed a ride anywhere. Luckily, Greg was busy with my upstairs neighbor's kids for the last half-hour or so, leaving me free to make phone calls.

Coincidentally, my friend Julie stopped over a few minutes later, and we commiserated. Her car had been stolen, damaged, and recovered twice in the past four months! She gave me the opportunity to vent some of my anger and verbalize all the things I wanted to do to whoever had attacked my car.

Just as Julie was leaving, at 2:30, the police arrived. The two officers and I walked over to the car. One was especially grim-faced, and they both looked like they'd rather be anywhere else. They looked bored; nonetheless, they asked me a few questions. They wanted to know if anybody held a grudge against me, or if I had cut someone off recently while driving. Then they asked whether my husband or I were teachers, having noticed my college parking sticker. The friendlier of the two patrolmen, a tall, slim, good-looking man of about forty-five, explained that it was common for students to do things like this to teachers who failed them! I said that neither of us were teachers, and I had no idea who could have done this. The other officer, shorter and stockier, wrote the report. He said that he believed the act of violence to have been deliberately aimed at us. He didn't think it was an early April Fool's Day prank, acted out by fun-loving teenagers; the damage was too extensive and it was unusual for such an old, beat-up car to be the random victim of this type of act.

Marty appeared at this moment, asking the police to see if they could get any fingerprints off the car. They made a call on their radio and said that the print team would come over later that day. (They did, but the effort proved fruitless.)

The police left before 3:00, and Marty and I went inside. I called the Mobil Auto Club, which sent someone over to inflate the tires. We had already determined that they didn't appear to be slashed. Then Marty drove the car to a nearby service station.

All in all, the car was "patched up" for $100.00, which I put on my Sunoco credit card. I had the Maverick back by the next afternoon. But for the next two weeks, I woke up every night at about 3:00 A.M. and stared out of my window, to see if my car had been vandalized again. The police had indicated that deliberate attacks are usually repeated, and I was as edgy as I could possibly be. I felt scared and terribly violated. I was also worried that this type of violence could extend to me or my family. I became increasingly suspicious of people. I wondered if a neighbor, with whom I had had a very vocal argument the year before, could possibly be responsible. I began to look squinty-eyed at the local teenagers, searching faces for signs of guilt or accomplishment. I really became extremely paranoid. I just couldn't rationalize that anyone would want to do this to me deliberately; on the other hand, I couldn't fathom anybody engaging in willful destruction for mere kicks.

I began to dwell on other menacing acts being inflicted on people by some members of society. People were pushing others in front of subway trains for no apparent reason. A man in California used a machine gun on a crowd of McDonald's patrons. And then there was the cyanide-laced Tylenol. What kind of society are we? Don't we all have enough unavoidable misfortune, without these useless, violent incidents? I remembered once seeing a group of young boys throwing rocks at passing cars from an overpass. Why? Who did they need to hurt? And I started to think about the people who go out of their way to witness misery. They'll rubberneck during the aftermath of a serious car accident, seeking out all the grisly details. People will gather for a fire or explosion. Media coverage of death is always extensive, death and dying being big attention-getters.

We live in a busy, overly competitive, violent world. Many individuals tend to range somewhere between rude and dangerous. I have no answers concerning unprovoked attacks on people and property. The aggressors may be frustrated, rebellious, insecure, unhappy, or unfulfilled. Or an attacker may turn out to be mentally deranged.

Being the victim of an intentionally injurious or destructive act changes a person somewhat. I, for one, am more frightened than I used to be. When I walk alone at night, I hold my keys in a position ready to defend myself, almost anticipating an intrusion.

On a more positive note, I'm happy to say that there has been no repeat performance concerning the vandalism of my car. But although nearly four months have passed since the incident, I still approach my car a little warily every morning. I don't understand senseless violence, and I don't think I ever will.

Adding. Adding—of words, phrases, or whole passages—is required when you neglect to put on paper information that the reader needs to know. Subconsciously, you may have assumed that because what you wrote was clear to you, it would be clear to the reader. Or some facets of your subject may simply not have occurred to you when you wrote your rough draft. However, your "other self," your peer group, or your instructor may now suggest that important additions be made.

Details may need to be added that will make your writing more concrete; perhaps you wrote something like "The experience was terrifying" without indicating to the reader what the terrifying elements of the experience were. Or perhaps you wrote something like "The situation impinged on the group in a negative fashion," thinking that you were writing impressively, but not realizing that your language was very abstract and did not present an actual picture to the reader of how the group felt about what was happening to them. By adding details, the writers of the two sentences above could create much more vivid writing: "Slipping into Professor Wout's class even one minute late turned my knees to jelly, my insides into a volcano, and my head into a pounding drum" and "Having been so eager to see the film, which was purported to be Woody Allen's best, my disappointed friends looked like their idol himself as they hunched sadly away from the darkened theater."

You may also need to add details that define the relationships between the ideas in your draft. Perhaps you wrote an essay on animals in comic strips and did not express clearly the differences between Garfield's and Snoopy's attitudes toward life. Finding even one word that crystallizes the view of each cartoon character may clarify this important point.

You may have neglected some important features of your subject and need now to expand your outline. Perhaps you wrote on the disappearing animal species of Kenya and neglected the elephant—a vital omission that you will now want to rectify.

In addition to considering the information that the reader needs to know, think also of his or her point of view on your subject. Does your voice build a bridge between your point of view and that of your reader, or should words and phrases be added that will create this rapport? For example, if you, as a college student, wrote to your younger brother about your new appreciation of Picasso and did not take into account his disparagement of those "funny figures" in Picasso's work, you might want to add phrases that would bring your attitude and his closer together. To the following sentence in your draft, "Picasso introduced the twentieth century to new perceptions of time and space," you might add, "as Einstein did in physics," as your brother is currently taking that subject in high school.

Whether you are adding information or building bridges between you and your reader, adding words, phrases, and even paragraphs is an important part of revision.

In adding to the rough draft of your essay for this task, decide whether you have enabled your audience to experience the incident as you did. If not, add details to make your narrative as vivid as possible or, as did the writer of "A Victim of Strangers?" to enable your reader to see the relationships between your ideas. Also, if any important aspect of the incident has occurred to you belatedly, add that aspect. Finally, create a tone of voice that indicates that you are responsive to your audience by adding analogies or explanations that will encourage your reader to see your point of view.

Editing

Editing is different from revising in that revising affects content and organization, whereas editing affects the surface features of the essay, such as transitions, word choice, and mechanics. Editing should be done only when your revisions are complete. Editing changes include the same processes, however, as revisions: adding, rearranging, substituting, distributing, consolidating, and cutting.

Adding.   Add words that further clarify the meaning of your phrases and sentences. These words, such as adjectives and adverbs, can provide additional details as well.

Transitions.   Make sure to add transitions to your rough draft so that your peers can easily grasp the connections between your thoughts and also follow your chronological sequence. Are there any transitions that the student who wrote "A Victim of Strangers?" might have added to her essay?

Mechanics.   At this point, forget *what* you are saying and concentrate on *how* you are saying it. Reread your first draft solely for mechanical errors such as spelling (use a good dictionary); grammar (refer to the handbook at the end of this text); punctuation (again, the handbook); and capitalization (handbook once again).

Now, revise and edit your rough draft.

BECOMING AWARE OF YOURSELF AS A WRITER

Make use of your journal to record your thoughts and feelings about the task for Chapter 2. As you write in your journal, consider the following questions:

1. How useful were the journalist's questions in generating ideas for the task? Did you rely on any other means of generating information? In what ways were these means useful?

2. Do you understand the concept of the audience's frame of reference? Under what writing circumstances do you think that you must analyze your audience's frame of reference?

3. What are the limitations of inference in trying to determine your audience's point of view?

4. How did you feel about writing for your peers? How helpful was it for you to evaluate the differences between their point of view and your own?

5. How did the writing process described in this chapter help or hinder the writing of your essay?

6. How helpful was the feedback you received on your rough draft? Did it lead to any significant improvements in your final draft?

7. What was the single most difficult aspect of the writing task for you? How did you resolve it?

3

Writing About
a Stage in
Your Life

PURPOSE

In writing for yourself, as in a journal (see Chap. 1), you can develop a unique, personal voice. When writing for others (see Chap. 2), usually it is necessary for you to make adjustments—in what you say and in how you say it—in order to be understood by a reader whose point of view is different from your own. Now we want to examine the problem of how you can retain the sincerity of your most private, authentic voice at the same time that you modify it in order to communicate fluently and intelligibly to your audience.

Different readers, of course, require that you modify your voice in different ways. In a sense, as a writer you assume a different voice in relation to each audience that you address. For example, when you write a letter of advice to your younger brother, you may sound helpful, self-assured, and experienced; when you write to your friends, asking them to lend you some money, you might plead or reason. The voice you use as an older brother or sister is different from the voice you use as a friend, because your role in relation to your audience is different.

The questions that this multiplicity of voices raises are complex. Can you express yourself freely and honestly and at the same time adopt a voice suited to your reader? To what degree can the voice that you adopt serve to bridge the gap between your point of view and that of your audience? These are questions addressed in Chapter 3.

Also in this chapter, you can experiment with the free-writing strategy that was introduced in Chapter 1 as a way to explore a personal experience as openly and as honestly as you can. We then ask you to identify a particular role that you played during or after that experience in order to see how writing in the voice of that role can be a means of accommodating yourself to your reader's point of view while still retaining your sincerity.

GENERATING IDEAS: FREE WRITING

Peter Elbow, in his book *Writing Without Teachers* (Oxford, 1973), explained what free writing is and how it can help you to find something to say about your subject. Free writing is writing about a subject without restrictions, writing whatever comes into your head, without concern for grammar, spelling, or organization. It is not prepared writing; it is not intended for a reader. Its only purpose is for you to explore on paper whatever thoughts and feelings you might have about your subject.

For example, the two students who wrote the following free-writing exercises were given a lemon and were asked to spend ten minutes in writing whatever came into their heads about it.

Writer 1

Lemon--a yellow lemon, the color of my bright yellow sweatshirt the color of yellow taxi cabs the color of the sun in a kid's coloring book my yellow paper on my test bananas are yellow. It feels smooth but has a soapy or waxy texture. The Lemon Ice King has good lemon ices. Lenny used to work at the Lemon Ice King, Lenny, Levy, and Mike used to rob a lot of money from Fat Pete. Lemons are yellow I had a yellow car that was a lemon. Bobby Pistilli's father used to call Bobby a lemon. He is a lemon driving in his Monte Carlo. I like lemons I hate the people who passed the lemon to me I don't want to see it. I like lemons, I like lemons in my iced tea, I like lemons over chicken cutlets, I like lemons raw, I like to take the lemon right out of the pitcher of iced tea and eat it raw. I love the sour taste, I love the expression on someone's face when they bite into a very sour lemon. I like lemon on seafood. My favorite is freshly squeezed lemon over freshly crumbed and baked shrimp or over fresh shrimp or over filet of any fish. Some lemons are round, others are oval-shaped--most lemons have a nipple at either end which is very small. One way to use a lemon (probably the most common way) is to slice it in half and squeeze it. Another way which is better is to first squeeze the lemon before you cut it open and roll it on a flat surface.

Notice how the first writer has relaxed and let his mind wander in any direction that the lemon has taken him; he touches on the appearance, the taste, and the feel of a lemon; its uses; and its emotional associations for him in the past and even in the present as he is writing. (Notice also that he has omitted much punctuation, perhaps in order to encourage the flow of his thoughts.)

Past associations engulf the second writer as she relaxes and writes about her subject:

Writer 2

Sometimes when I see a lemon, it brings back memories of my child-hood. I remember the lemon tree my family and I used to have in our backyard. There were other trees but the lemon tree was my favorite. No other house in our neighborhood had one. My mother had put nicely formed bricks around the trunk in a circle. It used to amaze me how those beautiful and nice-smelling flowers turned into lemons. This may sound ridiculous, but when I remember that lemon tree, it brings back nostalgic feelings. This may be because of how pleasant life used to be at that time.

SOME PRACTICE WITH FREE WRITING

1. As a way of getting started in free writing, begin with a subject that emphasizes a particular sense; for example, begin with the taste of a favorite food or dish and let go all your associations with it. Then, move on to the other senses—touch, sight, sound, smell—and write freely about the subjects and associations each evokes.

   As another way of stimulating free writing, write about one subject and try to include associations with all five senses.

2. Write for ten minutes about an impersonal object: a pencil, a pen, or a piece of chalk, for example. Then read the free writing that follows. Have you stretched your mind as much as or more than the student who wrote this piece?

Pen is an object, invented and created by man. It can make peace or start wars with just a simple wave from its point. It can teach people and help write important papers it can invent books, technology and create a picture of the universe. But yet we see what is a simple object which permits us to write as a worthless thing when really it holds the destruction of man or the creation of peace and love in the world in a small little tip. Down through time there have been different types of pens and pencils but all they did was to record our history and carry it down to each generation. A pen can be noble or very bad it all depends on who uses it. It has been called the sword of man or the staff of peace.

Free Writing as a Source of Ideas for Writing an Essay

Free writing can serve as a way of generating ideas once your imagination has really expanded, for you can discover ideas about subjects that you never realized were even in your mind. Peter Elbow said, "Free writing is a way to end up thinking something you couldn't have started out thinking." By examining the free writing that you do in class and at home in your journal, you can find thoughts or feelings to expand into prepared essays.

For example, read over the following free-writing sample:

Well, trick or treat, it is Halloween today. How I used to love that saying. Well I guess that I am growing up because I really do not feel that way anymore. But of course that is normal.

The hoodlums on the corner were throwing eggs at everybody today. It was so much fun to observe the action. It was hilarious to see the dumb fools getting bombarded with eggs.

Nobody, of course, ever tried throwing an egg at me. If they had, I swear that I would definitely have flipped out. But I am a familiar face and one does not throw eggs at the people he knows.

At home, I packed the little candy bags and it was fun distributing candy to all the really cute little kids dressed in their costumes coming to the door. I felt sad for a while there, it reminded me of how much fun my sister and I used to have on Halloween.

Oh well, the advantages of being an adult beat anything--even the fun kids have on Halloween.

Well, it's Tuesday and it seems as though I am not going to go any-

where again. Last night I decided to sleep over at Aggie's house, me &
that girl are so compatible that we have so much fun together.

I love Aggie, and she's been my best friend ever since I was little,
and she'll always be. We have been friends ever since we were little
and I have always thought of her as I would a sister.

Her parents really like me, they are always asking me about how I
am doing and how my parents are doing. We've been through a lot of
garbage together, and after all our messed-up years I really don't know
how we are alive after all the drugs that we have done.

It is true that we had both flipped out once but now, thank god, we
are all right.

Aggie though it seems to me is still a little shaky at times. I sometimes think that maybe the drugs did affect her more than any of us
would ever care to admit to ourselves or of course to her.

Why do you think that the writer associated Halloween with her friendship
with Aggie? What would you say was the primary topic, the main pattern of
thought, that this writer had on her mind? What sort of thoughts and feelings
might this writer expand into a formal essay, one that is organized, fully developed, and grammatically correct?

Free writing can be used to recall personal experiences, and it is also a good
technique for getting down on paper all the material on a recently studied
topic. It is a useful antidote to writer's block, or the "I don't know where to
start" syndrome. If you have given considerable thought to, and perhaps even
done some research on, an assigned topic but do not know where to begin in
writing about it, free writing of your thoughts or your recollections of what
you have read will get your material on paper. From this important first stage,
you can move on to organizing what you have written.

MORE PRACTICE WITH FREE WRITING

3. Write freely for thirty to forty-five minutes about a holiday you went on and
   the memories that you associate with it. When you are finished, make a list of
   the aspects of your subject that you might develop into a prepared essay. How
   are these aspects related? What pattern of thought or feeling do they trace?
   Which of them fit the least well into the pattern? Might these latter aspects be
   the start of a different pattern?

4. Think of a subject that you have recently studied for one of your classes or one
   that you have read about rather extensively. Without thinking too hard about

the subject, start writing freely about it. After writing for thirty to forty-five minutes, consider how many aspects of the subject you covered. Have you sufficient ideas for an essay? What pattern do these ideas form? Now that you have taken stock of what you have written, would more free writing serve a useful purpose?

Free Writing and the Writing Process

Free writing can help you to locate worthwhile ideas for a prepared paper. Perhaps it can do so most effectively if developed through several stages. In order to generate a maximum amount of material with free writing, before moving on to work on the rough draft of an essay, Peter Elbow suggests completing two free-writing stages, each of which takes an hour.

Hour 1   Freely write on your subject for forty-five minutes. Sum up the pattern that emerges for fifteen minutes.

Hour 2   Freely write about the emerging pattern for sixty minutes.

The free writing that you practice in these two hours can then be shaped into the rough draft of an essay.

MORE PRACTICE WITH FREE WRITING

5.   **Hour 1**   Using the topic about which you wrote freely in Exercise 3 or 4, sum up the pattern that emerges for fifteen minutes.

Hour 2   Freely write about the emerging pattern for sixty minutes.

Has the free writing that you produced in these two hours provided you with the material for a prepared essay? As a means of checking your answer, construct a rough outline for an essay.

ADDRESSING YOUR AUDIENCE: SELECTING A VOICE FOR YOUR READER

Selecting a Voice as a Means of Self-Expression

When we say that someone is playing a role, we usually mean that they are not being honest. They are pretending to be something that in reality they are not, and they may thus speak in a voice that masks rather than reveals who they are. But sometimes, when we say that people are playing a role, we mean only that they are acting in a manner typical of a certain stage of life that they are in or a certain position that they hold. In this case, they *are* expressing themselves, telling us something true about who and what they are, communicating an aspect of their identity through a voice they select.

We all select different voices during our lives, voices that are expressions of one or another aspect of ourselves. We are children and parents; we work for people and we hire people to work for us; we can be hosts or guests, friends or relatives or strangers. Because our lives have many aspects, we select different voices with which to speak at different times. A change in voice can reflect a change in our point of view, and often we change our voice any number of times in a single day. When we select among our various voices, we do not, however, lose our honesty or our individuality.

For example, consider a man who is both a father and a college student. At home, with his children, the man speaks knowledgeably, answering his children's questions with authority. At school, as a student, however, the man may speak less authoritatively; he may prefer asking questions to answering them; his manner, his tone of voice, the whole style with which he expresses himself may be different. Perhaps the man is more casual, more playful with his children, and more formal, more serious with his teachers. On the other hand, perhaps the man acts more seriously with his children than with his fellow students.

The fact that the man is selecting different voices does not necessarily mean that he is being insincere about expressing himself. In fact, selecting a voice can be a most effective means of expressing one or another of the many sides of one's complex human character.

SOME PRACTICE WITH SELECTING A VOICE AS A MEANS OF SELF-EXPRESSION

1. Determine your point of view on each of the following subjects: the women's movement, military spending, the criminal justice system, the wisdom of adults, and the sexual revolution. Then determine the role you were playing as you thought about each subject. How many voices might you select in order to express the complexity of your feelings on each subject? Does any particular voice express your feelings more fully than others?

2. Review the free-writing exercises in which you wrote about a holiday or about a subject of study (see pp. 93–94). Can you identify a specific voice that you selected as you wrote? What role were you playing that influenced you to select this voice?

Selecting a Voice as a Bridge Between the Writer and the Reader

Because we do live out roles in life, selecting a voice to reflect each role can be a legitimate and honest means of expressing how we really feel and think. Also, because playing roles is a primary human experience, something that everyone does, selecting a voice to communicate a role can serve as a most effective bridge between a writer and a reader whose points of view may be quite different.

Consider the girl who wrote the free-writing exercise about Halloween. What sort of voice had she selected? What stage of life had she reached? Might an elderly or middle-aged person, one of her peers, and someone younger than she react differently to her attitude about "the advantages of being an adult"? Might she choose a different voice for each different audience?

For example, suppose the girl, after reviewing her free-writing exercise, decides that her focus seems to be her feeling that she is not a kid anymore, that she is growing up. How is she going to write convincingly about this feeling? If she is writing for her peer, Aggie, who might feel similarly, she might simply use the casual style of one friend to another. But what if she is writing for her English teacher? If she plays the role of student, she is likely to adopt a voice that sounds less like a grown-up and more like a subordinate than she, in fact, feels.

A primary reason for her feeling more adult is that, having passed through a period of time in which she was "flipped out" on drugs, she has learned how much better off she is without drugs. Perhaps she will be most understandable, as well as most convincing, if she writes in the role of a former drug user. She can speak from experience about the growing up that one does in passing through such a phase. She can explain her subject with authority, even expertise. She can adopt a more grown-up voice if, as she writes, she thinks of herself in this role.

In doing so, she will be expressing her feelings honestly and reliably, even though her most private and original self is not identical with and is much more complex than the voice of a former drug user. Moreover, she will be giving her teacher a concrete image of the thoughts that she wishes to express.

The points of view of the girl and her teacher may be radically different. But the voice of someone who has recovered from a self-destructive habit is a typical voice in human experience, and even if the teacher has never adopted such a voice herself, it is likely to be familiar. Like most of the voices that we select in life, it is something of a stereotype. We can personalize any voice by the way in which we express it, even as we rely on its stereotypical nature to narrow the distance between us and our audience.

SOME PRACTICE WITH SELECTING A VOICE AS A BRIDGE BETWEEN WRITER AND READER

1. What sort of role and what corresponding voice might be most effective for you to assume if you want to express your point of view about violence on television to the sponsor of a particularly violent program? How might you alter your voice if, instead, you intend to address your eight-year-old nephew who enjoys watching the program? Might you select a different voice if you

are writing to the star of the program, who happens to be one of your favorite actors?

2. What is your point of view on the Moral Majority? As a voter, how might you convey your point of view to a liberal Democratic member of Congress who is campaigning for reelection in your neighborhood? How might your voice change if, instead, you want to address your next-door neighbor, who is an ultraconservative Republican?

3. To what sort of audience might the voice that you adopted in the free-writing exercise on a holiday appeal? If you were to write an essay based on this exercise and the audience was to be your English teacher, would you change your voice in any way?

TASK: WRITING ABOUT A STAGE IN YOUR LIFE

The task for this chapter is to write about a stage in your life, a time or an episode that represented a break from your earlier behavior or outlook. Unlike the incident that you were asked to write about in Chapter 2, this stage should have occurred over a lengthy period of time and may have involved any number of incidents. Many students choose to write about a phase that they went through; but some have responded to the task by focusing on an episode in which they made (or did not make) a choice or took (or did not take) advice, detailing the consequences that followed as they experienced a change of perspective on some aspect of their life. We will ask you to record the stage in such a way as to indicate how it represented a break or change in your life, what happened during it, and what you think its significance has been for you.

To do this task, you will probably want to strike a balance between narration and exposition. You can employ chronological development to tell the story of what happened before, during, and perhaps after the stage; at the same time you will need to explain just how and why the stage was a meaningful one.

As your audience for this task, we suggest your present English instructor. There is a practical reason for designating such an audience; probably you will be writing to teachers a good deal more than to anyone else over the next few years. But that is not the only reason that we ask you to address your instructor. Your instructor's point of view is bound to differ from your own in more ways than does the point of view of your peers. You will begin to learn here that you have a variety of options open to you that will help you bridge the distance between you and an audience whose perspective and ideas may be quite different from your own. Here, you can stress your voice as student, of course, and rely on your instructor's training and experience to narrow the gap between you. But you can also select a voice other than that of a student, a voice that more specifically expresses the role that you are playing, such as authority on a particular subject or someone sadder but wiser because of a particular choice.

In the remaining selections of this chapter, we will discuss how you can use free writing to generate ideas about your subject; how you can adopt a particular voice to express yourself intelligibly to your audience; how you can arrange your free writing to produce a rough draft of an essay based on both narration and exposition; and what considerations enter into the rewriting of this draft and its shaping into a final product.

WRITING THE ESSAY

Using Free Writing as a Source of Ideas

Earlier in this chapter, you were introduced to free writing and how it can help you discover what you think and feel about a given subject. Over the next few days, you might try free writing in your journal about different stages that represented a break from your past. You can tell stories of phases you have been through, or choices you have made, or advice you have benefitted from. This will give you the advantage of being able, a few days from now, to read back over and select from a group of possible topics for your next essay. It will also give you the chance to begin setting down your thoughts about the significance for you of a stage in your life, by writing your comments on and reactions to each story as you read over it in your journal.

Whether or not you choose to work with your journal this way, you can try using the two stages of the free-writing exercise to develop what will become the first draft of your essay. With Peter Elbow's two-step process, you can begin writing about your episode:

Hour 1   Write freely for forty-five minutes on the stage. Sum up the pattern that emerges for fifteen minutes.
Hour 2   Using the summing-up statement of Hour 1, write freely about your emerging pattern for sixty minutes longer.

At the end of this two-hour period, you will have two pieces of writing on the same topic. Hour 1 has hopefully produced a narrative culminating in a main point. Hour 2, on the other hand, has begun with the statement of the main point, and has then explained and discussed it. The next step will be to incorporate these two separate pieces into one piece of prose, thus producing a rough draft. That step is a long one and requires much thought; we will explore it in the section on arrangement.

Here is the work produced by one student in two hours of free writing on a phase:

Hour 1

The phase that I still remember is the one in which I was afraid of the devil. At that time, I was seven years old. I remember the bad dreams I had. I used to live in a small town with many superstitious people. They were talking to me of the devil as a red creature that likes bad boys and girls. I used to go to sleep with the light on because I was afraid of the dark. For me, darkness was the devil's hiding place. Once asleep, I used to dream of the devil coming at night to my town to take away bad children. I remember the dream that I had for so many nights. I was hiding in the basement of my house under three blankets, but still the devil found me and brought me into his world. There he cooked me, with some other boys and girls, for his daily dinner.

During that phase, many friends of mine used to invite me to the movies, but I always had an excuse to stay away. Frightening movies meant to me bad dreams and sleepless nights.

The devil was so impressed in my mind that when my father sent me into the basement to do something I almost cried. My grandfather used to tell me that there was a place in the valley where spirits and ghosts were having fun. The devil was their host. That statement always stood in my mind. The priest used to tell children that if they do bad things they will go to hell. I used to dream of hell as a place with flames where bad people suffered. They were surrounded by red creatures with horns on their heads and forks in their hands. I also dreamed I was on a high cliff where I was standing on the top and looking down in hell where many people were getting roasted. This phase lasted for more than two years.

Summary of Hour 1

I think this phase was caused by the community in which I was living. Also, I'm a very pessimistic individual now who always takes into consideration the negative aspects of life before the positive as a result of this experience.

But also, I'm a mature person. I try to obey my parents and respect other people, and I think this phase had a lot to do with making me that way.

Hour 2

Until I was fifteen I lived in a small town. I knew all the people who lived there. My community was like a big family. The people were very religious and superstitious. They believed in ghosts, devils, and spirits. They influenced my thinking very much. Many times I was told that the devil will take bad boys to hell. That statement stayed in my mind during my childhood and was the cause of many bad dreams. At night the town was very quiet and dark and very scary.

I'm a very pessimistic individual. Every time I watch a ball game, I think that my team is going to lose. Sometimes I even think of myself as a loser because I had so many painful experiences during my childhood.

But I'm not just pessimistic. I think this phase also had a positive effect on me because it made me more mature.

I think I became a more responsible person because of my phase with the devil. I tried to obey my parents and respect other people. When my father asked me to run an errand for him, it made me feel better about myself to do it.

This phase had a lot to do with making me that way. Now, I'm not afraid of hell or devils because I'm a secure individual with a future to think about.

The student now has a considerable amount of material with which to begin his work on a formal essay.

Selecting a Voice as a Bridge Between You and Your Audience

Your audience for this task is your present English instructor. Using inference, try to determine what your teacher's point of view might be with regard to the stage that you will be writing about. Once you have done so, your next step is to consider what voice you might best select in order to bridge the gap between your point of view and your teacher's.

Of course, you can address your teacher simply from the point of view of a student. But you may wish to play a less traditionally subordinate role and to adopt a less formal voice. In writing about a break in your behavior or outlook, you are probably going to focus on a change from one sort of role that many people play in life to another. Perhaps you will be able to express your ideas and feelings about this change most authentically if you select the voice expressing one of these roles, either the earlier one or the one developed by the change. Or perhaps you will do better to take a stance that represents the distance you have traveled since the stage, looking back on it from a role that you identify with now. In making the choice of voice, keep your teacher in mind. Which voice will most effectively communicate to your reader?

Once you identify your voice, review your two free-writing exercises. Where do you sound most in character? Are there thoughts expressed that seem out of character for the voice you wish to emphasize? Make whatever changes seem appropriate to the voice you have selected.

What voice might the student who wrote about his phase with the devil select in order to present his experience more intelligibly? What would be the effect, for example, if he acted the pessimist who looks back on his phase with some resentment about the harm he experienced? How might the essay be different if he acted the secure individual who looks back on his childhood fears with a certain amusement? Which voice would appeal most to his reader?

You now want to continue to think and write as honestly and completely as you can in the voice you have selected, as you set about arranging your material into a rough draft.

Answering the following questions of the "Audience Analysis Guide" will help you to prepare to write for your audience.

——— AUDIENCE ANALYSIS GUIDE ———

1. Who is my audience?
2. What is the frame of reference of this audience?
3. What point of view is my audience likely to have on my subject?
4. How do my own frame of reference and point of view differ from those of my reader?
5. How can I bridge any gap that exists between my reader's point of view and my own?
6. Which of my voices am I selecting as I write on this subject? How can the voice that I select bridge the gap between my audience and me?

Arranging Your Essay: The Shaping Idea, Narration, and Exposition

Let's begin to shape the two pieces of free writing that you have produced into a rough draft of a prepared essay. At this point, you might focus on the problem of developing an effective arrangement strategy. You should try to come up with a shaping idea. You might also begin to decide at what points in the essay you will use narration to convey your experiences during the stage and at what points you will use explanation to relate how these experiences represented a break from your previous behavior or outlook.

The Shaping Idea.   In devising a shaping idea for this task (see Chapter 1, "Focus: Shaping a Subject," pp. 37–41), one of the key questions that you need to address is "What is the particular significance of this stage?" Your statement of your shaping idea will embody the answer to this question.

One possible way to determine the answer is to take the two pieces of work produced in the two-step free-writing exercise and do the following:

1. Examine your statement about the emerging pattern made at the end of Hour 1 and used at the start of Hour 2.
2. Identify a sentence that captures the unique quality (feeling, mood, tone, experience) of the stage.
3. If there is no such sentence, write a new sentence that does capture this unique quality.
4. Then, expand or refine the chosen sentence so that it includes (a) a clearly defined time period and (b) words that describe the significance of the stage.
5. Now check the sentence to see if it meets the other requirements of the statement of an organizing idea: precision, lack of ambiguity, and grammatical correctness.

Of course, many writers do not know precisely how to organize their thoughts until after they have written the rough draft, and you may find that your shaping idea isn't clear to you until this later stage. The final version of your essay, however, should be clearly guided by one well-defined idea.

Now evaluate the following statements of the shaping ideas that some students used while writing drafts in the fulfillment of this task. If you have devised your own statement at this point, compare it with these:

1. <u>Title:</u> My Dental Hygiene Phase

   <u>Shaping Idea:</u> Looking back on the years 1976-1978, I laugh when I remember the neurotic behavior that marked my dental hygiene phase.
2. <u>Title:</u> My Brief Career

   <u>Shaping Idea:</u> Years of listening to my mother's stories of her days spent in the theater launched me on my exciting but brief theatrical career.

3. Title: Learning to Live in New York City

   Shaping Idea: My trip from Bogota, Columbia, to Queens, New York, two years ago covered a distance I have only begun to take in stride.

4. Title: Two Generations Going Through Changes

   Shaping Idea: Psychologists say that girls experience tremendous changes in their lives between the ages of fifteen and sixteen and that women experience their change of life, or menopause, between forty and fifty-five; in my case, my mother's changes and mine clashed.

Narration and Exposition in the Service of Narration.   Once you have identified and stated your shaping idea, a second key question in writing about a stage is "How do you order or arrange experiences that occurred over a period of time in such a way as to convey their realness to your audience, at the same time showing how they represented a break in your earlier behavior or outlook?" In answering this question, you may employ at least two modes of writing: narration and exposition.

As we saw in Chapter 2, the narrative mode is a natural method of telling a story step by step. It is obviously a valuable mode to use in the retelling of experiences. An additional mode, exposition, will also be useful in writing this task. Exposition explains, summarizes, or interprets an experience. Because the task for this chapter is more complex than the task for Chapter 2, you will need to use exposition as well as narration.

In Chapter 2, you wrote about an incident of short duration. Here, you will be writing about a period of longer duration: three months, six months, even two years. You will want to decide when to come in for a close-up of a particular event or experience that occupies a short period within the stage and therefore to use narration. You must also decide when to move back for a wider view or when to plunge into a deeper examination, both of which require exposition. Narration expands time and provides emphasis; exposition contracts time and comments on significance.

Using Narration in Writing on a Significant Stage.   Review the section in Chapter 2 on narration (pp. 65–75). Now turn to the writing you produced during Hours 1 and 2 of the free-writing exercise. In all likelihood, the dominant mode of the work produced in Hour 1 is narrative. (This may or may not be true of Hour 2.) Hence, much of what you have already produced is arranged in chronological sequence.

You might start with this sequence as a kind of scaffolding and build a rough draft with its aid. One way to do this is simply to start writing, keeping your sequence and your possible shaping idea in mind as you do so. Or, you could try placing the statement of your organizing idea at the top of a sheet of paper. then, take the following steps:

1. Read Hours 1 and 2 of your free-writing exercise.
2. Identify the narrative sections.
3. Check the chronology of the narrative sections for accuracy of sequence, effectiveness of writing, and time indicators (transitions, dates, and so on).
4. Consider your audience. Does your audience require a lot of background through a narrative account of the stage? Where is background most needed in the narrative?
5. Evaluate the narrated events. Are all the events of equal importance? If not, identify the events and experiences that you would like to zoom in on for a close-up, as well as those that might best be left in the background. This decision moves you toward identifying what should be narrated and what should be explained by exposition.
6. Now rewrite the ''close-up'' sections, providing them with vivid and concrete details.
7. As you rewrite, add time indicators (dates and transitions) to provide continuity.
8. Write on one side of your paper only.

At this point, let's move on to the matter of exposition.

Exposition in the Service of Narration.   Unlike the purely narrative mode, the expository mode, when used in a narrative framework, does not recount events in chronological order; rather, it summarizes, explains, or interprets them. The skill that is required in the development of exposition in the service of narration is one that will test your ability to condense into a meaningful whole experiences that have occurred over long periods of time. Narration shows what your experience was like, and exposition tells about it. Both have their place.

The technique of summarizing is not something new to you. In our day-to-day activities, we all constantly condense experiences, conversations, and happenings, because doing so allows us to extract the essence of an experience from all of the unnecessary details. Thus, when we summarize, we engage in heavy editing by asking ourselves, ''What information can I omit without significantly changing the experience I am telling about?''

As an example, what is your favorite spectator sport? Have you ever noticed the difference between the sportscaster's on-the-air report on the action of a sporting event while it is occurring and the report of the event prepared for a newspaper the next day? The first is a blow-by-blow account, detailed and unedited, and if recorded, it would take up as much time as the game itself. The second account is condensed. It is likely to be heavily edited, with details only of highlights, and will probably also include interpretation or explanation. The impulse to comment (explain or interpret) is one that comes almost automatically from the writer's attempt to fuse highlights with selected details.

The opportunity to have some distance (time) between the actual event and the reporting of the event is valuable in the use of exposition for it forces you to ask yourself how you felt about the event when it happened and how you feel about it now. The differences between the two sets of feelings can provide the basis for a dynamic interpretation of the event. During narration, you are getting close to the action, capturing its immediacy through sensory details. During exposition, you are getting away from the action and applying your powers of interpretation and analysis to the event.

There are then several forms that exposition can take in the service of narration: (1) straight summary, which retains narration's effect of placing the reader in the scene and which is a condensed telling of what happened, and (2) explanation and interpretation, which remove the reader from the action and ask him or her to contemplate its meaning or significance. Explanation and interpretation both clarify, increasing our understanding of an event; but the former is more emphatically objective and factual, whereas the latter tends to have a greater element of subjectivity and hence is more open to argument.

By way of example, think again of a sportswriter. If, when reporting on a track meet, the sportswriter tells you that Smith beat Jones in the mile, that the race was close, and that the winning time was 3:58, he or she is summarizing the event. If the sportswriter tells you that Smith, who was expected to break the record, failed, he or she is explaining. If the sportswriter suggests that the poor condition of the track was the main reason that Smith failed to set a new record, he or she is interpreting.

Following is an essay on a stage that a student writer went through. Notice how he placed his shaping idea and blended narration with exposition.

DAYDREAM BELIEVER

One of the advantages of youth is that you may indulge yourself in the wildest of fantasies. When I was young, I was an avid comic-book reader. You might say I was a fanatic. Wherever I went, my comics went with me. I anxiously awaited every new issue. My superheroes depicted adventurous deeds that I could easily identify with. Their experiences were for me, at the age of ten, very real. I portrayed, moreover, every character that I read.

Every one of them was capable of performing superhuman acts. Each was unique, possessing specialized powers. Some were able to fly, to become invisible, or to change their form, and some had strength far beyond that of mortals. Each superhero was easily identifiable by his name and costume, which added to the story line of the particular plot.

I remember one particular afternoon I was with my parents in the country. I was reading my favorite comic, Spider Man. Nearby some rocks towered above me. I instantly sensed danger and immediately scaled the rocks as the "wild web slinger." When I reached the top, my "spider sense" was tingling. I found myself face to face with my arch enemy, "The Lizard." We immediately became locked in a ferocious hand-to-hand, life-and-death struggle. A large crowd gathered below, watching in suspense. I blinded the reptilian creature with a face full of web. With a swift kick, I knocked him off the cliff in defeat.

It seemed as if I was continually reprimanded for living vicariously. My mother, as all mothers, was always concerned for my well-being. She apparently misconstrued my mysterious behavior. She also, however, seemed to possess the understanding and the realization that one day I would outgrow it.

All of my allowance was used to purchase comic books. On many occasions, I read my comic book in class. I would secretly place the comic in a text and read and dream while the class was in session. Although I managed to maintain a normal class standard, I had to expend more effort while dividing myself between two worlds. My teacher was suspicious of my actions and thus felt I was not giving my all. She felt I had a better academic potential than I was showing, and she periodically referred me to the dean for special counseling.

I recall that once in my sixth-grade math class I was very bored. In the next moment, I was Dr. Bruce Banner, walking the streets of New York. Suddenly people were running toward me in panic. They were screaming hysterically, fearing for their lives. They were running from a monster terrorizing the city. I, too, started to run away, but I was thrown to the ground by the crowd and lay helpless as the monster approached. With my heartbeat ever increasing, I knew that transformation would soon occur. In seconds, I was eight feet tall, with green skin and solid muscle. Dr. Bruce Banner once again became the Incredible Hulk.

In this period of my life, I did not have the same interests as my friends. As my friends emulated their sports heroes, I had my super-heroes. Sometimes, in the midst of a game, I would be criticized for my lack of attention. I would let a ball slip by me, or I would miss a throw. This angered my teammates as it sometimes led to the loss of a game.

Despite any obstacles placed before me, I persevered. My world was filled with fantasy, and superheroes fired my imagination with adven-ture. Over the years, I have retained my vivid imagination. However, I now apply it to more practical ends.

What was the writer's attitude toward the daydream period of his youth? To what degree did he still identify with the role of "daydream believer"? To what degree had he distanced himself from that role? How would you describe the voice that he selected in order to write his essay?

Using Exposition in Writing on a Significant Stage. It is possible that the student who wrote on his daydream period blended his passages of sum-mary, explanation, and interpretation into his narrative freely, without much planning, simply by sitting down and writing a draft. You can do the same, of course. Or, if you like, you can continue with the procedure that we intro-duced in the preceding section on "Using Narration in Writing on a Significant Stage."

In the second case, turn again to the two hours of free writing from which you have already taken and rewritten your close-up narrative sections. Now you will want to identify the sections that summarize, explain, and interpret. If you started your writing in Hour 2 with a statement of the pattern that emerged in Hour 1, you will probably have in the Hour 2 material a fair amount of writing that already summarizes, explains, and interprets. The instructions that follow will serve as your guidelines for rewriting the sections from Hours 1 and 2 that have the expository impulse. Again, place the refined statement of your shaping idea at the top of a sheet of paper. Now, do the following:

1. Read Hours 1 and 2 of the work you produced by free writing.
2. Identify the sections with the expository impulse.
3. Evaluate these sections to see whether they (a) summarize narrative por-tions of the stage; (b) explain a particular action, conversation, or pattern of behavior that occurred during the stage; or (c) interpret any part of the stage. Note the specific function of each section of your free-writing in the margins.
4. Now evaluate also those sections that you decided during your narrative rewrite would serve you better as background. They too will be turned into expository sections.

5. Now rewrite all the identified sections of summary, explanation, and interpretation, using the refined shaping idea to get started. As you write these expository sections, remember that you are striving to summarize gaps of time not accounted for during the close-up sections; to explain specific situations; and to interpret individual experiences, conversations, events, and actions, as well as to interpret the significance of the stage as a whole. Additionally each section should show its relatedness to your shaping idea.

6. Again, write on one side of your paper only.

Writing the Rough Draft: Cutting and Pasting

Now you may again decide to read through your material and compose a rough draft on fresh, blank paper. Or, you can try splicing the rewritten narrative and expository sections that you already have to form a first draft.

If you choose to splice, you will need (1) your rewritten narrative and expository sections (put away your Hours 1 and 2 of free writing but do not discard them); and (2) more paper, a pair of scissors, and some rubber cement or tape. You will also need all the courage you can muster, for many people are timid about cutting up their work. Do not be timid; out of this seeming destruction will emerge a new construction. Furthermore you can feel flattered that you are in the good company of many published writers who engage in cutting and pasting at some point in their writing process. Now do the following:

1. Read through the two rewritten sections, identifying and labeling potential parts of the essay, starting with the introduction and conclusion. Label them in the margins with a colored pencil. Use either letters or numbers to mark the sequence.

2. Decide what will follow your introduction, and label it in the margin also.

3. Continue this labeling process until you have labeled everything from these two narrative and expository sections. (This whole process requires a great deal of reading and rereading.)

4. Now that you have labeled all the sections numerically or alphabetically, cut out the introductory section and paste it on a new sheet of paper, which will become page 1 of your rough draft. Next, cut out the section labeled 1 or A, which is to follow your introduction, and paste it below, leaving three or four lines between the end of the introduction and the beginning of this new section. Continue in the same way until you have cut and pasted all the labeled sections through to your conclusion.

Now, whether by cutting and pasting or by simply reading over your notes and then writing a fresh draft, complete your rough draft. Then take a break from your essay.

During your break, take a look at the following essays by two professional writers, Russell Baker and Patrick Fenton. Where does each writer place his shaping idea? How thoroughly does each rely on exposition in the service of narration?

My Lack of Gumption
Russell Baker

I began working in journalism when I was eight years old. It was my mother's idea. She wanted me to "make something" of myself and, after a level-headed appraisal of my strengths, decided I had better start young if I was to have any chance of keeping up with the competition.

The flaw in my character which she had already spotted was lack of "gumption." My idea of a perfect afternoon was lying in front of the radio rereading my favorite Big Little Book, *Dick Tracy Meets Stooge Viller*. My mother despised inactivity. Seeing me having a good time in repose, she was powerless to hide her disgust. "You've got no more gumption than a bump on a log," she said. "Get out in the kitchen and help Doris do those dirty dishes."

My sister Doris, though two years younger than I, had enough gumption for a dozen people. She positively enjoyed washing dishes, making beds, and cleaning the house. When she was only seven she could carry a piece of short-weighted cheese back to the A&P, threaten the manager with legal action, and come back triumphantly with a full quarter-pound we'd paid for and a few ounces extra thrown in for forgiveness. Doris could have made something of herself if she hadn't been a girl. Because of this defect, however, the best she could hope for was a career as a nurse or schoolteacher, the only work that capable females were considered up to in those days.

This must have saddened my mother, this twist of fate that had allocated all the gumption to the daughter and left her with a son who was content with Dick Tracy and Stooge Viller. If disappointed, though, she wasted no energy on self-pity. She would make me make something of myself whether I wanted to or not. "The Lord helps those who help themselves," she said. That was the way her mind worked.

She was realistic about the difficulty. Having sized up the material the Lord had given her to mold, she didn't overestimate what she could do with it. She didn't insist that I grow up to be President of the United States.

Fifty years ago parents still asked boys if they wanted to grow up to be President, and asked it not jokingly but seriously. Many parents who were hardly more than paupers still believed their sons could do it. Abraham Lincoln had done it. We were only sixty years from Lincoln. Many a grandfather who walked among us could remember Lincoln's time. Men of grandfatherly age were the worst for asking if you wanted to grow up to be President. A surprising number of little boys said yes and meant it.

I was asked many times myself. No, I would say, I didn't want to grow up to be President. My mother was present during one of these interrogations. An elderly uncle, having posed the usual question and exposed my lack of interest in the Presidency, asked, "Well, what *do* you want to be when you grow up?"

I loved to pick through trash piles and collect empty bottles, tin cans with pretty labels, and discarded magazines. The most desirable job on earth sprang instantly to mind. "I want to be a garbage man," I said.

My uncle smiled, but my mother had seen the first distressing evidence of a bump budding on a log. "Have a little gumption, Russell," she said. Her calling me Russell was a signal of unhappiness. When she approved of me I was always "Buddy."

When I turned eight years old she decided that the job of starting me on the road toward making something of myself could no longer be safely delayed. "Buddy," she said one day, "I want you to come home right after school this afternoon. Somebody's coming and I want you to meet him."

When I burst in that afternoon she was in conference in the parlor with an executive of the Curtis Publishing Company. She introduced me. He bent low from the waist and shook my hand. Was it true as my mother had told him, he asked, that I longed for the opportunity to conquer the world of business?

My mother replied that I was blessed with a rare determination to make something of myself.

"That's right," I whispered.

"But have you got the grit, the character, the never-say-quit spirit it takes to succeed in business?"

My mother said I certainly did.

"That's right," I said.

He eyed me silently for a long pause, as though weighing whether I could be trusted to his confidence, then spoke man-to-man. Before taking a crucial step, he said, he wanted to advise me that working for the Curtis Publishing Company placed enormous responsibility on a young man. It was one of the great companies of America. Perhaps the greatest publishing house in the world. I had heard, no doubt, of the *Saturday Evening Post*?

Heard of it? My mother said that everyone in our house had heard of the *Saturday Post* and that I, in fact, read it with religious devotion.

Then doubtless, he said, we were also familiar with those two monthly pillars of the magazine world, the *Ladies Home Journal* and the *Country Gentleman*.

Indeed we were familiar with them, said my mother.

Representing the *Saturday Evening Post* was one of the weightiest honors that could be bestowed in the world of business, he said. He was personally proud of being a part of that great corporation.

My mother said he had *every* right to be.

Again he studied me as though debating whether I was worthy of a knighthood. Finally: "Are you trustworthy?"

My mother said I was the soul of honesty.

"That's right," I said.

The caller smiled for the first time. He told me I was a lucky young man. He admired my spunk. Too many young men thought life was all play. Those young men would not go far in this world. Only a young man willing to work and save and keep his face washed and his hair neatly combed could hope to come out on top in a world such as ours. Did I truly and sincerely believe that I was such a young man?

"He certainly does," said my mother.

"That's right," I said.

He said he had been so impressed by what he had seen of me that he was going to make me a representative of the Curtis Publishing Company. On the following Tuesday, he said, thirty freshly printed copies of the *Saturday Evening Post* would be delivered at our door. I would place these magazines, still damp with the ink of the presses, in a handsome canvas bag, sling it over my shoulder, and set forth through the streets to bring the best in journalism, fiction, and cartoons to the American public.

He had brought the canvas bag with him. He presented it with reverence fit for a chasuble. He showed me how to drape the sling over my left shoulder and across the chest so that the pouch lay easily accessible to my right hand, allowing the best in journalism, fiction, and cartoons to be swiftly extracted and sold to a citizenry whose happiness and security depended upon us soldiers of the free press.

The following Tuesday I raced home from school, put the canvas bag over my shoulder, dumped the magazines in, and, tilting to the left to balance their weight on my right hip, embarked on the highway of journalism.

We lived in Belleville, New Jersey, a commuter town at the northern fringe of Newark. It was 1932, the bleakest year of the Depression. My father had died two years before, leaving us with a few pieces of Sears, Roebuck furniture and not much else, and my mother had taken Doris and me to live with one of her younger brothers. This was my Uncle Allen. Uncle Allen had made something of himself by 1932. As salesman for a soft-drink bottler in Newark, he had an income of $30 a week; wore pearl-gray spats, detachable collars, and a three-piece suit; was happily married; and took in threadbare relatives.

With my load of magazines I headed toward Belleville Avenue. That's where the people were. There were two filling stations at the intersection with Union Avenue, as well as an A&P, a fruit stand, a bakery, a barber shop, Zuccarelli's drugstore, and a diner shaped like a railroad car. For several hours I made myself highly visible, shifting position now and then from corner to corner, from shop window to shop window, to make sure everyone could see the heavy black lettering on the canvas bag that said the *Saturday Evening Post.* When the angle of the light indicated it was suppertime, I walked back to the house.

"How many did you sell, Buddy?" my mother asked.

"None."

"Where did you go?"

"The corner of Belleville and Union Avenues."

"What did you do?"

"Stood on the corner waiting for somebody to buy a *Saturday Evening Post.*"

"You just stood there?"

"Didn't sell a single one."

"For God's sake, Russell!"

Uncle Allen intervened. "I've been thinking about it for some time," he said, "and I've about decided to take the *Post* regularly. Put me down as a regular customer." I handed him a magazine and he paid me a nickel. It was the first nickel I earned.

Afterwards my mother instructed me in salesmanship. I would have to ring doorbells, address adults with charming self-confidence, and break down resistance with a sales talk pointing out that no one, no matter how poor, could afford to be without the *Saturday Evening Post* in the home.

I told my mother I'd changed my mind about wanting to succeed in the magazine business.

"If you think I'm going to raise a good-for-nothing," she replied, "you've got another think coming." She told me to hit the streets with the canvas bag and start ringing doorbells the instant school was out next day. When I objected that I didn't feel any aptitude for salesmanship, she asked how I'd like to lend her my leather belt so she could whack some sense into me. I bowed to superior will and entered journalism with a heavy heart.

My mother and I had fought this battle almost as long as I could remember. It probably started even before memory began, when I was a country child in northern Virginia and my mother, dissatisfied with my father's plain workman's life, determined that I would not grow up like him and his people, with calluses on their hands, overalls on their backs, and fourth-grade educations in their heads. She had fancier ideas of life's possibilities. Introducing me to the *Saturday Evening Post,* she was trying to wean me as early as possible from my father's world where men left with their lunch pails at sunup, worked with their hands until the grime ate into the pores, and died with a few sticks of mail-order furniture as their legacy. In my mother's vision of the better life there were desks and white collars, well-pressed suits, evenings of reading and lively talk, and perhaps—if a man were very, very lucky and hit the jackpot, really made something important of himself—perhaps there might be a fantastic salary of $5,000 a year to support a big house and a Buick with a rumble seat and a vacation in Atlantic City.

And so I set forth with my sack of magazines. I was afraid of the dogs that snarled behind the doors of potential buyers. I was timid about ringing the doorbells of strangers, relieved when no one came to the door, and scared when someone did. Despite my mother's instructions, I could not deliver an engaging sales pitch. When a door opened I simply asked, "Want to buy a *Saturday Evening Post?*" In Belleville few persons did. It was a town of 30,000 people, and most weeks I rang a fair majority of its doorbells. But I rarely sold my thirty copies. Some weeks I canvassed the entire town for six days and still had four or five unsold magazines on Monday evening; then I dreaded the coming of Tuesday morning, when a batch of thirty fresh *Saturday Evening Posts* was due at the front door.

"Better get out there and sell the rest of those magazines tonight," my mother would say.

I usually posted myself then at a busy intersection where a traffic light controlled commuter flow from Newark. When the light turned red I stood on the curb and shouted my sales pitch at the motorists.

"Want to buy a *Saturday Evening Post?*"

One rainy night when car windows were sealed against me I came back soaked and with not a single sale to report. My mother beckoned to Doris.

"Go back down there with Buddy and show him how to sell these magazines," she said.

Brimming with zest, Doris, who was then seven years old, returned with me to the corner. She took a magazine from the bag, and when the light turned red she strode to the nearest car and banged her small fist against the closed window. The driver, probably startled at what he took to be a midget assaulting his car, lowered the window to stare, and Doris thrust a *Saturday Evening Post* at him.

"You need this magazine," she piped, "and it only costs a nickel."

Her salesmanship was irresistible. Before the light changed half a dozen times she disposed of the entire batch. I didn't feel humiliated. To the contrary. I was so happy I decided to give her a treat. Leading her to the vegetable store on Belleville Avenue, I bought three apples, which cost a nickel, and gave her one.

"You shouldn't waste money," she said.

"Eat your apple." I bit into mine.

"You shouldn't eat before supper," she said. "It'll spoil your appetite."

Back at the house that evening, she dutifully reported me for wasting a nickel. Instead of a scolding, I was rewarded with a pat on the back for having the good sense to buy fruit instead of candy. My mother reached into her bottomless supply of maxims and told Doris, "An apple a day keeps the doctor away."

By the time I was ten I had learned all my mother's maxims by heart. Asking to stay up past normal bedtime, I knew that a refusal would be explained with, "Early to bed and early to rise, makes a man healthy, wealthy, and wise." If I whimpered about having to get up early in the morning, I could depend on her to say, "The early bird gets the worm."

The one I most despised was, "If at first you don't succeed, try, try again." This was the battle cry with which she constantly sent me back into the hopeless struggle whenever I moaned that I had rung every doorbell in town and knew there wasn't a single potential buyer left in Belleville that week. After listening to my explanation, she handed me the canvas bag and said, "If at first you don't succeed . . ."

Three years in that job, which I would gladly have quit after the first day except for her insistence, produced at least one valuable result. My mother finally concluded that I would never make something of myself by pursuing a life in business and started considering careers that demanded less competitive zeal.

One evening when I was eleven I brought home a short "composition" on my summer vacation which the teacher had graded with an A. Reading it with her own schoolteacher's eye, my mother agreed that it was top-drawer seventh grade prose and complimented me. Nothing more was said about it immediately, but a new idea had taken life in her mind. Halfway through supper she suddenly interrupted the conversation.

"Buddy," she said, "maybe you could be a writer."

I clasped the idea to my heart. I had never met a writer, had shown no previous urge to write, and hadn't a notion how to become a writer, but I loved stories and thought that making up stories must surely be almost as much fun as reading them. Best of all, though, and what really gladdened my heart, was the ease of the writer's life. Writers did not have to trudge through the town peddling from canvas bags, defending themselves against angry dogs, being rejected by surly strangers. Writers did not have to ring doorbells. So far as I could make out, what writers did couldn't even be classified as work.

I was enchanted. Writers' didn't have to have any gumption at all. I did not dare tell anybody for fear of being laughed at in the schoolyard, but secretly I decided that what I'd like to be when I grew up was a writer.

What sort of stage does Baker focus on? Is he writing about a phase in his life, or would you say that the story he narrates is significant to him in some other way? What sort of role does he play in the essay? How much is the voice in which he writes a reflection of this role?

The next essay was written by Patrick Fenton especially for this chapter. How does Fenton choose to fulfill the task? What kind of voice does he adopt in order to bridge the gap between his readers' point of view and his own? Would you say that he identifies himself with a stereotypical role, either in the past, in the story he tells, or now, as the narrator of the story?

Still the Same
Patrick Fenton

The old neighborhood, an Irish working-class section of Park Slope, was called the "Hill" because it stood on the highest point of Brooklyn. Inside the tenement of 483 17th Street, where I grew up, ballads of Irish music would drone from radios and the sound would drift through the darkness of the hallways: "Some boys when they go out a courting, sure they haven't the spunk of a mouse. They stand on the corner and . . ." The songs would fill my head with a sadness that I never quite understood. To escape it I would line up my stacks of comic books on the oil-cloth of our kitchen floor and flip through them looking for doubles to trade. Soon I would be lost in the world of Daredevil and his friends, Scarecrow, Jock, and Slugger, as they danced across a bright red, blue, and yellow logo.

There were other forms of dreaming that filled the head with hazy visions of other places, places where heroes lived. On gray, wintry Saturday afternoons, hordes of kids would leave the tenements of 17th Street and head down the hill to the Globe Theater for an afternoon of cowboy movies. For twenty-five cents, the image of our hero, Tom Mix, would ride endlessly across the screen in the darkness of the fetid movie house. Over on 9th Street and 6th Avenue, there was the Brooklyn Public Library, a great stone building surrounded by rows of black picket fence. Its insides were filled with a pale yellow light, and rows of dark-covered books that led up to a balcony that I loved to get lost in. It was here that I read my first book, felt that first stirring of affection for words as I read the description of the waterfalls of Exmoor in Richard Blackmore's *Lorna Doone*.

On Sundays the great stone steps that led up to the front doors of Holy Name Church, over on Prospect Avenue, would be filled with altar boys. Through sun and rain I stood on these long steps as I took part in communions and funerals. Behind the great oak doors of the church were the dark reds and greens of the frescoes that covered the walls of the altar. Each Sunday morning, I would have to pass under the painted stare of fierce, armor-clad Roman soldiers as I marched up to the rail to receive communion.

For the most part, life in our parish passed with a certain amount of predictability: Children made plans for Christmas trips down to the five and dime stores on 5th Avenue and 9th Street. When they got older there would be plans for large, rowdy Irish weddings at the McFadden Brothers Post of the American Legion on 9th Avenue. Plans were made for christenings at Holy Name Church, and in sad times there would be plans made for Irish wakes in Pete Smith's Funeral Home, which was just across the street.

Then, in the mid 50s, life started to change in the neighborhood, as the era of the street gang spread across Brooklyn. Cars loaded with vicious kids from rival gangs, the Jokers, the South Brooklyn Boys, started to cruise 9th Avenue. A few doors down from where I lived, there was a brutal stomp killing that made the front pages of all the newspapers. That summer, Skinny Sterling, a 14-year-old kid that I knew from school, was shot dead by a cop in front of 483 17th Street. I remember looking down at his frail body from the top floor of our tenement, crowds surrounding him, windows opening up and down 17th Street as people yelled out, "What happened, what happened?" In the days that followed his death, there was no talk of treating his classmates for trauma, like there would be today. The school just marched us all off to his wake.

It became clear to me that the only way to survive was to toughen up. The first day I showed up at Manual Training, a high school on 5th Street in South Brooklyn that had the dubious distinction of having the same name as the school in the movie *Blackboard Jungle,* I turned up the collar of my black cotton shirt and swung into a bop walk that I had copied from One-Eyed Welsh.

One-Eyed Welsh was a tough kid who lived across the street from me. He had one bad eye that turned to the side, giving him the most menacing look of any kid in our neighborhood. His hair was the color of rust and his teeth had become green from years of neglect. He became my hero. Naturally, he never had any girls interested in him, but who cared. Each day I would be envious of him as I watched him prowl our neighborhood with all the freedom of a wildcat.

As I went deeper into this phase of my life, I was slowly changing. When I looked in the mirror, I didn't see an innocent kid who spent the most impressive part of his youth learning about virtue from the Saint Joseph Brothers at Holy Name Parochial School; I saw Vic Morrow pushing back his baseball cap as he got ready to give Glenn Ford, the teacher in *Blackboard Jungle,* trouble.

That summer I joined the junior division of the Gremlins, a street gang from the Park Circle area of our neighborhood. There wasn't much of an induction. I swore my allegiance in the darkened courtyard of the Pilgrim Laundry one night, in front of Skippy, a tough, fat kid who controlled the junior Gremlins. Most of the summer was spent talking tough and having mock flights with each other. "Come on, man. You think you're a diddley bop? I'll hit you so hard you'll have to back up a mile to blow your nose." I soon learned that there was a price you had to pay if you really wanted to act out this toughness. The toughest members of the Gremlins could spin off a litany of reform schools that they had spent time in: Lincoln Hall, Youth House, Warwick.

Before the summer was over, I found myself on the battlefield of the long meadows of Prospect Park as a soldier in a gang war. The battle took place just a few feet from the old Quaker Cemetery, a historical burial ground set in the darkness of the woods that surround the meadow. Like young men in a Civil War skirmish, we marched across the green of the meadow toward each other, about fifty in all. Some years later, I found a description of a Civil War battle that the poet Walt Whitman had witnessed, and it brought me back to that day in the park: "The shouts and curses of men—the orders from the officers. The wild cry of a regiment charging . . . The groans of the wounded, the sight of blood. O the hideous hell, the damned hell of war."

Why we were fighting is all vague to me now. A quick phrase like "There's going to be a rumble in the park" was enough to pull me along. As I remember it, I'm so far in the back ranks that I'm almost out of the park. It's late in the evening, and the few people who are still in the meadow are running frantically toward the street with their children in tow. I'm safe in the back ranks, filled with excitement as I march forward with groups of teenagers whipping the air with broken car aerials.

There's someone shouting orders up front, and we're all moving up faster now; we're starting to trot. The front lines start to split open like a broken daisy chain. All I can hear is shouting and the thud of chains and baseball bats landing on backs and heads. Then the front lines have a clear break in them, and as I turn to run, I can see guys stumbling in the dust; some of them are crying. "God help me," somebody yells. "Please dear God, help me." Police sirens are wailing as the cars bounce over the dividers of the meadows.

I remember running out of the park like a wild horse, my feet tripping over the discarded baseball bats, the lengths of lead pipe, the broken ends of Coke bottles that cover the dirt. "Please God," I pray. "I'll never return if I can make it to the safety of the streets."

I've thought about that phase of my life many times, wondering how it changed me, how it helped to form me into what I am today, what it taught me. There's still a part of me that's stirred by causes, some political, some matters of principle, but I'm not as quick to rush to battle with pen or fists to defend them. How easily we pick the wrong heroes when we're young, fight the wrong battles with a stubborn determination that defies reason.

Some of the things this phase of my life taught me I'm not proud of. But I am proud that the gentle part of me, the part that loved words, the part of me that loved cowboy movies, was still there when it was over.

Finally, before you get to the "focus" section in this chapter, you can read through the first draft of the essay written from the free-writing exercises on the student's phase with the devil. Notice how he has combined the two exercises on pp. 99–100 in writing his draft.

MY PHASE WITH THE DEVIL

I still remember the days when I was afraid of the devil. During this period, I learned to be a responsible individual.

I lived in a small town with many superstitious individuals. I knew all the people that lived there. My community was like a big family that shared the good and the bad things in life. There, the old people influenced my thinking very much. They used to tell me stories about the devil that stayed on my mind for months. By the time I was seven, I had started to have bad dreams. I used to dream of the devil as a huge red creature, half human and half animal. I used to go to sleep with the light on because I was afraid of the dark. For me, darkness was the devil's hiding place. Once asleep, I used to dream of the devil coming at night to my town and taking away bad children. Some of the children in town were my best friends, and seeing them alive each morning was a great relief to me.

.I remember a dream that I had for many nights. I was hiding in the basement in an empty barrel. The devil searched my house until he found me and brought me into his world of flames. There, he cooked me with some other boys and girls for his daily dinner.

During that phase, many friends used to invite me to the movies, but I always had an excuse to stay away from the theater. To me, horror movies meant dreams and sleepless nights. The devil was so impressed on my mind that when my father sent me to the basement to do something, I almost cried. My grandfather used to tell me that there was a place in the valley where ghosts were having fun. The devil was their host.

That story always stayed in my mind, and many times I dreamed about it. I dreamed of standing at the top of a high cliff and looking down into hell, a valley where many people roasted. The town priest used to tell children that if they did well they would end up in heaven. Otherwise, they would go to hell.

These dreams considerably affected my character. I became a more responsible individual. I tried to obey my parents and respect other people. I also became pessimistic, but in a positive way. What I mean is that I tried to do my best in defeating my pessimism. My dreams were very painful, but they helped me to become a mature person.

This period of unpleasant dreams ended when I was about ten years old. Now, I'm not afraid of hell or devils because I'm a secure individual with a future to think about.

Where in this draft did the student use narration? Where did he use summary or explanation or interpretation? How would you advise him to revise? Where does he need more detailed narration? Where does he need to explain or interpret more thoroughly?

FOCUS: PARAGRAPH STRUCTURE

Essays are divided into paragraphs as an aid to both the reader and the writer. The paragraph breaks in an essay help the reader to follow the flow of thought from point to point and of conversation from speaker to speaker. In addition, some paragraphs serve to emphasize for the reader the writer's major points by repeating a point developed in a previous paragraph.

Dividing an essay into paragraphs also helps the writer to develop his or her shaping idea sequentially throughout an essay and to emphasize special points. The writer of narrative may wish to use paragraph breaks to separate the major stages of the event, whereas the writer of exposition will use paragraphs to develop the primary aspects of his or her subject. Reexamine "Daydream Believer" in the previous section (pp. 105–107) for the paragraph structure. What rationale had the writer for his paragraph breaks?

Because of the importance of the paragraph, in writing your essay you will want to pay attention to the structure of each paragraph. Just as essays have a beginning, a middle, and an end, so most effective paragraphs have a beginning, a middle, and an end. You state the point of the paragraph in what can be called a *topic sentence* and then develop that point or topic in several other sentences. If the paragraph is sufficiently long, or if you want added emphasis, you may want a concluding sentence as well.

Notice in the following paragraph that the third sentence introduces the paragraph (after two initial background sentences), the next five develop the topic, and the last concludes emphatically by restating the topic sentence.

I have long wondered just what my strength is as a writer. I am often filled with tremendous enthusiasm for a subject, yet my writing about it will seem a sorry attempt. *Above all, I possess a driving sincerity, that prime virtue of any creative worker.* I write only what I believe to be the absolute truth—even if I must ruin the theme in so doing. In this respect, I feel far superior to those glib people in my classes who often garner better grades than I do. They are so often pitiful frauds, artificial, insincere. They have a line that works. They do not write from the depths of their hearts. Nothing of theirs was ever born of pain. *Many an incoherent yet sincere piece of writing has outlived the polished product.*

—**Theodore Roethke,** *On the Poet and His Craft*

The following paragraph begins with the topic sentence but has no conclusion, as the writer was more interested in the details of his day than he was in emphasizing the general idea of how he passed his time:

Do you want to know how I pass my time? I rise at eight or thereabouts—& go to my barn—say good-morning to the horse, & give him his breakfast. (It goes to my heart to give him a cold one, but it can't be helped.) Then, pay a visit to my cow—cut up a pumpkin or two for her, & stand by to see her eat it—for it's a pleasant sight to see a cow move her jaws—she does it so mildly & with such a sanctity.—My own breakfast over, I go to my workroom & light my fire—then spread my M.S.S. on the table—take one business squint at it, & fall to with a will. At 2½ P.M. I hear a preconcerted knock at my door, which (by request) continues till I rise & go to the door, which serves to wean me effectively from my writing, however interested I may be. My friends the horse & cow now demand their dinner—& I go & give it them. My own dinner over, I rig my sleigh & with my mother or sisters start off for the village—& if it be a Literary World day, great is the satisfaction thereof.—My evenings I spend in a sort of mesmeric state in my room—not being able to read—only now & then skimming over some large-printed book.

—Herman Melville

In the following paragraph, the writer has only a conclusion, or one could say that he placed his topic sentence at the end. This arrangement creates a dramatic, climactic effect.

When I first began to describe the little world of yesteryear that lives again in my books, that small corner of a French province, scarcely known even to Frenchmen, where the vacations of my school days were spent, I had no idea that I would attract the attention of foreign readers. We are all quite convinced of our utter singularity. We forget that the books which we ourselves found enchanting, those of George Eliot or of Dickens, of Tolstoy or Dostoevsky, or of Selma Lagerlöf, describe countries very different from our own, people of another race and another religion; and yet we loved them, because we recognized ourselves in them. All humanity is in this or that peasant back home, and all the landscapes in the world coalesce in the horizons familiar to our childish eyes. The novelist's gift is precisely his power to make plain the universal quality concealed in that sheltered world where we were born, and where we first learned to love and suffer.

—Francois Mauriac

Joan Didion's topic sentence in the following paragraph asks a question, and her conclusion summarizes the answers given in the developing sentences. This arrangement also creates a climactic effect:

Why did I write it down? In order to remember, of course, but exactly what was it I wanted to remember? How much of it actually happened? Did any of it? Why do I keep a notebook at all? It is easy to deceive oneself on all those scores. The impulse to write things down is a peculiarly compulsive one, inexplicable to those who do not share it, useful only accidentally, only secondarily, in the way that any compulsion tries to justify itself. I suppose that it begins or does not begin in the cradle. Although I have felt compelled to write things down since I was five years old, I doubt that my daughter ever will, for she is a singularly blessed and accepting child, delighted with life exactly as life presents itself to her, unafraid to wake up. Keepers of private notebooks are a different breed altogether, lonely and resistant rearrangers of things, anxious malcontents, children afflicted apparently at birth with some presentiment of loss.

—**Joan Didion,** "On Keeping a Notebook"

The following paragraph has no distinct topic sentence. The writer's point is understandable, however. Her topic sentence might have been, "Because the eyes can communicate in an instant, communication between two people in our fast-paced technological age is possible, but how can we learn to communicate in this way?" The topic sentence has been omitted because the writer was following a line of thought—delineating the aspects of a problem—rather than making a point:

Messages are conveyed by the eyes, sometimes by no words at all. It is no excuse to say that technology has accelerated our life to the point where we pass others without noticing them, without contacting, or without a real meeting. A real meeting can take place in one instant. But how does that come about? How do we reach a moment when in one instant we can communicate with another human being?

—**Marya Mannes,** "Television: The Splitting Image"

SOME PRACTICE WITH PARAGRAPH STRUCTURE

1. Three topic sentences are given for each of the paragraphs below. Can you decide which one is the actual topic sentence written by the author of the paragraph? Explain your choice in each case.

a. _____

_____

Where is Johnny? He is, you will recall, a college undergraduate, let's say a freshman. He has typically been exposed to a number of years of drill founded on a traditional and dubious grammar; he has done some writing of quite variable amount and character; he has read a few standard works of literature and probably a slender but startling miscellany of contemporary fare; he doesn't know how to pursue an idea through a piece of prose that has one; he concocts what he considers English for his English teacher and is shocked if anybody else expects this odd behavior of him; and, as there is no guarantee that he spells correctly, Professor Stackblowe is quite likely to be displeased with him. He has grown up believing that English means literacy because that is what he has been taught, and if it hasn't taken very well he is rather apologetic about it. Probably nobody has had time, strength, or inclination to help him very far toward competence. But, perhaps just because he is now eighteen or thereabouts, he can be helped toward competence and, if necessary, literacy into the bargain.

—"Why the Devil Don't You Teach Freshmen to Write?" *Saturday Review*

1. Literacy is the goal of Johnny's education.

2. Johnny has been given an incorrect definition of literacy.

3. The beginning of wisdom is to "take the student where he is."

b. From kids stealing candy bars to multi-million-dollar frauds, property crimes manifest a lack of concern for other people. _____

_____

Children living in places where people have no rights that they are capable of enforcing will rarely have a regard for rights of others. Since legal rights tend to reflect important values of society, such individuals have little regard for things society considers important. To know that police take bribes, the church treasurer ran off with the building fund, the construction contractor swindled your father out of the cost of new roofing, and three of your friends make more in a night stripping cars than you make in a week washing them is not conducive to respect for the law. Some finally rationalize that they would be fools to play it straight when everyone they know is on the make. The next step may be rolling a drunk. For suburban youth living in materialistic abundance the motivations for rapidly increasing property crime are different, diverse, and more difficult to identify. Neglect, anxiety, family breakup, emptiness, the loneliness of the individual in huge high schools and lack of identity contribute. Faceless youngsters of affluent families steal cars, burglarize suburban homes, and commit acts of malicious destruction most often because nothing else in their lives seems important.

—**Ramsey Clark**, "The Many Faces of Crime"

1. While the contributory factors are many and varied, crime is chiefly the result of poverty.

2. While the contributory factors are many and varied, the effects of property crimes cost billions annually.

3. While the contributory factors are many and varied, the capability for crime develops in early childhood when character is forming.

c. _____

_____

Deep-well disposal of chemical wastes by the U.S. Army near Denver led to earth tremors and small earthquakes as well as to contamination of the sub-soil. The Navy dumps tons of raw sewage into offshore waters, and its facili-ties, such as the notorious Fire Fighting School in San Diego, throw off pol-lutants into the air. Vessels carrying herbicides to Viet Nam and other areas of the world could possibly provoke one of history's greatest catastrophes. Should one ship sink and should the drums containing the chemicals be ruptured, marine organisms for miles around would be destroyed, thus reducing the oxygen supply available to mankind. The transfer of these herbicides through food to humans is another specter, given the fantastic geometric progress of the concentration of these chemicals from plankton on up the food-chain to man himself. Municipal waste disposal practices are, for many towns and cit-ies, primitive; and where waste is treated, effluents still upset the ecology of lakes, streams, and bays.

—from *Ecotatics*

1. Waste disposal is a great threat to mankind.
2. Government activity in sewage and solid waste disposal and in defense research has also burgeoned into environmental violence.
3. Governmental supervision of sewage and waste disposal is inadequate.

2. Write a topic sentence for each of the following paragraphs.

a. _____

_____

There were four of us in the long piroque, all of an age. For a long moment we were speechless. At last we said hello, and they answered in warm gay voices. We drifted the boat into the cove and began to speak to them. Two of the girls were sisters. The three of them had come to visit a relative who kept a fine summer lodge in the woods across the bayou from the camp. One of the sisters was fifteen and the others were seventeen. They were aglow with fresh and slender beauty, and their bathing suits were bright flags of color. Their impact upon us was overwhelming. We grew silly, tongue-tied, said foolish things we did not mean to say, shoved one another about in the boat, and finally overturned it. The loreleis laughed musical little laughs. They seemed unbearably beautiful. We had no idea what to do about it.

—**Thomas Sanction,** "The Silver Horn," *Harper's Magazine* (Feb. 1944)

b. _____

_____

For example, did they go to live in his father's castle? If so, how did she get on with the queen who was, incidentally, her mother-in-law? How many children did she have? Were they well adjusted or did she have to seek "professional help" for them? How did she handle the problem of sibling rivalry, which in this case may have been over no smaller a goal than the throne itself? How much did she see of her husband? Did wars, affairs of state, and commuting time ruin his family life? How could she possibly keep house without detergents? What did she do with herself when the children were all in school? She couldn't very well spend her time cleaning out the closets, as is sometimes the refuge of nonprincesses. Did she grow old gracefully? Did she outlive her husband and, if so, by how many years? What kind of pension could she claim in an era that preceded the advent of Social Security? In short, what was it like to live happily ever after?

—**Juanita Kreps,** *"What Was It Like to Live Happily Ever After?" Vital Speeches* (Dec. 15, 1964)

c. _____

_____

We know that, far from attracting her, whiskers and mustaches only make her nervous and gloomy, so that man had to go in for somersaults, tilting with lances, performing feats of parlor magic to win her attention; he also had to bring candy, flowers, and the furs of animals. It is common knowledge that in spite of these "love displays" the male is constantly being turned down, insulted, thrown out of the house. It is rather comforting, then, to discover that the peacock, for all his gorgeous plumage, does not have a particularly easy time of courtship; none of the males in the world do. The first peahen, it turned out, was only faintly stirred by her suitor's beautiful train. She would often go quietly to sleep while he was whisking it around. The *Britannica* tells us that the peacock actually had to learn a certain little trick to wake her up and revive her interest; he had to learn to vibrate his quills so as to make a rustling sound. In ancient time man himself, observing the ways of the peacock, probably tried vibrating his whiskers to make a rustling sound; if so, it didn't get him anywhere. He had to go in for something else; so, among other things he went in for gifts. It is not unlikely that he got this idea from certain flies and birds who were making no headway at all with rustling sounds.

—**James Thurber,** "Courtship Through the Ages," *My World and Welcome To It*

d. _____

_____

Consider the beer can. It was beautiful—as beautiful as the clothespin, as inevitable as the wine bottle, as dignified and reassuring as the fire hydrant. A tranquil cylinder of delightfully resonant metal, it could be opened in an instant, requiring only the application of a handy gadget freely dispensed by every grocer. Who can forget the small, symmetrical thrill of those two triangular punctures, the dainty pffff, the little crest of suds that foamed eagerly in the exultation of release? Now we are given, instead, a top beetling with an ugly, shmooshaped "tab," which after fiercely resisting the tugging, bleeding fingers of the thirsty man, threatens his lips with a dangerous and hideous hole. However, we have discovered a way to thwart Progress, usually so unthwartable. Turn the beer can upside down and open the bottom. The bottom is still the way the top used to be. True, this operation gives the beer an unsettling jolt, and the sight of a consistently inverted beer can might make people edgy, not to say queasy. But the latter difficulty could be eliminated if manufacturers would design cans that looked the same whichever end was up, like playing cards. What we need is Progress with an escape hatch.

—**John Updike,** "Beer Can," *Assorted Prose*

3. Which paragraphs in Exercises 1 and 2 have concluding sentences? Why has a conclusion been added in each case?

4. Develop the following topic sentences into paragraphs, experimenting by placing the topic sentence in different positions in the paragraphs. Use details or examples to support your point. Add a conclusion where you think one advisable.

> **a.** Registration for courses each semester is a hassle.
>
> **b.** Because of their desire for higher ratings, television news programs have become mostly entertainment.
>
> **c.** Instead of fulfilling their traditional role of providing fun, sports have deteriorated into hostile, often violent, competition.

5. Develop well-structured paragraphs based on the following topics. Word the topic sentence in each as clearly as possible. Add a concluding sentence if you think it effective.

> **a.** A free time pursuit.
>
> **b.** A recent observation of honesty.
>
> **c.** A current fad.
>
> **d.** The therapeutic value of a pet.

REWRITING

Obtaining Feedback on Your Rough Draft

Before you move into the revision of your first or rough draft, be sure that you have rested. You may have spent at least four hours moving through the rough draft, so if you worked continuously, take a break of twenty-four hours, unless, of course, the deadline is imminent. A break of a day can help to distance you from your work and can provide the objectivity that you will need in the reworking of your essay. You may also need this time for your peers or your instructor to evaluate your first effort. Before reading further, refer to the rewriting sections in Chapters 1 and 2 for comments on cutting, adding, and editing.

Your evaluators—yourself, your instructor, your peers—should organize their evaluations as before, according to the four questions of the "Audience Response Guide." Play the role of your intended audience (your instructor) as you read.

——— AUDIENCE RESPONSE GUIDE ———

1. What do you think the writer wanted to say in this paper? What is his or her purpose in writing? What does he or she want the paper to mean?
2. How does the paper affect the reader for whom it was intended?
3. How effective has the writer been in conveying his or her purpose and meaning? What are the strengths of the paper? What are the weaknesses?
4. How should the paper be revised to better fulfill its purpose and meaning?

Consider at this time the following peer evaluation of the rough draft of the student essay "My Phase With the Devil" (pp. 116–117). Compare your own evaluation of the draft with that of the peer group by answering the four questions of the "Audience Response Guide" before reading their answers.

1. The group felt that the writer wanted to convey how his fear of the devil had made him a more mature and responsible individual.
2. Playing the role of teacher, the group felt that the writer was writing as an adult who, perhaps like many adults, had matured because of a bad experience. His voice thus helped to create a bridge between him and his intended audience.
3. The group liked the writer's vivid use of detail, although they would have liked him to draw in closer to one of his dreams for a more thorough, blow-by-blow account that might have let them experience his fear more fully.
4. The group felt that he could have explained more clearly just how the phase led him to become more responsible, because the

connection between his pessimism and his responsibility was vague. As they felt the essay's organization was haphazard and did not seem to lead logically to the conclusion, they suggested that the writer rearrange his material by grouping together all of the stories told him by his elders, then all of his dreams, followed by their effects on him at the time they occurred, as well as their effects on him now.

Following is a revised version of "My Phase With the Devil." How well have the peer group's suggestions been incorporated? Did the writer make any additional changes himself? To what degree, for example, has he improved the paragraphs by rebuilding them around identifiable topic sentences? What additional changes might he have made?

MY PHASE WITH THE DEVIL

I still remember the days when I was afraid of the devil. Although this was a painful period for me, it helped me to become a more responsible individual.

I lived in a small town with many superstitious individuals. I knew all the people that lived there. My community was like a big family that shared the good and the bad things in life, including a belief in the devil.

The old people influenced my thinking very much. They used to tell me stories about the devil that stayed on my mind for months. My grandfather used to tell me that there was a place in the valley where ghosts were having fun. The devil was their host. Even the town priest spoke of the devil. He used to tell children that if they did well they would end up in heaven. Otherwise, they would go to hell.

My grandfather's story always stayed in my mind, and many times I dreamed about it. I dreamed of standing on a high cliff and looking down into hell, a valley where many people roasted. The devil was there, a huge red creature, half human and half animal. He stood over the people and laughed and stabbed their bodies with a pitchfork of flames.

I had other bad dreams as well. Sometimes I dreamed that I was hiding in the basement in an empty barrel. The devil searched my house until he found me and brought me into his world of flames. There, he cooked me with some other boys and girls for his daily dinner. I often dreamed of the devil coming at night to my town and taking away bad children. Some of them were my best friends, and seeing them alive each morning was a great relief to me.

Of course, I used to go to sleep with the light on because I was afraid of the dark. For me, darkness was the devil's hiding place. The devil was so impressed on my mind that when my father sent me to the basement to do something, I almost cried. And when my friends used to invite me to the movies, I always had an excuse to stay away from the theater. To me, horror movies meant bad dreams and sleepless nights.

These fears affected my character very much. I became a pessimistic individual. Every time I watched a ball game, I'd think that my team was going to lose. Sometimes I'd even think of myself as a loser because I had had so many painful experiences during my childhood.

But I tried to be pessimistic in a positive way. What I mean is that I tried to do my best in defeating my pessimism by working harder to make things turn out for the best. I became a more responsible individual because of my bad dream period. I tried to obey my parents and respect other people. My dreams were very painful, but they helped me to become a mature person.

This bad dream period ended when I was ten years old. Now, I'm not afraid of hell or devils because I'm a secure individual with a future to think about.

Rearranging

In revising your rough draft, you should decide whether the pattern of arrangement you have devised is effective. Start by testing your shaping idea once again. Does it suggest a pattern of organization for your essay, and if it does, does your essay's arrangement parallel the pattern it suggests? If it does not, rephrase your statement of your shaping idea so that it reflects the essay's arrangement pattern.

Next, examine the essay to see if the paragraphs follow each other in the most effective order. If sequences are askew, rearrange them.

Now, inspect the structure of your paragraphs. Does each have a topic sentence that is clearly related to the organizing idea of the essay? Do all the sentences in each paragraph develop the topic sentence? Is the topic sentence developed fully? Now rearrange any sentences that do not follow a logical pattern within your paragraphs. (Often narrative paragraphs do not have topic sentences because the subject is constantly changing through the passing of time.)

Finally, in completing the task for this chapter, evaluate the essay to see that it reflects an artful balance of narration, typified by specific details, and exposition, typified by summary, explanation, and interpretation. Evaluate the balance by counting first the paragraphs in which the dominant mode is narration and then those in which the dominant mode is exposition. If one or the other mode dominates overwhelmingly, ask yourself the following questions:

1. Have I included too many close-up narratives at the expense of the broader picture: If your answer is "no," do nothing and move on. If your answer is "yes," determine what close-ups can be omitted without damaging the essay and cut them out. Add the necessary exposition.

2. Have I tended to be too general, thus sacrificing the close-up? If your answer is "no," do nothing and move on. If your answer is "yes," determine what general exposition can be omitted and cut it out. Go into more detail to bring your narrative to life.

3. Have I written consistently in a voice that works as an effective bridge between my point of view and that of my reader? If your answer is "no," rephrase those passages in which you sound out of character.

Editing

Transitions.   The most well-organized paragraph may appear disorganized if transitions have not been used or if those used are imprecise. Effective transitions point out for the reader the essential unity of the sentence, the paragraph, and the essay. Reread the student essay "My Phase With the Devil" for the transitions that unify these various elements of writing. (For a review of transitions, read the discussion in Chapter 2, pp. 76–81.)

Topic Sentences.   Once again, review your topic sentences. Should transitions be added to relate the paragraph to the essay? Should any other words or phrases be added to make this important sentence as precise a summary of the paragraph as possible?

Mechanics.   Review earlier samples of your writing on which mechanical errors have been noted for guidelines to the spelling, punctuation, and grammatical errors common in your writing. Work with the handbook at the back of the book, if necessary, in making these corrections.

Finally, rewrite your draft, bearing in mind that even at this stage new material can be generated by the act of writing. In other words, do not mechanically rewrite or edit only, but continue to develop new ideas about your subject to include in your essay.

Now, revise and edit your rough draft.

BECOMING AWARE OF YOURSELF AS A WRITER

Now you might want to turn to your journal and write down your feelings about your progress as a writer, using if you like the following questions as guidelines:

1. Has free writing really "freed" you to think and write more clearly and fully about your subject? In what ways has free writing helped you in your writing thus far? In what ways might it be helpful in the future?

2. How easy was it for you to play a role as you wrote? Did the experiment of "selecting a voice" help you to express yourself more understandably? Would you be able to "select a voice" in another writing situation?

3. What new perspectives on yourself did you gain in writing about a significant stage in your life?

4. How did the writing process suggested in this chapter help or hinder the writing of your essay?

5. What was the single most difficult aspect of the writing task for you? How did you resolve it?

6. How much total time did you spend in the writing of the essay assigned in this chapter? Was this more time than you usually spend on an essay? How did you spend this time? Was this extra time beneficial?

7. Jot down below any additional observations you may have at this point about your behavior as a writer. Has your behavior been changed in any way by what you have learned so far?

PART II

Exploration

INTRODUCTION

It is a close play at the plate. The runner starts his slide just as the catcher gets the ball that has been thrown in from right field. The two players meet in a cloud of dust. The catcher is certain that he has tagged the runner out. The runner is equally certain that he has slid safely underneath the catcher's outstretched mitt. Each man looks toward the umpire . . .

Someone is likely to disagree with the umpire's decision. Whichever way he calls the play, someone in the stands or on the field is likely to say he is blind. Someone—the second baseman perhaps, or the manager in the dugout, or a fan in a box seat behind first base—is likely to feel that the angle from which he or she saw the play gave him or her a clearer view of what really happened, a clearer view than the one the umpire had in the midst of all the dust and confusion at home plate.

Yet the umpire's view is taken as final, because it is his role to play an objective observer. Unlike the fan or the manager or the second baseman, he has nothing to gain or lose as a result of his decision. His decision is always more impartial and less prejudiced, even if his perspective is often equally limited.

The umpire's view is limited: he attempts only to call the play as *he sees it*. Similarly, when you as a writer attempt simply to describe the world as you see it, as it appears from your personal angle of vision, you offer a limited perspective, a perspective that perhaps tells as much about you yourself as it tells about whatever you describe.

But what if you want to broaden your angle of vision and see the world more fully, not only as it looks to you but as it actually is in all its richness and complexity? What if you intend to write about the close play at the plate? Deciding whether, from your vantage point, the runner was safe or out, and thus whether you agree with the umpire's decision, may not be your first concern. You may be more interested in explaining why that decision is controversial, in comparing the play at the plate to other close plays you have seen, in speculating about the effect of the umpire's call on the outcome of the game, in evaluating the power of the right fielder's throwing arm or the agility with which the runner executed the mechanics of a slide into home plate. Of course, if you are watching the game on television, you may study videotaped replays of the tag as it is pictured by a variety of different cameras in different parts of the stadium. In each of these cases, you are exploring the world beyond any single self, any single perspective.

Your goal in the tasks that follow will be to explore the world from a perspective broader than that open to you when your concern is primarily self-expression, and then to inform your audience of the discoveries you have made.

4

Writing About a Place

PURPOSE

In working through the tasks for the next two chapters, you will find that you are moving away from the type of writing you have been doing thus far. Rather than expressing the experience of the self, as in Chapters 1 through 3, you will begin to explore the world of experience beyond the self. Instead of asking, "What does this experience that I have had mean?" you will find yourself asking, "What do I perceive about the world and how can I explain my perceptions as fully and richly as possible to others?" Your role will also shift from participant to interested observer, and your purpose will no longer be expressive but expository.

In moving on to this more objective, expository writing, you will continue to use, of course, the skills developed in the first three chapters, such as keen observation of what you see, a sense of ordering an experience chronologically, and an ability to analyze the significance of that experience. To these skills, now directed toward the world of others, you will begin to add other techniques, to be learned here, such as describing people, places, and objects and interviewing people to learn of their knowledge about your subject. Your focus will shift from narration and from exposition in the service of narration (Chapters 2 and 3) to exposition and narration in the service of exposition.

Because you will be seeking information about your subject, your method of generating ideas will be that of an explorer who asks, "How shall I learn

133

about this subject?" Your audience, too, will be seeking information, rather than your personal interpretation, and therefore the most important audience question for you to answer will become "What information about my subject does my audience both want and need?"

Although the aim in expository writing is to explore (Chapters 4 and 5) and inform (Chapters 6 and 7), and the emphasis is therefore on the subject rather than on the writer, as in expressive writing, your presence will still be felt. You will remain as both the guiding intelligence of what you write and a fervent believer in what you say.

GENERATING IDEAS: THE EXPLORER'S QUESTIONS

To generate ideas when exploring almost any subject, whether it is an object, a place, a person, an experience, or an idea, you can ask yourself the following five questions.

1. What features characterize it? In other words, what is it, and what does it look like?
2. How does it differ from others in its class? How is it similar to them?
3. How does it fit into larger systems of which it is a part: a larger category, an enterprise, a neighborhood, or a community?
4. How does it change? How has it changed since its inception? What was its high point? What will it be like in the future?
5. What are its parts, and how do they work together?

The first question asks for a description of the subject, whether it is a physical description of a place, an object, or a person, or the characterization of an idea or an abstract object, such as a poem. The intent in answering this question is to describe the thing in itself, the object in its unique existence. In describing a particular classroom on campus, for example, you might describe the old wooden desk tops on which past students have carved their initials, the poor ventilation that results in a stuffy atmosphere, the green color of the blackboards, and the other characteristics of this particular classroom.

Question 2 asks for a comparison of your subject with others like it—others in the same class. To continue with the example of the classroom, Question 2 asks how it compares with other classrooms, or perhaps with other places of study, such as a library. Is it a typical example of a classroom, or does it distinguish itself in some way? Is it, for example, smaller and more intimate than the typical classroom, perhaps having a large table around which students sit rather than individual desks? Or is it a room in which only science classes are held? Or is it a room in which you have been more bored or more stimulated intellectually than in other classrooms you have entered?

Question 3 wants to know about the many systems that most subjects fit into. Any classroom fits into a number of different systems. It is a part of a campus building, a reflection of the architectural and engineering systems of the building. It is a part of an educational system, a reflection of the philosophy and techniques of educating students at a particular school. It is a part of a college community, a reflection of the professional and social relationships at the school, a place where learning occurs but also where friendships are formed, ambitions are tested, and so forth.

Question 4 investigates the subject as dynamic—as it changes or has changed or will change. A classroom may seem a very different place at different times of the day or of the semester. It ages, of course, over time and may be subject to renovation on occasion. Its high point might have been when it was brand new or when a particularly effective teacher taught in it. Its future may be dark or bright, depending perhaps on the fate of the school of which it is a part.

Finally, Question 5 asks how the subject works—what parts it is composed of, which together comprise its whole and perform its function. Classrooms are composed of tables, desks, chairs, blackboards, chalk, and erasers, of course, but also of books, students, teachers, and so forth.

To cite another example, let's look at an idea that might be discussed in a classroom. Suppose that in a political science class you are studying the constitutional principle of free speech. Finding answers to the explorer's questions can help you to learn and write about this principle.

What is this principle? It is a right guaranteed to Americans by the First Amendment. It prohibits the government from censoring or in any other way limiting our right to say what we think whenever and to whomever we want. But it does not give us blanket permission to speak out: the right to free speech does not include, for example, a sanction to shout ''Fire!'' in a crowded place when there really is no fire or a right to commit libel against someone else.

How does our right to free speech compare with other rights enjoyed by American citizens? It can excite as much controversy as our right to bear arms. It can conflict with our right to privacy. It also can be compared with the principle of free speech as practiced (or not) in other nations.

This principle is a part of the system of government by which we live, but it is also a part of other systems. You might write about the role that free speech plays in our philosophy of individualism, or in our capitalist economic system, or in our artistic community.

Although the actual wording that guarantees the right to free speech in the Constitution has not changed over time, our attitudes toward this right have changed. At some points in our history, for example, the Supreme Court has interpreted this right less broadly than at other times. Private attitudes toward this right, toward who should be allowed to speak freely about what, often change. Have Americans enjoyed this right more or less thoroughly in the past? How strong will this right remain in our future? Answers to these questions can help you explore the meaning of the principle, as can an examination of the parts that compose it.

Of what parts is a principle or an idea composed? The right to free speech is composed, to a degree, of the laws passed by Congress over the years to defend it. It is also composed of the moral and political ideals used by its defenders to justify their position.

SOME PRACTICE WITH THE EXPLORER'S QUESTIONS

1. As you write in your journal, select a simple object—a lamp, a book, a picture—and analyze it according to the explorer's five questions.

2. Recall a place that you visited recently where people were involved in some mutual experience or enterprise. Analyze this place using the five questions as your guide.

3. Using the five explorer's questions, construct a dialogue between two people whose questions and answers provide information about a subject. For example, in the following dialogue, one person is trying to learn about the other by asking these questions:

   Lou: Who are you? I've never seen you here before.
   Sue: That's for you to find out.
   Lou: That's pretty funny. It's dark in here. Do you have red hair or is that the lights?
   Sue: I'm six feet tall and look like Susan Anton.
   Lou: Are you like all the other girls who come to this place?
   Sue: Of course. They're beautiful and so am I. But I'm also brilliant.
   Lou: Boy, you're pretty high on yourself. What are you doing here if you are so terrific?

   Most likely, you can also guess where they are. In your dialogue, try to create a situation that will allow the characters to arrive at an understanding of a subject of your choice. Some suggestions: landing on the moon, the first day of the semester, choosing a teacher at registration, arguing about a team's prospects for the new season.

4. Create a riddle by having the subject define itself by giving information that answers the five explorers' questions. For example:

   I am long and blond, but that's not the point. Some think that I'm too soft, others think I'm hard enough but that I snap under pressure. Although I look like a lot of others in my class, I often have a distinctive name tattooed all over my body. Many people say I'm not as important as I was years ago, that I've been made obsolete. But let me tell you, buddy, I can still go a long way. Get the message?

   Answer: a pencil

5. You have been sent by your employer in marketing research to do some field research for Dr. Fu's Spicy Hot Chicken, a new fast-food chain that is thinking of opening up a branch in your neighborhood. You are to do an analysis of their chief competitors, located across the street on a busy intersection in your community. Write a brief report using the explorer's five questions on two restaurants in your neighborhood that would be competitors for Dr. Fu's.

6. Select from one of your courses a topic that you have been asked to investigate. For example, in history you may have been asked to explain the changes in American attitudes toward politics in the 1960s. How could you use the explorer's questions to find an approach to this subject?

ADDRESSING YOUR AUDIENCE: DEPTH OF INFORMATION

As we have discussed already, an analysis of your audience's frame of reference and corresponding point of view makes it easier for you to plan and write an essay that bridges the gap between your point of view and that of your reader. In this chapter, we will discuss how knowing your audience's frame of reference can help you in determining how much and what kind of information to supply. We will discuss how to answer the question "What information about my subject does my audience both want and need?"

Some audiences require more information; some require different information. As we suggested in Chapter 2, if you were writing to a group of grade-school children, you would write differently from when you were addressing college students. Here are two passages on the same subject written for two different audiences, one (A) a class of college English students, the other (B) an English professor:

A. *Preparation.* For writers, there are probably two parts to the preparation stage. The first includes just about everything a person has engaged in before he or she starts on a writing assignment—education, personal experiences, sports, work, reading, family life. All these areas of one's life provide potential writing material, and the more alert and thoughtful one is about his or her experiences, the better prepared that person is to write.

The second part of the preparation stage in writing begins when the writer identifies the writing task. This stage may include choosing and narrowing a topic or clarifying an assignment made by someone else. It also requires identifying audience and purpose: for whom are you writing and why are you writing? When the writer has answered those questions, he or she can begin to employ various strategies for generating material. The writer may also start to develop it. The activity at this stage of the process might be compared to feeding information into a computer from which one will later write a program or solve a problem.

B. In preparation, the starting point for a writer is recognizing a problem worthy of honest inquiry. There must be reasonably substantial personal experience, observation, education, or reading to supply the subject matter or situation within which the student can recognize, formulate, and explore such a problem. Original thinking may grow out of recalling old and comfortable knowledge and integrating it with new or previously separate elements in a new combination. Students probably will demonstrate greater motivation and originality in their writing if they aim at something they find worth investigating on their own. But even that supposition needs qualifying, in that too many students seem conditioned to look for easy answers instead and avoid problems if they can. Students typically choose an idea acquired from someone else to write about, perhaps because they like it, not because there is any problem in it for them and not because they have anything original to say about it, at least at the moment of choosing. The most common curricular approach, to include challenging reading materials in a writing course, whether poetry by Dickinson and Plath or essays by Bruner and Eiseley, offers opportunities for problems, but only if the student reads attentively and competently enough to see the difference between a problem worthy of exploration and rather easily resolved factual ignorance. Richard Young, following John Dewey, suggests that the source of a problem lies in a clash of some sort contributing to an "uneasy feeling" in one's personal reaction to a situation. The clash may be explained as a logical inconsistency or a conflict with one's cultural values or educational training. But whatever the cause, awareness, curiosity, and a sort of discomfort usually stimulate strong motivation to correct or clarify the situation. The starting point, at any rate, is not with problems patiently waiting for any qualified researcher to come and seize them; rather it is with particular individuals recognizing and creating their own problems in the material they are working with. But students must not only be taught to look for problems; even at this early stage, they should define their problems so that the problems look potentially solvable and so that students will know when, and if, they have solved them.

> —**David V. Harrington,** "Encouraging Honest Inquiry in Student Writing,"
> *College Composition and Communication* (May 1979)

The first paragraph of Passage A, written for college students, roughly corresponds to Sentences 2 and 3 of Passage B, written for a professor. However, the second paragraph in Passage A offers much less information than the corresponding section in Passage B (the rest of the paragraph), which includes a more detailed discussion of selecting a writing task, generating material for writing about it, and planning the evolution of the paper. (Other characteristics of the two passages indicate their differing audiences as well, such as language level and paragraph length, but we are concerned here only with differences in depth of information.)

Here are two other passages written on the same subject—the Oedipus complex—for two different audiences, in this case, one a lay audience, the other a highly technical or professional one:

C. There is another typical dream dealing with the death of the father that we find particularly among young sons. We have to consider here the primitive state of the human being. There is always a rivalry between father and son for the love of the mother, and this, despite the fact that the father may love his boy very dearly. The son has learned that he receives much more attention and love from his mother, and is treated more leniently in the father's absence. In this type of dream, therefore, we see the desire on the part of the child to get rid of his father. It is really surprising to note how many boys dream openly as well as disguisedly of the death of their father. These dreams are even more common than those dealing with the death of the teacher, for the latter plays a smaller part in the child's psychic life than the father. For one thing, the teacher comes into his life at a later period, and as he is not surrounded with the halo of parental sanctity, hostile feelings against the teacher are generally quite conscious.

We call such dreams of the death of the father Oedipus dreams, because, according to Professor Freud, to whom we are indebted for the name, they bring to light an essentially human situation that has found most fitting expression in Sophocles's noted tragedy of *Oedipus Tyrannus*.

—**A. A. Brill,** from *Freud's Principles of Psychoanalysis*

D. Incest with the mother is one of the crimes of Oedipus and parricide the other. Incidentally, these are the two great offences condemned by totemism, the first social-religious institution of mankind. Now let us turn from the direct observation of children to the analytic investigation of adults who have become neurotic; what does analysis yield in further knowledge of the Oedipus complex? Well, this is soon told. The complex is revealed just as the myth relates it; it will be seen that every one of these neurotics was himself an Oedipus or, what amounts to the same thing, has become a Hamlet in his reaction to the complex. To be sure, the analytic picture of the Oedipus complex is an enlarged and accentuated edition of the infantile sketch; the hatred of the father and the death-wishes against him are no longer vague hints, the affection for the mother declares itself with the aim of possessing her as a woman. Are we really to accredit such grossness and intensity of the feelings to the tender age of childhood or does the analysis deceive us by introducing another factor? It is not difficult to find one. Every time anyone describes anything past, even if he be a historian, we have to take into account all that he unintentionally imports into that past period from present and intermediate times, thereby falsifying it. With the neurotic it is even doubtful whether this retroversion is altogether unintentional; we shall hear later on that there are motives for it and we must explore the whole subject of the "retrogressive phantasy-making" which goes back to the remote past. We soon discover, too, that the hatred against the father has been strengthened by a number of motives arising in later periods and other relationships in life, and that the sexual desires towards the mother have been moulded into forms which would have been as yet foreign to the child. But it would be a vain attempt if we endeavoured to explain the whole of the Oedipus complex by "retrogressive phantasy-making," and by motives originating in later periods of life. The infantile nucleus, with more or less of the accretions to it, remains intact, as is confirmed by direct observation of children.

—**Sigmund Freud,** from *A General Introduction to Psychoanalysis*

The first passage was written for an audience unfamiliar with psychology and its terminology. The writer, therefore, in simple language, explained first the causes and frequency of boys' dreams of the death of their fathers and then why Sigmund Freud termed these *Oedipal dreams*. In the second passage, the author, Sigmund Freud himself, was writing for other psychologists, explaining in depth the adult consequences of such dreams in highly technical terms *(totemism, neurotic, death wishes, retroversion)*. Furthermore he assumed that the reader knows who Oedipus (and Hamlet) is.

In order to analyze the information needs for your audience, make an exhaustive list of the aspects of your subject. Then, using your audience's frame of reference as a guide, try to determine which aspects your audience is familiar with and which represent unfamiliar territory. Group those in the first category under the heading "Familiar" and the second under the heading "Unfamiliar." If you have more aspects grouped under "Familiar" than under "Unfamiliar," you know you are writing for an informed audience that will not require much in the way of a general introduction to your subject and that you can therefore concentrate on giving new, in-depth information about the unfamiliar aspects. If, on the other hand, you have very few aspects of your subject grouped under the heading "Familiar," your audience is uninformed, and you will give basic background on your subject and present little specialized information.

For example, the author of Passage C above went into depth at some points but skimmed over others. Outlined, his passage looks like this:

Background
1. A young boy dreams of the death of his father.
2. The reason is that his mother gives him more attention and treats him more leniently.
3. These dreams are called *Oedipal dreams* because Sophocles wrote about this situation in a tragedy called *Oedipus Tyrannus*.

New Material
1. It is really surprising to note how many boys dream openly, as well as disguisedly, of the death of their father.
2. This dream is even more common than that of the death of the teacher.

Passage D, if outlined, would look like this:

Background
1. Incest with the mother is one of the crimes of Oedipus and parricide the other.

New Material
1. Adult neurotics were themselves Oedipuses.
2. The adult Oedipus complex is enlarged and accentuated by retroversion.
3. The infantile nucleus also remains in adulthood.

As we have seen, the writer of Passage C was writing to an audience that was unfamiliar with this subject, and he therefore found it necessary to give much background information. The writer of Passage D, whose readers were more informed, was able to discuss the Oedipus complex in some depth after giving only the briefest of introductions.

SOME PRACTICE WITH AUDIENCE DEPTH OF INFORMATION

1. You are a carpenter and have been asked to write an article for homeowners on how to build wooden shelves. You have been told that the publication for which you are writing appeals mostly to young couples. What would be the proportion of familiar to unfamiliar or new material? Would the article include more background or more new information?

    You are later asked to write on the same subject for a journal called *Craftsmanship*. Those who subscribe to this journal are craftspeople of many trades, not only carpentry. What would be the proportion of new material to background material? How would the proportion compare with that in the first article above?

2. You are the head of the art history department at your school, and one art history course is required in the first semester for all incoming freshmen. However, most freshmen are not art majors, and you want to write them a letter at the end of the first semester, hoping to get them interested in taking other art courses in addition to the required one. How much depth of information would you include? You want to write a letter to declared art majors at the same time informing them of second-semester course offerings. How would this letter differ in depth of information?

3. Prepare to write two letters on some aspect of college life, one to your college classmates and one to some friends still in high school. How do the frames of reference of the two audiences differ? With what aspects of your subject is each group familiar? Unfamiliar? What background information must you give each

group? What new material can you present? Once you have determined the answers to these questions, write the letters.

TASK: EXPLORING A PLACE

The task for this chapter asks you to visit a place closely or tangentially related to your major, to a hobby, or simply to an interest, a place you have not visited before, one that you know about only through the opinion of others. This should be a place for which you have high regard because of its reputation. You will want to observe its appearance and what is going on there, and to interview the people you meet there so that you can come to some overall impression of the place that does or does not justify your initial good opinion.

The purpose of this assignment is to give you the opportunity to explore a place about which a myth may have been created for you by others. Essentially, you will be answering the question "What do I perceive and how can I explain my perceptions to others as fully and richly as possible?" Do this by asking yourself a more specific writing question: "Is this place as vital as everyone led me to believe?" or "What can I discover about this place that will either support or negate my earlier opinion?"

You might, for example, plan to be a children's librarian, and you may always have wanted to visit the main branch of the public library in your city. The local librarians have cited as their models the procedures followed in the main branch, and you wish to visit to see if efficiency does indeed reign there. Or, as a future aerospace engineer, you may have read about Grumman or Boeing or McDonnell Douglas as the giants in the field. A visit might confirm your sense of admiration, but the industry is facing strong competition from abroad, and a visit might also explain why the once-proud aircraft industry is faltering. By asking yourself the question "Does this place justify my regard?" you leave yourself open to an honest evaluation of what you have discovered.

The audience for this task should be someone like you who is interested in your findings about this place, so we suggest that you write for a group of like-minded people, such as a class in your curriculum or a group of people who share your hobby or interest. This audience will know more about your subject than either a random selection of college students or your English class or possibly your English teacher. By adopting the explorer's questions, you can amass information about this place, and by evaluating the depth of information needs of your audience, you can determine what about your subject the audience needs to know.

The next section, "Writing the Essay," will help to answer the arrangement question, "How can I weave chronology, description, exposition, and dialogue together to create an overriding impression of my subject?"

WRITING THE ESSAY

Using the Explorer's Questions

To generate information and ideas for this assignment, try using your powers of observation to answer as many of the explorer's questions as time and access permit. You might want to take some notes about your observations, for example, a description of some unusual object or procedure that caught your attention or some person whose appearance or manner struck you as unusual. An old office building might have some unusual decorative feature that seems to you to contrast with the high-tech, architectural design of the employees' work area. Although you might not see the immediate practical use of small details, when you begin to write your essay after having thought about your subject for a while, some of these details might be useful to characterize a place, reveal some interesting feature, or highlight an important process that goes on at this place.

Another method for answering the explorer's questions is to seek help from others who already know the way this place works or who have some connection to the place. That is why we suggested in the task that you interview people in the place you visit. Don't be intimidated at the thought of engaging strangers in a question-and-answer conversation. Most people are flattered that you think they have information worthwhile imparting. It would be helpful for you to try to anticipate some of these questions ahead of time. Therefore, you might want to prepare a list of questions that would elicit information you need in order to know how this place works. Be specific—a question like "Can you tell me how your job task contributes to the overall process here?" is more effective than "Can you tell me about this place?"

Some explorer's questions may generate fuller answers than others, and some may be more crucial to the particular place you are writing about than others. For example, a place not similar to others in its class may require more description than a place comparable to others. A unique place will demand the most description of all.

Ask yourself which questions are the most important in writing about your place, which you can answer yourself, which you will need to interview people to answer, and how full an answer you require in each case. Note that you may want to reshape the five questions to elicit the most appropriate information about your subject. You may want to add questions, make them more specific, or redirect them in some way.

Following is the approach of a student who plans to write about the geology exhibit of a museum.

Question 1
What does this geology exhibit look like?

Question 2

How does it differ from the other exhibits in the museum? Why has the museum arranged it in this way? How does it compare with other geology exhibits I have seen?

Question 3

How does it fit into the layout of the museum? As this is a museum of natural history, how does a geology exhibit fit into the overall purpose of the place? What role does the exhibit play in the education of those who view it?

Question 4

How has the exhibit changed since the museum first created it? How will it change in the future, based on what I know or can learn about geological findings? Was the acquisition of moon rocks the high point of the exhibit? If not, what was?

Question 5

How is the exhibit arranged? What specific categories are there? What special exhibits exist?

Like this student, you may need to reshape the explorer's questions to suit the needs of your task.

Audience Depth of Information

You will want to compose a frame of reference for your audience and analyze how much depth of information your audience will need. Answer the questions "What points can I skim over?" "What knowledge can I take for granted?" and "Where and how much can or should I go into depth?"

In answering these questions, refer to the material you have generated through the explorer's method of inquiry. Ask yourself if any of the answers to the explorer's questions, or parts of the questions, should be given to your audience as necessary background. If so, should the answers be detailed or brief? Which questions, or parts of questions, should be answered in depth for this audience? How much depth can the audience absorb?

For example, the student writing about the geology exhibit composed the following frame of reference for her audience:

- **Audience:** A Geology I class.
- **Characteristics:** Interested in geology, although not necessarily planning to major in it.

- Did well in high-school science courses.
- Two are creationists; the rest are evolutionists.
- Most have not visited the geology exhibit.

The frame of reference helped her to understand the depth of information that her audience required:

Background (Brief)
1. What does the exhibit look like?
2. How does it differ from the other exhibits in the museum? From geology exhibits in other museums?
3. How does it fit into the museum? Into the interests of geologists and geology students in the area?

New Material (in Depth)
4. How has the exhibit changed over the years since it was first introduced into the museum? What was its high point? How might it change in the future?
5. What method of arrangement of exhibits has been used? What special exhibits are there?

Answering the following questions of the "Audience Analysis Guide" should help you to write more effectively for your audience.

—— AUDIENCE ANALYSIS GUIDE ——

1. Who is my audience?
2. What is the frame of reference of this audience?
3. What point of view is my audience likely to have on my subject?
4. How do my own frame of reference and point of view differ from those of my reader?
5. How can I bridge any gap that exists between my reader's point of view and my own?
6. Which of my voices am I selecting as I write on this subject? How can the voice that I select further help me to bridge the gap between my audience and me?
7. How much depth of information does my audience need and want on the background of my subject? On the new material I wish to present?

Arranging Your Essay

As you answer the explorer's questions, you will find yourself using different patterns of paragraph development. Question 1 calls for description; Questions 2 through 4 suggest patterns of exposition, such as comparison, contrast, classification and analysis; and Question 5 requires a form of narration that describes a process. You will therefore be weaving together patterns of narration, description, and exposition.

Narrative Patterns.   Although in this chapter you are writing about a place involving others, you should not disappear from the essay entirely, as you have chosen this place to write about because of its vital interest to you. As an observer of the place and the activities there, you can put yourself in the essay by giving a chronological account of your visit as an unobtrusive narrative framework to the essay. The question of arranging the essay then becomes "How can I frame the essay with a narrative account of my visit so that I can convey my considerable interest and at the same time keep the atmosphere and action of the place in the foreground?"

One way to answer this question is to develop a second narrative that, in answer to the fifth question of the explorer's method of inquiry, relates the process by which the systems of the place work together. Process analysis is a type of chronology that indicates how a person or mechanism accomplishes a task from the beginning of the operation to its completion. Whenever one discusses how anything works—from a simple can opener to the writing of an essay—one is dealing in time: in beginnings, middles, and endings.

A narrative account of the operation may be most effective in answering the question "How does this place operate?" The period of time covered, of course, will depend on the cycle or cycles of operation. Processes can be completed in an hour, in a day, on a weekly basis, monthly, annually, or seasonally. Once you have determined what processes need explanation, the objective is to narrate them sequentially (see Chapter 5, pp. 187–188, for more on process analysis).

Here is an example of a process:

It's seven in the morning and the day shift is starting to drift in. Huge tractors are backing up to the big-mouth doors of the warehouse. Cattle trucks bring tons of beef to feed its insatiable appetite for cargo. Smoke-covered trailers with refrigerated units packed deep with green peppers sit with their diesel engines idling. Names like White, Mack, and Kenworth are welded to the front of their radiators, which hiss and moan from the overload. The men walk through the factory-type gates of the parking lot with their heads bowed, oblivious of the shuddering diesels that await them.

Once inside the warehouse they gather in groups of threes and fours like prisoners in an exercise yard. They stand in front of the two time clocks that hang below a window in the manager's office. They smoke and cough in the early morning hour as they await their work assignments. The manager, a nervous-looking man with a stomach that is starting to push out at his belt, walks out with a pink work sheet in his hand.

—**Patrick Fenton**, *"Notes of a Working Stiff"*

Patterns of Exposition.   The answers to the explorer's Questions 2, 3, and 4 call for exposition. As we saw in Chapter 3, exposition is the presentation and explanation of ideas. In contrast to narration, which presents the world of time, and to description (which we will discuss below), which presents the world of space, exposition presents the world of the mind as it exists apart from time and space and interprets their relationships and analyzes their meanings.

The ideas presented by exposition may be concrete: an analysis of a beaver dam, a comparison of race tracks, a classification of the foods eaten by the athletes in various sports. They may also be abstract: a classification of the psychologies of different groups in America, an analysis of the international banking system, a comparison of Eastern and Western philosophies of religion. Whether concrete or abstract, or a mixture of the two, exposition classifies, analyzes, and compares ideas about ideas, objects, places, and emotions. (These and other purposes of exposition will be explained more fully in subsequent chapters.)

In fulfilling the task for this chapter, you will want to use exposition in answering the explorer's Question 2, which asks you to compare your subject with others like it; Question 3, which asks you to analyze what larger systems it is a part of; and Question 4, which requires you to analyze how it has changed, does change, and will change.

Understanding the differences between comparison and analysis will help you to organize your answers. Comparison and its corollary, contrast, ask you to point out the similarities and differences between two objects or among three or more objects. You can do this either (1) by presenting the similarities and then the differences or (2) by comparing and contrasting your subject point by point (see Chapter 5, pp. 186–187, for further discussion of comparison and contrast). An example of comparison and contrast follows. Which method of arrangement does it use, (1) or (2)?

We know from our work hundreds of outstanding competitors who possess strong character formation that complements high motor skill. But we found others who possessed so few strong character traits that it was difficult on the basis of personality to account for their success. There were gold-medal Olympic winners at Mexico and Japan whom we would classify as overcompensatory greats. Only magnificent physical gifts enabled them to overcome constant tension, anxiety, and self-doubt. They are unhappy, and when the talent ages and fades, they become derelicts, while someone like Roosevelt Grier just goes on to bigger mountains. We often wonder how much higher some of these great performers might have gone if they had, say, the strong personality structure that characterized our women's Olympic fencing team.

> —**Bruce C. Ogilive and Thomas A. Tutjo**, *"Sport: If You Want to Build Character, Try Something Else"*

Analysis calls for a breaking down of the subject into parts. It calls for probing beneath a solid surface to discover what a thing is composed of or how it changes (has changed or will change). Analysis also seeks to discover the larger pattern to which a thing belongs. The arrangement pattern of analysis is the presentation of the parts in a systematic order. What parts does the author of the following passage delineate in the origin of *Y'know?*

We know less about the origin of Y'know than about the origin of Boola boola, but there is some reason to believe that in this country it began among poor blacks who, because of the various disabilities imposed on them, often did not speak and for whom Y'know was a request for assurance that they had been understood. From that sad beginning it spread among people who wanted to show themselves sympathetic to blacks, and among those who saw it as the latest thing and either could not resist or did not want to be left out.

> —**Edwin Newman**, *"A Protective Interest in the English Language"*

Patterns of Description.   Description presents the appearance of things that occupy space, whether they be objects, people, buildings, or cities. The aim of description is to convey to the reader what something looks like. It attempts to paint a picture with words.

In order to clarify the appearance of your subject for your reader, you should develop the tools of the visual artist and describe shapes, colors, positions, and relationships. Following a particular order—left to right, top to bottom, inside to outside—also aids the reader. Selecting your details with an eye to creating a main impression simplifies your task and at the same time enhances the description.

The question to be answered in description is "How can I best describe my subject so that my readers can visualize what I want them to see?"

Here is an example of description:

In winter, the warehouse is cold and damp. There is no heat. The large steel doors that line the warehouse walls stay open most of the day. In the cold months, wind, rain, and snow blow across the floor. In the summer, the warehouse becomes an oven. Dust and sand from the runways mix with the toxic fumes of forklifts, leaving a dry, stale taste in your mouth. The high windows above the doors are covered with a thick, black dirt that kills the sun. The men work in shadows with the constant roar of jet engines blowing dangerously in their ears.

—**Patrick Fenton,** *"Notes of a Working Stiff"*

Description may be used as an end in itself but it often serves other purposes. In fulfilling this task, in fact, you will describe your place in answering Question 1, but you will combine description with process narration in answering Question 5, as the reader will better understand the process if she or he knows what the machinery, equipment, props, uniforms, and so on look like.

Dialogue.   *Dialogue* literally means the conversation of two people. In fulfilling this task, you will be interviewing one or more people in the place visited, and therefore dialogue will be a part of your arrangement. In writing the paper, you may want to include part of an exchange you had with someone, or you may want simply to quote the person interviewed. Your guide will be to select comments that highlight an aspect of your subject. The question you will be answering is "What comments were made that are particularly useful to my purposes because they succinctly state the answers to the explorer's questions?"

Following are two examples of quotation, one including only one speaker, the second the dialogue of two speakers. Notice the use of paragraphs for each speaker in the dialogue and the use also of quotation marks:

"Some of these activities are very, very appealing to people who've been turned off by team sports," William H. Monti, a physical education reform leader at San Rafael High, explained. "A number of students who rebelled against all forms of physical education have gravitated toward rock climbing. These were the types who said that they didn't like team sports of any kind. Later, of course, they found out that rock climbing involves as much teamwork as the traditional team sports, or more. They still love it."

—**George Leonard,** *"Why Johnny Can't Run"*

Banke, a red-haired, red-faced man, takes a special interest in the Elmhurst tanks because he lives in Maspeth, which borders Elmhurst.

"This is a natural landmark," he said. "It's our version of the Statue of Liberty."

"Anything that goes wrong here, I yell at him," said Trieste.

"I get the neck of the chicken," said Banke. "But, being a local resident, I make sure things go right."

—**"Tanks,"** *The New Yorker*

The Overriding Impression.   So far you have been asking and answering
questions about the parts of this task: the five explorer's questions, the four
types of arrangement spelled out. You now need to ask, "What is my overriding impression about this place? What ties all these parts together?" Included
in your overriding impression will no doubt be an answer to the specific question of the task: "Is this place as vital as everyone has led me to believe?" A
sentence clearly stating this impression will serve as the shaping idea of your
essay (see Chapter 1) and will help you write the rough draft.

Following is a professional essay that attempts to answer the same questions
that you are answering in terms of the description of place, narration of visit
and the place's processes, and exposition of the more abstract facts about systems and dynamics, including dialogue between the observer and people in the
place. Most important, the author, Saul Bellow, explored the question "How
vital (and how safe) is a kibbutz?"

Developed in Israel, the kibbutz is an autonomous, self-sustaining com-
munal settlement usually engaged in agriculture. All its members participate in
the many duties of the kibbutz, even the elected leaders. The children are generally reared and educated apart from their parents, although recently this practice
has changed in many kibbutzim.

On a Kibbutz
Saul Bellow

On a kibbutz.

Lucky is Nola's dog. John's dog is Mississippi. But John loves Lucky too, and
Nola dotes on Mississippi. And then there are the children—one daughter in the
army, and a younger child who still sleeps in the kibbutz dormitory. Lucky is a
woolly brown dog, old and nervous. His master was killed in the Golan. When
there is a sonic boom over the kibbutz, the dog rushes out, growling. He seems
to remember the falling bombs. He is too feeble to bark, too old to run, his teeth
are bad, his eyes under the brown fringe are dull, and he is clotted under the tail.
Mississippi is a big, long-legged, short-haired, brown-and-white, clever, lively, affectionate, and greedy animal. She is a "child dog"—sits in your lap, puts a paw
on your arm when you reach for a tidbit to get it for herself. Since she weighs
fifty pounds or more she is not welcome in my lap, but she sits on John and Nola
and on the guests—those who permit it. She is winsome but also flatulent. She
eats too many sweets but is good company, a wonderful listener and conversa-
tionalist; she growls and snuffles when you speak directly to her. She "sings"
along with the record player. The Auerbachs are proud of this musical yelping.

In the morning we hear the news in Hebrew and then again on the BBC. We
eat an Israeli breakfast of fried eggs, sliced cheese, cucumbers, olives, green on-
ions, tomatoes, and little salt fish. Bread is toasted on the coal-oil heater. The
dogs have learned the trick of the door and bang in and out. Between the rows
of small kibbutz dwellings the lawns are ragged but very green. Light and warmth
come from the sea. Under the kibbutz lie the ruins of Herod's Caesarea. There

are Roman fragments everywhere. Marble columns in the grasses. Fallen capitals make garden seats. You have only to prod the ground to find fragments of pottery, bits of statuary, a pair of dancing satyr legs. John's tightly packed bookshelves are fringed with such relics. On the crowded desk stands a framed photograph of the dead son, with a small beard like John's, smiling with John's own warmth.

We walk in the citrus groves after breakfast, taking Mississippi with us (John is seldom without her); the soil is kept loose and soft among the trees, the leaves are glossy, the ground itself is fragrant. Many of the trees are still unharvested and bending, tangerines and lemons as dense as stars. "Oh that I were an orange tree/That busie plant!" wrote George Herbert. To put forth such leaves, to be hung with oranges, to be a blessing—one feels the temptation of this on such a morning and I even feel a fibrous woodiness entering my arms as I consider it. You want to take root and stay forever in this most temperate and blue of temperate places. John mourns his son, he always mourns his son, but he is also smiling in the sunlight.

In the exporting of oranges there is competition from the North African countries and from Spain. "We are very idealistic here, but when we read about frosts in Spain we're glad as hell," John says.

All this was once dune land. Soil had to be carted in and mixed with the sand. Many years of digging and tending made these orchards. Relaxing, breathing freely, you feel what a wonderful place has been created here, a homeplace for body and soul; then you remember that on the beaches there are armed patrols. It is always possible that terrorists may come in rubber dinghies that cannot be detected by radar. They entered Tel Aviv itself in March 1975 and seized a hotel at the seashore. People were murdered. John keeps an Uzi in his bedroom cupboard. Nola scoffs at this. "We'd both be dead before you could reach your gun," she says. Cheerful Nola laughs. An expressive woman—she uses her forearm to wave away John's preparations. "Sometimes he does the drill and I time him to see how long it takes to jump out of bed, open the cupboard, get the gun, put in the clip, and turn around. They'd mow us down before he could get a foot on the floor."

Mississippi is part of the alarm system. "She'd bark," says John.

Just now Mississippi is racing through the orchards, nose to the ground. The air is sweet, and the sun like a mild alcohol makes you yearn for good things. You rest under a tree and eat tangerines, only slightly heavy-hearted.

From the oranges we go to the banana groves. The green bananas are tied up in plastic tunics. The great banana flower hangs groundward like the sexual organ of a stallion. The long leaves resemble manes. After two years the ground has to be plowed up and lie fallow. Groves are planted elsewhere—more hard labor. "You noticed before," says John, "that some of the orange trees were withered. Their roots get into Roman ruins and they die. Some years ago, while we were plowing, we turned up an entire Roman street."

He takes me to the Herodian Hippodrome. American archeologists have dug out some of the old walls. We look down into the diggings, where labels flutter from every stratum. There are more potsherds than soil in these bluffs—the broken jugs of the slaves who raised the walls two thousand years ago. At the center of the Hippodrome, a long, graceful ellipse, is a fallen monolith weighing many tons. We sit under fig trees on the slope while Mississippi runs through the high smooth grass. The wind is soft and works the grass gracefully. It makes white air courses in the green.

Whenever John ships out he takes the dog for company. He had enough of solitude when he sailed on German ships under forged papers. He does not like to be alone. Now and again he was under suspicion. A German officer who sensed that he was Jewish threatened to turn him in, but one night when the ship was only hours out of Danzig she struck a mine and went down, the officer with her. John himself was pulled from the sea by his mates. Once he waited in a line of nude men whom a German doctor, a woman, was examining for venereal disease. In that lineup he alone was circumcised. He came before the woman and was examined; she looked into his face and she let him live.

John and I go back through the orange groves. There are large weasels living in the bushy growth along the pipeline. We see a pair of them at a distance in the road. They could easily do for Mississippi. She is luckily far off. We sit under a pine on the hilltop and look out to sea where a freighter moves slowly toward Ashkelon. Nearer to shore, a trawler chuffs. The kibbutz does little fishing now. Off the Egyptian coast, John has been shot at, and not long ago several members of the kibbutz were thrown illegally into jail by the Turks, accused of fishing in Turkish waters. Twenty people gave false testimony. They could have had a thousand witnesses. It took three months to get these men released. A lawyer was found who knew the judge. His itemized bill came to ten thousand dollars—five for the judge, five for himself.

Enough of this sweet sun and the transparent blue-green. We turn our backs on it to have a drink before lunch. Kibbutzniks ride by on clumsy old bikes. They wear cloth caps and pedal slowly; their day starts at six. Plain-looking working people from the tile factory and from the barn steer toward the dining hall. The kibbutzniks are a mixed group. There is one lone Orthodox Jew, who has no congregation to pray with. There are several older gentiles, one a Spaniard, one a Scandinavian, who married Jewish women and settled here. The Spaniard, an anarchist, plans to return to Spain now that Franco has died. One member of the kibbutz is a financial wizard, another was a high-ranking army officer who for obscure reasons fell into disgrace. The dusty tarmac path we follow winds through the settlement. Beside the undistinguished houses stand red poinsettias. Here, too, lie Roman relics. Then we come upon a basketball court, and then the rusty tracks of a children's choochoo, and then the separate quarters for young women of eighteen, and a museum of antiquities, and a recreation hall. A strong odor of cattle comes from the feeding lot. I tell John that Gurdjiev had Katherine Mansfield resting in the stable at Fontainebleau, claiming that the cows' breath would cure her tuberculosis. John loves to hear such bits of literary history. We go into his house and Mississippi climbs into his lap while we drink Russian vodka. "We could live with those bastards if they limited themselves to making this Stolichnaya."

These words put an end to the peaceful morning. At the north there swells up the Russian menace. With arms from Russia and Europe, the PLO and other Arab militants and the right-wing Christians are now destroying Lebanon. The Syrians have involved themselves; in the eyes of the Syrians, Israel is Syrian land. Suddenly this temperate Mediterranean day and the orange groves and the workers steering their bikes and the children's playground flutter like illustrated paper. What is there to keep them from blowing away?

1. Bellow provided a loose narrative framework by telling the story of his morning tour of the kibbutz. What features of the kibbutz did he describe during his exploration? How complete a picture did he paint? Did he offer any points about the philosophy on which the kibbutz operates?

2. Bellow did not compare this kibbutz to others that he may have visited. Where did he make comparisons that help us to understand the nature of life on this kibbutz better? What do you make, for example, of the opening contrast that he draws between the two dogs?

3. How does the kibbutz fit into the larger system of Mideast politics? How did the answer to this question alter Bellow's view of the kibbutz?

4. In what ways have the kibbutz and the life of its inhabitants changed over time? What do the answers to this question reveal about the inhabitants of the kibbutz?

5. What overriding impression of the kibbutz did Bellow finally offer? How does the dialogue in Paragraph 5 contribute to this impression?

In the next essay, Paul Engle uses many descriptive details to convey an overriding impression of an Iowa state fair as the "best of all possible worlds." How do these details contribute to Engle's overriding impression? What unusual organizing device does he use to express many of the sense impressions one might encounter at the fair? Engle's enthusiasm for the fair contrasts with Bellow's objectivity. How would you account for the difference?

The Iowa State Fair

Paul Engle

If all you saw of life was the Iowa State Fair on a brilliant August day, when you hear those incredible crops ripening out of the black dirt between the Missouri and Mississippi rivers, you would believe that this is surely the best of all possible worlds. You would have no sense of the destruction of life, only of its rich creativeness: no political disasters, no assassinations, no ideological competition, no wars, no corruption, no atom waiting in its dark secrecy to destroy us all with its exploding energy.

There is a lot of energy at the Fair in Des Moines, but it is all peaceful. The double giant Ferris wheel circles, its swaying seats more frightening than a jet plane flying through a monsoon. Eighty thousand men, women, and children walk all day and much of the night across the fairgrounds. Ponies pick up their feet in a slashing trot as if the ground burned them. Hard-rock music backgrounds the soft lowing of a Jersey cow in the cattle barn over her newborn calf, the color of a wild deer. Screaming speeches are made all around the world urging violence; here there are plenty of voices, but they are calling for you to throw baseballs at Kewpie dolls, to pitch nickels at a dish which won't hold them, to buy cotton candy, corn dogs, a paring knife that performs every useful act save mixing a martini.

Above all, you would believe there was no hunger in the world, for what the Iowa State Fair celebrates is not only peace but food. This is one of the few places in the world where you see every condition of food. It walks by you on the hoof, the Hereford, Angus, Charolais, Shorthorn steer, the meat under its hide produced by a beautifully balanced diet more complicated than a baby's formula. These thousand-pound beef animals look at you with their oval, liquid eyes, not knowing that in human terms they are round steak, rib roast, tenderloin, chuck, and hamburger.

The Fair has always specialized in show-ring competition for swine and cattle, but in recent years this has been extended to the slaughtered and dressed carcass. Often the animal which won on the hoof will not actually be as good a meat specimen as one graded lower on its "figure." Probably the most important single event at the Fair is also the quietest and most hidden: the judging of the carcass by experts in white coats in a refrigerated room. The months of elaborate feeding, of care to prevent injuries, all have their meaning when the loin eye is measured and the balance between fat and lean is revealed. At the 1974 Fair, Roy B. Keppy's crossbred hog placed second in the live competition, but first in the pork carcass show. It yielded a chop which measured 6.36 square inches, one of the largest in the history of the Fair. A little more than an inch of fat covered the rib (loin-eye) area.

If you saw close up the boys and girls of 4-H, you would also believe that this world was lived in by the best of all possible people. These are not the drugged youth of the newspapers. They are intelligent and sturdy and have carried into the present the old-fashioned and sturdy ideas: the four-H concept means thinking HEAD, feeling HEART, skilled HAND, and strong HEALTH. They walk with the ease of the physically active and the confidence of people who have done serious and useful projects. They understand animals, machines, fibers.

Nor are they the "hicks" of rural legend. Newspapers, radio, television have brought the world into their home; before their eyes they see what is happening not only in the nearest city but in a country five thousand miles away. Nor are they dull. Often a 4-H boy and girl will work together washing down their steers, shampooing the tails and polishing the hooves, and then go off to spend the evening dancing or at a rock concert.

One of the great sights in 4-H at the Fair is the weeping face of a bright, attractive farm girl whose steer has just won a championship. She has raised the animal herself. She has kept a daily record of how much she fed it each day, of how many pounds of feed it took to make pounds of grain (a corn-fed beef steer's daily growth is frightening and fattening). She has washed and brushed and combed it, taught it to lead with a halter, to stand still on order.

The final moment of truth comes when she leads it into the show ring and the judge examines it with a hard and expert eye. If a Blue Ribbon is awarded, tears of joy on the cheeks of the 4-H girl, after her months of loving care and the tension of competing. Then the auction, for which she receives much more per pound than the average because she has the champion, with tears of sadness because the creature who had become a pet at home is led off to be slaughtered. Head, Heart, Hand and Health of that devoted girl went into the profitable health of that sexless steer.

One of the dramatic examples of energy at the Fair is in the tractor, draft team and pony "pulls," in which the machine and the animals rear up as they try to pull a weighted sledge. The tractor is the usual case of a souped-up engine performing a task it would never do on a farm, with a great snorting and straining. The fun is in the horse and pony pulls, where the animals dig into the turf and drive themselves beyond their real strength, as if they understood the nature of competition.

Above all, the Fair gives a workout to the body's five senses they could get nowhere else in the U.S.A. Apart from the fact that most people walk far more than they realize in their four-wheeled daily life, one reason for the healthy tiredness at the end of a morning-afternoon-evening at the Fair is that eye, hand, ear, tongue, and nose are exercised more than in all the rest of the year.

Eye sees the great, full udders of Holstein cows swaying between those heavy legs, the rounded bellies of hogs unaware that the symmetry will lead to an early death, the sheep struggling under the shearer's hand as he draws red blood on their pink skin in his haste, the giant pumpkin glowing orange as an autumn moon, the Ladies' Rolling Pin Throw contest (you wouldn't argue with one of them), the blue-red-purple-white stalks of gladioli from home gardens, the harness horses pulling goggled drivers as they trot and pace frail sulkies in front of the grandstand.

Hand touches surfaces it never meets at home unless it belongs to a farmer: softness of Guernsey hide or of the five-gaited saddle horse sleek from the currycomb, the golden feel of new oat straw, the fleece of Oxford Down or Shropshire lambs, the green surface of a John Deere eight-row corn picker, smooth as skin and tough as steel, the sweet stickiness of cotton candy.

Ear has almost too much to take in: the hog-calling contest with its shrill shrieks, the husband-calling contest combining seduction with threats, the whinnying of Tennessee walking horses, the lowing of cattle bored with standing in the show-ring, the male chauvinist crowing of roosters at the poultry barn, loudest at daybreak (the champion crowed 104 times in half an hour), the merry-go-round playing its old sentimental tunes, the roar of racing cars, the barkers praising the promised beauty to be revealed at the girlie show, the old fiddler's contest quivering the air with "Buffalo Gal," "Texas Star" and "Tennessee Waltz," the clang of horseshoes against each other and against the stake.

Tongue learns the taste of hickory-smoked ham, the richness of butter on popcorn with beer, the tang of rhubarb pie, sour elegance of buttermilk served ice cold, the total smack of hamburger with onion, pickle, mustard and horseradish, many-flavored ice cream, chicken fried in sight of their live cousins in the poultry barn, barbecued pork ribs spitting their fat into the fire as fattened hogs waddle by on their way to be judged.

Nose has an exhausting time at the Fair. It smells the many odors rising from the grills of men competing in the Iowa Cookout King contest, grilling turkey, lamb, beef, pork, chicken, ham with backyard recipes which excite the appetite, the delicate scents of flowers in the horticulture competition, the smell of home-made foods, the crisp smell of hay. People drive hundreds of miles in airconditioned cars which filter out smells in order to walk through heavy and hot late summer air across the manure-reeking atmosphere of the hog, cattle, horse and sheep barns, to sniff again the animal odors of their childhood.

You can watch the judging of home-baked bread or listen to the latest rock group. You can watch free every day the teenage talent search or pay money to hear the same nationally known acts you can watch free on television. The 4-H sewing contest, in which contenders wear the clothes they made, was startled in 1974 to have a boy enter himself and his navy blue knit slacks and jacket with white trim (he grew up on a hog farm, but wants to design clothes). A girl won.

The Iowa State Fair is a great annual ceremony of the sane. Young girls still stand all night behind dairy cows with pitch forks to keep the freshly washed animals from getting dirty before being shown in the morning. Boys milk cows at 10 P.M., 2 A.M., and 3 A.M. to be sure their udders are "balanced" when judges look at them. This is hardly the view of teenagers we often hear. A six-year-old boy wins the rooster crowing contest. There is Indian Wrestling (arm-hand wrestling) with a white and black sweating in immobile silence; the judge was John Buffalo, a real Indian from the Tama reservation.

Year after year this rich and practical ritual of life is repeated. Animals whose ancestors competed many Fairs ago come back. So do people, returning by plane and automobile to the grounds their grandparents visited by train and buggy. Three-hundred-and-fifty-horsepower internal-combustion engines have replaced the one-horse hitch or the two-horse team, but the essential objects of life are the same: the dented ear of corn, the rounded rib of steer and pig, that nourishment of the human race which is the prime purpose of the plowing and harvesting State of Iowa.

To some, the Fair seems corny. To others, the world still needs to catch up to the human and animal decency which each year dignifies a corner of this corrupt world. A few hundred acres of human skill and animal beauty in Des Moines, Iowa, prove to the space capsule of Earth how to live.

Like Bellow, Engle uses descriptive details to reveal the process of his subject. What does he wish to emphasize about the process of the fair? Why does Engle refer to the fair as a "ritual of life"? What does this explain about his attitude toward the fair? How does Engle combine narrative, exposition, and description in his essay?

Writing the Rough Draft

The question at this point is how to weave together the various answers to the explorer's questions and the elements required by the task: narration, exposition, description, and dialogue.

One approach, of course, is to use the explorer's questions as an outline for your essay, working description in naturally in answering Question 1, exposition for the answers to Questions 2 through 4, and process narration for Question 5. Appropriate dialogue or quotations can be tucked in at any point. And the chronological account of your visit can frame the essay, providing the content of the introduction and the conclusion.

You might want to follow the method of Saul Bellow and weave a more intricate design by interspersing the elements throughout the essay. Or, like Paul Engle, you could emphasize the process of the place by focusing your reader's attention on the many sense impressions you observed. Notice, however, that Bellow did use a narrative framework and that Engle found narrative generally unnecessary for his purpose.

To begin organizing your essay, write down the overriding impression that you wish to convey about the place you visited. This shaping idea may also suggest a pattern of arrangement. If not, this pattern will occur to you as you forge an outline before beginning to write, or you may need actually to immerse yourself in writing for a pattern to emerge. Regardless of your method—preoutlining or immersion outlining—you will want to arrive at a coherently presented essay.

Here is one student's rough draft. What patterns of arrangement did the student use?

THE ASSEMBLY-LINE METHOD OF REPRODUCTIVE HEALTH

The walk from the subway seemed long. A strong, cold wind was at my back, pushing me down Twenty-third Street. It was a nice part of the city. There were lots of auxiliary cops around because I was near the Police Academy. I noticed lots of kids with portfolios who were coming from the School of Visual Arts. The wind kept pushing me toward Second Avenue. From a distance, I could see my destination. A dirty, blue and white banner hung from the second story of 380 Second Avenue, proudly announcing the Margaret Sanger Center of Planned Parenthood, New York City.

Planned Parenthood has quite a reputation. It is where young girls can go to get information about birth control, pregnancy, abortion, and venereal disease. The outstanding feature is the clinic's promise of confidentiality. The organization is funded by private donations, and federal subsidies make up less than fifteen percent of its budget.

I entered the reception area and asked for an appointment. Without looking up, the secretary said, "Go down the hall, turn right, and pick up one of the beige phones to make an appointment." Although I was taken aback by her indifference, I did as she said. The woman on the phone said I could have an appointment that morning, and she sent me back to the reception desk.

This time the woman looked up. She gave me forms to fill out and said that I would have to pay in advance. A pelvic exam was fifty dollars. I filled out the form, paid the fifty bucks and waited.

The waiting room was comfortable. There were eight loveseats arranged in a rectangle with small tables at the corners. Five women hid behind magazines and newspapers. One guy sat staring out the window. I was the only person who wasn't nervously puffing away at a cigarette. It was uncomfortably silent. Nothing happened for half an hour. Then my name was called.

A robot of a woman directed me to a laboratory. My urine was tested for sugar and my blood for iron. The robot directed me to another waiting area, and once again I was told to listen for my name to be called. I sat and waited in disgust. There wasn't a friendly face around. My finger was bleeding from the blood test. I hadn't realized it, so there was blood on my purse and my notebook. It was embarrassing, and I could feel the heat in my face as I blushed. My stomach was queasy, and I hoped it would not take much longer.

The girl across from me offered me a tissue. Finally, I thought, a human! I asked her what she thought of the place, and she said exactly what I expected: "It's not cheap, the people aren't very nice, and I can't wait to get this over with." Other women in the room were listening to us and agreed with a chorus of "Me, too" and "They're too slow."

I waited for over twenty minutes before I was called. A very young girl led me to her office. We went over my family's medical history and she took my blood pressure. She seemed nice, but she was in a hurry. She led me to a changing room and told me to don the traditional paper robe and slippers. Then, I couldn't believe it, another waiting room!

This room was a small cubicle with chairs lining the walls. There were three women already waiting there, dressed as I was and looking very silly. Again, I asked opinions about the clinic. One woman complained that she had been there for over an hour--so had I. Another girl said she'd been to better clinics--so had I. We all agreed that fifty dollars for a pelvic exam was not the going rate. My clinic, the Flushing Women's Health Organization, charges forty dollars on the first visit and thirty dollars every time after. This wait was the longest. We talked for over half an hour.

When the doctor called me, I sighed with relief. She introduced herself as Irma and smiled. We discussed the advantages and disadvantages of different methods of birth control, and I began to feel at ease. I told her how disappointed I was with Planned Parenthood, and she didn't seem surprised. She said that up until a year ago, they had heard no complaints, but because they've become increasingly popular, they've had more patients than they're equipped to handle. "Yet," she defended, "we do our best."

Given a choice, I would go to my usual doctor. It is closer to home, cheaper, and much faster. I spent over two and a half hours at Planned Parenthood--I'm not impressed.

Now begin writing your rough draft. When you have completed it, take a day's rest.

FOCUS: PARAGRAPH DEVELOPMENT

As individual paragraphs have beginnings, middles, and endings, so do these paragraphs take their place in the structure of the essay as a whole. If the experience of many writers is any guide, some of the most difficult moments of the writing process center around writing introductions and conclusions. The reasons seem clear: We're not sure how to begin and we're reluctant to say we have finished. We could look at the practice of many writers and point to countless strategies for creating beginning and concluding paragraphs. Since this would be impractical, we can offer a few general suggestions and examples here.

Because the introductory paragraph is your first encounter with your readers, you want to interest them, to set in motion some energy current of an idea, incident or issue that will be completed only by reading the rest of the essay. This might take the form of an anecdote, a question, a statement of a problem or a contradiction, the background of an issue or event, or a striking image or impression. The scope and depth of your topic will also influence the extent of your introduction. As the introduction is so vital to a good essay, you might feel more at ease by writing it after you have finished the body of your essay. Many writers do this, for it is often only when we have completed expressing an idea that we have an overall grasp of how we should approach it.

Concluding paragraphs generally work in the opposite direction of introductions. Rather than narrowing the readers' focus toward the specific topic of the essay, conclusions try to open them up to the larger context or possibilities of ideas and issues, to lead them to the connections that might exist between your specific topic and some larger generalization that might be inferred from it. This will remind the reader of the importance of your topic and send the reader back to your essay with a larger perspective on the topic. For example, the concluding paragraph of Paul Engle's essay suggests that we look upon the Iowa state fair as a model of decency and beauty for human beings to follow. For Engle, the fair has a moral quality that contrasts with "this corrupt world."

Whether we look at paragraphs that function as beginnings, middles, endings, there is another way of examining how paragraphs are developed—the way they are formed to express ideas. Just as sentences are structured to coordinate ideas or subordinate them, so are most paragraphs. Coordination occurs when two or more equal ideas are enumerated or an idea is repeated for emphasis. Subordination offers one idea in explanation of another. Coordination enumerates or emphasizes; subordination explains. In developing your topic sentence, therefore, determine the needs of your readers. Do they require you to enumerate or list points about your subject, or do they need an explanation of it? This method of inquiry should help you to develop any topic into a paragraph once you have determined your readers' needs.

For example, the following paragraph utilizes coordination:

When a society's values and institutions are seriously questioned, life transitions become anxious and traumatic. What does it mean to face the time of marriage when divorce is so common and alternative living arrangements, such as communes and cohabitation, are so widely explored? What does it mean to choose a vocation when all forms of work, and the idea of work itself, are so severely criticized? What does it mean to grow up when adulthood implies being locked into support of a violent, directionless culture? What does it mean to grow old when old people are isolated, put off by themselves in "homes" or institutions, apart from family and ongoing community? What does it mean to die when science has challenged sacred religious beliefs and in the place of spiritual comfort has left only the "scientific method"?

Robert Jay Lifton and Eric Olson, *"Death—the Lost Season," from* Living and Dying

An outline of this paragraph would look like the following:

Topic sentence: When a society's values and institutions are seriously questioned, life transitions become anxious and traumatic.

1. What does it mean to face the time of marriage when divorce is so common and alternative living arrangements, such as communes and cohabitation, are so widely explored?
2. What does it mean to choose a vocation when all forms of work, and the idea of work itself, are so severely criticized?

3. What does it mean to grow up when adulthood implies being locked into support of a violent, directionless culture?

4. What does it mean to grow old when old people are isolated, put off by themselves in "homes" or institutions, apart from family and ongoing community?

5. What does it mean to die when science has challenged sacred religious beliefs and in the place of spiritual comfort has left only the "scientific method"?

Note the use of the repetitive "What does it mean" phrase to emphasize the equality of all five points. Coordination often employs repetition, thus creating a dramatic effect.

The following is an example of subordination, in that Sentence 3 develops the topic sentence by explaining why the order of the city streets is complex, and Sentence 4 compares city street life to a ballet, explaining the topic sentence further. Sentence 5 continues the analogy:

Under the seeming disorder of the old city, wherever the old city is working successfully, is a marvelous order for maintaining the safety of the streets and the freedom of the city. It is a complex order. Its essence is intricacy of sidewalk use, bringing with it a constant succession of eyes. This order is all composed of movement and change, and although it is life, not art, we may fancifully call it the art form of the city and liken it to the dance—not to a simple-minded precision dance with everyone kicking up at the same time, twirling in unison and bowing off en masse, but to an intricate ballet in which the individual dancers and ensembles all have distinctive parts which miraculously reinforce each other and compose an orderly whole. The ballet of the good city sidewalk never repeats itself from place to place, and in any one place is always replete with new improvisions.

—**Jane Jacobs,** *The Death and Life of Great American Cities*

Outlined, the paragraph looks like this:

Topic sentences: Under the seeming disorder of the old city, wherever the old city is working successfully, is a marvelous order for maintaining the safety of the streets and the freedom of the city. It is a complex order.

I. Its essence is intricacy of sidewalk use, bringing with it a constant succession of eyes.
    A. This order is all composed of movement and change, and although it is life, not art, we may fancifully call it the art form of the city and liken it to the dance—not to a simple-minded precision dance with everyone kicking up at the same time, twirling in unison and bowing off en masse, but to an intricate ballet in which the individual dancers

and ensembles all have distinctive parts which miraculously reinforce each other and compose an orderly whole.

1. The ballet of the good city sidewalk never repeats itself from place to place, and in any one place is always replete with new improvisions.

Most paragraphs are a mixture of coordination and subordination, because most lists need explanation and explanations often require lists of examples. In the following paragraph, subordination follows coordination, as the first four sentences are coordinate, and the fifth is subordinate to the fourth.

This man made no flourishes to attract anybody. He never drove a fast horse. He never wore trousers with checks any larger than an inch square—which, for the time, was conservative. His house never got afire and burned down just after the fire insurance had run out. Not one of his boys and girls ever got drowned or run over by the steamcars. The few that died growing up died of diphtheria or scarlet fever, which were what children died of then, the usual ways.

—**Robert P. Tristram Coffin,** *"My Average Uncle," from* Book of Uncles

An outline of Coffin's paragraph clearly shows the mixture of subordination with coordination:

Topic sentence: This man made no flourishes to attract anybody.

1. He never drove a fast horse.
2. He never wore trousers with checks any larger than an inch square—which, for the time, was conservative.
3. His house never got afire and burned down just after the fire insurance had run out.
4. Not one of his boys and girls ever got drowned or run over by the steam-car.
   a. The few that died growing up died of diphtheria or scarlet fever, which were what children died of then, the usual ways.

The following paragraph, on the other hand, illustrates the mixture of coordination with subordination. Two parallel examples in Sentences 4 and 5 provide the coordination in an otherwise subordinate organization:

I have an increasing admiration for the teacher in the country school where we have a third-grade scholar in attendance. She not only undertakes to instruct her charges in all the subjects of the first three grades, but she manages to function quietly and effectively as a guardian of their health, their clothes, their habits, their mothers, and their snowball engagements. She has been doing this sort of Augean task for twenty years, and is both kind and wise. She cooks for the children on the stove that heats the room, and she can cool their passions or warm their soup with equal competence. She conceives their costumes, cleans up their messes, and shares their confidences. My boy already regards his teacher as his great friend, and I think tells her a great deal more than he tells us.

—**E. B. White**, *"Education," from* One Man's Meat

Again, an outline reveals the pattern:

Topic sentence: I have an increasing admiration for the teacher in the country school where we have a third-grade scholar in attendance.

I. She not only undertakes to instruct her charges in all the subjects of the first three grades, but she manages to function quietly and effectively as a guardian of their health, their clothes, their habits, their mothers, and their snowball engagements.
  A. She has been doing this sort of Augean task for twenty years, and is both kind and wise.
    1. She cooks for the children on the stove that heats the room, and she can cool their passions or warm their soup with equal competence.
    2. She conceives their costumes, cleans up their messes, and shares their confidences.
      a. My boy already regards his teacher as his great friend, and I think tells her a great deal more than he tells us.

When composing a paragraph, of course, a writer is also choosing a pattern of exposition. In a coordinate paragraph, he or she may be listing reasons, examples, definitions, or effects. In a subordinate paragraph, he or she may also use definition, example, cause, and effect to explain the points. And in a mixed paragraph, lists and explanations may be based on any combination of patterns (see Chapter 5, pp. 185–188, for further discussion of patterns of exposition).

For example, Robert Jay Lifton's coordinate paragraph, preceding, lists causes, or reasons why; Jacobs uses analogy to explain her point; Coffin uses a list of examples followed by a contrastive explanation; and White combines a cause-and-effect explanation ("She has been doing this sort of Augean task for twenty years, and is both kind and wise") with a list of causes and concludes with an explanation that is an example.

SOME PRACTICE WITH DEVELOPING PARAGRAPHS

1. Analyze the following paragraphs to determine whether their organization is coordinate, subordinate, or mixed. Outline the paragraph, if an outline is helpful.

   a. Besides, aren't commercials in the public interest? Don't they help you choose what to buy? Don't they provide needed breaks from programming? Aren't many of them brilliantly done, and some of them funny? And now, with the new sexual freedom, all those gorgeous chicks with their shining hair and gleaming smiles? And if you didn't have commercials taking up a good part of each hour, how on earth would you find enough program material to fill the endless space/time void?

   —**Marya Mannes,** *"Television: The Splitting Image," from* The Saturday Review
   of Literature *(Nov. 1970)*

   b. The mother wasp goes tarantula-hunting when the egg in her ovary is almost ready to be laid. Flying low over the ground late on a sunny afternoon, the wasp looks for its victim or for the mouth of a tarantula burrow, a round hole edged by a bit of silk. The sex of the spider makes no difference, but the mother is highly discriminating as to species. Each species of Pepsis requires a certain species of tarantula, and the wasp will not attack the wrong species. In a cage with a tarantula which is not its normal prey, the wasp avoids the spider and is usually killed by it in the night.

   —**Alexander Petrunkevitch,** *"The Spider and the Wasp,"*
   from Scientific American *(Aug. 1952)*

   c. Tell General Howard I know his heart. What he told me before I have in my heart. I am tired of fighting. Our chiefs are killed. Looking Glass is dead. Toohoolhoolzote is dead. The old men are all dead. It is the young men who say yes or no. He who led on the young men [Ollokot] is dead. It is cold and we have no blankets. The little children are freezing to death. My people, some of them, have run away to the hills, and have no blankets, no food; no one knows where they are—perhaps freezing to death. I want to have time to look for my children and see how many of them I can find. Maybe I shall find them among the dead. Hear me, my chiefs! I am tired; my heart is sick and sad. From where the sun now stands I will fight no more forever.

   —**Chief Joseph,** *U.S. Secretary of War Report, 1877*

   d. It is thus no exaggeration to say that Americans have taken to mechanical cooling avidly and greedily. Many have become all but addicted, refusing to go places that are not air-conditioned. In Atlanta, shoppers in Lenox Square so resented having to endure natural heat while walking outdoors from chilled store to chilled store that the mall management enclosed and air-conditioned the whole sprawling shebang. The widespread whining about Washington's raising of thermostats to a mandatory 78°F suggests that people no longer think of interior coolness as an amenity but consider it a necessity, almost a birthright, like suffrage. The existence of such a view was proved last month when a number of federal judges sitting too high and mighty to suffer 78°F, defied and denounced the Government's energy-saving order to cut back on cooling. Significantly, there was no popular outrage at this judicial insolence; many citizens probably wished that they could be so highhanded.

—**Frank Trippett,** *"The Great American Cooling Machine,"* Time *(1979)*

2. What patterns of exposition—definition, contrast, comparison, exemplification, cause and effect, analogy, and so on—did each writer of the paragraphs above use?

3. Develop the following topic sentences into paragraphs. Write for a reader unfamiliar with the subject. Decide before writing whether you wish to proceed through coordination, subordination, or a combination of the two:

   a. Sports figures are admired by everyone.

   b. Many young children understand the computer better than most adults.

   c. You can tell a person's lifestyle by the tee-shirt he or she wears.

   What pattern of arrangement did you use in each paragraph you wrote?

REWRITING

Obtaining Feedback on Your Rough Draft

By now, you should have developed one or more successful channels for obtaining responses to your rough draft: your "other self," your peers, or your teacher. Again, use these channels for obtaining answers to the "Audience Response Guide" about your draft of your essay on a place.

—————— AUDIENCE RESPONSE GUIDE ——————

1. What is the writer's purpose in writing about this place? What overriding impression does the writer wish to convey?

2. How does the paper affect the audience for whom it is intended?

3. How effective has the writer been in conveying an adequate and accurate impression of the place through observation and interviews?

4. How should the paper be revised to better convey a sense of the place and its significance?

The following is a peer evaluation of the rough draft of the student essay "The Assembly-Line Method of Reproductive Health," in response to the four questions above:

1. The writer wants to convey her disappointment with the Planned Parenthood Center. She feels that she could have received as good if not better treatment from her own doctor, who would not have charged her as much or kept her waiting as long.

2. A reader can identify with the writer's feelings about the way patients are treated in a health clinic, particularly with her complaints about the indifference of some of the employees and the amount of time she had to wait. A reader who is interested in going into the health care profession might want to know more about how the clinic is run.

3. The group felt that the writer had been quite effective. She might, however, have tried to show in more detail what the other patients were like and what they were feeling. Also, the group felt that the writer did not give enough information to account for the clinic's popularity.

4. The group suggested that the writer include more dialogue between herself and the other patients. They also suggested that more details about the positive aspects of her experience might help complete the picture.

Here is a revised version of "The Assembly-Line Method of Reproductive Health." How has the writer responded to the group's suggestions that she add more dialogue and more details? What other changes has she made?

THE ASSEMBLY-LINE METHOD OF REPRODUCTIVE HEALTH

The walk from the subway seemed long, and a strong, cold wind was at my back, pushing me down Twenty-third Street. It was a nice part of the city, however, as there were lots of auxiliary cops around from the nearby Police Academy, and lots of kids with portfolios were coming from the School of Visual Arts. The wind kept pushing me toward

Second Avenue. From a distance, I could see my destination. A dirty, blue and white banner hung from the second story of 380 Second Avenue, proudly announcing the Margaret Sanger Center of Planned Parenthood.

Planned Parenthood has quite a reputation. It is where young women and men can go to get information about birth control, pregnancy, abortion, and venereal disease. The outstanding feature is its promise of confidentiality. Although other women's health organizations also offer confidentiality, Planned Parenthood was the first to do so.

I entered the reception area and asked for an appointment. Without looking up, the secretary told me to "Go down the hall, turn right, and pick up one of the beige phones on the wall to make an appointment." Although I was taken aback by her indifference, I did as she said. The woman on the phone said I could have an appointment that morning and told me to return to the reception desk.

This time, the woman looked up. She gave me forms to fill out and said I would have to pay in advance. A pelvic exam would be fifty dollars. I filled out the forms, paid the money, and waited.

The waiting room was comfortable. There were eight loveseats arranged in a rectangle with small tables at the corners. Five women hid behind newspapers and magazines. One man sat staring out the window at the street below. I was the only person who was not puffing away nervously at a cigarette. The silence was uncomfortable.

Nothing happened for twenty minutes, and then my name was called. A robot of a woman directed me to the laboratory, where my urine was tested for sugar, and my blood was examined for iron. The robot then directed me to another waiting area, and once again, I was told to wait and listen for my name to be called. I sat and waited in disgust. There wasn't a friendly face to be found. My finger was bleeding from the blood test, and I hadn't realized it, so there was blood on my purse and my notebook. It was embarrrassing, and I could feel the heat in my face as I blushed. I reached into my purse for a tissue but didn't find one. I felt very uneasy, and I hoped it wouldn't be much longer before I was through.

The girl across from me offered me a tissue. Finally, I thought, a human! I asked her what she thought of the place, and she said exactly what I expected: "It's not cheap, the people aren't very nice, and I can't wait to get out of here." Other women in the room were listening to us and agreed with what she said. Another girl spoke up, "I think their prices are pretty good. My abortion would cost more anywhere else." All the other women said they were there for mere pelvic exams and seemed to feel sorry for this woman. She explained, "I already have two children and my husband can't find a job." We talked for over twenty minutes. She said she would love to have the child if she thought she could offer it a decent life. "Times are tough," she said. When she left, the room became quiet again. It was sad to watch her walk away.

I waited for another twenty minutes until my name was called. A very young girl led me to her office on the other side of the building. We went over my personal and family medical history, and she took my blood pressure. I asked her who pays for the organization and found out that most of its funding comes from private donations. Federal subsidies make up only fifteen percent of its budget. She said that if proposed legislation by the government was passed, they could use the federal money only to service women over eighteen. They are well prepared for anything that the laws may do to stop them from helping minors, however. This consultant was obviously interested in her work but couldn't talk long because of her busy schedule. She led me to a dressing room to don the traditional paper robe and slippers and then-- I couldn't believe it--another waiting room!

This room was a small, white cubicle with chairs lining the walls. There were three women already waiting there, dressed as I was and looking, as I did, very silly. Again, I asked for opinions about the clinic. One woman complained that she had been there for over an hour--so had I. Another girl said she had been to better clinics--so had I. We all agreed that fifty dollars for a pelvic exam was not the going rate. My clinic, the Flushing Women's Health Organization, charges forty dollars for the first visit and thirty dollars for every visit after that. One middle-aged woman said that it wasn't so bad a year ago. She said that it had never taken more than one hour as long as you had an appointment. By the time I was called by the doctor, I had already been there two hours!

When the doctor called me in, I sighed with relief. She introduced herself as Irma and smiled. We discussed the advantages and disadvantages of different methods of birth control, and I began to feel at ease. I then told her of how disappointed I was with Planned Parenthood, and she didn't seem surprised. She said that up to a year ago they had heard no complaints. However, as they've become increasingly popular over the past year, they have more patients than they're equipped to handle. "Yet," she defended, "we do our best."

Given a choice, I would go back to my usual doctor. He's closer to home, cheaper, and much faster. I spent over two and a half hours at Planned Parenthood--I'm not impressed.

Substituting

A fourth method of revision, in addition to cutting (p. 46), adding (pp. 86–87), and rearranging (pp. 127–128), is substituting. Substituting means trading words, phrases, and/or whole passages that do not contribute to the meaning of your essay for those that do.

Substitutions may be desirable for several reasons. One is that a word you have used may seem, when you are reading your essay over, to be not concrete enough: Why say the sky is gray when you can say it is leaden? Another is that a word may be inexact: you may have told your parents that your campus is far from the airport, leaving them to draw their own conclusions as to how much time they should leave for the taxi drive; to say that it is thirty minutes away is much more exact. You may also decide that one word conveys your tone of voice more successfully than another: "Teachers are stern" may convey the tone you want to establish more successfully than "Teachers are mean."

You may also want to substitute details if you find that your original detail does not create the impression that you wish to convey of your subject to your audience: When you are delineating the problems you are having with your car, for example, a description of its good features is out of place and should be replaced with further complaints, especially if your audience is the mechanic whom you paid to fix the car in the first place.

The structure of your essay may require substitutions as well. Whole paragraphs may be substituted if you discover that one point serves your purpose better than another. An item erroneously classified, for example, may be replaced with an item that does belong in the class you are writing about: Were you to classify the Kodak Instamatic as one of the types of 35mm cameras and omit the Leica, then a substitution would clearly be in order.

The student writer of "The Assembly-Line Method of Reproductive Health" has substituted some extensive dialogue in her revised version for the brief dialogue offered in her rough draft. Compare the revised version with the rough draft that appeared on pages 157–159. Can you point out other substitutions that the writer has made, more exact for less exact words, for example, or more appropriate for less appropriate details?

In writing the task for this chapter, you may want to substitute some dialogue that is especially pertinent for some that is lackluster. Some description may be extraneous to the operation of the place, and you may want to trade that for description that clarifies the process of the place. Or perhaps you have included too much narration of your visit and wish to substitute more information about the place.

Editing

Substitutions. Substitutions can also be made when you are editing. A word or a phrase can be traded for another word or phrase for a number of reasons: More formal language is needed, more precise words are available, more colorful expression is desirable, or a different grammatical construction is required.

Transitions. You are now combining your sentences nicely with conjunctions and conjunctive words and phrases. Scan your draft for these transitions. Are you using too many *and's* and *but's?* Try substituting more precise transitions—those that convey the exact relationship between ideas. *And* and *but,* particularly, are easily overdone.

For this particular assignment, substitute transitions of place when you are describing: "in the right-hand corner," "above me," "to my left," "on top." These prepositional phrases visually orient your readers and lead them from space to space.

Paragraphs. Although rewriting paragraphs is usually a revising chore affecting meaning, paragraphs can also be edited. On the surface, in other words, does each paragraph have a clear structure, or does the topic sentence need a few additions or substitutions to clearly characterize the content of the paragraph? Are transitions included between thoughts? Are they, moreover, precise?

Mechanics. By now, you know what mechanical errors you are inclined to make. Proofread your rough draft for these habitual mistakes and for any others that may have crept in.

Now revise and edit your rough draft.

BECOMING AWARE OF YOURSELF AS A WRITER

1. How did the explorer's method of inquiry aid you in thinking about your subject? For what other subjects might this be a useful inquiry method?

2. How did writing for a class in your curriculum differ from writing for your peers in general (or your English class) in the task for Chapter 2? How did it differ from writing for your instructor in the last chapter? To what extent do you think your audience affects the way you write?

3. Was interweaving the exposition, narration, description, and dialogue difficult for you? Do you understand the differing functions of exposition, narration, and description? Can you think of other writing assignments in which you have interwoven or might interweave the three?

4. What more have you learned about your own writing process from completing the task in this chapter? For example, are you more comfortable outlining before writing, or does an outline emerge only after you have completed your rough draft? Or does some other method of arranging your essay work for you?

5. What did you learn from writing about a place that was meaningful to you when you began the assignment? How did exploring the subject affect your perception of the place? What other subjects might you explore in the same way?

6. What kind of feedback are you receiving from your evaluators? Is it helpful? How could it be more helpful? What role do you play in its helpfulness?

7. How are you as an evaluator of the writing of others? To what extent does your reading of the writing of others affect your own writing?

8. What problems are you facing as a writer at the present? What steps have you plotted to solve them?

9. What are you satisfied with in your writing?

5

Writing a Case

In this chapter, you will continue the activity of the previous chapter: exploring the answer to a question. Whereas in Chapter 4 you asked the question "Is my visit to this place going to corroborate the high opinion others have of it?" here you will be asking, "After frequent observation of a situation that I have prejudged, will I prove my prejudgment or prejudice to be, in fact, an accurate evaluation, or will I find that I must discard it in favor of a new conclusion?"

Observing a situation—an ongoing event or a person—over a period of time is called *casing the subject,* much as, in the popular use of the term, a thief "cases a joint" before breaking in to determine employee or resident patterns of behavior, or police "case" a location to catch criminals. Probably the most common use of the term *case* is found among social workers, who write case studies about the families they visit to explain their financial, physical, and emotional needs. And psychiatrists use the term to refer to their written narratives about the lives of their patients. The task for this chapter will be to observe a situation of some kind over a period of time and to write your own case study.

The main thrust of the chapter lies in testing a prejudice by acquiring facts about the subject. Prejudice is by definition an evaluation arrived at before one knows the facts of a situation. Although we form these hasty conclusions all too often throughout our lives, thoughtful people attempt to decrease their

172

tendency to prejudge and attempt instead to form a conclusion based on a thorough examination of the subject.

In the first four chapters, we presented four methods of generating ideas: the journal (Chapter 1), free writing (Chapters 1 and 3), the journalist's questions (Chapter 2), and the explorer's questions (Chapter 4). In this chapter, we are going to present another series of questions, the classical questions, as further probes into your material.

The classical questions were devised by Aristotle during the Classical Age of Greece. As Athenians needed material for oral presentations at court and on ceremonial occasions, Aristotle devised a list of "topics" that would provide various ways of looking at any subject and generating ideas about it. These classical topics have been used in the study of rhetoric—both speech and writing—ever since. They have thus influenced Western patterns of thought for over two thousand years.

As you observe your situation, you may find some of the classical questions helpful in generating material for your case study. These questions, as used over the years, have also generated corresponding methods of arrangement of the material they generate, and they thus become a primary tool for the writer at various stages in the writing process.

After testing a prejudice through actual and frequent observation, and after writing about it with the aid of the classical questions, you should consider publishing your essay. In order to affect others' opinions about the situation you observed, we suggest you select an audience that would be most interested in the outcome of your case and an appropriate vehicle for publishing your findings—your student newspaper, for example.

GENERATING IDEAS: THE CLASSICAL QUESTIONS

Ten of the questions that Aristotle and other classical rhetoricians devised to generate ideas are the following:

1. What is it?
2. What class does it belong to, or what classes can it be divided into?
3. How is it like or unlike other objects, events, or ideas?
4. What caused it?
5. What did (will) it cause?
6. What process does it go through (has it gone through)?
7. What general ideas and values does it exemplify?
8. What examples are there of it?
9. What has been said about it by others?
10. What can be done about it?

In this chapter, we will consider Questions 3 through 6. (You might have realized that Questions 1 and 2 overlap with two of the explorer's questions discussed in the last chapter. For a discussion of how these two sets of questions differ, see pp. 175–176.) Questions 7 and 8 will be used in Chap. 6; Question 9, in Chap. 7; and Question 10, in Chap. 8.

In order to develop your topic fully, you will want to inquire into your subject at as many points as possible. Therefore, by forming subquestions about each of the classical questions, you can generate fuller answers. Some possible subquestions for Questions 3 through 6 are these:

III. How is *X* like or unlike other objects, events, or ideas?
   A. Am I equally interested in the other objects, events, or ideas, or am I using comparison and contrast as a device to describe *X* alone?
   B. If I am interested in all, then what points do they have in common? How are they different?
   C. If I am interested in describing *X* alone, then what objects, events, or ideas can I compare it with?
      1. Is there an analogy that usefully conveys *X*?
      2. How is *X* like *Y*, or like *Y* and *Z*?
   D. What can I contrast *X* with? How are these objects or ideas unlike *X*?

IV. What caused *X*?
   A. What is the most probable cause(s)?
   B. How far can I push the cause-and-effect relationship without committing one of the following logical fallacies? (See also Chap. 8, pp. 315–331.)
      1. Oversimplification
         a. Is it reasonable to assume *X* caused *Y*? Am I linking *X* and *Y* only because *X* happened just before *Y*?
         b. Is *X* the only cause of *Y*?
      2. Scapegoating
         a. Am I unfairly blaming an individual or a group for causing an effect that they did not actually cause?

V. What will *X* cause?
   A. Is the effect inevitable?
      1. Will *X* led to this effect and this effect, alone?
      2. Has *X* been the only cause of this effect?
   B. What reasonable effect(s) can I postulate?
   C. What analogies can I devise to show what the outcome might be?

VI. How does *X* work?
   A. What does *X* do?
   B. How is *X* put together?

    C. What was *X* intended to do?
    D. How well does *X* fulfill its intention or purpose?

One way to illustrate the use of the classical questions is to compare and contrast them with the explorer's questions from Chapter 4 to see whether each set of questions yields similar or different results. Let's say that you are thinking of writing about your prejudice toward your uncle, a person you had always disliked because he would embarrass you with his comic remarks and silly behavior. What can your uncle be compared to? The explorer's questions would ask how your uncle compared and contrasted with others in his class. For example, you might have envied your friend's uncle, who always behaved so properly and brought her presents. Or you might compare your uncle with other relatives or adult friends of the family. The classical questions would also generate this material but would allow for analogy as well. Analogy, which discovers the similarities between two unlike things, creates a tension and interest by going beyond the limits of a specific object to reveal its hitherto unnoticed connections to other abstract or concrete things. For example, your uncle might have seemed to you as a child like a blemished, irregularly shaped, tart Macintosh apple sitting in a bowl of perfectly shaped, glossy, sweet Delicious apples. At first this difference disturbed and embarrassed you, but now your mental and emotional maturity suggest to you that the "misfit apple" of your childhood might be more interesting and valuable than you previously thought. An analogy can reveal to the writer subtle and complex relationships that might not otherwise be disclosed.

    Another example of the differences between the classical and explorer's questions is illustrated by the question "What caused it?" The explorer's questions do not search for a causal relationship. They do not help us to see, for example, that your uncle's comic behavior might have been his way of facing some personal setbacks encountered in his life, or that his intention might have been to encourage you to develop your own sense of humor. The classical questions are not only concerned with such immediate causes but also with ultimate or more general causes or purposes. Using our example, you might be struck with the universal need of children for adult models outside the immediate family, or the significance for the child of comic language as a means of learning to interpret reality as ultimate causes of your uncle's behavior.

    "What will it cause?" The explorer's method does not look for effects, and so it isn't very helpful to you in demonstrating how your uncle's outlook on life has helped you to deal with your own personal failure or misfortune in your own experience. Nor can it suggest that you will want to carry over to your own children some of his playfulness and distrust of conventions.

    "How does it work?" Here the classical and the explorer's questions are very close (just as the classical questions "What is it?" and "What class does it belong to?" are very close to two of the explorer's questions).

Explorer's	*Classical*
• What larger system is it part of?	• What was it intended to do?
• How do the parts work together?	• What does it do? How is it put together?

The classical approach also adds an evaluative dimension in asking, "How well does it fulfill its intention or purpose?"

From the comparisons and contrasts between the two sets of questions, their differing thrusts should be clear: the explorer's questions seek out new facts about the subject—as a static entity, as a dynamic entity, and as part of a larger system—whereas the classical questions relate the subject to past or current knowledge and values by comparing and contrasting it with unlike subjects, by explaining its causes and effects, and by evaluating it. Both sets of questions, used separately or together, can aid you in generating an almost infinite number of ideas about your subject.

SOME PRACTICE WITH THE CLASSICAL QUESTIONS

1. Choose an everyday event, process, or condition—for example, traveling to school, working a computer, terrorism—and generate ideas in your journal, using the classical questions. Compare your ideas with the ideas of members of your group and compose a master list of results. Write a paragraph on one or more of the ideas you generated.

2. Identify the logical fallacies of the following causal statements. Which are examples of oversimplification and which of scapegoating?

   a. The size of Cleopatra's nose caused the fall of the Roman Empire. If her nose had been longer, she would have been less beautiful, and Marc Antony would not have fallen in love with her. He would not then have neglected his military duties and lost the battle of Salamis, thus setting in motion the decline in might and authority of Roman rule.

   b. Johnny caused his teacher to go crazy. When he accidentally hit her with a board eraser he had thrown across the room, Mrs. Gorp became hysterical and had to leave school. She never returned. It was later reported that she had been institutionalized.

   c. The headline read, "Pac Man Kills. Enraged Youth Kills Friend After Losing at Video Game."

   d. The student was asked, "Why did you fail math?" The student replied, "Because the teacher was boring. If the class had been more interesting, I'd have been more attentive to my work."

3. Which pairs of items seem most promising as subjects for comparison or contrast? Explain why some are promising but not others. How do comparison and contrast help you to understand each item in the pair better than if it were described alone?

   a. Nicaragua/Vietnam

   b. Rental apartment/private home

   c. The Beatles/the Marx Brothers

   d. Compact discs/video cassettes

   e. NHL hockey games/street fighting

   f. Cigarette smoking/drug addiction

4. Complete the following statements by devising an analogy to fit each example. How does each analogy help to describe the subject?

   a. My love is like . . .

   b. This politician was as smooth as . . .

   c. He captained the basketball team like . . .

   d. Her hamburger tasted like . . .

   e. He strode down the street like . . .

ADDRESSING YOUR AUDIENCE: WRITING FOR PUBLICATION

When writers write for publication, they usually write for one of two audiences. Either the magazine or journal is directed toward a very specific audience, or it has a general readership. In the last chapter, we discussed writing for a specific audience, one that is interested in your subject matter and knowledgeable about it. In this chapter, we are going to discuss how to write for a very general audience, an audience that may or may not be interested in your subject and may or may not know much about it.

The writer who writes for a large audience that is comprised of many different groups of people must therefore extrapolate those interests and qualities that these readers share and use this composite frame of reference in deciding how to write for this audience. How this can be done is the subject of this section.

No matter what magazine or newspaper you may read, none is written for everyone, no matter how unspecialized the content may appear to be. Each publication has a readership that can be fairly well defined, even though it may not be a technical journal, an entertainment rag, or a musician's bible. The reader of one publication is not necessarily the reader of another.

Think, for example, of the newspapers that are sold on the newsstands in your town. Newspapers with national circulations like *The Wall Street Journal* and even *The New York Times* have audiences that can be fairly well defined. Businesspeople probably read *The Wall Street Journal,* and many people who buy *The New York Times,* with its sections on cultural affairs and informed opinion, are college educated. Consider next the paper with the largest distribution in your state. Its readership may include these two audiences, but it may also number many who read neither *The Journal* nor *The Times.* And when you add your local neighborhood daily or weekly to the list, you find still another reader emerging, one who may read none of the other newspapers, one interested only in news that is close to home, like local marriages and births, sports, and politics. Finally, the reader of your college newspaper is still another composite, based on the interests and knowledge shared by the students on your campus.

How does one determine the frame of reference of the readership common to a particular publication? The following aspects of the publication should provide some guidelines: the types of subjects covered, the depth of the information given, the editorial perspectives delineated, the level of vocabulary used, the number and type of visuals printed (such as photographs and comics), and the advertisements included.

Take *The New York Times,* for example, which is available in all college libraries if not on your local newsstand. Why do we assume that it is for a reader who has a college education? Look first at the subjects covered. We find in Section 1 world and U.S. news and two pages of editorials, usually of a liberal bent, and informed opinions; in Section 4, we find extensive treatment of the stock market; and there are various daily supplements on sports, business, science, education, and entertainment. Although the types of information do not necessarily set *The Times* aside as aimed at the educated reader, the depth of information clearly does so. Also, the vocabulary level is high (it is estimated to be at a 12th-grade reading level). The number and type of visuals are a further indication, because the headlines are small, the pictures are few, and no comic strips are included. And although middle-priced items are advertised in its pages, luxury items tend to predominate.

At the other extreme are the tabloids. The topics covered in their pages are news, sports, and entertainment, with an emphasis in each case on the sensational aspects. The size of the headlines is very large, as are the pictures. The articles, on the other hand, are very short, and their depth of information is shallow. They are written on about an 8th-grade reading level. The advertisements are for products that are in a low to middle price range.

Once a writer has scanned his or her chosen publication from these angles, he or she can begin to assemble a reader frame of reference. The typical reader of the tabloid, we can assume, has perhaps a high-school education but often less; has a lower to middle income; is interested in the easily understood, often flamboyant aspects of the news rather than an in-depth analysis; and spends as much time on the sports, human interest, and comic sections as on the news. The reader of *The New York Times,* we can assume, not only is educated but is also inclined to be fairly prosperous, interested in understanding the news as well as in keeping abreast of it, liberal in political views, and willing to read the news on a daily basis. Anyone writing for either publication must take all of these factors into account if he or she wishes to reach the intended readership.

Of course, a writer does not always know what publication a given piece of writing should best be directed toward. Often one must select a publication after a piece has been written. The question then becomes "What publication has an audience similar to the one I have written for?" The first step in the process of finding an appropriate home for your writing is to make a list of the publications with which you are familiar. In addition to newspapers on the national, state, local, and campus levels, consider newsletters as a likely vehicle for publication. Newsletters are published by most agencies—by libraries, schools, department stores, homeowners' associations, athletic associations, and theater groups. The advantages of writing for a newsletter are many: The audience in most cases is specialized, and if you are yourself familiar with the specialization, their frame of reference will be easy for you to discover. Also, newsletters will be more likely than a more professional publication to publish the work of a beginning writer. Finally, the editor might work with you in shaping your piece for publication.

After you have considered the likely vehicles for the publication of your essay, such as newspapers and newsletters, begin to think of magazines that might publish your work. If you are serious about being published, think realistically about which magazines, such as small specialty magazines, might be likely to publish the work of a student writer. You can arrive at the frame of reference of the readers common to magazines by analyzing the same features as were analyzed above for newspapers and newsletters.

SOME PRACTICE WITH WRITING FOR PUBLICATION

1. Analyze the audiences of the following publications. What groups in America are excluded by the audience appeal of any of these magazines? Which magazines are addressed to the same audiences?

   Life Magazine   *TV Guide*
   Time Magazine   *People Magazine*
   National Enquirer   *Atlantic Monthly*
   Reader's Digest

2. Compare the audiences of *The New York Times*, your state's largest daily newspaper, and your hometown newspaper. To what extent do their audiences overlap? How are they different?

3. Take the frame of reference assembled above for the readers common to *The New York Times* and determine how they would best be approached on the following topics in terms of their attitude toward the subject, the depth of information they would require, and your role in relation to them:

> The CIA in Central America
> Glasnost
> The New York Yankees
> Disarmament
> Princess Di
> Unemployment

4. Select one of the following topics, find a shaping idea for it, and determine what audience you would best like to reach. Then choose a publication that reaches that audience, explaining why you think it does:

> The American auto industry
> Cable television
> The value of an education in America
> Young people and the job market
> Automation

5. Analyze the frame of reference of the audience for your college newspaper suggested by a perusal of a few issues. How similar is this frame of reference to that you devised for your peers in Chapter 2? On the basis of any dissimilarities, what suggestions would you make to the editors about the appropriateness of the newspaper for its audience?

TASK: WRITING A CASE

As the writing task for this chapter, choose an ongoing situation—an event, a person, a process, or a condition—about which you have made a prejudgment of some sort, and through a series of visits, observations, and/or interviews, write a case study in which you test your prejudgment or prejudice against the information that you have amassed. Your subject must be one that you have not observed sufficiently to form a legitimate conclusion about and that you have prejudged for one reason or another, either from past experience with similar subjects, because of hearsay, or because you judged hastily. This subject must be one that you can frequently observe while you are preparing to write the essay.

Logical areas in which to search for the subject of your case study are school, work, or your neighborhood. You might, for example, observe a sports team at practice or in the first two weeks of play to determine if the players are as bad as your prejudice tells you they are; a class after a difficult exam to determine if they will, as you suspect, blame only the teacher; a new arrangement at work that you believe will prove counterproductive; a noisy group in the local library who you think cannot possibly be accomplishing any work; public transportation that you have always assumed to be inefficient although you have never used it; or a person with whom your first encounter was unpleasant.

In order to successfully test your prejudice, you will want to observe your situation frequently and with objectivity. You will be following much the same procedure that a scientist engages in when testing a hypothesis: Through the gathering of many facts, she or he either corroborates the hypothesis or rejects it. Because a prejudice, like a hypothesis, precedes the acquisition of actual knowledge, testing it is absolutely essential for the thoughtful, educated person. As you embark on this task, play the role of the scientist—that of a disinterested, objective observer who is always willing to reject her or his own hypothesis if the facts demand it.

Use the questions of the classical method of inquiry in generating material for your case study. Different questions will be useful for different topics, so you will want to choose those that seem like they are going to prove most useful for you in gathering information and evaluating your reaction.

Obviously, other people may share your prejudice about your subject, and you may want to prove to them that you and they have been either wrong or completely justified. Choose a publication whose readership would be interested in your case study and that would actually consider publishing your essay. You might try for the school newspaper, for example, or a newsletter at work or the neighborhood weekly. Because most such publications are addressed to an homogeneous audience, the discussion on pp. 177–179 should be helpful in determining what your readers' background and point of view are and what depth of information they require. If you are not serious about publication at this point, then select any magazine that you are familiar with, and do your best to analyze and write for its audience.

In the sections that follow, we will discuss how to choose the most appropriate classical questions for your topic, how to construct a frame of reference and evaluate the depth of information needs of the reader common to a particular publication, and how to arrange your essay according to the arrangement patterns that correspond to the classical questions you have asked.

WRITING THE ESSAY

Generating Ideas With the Classical Questions

Before beginning the observations of your subject, you might want to review the classical questions discussed in the first section of this chapter as a way of deciding what to look for while you observe. Although all of the listed questions are at your disposal, and all subjects will suggest answers to some questions better than others, four seem to be most useful in completing this task. Each of these four questions generates others in responding to the task in general and may generate still others in response to your particular subject:

1. *How is it like or unlike other objects, events, or ideas?*
   How is it like or unlike other similar situations?
   How is it like or unlike the ideal of its situation?
   How is it like or unlike what I thought of it before observing it?
2. *What caused it?*
   What brought about the situation or an aspect of the situation?
   What caused the prejudice that I originally had (or the conclusion I still have) about the situation?
3. *What did (will) it cause?*
   What effect(s) has this situation I am observing caused?
   What effect(s) do my observations suggest it might cause in the future?
4. *What process does it go through (has it gone through)?*
   What process is the situation going through as I am making my observations?
   How is the situation changing from observation to observation?

Jot down any other variations on these questions that occur to you to ask about your subject. A student writing about the Soho Soccer Club, a Manhattan-based team, which he felt lacked cohesion, asked the following questions:

1. *How is it like or unlike other objects, events, or ideas?*
   How does the Soho Soccer Club compare and contrast with a professional soccer team?
   How does their coach compare with professional coaches?
2. *What caused it?*
   Why does the team lack cohesion?
   Why is the coach unable to achieve this cohesion?
3. *What did (will) it cause?*
   Will the team improve in the next two weeks under this coach's supervision?

Will the team suffer loss of morale?

Will team discipline be affected?

4. *What process does it go through (has it gone through)?*

What will the coach encourage his team to do in the practices I observe?

Will he teach transition before he teaches the proper passing techniques?

Will he teach them how to kick properly?

Do his players like and respect him?

Addressing the Reader of Your Publication

Think of a publication that might conceivably publish your essay, such as your college newspaper, a neighborhood weekly newspaper, a newsletter connected in some way with the situation you have chosen to write about, or some similar journal. Although actually publishing an essay is worth trying and would certainly be rewarding, if no such publication occurs to you, then choose any publication whose readers you think would be interested in your subject matter.

If you are not well versed in the particulars of your publication, then browse through it at some length now, looking at the types of articles and reading some of them to determine the depth of information they contain; examining the editorials, if any, for the editors' point of view; noting the products advertised and any other visuals (how large are the headings, are pictures or photographs included, are there any cartoons and, if so, of what nature: political, comic strip, other?); and surveying the feature columns for subject and focus. Ask yourself throughout this get-acquainted period whom each article and editorial is intended for: Is the reader being addressed educated, and if so, how much? Is a special hobby or career being presupposed? What social class does the publication seem aimed at? Is religion or sex or political persuasion being appealed to?

Once you have a knowledge of the publication you are writing for, answer the questions of the "Audience Analysis Guide" developed for this task.

────── AUDIENCE ANALYSIS GUIDE ──────

1. **What is the frame of reference of the readers common to this publication for which I am writing?**

2. **What will be their point of view on my subject? Will they share my initial prejudice?**

3. **What voice am I selecting as I write this essay? How can or will my voice selection affect my audience's point of view? If through observation I have decided that I no longer believe what I once did about my subject, but I suspect that my audience is still prejudiced about it, what voice can I use to bridge the gap?**

4. What depth of information about my subject does my audience need and want: (a) are they prejudiced as I was; (b) have we both observed the situation sufficiently to form a valid conclusion; or (c) have they formed no opinion on my subject at all. In each case, a different depth of information will be needed: The first reader will need much depth of new material gleaned from your observations; the second reader will be interested in both why you formed the prejudice in the first place (background) and why you subsequently changed your mind (new information); and the third reader will need to know both what the situation is and why you formed a prejudice about it (mainly background).

For example, a student interested in the Thalia Spanish Theater wrote about its "innovative" director, who "encourages the creativity of the actor." The publishing "home" for his essay was the Thalia Program, which audiences receive at the beginning of each performance. He decided that the frame of reference of his readership was that they were Catholic, were of Spanish descent (although some might be simply devotees of the Spanish theater), were middleclass, had received a secondary education in their native countries or had a background in the performing arts, and were of both sexes and all ages.

He felt that his audience loved the theater and would share his excitement about the director. The role he was playing was that of a student of the Spanish theater who hoped one day to be a a leading actor in the Thalia Company. He felt that the audience would respond to the voice of someone who shared their love of the theater and knew something about it.

Because his audience was familiar with his subject, at least in its general outlines, he knew he could devote his essay to an in-depth discussion of the techniques employed by the director which he observed over a period of time.

Arranging the Essay

The Shaping Idea.   There are several arrangement patterns you might use in fulfilling this task: cause and effect, comparison and contrast, and process analysis. These may be used separately or in combination, depending on the shaping idea that you have chosen for your essay. If you have not yet chosen a shaping idea, you will want to compose one now, one that reflects the situation that you are casing, your prejudice toward it, and the classical questions that you chose to answer in generating ideas for your paper. Here are some examples of students' shaping ideas:

1. I have heard that the process of creating a character is always challenging when working with Mr. Davila, who has developed a

number of innovations on the Stanislavsky method that have proven stimulating to the creativity of the actor.

2. Although some of the players have a good sound knowledge of the game, the team lacks cohesion because of the coach's poor tactical methods.

3. I have always thought that the public library is like a zoo and that students cannot accomplish very much there.

The student writing on the first shaping idea will no doubt discuss the process that Mr. Davila goes through in directing his actors, perhaps also discussing why this approach is so stimulating to the actors, and perhaps comparing him with other directors as well. The second shaping idea calls for a discussion of the coach's poor process of teaching tactical methods, of the effects of this process on the players, and of the ways in which he compares with other coaches. The last shaping idea intends to present the effects on students of studying in the public library and perhaps to contrast this place of study with other, quieter ones.

These classical questions all have corresponding patterns of arrangement, and we will now discuss cause and effect, comparison and contrast, and process analysis.

Cause and Effect.   The pattern of arranging your material when discussing causes and effects depends entirely on your subject matter and how many causes and effects you are discussing. The basic patterns are these:

- A caused B (and C and D, depending on the number of effects).
- A is caused by B (and C and D, depending on the number of causes).
- A caused B, B caused C, and C caused D.

These patterns can be used to apply to a single paragraph or to an entire essay. When applied to a paragraph, A, B, C, and D may each be contained in one or two sentences; when applied to an essay, each letter may be the subject of an entire paragraph. Here is a student paragraph developed according to one of these causal patterns (A caused B, and B caused C):

Eight books were assigned from the course, and I found myself reading from four at a time. As if that wasn't difficult enough, the reading material never seemed to be fully explained in class. Something was always left hanging. For a while, I figured that perhaps it was just I who was having difficulty and that I wasn't putting enough effort into my work. No one asked questions as "Mrs. Doe" went along through the battles between lords and vassals, popes and kings. Thus I figured that everyone else understood the work, and that I just had to devote more time and effort to my studies. So read and study I did, until I was down to four hours' sleep per night.

Comparison and Contrast.   Two basic patterns are available when you are comparing and contrasting subjects. One is the "whole-by-whole" method, in which each subject is presented separately, and then comparisons and contrasts are delineated; the other is the "part-by-part" method, in which the two subjects are compared and contrasted point by point throughout the paragraph or essay.

When applied to a paragraph, the whole-by-whole method requires that two or three sentences at the beginning of the paragraph be devoted to the first subject, two or three in the middle deal with the second subject, and the final third of the paragraph point out the similarities and differences. The part-by-part method for a paragraph calls for every sentence to explore a different point at which the two subjects either compare or contrast.

When applied to an entire essay, the whole-by-whole method would suggest that the first section of the essay discuss one subject, the middle section present the other, and the final section directly compare and contrast the two. In using the part-by-part method for an essay, one would probably assign to each paragraph a different point on which the two subjects would be compared and/or contrasted.

Below are two student paragraphs illustrating these two methods of comparison and contrast:

Part-by-part

The roles of the candidates' wives finally convinced me who would win. Louise Lehrman sent a "woman-to-woman" message telling of the faith she had in her husband. This may have been a good idea, but unfortunately Matilda Cuomo beat her to the punch. Days earlier, Mrs. Cuomo was seen on TV giving virtually the same message. Also, Matilda Cuomo was on the campaign trail with and without her husband. Louise Lehrman's lack of involvement in her husband's campaign may have hurt him very much.

Whole-by-whole

When the public library is busy, which is most of the time, all the tables are full, and the majority of people are engrossed in conversation. The smaller kids are running around wildly. High-school kids are noisily putting the books back on the shelves. The elderly talk louder because many of them are hard of hearing. Long lines have formed at the reference desk and checkout counters. On the other hand, the library at the local college has lots of space for students who want to study. It is equipped with several small, comfortable, soundproof rooms for people who need peace and quiet. These rooms have glass all around them, and you can see people talking but you can't hear them. The college library is more spacious, more quiet, and more accommodating.

Process Analysis.   Process analysis combines elements of narration and exposition: narration because a process usually occurs in chronological order, exposition because one is explaining how something is done. The logical pattern for process analysis is to break up the stages of a process into their proper or logical order: Step A, Step B, Step C, Step D, and so on. If you are describing a process that others must attempt to follow, you'll want to take care in presenting the correct order of the steps in the process as well as in describing what takes place at each step.

Again, as in the cause-and-effect and the comparison-and-contrast patterns, if you are writing a paragraph on a process, each sentence will depict a different step; if you are writing an essay, each paragraph will describe a step or a unified series of steps. Here is a paragraph developed according to the process pattern:

Our defense is an intelligent and coordinated one. I drop back ten yards to break up a pass over the middle. Danny Romero, a solid defensive player, moves to the deep right side as safety. Left-side safety Eddie Dietrick, who leads the team in interceptions with four, tears across his side of the field. Short left-side safety Jimmy White, who has the reactions of a cat, watches the opposing quarterback intently. On the short right-hand side, John Sullivan, the most physical player on the team, prepares for a receiver foolish enough to run into his orbit. Jeff Marconi and Frank Roberto, two solid backup defensive players, dig their cleats in and tense their bodies. This is the way our shifting zone defense works.

Model Essays.   The first essay that follows, "Workers," from Richard Rodriguez's autobiographical *Hunger of Memory* (1982), exemplifies the chapter task in many significant ways. The author recounts his experiences as a manual laborer at a summer construction job. Expecting at first that his work would gain him "admission to the world of the laborer," he finds instead that a wide gap separates him from the lives of *los pobres,* the real working poor he would never come to know because of his education and class difference. He "cases" his subject by showing us his reactions to the work over a short period of time, his attitude changing as he becomes familiar with his fellow workers and the demands of physical labor.

Workers
Richard Rodriguez

It was at Stanford, one day near the end of my senior year, that a friend told me about a summer construction job he knew was available. I was quickly alert. Desire uncoiled within me. My friend said that he knew I had been looking for summer employment. He knew I needed some money. Almost apologetically he explained: It was something I probably wouldn't be interested in, but a friend of his, a contractor, needed someone for the summer to do menial jobs. There would be lots of shoveling and raking and sweeping. Nothing too hard. But nothing more interesting either. Still, the pay would be good. Did I want it? Or did I know someone who did?

I did. Yes, I said, surprised to hear myself say it.

In the weeks following, friends cautioned that I had no idea how hard physical labor really is. ("You only *think* you know what it is like to shovel for eight hours straight.") Their objections seemed to me challenges. They resolved the issue. I became happy with my plan. I decided, however, not to tell my parents. I wouldn't tell my mother because I could guess her worried reaction. I would tell my father only after the summer was over, when I could announce that, after all, I did know what "real work" is like.

The day I met the contractor (a Princeton graduate, it turned out), he asked me whether I had done any physical labor before. "In high school, during the summer," I lied. And although he seemed to regard me with skepticism, he decided to give me a try. Several days later, expectant, I arrived at my first construction site. I would take off my shirt to the sun. And at last grasp desired sensation. No longer afraid. At last become like a *bracero.* "We need those tree stumps out of here by tomorrow," the contractor said. I started to work.

I labored with excitement that first morning—and all the days after. The work was harder than I could have expected. But it was never as tedious as my friends had warned me it would be. There was too much physical pleasure in the labor. Especially early in the day, I would be most alert to the sensations of movement and straining. Beginning around seven each morning (when the air was still damp but the scent of weeds and dry earth anticipated the heat of the sun), I would feel my body resist the first thrusts of the shovel. My arms, tightened by sleep, would gradually loosen; after only several minutes, sweat would gather in beads on my forehead and then—a short while later—I would feel my chest silky with sweat in the breeze. I would return to my work. A nervous spark of pain would fly up my arm and settle to burn like an ember in the thick of my shoulder. An hour, two passed. Three. My whole body would assume regular movements, my shoveling would be described by identical, even movements. Even later in the day, my enthusiasm for primitive sensation would survive the heat and the dust and the insects pricking my back. I would strain wildly for sensation as the day came to a close. At three-thirty, quitting time, I would stand upright and slowly let my head fall back, luxuriating in the feeling of tightness relieved.

Some of the men working nearby would watch me and laugh. Two or three of the older men took the trouble to teach me the right way to use a pick, the correct way to shovel. "You're doing it wrong, too hard," one man scolded. Then proceeded to show me—what persons who work with their bodies all their lives quickly learn—the most economical way to use one's body in labor.

"Don't make your back do so much work," he instructed. I stood impatiently listening, half listening, vaguely watching, then noticed his work-thickened fingers clutching the shovel. I was annoyed. I wanted to tell him that I enjoyed shoveling the wrong way. And I didn't want to learn the right way. I wasn't afraid of back pain. I liked the way my body felt sore at the end of the day.

I was about to, but, as it turned out, I didn't say a thing. Rather it was at that moment I realized that I was fooling myself if I expected a few weeks of labor to gain me admission to the world of the laborer. I would not learn in three months what my father had meant by "real work." I was not bound to this job; I could imagine its rapid conclusion. For me the sensation of exertion and fatigue could be savored. For my father or uncle, working at comparable jobs when they were my age, such sensations were to be feared. Fatigue took a different toll on their bodies—and minds.

It was, I know, a simple insight. But it was with this realization that I took my first step that summer toward realizing something even more important about the 'worker.' In the company of carpenters, electricians, plumbers, and painters at lunch, I would often sit quietly, observant. I was not shy in such company. I felt easy, pleased by the knowledge that I was casually accepted, my presence taken for granted by men (exotics) who worked with their hands. Some days the younger men would talk and talk about sex, and they would howl at women who drove by in cars. Other days the talk at lunchtime was subdued; men gathered in separate groups. It depended on who was around. There were rough, good-natured workers. Others were quiet. The more I remember that summer, the more I realize that there was no single *type* of worker. I am embarrassed to say I had not expected such diversity. I certainly had not expected to meet, for example, a plumber who was an abstract painter in his off hours and admired the work of Mark Rothko. Nor did I expect to meet so many workers with college diplomas. (They were the ones who were not surprised that I intended to enter graduate school in the fall.) I suppose what I really want to say here is painfully obvious, but I must say it nevertheless: The men of that summer were middle-class Americans. They certainly didn't constitute an oppressed society. Carefully completing their work sheets; talking about the fortunes of local football teams; planning Las Vegas vacations; comparing the gas mileage of various makes of campers—they were not *los pobres* my mother had spoken about.

On two occasions, the contractor hired a group of Mexican aliens. They were employed to cut down some trees and haul off debris. In all, there were six men of varying age. The youngest in his twenties; the oldest (his father?) perhaps sixty years old. They came and they left in a single old truck. Anonymous men. They were never introduced to the other men at the site. Immediately upon their arrival, they would follow the contractor's directions, start working—rarely resting—seemingly driven by a fatalistic sense that work which had to be done was best done as quickly as possible.

I watched them sometimes. Perhaps they watched me. The only time I saw them pay me much notice was one day at lunchtime when I was laughing with the other men. The Mexicans sat apart when they ate, just as they worked by themselves. Quiet. I rarely heard them say much to each other. All I could hear were their voices calling out sharply to one another, giving directions. Otherwise, when they stood briefly resting, they talked among themselves in voices too hard to overhear.

The contractor knew enough Spanish, and the Mexicans—or at least the oldest of them, their spokesman—seemed to know enough English to communicate. But because I was around, the contractor decided one day to make me his translator. (He assumed I could speak Spanish.) I did what I was told. Shyly I went over to tell the Mexicans that the *patrón* wanted them to do something else before they left for the day. As I started to speak, I was afraid with my old fear that I would be unable to pronounce the Spanish words. But it was a simple instruction I had to convey. I could say it in phrases.

The dark sweating faces turned toward me as I spoke. They stopped their work to hear me. Each nodded in response. I stood there. I wanted to say something more. But what could I say in Spanish, even if I could have pronounced the words right? Perhaps I just wanted to engage them in small talk, to be assured of their confidence, our familiarity. I thought for a moment to ask them where in Mexico they were from. Something like that. And maybe I wanted to tell them (a lie if need be) that my parents were from the same part of Mexico.

I stood there.

Their faces watched me. The eyes of the man directly in front of me moved slowly over my shoulder, and I turned to follow his glance toward *el patrón* some distance away. For a moment I felt swept up by that glance into the Mexicans' company. But then I heard one of them returning to work. And then the others went back to work. I left them without saying anything more.

When they had finished, the contractor went over to pay them in cash. (He later told me that he paid them collectively—"for the job," though he wouldn't tell me their wages. He said something quickly about the good rate of exchange "in their own country.") I can still hear the loudly confident voice he used with the Mexicans. It was the sound of the *gringo* I had heard as a very young boy. And I can still hear the quiet, indistinct sounds of the Mexican, the oldest, who replied. At hearing that voice I was sad for the Mexicans. Depressed by their vulnerability. Angry at myself. The adventure of the summer seemed suddenly ludicrous. I would not shorten the distance I felt from *los pobres* with a few weeks of physical labor. I would not become like them. They were different from me. . . .

That summer I worked in the sun may have made me physically indistinguishable from the Mexicans working nearby. (My skin was actually darker because, unlike them, I worked without wearing a shirt. By late August my hands were probably as tough as theirs.) But I was not one of *los pobres*. What made me different from them was an attitude of *mind*, my imagination of myself.

I do not blame my mother for warning me away from the sun when I was young. In a world where her brother had become an old man in his twenties because he was dark, my complexion was something to worry about. "Don't run in the sun," she warns me today. I run. In the end, my father was right—though perhaps he did not know how right or why—to say that I would never know what real work is. I will never know what he felt at his last factory job. If tomorrow I worked at some kind of factory, it would go differently for me. My long education would favor me. I could act as a public person—able to defend my interests, to unionize, to petition, to speak up—to challenge and demand. (I will never know what real work is.) I will never know what the Mexicans knew, gathering their shovels and ladders and saws.

Their silence stays with me now. The wages those Mexicans received for their labor were only a measure of their disadvantaged condition. Their silence is more telling. They lack a public identity. They remain profoundly alien. Persons apart. People lacking a union obviously, people without grounds. They depend upon the relative good will or fairness of their employers each day. For such people, lacking a better alternative, it is not such an unreasonable risk.

Their silence stays with me. I have taken these many words to describe its impact. Only: the quiet. Something uncanny about it. Its compliance. Vulnerability. Pathos. As I heard their truck rumbling away, I shuddered, my face mirrored with sweat. I had finally come face to face with *los pobres*.

1. How does Rodriguez's use of comparison and contrast help the reader to understand the meaning of his experience with physical labor?

2. What prejudgment of workers had Rodriguez made before he started the job? What accounts for his change in attitude?

3. Why does the author devote almost half his essay to the Mexican workers he didn't even know? How does he contrast himself with them?

4. How does the knowledge that Rodriguez has gained by his concluding paragraph contrast with the expectation about work that he expresses in his introductory paragraphs?

5. How could the author's summer experience have significance later in his life with regard to what he calls his "imagination of myself"?

In the next essay, Jane Jacobs turns her attention to an abstract idea, the dynamic order of the city, which she humanizes by recreating the process of

Hudson Street, an older neighborhood in New York City. By showing us the movement and change that take place in the course of one day, she composes what she calls a "sidewalk ballet" in which everything that happens contributes to the vibrant life of the city.

Sidewalk Ballet

Jane Jacobs

Under the seeming disorder of the old city, wherever the old city is working successfully, is a marvelous order for maintaining the safety of the streets and the freedom of the city. It is a complex order. Its essence is intricacy of sidewalk use, bringing with it a constant succession of eyes. This order is all composed of movement and change, and although it is life, not art, we may fancifully call it the art form of the city and liken it to the dance—not to a simple-minded precision dance with everyone kicking up at the same time, twirling in unison and bowing off en masse, but to an intricate ballet in which the individual dancers and ensembles all have distinctive parts which miraculously reinforce each other and compose an orderly whole. The ballet of the good city sidewalk never repeats itself from place to place, and in any one place is always replete with new improvisions.

The stretch of Hudson Street where I live is each day the scene of an intricate sidewalk ballet. I make my own first entrance into it a little after eight when I put out the garbage can, surely a prosaic occupation, but I enjoy my part, my little clang, as the droves of junior high school students walk by the center of the stage dropping candy wrappers. (How do they eat so much candy so early in the morning?)

While I sweep up the wrappers I watch the other rituals of morning: Mr. Halpert unlocking the laundry's handcart from its mooring to a cellar door, Joe Cornacchia's son-in-law stacking out the empty crates from the delicatessen, the barber bringing out his sidewalk folding chair, Mr. Goldstein arranging the coils of wire which proclaim the hardware store is open, the wife of the tenement's superintendent depositing her chunky three-year-old with a toy mandolin on the stoop, the vantage point from which he is learning the English his mother cannot speak. Now the primary children, heading for St. Luke's, dribble through to the south; the children for St. Veronica's cross, heading to the west, and the children for P.S. 41, heading toward the east. Two new entrances are being made from the wings: well-dressed and even elegant women and men with briefcases emerge from doorways and side streets. Most of these are heading for the bus and subways, but some hover on the curbs, stopping taxis which have miraculously appeared at the right moment, for the taxis are part of a wider morning ritual: having dropped passengers from midtown in the downtown financial district, they are now bringing downtowners up to midtown. Simultaneously, numbers of women in housedresses have emerged and as they crisscross with one another they pause for quick conversations that sound with either laughter or joint indignation, never, it seems, anything between. It is time for me to hurry to work too, and I exchange my ritual farewell with Mr. Lofaro, the short, thick-bodied, white-aproned fruit man who stands outside his doorway a little up the street, his arms folded, his feet planted, looking solid as earth itself. We nod; we each glance quickly up and down the street, then look back to each other and smile. We have done this many a morning for more than ten years, and we both know what it means: All is well.

The heart-of-the-day ballet I seldom see, because part of the nature of it is that working people who live there, like me, are mostly gone, filling the roles of strangers on other sidewalks. But from days off, I know enough of it to know that it becomes more and more intricate. Longshoremen who are not working that day gather at the White House or the Ideal or the International for beer and conversation. The executives and business lunchers from the industries just to the west throng the Dorgene restaurant and the Lion's Head coffee house; meatmarket workers and communications scientists fill the bakery lunchroom. Character dancers come on, a strange old man with strings of old shoes over his shoulders, motor-scooter riders with big beards and girl friends who bounce on the back of the scooters and wear their hair long in front of their faces as well as behind, drunks who follow the advice of the Hat Council and are always turned out in hats, but not hats the Council would approve. Mr. Lacey, the locksmith, shuts up his shop for a while and goes to exchange the time of day with Mr. Slube at the cigar store. Mr. Koochagian, the tailor, waters the luxuriant jungle of plants in his window, gives them a critical look from the outside, accepts a compliment on them from two passersby, fingers the leaves on the plane tree in front of our house with a thoughtful gardener's appraisal, and crosses the street for a bit at the Ideal where he can keep an eye on customers and wigwag across the message that he is coming. The baby carriages come out, and clusters of everyone from toddlers with dolls to teen-agers with homework gather at the stoops.

When I get home after work, the ballet is reaching its crescendo. This is the time of roller skates and stilts and tricycles, and games in the lee of the stoop with bottletops and plastic cowboys; this is the time of bundles and packages, zigzagging from the drug store to the fruit stand and back over to the butcher's; this is the time when teen-agers, all dressed up, are pausing to ask if their slips show or their collars look right; this is the time when beautiful girls get out of MG's; this is the time when the fire engines go through; this is the time when anybody you know around Hudson Street will go by.

As darkness thickens and Mr. Halpert moors the laundry cart to the cellar door again, the ballet goes on under lights, eddying back and forth but intensifying at the bright spotlight pools of Joe's sidewalk pizza dispensary, the bars, the delicatessen, the restaurant and the drug store. The night workers stop now at the delicatessen, to pick up salami and a container of milk. Things have settled down for the evening but the street and its ballet have not come to a stop.

I know the deep night ballet and its seasons best from waking long after midnight to tend a baby and, sitting in the dark, seeing the shadows and hearing the sounds of the sidewalk. Mostly it is a sound like infinitely pattering snatches of party conversation and, about three in the morning, singing, very good singing. Sometimes there is sharpness and anger or sad, sad weeping, or a flurry of search for a string of beads broken. One night a young man came roaring along, bellowing terrible language at two girls whom he had apparently picked up and who were disappointing him. Doors opened, a wary semicircle formed around him, not too close, until the police came. Out came the heads, too, along Hudson

Street, offering opinion, "Drunk . . . Crazy . . . A wild kid from the suburbs" *

Deep in the night, I am almost unaware how many people are on the street unless something calls them together, like the bagpipe. Who the piper was and why he favored our street I have no idea. The bagpipe just skirled out in the February night, and as if it were a signal the random, dwindled movements of the sidewalk took on direction. Swiftly, quietly, almost magically a little crowd was there, a crowd that evolved into a circle with a Highland fling inside it. The crowd could be seen on the shadowy sidewalk, the dancers could be seen, but the bagpiper himself was almost invisible because his bravura was all in his music. He was a very little man in a plain brown overcoat. When he finished and vanished, the dancers and watchers applauded, and applause came from the galleries too, half a dozen of the hundred windows on Hudson Street. Then the windows closed, and the little crowd dissolved into the random movements of the night street.

The strangers on Hudson Street, the allies whose eyes help us natives keep the peace of the street, are so many that they always seem to be different people from one day to the next. That does not matter. Whether they are so many always-different people as they seem to be, I do not know. Likely they are. When Jimmy Rogan fell through a plate-glass window (he was separating some scuffling friends) and almost lost his arm, a stranger in an old T-shirt emerged from the Ideal bar, swiftly applied an expert tourniquet and, according to the hospital's emergency staff, saved Jimmy's life. Nobody remembered seeing the man before and no one has seen him since. The hospital was called in this way: a woman sitting on the steps next to the accident ran over to the bus stop, wordlessly snatched the dime from the hand of a stranger who was waiting with his fifteen-cent fare ready, and raced into the Ideal's phone booth. The stranger raced after her to offer the nickel too. Nobody remembered seeing him before, and no one has seen him since. When you see the same stranger three or four times on Hudson Street, you begin to nod. This is almost getting to be an acquaintance, a public acquaintance, of course.

I have made the daily ballet of Hudson Street sound more frenetic than it is, because writing it telescopes it. In real life, it is not that way. In real life, to be sure, something is always going on, the ballet is never at a halt, but the general effect is peaceful and the general tenor even leisurely. People who know well such animated city streets will know how it is. I am afraid people who do not will always have it a little wrong in their heads—like the old prints of rhinoceroses made from travelers' descriptions of rhinoceroses.

On Hudson Street, the same as in the North End of Boston or in any other animated neighborhoods of great cities, we are not innately more competent at keeping the sidewalks safe than are the people who try to live off the hostile truce of Turf in a blind-eyed city. We are the lucky possessors of a city order that makes it relatively simple to keep the peace because there are plenty of eyes on the street. But there is nothing simple about that order itself, or the bewildering number of components that go into it. Most of those components are specialized in one way or another. They unite in their joint effect upon the sidewalk, which is not specialized in the least. That is its strength.

---

* He turned out to be a wild kid from the suburbs. Sometimes, on Hudson Street, we are tempted to believe the suburbs must be a difficult place to bring up children.

1. Why does Jacobs create the metaphor of the ballet? What aspects of the ballet does she have in mind by relating it to the city? What other analogies might she have made? Do you agree with her choice of analogy?

2. To what extent is Jacobs' testing a prejudgment about life on Hudson Street, and to what extent is she presenting her observations as evidence for a point of view she does not wish to question? What hints does Jacobs include that her view of Hudson Street might be slanted? How might she revise her essay to reflect life on city streets more objectively?

3. Jacobs published her essay in a book entitled *The Life and Death of Great American Cities,* in effect selecting her own audience. What publication with which you are familiar might have chosen this for its readers?

Writing the Rough Draft

Once you have made your observations with the aid of the classical questions, have decided what audience you are addressing, and have planned what arrangement patterns you will use, you are about ready to begin your rough draft. At this point, if you have not already done so, you will also want to decide whether your observation of your subject has supported your prejudice. Although your shaping idea has announced your prejudice, it will not necessarily indicate your final decision about it, especially if you have changed your mind in the course of your observations. Your verdict can emerge in your essay at various junctures: in the introduction, in the course of presenting your observations, in your conclusion, or in all three. Knowing your verdict about your situation is important before beginning to write: Whether or not your reader agrees with your prejudice will shape what you say and how you say it.

Following is the rough draft of a student's essay in fulfillment of this task. Where did she state her shaping idea? At what point do you know whether she felt her initial prejudice was justified or not? What questions did she ask in generating material? How did she arrange her paragraphs? Her audience comprised other women who might be amused to read about her encounter with a modern home appliance. She addressed them in the college newspaper, writing specifically for evening students who are generally older and often have to juggle the demands of home, work, and school.

A BOTHERSOME CONVENIENCE

Somewhere in the back of my mind, I always felt that the new contraption in my kitchen was more bother than it was worth. The dishwasher was a gift from my mother-in-law for my remodeled kitchen three years ago. Still today, this lovely color-coordinated appliance with its push-button everything and a cycle for every imaginable type of dish is shiny and new. I never wanted the thing, but I relented and let my mother-in-law buy it for me after all my dishwasher-owner friends and family insisted that it was senseless to remodel the kitchen and not get one. Their reasons for owning one were endless: It would be easier to sell the house. (I have no intention of moving anytime in the near future.) I could be doing other things instead of slaving over the sink. (My husband is a great dishwasher and the children are getting good.) The dishes would be cleaner. (I never really checked that closely, but the family is still very healthy so they must have been clean enough.) As numerous as their reasons for using it were, I have even more for discontinuing after two weeks of constant use.

For one thing, before I got that lovely gift, the dishes were washed, dried, and put away after every meal, so my service for twelve for my family of six was quite sufficient. Not so with this new gadget for which I need twenty-four of everything or at least of cereal bowls and teaspoons, which the children use for everything. They need these for everything--breakfast, lunch, between-meal snacks, dinner, dessert, popcorn. Numerous times during the last two weeks I have had to go to the dishwasher, get out a dirty teaspoon, and wash it so that I could fix myself a cup of tea.

As if all this were not bad enough, there were times when I forgot to run the dishwasher and had to use the good china to eat pizza from. Other times I would start to run it and almost instantly hear a scream from the shower of "Ma, there's no hot water in here." I would shut it off and tell whoever it was to continue. Because it only uses hot water, I also can not do a wash while it is operating or I will finish with murky-looking clothes and, heaven forbid, spotted glasses.

Another thing--since we are a fairly large family with growing, hungry children, I need to use large pots when cooking. Now these big pots do not fit in the dishwasher, because the water arms will get stuck on them and nothing will be clean.

This thing has also made a bit of a liar out of me. Since my mother-in-law gave it to me, I don't have the heart to let her know that I don't use it. When they dine with us I just pile the dishes on the counter and say, "Oh, don't worry, I'll just stick them in the dishwasher later." I really miss the comradery of standing in front of the sink with her, washing, drying, and catching up on the latest gossip.

Also, some of the antics of the dishes while they are being washed in it have helped to take me back to the old-fashioned method. Plastic bowls have a tendency to turn upside down during the cycle, and when I open it they are filled with boiling hot water and particles of food from all the other dishes, so I have to wash and dry by hand again anyway. And when food like mashed potatoes or rice is not properly scraped, it gets propelled up inside cups and glasses and becomes permanently glued there.

To my original suspicion that this is a bothersome machine, I now have a new one, which is that those who extoll its virtues do not want to confess to its uselessness. After all, who would want others to know that you spent a lot of money on a good-for-nothing gadget. Therefore, the myth continues.

Since I started using the machine, it seems that every dish in the house has become my sole domain. Conveniently, the rest of the family have failed to master the art of loading and unloading it.

Maybe someday I will find a place for this invention in my life, but for now I am returning it to its previous function as a catchall for those seldom-used things around the kitchen.

FOCUS: SENTENCE COMBINING

The sentence, like the paragraph, is a basic unit of thought. How one phrases one's sentences—their language, their structure, their punctuation, and even their length—indicates one's level of maturity as a writer. In this section, we suggest exercises that will help you to improve the structure and therefore the maturity of your sentences by giving you options for shaping them with which you be unfamiliar. The first exercises work with the simple base sentence. These exercises gradually lead into longer, combined sentences. Other exercises show the relationship of punctuation to sentence structure. Still others show how sentence structure can help build transitions between thoughts, on both the sentence level and the paragraph level.

The Base Sentence

The base sentence is a simple sentence that includes a subject, a verb, and often either an object, a predicate nominative, or a predicate adjective. Examples of these four base sentence patterns are the following:

The girl cried. (SUBJECT AND VERB)

The girl takes calculus. (SUBJECT, VERB, AND OBJECT)

The girl is a mathematics major. (SUBJECT, VERB, AND PREDICATE NOMINATIVE)

The girl is smart. (SUBJECT, VERB, AND PREDICATE ADJECTIVE)

SOME PRACTICE WITH BASE SENTENCES

1. Write a paragraph on any subject, using only simple sentences. Base your sentence patterns on the four base sentences above.

2. Rewrite the paragraph from Exercise 1, placing each sentence on a separate line and leaving three spaces between each sentence. Then list three adjectives, three adverbs, and three prepositional phrases that will add information to each base sentence. Finally, combine all the new elements with each simple sentence and rewrite the four sentences as a paragraph.

   Example
   Base sentence: The boy eats chocolates.
   Adjectives: plump, young, expensive
   Adverbs: slightly, hastily, greedily
   Prepositional phrases: in the cafeteria, of his school, during lunchtime
   Combined: The slightly plump young boy hastily and greedily eats
       expensive chocolates in the cafeteria of his school during lunchtime.

3. Write a second paragraph on any subject. Again, write in simple sentences based on the four simple patterns above. Combine two or more base sentences with coordinating conjunctions such as *and, or, but, for,* and *yet,* adding adjectives, adverbs, and prepositional phrases where appropriate as you go along (see Handbook, pp. 428–429, 431).

Subordinate Clauses

You can turn a base sentence into a subordinate clause by adding subordinating conjunctions before it, such as *although, as, because, since, when, that, after, before, how, if, though, unless, until, what, where, while, in order that, provided that, as long as, as though,* and *so (that).*

Example

Base sentence 1: Television is no longer slavishly watched.

Base sentence 2: The network executives are becoming worried.

Combined: Because television is no longer slavishly watched, the network executives are becoming worried. (The addition of the subordinating conjunction *because* creates a subordinate clause out of the first base sentence, and the second sentence remains "independent." Note: subordinate clauses cannot stand alone as sentences; they must be joined to an independent base sentence for the completion of their meaning.)

SOME PRACTICE WITH SUBORDINATE CLAUSES

4. Combine the sentences in the paragraph in Exercise 3 so that some base sentences become subordinate clauses.

Example

Base sentence 1: The husky coach calmly and quietly announced the lucky winner of the first prize for boxing at the college.

Base sentence 2: My usually courageous brother shook.

Combined: As the husky coach calmly and quietly announced the lucky winner of the first prize for boxing at the college, my usually courageous brother shook.

Free Modifiers

Base sentences can also be turned into "clusters" of words that act as free modifiers coming before, after, or in the middle of base clauses and set apart by punctuation. These clusters can act as nouns, verbs, adjectives, or adverbs in reference to another base sentence.

Noun Cluster

Example

Base sentence 1: Wally is a jokester.

Base sentence 2: He finds that his pranks are funny only to him.

Combined: A jokester, Wally finds that his pranks are funny only to him.

Verb Cluster

Example

Base sentence 1: Wally hooted with laughter at the absurd dilemma of his friend.

Base sentence 2: He was not appreciated.

Combined: Hooting with laughter at the absurd dilemma of his friend, Wally was not appreciated.

Adjective Cluster

Example

Base sentence 1: Wally is disliked.

Base sentence 2: Most of his fraternity brothers avoid him whenever possible.

Combined: Disliked, Wally finds himself avoided by most of his fraternity brothers whenever possible.

Adverb Cluster

Example

Base sentence 1: Wally is scarcely aware of their antipathy.

Base sentence 2: This is hard to believe.

Combined: Unbelievably, Wally is scarcely aware of their antipathy.

Subordinate clauses are also free modifiers.
When two or more free modifiers modifying the same word are used in a sentence, they should be in the same or parallel form.

Example

Base sentence 1: The April sun shone *weakly*.

Base sentence 2: Intermittently, the sun shone.

Base sentence 3: The sun, *while the rain fell,* shone.

Base sentence 4: While storm clouds threatened to eclipse it, the sun shone.

Combined: Weakly and intermittently, the April sun shone while the rain fell and storm clouds threatened to eclipse it.

SOME PRACTICE WITH FREE MODIFIERS

5. Write three sentences, each of which contains parallel free modifiers. Use a different type of free modifier in each sentence.

6. Rewrite the paragraph from Exercise 3, turning each subordinate clause into another type of free modifier.

Example

Subordinate Clause: Because television is no longer slavishly watched, the network executives are becoming worried.

Verb Cluster: Noticing that television is no longer slavishly watched, the network executives are becoming worried.

7. Write as long a sentence as you can by adding all types of free modifiers to the base clause. Remember to keep the free modifiers in parallel form. Structure the sentence so that it does not sound strung together. As an example, examine the sentences in the paragraph that follows, some of which continue for five or six lines, but none of which sounds tedious or run-on:

> About ten years ago a well-known literary critic and essayist, a good friend of long standing, told me that a wealthy widely-circulated weekly pictorial magazine had offered him a good price to write a piece about me—not about my work or works, but about me as a private citizen, an individual. I said No, and explained why: my belief that only a writer's works were in the public domain, to be discussed and investigated and written about, the writer himself having put them there by submitting them for publication and accepting money for them; and therefore he not only would but must accept whatever the public wished to say or do about them from praise to burning. But that, until the writer committed a crime or ran for public office, his private life was his own; and not only had he the right to defend his privacy, but the public had the duty to do so since one man's liberty must stop at exactly the point where the next one's begins; and that I believed that anyone of taste and responsibility would agree with me.
>
> —**William Faulkner**, "On Privacy," *Harper's Magazine*, July 1955

Varying Sentence Length and Rhythm

Base or simple sentences need not always be combined; they remain useful to the mature writer, usually to introduce a new topic or to emphasize a point or to make a dramatic statement. Examine the use of varying sentence structures in the following paragraphs, paying attention to the rationale with which the writers used simple sentences as well as combined sentences. How are both sense and rhythm affected in each case?

> It is the traffic that makes it all unique. A traffic in trams grinding round corners, a traffic in approximately London buses whose radiators seem ready to burst, in gypsy-green lorries with "Ta-ta and By-by" and other slogans painted on the back, in taxis swerving all over the road with much blowing of horns, in rickshaws springing unexpectedly out of sidestreets, in bullock carts swaying ponderously along to the impediment of everyone, in sacred Brahmani cows and bulls nonchalantly strolling down the middle of the tram-tracks munching breakfast as they go. A traffic, too, in people who are hanging on to all forms

of public transport, who are squatting cross-legged upon the counters of their shops, who are darting in and out of the roadways between the vehicles, who are staggering under enormous loads, who are walking briskly with briefcases, who are lying like dead things on the pavements, who are drenching themselves with muddy water in the gutters, who are arguing, laughing, gesticulating, defecating, and who are sometimes just standing still as though wondering what to do. There never were so many people in a city at seven o'clock in the morning. Patiently the driver of the limousine steers his passage between and around them, while they pause in mid-stride to let him through, or leap to get out of his way, or stare at him blankly, or curse him roundly, or occasionally spit in the path of his highly polished Cadillac. Presently, and quite remarkably, he comes to the end of the journey without collision and deposits the traveler and his luggage upon the pavement in front of an hotel. And here the traveler has his first encounter with a beggar. He had better make the best of it, for beggary is to be with him until the end of his days in Calcutta.

—**Geoffrey Moorhouse**, *Calcutta*

Now when I had mastered the language of this water and had come to know every trifling feature that bordered the great river as familiarly as I knew the letters of the alphabet, I had made a valuable acquisition. But I had lost something, too. I had lost something which could never be restored to me while I lived. All the grace, the beauty, the poetry, had gone out of the majestic river! I still kept in mind a certain wonderful sunset which I witnessed when steamboating was new to me. A broad expanse of the river was turned to blood; in the middle distance the red hue brightened into gold, through which a solitary log came floating, black and conspicuous; in one place a long, slanting mark lay sparkling upon the water; in another the surface was broken by boiling, tumbling rings that were as many-tinted as an opal; where the ruddy flush was faintest was a smooth spot that was covered with graceful circles and radiating lines, ever so delicately traced; the shore on our left was densely wooded, and the somber shadow that fell from this forest was broken in one place by a long, ruffled trail that shone like silver; and high above the forest wall a clean-stemmed dead tree waved a single leafy bough that glowed like a flame in the unobstructed splendor that was flowing from the sun. There were graceful curves, reflected images, woody heights, soft distances, and over the whole scene, far and near, the dissolving lights drifted steadily, enriching it every passing moment with new marvels of coloring.

—**Mark Twain**, *Life on the Mississippi*

SOME PRACTICE WITH SENTENCE LENGTH AND RHYTHM

8. Now write a paragraph, again on a subject of your own choosing, in which you use a variety of sentence structures: simple sentences, sentences with a variety of free modifiers, including subordinate clauses, and base sentences joined with coordinating conjunctions. What function does each type of sentence play in conveying the meaning of the paragraph?

Punctuation

Once you understand the concept of base clauses, subordinate clauses, and verb, noun, adverb, and adjective clusters, the punctuation of sentences becomes much clearer. Below are four rules for sentence punctuation.

1. A comma either separates elements in a series or sets off a base clause from a free modifier. With a conjunction, it can separate two base clauses.

   Examples
   The rain, fog, and humidity did not deter them from making the trip.
   Quietly and furtively, he approached the abandoned car.
   Children are growing up very fast, and their parents must be partly responsible.
   Because children are growing up very fast, their parents must be partly responsible.

2. A semicolon can separate two base clauses.

   Example
   Children are growing up very fast; their parents must be responsible.

3. A colon can appear only at the tail end of a base clause; it introduces either a list or a restatement of the base clause.

   Examples
   The economy has been sluggish in many ways: employment, construction, and trade.
   I would like to invite you to dinner: I would like to see you very much.

4. A dash acts as a strong comma, setting off middle- and final-position free modifiers from a base clause.

   Examples
   The man left the office—at once.
   The man—who could scarcely wait to don his coat—left the office.

Transitions

Free modifiers are also useful as transitions between thoughts, whether these thoughts occur in sentences or in paragraphs. When placed at the beginning of a sentence, the free modifier connects the sentence to the preceding one.

Example
Farm prices are down from what they were five years ago. As a result, farmers are angry.

Notice in the following paragraphs the use of free modifiers to connect thoughts between parts of sentences, between sentences themselves, and between paragraphs.

Why is that woman laughing so early in the morning? I keep trying to put myself in her place, but she always surprises me. From somewhere else in the building, sound waves echoing around the courtyard to disguise their origin, comes a brutal argument. So I must wonder what makes that couple fight so furiously and, even more, what makes them continue living together despite their rage.

I live in an apartment, but not totally apart. I can tell a body not to enter my space, but I cannot command the sound waves. They enter as they will. And not only that, but they force their way into my head and, with no regard for my own volition, tie me into the lives of my neighbors.

Accosted also by sounds from the street, I am pulled into the activity there. A youngster tries to call his friend down from a high floor, and calls and calls his name, unaffected by lack of response. Soon I yearn for Henry to come down as much as the caller does. A transistor blares with a volume that bothers my ears. Drawn to the window, I marvel that the teenage boy, dancing alone on a stoop, can stand it right beside him. The sound must anesthetize like a drug. Now someone double parked is blocking a man who wants his car out. He honks, and makes me turn from whatever I'm thinking about to share his frustration, which is intense.

Back inside, I hear a young woman in an apartment next to mine practicing her clarinet. She is pretty good, beginning a professional career, I've learned, getting jobs with an orchestra here and there. Her practice hours give the building a cool, classical sound. I'm also brought into the anxieties of her young career. I hear the answering machine she has installed, asking whoever it is please to leave a message. Maybe it will mean another break for her.

—**Tracey Early,** "Sounds That Bring Us Closer Together,"
Christian Science Monitor, Jan. 1980

SOME PRACTICE WITH SENTENCE COMBINING

9. Write two paragraphs in which you use free modifiers to connect the thoughts within sentences, between sentences, and between paragraphs. Use the appropriate punctuation.

10. Combine the following sentences into an effectively written essay. The breaks between sentence groups represent paragraphs in the student's original essay,

but ignore them if you think it advisable. Add words when necessary to combine the sentences but do not change the meaning:

Imaginary Jane

1. I moved into the house I am living in now.
2. I was only three years old.
3. We bought the house from my grandfather.
4. We have been living there for about fifteen years now.
5. There were no other children on my block.
6. There were no children to play with.
7. The other families were mostly old people.
8. The other families lived on my block.
9. Their children were already grown up.
10. This left me with no choice.
11. I had to play by myself.

12. I found many things to do on my own.
13. I would play house alone and dolls alone also.
14. I played with my parents.
15. My parents were often too busy.
16. The day was really long and boring.
17. This went on for a couple of years.
18. Then kindergarten started.

19. School was a relief.
20. I made new friends.
21. I had a lot of classmates.
22. This did not, of course, help me with my problem of staying alone.
23. I continued to stay by myself at home.

24. I became six years old.
25. A little girl named Diane moved next door.
26. I did not like to play with her.
27. I was so used to staying alone.
28. I did not want her to touch any of my things.
29. I was afraid.
30. She was going to take my toys away from me.

31. Staying alone was not such a good idea.
32. I started to make things up.
33. I started to pretend.
34. I had an imaginary friend.
35. My friend's name was Jane.
36. I have no idea where the name came from.
37. I do not know anyone with that name.

38. Jane lived in the bathroom and in many of the closets around the house.
39. I used to talk to her.
40. I pretended that she answered me.

41. We would play house together.
42. My mother used to give me cookies and milk.
43. I, of course, ate my cookies.
44. So did Jane.
45. I ate her cookies.
46. I pretended she ate her cookies.
47. This went on for about a whole year.
48. I would play with Jane.
49. I went to bed in the evening.

50. My parents began to get worried.
51. They asked my doctor about Jane.
52. They asked my doctor about this imaginary friend.
53. The doctor said it was normal.
54. A lonely child creates an imaginary friend.
55. He made a recommendation.
56. I should play with a real friend.
57. I should play with Diane.

58. My mother would make me play with Diane.
59. I would call for Diane.
60. Diane and I would play togehter.
61. We would play for a little while.
62. I forgot about Jane little by little.
63. I played with Diane all the time.

64. This was not an unusual phase to go through.
65. This went on for a whole year.
66. I rarely thought about Jane again.
67. That is, until now, for this essay.

REWRITING

Obtaining Feedback on Your Rough Draft

In order to give you the proper response to your rough draft, your evaluators will want to role-play the reader to whom your essay is directed. Your "Audience Analysis Guide" should give them sufficient information about your audience to successfully look at your essay from its point of view. If you yourself are evaluating your rough draft, then you too will want to role-play your audience as you do so.

The "Audience Response Guide" can then be filled in.

———— AUDIENCE RESPONSE GUIDE ————

1. What do you think the writer wanted to say in this paper? What is his or her purpose in writing? What does he or she want the paper to mean?

2. How does the paper affect the audience for which it was intended?

3. How effective has the writer been in conveying his or her purpose and meaning? What are the strengths of the paper? What are the weaknesses?

4. How should the paper be revised to better fulfill its purpose and meaning?

Below are two peer responses to the rough draft of "A Bothersome Convenience" (pp. 195–197). Each evaluator responded to the four questions of the "Audience Response Guide."

Question 1

Evaluator A: The writer wishes to convey how her worst suspicions about the dishwasher's relative uselessness have been confirmed.

Evaluator B: The writer now believes that for her a dishwasher is ineffective and an absolute waste of time.

Question 2

Evaluator A: It had humor in it that almost all women can relate to, and I got an insight into the writer's family structure and life.

Evaluator B: Many housewives will agree about the problems the writer encountered.

Question 3

Evaluator A: The writer's use of underplayed sarcasm complements the comfortable homelike atmosphere created in the essay.

Evaluator B: The humor puts the topic into clear perspective. The writer makes her subject seem worthwhile and important.

Question 4
Evaluator A: Some sentence revision would improve the clarity and effectiveness of paragraphs. The shaping idea could be more
concise and evident.
Evaluator B: The concluding paragraphs seem unnecessary and unconvincing. Some details are extraneous.

Here is a revised version of the student's essay. How has the writer responded to the suggestions of the two evaluations?

A BOTHERSOME CONVENIENCE

Somewhere in the back of my mind lurked the sneaky suspicion that
the new contraption in my kitchen was more bother than it was
worth. The dishwasher was a gift from my in-laws for my newly remodeled kitchen. Though I never yearned for one, I relented after my
persistent, dishwasher-owner friends insisted that it would be senseless not to have it in a new kitchen. After three years, this lovely,
color-coordinated appliance with its push-button everything and a
cycle for every imaginable dish from pots to crystal is still shiny
and new.

My friends' reasons for owning this modern convenience were
many: It would be easier to sell the house, I could be doing other
things instead of slaving over the sink, the dishes would be so clean
they would be sterilized. Somehow these reasons do not justify for me
ownership of a dishwasher. After all, I have no intention of selling the
house anytime in the near future. Too, my husband is a great dishwasher, and the children are improving every day. As for how clean
the dishes were, I never checked that closely, but the family is still
quite healthy, so they must have been clean enough. After experimenting with two weeks of constant use, I have found my suspicion confirmed; that contraption is much more bother than I or my family
wish to endure. Since I instituted its regular use, the problems I encountered were even worse that I had anticipated.

The shortage of everyday dishes was a big problem. There were
times when we had to resort to using good china to eat pizza from.
With the old-fashioned method dishes were washed, dried, and put

away (or at least on the drainboard), so there was always a clean, ready supply. That way my service for twelve for my family of six was quite sufficient. Not so with this new gadget, which seems to hold twenty-four of everything, which I do not own. Then too, each child has a favorite cup or mug that at mealtime was usually in the half-full dishwasher. He or she would stare hatefully at the machine and whine, "Where's my Bear mug?" I could, of course, buy extra dishes, install extra cabinets to hold them, and insist the children cultivate a love of more than one mug, but first I'll have to win the lottery.

Another annoyance is the propensity of this gadget to use only hot water and instantly cut off the supply to the rest of the household. Nearly everyone in the house has had a cold-water shock in the shower. Without thinking I would start to run it and, almost immediately, hear the scream of, "Ma, there's no hot water in here." Also, if I do laundry while it is operating, I get murky-looking clothes and, heaven forbid, spotted glasses because the water is not hot enough. Not only this, but tepid water causes the dishwasher detergent to become an icky blob, which has to be scraped out of the dispenser.

This machine is aptly named dishwasher. Dishes are the only things it washes well. Pots, pans, and casserole dishes have to be washed again by hand when they come out of it. Since these are the items that I dislike washing anyway, I had hoped that it would prove itself worthy of continued use by doing a respectable job on them. Well, it did not. If I have to rewash them, then I may as well do everything by hand and save myself the bother.

The worst problem of all is that the dishwasher has made me into a bit of a liar. For years, I never admitted to anyone, especially my in-laws, that I did not use it. I had to go to great lengths to keep my secret. When the family dined with us, I would pile the dishes on the counter and say, "Oh, don't worry. I'll just stick them in the dishwasher later." Then when they left, I really did have to slave over the sink all by my lonesome self. Gone was the comradery of sharing the family ritual of dishwashing while catching up on the latest gossip. Further, since I originated the use of this gadget, it seems that all dishes in the house, clean and dirty, have become my sole domain. Con-

veniently or purposely, the family has failed to master the art of loading, running, and unloading it. I hope they relearn their old habits
soon, as we are headed back to the old method.

The family is anxious to return to the old-fashioned way. No longer
will they be deprived of favorite mugs, or have to endure shocking,
cold-water showers. Again I will be able to do the laundry at my whim
and know it will be sparkling clean. I am very confident that we can
all survive less-than-sterilized dishes, as mankind has done through
the ages. Already I can visualize my mother-in-law and me at the sink
catching up on the latest family gossip. I can't wait!

Maybe someday I will find a place for a dishwasher in my life. For
now at least, I am returning it to its previous function as a catchall for
all the seldom-used things like the ice bucket, the mixer and all gad-
gets for which I need a hiding place.

Distributing

Distribution is a form of addition in which material on one aspect of your
subject is added to more than one segment of the original draft, usually as a
means of achieving unity. A key word may bear repeating (see Chap. 2 on
Transitions, p. 76–81). By distributing words like gadget, family, and contraption throughout her essay, the writer of "A Bothersome Convenience" provided bridges between thoughts that unified the essay.

By examining the early paragraphs of a piece that you are writing, you may
discover structures that should be distributed throughout; for example, a metaphor worked out early in the essay might well be extended throughout in
order to create a coherent and unified pattern. If at one point in your essay,
you compare your car to an old friend because it is so reliable, you might
consider extending the comparison to your entire description of your car.

In general, do not start an approach to your subject and then drop it. Rather,
distribute that approach throughout your work. If the smell of a place over-
whelms you, then that odor should permeate your entire essay. If your tone of
voice is playful in your introduction, then the words and details that support
that tone should be distributed from beginning to end, unless, of course, you
have a reason for changing your attitude and indicate that reason to the reader.

Editing

Once you have gone through the steps of revising your essay—cutting (Chap.
1); adding (Chap. 2); rearranging (Chap. 3); substituting (Chap. 4); or distributing (above)—you should turn to editing to determine correct word choice
and grammatical precision.

Distributing.   Distributing can be an editing exercise also. For example, if you decide to alter your word choice, you may decide to distribute that alteration throughout the essay wherever you have used that word. Or you may need to distribute a change in verb tense or pronoun reference. Distribution, whether in revising or in editing, asks that you look at the larger picture, at the total essay, rather than tinkering with isolated parts only.

Sentence Combining and Transitions.   A very important part of editing, as we have stressed in each chapter so far, is the use of transitions. To combine sentences is another way to establish connections between thoughts. Sentence combining also keeps your essay from having the "choppy" rhythm of strung-together simple sentences and achieves instead the flowing rhythm of the mature combined sentence. Reviewing your writing from the point of view of sentence combining is one of the most important of the editing techniques.

Paragraphs.   Continue to regard your paragraphs closely. Are they structured tightly around some clearly defined unit of thought? Have you developed them with sufficient coordinate accumulation of detail or subordinate provision of example and explanation? Review as often as you need to the paragraph sections in Chapters 3 and 4.

Mechanics.   What mechanical errors of grammar or spelling have persisted in your writing? Perhaps it is time now to make a list of those errors that have constantly defied your attempts to correct them. Now turn this list into a chart by indicating next to each error a definition of the problem and then a method of solution. Finally, in a fourth column, analyze why the method of solution has escaped you. As you go about editing the rough draft for this task, develop this analysis further in the hope of finding a way of implementing the solution.
Now, revise and edit your rough draft.

BECOMING AWARE OF YOURSELF AS A WRITER

You might want to make use of your journal to record your thoughts and feelings about the tasks for this chapter. As you write in your journal, consider the following questions.

1. In what future situations can you foresee writing cases? What appear to be the important features of case writing?

2. Do you feel satisfied that you know how to analyze the frame of reference and the point of view of the readers common to a particular publication? When in the future can you imagine yourself writing to the reader of another publication? How did you analyze your reader's frame of reference when you wrote the essay for this chapter?

3. How useful is the sentence-combining approach to your own writing? Are your ideas combined already, or do you feel that you need to pay attention to this aspect of your writing?

4. Did you "enjoy" learning about your subject as you tested a prejudice while writing? How important do you think writing is or should be as a way of learning, as well as of expressing what you already know?

5. How often in the past have you used the classical questions without being aware of having used them? Have you observed others using them? The explorer's questions have been devised in this century out of a need to supplement the classical ones. What roles can you foresee both sets of questions playing in your thinking and writing?

PART III

Explanation

INTRODUCTION

Writing as an interested observer, you invited your readers to explore a subject along with you, to experience your own curiosity and the broader perspective that it led to. Now we are going to ask you to write instead in order to explain a subject to your readers that you have already explored yourself.

The difference between exploration and explanation is subtle. It is a difference, in part, of tone and emphasis. In the former case, you are likely to adopt the attitude of a peer as you share your discoveries with your audience. In the latter case, you may take on a more knowledgeable, authoritative tone, drawing conclusions based on your broadened perspective and offering information that has a general application and validity.

One subject that we all have explored sufficiently enough to render us experts is the media. Whether we speak of television, radio, film, newspapers, magazines, or popular books, the chances are very good that we are familiar with some aspect of one or all of these visual or print influences on our lives. Whereas the explorer examines a new subject or a subject from a new perspective, the writer who would explain some aspect of the media has only to form a generalization: through years of exposure, the research has already been done. The task for Chapter 6 will be to gather your media experiences and explain their significance to your readers.

Your own ideas about a subject may gain more validity the more you take into account the ideas of others who are knowledgeable about the subject. To explain a subject well, it is often helpful to inform your audience not only of your own explorations but of the explorations and discoveries, the observations and conclusions of others. As the explorer of a place, you may have interviewed people whom you met there in order to evaluate and understand the place better. But to see the place from the broadest possible perspective, and to explain its significance as fairly and fully as you can, you also want to take into consideration the views of others who have made similar explorations.

The most obvious way to gather a wide range of such information is to read what has been written by others about your subject. The more you learn of what others have said about a subject, the more informed you make yourself, and hence the more informative your explanations become.

In Chapter 7, we will ask you to include library research in explaining your subject. In the next two chapters, we will ask you to write in as informative a manner as you can.

6

Writing About the Media

PURPOSE

To the extent that your discoveries as an explorer of the world beyond yourself broaden your perspective on that world, you may gain a greater capacity to understand and appreciate widely different patterns of behavior and thought. In a sense, you learn to look with new eyes, to comprehend what once might have puzzled you, and to see the value in what you once might have thought valueless. It is a natural impulse to seek to tell others what you have learned in this fashion. In this chapter and the next, we would like you to act on such an impulse, and inform your readers, broadening their knowledge by explaining a subject to them so that they understand and appreciate it more fully than they otherwise might.

A common way of understanding ourselves is to assume a separation between our private and our public lives. We say we live one life at school, work, or wherever we act in a formal or official capacity, and another life with our family, friends, or ourselves. But in a real sense it is no longer possible to make a clear distinction between our private and public lives, for as soon as we enter our homes we are met with all the signs of our involvement with the public world—more specifically, the world of the media. Newspapers, magazines, books, television, film, videos, tapes—how could we possibly turn off their influence on us even if we wanted to?

Few consumers of these media remain neutral about the nature and quality

215

of the products that result. Whether we love them or loathe them, we are fascinated by their hold on us and by the ways they provoke us to respond. We often move quickly from an attraction to the "what" of the media, that is, our observations and experiences with them, to an interest in the "how," the methods and ideas that comprise them. Thus we try to arrive at an understanding of the media for ourselves and others. In this chapter, we shall direct your attention to the media and how your already impressive knowledge of the subject can be focused toward writing an essay that interprets and explains your encounters with the media for a broad audience that shares a similar experience but has not analyzed it.

In writing this essay, you can continue to rely on your personal experiences and observations in order to gather information. You will want to generalize, to point out the broader, more universal interest inherent in your specific observations and knowledge of the media. We will suggest in this chapter that you attempt to answer the classical questions "What have I seen or heard that can offer support as examples?" and "How can I generalize about what has been said?" (See Chap. 5, pp. 173–176.)

Because the audience for the media is so broad, encompassing your school, community, and culture, we shall ask you to write for one particular group of this large media-consuming public. In contrast to the personal, private voice you used earlier in your journal and in writing essays about your own experiences, you will be asked here to develop a more formal, more public voice with which to express your generalizations and narrative examples on the media to the segment of the public you have selected to be your readers.

GENERATING IDEAS THROUGH GENERALIZATION

In thinking about our experiences and observations, we generalize about them; that is, we attempt to see a linked significance to them, a meaning. When something happens to us or we observe an event, we attempt to relate the experience or observation to others that we have had or seen and to see a pattern. Without the ability to generalize our lives would appear to be a series of random events, with no significant connections. We would not be able to learn anything about ourselves or about the world; in fact, the ability to form generalizations is crucial to our survival and growth. A child who cannot learn after touching a hot stove three times that hot stoves should not be touched is doomed to a life of suffering, just as is the unemployed mill worker who observes that mills are closing down but does not conclude that there will be no job for him or her.

On the other hand, we often make generalizations that we cannot find adequate experience or observation to justify. Of what real use is it to make an assertion when it cannot be supported? We have either lost our argument or at the very least bored our audience. Who, for example, is impressed with the generalization that someone is a good cook when the speaker cannot cite one good dish that that person has produced? And who wants to know that a book or film is a good one if the speaker cannot support this claim with examples?

Generalizations and their supporting examples must be part of the same process. A writer who wishes to write an essay on how black children are represented on TV sitcoms must both point to specific incidents on these programs and then attempt to generalize about the meaning and significance of these incidents. A writer may begin by asking questions such as "What happens?" and "How does it turn out?" but he or she will then try to answer questions that impose a pattern of coherence on the narrative, questions like "What do these incidents mean? What do they have in common? What are they all about?"

In a sense it is our attraction to narrative examples or stories that gets us started in the process of explaining ourselves to others in the first place. Television news anchor persons refer to their news items as "stories," that is, events that contain strong narrative interest and have clearly distinguishable beginnings, middles, and endings. Listen to a friend tell a personal story or relate a joke, and you will recognize something of the same narrative strategy. The teller selects to relate only the essential plot elements of the story; characterization is given only if it is directly connected to the outcome of the story. Television commercials are also examples of economical story telling that selects those incidents and images that produce the anticipated ending.

In response to the classical question "What have I seen or heard that can offer support as examples?" your experiences and observations in life have provided you with a large repository of stories. If writing about the media, for example, your knowledge of the popular media would provide you with a large selection of images, stories, references to contemporary fashions, ideas, persuasive methods, and language. You might determine from your viewing of television soap operas that women are portrayed in stereotype—they are either wonderfully warm and good or hopelessly cold and evil. You will surely want to relate some examples to your readers who, although they may not have seen these incidents, will be informed by your brief narratives.

But you will probably also want to tell your readers what you think this all adds up to. Why are women represented in this way? What caused it? How does this compare to your real-life experience? How do these characters compare to women characters in other media? By answering these questions, you will also be responding to the classical question "How can I generalize about what has been said?" An ability to explain the general significance of information is important to writers who would inform their audience. For one thing, it is often intelligent generalization that gives relevance and significance to the specific details that you have just related. Without a generalization that is adequate, reasonable, and convincing, you are left with a headless body of prose, an essay without coherence or purpose.

Suppose you wrote an essay about the persuasive, manipulative techniques of TV commercials and print advertising. In this paper, you gave examples of different products, showing how each makes its appeal to the apparently unknowing viewer. But suppose also that you failed to tell your readers what this all adds up to? Is it bad to advertise this way? What does it suggest about the psychology of viewers or readers? What does it reveal about American consumers? In other words, what do your examples tell us about such advertising? We already know it is manipulative; what we want to know is the general significance of the information you have given us. Here are some questions to keep in mind when creating a generalization:

1. Does the generalization seem too broad (or narrow) for the examples given?
2. Are there sufficient examples to support this generalization?
3. Does the generalization follow logically from your examples?
4. Does the generalization create a pattern of coherence for the supporting examples?

SOME PRACTICE WITH GENERALIZATION AS A WAY OF GENERATING IDEAS

1. For a week, keep a record in your journal of your reading, viewing, and listening experiences with the popular media. What experiences particularly impressed you, either positively or negatively? Why?

2. Read every article on the front page of your daily newspaper; then write a paragraph about one general condition of contemporary life that the information you have read illustrates. In what way might information from other sources change the generalization that you have made?

3. Take a survey of the reading habits of your friends, family, and classmates. Inquire as to the kinds of material they read regularly, the articles and books they find most appealing and/or informative, and the criticism they have of those they find less worthwhile. How typical do you think their responses are? Did any of their responses surprise you? Why? How do their preferences compare to yours?

4. Joan Didion generalized about John Wayne that he symbolized "the inarticulate longings of a nation wondering at just what pass the trail had been lost." What specific things do you know about Wayne that might support this generalization? What general ideas and values does Wayne symbolize in your eyes?

5. Ben Franklin, writing in his *Autobiography* about his difficulty in correcting his moral faults, compared himself to a man who goes to a blacksmith to buy an ax. The man, Franklin wrote,

> desired to have the whole of its surface as bright as the edge; the smith consented to grind it bright for him if he would turn the wheel. He turned while the smith pressed the broad face of the ax hard and heavily on the stone, which made the turning of it very fatiguing. The man came every now and then from the wheel to see how the work went on; and at length would take his ax as it was, without further grinding. "No," says the smith, "turn on, turn on; we shall have it bright by and by; as yet 'tis only speckled." "Yes," says the man, *"but I think I like a speckled ax best."*

What generalizations about human nature might you draw from Franklin's tale of the man and his ax? How might you incorporate the general ideas represented by the tale into a paper of your own?

ADDRESSING YOUR AUDIENCE: ADOPTING A PUBLIC VOICE

For a writer who intends to explain a subject for a large, general audience, there is an important point to consider, "What voice will I adopt in presenting my ideas to my readers?" Writing in your journal encouraged you to practice developing an expressive personal voice. Writing about personal experiences, observations, and attitudes made more demands on your personal voice as you moved outward to an audience that most likely shared your experiences and outlook. Your readers required you to think more deeply about what ideas to express and how they could be arranged more effectively. In short, you became more aware of what we might call the conventions of public discourse—what is expected of a writer who purports to reason and explain to a large audience.

In deciding how to address such a readership, you might think first of yourself as a writer reaching out to communicate with an ever-increasing audience—from your school to your community to the larger general culture of readers and viewers. These readers will have little direct personal knowledge of you or your experiences; they will be able to judge the worth of your thought and expression only by the power of your "argument"—a word used here to refer to the coherent pattern of generalization and narrative incident explained in the "Generating Ideas" section. Acquiring this "public voice" does not mean your voice will lack personal feeling or opinion, but it suggests that the writer must demonstrate to readers that his or her point of view is valid and convincing because of the way it is presented, not merely because the writer is sincere and well intentioned.

A public voice is not a substitute for a private voice; it is really different in degree rather than in kind. All the qualities that you associate with good personal writing—authenticity, truthfulness to your experiences, self-revelation, and understanding—hold true for writing directed to a broader public purpose. It is mainly a matter of emphasis: A public voice generally leads the audience to observations and reasoned conclusions that have relevance to broader, more socially significant questions and concerns than your own limited personal experiences and opinions. For example, note the subtle difference in voice between Anne Morrow Lindbergh's account of her busy life in her journal and in her essay "Channelled Whelk."

Why can I not write as much as (my husband), when he is holding down a war job as well? It is four children and a household to run, I explain. But I have people to help. Yes, and they fight. I sometimes feel it would be better to do it all oneself. (I shall have to no doubt before long.)

—*War Within and Without: Diaries and Letters 1939–1944*

With a new awareness, both painful and humorous, I begin to understand why the saints were rarely married women. I am convinced it has nothing inherently to do, as I once supposed, with chastity or children. It has to do primarily with distractions. The bearing, rearing, feeding and educating of children; the running of a house with its thousand details; human relationships with their myriad pulls—woman's normal occupations in general run counter to creative life, or contemplative life, or saintly life. The problem is not merely one of *Woman and Career, Woman and the Home, Woman and Independence*. It is more basically: how to remain whole in the midst of the distractions of life; how to remain balanced, no matter what centrifugal forces tend to pull one off center; how to remain strong, no matter what shocks come in at the periphery and tend to crack the hub of the wheel.

—*Gift from the Sea*

Note the complaining, self-pitying tone in her journal, as compared with the more objective, even humorous, tone of the passage from her essay. In the journal, furthermore, she refers only to her own life, while in the essay she considers the lives of all women. Finally, in the journal she does not document as thoroughly as she does in the essay the duties and "distractions" that a working woman has.

Another characteristic of an effective "public voice" is one we might call appropriateness, that is, an attitude or tone that is appropriate for the subject being explained. Anne Morrow Lindbergh's tone in her essay is serious because her subject is serious. The writers of the professional essays in this chapter realize that on a scale of relative importance the advertising for an antacid and the contents of drugstore novels are not matters of grave national security.

Their language often takes on an ironic, slightly comic tone of voice that intends to entertain as much as inform the reader:

Where they [Alka-Seltzer commercials] once leaned toward the ridiculous, they now seem headed for the sublime.

In stark contrast, the virtuous virginals generally feature saccharine-sweet, submissive heroines, chaste unto their inevitable marriages when, in a euphemism for sexual intercourse, the heroes transport them "up to the stars."

Of course, this tone of voice is also due in part to the publications these essays originally appeared in and to the audience that might read them. As a writer addressing an audience that might include school, community, and culture, you too realize that you might need to consider how and for whom this public voice is created. Here is an example of a public voice writing on TV for a large, educated audience. How effectively does the writer present his views? What characteristics of a public voice does the writer exemplify?

What Effect Is TV Having on the Evolution of English?
Edwin Newman

Tomorrow evening at 9 on Channel 13, "The Story of English" will begin; the nine-part series, with Robert MacNeil as host, traces the history of the language from its beginnings to the present day. To one who has made a career in broadcast news, and a companion career in seeking to preserve the language in a reasonable state of health, it is encouraging that such a series should find its way onto television. It might also be taken as encouraging that the programs reflect the view that worry about the decline of English is unwarranted and misplaced. English, so Mr. MacNeil has concluded after three years of work on the series, is a mighty river that grows ever wider and richer.

If this is so, then television, which is so vastly influential, must itself contribute to the growing width and richness. Unfortunately, there's a good deal of evidence that points in the opposite direction. Television provides much that is informative and entertaining, and occasionally something that is splendid and notable. It does not, however, do much for the language.

Consider the "chat show." The name—chat is easy, informal, familiar—could not be more accurate. I know from my own experience that once you find yourself on camera, with a beaming host and an expectant studio audience, the pressure to tell an anecdote becomes almost irresistible. The exposition of ideas is frowned on. There isn't time. Besides, the audience isn't interested in talking heads.

Consider, then, "talking heads." You might think that what mattered was how well a head talked, whether it did any productive thinking before it talked. Yet, the very term is pejorative, dismissive.

That leads to something else television dislikes—"dead air," meaning the absence of talk and chat. There is a connection between thought and useful speech, between thought and interesting language. A period of silence would permit that, for both broadcaster and audience. Television has made periods of silence unacceptable. In the early days of radio, the World Series would be broadcast by one man. A second might be called in briefly. Now, on television, where far less description and explanation ought to be necessary, the job is done by four or five or half a dozen. The drone is incessant.

The fear that television would homogenize American speech has not been borne out. Anyone who travels around the United States knows that regional accents and expressions are as strong as ever. Television does, however, spread fashionable words and phrases across the country and make them tiresome. And not only across this country. Go to England and you will hear someone described as for real, an expert talking about a dynamic-type environment, and someone else referring to a pre-planned effort by a person who had everything going for him.

An opposition politician will tell a government minister to get his act together, and the minister will warn against a quick fix even though there are Brownie points to be had for giving it his best shot within a given time frame, because that is how he wants to play it. All of this is far too easy. Catch phrases are used as a labor-saving device: Nobody need be explicit.

Some critics make weightier charges against television. One is that staring at the screen has replaced conversation, and that it has replaced storytelling by parents, with predictable consequences for the language. There is something in this. Children are led to speak as characters in animated cartoons do, a horrifying thought. Nor is that all. On local news programs, "happy talk" passes for wit. In sitcoms, wit is represented by a gag line followed by a burst from a laugh track. On cops-and-gangsters programs, a battle of wits is a car chase. Soap-opera characters, explaining their problems speak a popularized version of psychiatric jargon, another blight on the language. And commercials, by making exaggerated claims, devalue the language, as do the claims that networks and stations put forward in promoting their programs.

Come now to the mistakes advertisers make deliberately, so as to seem friendly and not "elitist." Here is a rent-a-car commercial: "Even us bigshots like Budget's low prices." Indeed us do. Here is quarterback Dan Marino of the Miami Dolphins in a glove commercial: "How can I pass, laying on my back?" Chevrolet had former Chicago Bears linebacker Dick Butkus opening a commercial with "Me and my buddies. . . ." Apparently, "my buddies and I" would depress sales. Jordache—this list of advertisers could go on for pages—had a young woman saying that she hated her mother. Why? "She's so much prettier than me." Burger King uses "Ain't nothing like the real thing" and "Don't it feel good?" though it also put on this:

"Who has the best darn burger in the whole wide world?"

"Burger King and I."

Evidently, correct English can be used without causing immediate bankruptcy.

Not all the mistakes on television are deliberate. "That should expire the clock," a football broadcaster may say. And another: "It's a race between he and Michael Downes." One may spot the ball "laying on somebody's head," another may venture the opinion that "next time he won't get so hard of a rush," and still another suggest that "it looks like he might could have had it." When members of the British royal family turned up at Wimbledon, they became "the sinecure of all eyes."

It isn't only the mistakes. There is also the level of English used. In a remarkable demonstration of devotion to duty, I once listened to John Madden for not quite the entire second half of an N.F.L. game. He repeatedly misused like, as in "he gets like five or six snaps a week." He said "I tellya" 11 times, "see" or "you see" 13 times, and "y'know" 39 times. That sets a fairly deplorable example for those listening.

Newsmen and newswomen on television? CNN reported: "The President said the bombing would not deter he or the United States." It described a group of demonstrators as "not large but noisome." Noisome means foul-smelling. One of the mightier members of NBC's Washington bureau came up with a new word: perplexion. A CBS correspondent, speaking of President Reagan and Mikhail Gorbachev before Geneva, said, "Neither one have met each other." A station in St. Louis offered advice on what to do when "it's lightning out." The advice was: "Lie yourself as low as possible."

A trivial matter? Not really. The language of television news and public affairs is generally correct, but television is a teacher, whether it intends to be or not. So, when a mistake is made, it may appear to millions to have been ratified. It is quickly picked up and widely used.

Television affects language also by what it does not do. The programs rest heavily on teamwork; the best language—by which I do not mean English that is inflated, obscure, and intended to impress and intimidate—usually comes from a single mind. Moreover, language needs time and space to make its effect. Television does not often provide them. It also tends to exclude the odd, the out-of-the-ordinary.

Perhaps it is as well that television provides no home for old-fashioned political oratory (although it does for evangelists) and that it has shortened the political speech. Still, many politicians, and businessmen, receive training in being comfortable before the cameras and in achieving the best, i.e., most sincere effect. The result? Similarity bordering on uniformity in manner and in language. In addition, television is a thing of snippets and of images, often compelling. Hence, the rise of "media advisers" and political commercials, with an accompanying reduction in the use of the candidate's own words and an increased use of words supplied by others.

Is television, then, to be condemned? Of course not. There would in any case be no purpose in condemning it. Television is part of the march of technology that is transforming our lives, and it does offer a form of education for those who would not read or write on their own.

There are also welcome signs that, apart from "The Story of English," television is beginning to understand that mass illiteracy and semi-literacy place the nation in peril. But sporadic bouts of conscience are not enough. Broadcasters owe the language more.

—*The New York Times* (September 14, 1986, Sec. 2, pp. 27, 31)

SOME PRACTICE WITH A PUBLIC VOICE

1. Write a brief narrative of a personal experience or take one of your previous journal entries that narrate an experience. Rewrite the incident from an objective point of view, and write a generalization that explains the meaning of this experience. How does this rewritten account take on a different voice? What kinds of changes were necessary?

2. Take an op-ed article from *The New York Times* or another newspaper and explain to what extent the author has adopted an effective public voice. Is there evidence of both private and public voices in the essay? Is the voice appropriate for its subject and its intended audience? How would you evaluate its objectivity?

3. Examine the public voice in class of one of your teachers. What characteristics of this voice are determined by the requirements of the lecture or discussion format? To what extent does the subject of the class influence the kind of voice you observed? To what extent does a private voice also come through?

4. How would you describe the public voices of the prominent TV network news anchor reporters? What characteristics do they appear to have in common? How successfully do they convey their credibility and authoritativeness to their audience? What do they do to accomplish this?

TASK: WRITING ON THE MEDIA

Your task for this chapter is to write an essay on your experience of the popular media. You are asked to explore some aspect of TV, film, video, radio, books, newspapers, and magazines and explain your findings to your audience. You will gather observations you have made about this aspect of the media, make generalizations about these observations, and draw a conclusion for your reader.

The best way to begin this task might be to take a brief inventory of your own reading and viewing habits in order to determine where your areas of interest and knowledge lie. You know best what kinds of TV programs you respond to, the newspapers and magazines in your home, the films that have moved or entertained or dismayed you. Because of your extensive experience with these media, you already possess a large storehouse of images, scenes, characterizations, stories, points of view, and ideas drawn from a variety of sources. Your task as a writer is to create from these materials a coherent pattern of connection—a theme. A theme emerges from the writer's demonstration of some significant general observation or conclusion, for example, what is the difficult role of the game show host or how is the image of the working woman in fashion magazines changing? You will want to explain what your theme is, how it is present in the examples you have chosen to discuss, and its significance.

In writing this essay, you may find yourself seeking a balance between the broad generalization and the narrative incidents you offer as examples for your theme. A pattern of arrangement may emerge from this alternation of the general with the specific, or one or more of the classical patterns of arrangement may prove an effective way of developing your explanation (see Chapter 5, pp. 185–188).

In choosing how to address your audience, it may be helpful to consider how pervasive the media are in our lives. In a sense, you will be writing to everyone, for few in our society choose to ignore the power or interest of the media. We suggest that you try to imagine your audience as one group within your school, community, or larger culture. The subject you choose will to some extent be determined by the audience you have in mind, for example, the homemakers in your community who watch afternoon soap operas or sports fans in your school who are dissatisfied with local newspaper coverage of sports events. Your audience may or may not be familiar with the narrative incidents you use as examples. You will have to decide how much of your own media experiences you will need to relate in order to provide support for the generalizations you arrived at.

The two professional essays in the next section are intended to offer you examples of public voices writing on the media. Both essays are rich with narrative examples drawn from the authors' reading and viewing experiences. Both essays arrive at generalizations that give significance to these specific examples. As did the authors of these essays, you will try to provide answers to the classical questions "What have I seen or heard that can offer support as examples?" and "How can I generalize about what has been said?"

In the "Writing the Essay" and "Focus" sections of this chapter, we discuss how to create generalizations for your narrative examples, how best to arrange your pattern of generalization and examples, and what kind of stylistic concerns enter into your developing a public voice.

WRITING THE ESSAY

Generating Ideas for an Essay on the Media

Setting out to write on the media can confront you with a formidable task. There is so much material surrounding you that the first problem would seem to be how to limit yourself to a topic that you can manage in a short paper. You might think of yourself as a media researcher, who, although expert in some ways with the images and strategies of the media, is not yet experienced with the formal methods of research (see Chapter 7). But, as you did in earlier tasks, you recognize the importance of gathering information relevant to your purpose.

You might begin with your own reading and viewing practices. What kinds of TV programs interest you? What magazines or periodicals do you read regularly? What recent or past films have you seen or read about? Examine your journal for references to your attitudes toward the media or your likes or dislikes. If you work in a group, you and your group members might make lists of striking media images or present trends. You might list also the subject matter you associate most with a particular medium, for example, the TV miniseries on modern historical events, the business magazine's treatment of Japanese competition with American industry, or the sports magazine's attitude toward the commercialization of college football.

You might also want to find other publications on the media than those with which you are already familiar. One approach is to go to your college or public library to obtain articles on the media that appear in periodicals not specifically limited to the media, for example, magazines like *Harper's, The Atlantic Monthly, The New Republic,* and *The New Yorker.* Or you can refer to Chapter 7, page 271 for information on *The Readers' Guide to Periodical Literature,* a reference work that will direct you to many articles on a wide variety of topics from many different periodicals.

Primarily, though, you can write your paper from your own media experiences, using any additional materials as supplementary to your own examples. What is it you are looking for? Most likely, some recurring or prevalent theme. If you are discussing TV or film drama, what kinds of stories or characters have you observed? Because the media seem often to rely on narrative formulas or stereotypical characters, such as we find in crime shows and sitcoms, you might explain them or discuss their implications for the audience. If you are drawn to narrative situations and characters that go against type, you might ask yourself what developments in TV and film seem to be going in interesting or imaginative directions. Of course, you can also explain what you perceive as unfortunate and misguided developments as well.

You might find that you hold views on some media images or ideas that are different from other people's. Your paper could then be built around showing how you perceive your topic differently from the way it is usually perceived. Thurston and Doscher, for example, in their article on the ''bodice-busters,'' following, write that their analysis of historical romances arrives at a different conclusion from critics of these books. They find these erotic novels to be quite similar in attitude to many of the prominent feminist ideas argued in the 1970s. The authors' purpose is to get their readers to look at these books in a more receptive way and not to write them off as drivel or soft porn.

Another approach you might want to use is to trace the development of some media work that you are knowledgeable about. This approach is similar to the explorer's question "How has it changed?" which you might have used in an earlier task (see Chapter 4, pp. 134–137). For example, if you have watched a TV program since its inception, you might be able to explain how and why certain changes in format or character have been undertaken. Or perhaps you have followed a rock or jazz group's development in subject matter or approach through several record albums. Bernice Kanner, in her essay on Alka-Seltzer, following, shows how the advertising campaign for this product has mirrored the attitudes of decades from the 1930s to the present. This technique also answers the classical question "What are its causes?" making connections between the recent Alka-Seltzer ads showing business executives suffering from the stress of their aggressive pursuit of success.

Addressing Your Audience in a Public Voice

Writing on the media to an audience of your school, community, or culture suggests that you have thought about the level of interest and the degree of understanding of your readers. There are many specific audiences for the media, and the public voice you choose for one may be inappropriate or confusing for another. In writing on the recent appearances of a rock group for a college audience, for example, you can assume that your readers will grasp your comparisons to other musical styles or performing techniques. If, however, your purpose is to explain this music to a broader, less-informed audience in the general culture, your voice will adapt to this fact; you will make fewer assumptions about their knowledge, and by means of reasoned explanation and examples, you will attempt to direct them to a different attitude toward music they may find strange or distasteful.

Perhaps the most difficult decision to make with regard to addressing your audience is how much of your personal voice should be expressed here. In other words, just where is the boundary between a personal and a public voice? Of course, there can be no precise dividing line, but we can generally assume that in an essay like this your main objective is to explain some aspect of the media to your audience, perhaps to get them to see their own reading or viewing in a new, more satisfying or knowledgeable way. If you let your own strong feelings intrude too much, you direct your reader more to your emotions than to, say, what the recent books of how-to advice for career women suggest about their success in the male-dominated business world. A public voice usually means a moderate, objective, restrained approach to a subject; the writer possessing this voice shows a secure grasp of the topic, has generalized in a convincing way, and has provided sufficient specific examples as support for any generalizations. Expressions of irony, sarcasm, enthusiasm, disdain, even anger are not out of place, but they should be justified by the subject matter and supported by the examples you offer as evidence for these emotions. After all, everyone has strong opinions on the media; we certainly would not want it otherwise. Let your own understanding of your audience determine just how this public voice is to be adapted to the topic you choose.

Arranging Your Essay: The Shaping Idea, Generalization, and Narrative Incidents

As you begin to write, you may by now have a small collection of notes detailing the media experiences you wish to describe and the generalizations that follow from them. These generalizations in turn form parts of one larger general statement, some overall pattern of significance that you derive from your reading or viewing encounters with the media. This theme—your shaping idea—might run through a series of TV dramas or a group of articles on the technological future you found in popular science magazines. Whatever the source, your purpose is to show how these materials embody this theme and what generalizations you can draw from it.

Your shaping idea might be, for example, that hospital dramas all distort the real experience of being in a hospital but that *St. Elsewhere* shows a concern for realism that sets it apart from others you describe. Or you might find that a group of articles on the future of technology do not take into account any of the social or economic changes that could affect the future use of technology. Your shaping idea will control the form of your essay and provide a manageable pattern with which to contain other general statements you make about your subject.

Although we discuss the shaping idea first, you may not be certain what shaping idea will emerge from the generalizations and examples that you have put together until you actually begin writing. Often writers do not really know what they want to say until they begin to see a larger pattern form from the sequence of generalizations and examples that they set in motion. You might look over your observations and ideas for the dominant idea or ideas that were most important to you. After examining these for awhile, you will most likely see the direction in which you want to go.

As you write down the results of your media research, you are faced with some of the same questions facing any other researcher engaged in the writing process: "What comes first? How much space do I give to each example? What links should I create between one part and another? In what order should I place my examples?" The answers to such questions cannot be given as rules or formulas. They really follow directly from your own research materials, the generalizations, and narrative examples you wish to offer your audience. As possible models, you might examine the media essays that follow to see how the authors arranged their generalizations and narrative examples into a coherent pattern of meaning.

Supermarket Erotica: "Bodice-Busters" Put Romantic Myths to Bed
Carol Thurston and Barbara Doscher

Much comment on paperback romances has appeared in the popular press of late. Critics on the culture beat alternately call the books the marketing success of the decade for the troubled publishing business or deride them as either "bodice rippers" or "virtuous virginals." Successful or sleazy, the books accounted for almost 40 percent of the mass-market paperbacks printed in the United States in 1980, bringing publishers an estimated $250 million.

The bodice rippers, or busters, depending on the whimsy of the critic-writer, get their labels either from the bodice-ripping sexual encounters they portray or the hyperventilation readers are said to suffer while reading about them. In stark contrast, the virtuous virginals generally feature saccharine-sweet, submissive heroines, chaste unto their inevitable marriages when, in a euphemism for sexual intercourse, the heroes transport them "up to the stars."

No one knows for sure what share of the lucrative market each type controls today, but throughout the 1970s, the erotic historical romance—the bodice ripper—was the unquestioned queen of the supermarket and newsstand. So much so, editors admit, that some of the tasteless tomes now on the stands were acquired about three years ago, when the market was so hot they were buying every manuscript they could get their hands on. And they agree that these inferior books may have contributed to the recent decline in bodice-buster sales.

Critics, especially feminist critics, tend to lump all paperback romances together and take great delight in aiming potshots at the archetypal submissive-pure heroine and macho-stud hero or in attacking the whole bunch as soft porn. At the same time, they dismiss readers of such drivel as mindless drones living in a fantasy world. But we recently looked at more than fifty erotic historical romances published between 1964 and 1981, and came to a different conclusion.

We found not simpering acquiescence but vehement protest against unequal treatment. The heroine of Lynn Bartlett's *Courtly Love* rails, "A woman has as much pride, as much honor as a man, but she is treated as if she had none." Over and over, we saw a drive for personal independence so strong that marriage seemed too compromising. "Ye may have my love, my body, my undivided attention . . . even my money!" says Scotswoman Janet Leslie in Bertrice Small's *The Kadin*. "But I'll nae wed again! It's extremely pleasant being your mistress, but 'tis even more pleasant being my own mistress." In short, we found that most of the books we looked at did not fit the mold—did not portray submissive women or focus only on degrading sexual acts. And the readers we queried appreciated the difference.

Recently asked to summarize the advances made by the women's movement in the last decade, Gloria Steinem responded, "We've come to understand that it is the power to choose that is important, not what we choose." Jeanne Williams, writing as Megan Castell, says much the same thing in *Queen of a Lonely Country,* a story set in Fifteenth Century Wales:

"Till now there has not been an hour in all these passing years, Cerri, when I would not have gladly made you my wife and mistress of Heriot. You know that very well!"

"As I know there has not been one moment when you would have left me my own person."

"Yes," he said, mocking, "You must be queen. Even if it is a lonely country where beasts and birds are your subjects along with those who serve you. . . ."

Cerridwen stood quiet and straight, unmoved by his attack. "Sir Rhys, my old friend-enemy, you have forgotten the loneliest country of all."

"What?" he challenged.

"The country of the self." She smiled and watched him with her sea-variable eyes until he scowled and looked away. "And there I will rule. If the price of that is living lonely, then I will live alone."

"Rubbish!"

"There have always been women who ruled themselves," she returned equably. "Men forced them to be goddesses, saints, or witches, or they took refuge on islands or in nunneries. Men have never known whether to worship or destroy them, and so have done both." She laughed and turned to Gillian. "But I have hope, my dear. Perhaps you, or at least your daughters, can love a man and be yourselves, too. Perhaps you won't have to rule to keep from being devoured or broken."

"It is not in nature," Rhys growled.

"Nor is it in nature—except in man's—to clip the wings of swans to bind them to earth and your territory."

Historical settings seem to give authors a chance to send messages about contemporary women's issues, and also to imply that the drive for individual dignity and respect has motivated women for hundreds of years.

The determination to be accepted in one's own right, not defined by sex, marriage, or family lineage, is a common theme in erotic historical romances, as in Marilyn Harris's *Women of Eden:* "What have you always wanted, from the very beginning, John, even when you were a little boy?" Failing to elicit a response, she provided him with one. "Freedom, dignity, the right to pursue your own destiny, the opportunity to make those decisions that affect and influence your spirit and soul and body." She paused. "We are not different from you, John. Oh, our physiology is different, but that's all. And the difference does nothing to alter our hearts or our minds or our needs. For years, centuries, we've tried to convince each other that it does. But it doesn't, not in any fundamental or profound way."

Another cornerstone of the feminist movement, the belief that women must have control over their own bodies, also crops up again and again. Historical romances have a mixed record on the issue, but we did find many attempts to come up with a successful contraceptive, from the special herbs of harem women in the Middle East to the sponges of the brothel ladies in the old American West. All were attempts to escape physical domination by men.

In Bertrice Small's *Skye O'Malley,* a Catholic nun mounts an especially strong attack against sexual dependence. She acts as midwife to her sister (Skye) twice in ten months and then tells her she must take an herb potion to regulate her fertility. "But doesn't the Church forbid such wicked practices?" she is asked. The nun responds, "The Church has not seen innocent babies dying of starvation because there are too many mouths in the family to feed. What do the well-fed priests and bishops, snug in their stone houses on this snowy night, know of these poor souls and their endless torments? The innocent and superstitious poor I offer a 'tonic' to help them regain their strength. If they knew what I offer them they would not take it because they truly believe the Church's threat of eternal damnation. You, sister, are not so foolish."

The bodice rippers, as expected, vend fairly explicit sex, but always in romanticized language, as in male author Elizabeth Bright's description of multiple orgasm in *Passion Heirs:* "The flames burst inward and upward. She gasped and clutched his arms, hearing him say, 'Godalmighty, what a woman you are,' just before she again erupted, harder and longer than the other times. . . . There were times after that when she wished that glowing spot, the ember of her passion, would go out. But it would not. As long as he remained hard within her and she could move her hips against him, she continued to erupt into flames which lit her inner explosions.''

Heroines in bodice busters know they have sexual needs as strong as their lovers', and they are not ashamed to seek satisfaction. Oral sex came up in almost half of the books we read; the heroine had intercourse before marriage in two-thirds of the stories, and with more than one man in almost half. She married more than once in a third of the books and was sexually enterprising outside her marriage in one out of five.

All this sexual activity by the protagonists smacks more of contemporary society than of Victorian England, in which so many of the books are set. Such behavior is so common, in fact, that the stories seem to be telling readers that it is to be expected, and normal, and not in conflict with the roles of good wife and mother assumed later on.

It would be easy to fit all sexually descriptive passages into some category of pornography. But if erotica is a ''celebration of the body'' (Gloria Steinem) and pornography is degrading to females, many of these books are both.

Still, erotica always wins the day because the heroine overcomes degradation and finds a partner with whom she can ''celebrate.'' That is the overall impression the reader is left with—that women who insist on self-determination, independence, and respect are ''winners.'' Rather than the abductions, rapes, and betrayals common to the genre, it is the overcoming of these misadventures that is the central focus of the stories.

Rapes did occur in about half the books we examined, but in most of those, the hero expressed today's view that rape is a physical and emotional assault, not a sexual act, and certainly not the fault of the woman. To call the readers of these books sick is far from fair, in our opinion. Such episodes portray the kinds of bodily and psychological threats that women, and especially feminists, now decry. Women's rage at their perceived vulnerability is echoed in the experiences and responses of the heroines of these stories.

In probably the most militantly feminist story we found, Michelle de Winter's *Janine,* the heroine is the captain of a pirate ship who accedes to a captured captain's plea for mercy by demanding that he satisfy her sexually or take his chances with her crew. In the events that follow, she turns the tables on the usual male-dominance scene. He found some difficulty performing under the circumstances: ''His face became bathed in perspiration, and trickles rolled down his neck. 'The—the circumstances make it difficult for me. The atmosphere isn't— well, it isn't right for making love. Please be reasonable.'

''Janine looked him up and down slowly, making him even more conscious of his nudity. 'I assume you've been intimate with a number of women on many occasions over the years. Am I correct?' He had no idea where her question might lead, but was forced to nod agreement. 'Surely you never stopped to wonder whether the circumstances were appropriate for the lady. You were interested only in your own pleasure and didn't think of her.' 'But that was different—' 'Nonsense,' she declared, her voice sharp. 'A man has such vanity that he believes a woman will be receptive to him at any time and under any circumstances. Now you begin to know better.' ''

In spite of cover illustrations and blurbs, heroes in these books are gentle and sensitive, or if they are not in the beginning, they change as they come to admire and desire the woman of independence and integrity. The macho male patterned after the Steve Morgan of Rosemary Rogers' books has fallen out of favor and now is more likely to be the villain of the piece. Heroes are not ashamed to reveal emotions or admit to limitations. They do not need to dominate; they have a desire to control events, yes (as do the heroines), but a sense of fairness, sexual security, and understanding usually lets them compromise. They admire the high-spirited heroines above all other women, prizing them as sexual partners, as friends, and even as business partners, whether in privateering or cattle ranching.

Since both the heroes and heroines are much more androgynous than romance story stereotypes would suggest, if these portrayals do have any influence on readers' thinking or behavior, it is probably through the redefinition of "masculinity" and "femininity" that pervades the interactions of the characters. The central message in the erotic historical romances rings loud and clear: Macho males and saccharine ingenues are the losers in society.

These stories also suggest that freedom and responsibility are prerequisites for a complete and fulfilling life, regardless of gender. And while the majority of the books we studied conform to a generalized romance story formula, in focusing on the male–female relationship and in portraying the love of the hero as the most important motivation in the heroine's life, the fundamental power relationships between men and women have begun to be changed or at least challenged. The hero's love for the heroine is also the most important element in *his* life, and he often is heard to say that he is not "whole" or complete without her.

Such changes probably have been helped along by the many women authors and editors of romances whose social views are "feminist" in character. Star Helmer, editor-in-chief at Richard Gallen Books, says, "The reason I got into [editing these kinds of romances] in the first place was because I hoped to achieve some subtle brainwashing for the women's movement. And most of the authors I have worked with have had strong feminist attitudes."

How do these books function for the estimated twenty million women who read them? (Unsubstantiated reports from publishers describe typical readers as women between eighteen and sixty, most in their mid-thirties, with some college education and annual incomes of $20,000 and up.) Psychologists say "nonvisual relationships"—what comes across on the printed page—are more sexually stimulating to women than men. A 1971 study at Purdue University found that women are more aroused than men by erotic writing, especially when the story is removed from reality, in the sense that a fairy tale is. "What seems to be critical in this male–female difference is the extent to which mental processes beyond the purely sensory are engaged," says Glenn Wilson of the University of London Institute of Psychiatry. "The more that imagination is activated by an erotic stimulus, the more it is women who respond." The Purdue researchers concluded that if imagination is such a simple, powerful sexual stimulant, "individual differences in sexuality, such as sex drive and preferred frequency of orgasm, may largely be due to the way we learn to use sexual fantasies."

Certainly there is little doubt that avid readers of erotic historical romances are encountering lots of sexual fantasy. Easy access to these books in supermarkets and drugstores allows many women for the first time to "legitimately" obtain material that is sexually stimulating and informative, and for many this may be their first opportunity to "learn to use sexual fantasy."

Now publishers of the short so-called "category" books report that even their readers want "more sex." (Category books are constructed around highly specific publishers' formulas. Because of both plot and length restrictions, these stories are generally unimaginative and repetitive.) Silhouette Romances editor Karen Solem told writers attending the Romance Writers of America meeting in Houston last June that Silhouette would come out with two new lines: Rendezvous Romances would be short but sexier and Special Editions (which reached bookstores this January) would be longer and sexier. But not too sexy. The author's tipsheet for Rendezvous Romances advises writers that "Sexual encounters—which may include nudity and lovemaking even when the protagonists are not married—should concentrate on highly erotic sensations aroused by the hero's kisses and caresses rather than the mechanics of sex." (Such specifications often leave little for a writer to "create," as with the admonition that, "The hero and heroine meet early in the book and are never apart for more than ten pages. Their involvement with other characters is only for the purpose of moving the story forward.")

The profile we drew of the bodice-ripper heroines was that of the independent "total" woman: passionate lover, wife-confidante, devoted mother, astute businesswoman, and social worker. She merges the virtues of the Gothic heroine and her sexy, "bad-girl" counterpart, with the independence and career expectations of contemporary heroines in mainstream fiction. She reminded us of the women Betty Friedan (in her new book, *The Second Stage*) says the first stage of the feminist movement has produced.

For too long, women who should know better have assumed that the gender-free concepts of equality of opportunity, responsibility, and respect were the exclusive property of a highly educated, liberated minority. Surely the new-era bodice rippers, with or without artistic defects, have helped spread these ideas throughout society. Whether knowingly or not, these books and the feminist movement have been moving toward the same end. Only their audiences have been different.

1. This essay has a relatively long introduction. It begins with a brief statement on the commercial success of paperback romances, then gives a definition of the "bodice-buster" novel, follows with a summary of critical comment, and concludes with the authors' contradiction of this criticism. Is there a shaping idea? If so, where does it appear? Do you think the lengthy introduction is necessary? If so, why?

2. Narrative examples range from lengthy quotations to fairly short ones. Explain the authors' use of quoted material. What kinds of quotations do they use? How do these quotations contribute to the making of a shaping idea? Are the authors' conclusions from these narrative examples valid? Should they have provided more examples?

3. Why do the authors not use the quotation from Michelle de Winter's *Janine* at the beginning of the essay?

4. Why do the authors also discuss the heroes of these novels? How does this discussion act as a bridge to the rest of the essay?

5. What are some of the broader generalizations about women that the authors make toward the end of their essay? What effect might this generalization have on the reader's view of the importance of erotic romances?

6. How successful have the authors been in persuading readers to change their minds about these novels? What else might they have done to accomplish this?

7. How would you explain the arrangement of the essay with regard to the sequence of generalizations and narrative examples? Was this arrangement effective in conveying the shaping idea?

The Fizz Biz: Tiny Bubbles

Bernice Kanner

The fact is, Americans just aren't overeating, overdrinking, and overindulging in general the way they used to. And while that may spell relief to millions of heads and stomachs, it has spelled only trouble for Alka-Seltzer. The well-known aid for gluttons, bingers, and all-purpose overdoers had become synonymous with a hangover cure in the public's mind, and therefore almost obsolete in the temperate 1980s. What would make today's consumers reach for the familiar blue-and-white packet, plop its two subway-token-size tablets in water, and wait for the fizz?

To find out, Miles Laboratories, the unit of A. G. Bayer that makes Alka-Seltzer, turned to McCann-Erickson, the advertising agency, last September. McCann came up with the strategy of presenting Alka-Seltzer as an upbeat product, a remedy for all the symptoms of stress that come with success—and a product with almost universal appeal. After all, who does not, as the new campaign states, suffer "the anxious upset stomach that comes with a thumping headache or the thumping headache that comes with an upset stomach"?

According to McCann's research, about 30 percent of the population uses antacids. But who are they? Very middle-American but extremely upwardly mobile types. "They're highly susceptible to advertising and believe literally the claims products make," says Paula Drillman, the agency's research director. "In no other category I've examined do consumers respond like this."

The research also revealed that people who used to pop Alka-Seltzer twenty times a year had begun taking other remedies that addressed more contemporary ailments, such as nervous tension. Furthermore, says Michael Sennott, senior vice-president and management representative at McCann, "people had stopped identifying with the shlumpy characters in the Alka-Seltzer commercials." Interview subjects asked to draw an Alka-Seltzer user invariably penned someone potbellied and tieless. Other antacid users sketched were well groomed. "We had captured the hearts and minds of people—but our message was no longer relevant," says Sennott.

The characters in those spots weren't up to the marketing task at hand. Remember the spicy-meatball man and the stupefied glutton who "can't believe" he "ate the whole thing"? They didn't speak to the masses yearning for success, and their message was more apropos to the permissive, pill-popping 1960s and 1970s than to the all-things-in-moderation 1980s. "The executive lunch that began with a couple of martinis is as much a relic as the weekly hangover," says Drillman. "Many business people don't even order wine at lunch anymore—it's spritzers and Perrier. If you position to the mind-set of overindulgence today, you're dead."

Alka-Seltzer's new commercials, which make their debut this week, may not have the hilarious situations and absurd characters that were long its trademark— and that made the spots part of America's pop-cultural heritage. But they do have drama and style. Where they once leaned toward the ridiculous, they now seem headed for the sublime.

In one almost surrealistic spot, a piano tinkles an Erik Satie melody as the camera focuses on two tablets, bobbing in a slow motion in a watercooler, that look more like sculpture than medication. A soothing voice-over salutes the junior executive who has vowed to become a vice-president by the end of the fiscal year, the vice-president who has vowed to become senior vice-president by the time she is 39, and the board chairman who must ultimately face the shareholders. Then the voice delivers the pitch "for the symptoms of stress that can come with success" as the tablets are released—they seem to float—into a glass of water and a sea of bubbles explodes. And in another spot, dedicated to the class of '84, a mortarboard is lofted into Magritte-type clouds, where it spins slowly.

Alka-Seltzer's new look has come to an old product. Miles Labs concocted the first—and only—product combining aspirin and an antacid in 1929. Hub Beardsley, then president of Miles, located in Elkhart, Indiana, had visited the local newspaper during a flu epidemic that mysteriously bypassed the paper's employees. Everyone credited the editor's home prescription—a dose of aspirin and bicarbonate of soda—and Beardsley asked Miles's chemists to imitate the formula. He then distributed Alka-Seltzer to fellow passengers on a Mediterranean cruise who had the flu, and in 1931 began promoting it on the radio, eventually sponsoring shows including *The Saturday Night Barn Dance* and *The Quiz Kids*. The product became associated with relieving hangovers, and in 1933, when Prohibition ended, its sales spurted.

Alka-Seltzer continued to grow through the 1940s and 1950s, when Speedy, the three-dimensional animated figure and precursor of the Pillsbury Doughboy, charmed TV audiences with "relief is just [pause] a swallow away [*ping*]." "Speedy was an unthreatening character who established the brand with viewers," says Bruce Nelson, executive vice-president of McCann. "He didn't dish out any parental stuff. Rather, his style was 'Oh boy, you've done it again, wink, wink.' " Adds executive vice-president Ira Madris, "To have a salesman liked is a wonderful foot in the door for a product. Speedy was a well-liked salesman."

His successor, in the early 1960s, was an animated talking stomach. A cartoon man sat in one chair while his irate little (though bloated) stomach sat in another and took him to task for all his pepperoni binges. About the same time, Alka-Seltzer aired what Miles Labs figures is its most remembered commercial: the stomach montage. The camera panned a universe of assorted abdomens, then, 55 seconds into the spot, a voice-over said, "No matter what shape your stomach is in, when it gets out of shape, take Alka-Seltzer."

The late 1960s were Alka-Seltzer's heyday. Americans guffawed as poor Jack suffered through 59 takes of a "commercial" for those spicy meatballs. They laughed as a waiter urged a hapless diner to "try it—you'll like it." And they so enjoyed the glassy-eyed, rumpled Ralph's lament, "I can't believe I ate the whole thing," that they made it part of the vernacular.

Those glory days for Alka-Seltzer and advertising came to a halt in late 1972 when the Food and Drug Administration, spurred by Ralph Nader, undertook a major regulatory review of over-the-counter drugs. Alka-Seltzer came in for a lot of negative publicity about aspirin's effects on the stomach, and "we could no longer promote it for upset stomachs alone," says Stephen Reim, brand manager for Alka-Seltzer.

Miles Labs defended Alka-Seltzer's formula in the scientific community, but introduced Alka-Seltzer Gold, a nonaspirin product just for stomachs. It has not caught on. The company also cut back on advertising the original Alka-Seltzer, and from 1973 through 1978 tried a slew of different campaigns. Sammy Davis Jr. crooned for the brand, and there was a series of dull testimonials. "We tried to show our critics we were living up to the F.D.A. regulations," explains Reim. But none of the campaigns clicked until Wells Rich Greene came up with "plop, plop, fizz, fizz—oh, what a relief it is" in 1976. That ran for three years.

In 1981, Miles's research confirmed that the public was still skeptical about the government review and Ralph Nader's attacks. "We had to tell more of a reassurance story," says Reim. The company's answer: America's Home Remedy, a campaign in which a disheveled-looking binger groped his way down a long corridor, or pawed through the medicine cabinet panic-stricken that the Alka-Seltzer wasn't there. Those spots worked briefly, but the field was growing increasingly more competitive. In 1982, antacid advertisers spent approximately $70 million, though most of their spots are the heavy-handed, claim-cluttered, comparative kind. (Sales for the upset-stomach-remedy category climbed 9.1 percent to $638 million last year. Liquids are the largest segment, followed by chewables. Alka-Seltzer remains the leader of the effervescents—a relatively small segment that also includes Bromo Seltzer and the regional brand Brioschi—and with a 14 percent share of the overall antacid market trails just Maalox liquid and chewables combined, which have a 15 percent share, and edges out Mylanta [13 percent], Pepto Bismol liquid and chewables combined [13 percent], Rolaids [12.5 percent], and Tums [7 percent], according to A. C. Nielsen figures.)

Alka-Seltzer, which spends about $15-million a year on advertising, stopped being a maverick in 1982 by coming out with its own comparative commercial. In Big Relief, a dyspeptic fisherman rejected offers of Rolaids and Tums before finally finding what he wanted in his hat: Alka-Seltzer, of course.

It was when that campaign also fizzled that Miles started looking around for another approach. Whether the arty new commercials will bring relief to Alka-Seltzer—and prove as memorable as some of their predecessors—remains to be seen. Meanwhile, I admit I was moved after previewing them to try the stuff for the first time. It tastes a lot like regular seltzer, except sharper. It's an acquired taste, they tell me.

1. Why does the first paragraph end with a question? How does it affect the paragraphs that follow?

2. Why does the narrative of the history of Alka-Seltzer advertising follow the discussion of new commercials rather than precede it? Would chronological order have made it more or less effective?

3. Many of the quotations are from interviews with the employees of an advertising agency responsible for Alka-Seltzer commercials. What purpose do these quotations serve? How authoritative are they?

4. How successfully has the author presented the results of her media research?

5. How would you explain the author's choice of language and style?

6. How would you account for the difference in tone of voice and pattern of arrangement in this essay from Thurston and Doscher's?

7. Which approach do you think might be more appropriate for your essay?

Now that you have studied these essays, you might have some idea how to arrange your own. Perhaps you have already decided on a cause-and-effect pattern of generalization and example. Or a pattern of narrative incidents that lead to a conclusion about a major theme in one of the media. Whatever the pattern you choose, it is the alternation of generalization and incident that will drive your essay forward and create the interest and significance you wish to convey to your audience.

Writing the Rough Draft

It is now time to write your rough draft. Once you have completed it, take a break. Before you begin to think about rewriting, look at the following essay written by another student in response to this chapter's task:

HORRORS

The evolution of horror films certainly doesn't compare to the wondrous and lengthy evolution of humankind. In fact, horror films might merely be a reflection of the twentieth century's every-changing morals, values, and fears. Indeed, horror films have certainly changed over the years; however, whether yesteryear's horror films are better than today's is as arguable as stating that modern humans are better than their ancestors. Do we not commit the same atrocities (rape, thievery, murder) that our ancestors did?

The year 1931 marked the coming age of the horror genre. Although there had previously been scattered examples of films that dramatized the horrible and the grotesque, the horror film did not flourish until the high-budgeted Frankenstein, based loosely on Mary Shelley's novel, was released by Universal amid tremendous fanfare.

Audience reaction proved so favorable that the major Hollywood studios (chiefly RKO and Universal) loosely adapted many other classic horror novels and certain legends to the silver screen in films such as Dr. Jekyll and Mr. Hyde (with Spencer Tracy as Robert Louis Stevenson's schizoid novel creation); Dracula (with Bela Lugosi as the irrepressible count of Bram Stoker's novel); Island of the Lost Souls (with Charles Laughton in this adaptation of H. G. Wells's novel); The Mummy (Karloff in tape); The Invisible Man (with Claude Rains); The Wolf Man (with Lon Chaney, Jr.); and King Kong. Not only was this new genre very successful, but it spawned a plethora of new stars who would become known as "horror stars" (such as Karloff, Lugosi, and Chaney, Jr.).

Curiously, Dracula, Frankenstein, and other assorted monsters achieved a weird kind of commercial immortality with their sudden success. It was necessary to resurrect them, no matter how thoroughly they had been killed off in the preceding film. They returned as themselves or as "sons," "daughters," and "ghosts" in such films as Son of Kong, The Invisible Man Returns, The Mummy's Ghost, and The Bride of Frankenstein.

However, there's a limit to human invention, if not human credulity. Horror films came out with the regularity of a monthly magazine. By the mid-1940s, Hollywood had gorged the public past horror satiety. In a desperate attempt to rejuvenate horror's sagging box office, Hollywood united horror filmdom's monsters (Frankenstein Meets the Wolf-

Man), a move that slowed down the erosion of box-office dollars but didn't stop it. Feeling that the imaginary horror of a film couldn't possibly compete with the true horror tales of Nazism and World War II circulating in the United States, Hollywood lamely blamed World War II for the continuing plummet of horror's box-office popularity. Finally, horror expired in self-parody as it was exploited for cheap laughs: Abbott and Costello Meet Frankenstein, The Dead End Kids Meet the Spook, and so on. Ironically, a genre in which death was a constant staple had died the most unkind of deaths itself by 1945.

In 1952, like a Phoenix rising from its own ashes, the horror genre entered its second cycle, but it took on a vastly different appearance. With the major studios generally abandoning horror, the small, independent film companies (ranging from the fairly big American International Pictures to the ultracheap Astor) became the most consistent suppliers of horror films. These independents specialized in making quick, contemporary horror films, all of which had assured profit potential because of minuscule budgets and sensationalized advertising. Indeed, AIP, in many cases, just made up an advertising campaign, and if they liked the campaign's look, they would make the film in three to six days.

From old myths of vampires, werewolves, and inhuman monsters, the horror genre veered into new angles as it married with science fiction in such films as I Married a Monster from Outer Space, It Conquered the World, and The Incredibly Strange Creatures Who Stopped Living and Became Mixed-Up Zombies. If one replaces the words monster, zombie, and it with Communist and the words outer space with Russia in the preceding film titles, it becomes evident that with these films, the independent shrewdy exploited the prevalent fear in the United States of being "taken over" by subversives.

The public's fear of imminent nuclear disaster was also skillfully exploited. Thus were born the "atomic age monsters," who were either normal living organisms turned into mutants by incessant human dabbling in the atomic field (Colossal Man, Attack of the Crab Monsters) or supposedly extinct dinosaurs unleashed from their "dormancy" deep below the oceans or ice caps because of atomic testing

(The Beast from 20,000 Fathoms). The independents also keenly
sensed that with the advent of fast cars and rock 'n' roll, the mood of
their basically youthful audience was shifting. Thus began the recycling of old horror monsters into romantic villains (I Was a Teen-Age
Werewolf, I Was a Teen-Age Frankenstein)--misunderstood and inarticulate but sympathetic to the underdogs (i.e., the young audience) and
irritants to authority (i.e., the establishment).

It was during this reincarnation of "old-time" monsters that the
genre was ushered into its third cycle as it looked on its old saviors to
return it to the prosperity that it had once tasted. In 1958, Hammer
Films, a small, fledgling independent film company, released Horror of
Dracula (with Christopher Lee and Peter Cushing). It was essentially a
remake of the 1932 Dracula with an authentic gothic look (which became a Hammer trademark). Buoyed by the film's enormous success,
Hammer recycled other horror films of the 1930s (Evil of Frankenstein, Curse of the Mummy, Curse of the Werewolf). AIP also delved
into gothic horror with the release of The Pit and the Pendulum (very
loosely based on Edgar Allan Poe's story and featuring Vincent Price)
as a counterpunch to Hammer. The success of this movie compelled
AIP to go through a wild rummage of Poe: Masque of the Red Death,
The Oblong Box, The Raven, and others (all with Price). Interestingly,
horror was once again spawning its own stars, as the names of Price,
Lee, and Cushing became synonymous with horror.

Besides Hammer's "British invasion" (which, incidentally, was not
only similar in popularity to the Beatles' but preceded them by six
years), Japan sent us Godzilla, who was actually a remnant of the
"atomic-age monster" period. Released in 1958, the film did so well
that Godzilla returned in numerous sequels with a slew of foes and allies to accompany him. The Japanese even reincarnated King Kong,
who inevitably did battle against Godzilla.

It was during the third cycle that the major studios returned, opting
for a more bold type of horror, which often paralleled reality--What-
ever Happened to Baby Jane? (mental illness), The Collector (sexual
perversion), and Repulsion (sexual obsession)--rather than the costumed period pieces of the independents. It was also during the third
cycle that blood and fairly explicit violence were used or, as director

Don Sharp said in a recent interview on the subject of Hammer Films, "They'd got into the pattern of making each film a bit bloodier than the one before it." It was with Alfred Hitchcock's Psycho in 1960 that horror achieved a new permissiveness in the limits on screen violence, as that film would forever shatter the invisible line of what was and was not acceptable on the screen. In 1968, that line was further annihilated when a small independent, Lavrel, released the ultragraphic Night of the Living Dead, a film which was unrated by the Motion Picture Association of America.

This film signified the beginning of the fourth cycle, a period in which both the major studios and the independents prospered and screen violence was given a new definition because the newly imposed film ratings freed movies from their hitherto self-imposed censorship. The major studios continued to reject such previously traditional subjects as vampires, werewolves, and mad scientists and now relied on common earth critters to provide ample terror (Jaws, Orca, The Swarm) and became fixated on the supernatural (The Exorcist, The Omen, Carrie). The burgeoning expansion of independents also continued in the fourth cycle, as they forayed into the unusual (Ilsa: She-Wolf of the SS, Gore, Gore Girls, I Dismember Mama). It was in 1974, as the independents continued to create unusual formulas for success, that the highly successful ultraexplicit Texas Chainsaw Massacre was released. This film not only set a new precedent in screen violence but created a formula (the indestructible killer) that still saturates the independent horror-film market today (Friday the 13th, Maniac!, Madman). Today independents in the fourth cycle continue to follow the "deranged slasher" theme (affectionately dubbed splatter film by its fans), while the major studios continue to opt for new formulas. In recent years, the major studios have returned to their "bankable stars," as can be witnessed by the current spate of werewolf movies (The Howling, American Werewolf in London) and vampires (The Hunger). It is evident that, like most of their monsters, horror films never die.

What media experiences provided the subject for this essay? What was the writer's shaping idea? What examples did he use? How did he move between the general and the specific?

FOCUS: STYLE

The Components of Style

A writer's style, according to E. B. White, might be defined as "the sound his words make on paper." Writers may sound proper and formal or relaxed and colloquial. They may write lyrically and poetically or logically and scientifically. Their words may seem simple and forthright or satirically double-edged. Although one's style changes, clarity is most often the key to an intelligent style in any age. The question for writers is rarely whether they want to be clear or unclear, but whether they want to achieve clarity through simplicity or complexity, through plainness or eloquence. In *The Elements of Style*, White advised inexperienced writers to write about their subject as directly, simply, naturally, and sincerely as they can. By doing so, they may develop a clarity of expression often sacrificed by those who use the extremes of ornate, pretentious locution or breezy, off beat slang.

Style is shaped by the writer's purpose in writing and by his or her audience. For example, a writer who has information to convey is likely to seek a plainer, less eloquent style than one who is writing to entertain or to argue. Thus, the author of a cookbook would be well advised to avoid writing like a poet: telling a reader to bake a cake in an oven "as hot as a jealous heart" would create pointless confusion. At the same time, a writer who is attempting to explain Einstein's theories of relativity will need to sound more erudite, and perhaps more poetic as well, than one who is explaining how to bake a cake.

Style is also shaped by the audience. For example, writing for a young, uneducated audience will affect the "sound your words make on paper" in a different way from writing for a peer audience (see Chap. 2) and from writing for an instructor (see Chaps. 3 and 9). Your style in writing for a sympathetic audience would be different from your style in writing for an unsympathetic audience.

Perhaps, the key would is *adjust*. Writers do not usually use radically different styles in different situations; rather they make subtle adjustments in the style that comes most naturally to them. They try to be a bit more concrete for one audience, a bit more abstract for another. Often a writer is wise to introduce some variety, a simple sentence in a paragraph of complex ones, a metaphor in a sea of scientific facts.

Ways of Adjusting Style

What sort of adjustments in sentence structure and diction can one make in order to simplify or embellish the sound of one's prose? Perhaps we can seek a few basic answers to this question.

Often simplicity of style stems from concreteness, complexity from abstraction.

Adjusting for Concreteness.   To simplify your style and to make it easier
to follow, write about your subject in concrete, specific terms. You may try
using a narrative mode, for example, even when you are explaining a principle
or a concept, as a dramatic situation is often more accessible than an abstract
explanation. Compare the following two passages, each of which explains why
Thoreau, the author of *Walden,* chose in 1845 to leave his home in the town
of Concord, Massachusetts, and to go off to live alone in a hut in the woods
by Walden Pond:

The principle of turning one's back on unpleasant facts—unpleasant, because
they were so deeply inessential, so foreign, in a way, to our essential Nature—is
one *naturally* congenial to the American mind. Thoreau gave this principle its
classic utterance. In his spirit, if not in his name, we still take to such woods as
we can find.

I think one reason he went to the woods was a perfectly simple and commonplace one. . . . [He was a] young man, a few years out of college, who had not
yet broken away from home. He hadn't married, and he had found no job that
measured up to his rigid standards of employment, and like any young man, or
young animal, he felt uneasy and on the defensive until he had fixed himself a
den. Most young men, of course, casting about for a site, are content merely to
draw apart from their kinfolks. Thoreau, convinced that the greater part of what
his neighbors called good was bad, withdrew from a great deal more than family.

The second passage, by White, is a bit easier to follow than the first, by Wright
Morris, because White dramatized the "principle of turning one's back on unpleasant facts." At the same time, in writing more abstractly, Morris offered a
more cogent summary statement of the general significance of Thoreau's action.

The Verbal Sentence.   When you narrate in order to explain, you involve
your reader in an action that illustrates the ideas you want your reader to
understand. You also write more concretely when you employ short sentences
that emphasize persons or things as their subject and active verbs as their predicate. Look at the following three sentences:

The boy knew every trick.
He grew up in the ghetto.
He was tough and streetwise.

Each one is what we call a verbal sentence: the focus is on a subject that is an
actor, a verb that tells what the action is, and modifiers that tell something
more about who the actor is and/or what he is doing. Each one is in the active
voice, which many style manuals argue is more direct than passive constructions, in which the actor becomes the object of the sentence and the verb is
turned into a past participle ("Every trick was known by the boy"). You may

not necessarily write more clearly if you favor short, active, verbal sentences, but your style will sound simpler and more concrete.

Of course, a piece of writing composed only of short, simple sentences is apt to be choppy and monotonous. Even the most concise and direct stylist wants to include longer, more complex sentence structures in her or his writing. In the "Focus" section of Chapter 5, you received some practice in sentence combining as a way of making your style more complex. A possible combination of the three sample sentences might be "Growing up tough and streetwise in the ghetto, the boy knew every trick." In this sentence, the noun *boy* is modified by the cluster "Growing up tough and streetwise in the ghetto," a cluster in which the verbal component "Growing up" is itself qualified by "tough and streetwise in the ghetto."

Adjusting for Abstractness. In the combined sentence above, attention has been directed to the ghetto toughness of the boy. The sentence is thus more abstract, focused as much on a concept, "ghetto toughness," as on an action. By modifying a noun or a verb, either with a string of adjectives and/or adverbs or with clusters of subordinate clauses, you draw the reader's attention to the distinctive qualities of the subject and/or the action you are writing about.

The use of modifiers and of long, involved sentences will not guarantee an intelligently complex style. But, especially in the service of abstract explanation, these rhetorical tools can lend clarity to the expression of complicated ideas. Thus, in the first sentence of the passage about Thoreau by Wright Morris, the subordinate clause, with its modifying adjectives *inessential* and *foreign*, does help to explain the concept of *unpleasant facts* and thus clarifies a reader's understanding of the subject of the sentence, the "principle of turning one's back on unpleasant facts."

The Nominal Sentence. Let's take the combined sentence about the boy in the ghetto and make one more alteration: "His growing up tough and streetwise in the ghetto is what taught the boy every trick." Note that "the boy" is no longer the subject of the sentence. We have nominalized the verbs and adjectives of the modifying cluster; that is, we have turned them into nouns that can function as the subject.

Nominal sentence structures, because they tend to create abstract subjects of verbs and adjectives, can be effective tools for the stylist interested in analyzing ideas. If you change the verbal construction "He loved the woods and felt free there and so went camping often" into a nominal construction, "His love of the woods and the freedom he felt there led him to go camping often," you are directing the reader's attention more emphatically to the idea that explains why the person went camping.

If you work in a more abstract, idea-oriented style, however, your writing will not necessarily be more profound than it you write in a more concrete, verbal style. Nor will you necessarily sound more eloquent. You may, in fact, choose plain, direct words because you want to explain a complex idea as clearly as you can.

How to Write More Eloquently

Whether your style is simple or complex, concrete or abstract, there are a few guidelines you might follow in attempting to write with more eloquence.

Balanced Phrasing. Balanced phrasing is an effective means of lending an eloquent sound to your style. "He ate scrambled eggs, buttered toast, and fresh-squeezed orange juice" would sound less polished if it were written, "He ate scrambled eggs, toast with butter, and orange juice that had been freshly squeezed." Particularly when you are writing long, complicated sentences, phrasing similar grammatical units and similar ideas in similar ways is an important means of achieving clarity. Note how repetition lends balance to the following sentence: "The difference between living today and living at any time in the past is the difference between living in fear of nuclear destruction and living free of such fear." This would be a more difficult sentence to understand without such a balanced effect: "The difference between living today and at any time in the past is fear of nuclear destruction."

Loose and Periodic Sentences. As you seek balance in your phrasing, seek variety in your sentence structuring. It is sometimes argued, for example, that periodic sentences, in which the modifiers precede the base, sound somehow better than loose sentences, in which the modifiers follow the base. But writing only periodic sentences is as dull as writing only short, simple sentences. The periodic sentence "having gone to the woods, he camped out" does place more dramatic emphasis on the subject than would a loose version of the same sentence. "He camped out, having gone to the woods." But there is really no justification for preferring one type of sentence over the other. A loose sentence may prove as effective as a periodic sentence, depending on what element in the sentence a writer wishes to emphasize and whether the emphasis will be best achieved by the placement of that element first or last. The context must always be taken into consideration.

Figurative Language. Skillfully and judiciously used, similes, metaphors, irony, understatement, and similar figures of speech will lend eloquence to your style.

A metaphor is an implied comparison between dissimilar things. To write "Our world is a ship without a helmsman on the dark sea of space" is to imply that our world, like a ship drifting on the sea, needs someone to guide and steer it. In a simile, the comparison is made explicitly by the use of *like* or *as*.

There are a number of dangers in using metaphors and similes. They may end up sounding trite, as does the example above. If they are used too frequently, they may actually distract a reader's attention from the point that the writer wishes to make instead of making the point more memorable. Also, novices who try to extend a metaphor often mix it up, with ludicrous results. Thus, if the writer who compared the world to a ship goes on to write, "If we are not careful, our ship may sink in the flames of a third world war," the "sea" has gone through a most awkward transformation. In general, use the occasional metaphor that comes to you naturally in the course of writing.

Irony. Irony involves undercutting a reader's expectations. To write "After Adam and Eve ate the apple, they found life a bit tougher" is to create an ironic effect through understatement. The reader expects you to say and knows that you mean that Adam and Eve found life very much tougher. Like any form of verbal humor, irony requires subtlety. The ironist is always in danger of falling flat on his or her face. Irony should not be overdone.

You may find yourself most eloquent when your language is as simple and direct as you can make it. Take the following advice from E. B. White:

The beginner should approach style warily, realizing that it is himself he is approaching, no other; and he should begin by turning resolutely away from all devices that are popularly believed to indicate style—all mannerisms, tricks, adornments. . . .

Style takes its final shape more from attitudes of mind than from principles of composition, for, as an elderly practitioner once remarked, "Writing is an act of faith, not a trick of grammar." This moral observation would have no place in a rule book were it not that style *is* the writer, and therefore what a man is, rather than what he knows, will at last determine his style.

—**William Strunk, Jr., and E. B. White,** *Elements of Style*

SOME PRACTICE WITH STYLE

1. Identify each of the following sentences as verbal or nominal. Restructure each verbal sentence into a nominal one, each nominal sentence into a verbal one:

   a. You take the high road, I'll take the low road, and I'll get to Scotland before you.

   b. Keeping physically fit has become a major preoccupation of many people today.

   c. Our capacity for wonder at the news has been lost because of television.

   d. I like the essay, have always liked it, and even as a child was at work, attempting to inflict my young thoughts and experiences on others by putting them on paper.

2. Identify each of the following sentences as periodic or loose. Recast each periodic sentence into a loose one, and each loose sentence into a periodic one. What are the differing effects?

   a. Having a thick coat of fur, the animal survived.

   b. Mercilessly goading the bully, our hero saved the day.

   c. Snowstorms make driving hazardous and thus endanger lives, even as they give countless children hours of gleeful play.

   d. Newsmagazines are popular, offering an artful combination of news, popular opinion, and gossip.

3. Identify each of the following sentences as active or passive. Restructure each active sentence into a passive one, each passive sentence into an active one:

   a. Paradoxically, in a free society, one is often worried and frustrated by government policy.

   b. The house was torn apart by the swirling winds of the tornado.

   c. The hard day's work at the factory tired him out.

   d. Don't count your chickens before they hatch.

4. Simplify the style of the following paragraph by rewriting in order to dramatize its central idea:

   > The mass of men lead lives of quiet desperation. What is called resignation is confirmed desperation. From the desperate city you go into the desperate country and have to console yourself with the bravery of minks and muskrats. A stereotyped but unconscious despair is concealed even under what are called the games and amusements of mankind. There is no play in them, for this comes after work. But it is a characteristic of wisdom not to do desperate things.
   >
   > —**Henry David Thoreau,** *Walden*

5. Write a paragraph of abstract generalizations that summarize the interactions between the media and Americans according to their essays in this chapter.

6. Analyze the following passages for their style: identify sentences as verbal or nominal, periodic or loose, simple or complex; indicate whether verbs are passive or active; determine how phrasing has been balanced, what figures of speech have been used, and if irony is a component. Finally, has clarity been maintained throughout? What would you say is the chief means by which the writer's style gave eloquence and meaning to each passage?

Springtime in the heyday of the Model T was a delirious season. Owning a car was still a major excitement, roads were still wonderful and bad. The Fords were obviously conceived in madness: any car which was capable of going from forward into reverse without any perceptible mechanical hiatus was bound to be a mighty challenging thing to the human imagination. Boys used to veer them off the highway into a level pasture and run wild with them, as though they were cutting up with a girl. Most everybody used the reverse pedal quite as much as the regular foot brake—it distributed the wear over the bands and wore them all down evenly. That was the big trick, to wear all the bands down evenly, so that the final chattering would be total and the whole unit scream for renewal.

The days were golden, the nights were dim and strange. I still recall with trembling those loud, nocturnal crises when you drew up to a signpost and raced the engine so the lights would be bright enough to read destinations by. I have never been really planetary since. I suppose it's time to say good-bye. Farewell, my lovely!

—**E. B. White,** "Farewell, My Lovely!"

In a newsreel theater the other day I saw a picture of a man who had developed the soap bubble to a higher point than it had ever before reached. He had become the ace soap bubble blower of America, had perfected the business of blowing bubbles, refined it, doubled it, squared it, and had even worked himself into a convenient lather. The effect was not pretty. Some of the bubbles were too big to be beautiful, and the blower was always jumping into them or out of them, or playing some sort of unattractive trick with them. It was, if anything, a rather repulsive sight. Humor is a little like that: it won't stand much blowing up, and it won't stand much poking. It has a certain fragility, an evasiveness, which one had best respect. Essentially, it is a complete mystery. A human frame convulsed with laughter, and the laughter becoming hysterical and uncontrollable, is as far out of balance as one shaken with the hiccoughs or in the throes of a sneezing fit.

—**E. B. White,** "Some Remarks on Humor"

7. Take a passage from your journal or from an essay that you have written, and recast the sentences to make your writing more abstract and complex. Assume, for example, that you are writing for *The New York Times*. If your original passage was a narrative, you can summarize it as an abstract statement. You might recast your sentences into the nominal form and combine the various elements into sentences of greater length. Do not, of course, sacrifice clarity in your revision.

8. Now, revise the passage again, this time aiming for concreteness. You might begin by developing a narrative to support the main point of the piece. Employ any figures of speech that seem to you to add vividness. Balance your complex sentences with shorter verbal structures in the active voice that give emphasis to the action.

9. Examine the passage for ways in which you can make your writing more eloquent. What balanced phrasing can be added, and what variations in sentence structure, to achieve both periodic and loose sentences? Would it be possible to revise your passage once again, aiming for an ironic slant toward your subject?

EWRITING

Obtaining Feedback on Your Rough Draft

Once you have taken sufficient time away from your rough draft so that you can review it with a measure of objectivity, turn to one or more of the channels you have developed for obtaining feedback on what you have written: your "other self," your peers, or your teacher. Again, use these channels for obtaining answers to the "Audience Response Guide" about your draft.

———— AUDIENCE RESPONSE GUIDE ————
---

1. **What do you think the writer wanted to say in this paper? What is his or her purpose in writing? What does he or she want the paper to mean?**
2. **How does the paper affect the audience for which it is intended?**
3. **How effective has the writer been in conveying his or her purpose and meaning? What are the strengths of the paper? What are its weaknesses?**
4. **How should the paper be revised to better fulfill its purpose and meaning?**

Consider at this time the following peer evaluation of the rough draft of the student essay "Horrors." Compare your own evaluation of the draft to that of the peer group by answering the four questions of the "Audience Response Guide" before reading their answers.

1. The readers disagreed on the purpose of the essay. One felt that the writer intended to give a historical survey of the development of horror films and its later offshoots, but the other said that the purpose was unclear, that the paper provided a lot of information but failed to explain why it was doing so.
2. The first reader believed that the paper was intended for an uneducated film audience--one that had not seen most of these

films and wasn't aware of the horror film's origins. The other
reader felt a bit overwhelmed by the information.

3. Both readers agreed that the essay included too much
   information and too little assimilation, and that the information
   lacked supplemental explanations of its intended purpose. Both
   were very impressed by the extent of the writer's knowledge.

4. The readers agreed that the writer should narrow his focus,
   concentrate more on some representative films, and explain his
   purpose further.

Here is a revised version of "Horrors." How well were the readers' suggestions incorporated? Did the writer make any additional changes himself? What
additional changes might he have made?

HORRORS

The evolution of horror films certainly doesn't compare to the wondrous and lengthy evolution of humankind. Horror films are, however,
a vivid reflection of the twentieth century's ever-changing morals, values, and fears. Although horror films have certainly changed over the
years, saying that yesteryear's horror films are better than today's is
as arguable as stating that humans are better now than they were a
half century ago. Do we not commit the same atrocities (rape, thievery,
murder) as our grandparents or our greatgrandparents did?

The year 1931 marked the coming of age of the horror genre. Although there had previously been scattered examples of films that
dramatized the horrible and the grotesque, the horror film did not
flourish until Universal released Dracula, featuring Bela Lugosi as the
irrepressible Transylvanian count of Bram Stoker's classic novel;
shortly after, Universal released Frankenstein, featuring Boris Karloff
as Mary Shelley's monstrous novel creation. As the genre prospered, in
1932 Karloff appeared in The Mummy; in 1933 Claude Rains was The
Invisible Man, and King Kong made a monkey of himself; and in 1940
Lon Chaney, Jr., was transformed into The Wolf Man to add to horror's

growing assemblage of monsters and spookes. Interestingly, this new genre, in which all of the major Hollywood studios were involved, spawned a plethora of new stars who would become known as "horror stars" (such as Karloff, Lugosi, and Chaney, Jr.).

The horror genre's sudden success was indeed puzzling, because these films succeeded during the economic depression that occurred after 1929. In fact, audiences relentlessly flocked to this macabre new genre. Perhaps the audiences of that era equated the grim stories of countless people and villages being destroyed by various creatures with the Great Depression, which in reality destroyed many people and cities. Perhaps they hoped that, like the films in which the creature dies at the end and a sense of balance is restored to the village, the poverty and despair induced by the Depression would also be conquered and a sense of order would be restored.

Curiously, Dracula, Frankenstein, and other assorted monsters achieved a weird kind of commercial immortality with their sudden success. Thus the studios set out on a steady and profitable progress through a series of sequels in which the creatures returned as themselves or as "sons," "daughters," and "ghosts" in such films as Son of Kong, The Invisible Man Returns, The Mummy's Ghost, and The Bride of Frankenstein.

However, there's a limit to human invention, if not human credulity. Horror films came out with the regularity of a monthly magazine. By the mid-1940s, Hollywood had gorged the public past horror satiety. In a desperate attempt to rejuvenate horror's sagging box office, Hollywood united horror filmdom's monsters (Frankenstein Meets the Wolf Man), a move that slowed down the erosion of box-office dollars but didn't stop it. Feeling that the imaginary horror of a film couldn't possibly compete with the true horror tales of Nazism and World War II circulating in the United States, Hollywood lamely blamed World War II for the continuing plummet of horror's box-office popularity. Finally, horror expired in self-parody as it was exploited for cheap laughs: Abbott and Costello Meet Frankenstein, The Dead End Kids Meet the Spook, and so on. Ironically, a genre in which death was a constant staple died the most unkind of deaths itself by 1945.

After the war, little was heard of horror until the advent of science fiction in 1950, when the genre, like a Phoenix rising from its own ashes, entered its second cycle. With the big Hollywood studios generally abandoning horror like a wounded, dying animal, various small, independent film companies, ranging from the fairly big American International Pictures (AIP) to the ultracheap Astor, became the most consistent suppliers of horror films. The independents shrewdly manipulated and exploited the prevalent fears and changing values of that era. The independents' skillful exploitation of the public's fear of imminent nuclear destruction, for example, gave birth to the "atomic-age monsters," who were either normal living organisms, transformed into mutants by incessant human dabbling in the atomic field (in such films as Colossal Man and Attack of the Crab Monsters), or supposedly extinct dinosaurs unleashed from their centuries' long "dormancy" deep below ocean floors or ice caps because of atomic testing, as in Beast from 20,000 Fathoms.

More subtle was the independents' shrewd, artful exploitation of McCarthyism for a generally unknowing audience. Such films as The Incredibly Strange Creatures Who Stopped Living and Became Mixed-Up Zombies, It Conquered the World, and I Married a Monster from Outer Space, although seemingly only crude productions dealing with aliens conquering us and/or infiltrating our very human existence, purposely paralleled (if somewhat indiscreetly) the shocking real-life aspects of McCarthyism. Indeed these films' menacing fictional aliens served as metaphors for the McCarthyite vision of Communists infiltrating and conquering our land.

The second cycle of horror was a time of high exploitation as the independents specialized in making quick contemporary horror films, all of which had an assured profit potential because of minuscule budgets and sensationalized advertising. In fact, AIP, in many cases, just made up an advertising campaign, and if they liked the campaign's look, they then made a film (usually in three to six days) pertaining to the poster's theme. As noted film historian Leslie Halliwell claimed, in The Film Goer's Companion, "Such crude and shoddy productions cheapened the genre considerably." Perhaps they were "crude and

shoddy," but they were attuned to their audience's whims, and the independents keenly sensed that with the advent of fast cars and rock 'n'
roll, the mood of its basically youthful audience was undergoing a dras-
tic shift. Thus began the recycling of familiar horror-film monsters
into "romantic villains" in such films as I Was a Teen-age Werewolf
and I Was a Teen-age Frankenstein, whose heroes were misunderstood
and inarticulate but, not uncoincidentally, sympathetic and identifiable
to these films' chiefly youthful audiences, who had the same problems
as these monsters; even less uncoincidentally, these monsters were irritants to authority, just as their youthful audiences were. By shrewdly
exploiting this new significance of the teen-ager, these independents
helped establish the now famous "youth market."

It was during this reincarnation of "old-time" monsters that the
genre was ushered into its third cycle as it looked on its old saviors to
return it to the prosperity that it had once tasted. In 1958, Hammer
Films, a small, fledgling independent film company, released Horror of
Dracula (with Christopher Lee and Peter Cushing). It was essentially a
remake of the 1932 Dracula with an authentic gothic look, a bold style,
and a new permissiveness in "screen blood." Buoyed by the film's enormous success, Hammer recycled other horror films of the 1930s (Evil
of Frankenstein, Curse of the Mummy, Curse of the Werewolf). AIP
also delved into gothic horror with the release of The Pit and the Pendulum (very loosely based on Edgar Allan Poe's story and featuring
Vincent Price) as a counterpunch to Hammer. The success of this
movie compelled AIP to go through a wild rummage of Poe: Masque of
the Red Death, The Oblong Box, The Raven, and others (all with Price).
Interestingly, horror was once again spawning its own stars, as the
names of Price, Lee, and Cushing became synonymous with horror. An
explanation for this new and sudden fixation on "old" values might be
linked to the presidency of that era. Just as America saw in the JFK
administration the past pleasant virtues of Camelot, so may people
have sought in Hammer's films the past virtues of the old horror
"look."

It was during the third cycle that the major studios returned, opting
for a more bold type of horror that often paralleled reality--Whatever

Happened to Baby Jane? (mental illness), The Collector (sexual perversion), Repulsion (sexual obsession)--rather than the costumed period pieces of the independents. It was also during the third cycle that
blood and fairly explicit violence were used or, as director Don Sharp
said in a recent interview in Fangoria on the subject of Hammer
Films: "They'd got into the pattern of making each film a bit bloodier
than the one before it." It was with Alfred Hitchcock's Psycho in 1960
that horror achieved a new permissiveness in the limits on screen violence, as that film would forever shatter the invisible line of what was
and was not acceptable on the screen.

In 1968, that line was further annihilated when a small independent, Laurel, released the ultragraphic Night of the Living Dead. This
film, which went unrated by the Motion Picture Association of America, signified the beginning of the fourth cycle, a period in which both
the major studios and independents prospered and screen violence was
given a new definition because the newly imposed film ratings freed
movies from their hitherto self-imposed censorship. Perhaps this new
permissiveness mirrored the fact that our society at the time equated
carnage with horror, what with television daily invading living rooms
showing the grisly effects of the Vietnam war. After seeing such real-
life bloody carnage in their homes, perhaps the public could no longer
accept the quaint gothic horrors of the past.

During the mid-1970s, the major studios seemed intent on reflecting
our ecological worries in such tales of ecological revenge as Jaws,
Orca, and The Swarm and became fixated on the supernatural (The Exorcist, The Omen, Carrie). Meanwhile the independents successfully
forayed into a variety of unusual subjects, including the return of Dracula and Frankenstein in the most unlikely of vehicles, such as Bla-
cula, Andy Warhol's Frankenstein, and Ilsa: She-Wolf of the SS. It was
in 1974, as the independents continued to create unusual formulas for
success, that the highly successful, ultraexplicit Texas Chainsaw Massacre was released. This film not only set a new precedent in screen
violence but created a formula (the indestructible killer) that still saturates the independent horror-film market today (Friday the 13th,
Maniac!, Madman). This type of film has been affectionately dubbed
splatter film by its fans, for obvious reasons.

One thing is certain: whether the monsters come from graveyards, outer space, or oceans, or are just plain homicidal psychotic killers, horror films, like the monsters they dramatize, will not die, and as the twentieth century continues to evolve, horror films will reflect our changing preoccupations.

Consolidating

Words, sentences, and whole passages often need consolidating to make a stronger impact. Consolidating occurs when the writer brings together ideas that in the rough draft were scattered throughout a sentence, a paragraph, or the entire essay. This scattering weakens the effect that the writer wishes to make by diluting the impact, whereas consolidating the material strengthens it by creating a concentrated effect.

Consider this sentence: "The health effects of all the different chemicals ingested by animals are well documented by impartial M.D.s, so this is not just hearsay from ASPCA people or the like." This is not a bad sentence as it is, but consolidating the two clauses on the health effects creates a more focused effect: "That animals' health is affected by all the different chemicals they ingest is not just hearsay from the ASPCA but is well documented by impartial M.D.s." (Refer also to the section on sentence combining on pages 197–206 for the different ways in which sentence elements can be consolidated.)

Consider the following introductory paragraph to an essay on fraternal orders:

As a youngster, I remember watching such shows as The Honeymooners and The Flintstones, during which, on many occasions, the main characters tried to deceive and lie to their wives in order to go bowling or play cards with their brother lodgemen. The lodges or fraternities that these men belonged to had funny names like "The Raccoons," which Ralph belonged to in The Honeymooners, and "The Loyal Order of Waterbuffaloes," which Fred was a member of in the Flintstones. All the members wore funny hats and had ridiculous handshakes. Unfortunately, that is where my education and that of many others about fraternal organizations began.

Although this first version presents some effective details, consolidating the information makes a stronger impact on the reader:

In order to go bowling or play cards, Fred Flintstone lied to his wife about his destination. Then he donned a funny hat and, with a ridiculous handshake, joined his brother lodgemen at "The Loyal Order of Waterbuffaloes." Ralph, in <u>The Honeymooners</u>, also had to stoop to deceit in order to participate in the activities of "The Raccoons." Unfortunately, these shows were where my education and that of many others about fraternal organizations began.

Look again at the final draft of "Horrors," the student essay on pages 250–255. Although on the basis of his peer-group analysis, the writer had consolidated much of the material that appeared in his rough draft (pp. 237–241), what additional consolidation might he have made? What segments of his sentences, paragraphs, and the whole essay might he have brought together to make his point more strongly?

Editing

Consolidating.   Consolidate words and phrases that ramble aimlessly in order to achieve a stronger impact. Why say "thin and sickly" when you can write "emaciated"? Or why write "Carrying the football, I lunged forward, the ball tucked snugly under my arm," when "I lunged forward, the football tucked snugly under my arm" consolidates your material for a sharper effect?

Style.   Review your essay with an eye to adjusting your style so that you have presented your ideas as clearly as possible. Are there sentences or phrases or words that you need to simplify? Might you turn a verbal sentence into a nominal one in order to focus your reader's attention on an abstract point? If you have employed figurative language, have you done so judiciously?

Mechanics.   Once again, review earlier samples of your writing in which mechanical errors have been noted, then check your draft for spelling punctuation, and grammatical errors common to your writing. Work with the handbook in the back of the book, if necessary, to make corrections.
   Now review and edit your rough draft.

BECOMING AWARE OF YOURSELF AS A WRITER

You might want to make use of your journal to record your thoughts and feelings about the task for this chapter. As you write in your journal, consider the following questions.

1. How did you use your media experiences in generating ideas for this essay? How did you obtain your sources of information?

2. Was the information you provided sufficient for your audience to understand your subject? What kind of information could you have added? If you had offered more information, how would it have helped your audience?

3. Did you find that the ability to generalize was of help to you when you sought to convey information to your audience? What purpose did the generalization serve?

4. How specifically were you able to support the generalization on which you based your essay? What concrete examples or details did you use?

5. What would you say are the major characteristics of a public voice? How would you differentiate your public voice from the private voice you used in writing about yourself?

6. How would you characterize the style of writing that comes most naturally to you? Did you find it necessary to make adjustments in your style in order to write an effective explanatory essay? What kind of adjustments did you make?

7

Writing About Research

PURPOSE

You enter a large room. You observe that approximately thirty males and females, mostly between the ages of eighteen and twenty-one, are seated facing a wide wall with a gray slate board mounted on it. In front of the wall, an adult male is seated behind a wood-grained metal desk. The young people in the room are looking directly at the seated male, who is speaking to the entire group. Occasionally an arm rises, followed by a comment from the person whose arm was raised. After about an hour, the adult male stops speaking, begins to collect his books and papers from the desk, and stands. Shortly after, the young people stand and walk toward the door.

Because these observations are so familiar, you don't have to think long before deciding on a generalization that explains the situation just described. Somewhere during your reading of this paragraph, the details cohered into a single conclusion: this is a description of a class. The process of reasoning that leads us to this conclusion is called *induction*. Induction is one of the major methods through which we arrive at the meaning of our observations and experience, providing us with a technique for verifying what we decide is the factual truth. Scientists in the laboratory and in the field use induction to arrive at conclusions about phenomena in nature and in society.

In this chapter, we will ask you to write with the specific purpose of explaining to your reader the nature and meaning of scientific conclusions on a topic of your choice; that is, we will ask you to write on interpretations of certain observed phenomena that can be accepted as valid because they have been verified by the experimentation of scientists and are convincingly explained according to the standards of accepted scientific discourse. Your task will be a research paper on a scientific subject organized according to the principles of inductive reasoning. Inductive reasoning relies on the assumption that collected data—the products of observation or experimentation—can produce reliable explanations of the physical world, provided that the data are relevant to the problem under consideration. The writer who wishes to provide valid scientific explanations must be able to produce evidence and to draw conclusions from it that the reader will recognize as "scientific" and thus will accept as valid.

In fulfilling the writing task in Chapter 5, you relied solely on your own powers of observation to give you authentic information on a place or an ongoing event. And what gave power to these observations was the use of the classical questions. These questions provided you with a mental framework on which you could construct your case. In this chapter, your emphasis will be on the implications for scientific inquiry contained in the questions "What examples are there of it?" and "What conclusions can we draw from these examples?" Whereas, in Chapter 6, you also responded to these questions, there you cited examples to support a generalization about the value of some knowledge that you possess. Here we will ask you to discuss scientific ideas arrived at by the scientific method. You will want to explain both examples and conclusions in a way that gives credibility to your method of investigation. You also will want to present a hypothesis or explanation that is meaningful, one that does not conflict with the accepted scientific model of the physical world. You could not expect to offer convincing evidence that there are unicorns in the municipal zoo or that the sun will literally rise or set tomorrow. Following from your reasonable hypothesis, you will need to provide, through your research, examples of investigations or experiments performed by scientists that pertain to your subject and that, taken together, prove your hypothesis: You will answer another classical question: "What has been said about it?" You will also want to know the methods that are used to create a piece of scientific research: finding and evaluating information; arranging materials into a meaningful, logical form; employing the conventions of scientific documentation; and using the voice and tone of objective discourse.*

Although your emphasis will be on using scientific materials, the methods of research that you employ to investigate your topic can be applied to many other subjects. Many subjects are assigned in college with the assumption that

---

*We are using the term *research* in two not unrelated ways: one refers to your research into the work of others, or academic research, and the other refers to the research of scientists in the laboratory or field. Essentially your task will be to research the research that scientists have done, and to use the inductive method in your presentation.

the student has the knowledge and the skill to apply certain methods of investigation to solving problems. A knowledge of the process of induction can lead you to insights in unexpected areas. One of these areas is simply your own personal observation. Although this is not on the same conceptual level as research performed in a laboratory, your informed observation of, for example, students applying for jobs at the college employment office is a method of arriving at an inductive understanding of the job prospects for potential college graduates. Similarly, an interview with the employment counselor, in which you learn that employment opportunities for liberal arts graduates have declined by 20 percent in the past five years, will give you inductive evidence for coming to a conclusion about where the future job opportunities will be found. You can then support these findings with the research you have done in books and periodical articles that investigate the topic of employment opportunities for college graduates. Through the combined use of library research, observation, and interview, you can arrive at a conclusion that is the result of original investigation.

Our brief discussion of the kind of discourse we recognize as scientific implies the existence of an audience for whom this discourse is intended. A scientific audience may be one that is interested primarily in the practical application of scientific principles (as in magazines like *Popular Mechanics* and *Popular Electronics*), or one interested in the explanation of current research and scientific theory for the science-educated nonspecialist (as in *Scientific American* or *Science*), or the audiences for the many specialized and highly technical publications in which such professional scientists as nuclear biologists or enzyme chemists report the results of their experiments. As we move up the pyramid of complexity, the audience becomes smaller and smaller, so that at the highest levels of abstraction only a relative handful of readers is capable of evaluating and validating the writer's conclusions. In the audience section of this chapter, we will discuss the kinds of audience to whom you might direct your investigation, as well as the nature of the discourse that you will want to adopt.

When you write in order to explain, you want to take into account other important elements of the writing process. In dealing with a large number of ideas or relevant examples, you are faced with the need to organize your materials and to form a preliminary framework on which to arrange them so that they can be presented most logically and efficiently. This outline also functions as a kind of screen on which you project the order of your evidence and the conclusions that result from it. You can then begin to see the emerging direction of your paper. The result of this process can be a paper that is credible and convincing. Although you will not be expected to make an original scientific discovery, you can, through the act of synthesizing (or combining already existing materials into a new arrangement), create a discourse that has the authority of skillful, objective research. You can lead your reader to a new insight.

GENERATING IDEAS THROUGH INDUCTION

In a sense, induction is not really a formal method of inquiry but an ongoing process of perception that gives us knowledge of the external world by imposing an order on the rush of sensations that we constantly experience. The more experiences we have and then file away in our active memories, the more order and understanding we can bring to bear on future experiences. Further experiences cause us to test the validity of our past experiences, and if necessary, we revise our mental maps to take into account new or additional information. Just as physical sensations must leap across nerve cells before they can be transmitted to our brains, experiences must undergo a kind of "leap," an inductive leap, before we can arrange them into a pattern of meaning.

If during several days of going from a dimly lit building into bright sunshine, you found the bright light dazzled you each day in succession, the chances are quite good that it will continue to do so unless you prepare for it in advance. One day you get the idea to put on your sunglasses just before you emerge from the building. You have reasoned from particular experiences and arrived at a general conclusion: sunlight dazzles. Further observations may cause you to refine your conclusion: Some days the sky is cloudy and the sun shines through only intermittently; if you leave the building on such a day, you might not need sunglasses. Or you calculate that if you leave after a certain hour, the sun will have shifted and will no longer dazzle your eyes when you emerge from your usual exit. In fact, there seem to be an endless number of variables that affect your actions, many of which you don't even give conscious thought to because they are so habitual.

Of course, we base our conclusions on a certain degree of probability. Although we cannot be absolutely certain that the sun will emerge tomorrow, we can be pretty sure that it will and that it will appear to rise in the east and set in the west. Our reasoning requires that we base our inductive leap on a limited but *adequate number of examples*. You can't be sure that the last pair of pants on a department-store clothing rack has a price tag on it, but if the other twelve pairs on the rack have such a tag, you can reasonably expect the last pair to have a tag. After you noticed that the first eight or ten pairs of pants had a price tag, you reasoned inductively and concluded, "All these pants have price tags." If you then decided to generalize further, claiming, "Every item in this store has an attached price tag," you would be guilty of making a *hasty generalization*. How can you be sure that every item has a price tag attached? Would you check every item in the store, spending the next two years of your life moving from department to department? Well, certainly not, but you might decide to check a number of items in every department, taking what you estimate to be a *representative sampling* of items in the store. And you must not avoid counting departments like fine china or baked goods, where you suspect that many dishes and pastries don't have attached price tags, for such an omission would indicate a tendency on your part to exclude *unfavorable evidence that would negate your conclusion.* You don't want to *distort or falsify your evidence* either, for again, that would put your conclusion in question. Finally, you must *evaluate your evidence for the reliability of its sources* to determine whether your conclusion is based on reliable information.

One source of evidence that would seem reliable is our own power of observation. But as was suggested earlier in the example of the "rising" and "setting" of the sun, personal observation is full of pitfalls, offering little assurance that we can always believe what we observe. Consider the account of an early-twentieth-century attempt to demonstrate that animals could perform human mental operations such as counting. Michael Polanyi, in his book *Personal Knowledge,* related the story of the horse "Clever Hans":

> The horse . . . could tap out with his hoofs the answer to all kinds of mathematical problems, written out on a blackboard in front of him. Incredulous experts from all relevant branches of knowledge came and tested him severely, only to confirm again and again his unfailing intellectual powers. But at last Mr. Oskar Pfungst had the idea of asking the horse a question to which he, Pfungst, did not know the answer. This time the horse went on tapping and tapping indefinitely, without rhyme or reason. It turned out that all the severely sceptical experts had involuntarily and unknowingly signalled to the horse to stop tapping at the point where they—knowing the right answer—expected him to stop. This is how they made the answers invariably come out right.

In this incident, we see how strongly observers can influence the results of observation by the strength of their own desire to have an experiment mean what they want it to mean, in effect to "prove" what they already believed at the outset of their scientific inquiry. This example suggests that scientific objectivity—the total impartiality of the observing scientist—is never a simple, unambiguous given that we can assume as the guiding principle of all scientific research, but that it is an ideal (some would say a myth) that needs to be understood in advance by the researcher who uses scientific evidence. Having acknowledged this fact, however, how are you, the student writer—lacking the technical knowledge or the scientific authority to evaluate your sources—to determine whether these sources have a definite "axe to grind"? To a large extent, you cannot. You must rely on the reputation of the authorities—the institution, the author, or the periodical—that stand behind the published results. And you can use the knowledge that you have of the reasoning process to aid you in determining how reliable a given source is, whether it is yourself, someone you interview, or sources that you locate in the library.

SOME PRACTICE WITH INDUCTION

1. Use your journal to record observations that are as objective as possible. Select a place from which to begin observing and recording examples, for instance, the student cafeteria, a bench in front of a bus stop, or the window in your room that overlooks the street. Record the details observed from this vantage point over a period of several days. Try observing the same object but from a different observation point. You might take a photograph of the scene or even tape-record the sounds that you heard for a limited period of time. What generalizations can you make from your observations? Was there any discernible pattern that emerged from these observations?

2. Assume you are a social anthropologist, one who observes the practices of cultures that are strange to us and tries to understand their meaning. Select some ritual of daily life that goes largely unnoticed, for example, a gathering of students at the campus lounge. Write down your observations very carefully, trying not to impose your views on what is taking place. Some other rituals that you might observe are lunchtime at a fast-food establishment or the behavior of customers in a supermarket. After gathering sufficient examples of behavior, arrive at a conclusion about the meaning of the ritual or the pattern of behavior observed.

3. Select a topic about which to poll student attitudes on campus. Prepare a series of questions. Determine what would be an adequate sampling of views and how the respondents should be selected. Next, conduct your poll, collecting answers to your questions from selected students. Evaluate your collected data and make some generalizations about the views of the students who contributed opinions. To what extent are your results accurate as a representation of student opinion? What criticisms might be made of your method of questioning or your sampling of opinions?

4. Basing your opinions on the evidence supplied, explain whether the generalizations in the examples below are valid:

   a. Everyone in the class has had at least one unpleasant experience in dealing with bureaucracies. The class overwhelmingly concludes that bureaucracies are terrible and should be abolished.

   b. In Steve's survey of students who smoke, 67 percent in two classes of business majors smoke, whereas only 48 percent of the students in two classes of English majors smoke. Steve concludes that business majors smoke more than English majors.

   c. When asked by a local newspaper, ten out of ten members of the college administration state that the evening students on campus are satisfied with the college's evening program, as enrollment has gone up from last year. The newspaper says that the unanimous agreement of the administration is conclusive evidence that they are right.

ADDRESSING YOUR AUDIENCE: THE LAY READER

On one of his morning television programs, Phil Donahue had as guests two of the most widely read scientist-writers of our time, Carl Sagan and Stephen Jay Gould. Here were two highly trained, technically skilled university professors explaining theories of evolution to a large television audience. Pointer in hand and standing before a large TV graphic, Sagan explained that all of geological time could be understood if we thought of it as if it were only a one-year calendar. According to this analogy, humankind makes its first appearance about December 25, almost at the very end of the "year." In this way, Sagan tried to show how recently our species had arrived on the planet. It was an imaginative comparison, one that his audience could grasp far more easily than if he had said that the evolutionary process was of several billion years' duration. Certainly Sagan would not have used this analogy if he were addressing a convention of the American Association for the Advancement of Science or a graduate seminar on the origins of the solar system. But for an audience of the scientifically unschooled, this was a highly effective learning device.

As this textbook is being prepared, the public consciousness of science is undergoing a minor revolution. Much of it may be due to the rise of the computer sciences and their startling grasp on the popular imagination. In addition, there are exciting discoveries that have altered our view of human genetics and its effects on the human species.

You need look no further for evidence of this ferment in scientific exploration and discovery than your nearest newsstand. Here are some of the many science magazines now being directed to relatively large audiences:

The Sciences	*Scientific American*
Omni	*Nature*
Science News	*Discover*
American Scientist	*Psychology Today*
Natural History	

Each of these magazines differs somewhat in style and substance. Some are weighted more heavily toward the behavioral and life sciences. Others, intended for a large reading public, are heavily illustrated and tend to focus on the future implications of scientific technology. *Scientific American* and *Nature* make rigorous demands on the reader and often report important new discoveries. All of these periodicals are aware of the level of interest and scientific abilities of their readers.

At the same time that more people are becoming interested in science, the technical language of scientific explanation is becoming more remote from the understanding of the ordinary—even if scientifically educated—reader. Thus the need exists for writers who can explain and interpret the world of scientific discourse in ways that are interesting yet not patronizing to their readers. Stephen Jay Gould, a professor of biology and geology at Harvard University, writes a monthly essay on a variety of biological topics for *Natural History,* a widely circulated magazine published by the American Museum of Natural History in New York. His writing is a combination of human curiosity and penetrating intelligence, supported by a fine writer's eye for the unexpected analogy and the offbeat allusion:

When I was 10 years old, James Arness terrified me as a giant, predaceous carrot in *The Thing* (1951). A few months ago, older, wiser, and somewhat bored, I watched its latest television rerun with a dominating sentiment of anger. I recognized the film as a political document, expressing the worst sentiments of America in the cold war: its hero, a tough military man who wants only to destroy the enemy utterly; its villain, a naively liberal scientist who wants to learn more about it; the carrot and its flying saucer, a certain surrogate for the red menace; the film's famous last words—a newsman's impassioned plea to "watch the skies"—an invitation to extended fear and jingoism.

Amidst all this, a scientific thought crept in by analogy and this essay was born—the fuzziness of all supposedly absolute taxonomic distinctions. The world, we are told, is inhabited by animals with conceptual language (us) and those without (everyone else). But chimps are now talking. All creatures are either plants or animals, but Mr. Arness looked rather human (if horrifying) in his role as a mobile, giant vegetable.

Either plants or animals. Our basic conception of life's diversity is based upon this division. Yet it represents little more than a prejudice spawned by our status as large, terrestrial animals. True, the macroscopic organisms surrounding us on land can be unambiguously allocated if we designate fungi as plants because they are rooted (even though they do not photosynthesize). Yet, if we floated as tiny creatures in the oceanic plankton, we would not have made such a distinction. At the one-celled level, ambiguity abounds: mobile "animals" with functioning chloroplasts; simple cells like bacteria with no clear relation to either group.

Taxonomists have codified our prejudice by recognizing just two kingdoms for all life—Plantae and Animalia. Readers may regard an inadequate classification as a trifling matter; after all, if we characterize organisms accurately, who cares if our basic categories do not express the richness and complexity of life very well? But a classification is not a neutral hat rack; it expresses a theory of relationships that controls our concepts. The Procrustean system of plants and animals has distorted our view of life and prevented us from understanding some major features of its history.

The style and tone of Gould's essay assumes that a reader interested in the subject of evolution and biological taxonomy (classification) need not possess a highly specialized vocabulary nor a graduate degree in order to understand and appreciate the subject. Gould began by recollecting a movie that terrified him as a child. It now suggested to him an analogy of how we divide living things into either plants or animals. This is a "Procrustean system," that is, a limited way to "express the richness and complexity of life." The last sentence points ahead to Gould's main intention: to show how our method of classifying living things prevents us from understanding their real nature.

Although he began with references to himself, Gould's purpose was not to draw attention to the terrors of his childhood or to his taste in films. He was simply using these references as an interesting, colorful introduction to the scientific ideas that are brought into the second paragraph. The author's main purpose was expository, not expressive. He was soon engaged in a serious discussion of the implications of scientific classification. As a scientist, he freely used the language of scientific discourse *(macroscopic organisms, functioning chloroplasts, taxonomists),* yet the overall voice in his language is that of a literate, interested writer making contact with a reader of similar qualities who can also perceive that his is a topic of importance. Both author and reader meet at a level of special knowledge and range of reference that should not be very difficult for a college student to attain.

In discussing a scientific topic in language that will be understandable and interesting to a lay audience, your writing will require the synthesis, or combining, of scientific knowledge into a coherent discussion that presents this knowledge in a convincing way. The language of your discussion must be adapted to the knowledge of the subject that your audience can reasonably be expected to possess. As Gould's writing shows, this approach does not have to result in oversimplification or in trivialization of the subject matter. You should see yourself as the reader's guide through a densely wooded forest, where your familiarity with the trails is the important factor that ensures everyone's safety.

SOME PRACTICE WITH WRITING FOR A LAY AUDIENCE

1. Select three of the science magazines listed in the audience section. Write an analysis of each magazine's intended audience. Does each magazine address its audience successfully? Which is the most successful and why? What changes in each publication would you recommend? How does the format of each magazine (layout, length of articles, amount of advertising, illustrations, special features, and so on) reveal a particular intended audience? How is the language different?

2. Select an author of one of the articles featured in any science magazine named above whose other works are named in the magazine. Look these up in your

college library. Write a brief analysis of the differences between the author's treatment of the same (or different) scientific subject in the magazine article and in the book or more specialized publication in which the writer's other work appeared. What differences in audience do you notice? What differences in research techniques do you notice?

3. College textbooks are excellent examples of how specialized technical material is adapted for a large audience. Analyze your own textbook from one of the natural, physical, or social sciences with regard to the methods it uses to teach technical material to a college audience. How has the author tried to interest students? Has the author been successful? Would you read this book if you were not a student? Contrast this text with another on the same subject and determine which is the more successful. Write a brief report for the department chairman on the book, either recommending it for further adoption or urging that it be dropped.

4. Prepare an outline describing a proposed college science magazine or newsletter. Organize your outline under the following headings: advertising techniques and products, general format of publication, and special features. Briefly explain how this magazine would have special interest and appeal for a college-aged population.

TASK: WRITING ABOUT RESEARCH

Your task for this chapter is to select a subject that you are familiar with, in either the natural or the social sciences; to devise a hypothesis about it based on your present knowledge; to investigate it; to analyze and interpret the materials you find; and to convey your information either as leading to a theory in support of your original hypothesis or to a new or revised interpretation. You will not yourself experiment with your hypothesis, but will synthesize the findings of others, recorded in books and periodicals, with information that you gather through your own observations and from interviews with others who are capable of providing you with authoritative comment on your subject. This synthesis of information will provide evidence that will help you formulate a conclusion.

   In this act of informing your readers by interpreting your findings and those of others, you are engaging in the activity of research. Although this process is one we undergo everyday—say, in the gathering, interpretation, and evaluation of the information needed to find a suitable gift for a friend or to buy a used car—in the more formal discourse of the college and professional worlds, research implies a specific kind of mental activity and a specific form for presenting this effort to others. In many of your college classes, you may be asked to write a paper showing that you understand how to use the methods and forms of academic research.

As a possible approach to the research task for this chapter, you might begin with your experiences with your cousin, who suffers from anorexia nervosa, and then form a hypothesis about the causes of the illness based on your initial observations of your cousin's behavior. In order to test your hypothesis, you will need to gather outside information on the subject, to analyze your sources to find scientifically convincing and acceptable statements on the causes of the illness, and to present your findings in a clear and accurate manner as either validating your own interpretation or indicating a revised or new hypothesis. Or, if you have developed a hypothesis about the effects on society of reduced tax rates for the rich, you might include in your essay the results of an interview with a member of your college's economics department, as well as the information that you acquire from the printed sources.

When you are writing such a paper, it is helpful to imagine an audience that would profit from your findings. An audience of your peers, readers of a college publication, for example, would be interested in the research activity of other students. And a publication that shares the results of such exploration with others would be a genuine source of information that others would profit from. For this task, try writing your researched essay as an article for a college magazine that presents the work of students exploring the natural and social sciences: Your audience will be interested in your findings and will profit from them but will be essentially a lay or nonscientific audience.

The extent of this article is something that your instructor will most likely wish to discuss with you. An investigative paper of approximately five to eight pages, using at least six printed sources, should provide you with an adequate introduction to the methods of inductive research.

In the "Writing the Essay" section that follows, we discuss how to generate ideas, find a topic, gather sources, take notes, organize your evidence, consider your audience, and finally put the paper together.

WRITING THE ESSAY

Using Induction as a Means of Generating Ideas

In writing your paper, it will help to make use of the classical questions "What examples are there of it?" and "What conclusions can we draw from these examples?" Not only will your task require you to provide examples of your topic through the research techniques of personal observation, interview, and library investigation, but you will also want to make some conclusions about the material you have presented, testing them against your starting hypothesis.

The personal observation that you want to include may have occurred before you begin your paper, or you may want to set about gaining such a personal experience after selecting your topic. Your observation may occur, of course, in conjunction with your interview. For example, if you plan to interview a coach for an essay on the group behavior of athletes, you may observe his or her team in action before or after the interview.

In seeking an interview, you need to decide who might be considered an authority on your subject, who would also be available for an interview, for example, a professor, a doctor, or a social worker.

We discuss how to obtain print sources in following sections, but in all cases—observation, interviews, books, and periodicals—you will want to apply the principles of valid induction to the data that you compile. You need, in other words, to gather examples that will constitute a sufficient sampling of evidence (avoid making hasty generalizations) and that will also constitute a representative sampling (do not ignore unfavorable evidence). Furthermore you will want to use reliable sources that, to the best of your knowledge, do not have an ''axe to grind,'' or if all your sources do appear to have subjective or at least differing attitudes, then you will want to make sure to present both or all approaches to the evidence (it is wishful thinking to assume that all scientific research can be interpreted in only one way).

You can then synthesize these data and arrive at your own conclusion, one that may or may not correspond to your original hypothesis.

Because you have already written essays in which you gathered information, interpreted its significance, and presented your results to an audience, you have already acquired much of the experience necessary for taking on the research paper. The major difference is that, in writing this article, you will derive much of your material from sources written by others.

Finding a Topic

Although your purpose is to write an article for a school publication, your topic should be one that interests you as well as others. Will you be able to learn from your topic in the process of explaining it to others? There is little point in writing on a topic that you yourself find uninteresting. But if you have been wondering why your cousin suffers from anorexia nervosa or why punk rockers dress as they do, this might be a good place to begin.

Quite possibly you may be drawn to a topic because you have heard a lot about it, have seen it featured on TV, or have read about it in a magazine or newspaper. Topics like these are often controversial as well; they provide the writer with a certain advantage in catching the attention of an audience. For the researcher, however, controversy poses some difficulty: some topics are so timely that you might have difficulty finding any information other than newspaper stories and a few scattered magazine articles. A subject needs to seep into the public consciousness and to be studied over a period of time before reasoned, reliable books begin to appear. You might be better off writing on a topic that has been the subject of considerable study. Here are some topics that you might find interesting and about which you should be able to find ample recent investigations. Some are fairly broad and, in forming your hypothesis, you will need to focus more narrowly.

Sciences

1. AIDS
2. Herpes simplex
3. Anorexia nervosa
4. Genetic engineering
5. Animals threatened with extinction
6. Toxic wastes
7. Organ transplants
8. The artificial heart
9. Animal intelligence
10. The aging process
11. The discovery of DNA
12. Cancer and diet
13. The debate over cholesterol and the heart
14. Vitamins and health
15. Nuclear power and the environment
16. Hypertension
17. Toxic shock syndrome
18. New diagnostic tools in medicine
19. The origins of the universe
20. Harnessing the sun's energy
21. The future of artificial satellites
22. Applications of laser technology
23. Microchips and semiconductors

Social Sciences

1. Occupational health and safety
2. Measuring human intelligence
3. Computer and child learning
4. Religious cults
5. Changing roles of men and women
6. The new immigration
7. The rise of the Sunbelt
8. Child abuse
9. The Japanese worker
10. Violence in sports
11. Creationism and the schools
12. The attack on psychoanalysis
13. Nursing homes
14. Nurse practitioners
15. Women executives
16. Children of divorce
17. Urban gentrification
18. Phobias: their causes and effects
19. The effect of video games on children
20. The battered-wife syndrome
21. The job outlook for the 1990s
22. Sex stereotypes on TV
23. The value of the hospice
24. Physical fitness: fad or revolution?

Your first attempt to find a topic will often begin with a question: What do I know about the extinction of the great whales? Why are some people subject to severe phobias? What are the most successfully treated malignancies? Not only can a question help to point you to a topic that interests you, it can also guide you through your first crucial choice: selecting a topic that is limited enough so that you can explain it in a short article. Your next step is to form a hypothesis. Your hypothesis will emerge from your reading or hearing about your subject or your own personal observations. For example, you may have observed a natural phenomenon, such as a shooting star or an illness, or read about a social phenomenon, such as the behavior of a cult, and you may have arrived already at a tentative interpretation of some aspect of this phenomenon: A shooting star is in actuality a comet, anorexia nervosa is caused by anxiety, punk rockers are motivated by alienation from society just as the beatniks of the 1950s were. This tentative conclusion is your hypothesis. Whether your hypothesis ultimately proves to be right or wrong is not the point; the point is that, like the scientist, you must begin somewhere. The scientific method begins with the most logical interpretation at the time, proceeds to gather evidence, and then makes a determination based on that evidence. It is the process and the conclusion that attest to a scientist's acumen.

Gathering Sources: Preparing a Preliminary Bibliography

Gathering sources—for many writers the most interesting part of the research process—takes you to the library and sends you through its vast maze of printed materials. Intimidating as it first is for many students, the library soon becomes a place where you feel more confident as you grow to have more and more authority in using its resources.

You might begin by looking at one of the magazines named in the audience section of this chapter. It may give you an insight into a topic that you are curious about or may lead you to a topic that you hadn't really been aware of. To find more magazines, often with more information, consult *The Readers' Guide to Periodical Literature.* For many years, this source has been an indispensable starting point for researchers. Arranged by author and subject, *The Readers' Guide* lists articles in more than 150 periodicals read by a relatively wide audience. For example, if you are interested in the subject of the brain, you will want to begin by looking at recent entries:

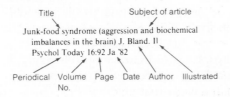

In addition to *The Reader's Guide,* there are a number of reference works that list more specialized articles in periodicals for particular fields in the sciences and the social sciences, such as:

Applied Science and Technology Index

Biological and Agricultural Index

Consumers' Index

Educational Index

General Science Index

International Index

Social Sciences and Humanities Index

Social Sciences Index

For recent developments and past events, a good place to begin is *The New York Times Index,* where you will find, listed by subject, summaries of news articles that have appeared in this important newspaper. Most college libraries have the *Times* in microfilm. Check yours to see if this service is available.

Once you begin to explore sources on your subject, you will need a method for recording essential information identifying those sources from which you will take your data. Although any scrap of paper will do for scribbling down a few words, such as "*Scientific American* May 1980," a more efficient method includes at least a full reference to the author, the title of the book or of the periodical, the title of the article, its date and pages, and some comment briefly stating the contents of the work, along with any identifying number for locating this source in the library. Having this information handy can save you additional trips to the library, especially once you have already begun to prepare your paper. A convenient way to record this information is to write all the important bibliographic data on a separate slip of paper or an index card. These separate bibliographic cards will—along with your note cards (see below)—contain the results of your investigations in the library stacks and periodical sections. Later, you can use these cards to prepare the final bibliography for your completed paper. At this stage of your research, your main concern is to acquire a sufficient number of sources from which to draw your information.

For an article of five to eight pages, you might begin with twenty or more periodicals and books. After some broad reading in your sources—skimming, in the case of books, to find usable material—you will most likely depend mainly on six to eight sources in preparing your article. If you use considerably more than this number, your topic is probably too broad, and you may not be able to organize your information coherently. If you are too dependent on one or two books or articles, you probably will write more of a summary or a report than a paper that investigates a variety of sources and synthesizes information to form a new whole. There is no formula for determining the right number of sources to use, but too many or too few tend to produce an uninteresting and unsatisfying paper.

Rorvik, David M. *Your Baby's Sex: Now You Can Choose*. New York: Dodd, Mead & Co., 1970.

— background of preselection
— research of L. B. Shettles
— effects on population control

QH 309
R 54

BIBLIOGRAPHY CARD

Taking Notes

Taking notes from your sources is one of the most important steps in preparing your paper. Not only are you recording information, but by turning another writer's language into your own, you are also selecting, analyzing, and interpreting this material with an eye to how it will be made into your own continuous discussion. You need to decide as you are reading over your material what is likely to be important to your topic. You can't always be certain that a particular passage will be of value, but it is better to take more notes than you will actually need than to realize later that some material that you decided not to take down was quite important. Nor can you rely on the duplicating machine to do your note-taking for you. Certainly duplicating is useful if you want to spend more time with materials like periodical articles or reference books that you cannot ordinarily take out of the library. But you will then still want to take notes from your information. Underlining or annotating the text of an article cannot substitute for extracting specific passages for quotation or summary and arranging them under subject headings that will later become the organizing plan of your article.

For your notes, you will want separate slips of paper or index cards. Because you will already have written the complete bibliographic information on a separate card, you will need only to write some identifying word, usually the

> *New developments on the horizon*
>
> Ray, 76.
>   Scientists experimenting with pills that stop one type of male sperm production
>
> Rorvik,
>   Shettles is experimenting with insemnation high into the cervical canal. The more motile male sperm reaches the egg first. He feels he can achieve a 90% success rate. Female sperm can be preselected since they are stronger and survive after aging for days in a petri dish.

author's last name, on your note card. You can leave room at the top of the card for a subject heading if you aren't sure at this time what your headings will be. If you are quoting directly, you can write the page number(s) next to your quotation. The quotation must be exact. If you wish to omit words or sentences that are unnecessary for your purposes, you can show this through the use of the ellipsis (see "Handbook," pp. 469–470).

A note card is more effective if it is limited to a single note. Even if you are taking notes from the same page of an article or the same chapter of a book, the quoted information may actually pertain to more than one of the main subjects of your paper. If you remember that you are always trying to anticipate how you can have ready access to your information when you are writing your paper, you will not bury a note in such a way that it will be difficult to find later. Efficient notes, for example, cannot be lumped together on a large notebook page. Also, because you will be taking notes from many sources, you will probably not want to copy lengthy quotations from all of them.

You will want to make sure to quote carefully and exactly the text you wish to use. Sometimes you may want to quote an author who has narrated a distinctive anecdote or has summed up his or her main purpose clearly and succinctly. Or perhaps an author has made a far-reaching conclusion that you would like to use as part of your closing paragraph. These are legitimate uses for quotations. Most of the time, however, it is best to use direct quotations—especially extended ones—sparingly. Therefore you may find it useful to develop the habit of combining these methods of taking notes: quotation, summary, and paraphrase. A summary is a substantially reduced note that records information that you may want to include in your paper but that you don't think

Values to preselection

Ray, 77
    Couples can limit family size to the children they desire. They can have only one girl if they so choose. This element of choice has important implications for limiting population growth.

PARAPHRASE

is necessary to quote directly. A paraphrase, like a summary, is written in your own words, but, unlike a summary, it approximates the form and content of the original. Whether you quote, summarize, or paraphrase, it is essential to refer to the source of your information in your footnotes, so you will want to be sure to take down the page numbers of all such material that comes from

Sperm separation

Pinkel, 904
    "The only ... difference on which to base sperm separation is chromosomal constitution." In mammals, sperm with X chromosomes result in females; Y chromosomes in males.

QUOTATION

your sources. Failure to provide such required documentation is plagiarism, a practice that many students imperfectly understand.

Many students feel that direct quotations are evidence enough that they have used specific sources. Actually this is not true. Anytime you use information that is not your own, you must credit your source. Paraphrasing or summarizing outside source material accurately (making sure to note the specific source and page numbers of your information) is one way to avoid using others' writings as if they were your own. In response to the student who asks, "You mean my whole paper will be continuous footnoting, as everything in it comes from other sources?" the answer is, "Yes, you will obviously need a large number of footnotes, but every statement or sentence need not be footnoted individually. Often one footnote will do for a series of sentences from one source." Remember also that your task for this writing assignment makes use of your own direct observations, interviews, or surveys of others who can provide you with information. This material also requires documentation, which will be discussed in the "Focus" section of this chapter.

Working through this stage in your task, you will accumulate a substantial number of notes, with some direct quotations that you think are highly informative, distinctively worded, or illustrative of some main idea that you intend to explain. Your next task will be to examine your notes and subject headings to see how they can be organized into a meaningful plan or outline. This plan, which forms the skeletal structure of your paper, will then be followed as you begin your first draft.

Outlining

An outline is the pattern of meaning that emerges from the body of notes you have taken. After you have given much thought to your notes and the main ideas under which you arranged these notes, you will begin to see how these main ideas are related to one another and which main ideas should precede or follow others. In other papers that you have written, you performed the same kind of organizing operations. But in a research paper, with its larger number of facts and statements, the need to organize in detail is essential. During the course of your research, you may find it helpful to make several outlines, beginning with a broad overview of your topic and ending with a more detailed plan once the direction of your investigation becomes clearer. At first you might write a broad outline such as this:

Topic: Choosing the sex of an unborn child

  I. Introduction

  II. X and Y chromosomes

III. Recent experiments

IV. Effects on society

After you have organized your notes, perhaps even gathering more information to fill what you think are gaps in your research, you will want to prepare a more detailed outline. This outline, listing the main topics of your article, as you foresee them emerging during the course of your writing, actually shows you what the paragraph structure of your paper will be. Each main topic or subtopic of your outline shows you that one paragraph or more will be needed to explain this idea. And the words that you use in your outline to describe each topic can later become the topic sentences for these paragraphs. Thus, when you prepare a fairly detailed outline, you are actually beginning the first draft of your paper. Here is a more detailed version of the previous outline, revealing a more advanced stage of a student's plan:

CHOOSING THE SEX OF AN UNBORN CHILD

I. Introduction
   A. Couples have always desired to choose the sex of their child
   B. Values to society of preselection
   C. Failed methods

II. Methods for choosing the sex of an unborn child
   A. The basis of all theories of sex determination: X and Y chromosomes
   B. The research of L. B. Shettles into X and Y chromosomes
      1. Differing sizes of X and Y sperm cells
      2. Need for ways to separate boy sperm from girl sperm
   C. R. J. Ericsson separated sperm for the first time
   D. S. Langendoen developed dietary programs for women prior to conception
   E. Selective abortion

III. New frontiers in the science of preselection

IV. Conclusion: Effects of preselection on society

In this outline the student has divided her plan into four main sections. Part II, the longest part of her paper, has been divided into five subtopics, one of which has been subdivided into two parts. Notice that each time you create a subheading, you need to supply two subtopics. For every A, there must be a B; for every 1, a 2. Notice also that each major division is indented to show that it is subordinate to the topic above. This student may yet modify her outline as she continues to organize her information and revise the plan of her article. But in preparing a fairly detailed outline, she has begun her next step, writing the first draft of her paper.

Considering Your Audience

When you begin to write your first draft, you will need to remind yourself that your audience comprises the teachers and students of your college. Although some of them may be quite well informed on your topic, many of them will not know the more detailed information that you present to them. In addition, you are including in your paper personal observations and interviews (possibly with some of these very same faculty) that will make your article an original piece of research.

This inclusion of your own experience, however, can create a difficulty when you address an audience for the task in this chapter. In earlier chapters, you were encouraged to write about yourself and your observations in a vivid, often imaginative style. In this chapter, however, you will need to restrain your expressive language, writing instead in a more objective, expository manner. Your purpose is to let the force of your material, gathered inductively, convey to your audience the importance of your subject and the validity of your conclusion. Although you may wish to explain to your audience scientific or psychological concepts that you have obtained from technical or specialized sources, you will want to explain these ideas in as nontechnical a way as possible, but without simplifying the material to the point where your audience will find your discussion superficial. You will want to avoid the use of jargon terms but to recognize also that there may be no substitute for some of the language of your sources. Most important, your purpose is not to try to direct attention to yourself. Because you are writing to inform your audience on a subject that they will find worthwhile, they will tend to believe what you say if you appear to be an objective, informed guide to the material you present.

SOME PRACTICE WITH RESEARCH METHODS

1. To write a paraphrase of this paragraph, fill in words that would adequately substitute for those in the original source.

The fast-growing field of research has even been given a new name—psychoneuroimmunology—and is finally beginning to win the respect of the modern medical establishment, which despite physicians like Dr. Osler, had scorned or ignored previous suggestions of a strong mind–body link. Many of the studies are now being supported by various branches of the National Institute of Health. More and more, as Dr. Osler recognized, the emotions are being considered necessary components of the cause as well as the treatment of most illness.

The quickly developing area of _____ has been _____ psychoneuroimmunology and is at last starting to _____ of today's medical _____ who had criticized or _____ former _____ of a _____. Much of the research is being _____ by _____ of the National Institutes of Health. Increasingly, as Dr. Osler _____, the _____ are _____ important _____ of the cause and _____ of most _____.

2. Write a summary and a paraphrase of the following paragraphs of an article written by Jane Brody that appeared in *The New York Times*, May 24, 1983.

Nearly a century after some leading physicians first recognized the powerful role of the mind in health and healing, scientists have begun to decipher exactly how stress and other emotional states can influence the onset and course of disease.
   Aided by new biochemical techniques and a vastly expanded understanding of immunology and neurochemistry, their studies show that emotions, acting through the brain, can affect nervous system function, hormone levels and immunological responses, thereby changing a person's susceptibility to a host of organic ills.
   Depending on the circumstances, animal and human studies have revealed that emotional reactions can suppress or stimulate disease-fighting white blood cells and trigger the release of adrenal gland hormones and neurotransmitters, including endorphins, that in turn affect dozens of body processes.

3. Compare the original source with the summary that follows. Did the student fail to change the original wording adequately? How effective will these notes be when the student prepares the paper?

Although the influence of mind on body was well-known to ancient healers and has dominated folklore to the present day, "scientific" medicine has until recently focused almost exclusively on physical causes for bodily illness. Only a few so-called psychosomatic diseases, such as asthma and ulcers, were said to have an emotional basis.
   The new studies strongly indicate, however, that virtually every ill that can befall the body—from the common cold to cancer and heart disease—can be

influenced, positively or negatively, by a person's mental state. By unveiling the mechanisms behind these effects, the studies point to new ways to prevent and treat some of the nation's leading killing and crippling diseases. They strongly suggest that psychotherapy and behavioral techniques should be an integral part of preventive and therapeutic medicine.

Summary: "Brody states that although the influence of mind on body was well known to ancient healers, modern medicine has given attention only to the physical causes of bodily illnesses. New research shows that almost all illness is affected by a person's psychological condition. By unveiling the mechanisms behind these effects, the studies point to new methods of stopping the country's leading illnesses. They show that psychotherapy and behavioral techniques should be considered essential to preventative and therapeutic medicine."

4. Read an article in one of the periodicals named in the audience section. Take notes from this article, making sure to provide complete bibliographic information and subject headings on your note cards.

5. Select one of the topics listed in this chapter and do the following:

   a. Prepare three questions that would give a focus to someone planning to investigate it.

   b. Develop a tentative shaping idea for the topic.

   c. Prepare a broad outline of a paper on this topic.

6. Select one of the topics listed in this chapter and explain how you would begin to investigate it in your library.

7. Prepare a preliminary bibliography of at least six items for the investigative paper that you are writing. Write each source on a separate index card or slip of paper.

8. Select a paragraph from one of your sources. Write a paraphrase and then a summary. How are they different? Compare your paraphrase with the original. Did you change the language sufficiently?

Putting Your Notes Together

In writing the rest of your paper, you will want to take your collected notes and work them into a continuous discussion of your own, based on your outline. It is important to avoid an unbroken chain of quotations, for they will require the reader to sort out the crowd of voices in such a paper. Try instead to turn these other voices into your single voice. That is, clarify in your own mind the relationships among your notes of quotations, summaries, and paraphrases, in order to transform them into sentences and paragraphs that will blend smoothly into a single, coherent discourse.

Here is one student's use of quoted material:

When alcohol begins to take effect in small amounts, feelings of happiness and lightness may occur, depending on the personality, mood, and expectations of the user. Alcohol offers an escape from the pressure and tension of everyday society. As the drinking continues, drowsiness, extreme boisterousness, or depression may occur, along with physiological discomfort. "Most people don't drink because they like the taste or smell of alcohol: they drink because they have been taught to do so by the advertisements and the examples of those around them."[3]

This student's use of quotation is inadequate. The student has not introduced the quotation or shown why it is important. If it were not quoted material but an original sentence, it would simply be incoherent, having no connection to the rest of the paragraph. Furthermore, the information conveyed in the quotation does not seem particularly noteworthy, as its main point—that drinkers are affected by outside influences—seems obvious.

Another student's paragraph reveals other problems in the use of quotations:

"Supporters of lie detector methods insist that the technique is more than 90 percent accurate, that it is difficult for most offenders to deceive an experienced polygraph operator." "Others contend that the polygraph has never been accepted by the scientific community, and libertarians question the fairness of the lie detector, arguing that it unjustly robs a person of his innermost secrets." But its main function is to clear the wrongly accused innocent, not to convict the guilty.

This writer relied on a quotation to provide a main idea sentence for the paragraph. Beginning a paragraph with a quotation leaves it up to the reader to determine what the paragraph is to be about and why the quotation is important. And using quotations in sequence without even a minimal bridge between them creates a paragraph of little value, because the relationship of its parts is not made clear, nor is its connection with the rest of the essay clarified.

In the following paragraph, the writer tried to avoid direct quotation, using it only once, but failed to really assimilate the source material as the sentences don't follow each other very clearly. The paragraph is mainly a series of loosely related facts:

> This pill works after egg implantation and technically produces an abortion. Louise Tyrer, M.D., says that "people should be aware of this." Although this would not be a problem for a majority of people, some would not feel comfortable with it. This four-day pill does not regulate the hormonal cycle. Instead it makes it temporarily impossible for the uterus to absorb progesterone.

In the next example, written by a professional writer, the author has skillfully worked others' material into a continuous discourse. Most of the paragraph is quotation, but through the use of ellipses and by carefully selecting the quoted material, the author has made it part of the structure of his own sentences:

> Viewing the society freshly, students often have a clearer insight into this (. . .) lack of human involvement (. . .) than older adults—though they tend, in oversimplified fashion, to blame it on the institutions. "We have just not been given any passionate sense of the excitement of intellectual life around here," said the editor of the Columbia *Spectator*. A student columnist in *The Michigan Daily* wrote, "This institution has dismally failed to inculcate, in most of its undergraduates at least, anything approaching an intellectual appetite." He spoke of the drift "towards something worse than mediocrity—and that is absolute indifference. An indifference towards perhaps even life itself." "We were all divided up into punches on an IBM card," a Berkeley student remarked. "We decided to punch back in the riots of 1964, but the *real* revolution around here will come when we decide to burn computer cards as well as draft cards."
>
> —**Rollo May**, *Love and Will*

Writing the Introduction

Once you have organized your information and prepared a working outline, you will be ready to begin writing your paper. As you did in the essays that you wrote in previous tasks, you will need to provide an introduction for your reader. The introductions to your other essays probably began with general approaches to your subject and concluded with your shaping idea. In a research paper, you may have to provide a more extensive introduction for your reader as you move from the general to the specific. Perhaps two or three paragraphs might be necessary to state your hypothesis, to give some necessary background to the uninformed reader, and to tell your reader what the plan of your paper will be. How you introduce your subject often determines how much confidence and belief your reader will have in your research. An introduction that makes the subject interesting, gives the reader an overview of the subject, and tells the reader how you are going to present your material will establish your credibility and give authority to your research.

To introduce your subject, you must first identify it, either directly or indirectly. Some questions you might ask yourself when preparing your introduction are

1. Why is my subject important?
2. What has been said about it?
3. What will I limit myself to?
4. How am I going to investigate it?
5. What hypothesis am I going to prove or set forth?
6. How might my subject change in the future?

It is often the practice of a writer to answer these questions in the introduction to his or her investigation. If you can answer them clearly and briefly in the opening paragraphs of your article, you will be able to write the rest of your investigation confident that you will be informing your reader in an interesting and persuasive way.

Writing the Rough Draft

After you have outlined your topic, have arranged your notes in a meaningful order, and have considered the information you wish to convey to your reader, begin your first draft. Make sure that you have exact references for all the sources you wish to cite. If you wish to use direct quotations, be certain that you have copied down the precise words and punctuation of your source. Remember also to use transitions as you move from one section of your article to another.

It is not necessary to divide your paper into sections or "chapters." Because you are writing a relatively short paper, you will be able to write a continuous prose discourse, moving clearly and efficiently from one main idea to the next. You might find it convenient, however, to work on one main section of your paper at a time. Once you finish one section and before you begin the next, reread your entire essay to ensure the direction in which you wish to go: you may find you want to alter your course now that you have actually begun working out your ideas through writing.

Following is a student's rough draft of her research paper. As you read through the paper, you will want to determine whether the writer has used her sources effectively. There should be a smooth transition from the sources to the author's own writing. Paragraphs especially need smooth transitions from one major idea to another. Most important, the paragraphs should flow from the author's own mastery of her sources and information rather than being a string of notes pieced together to form pseudoparagraphs. No less than in the other tasks that you have completed, the voice in the research essay should emerge as coherent, authoritative, and interesting.

You might also want to determine the writer's beginning hypothesis and the extent to which her research supports it. What claims has she made as to the scientific validity of her approach?

NOT THE WEAKER SEX:
A COMPARISON OF GIRLS AND BOYS

For many years "they" have said that little girls are brighter, faster, quicker, and/or smarter, than little boys. Old wives' tales have stated that little girls talk earlier and better than their brothers. Teachers I've spoken to in the lower grades seem to feel that boys don't do as well as girls in the early years of school. No young boys, and few men, will easily admit to this. Most males will dismiss the theory of female intellectual superiority at any stage as nothing but unsubstantiated hogwash. Sorry guys, but it seems that science is not on your side!

Studies have shown that girls begin to talk at an average age of eleven months, while boys do not start speech until they reach about thirteen months. In a study conducted at Our Lady of Victory Home in Lackawanna, New York, the results clearly pointed out this difference. At the age of 15 months, girls were ahead of boys in their verbal skills, and at the age of 27 months, surpassed the boys in social and personal skills. My own observances of children--my own and others--had already convinced me of this. Shortly after their second birthdays, my daughter and her friend were almost obsessed with keeping themselves neat and clean; both little girls could eat in a very civilized, adultlike manner. My sons and their friends at the same age, however, were quite content to live with gray hands and sticky fingers and didn't care if they wore half their meals on their shirts. I also noticed this at a later age, through my work as a Brownie and Cub Scout leader. After snack time was over, the girls, though a much larger group, required far less clean up than did the boys! The Brownies' conversation tended to be more adultlike, with a higher level of complexity and more variety of subject than that of the Cub Scouts. In both groups, the age range was seven to nine.

In a tape put out by the Christian Broadcasting Services, a possible explanation for this dramatic difference is discussed. Studies done by Dr. Donald Joy have led him to believe that these differences are inborn. According to him, as the brain develops in a fetus, both halves grow at the same rate. During the fourth month, those fetuses that are to be boys start producing testosterone, the male sex hormone. Testosterone somehow slows the growth rate of the left hemisphere of the brain. It is the left half of this marvelous organ that controls the main language and learning centers. During the miracle that causes the sexually neutral fetus to become a boy, the brain must suffer a bit--the left half remains slightly smaller than the right side, and the corpus callosum, the connecting wall between hemispheres, develops fewer electro-impulse areas to allow communication between halves. Joy also uses this argument to explain so-called female intuition. The corpus callosum, more well developed in females, allows for a much quicker recall and processing of information; women, therefore, often can make an accurate judgment or decision more quickly than men can. If questioned on how she arrived at her answer, however, the average woman would not be able to tell exactly how she reached it, but would be likely to say something like "I just knew."

The brain works across the body; that is, the left brain controls the right side of the body, and the right brain controls the left side. This fact does give some boys an even chance. Left-handed males tend to be "right brained"--the right side of their brains contain the centers normally found in the left side of right-handed males. There does not seem to be as great a difference between left-handed and right-handed females, which Dr. Joy attributes to the better developed female corpus callosum. Thus, left-handed males tend to be quick to begin speech and can be said to be brighter and more verbal than their right-handed brothers. We can see proof of this in that many of the world's greatest artists, such as Michelangelo, da Vinci, and van Gogh were left-handed, as were our own American heroes Thomas Jefferson and Ben Franklin. It makes no sense to me, then, that the word sinister--meaning wicked, evil, or dishonest--means left-handed in Latin; the lefties mentioned above were anything but evil!

In addition to causing the growth-rate change in the brain that Dr. Joy mentioned, the presence of the hormone testosterone also tends to make males more aggressive, while the presence of the female hormones produces a more passive individual. I think this, too, could be a strong factor in the intellectual differences. Boys must channel or work off their aggressiveness, which can distract them from the learning tasks, while girls, with the more passive tendency, are able to concentrate on and master the tasks more easily.

The superiority does not last indefinitely. Although women do tend to retain the better linguistic verbal and intuitive power, men as well have areas in which they excel. When children reach the age in which math, science, and related fields are taught, boys almost always surpass girls. This gap widens even further at and beyond puberty.

Pediatrician Leonard T. Goslee, in an interview May 3, 1985, told me that little girls have a much greater curiosity than that of little boys. A boy tends to take things pretty much at face value, but a girl will usually probe deeper, especially in more abstract areas. Where a boy might ask, "Why are leaves green?" a girl is more likely to add to that question "How does the tree know it's supposed to make the leaves green and the flowers red?" Dr. Goslee also told me that he has less trouble with little girls. "The boys fight. They don't want shots, they don't want an examination. It can be a real struggle to give a boy a physical, because if he's not willing to go along with it, he'll put up a good struggle. Girls cry. They may cling to mother, they may refuse, verbally, to follow my instructions, but they will go along with what they're told to do, and if I explain what I'm doing, they'll often get interested in the procedures. But they do cry more." Dr. Goslee also told me that boys are much more likely to come in for emergency treatment of cuts, bruises, broken bones, and the like. He feels that girls are more sensible. It isn't too common to find girls doing such things as jumping off roofs or climbing trees as it is to see boys doing these things, and even if a girl is a "tomboy," she'll still hold back and leave the big risks to the boys.

Most of the experts, then, concur. For the first dozen years or so, the average girls do outperform average boys in intellectual and social development. Although the age at which they finally become "even" is about six years beyond that which I first thought, I knew all along that little girls have a clear advantage.

Three teachers and a social worker I interviewed also backed up my theory. All four cautioned against absolutes-- a group study may bear out my findings, but I must never forget that all children are individuals and many boys are competent in the traditional "girlish" areas, and vice versa.

The teachers, Mrs. Argis, Mrs. Cancienne, and Mrs. Denara, were all emphatic in their feelings that little girls were usually more mature and settled into school life more easily. They all think, as experience has shown them, that this tends to be so up until junior high. As stated before, they agree with me that girls excel in the language-related subjects. Both sexes are nearly equal in math and science until about halfway into second grade, then boys jump ahead and stay in front. Mrs. Argis told me that differences disappear as maturity and special interests develop and said "All children can excel in areas in which they have talent, inclination, and perhaps most important, encouragement."

Mrs. Denara and Mrs. Cancienne agreed wholeheartedly with that statement, as do I, but both still feel the female populations of their classroom outshine the male.

Dr. Frank Denara, social worker, feels that, while girls do speak earlier and are slightly more mature at kindergarten and first grade age, any differences from that point on are largely environmental. "In my cases, I have seen brilliant boys and girls ruined by uncaring, disinterested parents, and slower, even marginally retarded kids of both sexes lifted to great heights of accomplishment by parents who fully and unquestioningly believe in their offspring." Well said, Frank. I totally agree that the degree of parental support can make or break an education, but the facts speak for themselves. Nine out of ten speech pathology patients are boys, as are eighty-five percent of the children in need of remedial reading! Girls require much less remedial help than boys until sixth or seventh grade, and then it's almost always in math or sciences!

SOURCES

Argis, Joanne--1st grade, 213

Baby Talk, <u>NOVA,</u> PBS, Videotape Feb. 1985

Cancienne, Margaret--3rd grade, 213

Casler, Lawrence--Supplementary Auditory and Vestibular Stimulation and Effects on Institutionalized Children-<u>Journal of Experimental Psych,</u> Vol 19, 1975 pp. 181-194

Denara, Frank J. PhD--Social Worker, Indiana Co, Penn, interview May 11, 1985

Denara, Cathy--2nd grade, SS. Simon Jude, Blairsville

Goleman, Daniel, <u>Introductory Psychology,</u> second edition, NY, Random House, 1982

Goslee, LT--pediatrician, May 9, 1985

Innate Differences Between Boys and Girls--<u>Focus on the Family,</u> Dr. James Dobson, host, Dr. Donald Joy, guest, Christian Broadcasting Network 1985

FOCUS: DOCUMENTATION

Using the Citation Method

As the writer of an investigative essay, you must identify the sources of your information. You should refer to the books and periodical articles cited in your paper by using "citations" and a list of works cited. A citation includes the author's name and the page number in parenthesis in the text itself. The list of "Works Cited" or bibliography is placed at the end of the essay and includes the name of the source and publishing information. To identify the source referred to, the reader can glance quickly from author and page number to the list of works cited. Here is an example of the citation method:

According to Frank, a mother may not wish to accept the rhythms of her infant (160). A child's development, however, is likely to be shaped by a number of forces, all of them interacting in ways that intensify or reduce the effect of any one of them (Frank 161).

Works Cited

Frank, Lawrence K. On the Importance of Infancy. New York: Random House, 1966.

As this example illustrates, you can either work the author's name into your own sentence or include it in the parentheses. You might also say:

As Frank states, . . . (160).
In Frank's view, . . . (160).
Frank reports that . . . (160).
One investigator notes . . . (Frank 160).

In recent years, the trend has been to develop forms of documentation that are clear, coherent, and simple. In the interests of simplicity and efficiency, this method seems preferable to the traditional method of documentation because it virtually eliminates the need for footnotes and places all the names and page references within the text, where they most logically belong. Your list of "Works Cited," arranged alphabetically, will show your readers all the sources that you referred to in your paper. With some practice, you will be able to work the authors' names into your text without undue repetition.

In your readings in scientific articles, you may have encountered a similar method of documentation. In specialized scientific research, it is common to place the author's name and the date of publication in parentheses: (Miller, 1980, p. 360). Because scientific research changes rapidly, the year of publication would be of great importance in an evaluation of the significance of a specific study. The reader turns from the text to a list of sources following the article to refer to the individual citation. If there is more than one work by an author referred to, the sources are listed by date of publication, starting with the oldest and ending with the most recent.

Before adopting any method of documentation, you will want to make sure that you have discussed with your instructor which form of citation is applicable to your assignment. The traditional or footnote method is discussed on pp. 291–293 and an example of its use can be found on pp. 300–306.

Using a Bibliography

A bibliography is an alphabetized list of works that you have used in preparing your paper. It is placed at the end of your text on a separate page. The bibliography may be synonymous with a list of works cited or your instructor may decide that you can include works that were consulted but that are not cited in your text. The bibliographic citation separates elements with periods and indents the second line. Some bibliographic entries that you are likely to use follow:

1. A book with more than one author:

> Mason, Jim and Peter Singer. Animal Factories. New York: Crown, 1980.

2. An edited book:

> Sacks, Sheldon, ed. On Metaphor. Chicago: University of Chicago Press, 1979.

3. A work with a corporate author:

> Health Effects of Air Pollutants. U.S. Environmental Protection Agency. Washington, D.C.: Government Printing Office, 1976.

4. An essay published in a collection of essays:

> De Man, Paul. "Intentional Structure of the Romantic Image." Romanticism and Consciousness: Essays in Criticism. Ed. Harold Bloom. New York: W. W. Norton, 1970, pp. 65-77.

5. An article in a periodical with continuous pagination:

> Branscomb, Lewis. "Taming Technology." Science 171 (12 March 1971), 963-975.

6. An article in a periodical with separate pagination:

> Begley, S. "How the Brain Works." Newsweek (7 Feb. 1983), pp. 40-47.

7. An article in a newspaper:

Brody, Jane E. "Emotions Found to Influence Nearly Every Human Ailment." New York Times (24 May 1983), Sec. C. p. 1.

8. Interview:

Denara, Frank. Social worker, Indiana County, Pennsylvania. Interview on 11 May 1985.

Using Footnotes

Footnotes—or endnotes, as they are called if they appear on a separate page at the end of the paper—are the traditional method of indicating to the reader that you have borrowed from your sources to back up your statements. The footnote or endnote includes the same information as the bibliographic entry as well as the page or pages of the source from which the material was borrowed. Note, however, that, unlike the bibliographic entry, the first line in a footnote is indented and the elements are punctuated with commas. A footnote number appears twice: once in the text of your paper (where the citation also appears) and again at the bottom of the page of text or on the separate page for notes. Footnotes are numbered consecutively throughout the text. Here is a typical footnote for a book:

[1] David M. Rorvik, Your Baby's Sex: Now You Can Choose (New York: Dodd, Mead, 1970), p. 48.

You should give this information the first time you cite this book. If you refer to it again, you need only give a short note:

[2] Rorvik, p. 49.

For periodical articles, the following would be typical first and subsequent references:

[3] John Lorber, "Disposable Cortex," Psychology Today (Apr. 1981), p. 126.

[4] Lorber, p. 127.

Other sources that you use may require different styles of documentation. Here are some of the possible citations that you are likely to encounter.

1. A book with more than one author:

> [1]Jim Mason and Peter Singer, <u>Animal Factories</u> (New York: Crown, 1980), p. 46.

2. A work without a specified author, often written by some corporate, governmental, or institutional agency:

> [1]<u>Health Effects of Air Pollutants,</u> by the U.S. Environmental Protection Agency (Washington, D.C.: Government Printing Office, 1976), p. 2.

3. A book made up of a variety of essays by a single author:

> [3]Lewis Thomas, "The Iks," <u>The Lives of a Cell: Notes of a Biology Watcher</u> (New York: Viking Penguin, 1974), p. 60.

4. A book made up of a variety of essays by several authors:

> [4]Donald Davidson, "What Metaphors Mean," <u>On Metaphor,</u> ed. Sheldon Sacks (Chicago: University of Chicago Press, 1979), p. 36.

5. An article in a periodical with continuous pagination:

> [5]Lewis Branscomb, "Taming Technology," <u>Science</u> 171 (12 March 1971), 970.

6. An article in a newspaper:

> [6]Jane E. Brody, "Emotions Found to Influence Nearly Every Human Ailment," <u>New York Times</u> (24 May 1983), Sec. C, p. 1.

7. An interview:

> [7]Dr. George Adams, Assoc. Prof. of Anthropology, Danville College, Interview on 20 June 1983.

SOME PRACTICE WITH DOCUMENTATION

1. Write a bibliographic entry for a magazine article entitled "The Compleat Eclipse-Chaser" that appeared in *The Sciences* in the May–June 1983 issue, on pages 24–31. The author is Laurence A. Marschall.

2. Write a bibliographic entry for an article entitled "Nerve Cells That Double as Endocrine Cells," written by W. K. Samson and G. P. Kozlowski. It appeared in Volume 31 of *Science*, the June 1981 issue, on pages 445–448.

3. Write a bibliographic entry for an essay by Loren C. Eiseley named "Charles Darwin." It appeared on pages 283–293 in a collection of essays entitled *Modern American Prose: A Reader for Writers*. The book was edited by John Clifford and Robert Di Yanni and was published in New York by Random House in 1983.

4. Write a footnote for each bibliographic entry above.

5. Write subsequent footnotes for each of the above sources.

REWRITING

Obtaining Feedback on Your Rough Draft

By now, you are accustomed to getting direct responses to your work. Hopefully, you have grown more comfortable in accepting the comments of others, and they have learned to be more specific about their responses. You may find, however, that your audience's reaction to your research article will be somewhat ambivalent. On the one hand, they may be reluctant to criticize a project that has occupied so much of your time and concentrated effort. On the other hand, you may notice immediately by their reaction whether you have adapted your research materials to their understanding. If they're not quite sure about what level of comprehension you were aiming at, you might have to give your approach to your audience some more thought when you revise your first draft.

──── AUDIENCE RESPONSE GUIDE ────

1. What do you think the writer wanted to say in this paper? What is her or his purpose in writing?
2. How does this paper affect the reader for whom it was intended?
3. How effective has the writer been in conveying her or his purpose and meaning? What are the strengths of the paper? What are the weaknesses?
4. How should the paper be revised to better fulfill its purpose and meaning?

Here is a peer evaluation of the rough draft of "Not the Weaker Sex: A Comparison of Girls and Boys."

1. Her peer group agreed that her hypothesis was very clearly stated: She believed in the intellectual superiority of girls over boys in the early years of development. Her purpose was to explain her research to her reader.

2. While one member of the group wished he knew more about developmental psychology, the majority of the group believed the essay was written for a nontechnical audience. As one member commented, "When the vocabulary is somewhat technical, technical terms are explained."

3. The writer received good comments for her research and inclusion of life experiences--her children and their friends-- from every member of the group. They felt she proved her hypothesis. Weaknesses include her reliance on interviews rather than on published studies. Several group members felt she should eliminate her slang.

4. The group felt she should support her research with additional examples from published studies; transitions should be inserted between formal research and personal experience; her language level should be balanced to eliminate slang, jargon, and unnecessary technical words; and her information about her sources should be arranged accurately.

What follows is the final draft of the student's research paper, "Not the Weaker Sex: A Comparison of Girls and Boys." In this final draft, the student has added citations in the text wherever she felt that it was necessary to document the sources of her information. She also has added a bibliography ("Works Cited") at the end of her paper.

Compare the rough draft of the student's research paper on pages 284–288 to the revised paper that follows. You might also want to review the peer group evaluation on pages 284–288, as well as your own response, before doing so. In comparing the two versions, you might look for rewritten sentences that have eliminated wordiness. Are there sentences in the revised paper that still need pruning? What other changes has the writer made in response to the suggestions on pages 306–307 for revising and editing scientific writing?

Following her revised essay, which uses the citation method of documentation, we have reprinted the essay, this time using the traditional footnote method, in order to present examples of both methods of documentation.

Citation Method

NOT THE WEAKER SEX: A COMPARISON OF GIRLS AND BOYS

For many years, it has been widely accepted that little girls are brighter, faster, quicker, and/or smarter than little boys. Old wives' tales have long stated that little girls talk earlier and better than their brothers. Primary-grade teachers I have spoken to seem to agree that boys do lag behind girls in the early years of schooling. No young boys, and few men, will easily admit this, preferring instead to dismiss the ideas as unsubstantiated rumor. As painful as it may be for these males to accept, my experience clearly shows that, until the third grade, girls have a definite advantage over little boys.

Studies of normal children have shown that girls begin to talk at an average age of eleven months while boys generally do not start speaking until two or four months later (Casler 460). Even when children reach the age of three or four, when language is well established, girls' speech is more complex and more easily understandable. In a study taken at Our Lady of Victory Home in Lackawanna, New York, the results clearly point out this difference. At the age of fifteen months, girls were ahead of the boys in verbal skills, and, at twenty seven months, surpassed the boys in social and personal skills as well (Casler 460-461).

My personal observations of children--my own and others--had already convinced me of this. Shortly after their second birthdays, my daughter and her friend were almost obsessed with keeping themselves neat and clean. Both little girls could eat in a very civilized and adult-like manner, and their play involved detailed, coherent conversation. My sons and their friends at approximately the same age were quite content to live with greasy hands and sticky faces, and did not care if they wore half their meals on their shirts. In their play, there was much less real conversation and more pure noise, such as airplane and motor sounds.

I even found this superior development later, through my work as a Brownie and Cub Scout leader. After snack time, the girls, though a much larger group, required far less clean-up time than did the boys. The Brownies' conversations tended to be more grown up, with higher levels of complexity on a wider variety of subjects than those of the Cub Scouts. And though quite common with the boys, there was never a food fight among the girls! In both groups, the age range was six and a half through eight.

Studies done by Dr. Donald Joy have led him to believe that these differences are inborn. According to Dr. Joy, in the early stages of fetal development, both halves of the brain grow at the same rate. During the fourth month, the male fetus starts producing testosterone, the male sex hormone. Testosterone slows the growth of the left hemisphere of the brain, the side that houses the main learning and language centers. During the miracle that causes the sexually neutral fetus to become obviously male, the brain suffers a bit; in addition to the left half remaining slightly smaller than the right, the corpus callosum, the connecting wall between brain halves, develops fewer electro impulse areas. These areas enable impulses to travel across the brain, thus allowing the signals to be transformed into useful information (Joy).

Dr. Joy refers to this as a form of "brain damage," but I think that is much too harsh a term; a better word would be "different." Joy also uses his findings to explain female intuition. Due to the absence of large amounts of the growth-inhibiting testosterone, the corpus callosum is more highly developed in females, allowing for a much more rapid recall and processing of information. This makes females able to reach often accurate judgments faster than most males. Because the process involves virtually no conscious thought processes, if questioned about how she arrived at her answer, the average female would not be able to tell, but would be likely to say something like, "I just knew" (Joy).

The brain works across the body; that is, the left brain controls the right side of the body, and the right brain governs the left. This fact gives some males an even start. Left-handed males tend to be right brained. The right sides of their brains contain the centers normally found in the left brains of right-handed males. Therefore, the linguistic information does not have to shift from one side to the other in order to be used. (There is not such a difference in left handed females, which Dr. Joy attributes to the better developed corpus callosum.) Left handed males tend to speak earlier and can often be said to be brighter, more creative and more verbal than their right handed brothers (Joy). We can see proof of this in that many of the world's greatest artists, such as Michelangelo, DaVinci, Van Gogh, and Picasso, were left handed, as were at least two of our American heroes, Thomas Jefferson and Ben Franklin.

In addition to the growth-rate change Dr. Joy mentioned, the presence of testosterone also tends to make males more aggressive, while the female hormones help to produce a more passive individual (Goleman 530). Boys must work off some of this aggressiveness, which can distract them from the learning task. Girls, with the more passive tendency, are better able to concentrate on and master the task more easily (Goleman 530).

Pediatrician Leonard Goslee, whom I interviewed on this subject, also finds a difference in how children learn. Since his patients are from a wide range of social and economic groups, I asked if there were any major influences due to class differences. He told me that learning cuts through social classes, given that the family lifestyles are normal (i.e., no alcoholic or abusive parents). Little girls, he says, generally have a deeper curiosity.

A boy may ask, "Why are the leaves green?" but a girl is likely to add to that question, "How does the tree know it's supposed to make the leaves green and the flowers red?" Girls tend to make easier patients. Though they may cry more and cling to their mothers, they are more easily convinced to submit to an exam than boys are. Girls are more pliable. Boys are much more likely to need a doctor's care for emergency treatment of broken bones, cuts, and bruises. Girls are much more cautious. It is not as common to find girls doing such things as jumping off a roof or climbing the high branches of a tree. Even if a girl is a tomboy, she is still likely to hold back and leave the really big risks to the boys (Goslee).

Dr. Joy also noted that girls are more cautious, and calls them "more sensible."

I interviewed three teachers--Joanne Argis, Margaret Cancienne, and Cathy Denara--who backed up my findings, though all three cautioned against absolutes. "Though a group study may bear out a theory, you must never forget that all children are individuals, and many boys are competent in the 'feminine' areas, and vice-versa" (Argis). Harold Stevenson confirms this by concluding that what and how much a child can learn depends largely on his or her maturity or reason to learn. There are very marked differences among normal children as to limits of educability (Stevenson 347-350).

Mrs. Argis, Mrs. Cancienne, and Mrs. Denara were all emphatic in their feelings that little girls are usually more mature, and are able to settle into school life more easily than boys. Experience has shown them that this tends to be so up until junior high school age. "Some differences, however, disappear as maturity and special interests develop, and all children can excel in areas in which they have talent, and, perhaps most important, encouragement" (Argis). When I spoke to Mrs. Denara, I mentioned that I was somewhat concerned that she may have different observations because she teaches at a rural school. I was reassured, however, when I realized that many of the textbooks her students use are the same ones my children have used in the New York City school system. "City kids, country kids, they're the same. The little girls are still more mature and more sociable than the boys" (C. Denara).

Social worker Frank Denara thinks that, while girls do speak earlier and are slightly more mature than boys at kindergarten age, any differences from that point on are largely environmental. "In my casework, I have seen bright children ruined by uncaring, disinterested parents, and slower, even marginally retarded kids of both sexes lifted to great heights of accomplishment by parents who fully and unquestioningly believe in their offspring" (F. Denara).

While I certainly agree with Dr. Denara's statement, I still believe that girls start out with an advantage. The superiority does not last indefinitely. Although women do retain an edge linguistically and intuitively, males have special areas in which they, too, excel. When children reach the age at which math and sciences are taught, around third grade, boys begin to surpass the girls. The gap widens steadily up to and beyond puberty ("Baby Talk"). Although girls require far less remedial work than boys do, at least until sixth or seventh grade, when girls do need help, it is almost always in math or science (Joy). Before sixth grade, boys make up the majority of those students needing special help. Nine out of ten speech pathology patients are boys, as are nearly eighty-five percent of the children in remedial reading classes ("Baby Talk").

Most of the experts agree, then, that girls do start out in life with a firm advantage over boys. They are ahead socially and intellectually before they start their formal education, as I had long suspected. I was surprised to find, however, that boys and girls never seem to become scholastically equal. I thought that, by third or fourth grade, any intellectual differences would be purely individual, but my research showed me this is not so. All the way up the educational ladder throughout junior high, there are specific areas in which one sex tends to dominate the other. The "battle of the sexes" rages on!

Works Cited

Argis, Joanne. First grade teacher, P.S. 213, Queens, New York.
    Interview on 11 May 1985.
"Baby Talk." <u>Nova</u>, Public Broadcasting Service. February 1985.

Cancienne, Margaret. Third grade teacher, P.S. 213, Queens, New York. Interview 13 May 1985.

Casler, Lawrence. "Supplementary Auditory and Vestibular Stimulation and Its Effects on Institutionalized Children." Journal of Experimental Psychology, 19 (1975), 456-463.

Denara, Cathy. Second grade teacher, SS. Simon and Jude Elementary School, Blairsville, Pennsylvania. Interview on 11 May 1985.

Denara, Frank. Social worker, Indiana County, Pennsylvania. Interview on 11 May 1985.

Goleman, Daniel, Trygg Engen, and Anthony Davids. Introductory Psychology. New York: Random House, 1982.

Goslee, Leonard, M.D. Pediatrician. Interview on 9 May 1985.

Joy, Donald. "Innate Differences Between Boys and Girls." Focus on the Family, James Dobson, host. Christian Broadcasting Services, 1983.

Stevenson, Harold W. Children Learning. New York: Appleton-Century-Crofts, 1972.

Traditional Method

NOT THE WEAKER SEX: A COMPARISON OF GIRLS AND BOYS

For many years, it has been widely accepted that little girls are brighter, faster, quicker, and/or smarter than little boys. Old wives' tales have long stated that little girls talk earlier and better than their brothers. Primary-grade teachers I have spoken to seem to agree that boys do lag behind girls in the early years of schooling. No young boys, and few men, will easily admit this, preferring instead to dismiss the ideas as unsubstantiated rumor. As painful as it may be for these males to accept, my experience clearly shows that, until the third grade, girls have a definite advantage over little boys.

Studies of normal children have shown that girls begin to talk at an average age of eleven months while boys generally do not start speaking until two to four months later.[1] Even when children reach the age of three or four, when language is well established, girls' speech is more complex and more easily understandable. In a study taken at Our Lady of Victory Home in Lackawanna, New York, the results clearly point out this difference. At the age of fifteen months, girls were ahead of the boys in verbal skills, and, at twenty seven months, surpassed the boys in social and personal skills as well.[2]

My personal observations of children--my own and others--had already convinced me of this. Shortly after their second birthdays, my daughter and her friend were almost obsessed with keeping themselves neat and clean. Both little girls could eat in a very civilized and adult-like manner, and their play involved detailed, coherent conversation. My sons and their friends at approximately the same age were quite content to live with greasy hands and sticky faces, and did not care if they wore half their meals on their shirts. In their play, there was much less real conversation and more pure noise, such as airplane and motor sounds.

I even found this superior development later, through my work as a Brownie and Cub Scout leader. After snack time, the girls, though a much larger group, required far less clean-up time than did the boys. The Brownies' conversations tended to be more grown up, with higher levels of complexity on a wider variety of subjects than those of the Cub Scouts. And though quite common with the boys, there was never a food fight among the girls! In both groups, the age range was six and a half through eight.

Studies done by Dr. Donald Joy have led him to believe that these differences are inborn. According to Dr. Joy, in the early stages of fetal development, both halves of the brain grow at the same rate. During the fourth month, the male fetus starts producing testosterone, the male sex hormone. Testosterone slows the growth of the left hemisphere of the brain, the side that houses the main learning and language centers. During the miracle that causes the sexually neutral fetus to become obviously male, the brain suffers a bit; in addition to the left half remaining slightly smaller than the right, the corpus callosum, the connecting wall between brain halves, develops fewer electro impulse areas. These areas enable impulses to travel across the brain, thus allowing the signals to be transformed into useful information.[3]

Dr. Joy refers to this as a form of "brain damage," but I think that is much too harsh a term; a better word would be "different." Joy also uses his findings to explain female intuition. Due to the absence of large amounts of the growth-inhibiting testosterone, the corpus callosum is more highly developed in females, allowing for a much more rapid recall and processing of information. This makes females able to reach often accurate judgments faster than most males. Because the process involves virtually no conscious thought processes, if questioned about how she arrived at her answer, the average female would not be able to tell, but would be likely to say something like, "I just knew."[4]

The brain works across the body; that is, the left brain controls the right side of the body, and the right brain governs the left. This fact gives some males an even start. Left-handed males tend to be right brained. The right sides of their brains contain the centers normally found in the left brains of right-handed males. Therefore, the linguistic information does not have to shift from one side to the other in order to be used. (There is not such a difference in left handed females, which Dr. Joy attributes to the better developed corpus callosum.) Left handed males tend to speak earlier and can often be said to be brighter, more creative and more verbal than their right handed brothers.[5] We can see proof of this in that many of the world's greatest artists, such as Michelangelo, DaVinci, Van Gogh, and Picasso, were left handed, as were at least two of our American heroes, Thomas Jefferson and Ben Franklin.

In addition to the growth-rate change Dr. Joy mentioned, the presence of testosterone also tends to make males more aggressive, while the female hormones help to produce a more passive individual.[6] Boys must work off some of this aggressiveness, which can distract them from the learning task. Girls, with the more passive tendency, are better able to concentrate on and master the task more easily.[7]

Pediatrician Leonard Goslee, whom I interviewed on this subject, also finds a difference in how children learn. Since his patients are from a wide range of social and economic groups, I asked if there were any major influences due to class differences. He told me that learning cuts through social classes, given that the family lifestyles are normal (i.e., no alcoholic or abusive parents). Little girls, he says, generally have a deeper curiosity.

A boy may ask, "Why are the leaves green?" but a girl is likely to add to that question, "How does the tree know it's supposed to make the leaves green and the flowers red?" Girls tend to make easier patients. Though they may cry more and cling to their mothers, they are more easily convinced to submit to an exam than boys are. Girls are more pliable. Boys are much more likely to need a doctor's care for emergency treatment of broken bones, cuts and bruises. Girls are much more cautious. It is not as common to find girls doing such things as jumping off a roof or climbing the high branches of a tree. Even if a girl is a tomboy, she is still likely to hold back and leave the really big risks to the boys.[8]

Dr. Joy also noted that girls are more cautious, and calls them "more sensible."

I interviewed three teachers--Joanne Argis, Margaret Cancienne, and Cathy Denara--who backed up my findings, though all three cautioned against absolutes. "Though a group study may bear out a theory, you must never forget that all children are individuals, and many boys are competent in the 'feminine' areas, and vice-versa."[9] Harold Stevenson confirms this by concluding that what and how much a child can learn depends largely on his or her maturity or reason to learn. There are very marked differences among normal children as to limits of educability.[10]

Mrs. Argis, Mrs. Cancienne, and Mrs. Denara were all emphatic in their feelings that little girls are usually more mature, and are able to settle into school life more easily than boys. Experience has shown them that this tends to be so up until junior high school age. "Some differences, however, disappear as maturity and special interests develop, and all children can excel in areas in which they have talent, and, perhaps most important, encouragement."[11] When I spoke to Mrs.

Denara, I mentioned that I was somewhat concerned that she may have different observations because she teaches at a rural school. I was reassured, however, when I realized that many of the textbooks her students use are the same ones my children have used in the New York City school system. "City kids, country kids, they're the same. The little girls are still more mature and more sociable than the boys."[12]

Social worker Frank Denara thinks that, while girls do speak earlier and are slightly more mature than boys at kindergarten age, any differences from that point on are largely environmental. "In my casework, I have seen bright children ruined by uncaring, disinterested parents, and slower, even marginally retarded kids of both sexes lifted to great heights of accomplishment by parents who fully and unquestioningly believe in their offspring."[13]

While I certainly agree with Dr. Denara's statement, I still believe that girls start out with an advantage. The superiority does not last indefinitely. Although women do retain an edge linguistically and intuitively, males have special areas in which they, too, excel. When children reach the age at which math and sciences are taught, around third grade, boys begin to surpass the girls. The gap widens steadily up to and beyond puberty.[14] Although girls require far less remedial work than boys do, at least until sixth or seventh grade, when they do need help, it is almost always in math or science.[15] Before sixth grade, boys make up the majority of those students needing special help. Nine out of ten speech pathology patients are boys, as are nearly eighty-five percent of the children in remedial reading classes.[16]

Most of the experts agree, then, that girls do start out in life with a firm advantage over boys. They are ahead socially and intellectually before they start their formal education, as I had long suspected. I was surprised to find, however, that boys and girls never seem to become scholastically equal. I thought that, by third or fourth grade, any intellectual differences would be purely individual, but my research showed me this is not so. All the way up the educational ladder throughout junior high, there are specific areas in which one sex tends to dominate the other. The "battle of the sexes" rages on!

End Notes

[1] Lawrence Casler, "Supplementary Auditory and Vestibular Stimulation and Its Effects on Institutionalized Children," Journal of Experimental Psychology, 19 (1975), 460.

[2] Casler, pp. 460-461.

[3] Donald Joy, "Innate Differences Between Boys and Girls," Focus on the Family, James Dobson, host. Christian Broadcasting Services, 1983.

[4] Joy.

[5] Joy.

[6] Daniel Goleman, Trygg Engen, and Anthony Davids. Introductory Psychology (New York: Random House, 1982), p. 530.

[7] Goleman, p. 530.

[8] Leonard Goslee, M.D., Pediatrician, Interview on 9 May 1985.

[9] Joanne Argis, First grade teacher, P.S. 213, Queens, New York. Interview on 11 May 1985.

[10] Stevenson, Harold W. Children Learning (New York: Appleton-Century-Crofts, 1972), pp. 347-350.

[11] Argis.

[12] Cathy Denara, Second grade teacher, SS. Simon and Jude Elementary School, Blairsville, Pennsylvania, Interview on 11 May 1985.

[13] Denara, Frank, Social worker, Indiana County, Pennsylvania, Interview on 11 May 1985.

[14] "Baby Talk," Nova, Public Broadcasting Service, February 1985.

[15] Joy.

[16] "Baby Talk."

Bibliography

Argis, Joanne. First grade teacher, P. S. 213, Queens, New York. Interview on 11 May 1985.

"Baby Talk." Nova, Public Broadcasting Service. February 1985.

Cancienne, Margaret. Third grade teacher, P.S. 213, Queens, New York. Interview 13 May 1985.

Casler, Lawrence. "Supplementary Auditory and Vestibular Stimulation and Its Effects on Institutionalized Children." Journal of Experimental Psychology, 19 (1975), 456-463.

Denara, Cathy. Second grade teacher, SS. Simon and Jude Elementary School, Blairsville, Pennsylvania. Interview on 11 May 1985.

Denara, Frank. Social worker, Indiana County, Pennsylvania. Interview on 11 May 1985.

Goleman, Daniel, Trygg Engen, and Anthony Davids. Introductory Psychology. New York: Random House, 1982.

Goslee, Leonard, M.D. Pediatrician. Interview on 9 May 1985.

Joy, Donald. "Innate Differences Between Boys and Girls." Focus on the Family, James Dobson, host. Christian Broadcasting Services, 1983.

Stevenson, Harold W. Children Learning. New York: Appleton-Century-Crofts, 1972.

Revising and Editing Scientific Writing

Revising.   As a writer of expository prose who is researching a scientific subject, you will want to be as objective and impartial as possible. In order to help you emphasize your objectivity, we ask questions below that you might apply to your scientific paper. These questions are based on the revising strategies discussed in this section in previous chapters—cutting (Ch. 1), adding (Ch. 2), rearranging (Ch. 3), substituting (Ch. 4), distributing (Ch. 5), and consolidating (Ch. 6).

1. **Cutting.** Have you digested your researched material thoroughly or, on closer scrutiny, have you either repeated points or included points that do not apply? If so, you will want to cut this material from your paper.

2. **Adding.** Have you included all the research on the subject that can affect your decision about your hypothesis? Have you included all the supporting research for your conclusion about your subject? A reexamination of your sources may indicate that you have material that should be added.

3. **Rearranging.** Do your major subdivisions present the material in the most useful order for your reader? Do you present background material first, followed by aspects of the research? Should these aspects be arranged in chronological order or in some other order such as those suggested in Chapter 5 (cause and effect, comparison and contrast, or process analysis)? If you cannot discern any logic to your organization, you may want to rearrange your points so that an order is apparent.

4. **Substituting.** If you have cut questionable points and replaced them with new ones, then you have already engaged in substituting. In addition, you may want to ask yourself if any of the sources you cited are questionable. For example, have you relied too heavily on popular sources or on outdated material? Rather than weaken your presentation by cutting too much supporting evidence, you may want to substitute more reputable or current scholarship.

5. **Distributing.** Have you constantly referred to your hypothesis or have you left it up to your reader to remember what it is? If the latter is true, you may want to distribute mention of it throughout your essay as a way of keeping your purpose clearly focussed for your reader.

6. **Consolidating.** Does your essay seem scattered because aspects of your major points reappear throughout? If so, gather them together and present them in one section. Have you made your points as forcefully as you would like? If not, it may be that you have not given sufficient information to establish their significance. If this information is elsewhere in your essay, consolidate it around your point for greater emphasis.

Editing. In writing on a scientific subject, you will want your language to be as clear and concrete as possible. You will want to define all technical terminology for your reader and for yourself as well to insure that you use all scientific terms accurately. You might also review the Focus section on Style in Chapter 6 for other suggestions about how to make your style concrete, such as the use of verbal sentences.

You will also want your language to be appropriate for your subject. You will want to avoid slang on the one hand because it is too informal for your subject and figurative language on the other because figures of speech do not meet the criteria of clarity and concreteness discussed above. You will probably want to avoid humor also because it may detract from your goal of impartiality. You may also want to write in the third person pronoun, rather than the first, in order to further convince your reader of your objectivity.

Finally, you will want your language to be economical. By eliminating "deadwood," you can pare your writing of words that are repetitious or add nothing to the sense of the sentence in which they appear. Below are some examples of how to make your writing sharper by getting rid of deadwood.

Eliminating Deadwood

> In my considered opinion, in the area of accuracy of steering, this driving machine performed in an erratic manner due to the fact that the road was of a wet condition. It is recommended by the inspector that in such a definitely damp and humid weather situation, the vehicle operator act in a manner that exercises extreme caution.

What is wrong with this language? Doesn't it have the sound of authority, of some official writing a report in an official style? If so, isn't it adequate for its intended audience, probably another official? But would the intended reader of such prose, even another inspector, make sense of it? Writers who use such language are really placing a barrier to communication between themselves and their audience. Part of the problem with this kind of writing is that we don't hear the *person* behind the language. Instead there is a mask of pretentiousness disguising a simple statement with lengthy connective expressions ("in the area of," "due to the fact that"); wordy substitutes for common nouns ("weather situation," "vehicle operator"); and the passive voice ("is recommended," "caution is exercised"). The writer wishes to sound important and to appear an expert by avoiding the simple language of clarity:

> Because the road was wet, the car was hard to steer. The driver should be careful when it rains.

In trying to explain, we also have a tendency to reach for an abstraction rather than a simple direct statement of fact. This tendency often results in our emphasizing an abstract noun over a verb, just as this writer did in the previous sentence by writing "have a tendency" rather than "tend." (See the discussion of style in Ch. 6, pp. 242–249.)

The term *deadwood* is a general label for language that obscures the meaning of a sentence. By cutting out deadwood, we sharpen and clarify our language. We learn to be more direct with our audience, more accurate in our choice of diction, and less tentative in our assertions. The writer who says, "In my opinion, I feel that abortion on demand can be considered counterproductive," is avoiding a direct commitment to a point of view. Instead of saying, "Abortion on demand is wrong," the writer tries to hide behind weak, unconvincing language that qualifies every assertion. A writer does not intend to write deadwood; it is a plain reminder to us all how difficult it is to write clearly and concisely.

Deadwood is often the result of awkward sentence structure as well as poor word choice. In this case, the writer must be more analytical, revising the sentence fully. The following sentences show how to revise statements that hinder communication between writer and audience:

Original: This woman who was boisterous and unruly was thrown out of the restaurant, which was French and therefore elegant, and in which we were eating dinner.

Revised: While we were eating dinner in an elegant French restaurant, a boisterous, unruly woman was thrown out.

This sentence was improved by the use of subordination and the omission of unnecessary modifying clauses.

Original: His car which was an antique, black Ford, moved in a creeping fashion toward the other cars.

Revised: His antique, black Ford crept toward the others.

The modifying clause is replaced by adjectives attached directly to the noun. *Car* is replaced by the more specific *Ford.*

Original: The pennant-bound club will seize every opportunity to win. They will hound the pitcher with stolen bases. They will punch singles through the infield. And they will always come through with timely hits.

Revised: The pennant-bound ball club will seize every opportunity to win, hounding the pitcher with stolen bases, punching singles through the infield, and always coming through with timely hits.

Too many separate sentences can be combined into one sentence with participial modifiers. The writer must remember to keep these modifiers parallel. (See discussion of sentence combining in Ch. 5, pp. 197–206.)

Original: Another theory has been set forth by Sally Langendoen, who has based her theory on the works of Dr. Joseph Stolkowski.

Revised: Another theory, based on the works of Dr. Joseph Stolkowski, has been set forth by Sally Langendoen.

Sally Langendoen has set forth a theory based on the works of Dr. Joseph Stolkowski.

In this example, the writer gets rid of repetitive phrasing and also more clearly emphasizes the subject (see also Chap. 1, pp. 14–22 and Chap. 5, pp. 197–206).

BECOMING AWARE OF YOURSELF AS A WRITER

1. How efficient were your methods of investigation in writing the research paper? What was the most helpful method you used?

2. Were you able to use your knowledge of other academic subjects to provide you with material for your paper? If so, how were you able to adapt this knowledge for your audience?

3. Was it difficult obtaining information on your topic? What could you have done to find more material?

4. How skillfully were you able to analyze and interpret the usefulness or validity of your sources? Did you encounter any contradictory information in your sources? If so, how did you decide what to accept or reject?

5. How did you convert your source material into your own words? Were there any rough spots that you found particularly difficult to work on? How would you account for them? How did you solve the problems they created?

6. if you are assigned an investigative paper in the future, might you pursue your research any differently? How might you proceed?

7. How does writing for an audience affect the preparation of an investigative paper? What adjustments did you make?

8. Do you see the writing of an investigative paper as mainly an exercise in acquiring factual information, or are there other skills to be learned? What are those skills? How do you think you can use these skills in other writing that you do?

9. What did the author of the student essay do to avoid making her paper an exercise in "sterile fact gathering"? Would her technique work for you?

IV

Persuasion

INTRODUCTION

Argumentation is perhaps the oldest form of discourse. Before our ancestors were able to form a clear enough sense of their own identity to express it, had time free from their efforts to survive to explore the world, or knew enough about what they discovered to explain their experiences to others, they would have engaged in rudimentary forms of verbal persuasion: this tool over that tool, this method of hunting over that one, my territory not your territory.

By the time of the Greeks, persuasion, which was still the primary form of public discourse, had become very sophisticated, and it is to the Greeks and the Romans, who followed, that we owe much of what we know about persuasive techniques today. Aristotle articulated three areas in which persuasive speakers and writers must appeal to the audience: They must appeal to their logic, their sense of ethics, and their emotions.

In this section on persuasion, we will study these three persuasive appeals. In Chapter 8, we will analyze each of them and present a task in which you are asked to utilize them in supporting an argument of your own. In Chapter 9, you will be asked to analyze several arguments that utilize these appeals in presenting the varying positions on an issue that is particularly controversial in our culture at the present time. You can then apply your critical thinking skills to the issue and attempt to formulate a synthesis of the varying points of view.

While various persuaders have emphasized the emotional appeal over the ethical and logical (advertisers come first to mind) or sincerity over the emotional and the logical (politicians often make this appeal), we can perhaps say that the logical appeal is a necessary ingredient in any successful argument. The Greeks developed the syllogism, a formula for developing logical thinking that provides a litmus test for the logic of any argument we might wish to make. A syllogism is a series of generalizations on a controversial issue to which various tests are applied to determine whether one generalization follows logically from the other and hence whether the argument is valid. The most famous syllogism is

> All men are mortal.
> Socrates is a man.
> (Therefore,) Socrates is mortal.

It is impossible to argue that Socrates is immortal because all men in human history have died; therefore, this is a logical argument.

In Chapter 8, we will discuss how to construct a syllogism that will test the validity of the argument you have chosen for your task; in Chapter 9, we will ask you to apply syllogistic reasoning to the varying viewpoints on a controversial issue in order to synthesize them into one coherent point of view.

8

Writing Persuasively

PURPOSE

In Chapter 8, we turn to a third type of writing, writing that has an aim and purpose different from those of both expressive writing and expository writing. The primary aim in writing to persuade is neither to express the writer nor to explain the subject but to convince the reader of the writer's point of view on a particular issue. In terms of the triangle diagram from Chapter 2, the focus is on the reader rather than on the writer or the subject.

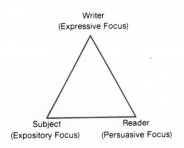

```
                    Writer
              (Expressive Focus)




        Subject              Reader
   (Expository Focus)   (Persuasive Focus)
```

Persuasion, or argumentation, is a common aim in our society. Newspaper editorials aim to persuade, politicians argue their positions in speeches, preachers persuade from the pulpit, advertisers lure readers in the pages of magazines

313

and newspapers. And in our everyday communication with others, we often wish to convince them of our point of view. To learn how to persuade or argue effectively in writing is the purpose of Chapter 8.

The tools of persuasion are the abilities to reason well and to use language effectively. But as you develop these abilities, you should take some care in how you use them to influence others. Often, in our society, the tools of persuasion are wielded as weapons, to influence the public through illogical reasoning and seductive language, as in many political speeches and in much advertising. In its extreme form, persuasion can become propaganda, in which a cause is supported regardless of the merits of the arguments used. When studying persuasive techniques, then, it is important to distinguish, as Aristotle himself did, among the different means of argumentation: You can appeal to an audience's logic, emotions, or sense of ethics. (In fact, a distinction is often made between persuasion and argumentation; the former is defined as an appeal to the emotions, and the latter as an appeal to reason.) When appealing to the logic of your readers, you should be careful to be indeed logical and not to mislead them; when appealing to their emotions, you should be careful not to manipulate them; when appealing to their ethical or moral sense, you should be ethical yourself and not lead your readers astray. Perhaps the best argument includes all three appeals, each a counterbalance for the other. In the "Generating Ideas" section of this chapter, we will discuss the forms of logical appeal, including induction and deduction.

Because the emphasis in persuasive writing is on the audience, we will concentrate in the "Audience" section on how you, as a writer, can establish a relationship with your readers so that you can best persuade them to adopt your point of view. From the outset, you must take care to respect your readers even if they differ from you, and especially if they are ignorant of the subject altogether. You should have their attitude uppermost in your mind throughout or seek to foster a positive attitude if none exists. It is also important that you seek to establish your own credibility as an authority on the subject, as well as your sincerity in presenting your point of view. All the facets of writing to an audience that we have discussed thus far should be brought to bear: understanding the audience's frame of reference, role playing the audience to understand their attitude, determining your voice, and, finally, ascertaining how much depth of information the audience needs about the subject.

The "Audience" section culminates in a discussion of how to appeal to your readers' sense of ethics, and the "Focus" section concentrates on how to phrase your essay in words that will appeal to your audience's emotions.

In the "Writing the Essay" section of this chapter, we present two of the most powerful arguments in American history, the American colonists's "Declaration of Independence" and Martin Luther King's support of his nonviolent tactics in "Letter from a Birmingham Jail." Studying these documents in the light of what you know about their effect on history will dramatize for you the mighty force wielded by an effective argument.

GENERATING IDEAS: INDUCTION, DEDUCTION, AND THE CLASSICAL QUESTIONS

Ideas for argument and persuasion can be generated on a number of levels; for example, one may think through the logic of an argument using inductive or deductive reasoning, then use many of the classical questions as a means to generate ideas to support that reasoning. Induction, deduction, and the classical questions, as they can be used in support of the persuasive aim, are discussed in this section.

Induction

Although inductive reasoning, as a product of the scientific age, arrived on the scene more recently than deduction, which was devised by the Greeks many centuries ago, we will discuss induction first for two reasons: (1) it is simpler than deduction, and (2) you are familiar with the concept of induction from Chapter 7.

In Chapter 7, you used induction as a way of arriving at scientific truth, answering the classical question "What examples are there of it?" Induction as a persuasive tool also answers this question, but the process of arriving at a conclusion is somewhat different from the process used by scientists. The scientific method begins with examples and then forms a conclusion; inductive argumentation uses examples to support a point of view. This distinction can, of course, be pushed too far, for the scientist begins with a hypothesis, and the persuasive writer, hopefully, has looked at the evidence before forming his or her point of view. But there are other differences as well: the scientific writer, for example, works with scientific subjects, whereas the persuasive writer works outside the laboratory with issues, emotions, and opinions.

The major difference is in intent. Scientific writers are more involved in their subject matter than with their audience, whereas persuasive writers marshal their evidence and present it in such a way as to convince their readers. Their emphasis is more on the reader, less on the subject (see the "Audience" section).

There are three types of persuasive induction: sampling, analogy, and causal generalization. Sampling is used to arrive at a conclusion about a group through reference to a certain percentage of that group rather than the entire membership, as discussing or even knowing about every member of a group would be impossible. For example, we might conclude through sampling that Americans want to view escapist movies because so many science-fiction movies have been so successful (for more on sampling, see Chapter 7, p. 261).

Analogy is helpful to an argument because it suggests that things alike in some ways must also be alike in others. You might argue by analogy that hecklers at public meetings are like political tyrants: They take ideas hostage.

This statement suggests that hecklers, like tyrants, prevent the free exchange of ideas.

Causal generalization generalizes about many members of a class in order to determine why one member of the class is different. Only one child in a family got measles, and because he was the only one to visit a cousin, the implication is that he contracted the measles while at his cousin's house.

All of these methods must be handled logically, for there are many pitfalls in their use. If you use too few examples or samples, you may not prove your position. Hasty generalizations—for example, we will have a recession every eight years because we had one in 1975 and another in 1983—tend to be unconvincing. Atypical examples also tend to undercut the effectiveness of an argument; thus it may not help much to interview those not on welfare if you wish to argue that the welfare system is working. Moreover it is unfair to ignore examples that contradict your line of reasoning; if some people on welfare feel that the system is not much help to them, there is a way of admitting this contrary evidence (see the section on "Arranging Your Essay," p. 343).

When you argue inductively, it is best to avoid claiming more for your examples than they merit and to avoid making sweeping generalizations as did the cigarette commercial "Everyone who knows smokes Kools." Analogies, too, should be drawn carefully so that there is a sound basis of comparison and not a fleeting or glamorous one: When politicians claim that Latin American refugees will become "feet people" just as the Vietnamese were "boat people" if we do not defend Central America, their analogy is less sound than it might be; what actually causes refugees in either case is war itself, not our unwillingness to become involved.

Finally, in ascribing causal generalizations, watch for the dangers, mentioned in Chapter 5, that can be encountered when using causation: Is X the real cause of Y, or did it just come before it in time? Or is the connection just coincidental? Or is X the only cause of Y? Perhaps the child with the measles contracted the disease in school, rather than from contact with his cousin, or perhaps both the cousin and the classmates had the disease.

The criteria for successful inductive reasoning, then, include the following:

1. Your examples should be of sufficient quantity.
2. They should be randomly selected.
3. They should be accurate and objectively presented.
4. They should be relevant to the conclusion drawn.
5. They should disprove the evidence of the opposition.

SOME PRACTICE WITH INDUCTION

1. Identify the type of induction used in the following passages:

   a. "Beasts abstract not," announced John Locke, expressing mankind's prevailing opinion throughout recorded history. Bishop Berkeley had, however, a sardonic rejoinder: "If the fact that brutes abstract not be made the distinguishing property of that sort of animal, I fear a great many of those that pass for men must be reckoned into their number." Abstract thought, at least in its more subtle varieties, is not an invariable accompaniment of everyday life for the average man. Could abstract thought be a matter not of kind but of degree? Could other animals be capable of abstract thought but more rarely or less deeply than humans? . . .

There is by now a vast library of described and filmed conversations, employing Ameslan and other gestural languages, with Washoe, Lucy, Lana and other chimpanzees studied by the Gardiners and others. Not only are there chimpanzees with working vocabularies of 100 to 200 words; they are also able to distinguish among nontrivially different grammatical patterns and syntaxes. What is more, they have been remarkably inventive in the construction of new words and phrases.

On seeing for the first time a duck land quacking in a pond, Washoe gestured "water bird," which is the same phrase used in English and other languages, but which Washoe invented for the occasion. Having never seen a spherical fruit other than an apple, but knowing the signs for the principal colors, Lana, upon spying a technician eating an orange, signed "orange apple." After tasting a watermelon, Lucy described it as "candy drink" or "drink fruit," which is essentially the same word form as the English "water melon." But after she had burned her mouth on her first radish, Lucy forever after described them as "cry hurt food." A small doll placed unexpectedly in Washoe's cup elicited the response "Baby in my drink." When Washoe soiled, particularly clothing or furniture, she was taught the sign "dirty," which she then extrapolated as a general term of abuse. A rhesus monkey that evoked her displeasure was repeatedly signed at: "Dirty monkey, dirty monkey, dirty monkey." Occasionally Washoe would say things like "Dirty Jack, gimme drink." Lana, in a moment of creative annoyance, called her trainer "You green shit." Chimpanzees have invented swear words. Washoe also seems to have a sort of sense of humor; once, when riding on her trainer's shoulders and, perhaps inadvertently, wetting him, she signed: "Funny, funny."

Lucy was eventually able to distinguish clearly the meanings of the phrases "Roger tickle Lucy" and "Lucy tickle Roger," both of which activities she enjoyed with gusto. Likewise, Lana extrapolated from "Tim groom Lana" to "Lana groom Tim." Washoe was observed "reading" a magazine—i.e., slowly turning the pages, peering intently at the pictures and making, to no one in particular, an appropriate sign, such as "cat" when viewing a photograph of a tiger, and "drink" when examining a Vermouth advertisement. Having learned the sign "open" with a door, Washoe extended the concept to a briefcase. She also attempted to converse in Ameslan with the laboratory cat, who turned out to be the only illiterate in the facility. Having acquired this marvelous method of communication, Washoe may have been surprised that the cat was not also competent in Ameslan. . . .

I would expect a significant development and elaboration of language in only a few generations if all the chimps unable to communicate were to die or fail to reproduce. Basic English corresponds to about 1,000 words. Chimpanzees are already accomplished in vocabularies exceeding 10 percent of that number. Although a few years ago it would have seemed the most implausible science fiction, it does not appear to me out of the question that, after a few generations in such a verbal chimpanzee community, there might emerge the memoirs of the natural history and mental life of a chimpanzee, published in English or Japanese (with perhaps an "as told to" after the byline).

If chimpanzees have consciousness, if they are capable of abstractions, do they not have what until now has been described as "human rights"? How smart does a chimpanzee have to be before killing him constitutes murder? What further properties must he show before religious missionaries must consider him worthy of attempts at conversion? . . .

The long-term significance of teaching language to the other primates is difficult to overestimate. There is an arresting passage in Charles Darwin's *Descent of Man:* "The difference in mind between man and the higher animals, great as it is, certainly is one of degree and not of kind. . . . If it could be proved that certain high mental powers, such as the formation of general concepts, self-consciousness, et cetera, were absolutely peculiar to man, which seems extremely doubtful, it is not improbable that these qualities are merely the incidental results of other highly-advanced intellectual faculties; and these again mainly the results of the continued use of a perfect language. . . ."

—**Carl Sagan,** *The Dragons of Eden*

b. When Lincoln at last determined, in July 1862, to move toward emancipation, it was only after all his other policies had failed. The Crittenden Resolution had been rejected, the border states had quashed his plan of compensated emancipation, his generals were still floundering, and he had already lost the support of great numbers of conservatives. The Proclamation became necessary to hold his remaining supporters and to forestall— so he believed—English recognition of the Confederacy. "I would save the Union," he wrote in answer to Horace Greeley's cry for emancipation. ". . . If I could save the Union without freeing any slave, I would do it; and if I could do it by freeing all the slaves, I would do it." In the end, freeing all the slaves seemed necessary.

It was evidently an unhappy frame of mind in which Lincoln resorted to the Emancipation Proclamation. "Things had gone from bad to worse," he told the artist F. B. Carpenter a year later, "until I felt that we had reached the end of our rope on the plan of operations we had been pursuing; that we had about played our last card, and must change our tactics, or lose the game. I now determined upon the adoption of the emancipation policy. . . ." The passage has a wretched tone; things had gone from bad to worse and as a result the slaves were to be declared free!

The Emancipation Proclamation of January 1, 1863, had all the moral grandeur of a bill of lading. It contained no indictment of slavery, but simply based emancipation on "military necessity." It expressly omitted the loyal slave states from its terms. Finally, it did not in fact free any slaves. For it excluded by detailed enumeration from the sphere covered in the Proclamation all the counties in Virginia and parishes in Louisiana that were occupied by Union troops and into which the government actually had the power to bring freedom. It simply declared free all slaves in "the States and parts of States" where the people were in rebellion—that is to say, precisely where its effect could not reach. Beyond its propaganda value the Proclamation added nothing to what Congress had already done in the Confiscation Act.

Seward remarked of the Proclamation: "We show our sympathy with slavery by emancipating the slaves where we cannot reach them and holding them in bondage where we can set them free." The London *Spectator* gibed: "The principle is not that a human being cannot justly own another, but that he cannot own him unless he is loyal to the United States."

But the Proclamation was what it was because the average sentiments of the American Unionist of 1862 were what they were. Had the political strategy of the moment called for a momentous human document of the stature of the Declaration of Independence, Lincoln could have risen to the occasion. Perhaps the largest reasonable indictment of him is simply that in such matters he was a follower and not a leader of public opinion. It may be that there was in Lincoln something of the old Kentucky poor white, whose regard for the slaves was more akin to his feeling for tortured animals than it was to his feeling, say, for the common white man of the North. But it is only the intensity and not the genuineness of his antislavery sentiments that can be doubted. His conservatism arose in part from a sound sense for the pace of historical change. He knew that formal freedom for the Negro, coming suddenly and without preparation, would not be real freedom, and in this respect he understood the slavery question better than most of the Radicals, just as they had understood better than he the revolutionary dynamics of the war.

For all its limitations, the Emancipation Proclamation probably made genuine emancipation inevitable. In all but five of the states freedom was accomplished in fact through the thirteenth amendment. Lincoln's own part in the passing of this amendment was critical. He used all his influence to get the measure the necessary two-thirds vote in the House of Representatives, and it was finally carried by a margin of three votes. Without his influence the amendment might have been long delayed, though it is hardly conceivable that it could have been held off indefinitely. Such claim as he may have to be remembered as an Emancipator perhaps rests more justly on his behind-the-scenes activity for the thirteenth amendment than on the Proclamation itself. It was the Proclamation, however, that had psychological value, and before the amendment was passed, Lincoln had already become the personal symbol of freedom. Believing that he was called only to conserve, he had turned liberator in spite of himself:

"I claim not to have controlled events but confess plainly that events have controlled me."

—Richard Hofstadter, *"Abraham Lincoln and the Self-made Myth"*

c. We should not conclude, either, that the child who has strong ties to his parents is insured against neurosis. We can only say that he will have the best possible measures within his personality to deal with conflict, which may then provide greater resistance to neurotic ills. But a neurosis is not necessarily an indictment of the parent–child relationship; a neurotic child is not necessarily an unloved child, or a rejected child. The child who has never known love and who has no human attachments does not develop a neurosis in the strict clinical meaning of the term. The unattached child is subject to other types of disorders. He might develop bizarre features in his personality, he might be subject to primitive fears and pathological distortions of reality, he might have uncontrollable urges that lead to delinquency or violence, but he would probably not acquire a neurosis because a neurosis involves moral conflicts and conflicts of love which could not exist in a child who had never known significant human attachments. The merit of a neurosis—if there is anything good to be said about it all—is that it is a civilized disease. The child who suffers a disturbance in his love relationships or anxieties of conscience offers proof of his humanity even in illness. But the sickness of the unattached child is more terrible because it is less human; there is only a primitive ego engaged in a lonely and violent struggle for its own existence.

Indeed, it can be argued that the real threat to humanity does not lie in neurosis but in the diseases of the ego, the diseases of isolation, detachment and emotional sterility. These are the diseases that are produced in the early years by the absence of human ties or the destruction of human ties. In the absence of human ties those mental qualities that we call human will fail to develop or will be grafted upon a personality that cannot nourish them, so that at best they will be imitations of virtues, personality façades. The devastating effects of two world wars, revolution, tyranny and mass murder are seen in cruelest caricature in the thousands of hollow men who have come to live among us. The destruction of families and family ties has produced in frightening numbers an aberrant child and man who lives as a stranger in the human community. He is rootless, unbound, uncommitted, unloved and untouchable. He is sometimes a criminal, whether child or adult, and you have read that he commits acts of violence without motive and without remorse. He offers himself and the vacancy within him to be leased by other personalities—the gang leaders, mob-rulers, fascist leaders and the organizers of lunatic movements and societies. He performs useful services for them; he can perform brutal acts that might cause another criminal at least a twinge of conscience, he can risk his life when more prudent villains would stay home, and he can do these things because he values no man's life, not even his own. All that he asks in return is that he may borrow a personality or an idea to clothe his nakedness and give a reason, however perverse, for his existence in a meaningless world.

We have more reason to fear the hollow man than the poor neurotic who is tormented by his own conscience. As long as man is capable of moral conflicts—even if they lead to neurosis—there is hope for him. But what shall we do with a man who has no attachments? Who can breathe humanity into his emptiness?

—**Selma H. Fraiberg,** *The Magic Years*

2. Observe the use of the types of induction in the following essay. Does the essay meet all of the criteria for effective induction?

I knew a man who went into therapy about three years ago because, as he put it, he couldn't live with himself any longer. I didn't blame him. The guy was a bigot, a tyrant and a creep.

In any case, I ran into him again after he'd finished therapy. He was still a bigot, a tyrant and a creep, *but* . . . he had learned to live with himself.

Now, I suppose this was an accomplishment of sorts. I mean, nobody else could live with him. But it seems to me that there are an awful lot of people running around and writing around these days encouraging us to feel good about what we should feel terrible about, and to accept in ourselves what we should change.

The only thing they seem to disapprove of is disapproval. The only judgment they make is against being judgmental, and they assure us that we have nothing to feel guilty about except guilt itself. It seems to me that they are all intent on proving that I'm OK and You're OK, when in fact, I may be perfectly dreadful and you may be unforgivably dreary, and it may be—gasp!—*wrong*.

What brings on my sudden attack of judgmentitis is success, or rather, *Success!*—the latest in a series of exclamation-point books all concerned with How to Make it.

In this one, Michael Korda is writing a recipe book for success. Like the other authors, he leapfrogs right over the "Shoulds" and into the "Hows." He eliminates value judgments and edits out moral questions as if he were Fanny Farmer and the subject was the making of a blueberry pie.

It's not that I have any reason to doubt Mr. Korda's advice on the way to achieve success. It may very well be that successful men wear handkerchiefs stuffed neatly in their breast pockets, and that successful single women should carry suitcases to the office on Fridays whether or not they are going away for the weekend.

He may be realistic when he says that "successful people generally have very low expectations of others." And he may be only slightly cynical when he writes: "One of the best ways to ensure success is to develop expensive tastes or marry someone who has them."

And he may be helpful with his handy hints on how to sit next to someone you are about to overpower.

But he simply finesses the issues of right and wrong—silly words, embarrassing words that have been excised like warts from the shiny surface of the new how-to books. To Korda, guilt is not a prod, but an enemy that he slays on page four. Right off the bat, he tells the would-be successful reader that

- It's OK to be greedy.
- It's OK to look out for Number One.
- It's OK to be Machiavellian (if you can get away with it).
- It's OK to recognize that honesty is not always the best policy (provided you don't go around saying so).
- And it's always OK to be rich.

Well, in fact, it's not OK. It's not OK to be greedy, Machiavellian, dishonest. It's not always OK to be rich. There is a qualitative difference between succeeding by making napalm or by making penicillin. There is a difference between climbing the ladder of success, and macheteing a path to the top.

Only someone with the moral perspective of a mushroom could assure us that this was all OK. It seems to me that most Americans harbor ambivalence toward success, not for neurotic reasons, but out of a realistic perception of what it demands.

Success is expensive in terms of time and energy and altered behavior—the sort of behavior he describes in the grossest of terms: "If you can undermine your boss and replace him, fine, do so, but never express anything but respect and loyalty for him while you're doing it."

This author—whose *Power!* topped the best-seller last year—is intent on helping rid us of that ambivalence which is a signal from our conscience. He is like the other "Win!" "Me First!" writers, who try to make us comfortable when we should be uncomfortable.

They are all Doctor Feelgoods, offering us placebo prescriptions instead of strong medicine. They give us a way to live with ourselves, perhaps, but not a way to live with each other. They teach us a whole lot more about "Failure!" than about success.

—**Ellen Goodman,** *"It's Failure, Not Success"*

Deduction

Deductive reasoning works quite differently from inductive reasoning: Rather than working from evidence to a conclusion, as does induction, deduction works from an assumption—a generalization that is generally accepted as true—to a specific conclusion. This assumption, called a *premise* in formal logic, leads to a specific conclusion with the help of a "linking statement." Here is an example of deductive thinking:

Assumption:	All college students should drink beer.
Linking Statement:	John is a college student.
Conclusion:	John should drink beer.

Of course, most of us usually do not think according to this process, called a *syllogism* in formal logic. Usually, we think only according to the last two steps of the process (formally called an *enthymeme*). For example, we might argue that because John is a college student, he should drink beer, taking for granted the assumption that all college students should drink beer.

If you decided to argue that we are going to war because we are having an army buildup, your argument similarly would rest on an unspoken assumption, in this case that an army buildup necessarily leads to war.

Assumption:	All army buildups lead to war.
Linking Statement:	We are having an army buildup.
Conclusion:	We are going to war.

You might find it a good idea to construct this syllogism to determine if the assumption on which your argument rests is a sensible (or valid) one. If it is valid that all army buildups lead to war (or that all college students should drink beer, for that matter), then your argument itself makes sense. To say that Peter is cold because he has no coat on is to assume that all people who have no coats on are cold. If the weather is cold, if the people are outdoors, and if they have no heavy sweaters on either, then your assumption is probably valid. And if your assumption is valid, then your argument is probably valid also.

Deduction is useful when you are trying to persuade your readers of a highly controversial conclusion because, if you can get them to agree with your assumption, you have a good chance of getting them to agree with your conclusion. It is worthwhile, therefore, to learn how to construct an informal syllogism. (Courses in logic instruct one in formal constructions.)

Each of the three statements in a syllogism has two parts, each of these parts appearing in one of the other statements according to the following pattern:

Assumption:	All that has a tendency to become stale needs renewing. 3 2
Linking Statement:	Slang has a tendency to become stale. 1 3
Conclusion:	Slang needs to be renewed. 1 2

Because your conclusion is usually your shaping idea, begin here to construct your syllogism. By adding a causal conjunction to your conclusion, you can usually arrive at your linking statement: *Slang needs to be renewed* because *it has a tendency to become stale*. You now have all three parts of your syllogism and can construct the third statement accordingly, as the assumption always contains Parts 3 and 2, in that order.

For example, suppose your shaping idea for your argument is "Our involvement in El Salvador is a no-win situation." By adding *because* to this sentence, you can arrive at your linking statement: "Our involvement in El Salvador is a no-win situation because it is a guerrilla war." Diagramming your enthymeme will give you your assumption:

Conclusion: Our involvement in El Salvador is a no-win situa-
                         tion. (because)   1   2

Linking Statement: El Salvador is a guerrilla war.
                         1   3

Assumption: Guerrilla wars are no-win situations.
                         3   2

We should add here that sometimes it is necessary to construct a series or
string of syllogisms, in order to clarify just what general assumption lies behind
a point that you wish to argue. For example, in a discussion of deductive logic
in one class, the students decided to construct an argument in support of handgun control. They found that they had to put together the following series of
syllogisms before they could determine the general assumption behind their
feeling that handgun possession is immoral:

Syllogism 1:
All persons who kill except in self-defense or in defense of others are im-
moral.
He killed neither in self-defense nor in defense of others.
He is immoral.
*(This syllogism does not establish that he has a handgun, so the students added
Syllogism 2 to their argument.)*

Syllogism 2:
All in possession of guns are readily equipped to kill in all situations (self-
defense, defense of others, and nondefense).
He is in possession of a gun.
He is readily equipped to kill in all situations.
*(This syllogism does not establish that the person equipped to kill is likely to kill, so
the students added Syllogism 3.)*

Syllogism 3:
All men readily equipped to kill are more likely to kill in nondefense situa-
tions, as well as in self-defense or in defense of others.
He is readily equipped to kill.
He is more likely to kill in nondefense situations.
*(This syllogism does not establish the charge of immorality, so the students added
still another syllogism.)*

Syllogism 4:

All men more likely to kill in nondefense situations are immoral.

He is more likely to kill in nondefense situations.

He is immoral.

(With Syllogism 4, the students felt that they had clarified the logic behind their argument that handgun possession is immoral.)

Do you think the students' assumptions are valid?

SOME PRACTICE WITH DEDUCTION

Reconstruct the assumptions on which the following arguments (enthymemes) are based. In each case, does the argument seem to rest on a valid assumption?

1. Business is a good major because you can get a job.

2. Toxic waste disposal is a vital issue because undisposed-of poisons can affect our health.

3. The government should continue to subsidize student loans because college tuitions can no longer be afforded by a sizable percentage of the middle class.

4. Playing video games should not be ridiculed because they encourage mind–body coordination.

5. Because high-technology firms promise employment, Americans should train or retrain to enter a high-technology profession.

6. The sexual revolution has been harmful because so many people are contracting sexually-transmitted diseases.

7. Bilingualism should not be encouraged because studies show that students in bilingual classes do not learn English well.

8. Advertising should not be considered worthless because buying an advertised product makes people feel good.

9. Women should resist the return to ultrafeminine fashions because this trend repudiates the philosophy of the women's movement.

10. Because it appears likely that young marrieds will not be able to afford the downpayment on a house due to rising interest rates, they should not hope to have a home of their own.

Deductive Fallacies

As we indicated previously, the reason for constructing a syllogism is to determine if your assumption is logical. Following are some of the problems that you might encounter in trying to make this determination.

1. *Faulty analogy:* There are not enough important similarities between the two subjects being compared to really support the conclusions that are being drawn. Although it is often said that the generation of the 1980s is just like that of the 1950s because both are silent, the differences between the two decades are greater than any similarities.
2. *False cause:* The ascribed cause is not really a cause at all or is just one of many factors. Although the women's movement has been blamed for the disintegration of the family, other societal factors are the chief causes.
3. *Begging the question:* The assumption takes for granted what ought to be established by proof. You cannot assume, for example, that a person cannot be believed because he has a reputation as a liar. You must establish proof that he is lying in a particular argument.
4. *Ad hominem:* An argument is formulated on the basis of a person's personal life rather than on the issue itself. To argue that because one is a Catholic one has no business talking about abortion is to stray from one's ideas about abortion to one's religious beliefs.
5. *Ad populum:* An argument is based on appeals to popular biases such as insisting that the nuclear freeze movement must be ignored because it is infiltrated by Communists.
6. *Either/or:* The implication is made that there are only the two options when, in fact, there may be several others. The argument that one is better off "dead than red" is a well-known example of the either/or fallacy.
7. *Red herring:* The audience is diverted from the real issue. Faced with laws insisting on the installation of pollution controls, a company might warn that employees will lose their jobs if the costly controls are installed, thus diverting attention from the legal and environmental issues.
8. *Genetic fallacy:* The class that a person is from, and not the person's own qualifications, becomes the focus of the argument. For example, many people argued that Ronald Reagan could not be a good president because he had been a movie actor.
9. *The bandwagon:* This argument asserts the value of its point of view because "everybody" is doing it. Advertisements often commit this fallacy:

"*Atlantic* Subscribers Never Miss" or "All Over the World People Have One Thing in Common: They Start the Evening with Red" (Johnnie Walker Red).

10. *Slanting:* Arguers sometimes use language unfairly to encourage the reader to take their view of the subject. To claim that over 30 percent of a class failed an exam when in fact nearly 70 percent had passed it for the highest percentage of passes ever is an example of slanting, because it emphasizes the small percentage that failed rather than the vast majority that passed.

SOME PRACTICE WITH IDENTIFYING DEDUCTIVE FALLACIES

1. Which assumptions in the exercise on pages 325–326 can be categorized by one of the logical fallacies?

2. Identify the fallacy in each of the following assumptions:

   a. He is an Italian; he must belong to the Mafia.

   b. Students, if you continue to protest this regulation, you will be encouraging anarchy in the schools.

   c. People who know use Product X.

   d. Ted doesn't use deodorant; how could he possibly be a good student-body president?

   e. The candidate has been divorced; therefore his qualifications for political office are questionable.

   f. If you do not learn computer languages, you will find yourself unemployed.

   g. His preposterous suggestion insults all red-blooded Americans.

   h. Foreign imports are destroying the U.S. economy.

   i. I cannot take this political speech seriously because politicians cannot be trusted.

   j. The Republicans are at it again: first Watergate and now "Iran-gate."

The Classical Questions in Support of Persuasion

Whether you develop an argument through inductive or deductive thinking, you need proof to support your position. The classical questions are useful in generating ideas that will supply proof for your argument. Because most arguments combine deduction and induction, we direct your attention here to questions that generate proof for both types of argument.

The classical question "What examples are there of it?" can generate a sampling to support an inductive argument. Other inductive questions are "What is it like?" (analogy or analogies) and "What factor not characteristic of others in its class may have caused it?" (causal generalization).

Deductive arguments or portions of arguments can be supported by the material generated by the classical question "What is it?" which may help you argue that your subject, as defined, has certain properties: characteristics, parts, and functions. For example, if you argue that "This gun is a product of human hatred and fear because it is a weapon," then you can base your argument on the assumption that "Weapons are products of human hatred and fear," and that the ownership of guns therefore should be abolished.

Another classical question to ask in support of deduction is "What is it like or unlike?" A variation on this question asks, "How does it compare with the ideal?" If, for example, the ideal is in your assumption that "All good deeds deserve rewards," then you can argue that what you have just done compares favorably with a good deed (and therefore you deserve a reward). Another variation on this question is "How does it compare with my opponent's view?" Explain why she or he disagrees either that you have done a good deed or that good deeds deserve rewards. Still another variation: "How does it compare with the alternatives?" Remind your reader that being rewarded will produce further good behavior, whereas being unacknowledged will lead to indifferent behavior.

A third classical question in the service of deductive proof asks, "How can it be classified?" Corresponding questions are "How can this group be defined?" "What characteristics of the group does my subject show?" and "How does it compare with others in its class?" Because we know that our recent purchase was made by a designer, we classify it as a designer fashion. We also assume that "All designer fashions are well made," and we can therefore argue that this purchase, which has a flaw in it, should be replaced.

SOME PRACTICE WITH THE CLASSICAL QUESTIONS AS MEANS OF GENERATING IDEAS FOR AN ARGUMENT

Which of the classical questions might be useful in generating ideas for the following arguments (deductive and/or inductive)?

1. Natural foods are healthier than processed ones.
2. Dogs are better pets than cats.
3. Crack is America's Number One social problem.
4. America should adopt more vigorous measures for feeding the hungry people of the world.

How to Apply the Principles of Induction and Deduction in Generating Ideas for a Persuasive Essay

In order to generate proof for your argument, we suggest that you take the following four steps:

1. Construct a logically sound argument using deduction and/or induction; summarize your main points. Research your issue if necessary to obtain the best proof. If you can find an argument developed by the opposition or one supporting your own point of view, such material should be helpful in constructing your own argument and in acquiring supporting proof.
2. Reevaluate your summary in the light of any conflict between your frame of reference and that of your audience and/or your opponent (your audience may not necessarily be opposed to your point of view, it may be neutral instead). Once you have understood how your audience and/or your opponent would view your argument, you have some idea of what the issues really are.
3. Weigh the merits of the various points of view underlying both sides of the issue, and make a case for the higher priority of the values of your case over those of your opponent. In order to do so, you may have to locate a new assumption that your opponent must agree with. Incorporate your new perspective into your argument by writing a new summary.
4. Use this final summary to write your argument.

For example, a student arguing against coed dormitories might work through the four steps in the following way:

1. **Formulate an Argument:** He formulates his main points using a combination of deduction and induction:

- **Shaping Idea:** Coed dormitories should be abolished because they introduce distractions and tensions into students' lives.
- **Inductive Proof by Example:**

   a. Ned, whose girlfriend lived on his floor, flunked math because he did not want to study.
   b. Jim, who organized nightly dormitory parties, had to leave school for a semester because he was suffering from exhaustion.
   c. Sarah, who developed a nervous condition because her boyfriend moved to another girl's dormitory, withdrew from her classes and her social relations as well.

- **Assumption:** Anything other than their studies that distracts and preoccupies students should be abolished.
- **Conclusions:** Coed dormitories should be abolished.
- **Argument Stated as a Syllogism:**
  Assumption: Anything that distracts and preoccupies students should be abolished.
  Linking Statement: Coed dormitories distract and preoccupy students.
  Conclusion: Coed dormitories should be abolished.

2. **Analyze Audience Frame of Reference:** His readers are new freshmen who either have no opinion on coed dorms or are anxious to try their social wings and are strongly in favor of them. The strongest argument of those supporting these dorms is that they encourage students to gain valuable social experience and thus help them to mature faster. Proof of their argument comes from examples supplied by their older brothers and sisters who have experienced living in coed situations.

    a. Susan, who had always felt awkward and unsure of herself on dates, learned to relax with the opposite sex by coming in contact with them in everyday situations.

    b. John gradually removed the pedestal from beneath women, stopped breaking up with every girl he went out with, and accepted Dorothy even though she didn't meet his ideal.

    c. Carol, who had attended an all-girl high school, enjoyed learning what men thought of her.

Assumption: Anything that encourages maturity should be maintained.

3. **Consider a Higher Priority:** Our writer recognizes that maturity is an important value and now knows that he must maintain that students have more to gain by doing well in their studies than by spending their study time in social pursuits, because this is a very competitive world, and a good education is a vital necessity.

4. **Reconstruct Your Argument:** He now reconstructs his argument in the following way:

- **Assumption:** In a competitive world, education must be students' first priority, and anything that interferes with that priority should be abolished.
- **Linking Statement:** Coed dorms interfere with education.
- **Conclusion:** Coed dorms should be abolished.

SOME PRACTICE WITH MAKING A CASE FOR THE HIGHER PRIORITY OF SOME VALUES OVER OTHERS

1. Review the passages by Sagan, Hofstadter, Fraiberg, and Goodman (pp. 316–322). Which, if any, of these authors have recognized the validity of their opposition's viewpoint and have argued for the higher priority of their own? What other attitudes have these authors taken toward their opposition? Can you explain why they have taken these attitudes?

2. Construct an audience frame of reference and the opposition point of view for the following deductive syllogisms; then reconstruct each syllogism so that it rests on an assumption of higher priority:

   a. **Assumption:** High-school teachers should help students to deal maturely with all of the pressures of adolescence.
   Linking Statement: Sex education is necessary if students are to deal maturely with the pressures of adolescence.
   Conclusion: Sex education should be taught by teachers in high school.

   b. **Assumption:** Anything that pollutes the atmosphere should be replaced by nonpolluting substitutes.
   Linking Statement: All gas-powered cars pollute the atmosphere.
   Conclusion: All gas-powered cars should be replaced by nonpolluting vehicles, such as battery- or solar-powered vehicles.

AUDIENCE: PERSUADING YOUR AUDIENCE

As the aim of persuasion differs from the aims of expressive and expository writing, so the role of the audience differs as well. When you engage in expressive writing, although you may wish to make yourself appealing to your audience and therefore may attempt to understand your readers through constructing their frame of reference, role-playing their point of view, and then deciding which of your own voices would be most effective, your purpose is not primarily to persuade your readers; you do not want your readers to adopt your point of view, but simply to accept you enough to enter into your experience.

In expository writing, your aim as a writer is to convey your subject matter, and your concern with your audience leads you to accommodate yourself to any disparity between their background and your own—in education generally and in the subject matter specifically. In order to be aware of any disparities, you must also construct a frame of reference and determine your own voice in writing—as an expert writing to a lay audience, for example.

For the most part, as a writer of persuasion, you can expect that your audience will be familiar with the subject matter already, although they may need some repetition of the basic facts and perhaps some in-depth treatment; what you want is for them to form an opinion about the subject matter, either their first opinion or a replacement opinion. In addition, you may want your readers to act on this newly formed opinion, either in a manner of their own choosing or in a very specific way determined by you. Thus you are demanding more of the audience than you might if you were writing expressive or expository prose, and you must use all the means at your disposal to accomplish your persuasive aim. You must first of all establish a relationship with your audience—you must establish your credibility as a writer, your role, and your voice. Then you must build bridges by establishing that you are aware of the attitude or the frame of reference of the audience and that you esteem your readers despite any differences in their point of view and your own. You must also be aware of how much depth of information your readers need. Although, of course, you must pay a considerable amount of attention to the subject matter itself and to the rational arguments for your point of view, you will also want to consider how to appeal to the emotions of your audience through your use of language and whether you have handled the ethical implications well: those of your own approach as well as those of the situation.

Establishing Credibility

How do you go about building a relationship with your audience? How do you establish bridges between your points of view? Whether your audience is neutral or hostile, a common ground can be established. The first thing that you will want to do is establish your credibility as someone who knows enough about the subject to have a worthwhile opinion about it. Professional writers, of course, have much less difficulty with this part of the task than does the average citizen or the college student. The editorial writers of *The New York Times* or of magazines with national circulation, like *Time* and *Newsweek*, have a built-in credibility by virtue of their position. Likewise, those in the professions arguing about issues in their fields are established authorities.

But how does the average citizen writing a letter to the editor or a student writing to a friend or speaking to his or her classmates establish credibility? One way is to indicate considerable experience with the subject. By narrating your encounters with the issue, you show yourself to be someone who has received firsthand knowledge. Another way is to research your subject thoroughly and to present this research to the reader. By giving background information, on the one hand, and inductive examples from research, as well as experience, on the other, you show yourself to be well versed in your subject matter.

Sometimes the role you choose to play will help you to establish your credibility. You should decide in which of your many roles you will appear most knowledgeable about your subject and select a voice that expresses that role. If you are presenting to your classmates the merits of soccer over lacrosse as a member of both teams, then the voice of a well-rounded athlete gives you added authority. If no knowledgeable voice is available to you, select a voice that indicates that you are involved in your subject. You might, for example, want to argue about state politics, and the voice that would best indicate that you are involved in the subject would be that of concerned citizen. Concerned citizen is, in fact, the most typical voice for the writer of argument to adopt, because it allows her or him to identify with her or his audience, who will no doubt want to be considered concerned citizens also.

Adopting the Proper Tone

Once you have chosen your issue and your voice in arguing that issue, you will also want to decide what tone—attitude toward subject matter—you should adopt. In most cases, your tone should be reasonable as opposed to strident or hostile. But once that is said, there are many combinations possible. As well as reasonable, you can be firm, distant, sarcastic, urgent, moral, full of righteous indignation, weary, chastising, disgusted, humorous, ironic, and so forth. The soccer and lacrosse player, for example, writing to his or her classmates on the merits of soccer, will adopt a tone consistent with his or her own attitude toward the two sports. After all, how much can one dislike lacrosse? His or her tone might, in fact, be humorous. And, too, this writer must take into account the audience's attitude toward lacrosse. Should they enjoy the sport, he or she must adopt a tone that will not offend them.

Thus your subject matter and your voice will help to determine your tone, and so will your audience. When arguing with politicians, for example, editorial writers often feel freer to adopt more extreme tones, such as sarcasm and disgust, than when writing to persuade private citizens. When persuading common citizens to change an opinion on a subject that is dear to their hearts, the writer often chooses a reasonable tone or combines it with humor or a "we're-all-in-this-together" camaraderie.

Analyzing Your Audience

This discussion leads us to the importance of analyzing your audience. You should know your audience's frame of reference in order to proceed. Once you have analyzed that, you know their point of view on the issue. If the audience has not yet formed a point of view, one strategy that you might take is to foster for them a perception of themselves as concerned, reasonable citizens who are willing to act in a reasonable way. If, however, the audience has a point of view, take it into account at all junctures in writing your argument: in deciding on your premises, in adopting your tone, in deciding what action you want the audience to take, and in choosing the language through which you phrase your appeals.

Often your best strategy in arguing is to show esteem for your audience, and to convey this esteem throughout. If you attack your opponents as ignorant or wrong, they probably won't listen to your argument. Instead, adopt the attitude that they are concerned citizens just as you are, and that you "are all in this together." Assume that they want to act in the right manner, just as you do. Be willing to compromise, above all. Very seldom are opposing positions on an issue right and wrong: both sides are right in certain ways and wrong in certain ways. Be willing to recognize this fact as you proceed.

Finally, analyze the depth of your audience's information needs. Do they require background because of lack of acquaintance with the issue? Are they lay readers who can absorb only so much in-depth information? Or are they willing to follow a long, detailed argument? How detailed an argument need you prepare? Analyzing their frame of reference should help you answer this question.

Presenting an Ethical Appeal

In the "Generating Ideas" section, we discussed how to appeal to your audience through the logical means of induction, deduction, and the classical questions. Two other appeals can be made. One is the ethical appeal, which depends on the writer's sincerity in approaching the topic; the writer seeks to involve his or her readers in the ethics of the situation as well. How can you establish your sincerity and honesty—your ethics—in approaching your issue? Many professional writers have a reputation that establishes their ethics for them, just as it establishes their credibility. On the other hand, no one quite believes in the honesty or the sincerity of politicians, because they usually feel obliged by their party affiliation to argue an issue from the party's point of view. They may sound sincere, sometimes to the point of making people believe in them, but the more dubious audiences often remain just that.

But as an average citizen or a student writer, you have no such baggage either to prove or to disprove your sincerity. You must rely on internal indications, such as your writing carefully, reasonably, and in a straightforward and clear style, making sure to support your points through careful research. Although these internal signs do not prove your honesty, they should appeal to most readers as honest attempts to present a credible argument.

The other appeal is to the emotions, which is made largely through your choice of language. The language of persuasion is discussed in the "Focus" section of this chapter.

SOME PRACTICE WITH PERSUADING YOUR AUDIENCE

Read the following argument and analyze who the writer's audience might be. How aware was the writer of his audience? What appeals has he made to his audience? Once you have read the essay, answer the questions at the end.

We are told that the trouble with Modern Man is that he has been trying to detach himself from nature. He sits on the topmost tiers of polymer, glass, and steel, dangling his pulsing legs, surveying at a distance the writhing life of the planet. In this scenario, man comes on as a stupendous lethal force, and the earth is pictured as something delicate, like rising bubbles at the surface of a country pond, or flights of fragile birds.

But it is illusion to think that there is anything fragile about the life of the earth; surely this is the toughest membrane imaginable in the universe, opaque to probability, impermeable to death. We are the delicate part, transient and vulnerable as cilia. Nor is it a new thing for man to invent an existence that he imagines to be above the rest of life; this has been his most consistent intellectual exertion down the millennia. As illusion, it has never worked out to his satisfaction in the past, any more than it does today. Man is embedded in nature.

The biologic science of recent years has been making this a more urgent fact of life. The new, hard problem will be to cope with the dawning, intensifying realization of just how interlocked we are. The old, clung-to notions most of us have held about our special lordship are being deeply undermined.

Item. A good case can be made for our nonexistence as entities. We are not made up, as we had always supposed, of successively enriched packets of our own parts. We are shared, rented, occupied. At the interior of our cells, driving them, providing the oxidative energy that sends us out for the improvement of each shining day, are the mitochondria, and in a strict sense they are not ours. They turn out to be little separate creatures, the colonial posterity of migrant prokaryocytes, probably primitive bacteria that swam into ancestral precursors of our eukaryotic cells and stayed there. Ever since, they have maintained themselves and their ways, replicating in their own fashion, privately, with their own DNA and RNA quite different from ours. They are as much symbionts as the rhizobial bacteria in the roots of beans. Without them, we would not move a muscle, drum a finger, think a thought.

Mitochondria are stable and responsible lodgers, and I choose to trust them. But what of the other little animals, similarly established in my cells, sorting and balancing me, clustering me together? My centrioles, basal bodies, and probably a good many other more obscure tiny beings at work inside my cells, each with its own special genome, are as foreign, and as essential, as aphids in anthills. My cells are no longer the pure line entities I was raised with; they are ecosystems more complex than Jamaica Bay.

I like to think that they work in my interest, that each breath they draw for me, but perhaps it is they who walk through the local park in the early morning, sensing my senses, listening to my music, thinking my thoughts.

I am consoled, somewhat, by the thought that the green plants are in the same fix. They could not be plants, or green, without their chloroplasts, which run the photosynthetic enterprise and generate oxygen for the rest of us. As it turns out, chloroplasts are also separate creatures with their own genomes, speaking their own language.

We carry stores of DNA in our nuclei that may have come in, at one time or another, from the fusion of ancestral cells and the linking of ancestral organisms in symbiosis. Our genomes are catalogues of instructions from all kinds of sources in nature, filed for all kinds of contingencies. As for me, I am grateful for differentiation and speciation, but I cannot feel as separate an entity as I did a few years ago, before I was told these things, nor, I should think, can anyone else.

Item. The uniformity of the earth's life, more astonishing than its diversity, is accountable by the high probability that we derived, originally, from some single cell, fertilized in a bolt of lightning as the earth cooled. It is from the progeny of this parent cell that we take our looks; we still share genes around, and the resemblance of the enzymes of grasses to those of whales is a family resemblance.

The viruses, instead of being single-minded agents of disease and death, now begin to look more like mobile genes. Evolution is still an infinitely long and tedious biologic game, with only the winners staying at the table, but the rules are beginning to look more flexible. We live in a dancing matrix of viruses; they dart, rather like bees, from organism to organism, from plant to insect to mammal to me and back again, and into the sea, tugging along pieces of this genome, strings of genes from that, transplanting grafts of DNA, passing around heredity as though at a great party. They may be a mechanism for keeping new, mutant kinds of DNA in the widest circulation among us. If this is true, the odd virus disease, on which we must focus so much of our attention in medicine, may be looked on as an accident, something dropped.

Item. I have been trying to think of the earth as a kind of organism, but it is no go. I cannot think of it this way. It is too big, too complex, with too many working parts lacking visible connections. The other night, driving through a hilly, wooded part of southern New England, I wondered about this. If not like an organism, what is it like, what is it *most* like? Then, satisfactorily for that moment, it came to me: it is *most* like a single cell.

—**Lewis Thomas,** *"The Lives of a Cell"*

1. How did the writer establish his credibility with the audience?

2. What role was the writer playing throughout?

3. What tone would you say he was taking in regard to the issue?

4. What attitude did the writer assume the audience has? To what extent do you think the writer created that attitude for the audience?

5. In what ways has the writer shown esteem for the reader?

6. How much depth of information has the writer supplied?

7. To what extent has the writer appealed to the ethics of the reader? To her or his sense of right and wrong?

8. What role does the writer's use of language play in making his point? What function, for example, does his use of analogy have?

TASK: WRITING A PERSUASIVE ESSAY

Your task for this chapter is to write a persuasive essay. Through your own combination of the methods of induction, deduction, and the classical questions, you should generate support for your point of view on an issue and present a well-reasoned, well-organized argument to your readers.

The issue, the audience, and your purpose in writing are to be selected by you. In order to give your task a context, we would like you to create a life situation or "case" in which you take the role of one of the participants in the situation and write an argument to convince one or more other participants of your point of view about an issue that has arisen. In creating your case, you will devise the context, the participants, the issue, your purpose in writing the argument, and the audience for whom it is intended.

Thus, in this task, you are to write not as yourself but as one of the participants in the case that you set up. For example, you might take the role of the manager of a local chemical plant that is considering the installation of costly pollution-control devices. You have been asked by the president of the company to present the company's argument for installing these devices to the other employees. You know that many of your readers may suffer pay reductions as a result of the high costs that the company will incur. How can you best argue your case?

The length of the case and its complexity are up to you. However, you should give your instructor and your peer group enough details about your role and that of your intended audience so that they can construct both frames of reference, and you should also give them enough information about the situation in general and the problem in particular so that they will know as much about your case as you do.

The audience that you select will be either undecided or hostile to your point of view; there is no point in selecting an audience that already agrees with you, as in that case you have no one to convince. Whether hostile or undecided, however, your audience should be interested in your subject and to some extent knowledgeable about it.

In constructing your case, you can proceed in one of two ways: (1) choose an issue that interests you and then build around it a situation containing a specific audience and a purpose for addressing that audience; or (2) choose a situation with which you are familiar, analyze the issues involved, and then select one issue to argue about.

For example, suppose that you want to argue that we should rely more than we do at present on nuclear power for local energy needs. By constructing a case around this issue, you can focus more sharply on whom you are addressing your argument to and why your argument is necessary. Your case might go something like this: You are a homeowner with a family to support in an area where energy costs are high. The local electric company has proposed building a nuclear facility that will lower energy costs to its customers, you and your neighbors. Many of your neighbors, however, are concerned about the dangers of such a facility, and some have formed an antinuclear group. You decide to attend a meeting of this group, to try to convince its members to see your side of the issue. First, you must write out your argument, so that you can present it clearly in what you realize will be a hostile setting. What do you write?

If you choose the second method, start with a situation that you know something about, perhaps one having to do with a job that you hold or with a subject that you are studying; decide what your role is to be; and then select your issue. You might, for example, be studying the period of the American Revolution in a history course, a period in which many important issues were fought over. Adopt a role for yourself from that era, say, the role of a merchant who has decided to back the rebel cause. The Boston Tea Party has just taken place. Write an essay for the local newspaper in which you state why your fellow citizens, many of whom feel that such an act of insurrection is immoral, should support those responsible for the Boston Tea Party.

In focusing on the issue, you might argue from one of the following points of view: You might argue about the merits of the situation, about whether it is "good or bad." Or you might argue about what your subject really means and how it should be interpreted. A third approach is to argue about what consequences will follow from a certain action. Finally, you may want to advocate a certain course of action. Of course, a combination of two or more of these approaches is also possible.

Construct your case before proceeding further. In the following section, "Writing the Essay," we discuss how to generate ideas for your argumentative essay, how best to address your audience, and how the arrangement patterns that correspond to the classical questions that you have asked can be used to help organize different sections of your essay. Most important, we present patterns of arranging a persuasive essay as a whole. In the "Focus" section, we discuss various considerations in choosing the language of your argument in order to best involve the emotions of your reader.

WRITING THE ESSAY

Generating Ideas Through Induction, Deduction, and the Classical Questions

Now that you have written your case, you know the issue that will form the subject of your essay and the point of view that you will take on that issue. If you have not phrased that point of view as a shaping idea, you will want to do so now. In order to clearly establish the purpose of your argument from the start, word it so that your reader knows whether you are arguing for a course of action ("This should be done"); a value judgment ("This is good/or bad"); an interpretation ("This is what it means and how it should be interpreted"); or a necessary consequence of certain actions or conditions ("This is what will happen").

Once you have your shaping idea, extend it into an enthymeme by linking it to a causal statement through the use of a causal conjunction such as *because* or *as*. Then work out the assumption on which your argument is based by constructing an informal syllogism according to the formula in the "Generating Ideas" section. Examine your assumption(s) for possible fallacious reasoning.

Next, determine the assumption of your opponent. Finally, revise your assumption to take his or hers into account by basing your assumption on a higher priority (see the "Generating Ideas" section).

As we have suggested, most arguments are a combination of induction and deduction. Do be aware, however, that some shaping ideas may not form the conclusion of a syllogism. If you are a scientist arguing that our water sources are plentiful, you may simply be marshaling evidence in a purely inductive argument. At the same time, the possibility that you will be developing a purely deductive argument is remote. Even though your argument may be based on a series of syllogisms in support of your basic conclusion or shaping idea, these conclusions will need inductive support.

You should find the classical questions discussed in the "Generating Ideas" section helpful in generating material for your essay. By making a list of those questions that will generate material on your subject, you can acquire proof for your essay. If you are arguing for a course of action, you might ask what the effects would be and how they would compare with the effects of not acting. If you are arguing the merits (or demerits) of your subject, then you might ask how it compares with the ideal or ask what analogy is effective. When arguing about what a subject means or how it can be interpreted, you might ask what it is, what it will cause, what class it is in, and what examples there are of it. Finally, arguments stating the consequences of a future action ("This is what will happen") can be supported through asking what the effects will be and what will cause those effects, through seeking an analogy, and through making comparisons with alternatives.

It is important that you seek through such questions concrete evidence to present in support of your position: specific examples, statistical information, and factual details. Try to avoid simply praising or condemning a point of view, without offering detailed evidence. And try to make your evidence as concrete as possible. If you give a general reason in support of an argument, back it up with specific details: Thus, if you argue that eighteen-year-olds should be allowed to drink by law because they are expected by society to act in general as responsible adults, back this argument up with references to specific ways in which society does expect eighteen-year-olds to act as responsible adults, and then illustrate your point in even more concrete detail by referring to specific eighteen-year-olds who act as responsible adults in specific ways.

Persuading Your Audience

As you have constructed a case, you virtually have the script for both playing your own role and role-playing that of your audience. Through role playing, you should be able to reconstruct your audience's frame of reference even more fully than you have done in writing the case. Know as thoroughly as you can their point of view on the issue, their education, their values, and the amount of information they have on the subject.

You will also want to analyze the frame of reference and the point of view of the character you are playing, of course, in order to clarify his or her role as well. If this role does not immediately establish your credibility, you might decide to do research on your subject to bolster your authority. Finally, you will want to select a voice that is consistent with your role, the subject, and your knowledge of your audience.

To the extent that the character you are playing is not yourself, keep in mind that you are writing as this character and use his or her voice consistently; as you write, make sure not to lapse into playing yourself at any point in the essay. Rather, develop the argument honestly and sincerely in this voice that you have selected, establishing how the subject engages your values, and remembering as well to relate your argument to the values of the audience.

Arranging Your Essay

The argumentative or persuasive essay has four main divisions: the introduction, the proof, the refutation of the opposing argument, and the conclusion. Following this pattern can help you to organize the material that you generate into an effective and clear presentation.

Introduction. The introduction to an argumentative essay fulfills the same functions as does any introduction (see Chapter 4, p. 159), although special care must be taken in developing some of its features. It must first of all establish who you are, as the writer—the role you are playing and how the role helps establish your credibility. You cannot introduce yourself, however, without knowing precisely who your audience is and how best to present yourself to them. At the outset, you must set the right tone for your subject and your audience in order to engage them. And then, of course, you must announce your shaping idea: the issue and your point of view on it.

Proof. The body of the paper should contain the proof of your argument and your refutation of your opponent's point of view. As we have discussed, you may garner proof through obtaining support for your arguments, whether inductive or deductive, by asking such classical questions as "What examples are there of it?" "What caused it?" "What is it?" "How can it be classified?" and "How does it compare with the ideal, with the opposing argument, with any alternatives, and with others in its class?" The arrangement of this proof thus should correspond to the patterns that we have discussed in previous chapters: cause and effect, comparison and contrast, and process in Chapter 5 and exemplification in Chapter 6 (general to specific) and Chapter 7 (induction).

Definition and Classification.   Two arrangement patterns not presented in earlier chapters are definition and classification. A definition may be as brief as that found in the dictionary, or you may extend it through attributing characteristics, analyzing the parts, stating functions, giving examples, and comparing and contrasting with other subjects. The arrangement pattern for definition may follow any ordering of these features. In the definition below, the nineteenth-century thinker John Stuart Mill argued for the equality of women by defining women's intuitive abilities. He began his argument by defining intuition, but he proceeded largely by comparing and contrasting the thought processes of women with those of men:

The Nature of Women
John Stuart Mill

What is meant by a woman's capacity of intuitive perception? It means, a rapid and correct insight into present fact. It has nothing to do with general principles. Nobody ever perceived a scientific law of nature by intuition, nor arrived at a general rule of duty or prudence by it. These are results of slow and careful collection and comparison of experience; and neither the men nor the women of intuition usually shine in this department, unless, indeed, the experience necessary is such as they can acquire by themselves. For what is called their intuitive sagacity makes them peculiarly. apt in gathering such general truths as can be collected from their individual means of observation. When, consequently, they chance to be as well provided as men are with the results of other people's experience, by reading and education (I use the word chance advisedly, for, in respect to the knowledge that tends to fit them for the greater concerns of life, the only educated women are the self-educated) they are better furnished than men in general with the essential requisites of skillful and successful practice. Men who have been much taught, are apt to be deficient in the sense of present fact; they do not see, in the facts which they are called upon to deal with, what is really there, but what they have been taught to expect. This is seldom the case with women of any ability. Their capacity of "intuition" preserves them from it. With equality of experience and of general faculties, a woman usually sees much more than a man of what is immediately before her. Now this sensibility to the present, is the main quality on which the capacity for practice, as distinguished from theory, depends. To discover general principles, belongs to the speculative faculty: to discern and discriminate the particular cases in which they are and are not applicable, constitutes practical talent: and for this, women as they now are have a peculiar aptitude. I admit that there can be no good practice without principles, and that the predominant place which quickness of observation holds among a woman's faculties, makes her particularly apt to build overhasty generalizations upon her own observation; though at the same time no less ready in rectifying those generalizations, as her observation takes a wider range. But the corrective to this defect, is access to the experience of the human race; general knowledge—exactly the thing which education can best supply. A woman's mistakes are specifically those of a clever self-educated man, who often sees what men trained in routine do not see, but falls into errors for want of knowing things which have long been known. Of course he has acquired much of the pre-existing knowledge, or he could not have got on at all; but what he knows of it he has picked up in fragments and at random, as women do.

In arranging the elements of classification, you may define the class, discuss how your subject fits into that class, and/or compare and contrast your subject with other members of the class. Another approach is taken by the authors of the following paragraphs in arguing that athletic competition has no more beneficial effects than intense endeavor in any other field. They first define their class as "problem athletes," then explain how the classification was arrived at, and finally contrast problem athletes with those outside the class.

Sport: If You Want to Build Character, Try Something Else
Bruce C. Ogilvie and Thomas A. Tutko

Types

The problem athletes who made up our original sample displayed such severe emotional reactions to stress that we had serious doubts about the basic value of athletic competition. The problems associated with sport covered a wide spectrum of behavior, but we were able to isolate major syndromes: the con-man athlete, the hyperanxious athlete, the athlete who resists coaching, the success-phobic athlete, the injury-prone athlete, and the depression-prone athlete.

When we confronted such cases, it became more and more difficult for us to make positive clinical interpretations of the effects of competition. In 1963, we established the Institute for the Study of Athletic Motivation to start research aimed at helping athletes reach their potentials. We wanted to examine normal players as well as problem athletes. To identify sport-specific personality traits, we and Lee Lyon developed the Athletic Motivation Inventory (AMI) which measures 11 traits common to most successful sports figures. We have since administered the AMI to approximately 15,000 athletes. The results of these tests indicate that general sports personalities do exist.

Traits

Athletes who survive the high attrition rate associated with sports competition are characterized by all or most of the following traits:

1) They have great need for achievement and tend to set high but realistic goals for themselves and others.
2) They are highly organized, orderly, respectful of authority, and dominant.
3) They have large capacity for trust, great psychological endurance, self-control, low-resting levels of anxiety, and slightly greater ability to express aggression.

Exemplification.   Although the evidence for your argument may be presented through one of the other classical arrangement patterns—as examples of the effects of a cause or as examples of how your subject compares with its alternative—your arrangement pattern may simply list the evidence in response to the question "What examples are there of it?" probably in an order that begins with the least convincing and ends with the most significant. Note the order of examples in this paragraph:

A Case for Rebellion

William O. Douglas

One reading American history and the stirring sentences of our Declaration of Independence would suppose that we would be on the side of the people and against the colonial rulers. *The contrary has been true.* The Dean Achesons who staffed our State Department stood firmly against Indonesian independence for five long years. The Henry Cabot Lodges who manned the United Nations stood resolutely against independence for Morocco or Algeria or Vietnam. By the mid-twentieth century we had become members of a rather plush club whose members wore homburgs, were highly respectable, and stood for the status quo. This was our consistent policy under Truman and Eisenhower. Not until the Kennedy administration did we change. On March 15, 1961, the tide turned when we supported the resolution in the United Nations in favor of Angola and against Portugal. Until that day we had either voted against independence resolutions or abstained. Until that day we stood with the respectable European colonial regimes and against those who pleaded for independence, at times with raucous voices. Indeed, without our financial support France would not have been able to subdue her subject peoples as long as she did.

Refutation.   Once you have established proof for your shaping idea, your next step is to refute the opposition. Refuting those factors that detract from your argument can gain you further credibility. Not only are you recognizing that another point of view exists, but if that point of view happens to be shared by your audience, then you are also giving them credit for their viewpoint. By stating the objections fairly and then refuting them fairly, you make your own argument more convincing.

Construct your opposing statements by concentrating on what you know about your audience. If your audience is hostile, then you will not want to further arouse their hostility; even a neutral audience will not respond well to a scathing attack. The most useful refutation may well be one that shows the opposition that a higher priority exists, as we discussed in the "Generating Ideas" section.

Sometimes it is also possible to deny the opposing argument by declaring it untrue or invalid under the circumstances. If an opponent has an erroneous grasp of the facts or if his or her facts do not apply in the situation, then you can point this out, remembering to do so tactfully.

Conclusion.   The fourth section of an argumentative essay is the conclusion. In this final section, you will want to summarize your proof and restate your major conclusion.

The Declaration of Independence is certainly one of the most famous arguments ever presented in America. An analysis of it will indicate how the writers went about organizing this important document:

The Declaration of Independence, July 4, 1776
The Unanimous Declaration of the Thirteen United States of America

When in the Course of human events, it becomes necessary for one people to dissolve the political bands which have connected them with another, and to assume among the powers of the earth, the separate and equal station to which the Laws of Nature and of Nature's God entitle them, a decent respect to the opinions of mankind requires that they should declare the causes which impel them to the separation.

We hold these truths to be self-evident, that all men are created equal, that they are endowed by their Creator with certain unalienable Rights, that among these are Life, Liberty, and the pursuit of Happiness. That to secure these rights, Governments are instituted among Men, deriving their just powers from the consent of the governed, That whenever any Form of Government becomes destructive of these ends, it is the Right of the People to alter or to abolish it, and to institute new Government, laying its foundation on such principles and organizing its powers in such form, as to them shall seem most likely to effect their Safety and Happiness. Prudence, indeed, will dictate that Governments long established should not be changed for light and transient causes; and accordingly all experience hath shown, that mankind are more disposed to suffer, while evils are sufferable, than to right themselves by abolishing the forms to which they are accustomed. But when a long train of abuses and usurpations, pursuing invariably the same Object evinces a design to reduce them under absolute Despotism, it is their right, it is their duty, to throw off such Government, and to provide new Guards for their future security. Such has been the patient sufferance of these Colonies; and such is now the necessity which constrains them to alter their former Systems of Government. The history of the present King of Great Britain is a history of repeated injuries and usurpations, all having in direct object the establishment of an absolute Tyranny over these States. To prove this, let Facts be submitted to a candid world.

He has refused his Assent to Laws, the most wholesome and necessary for the public good.

He has forbidden his Governors to pass Laws of immediate and pressing importance, unless suspended in their operation till his Assent should be obtained; and when so suspended, he has utterly neglected to attend to them.

He has refused to pass other Laws for the accommodation of large district of people, unless those people would relinquish the right of Representation in the Legislature, a right inestimable to them and formidable to tyrants only.

He has called together legislative bodies at places unusual, uncomfortable, and distant from the depository of their Public Records, for the sole purpose of fatiguing them into compliance with his measures.

He has dissolved Representative Houses repeatedly, for opposing with manly firmness his invasions on the rights of the people.

He has refused for a long time, after such dissolutions, to cause others to be elected; whereby the Legislative Powers, incapable of Annihilation, have returned to the People at large for their exercise; the State remaining in the mean time exposed to all the dangers of invasion from without, and convulsions within.

He has endeavoured to prevent the population of these States; for that purpose obstructing the Laws of Naturalization of Foreigners; refusing to pass others to encourage their migration hither, and raising the conditions of new Appropriations of Lands.

He has obstructed the Administration of Justice, by refusing his Assent to Laws for establishing Judiciary Powers.

He has made Judges dependent on his Will alone, for the tenure of their offices, and the amount and payment of their salaries.

He has erected a multitude of New Offices, and sent hither swarms of Officers to harass our People, and eat out their substance.

He has kept among us, in times of peace, Standing Armies without the Consent of our legislatures.

He has affected to render the Military independent of and superior to the Civil Power.

He has combined with others to subject us to a jurisdiction foreign to our constitution, and unacknowledged by our laws; giving his Assent to their acts of pretended legislation;

For quartering large bodies of armed troops among us:

For protecting them, by a mock Trial, from Punishment for any Murders which they should commit on the Inhabitants of these States:

For cutting off our Trade with all parts of the world:

For imposing Taxes on us without our Consent:

For depriving us in many cases, of the benefits of Trial by Jury:

For transporting us beyond Seas to be tried for pretended offences:

For abolishing the free System of English Laws in a neighbouring Province [Quebec], establishing therein an Arbitrary government, and enlarging its Boundaries so as to render it at once an example and fit instrument for introducing the same absolute rule into these Colonies:

For taking away our Charters, abolishing our most valuable Laws, and altering fundamentally the Forms of our Governments:

For suspending our own Legislatures, and declaring themselves invested with Power to legislate for us in all cases whatsoever.

He has abdicated Government here, by declaring us out of his Protection and waging War against us.

He has plundered our seas, ravaged our Coasts, burnt our towns, and destroyed the Lives of our people.

He is at this time transporting large armies of foreign mercenaries to compleat the works of death, desolation and tyranny, already begun with circumstances of Cruelty & perfidy scarcely paralleled in the most barbarous ages, and totally unworthy the Head of a civilized nation.

He has constrained our fellow Citizens taken Captive on the high Seas to bear Arms against their Country, to become the executioners of their friends and Brethren, or to fall themselves by their Hands.

He has excited domestic insurrections amongst us, and had endeavoured to bring on the inhabitants of our frontiers, the merciless Indian Savages, whose known rule of warfare, is an undistinguished destruction of all ages, sexes and conditions.

In every stage of these Oppressions We have Petitioned for Redress in the most humble terms: Our repeated Petitions have been answered only by repeated injury. A Prince, whose character is thus marked by every act which may define a Tyrant, is unfit to be the ruler of a free People.

Nor have We been wanting in attention to our British brethren. We have warned them from time to time of attempts by their legislature to extend an unwarrantable jurisdiction over us. We have reminded them of the circumstances of our emigration and settlement here. We have appealed to their native justice and magnanimity, and we have conjured them by the ties of our common kindred to disavow these usurpations, which would inevitably interrupt our connections and correspondence. They too have been deaf to the voice of justice and of consanguinity. We must, therefore, acquiesce in the necessity, which denounces our Separation, and hold them, As we hold the rest of mankind, Enemies in War, in Peace Friends.

We, therefore, the Representatives of the United States of America, in General Congress, Assembled, appealing to the Supreme Judge of the world for the rectitude of our intentions, do, in the Name, and by Authority of the good People of these Colonies, solemnly publish and declare, That these United Colonies are, and of Right ought to be Free and Independent States; that they are Absolved from all Allegiance to the British Crown, and that all political connection between them and the State of Great Britain, is and ought to be totally dissolved; and that as Free and Independent States, they have full Power to levy War, conclude Peace, contract Alliances, establish Commerce, and to do all other Acts and Things which Independent States may of right do. And for the support of this Declaration, with a firm reliance on the Protection of Divine Providence, we mutually pledge to each other our Lives, our Fortunes and our sacred Honor.

1. Discuss the assumptions made in the second paragraph. Are they valid? Under what conditions can such assumptions be considered not valid?

2. On what assumption does the argument for independence rest? Reconstruct the argument as an informal syllogism.

3. Does the Declaration conform to the four-part organization of introduction, proof, refutation, and conclusion? Explain.

4. What are the arguments of the opposition? How does the Declaration refute them and/or appeal to a higher authority?

5. Why have so many examples of America's grievances against the British king been listed? Does this appear to be a sampling or is it presented as an exhaustive list? To what extent do you think it was meant to inform the audience as well as to prove the argument?

6. How did the writers establish their credibility? In what voice did they speak and how did it affect their credibility?

7. Who was the audience for the Declaration? What was their frame of reference and point of view on the issue? What effect do you think the Declaration had on them? What effect does it have on present-day readers?

8. What was the attitude of the writers toward their audience? How did this attitude affect the tone of the piece? How did it affect the writer's ethical appeal?

Writing the Rough Draft

Once you have thought out your argument and assembled your proof for your audience, you are ready to begin writing your essay. Following is the case created by a student and the rough draft of her argument.

Case. I am Rachel McLish, two-time Miss Olympia, and a fervent believer in and practitioner of bodybuilding. You have probably seen me on the Diet Rite commercials with Lee Majors. I have recently been asked by the editors of Redbook Magazine to write an article for their readers arguing that bodybuilding is good for women. I have agreed to do so because I think their readers can be persuaded of my point of view. If I were to write for some other women's magazines, on the other hand, I might not be able to convince their readers, who are more traditional. Of course, I know that there are still other magazines for women whose readers, like me, are already working out in the gym. Redbook readers are adventurous without being in the avant-garde, and I should be able to win them over.

BODYBUILDING: THE SHAPE OF THE FUTURE

I am a female bodybuilder who has been actively engaged in the sport for many years. When you hear the word bodybuilding, the first thing that comes to your mind is probably a masculine man who is said to be clumsy or muscle-bound. Or a woman who looks manly. Most people's attitudes toward bodybuilding have come a long way, but there are still some who are unaware of its benefits. It is now a respected sport for men and women. A woman bodybuilder does not lose any of her femininity; she gains sexuality.

What would you rather have--fat or muscle? A shapely, firm body or a spongy, saggy one? I am sure everyone would pick muscle and a shapely, firm body. You don't gain large rippling muscles like the manly woman athletes whom you have seen unless you want them. But you will gain a strong, sleek, sexy body. If you lead a sedentary life, your youthful curves will quickly lose their shape and turn into fat. But if you choose the bodybuilding lifestyle, you will stay young and firm.

Bodybuilders have long had a reputation for being muscle-bound and clumsy. But in reality, bodybuilders build their agility along with their muscles. It is important for a bodybuilder to be agile and flexible in order to help prevent injuries. That is why all professional bodybuilders do stretching exercises as part of their exercise routine.

Another part of their routine is aerobic exercise. This is running, swimming, and cycling. This form of exercise strengthens your heart and lungs.

The most essential part of their routine is weightlifting. This exercise increases your strength and power and gives you a defined, firm body.

Bodybuilders eat only the most nutritious foods. They live on a high-protein diet. The foods that they are allowed, especially when in training for competition, are very restricted.

Bodybuilding is becoming more widely accepted. Because of the American Federation of Woman Bodybuilders, women's bodybuilding especially is a fast-growing sport. I am sure everyone knows Lou Ferrigno and Arnold Schwarzenegger, thanks to their total dedication to the sport.

Bodybuilders are specimens of perfect health. They are fit in all areas, such as strength, agility, flexibility, and muscular and cardiovascular endurance. Let's think of total physical fitness as a chair. One of the chair legs is stretching exercises, the second is aerobic exercises, the third is weight training, and the fourth is nutrition. Each leg needs the other to hold up the chair. If one element is missing, the chair falls. Bodybuilders do not confine themselves to lifting weights. They do all the exercises to keep themselves in the highest physical condition possible.

1. On what assumption did "Rachel McLish" base her argument? What did she hope to accomplish?

2. What proof did she offer to support her argument? What arrangement patterns did she use?

3. What is the view of the opposition? Has she refuted it? What method of refutation did she use, higher priority or denial?

4. How did she take her audience into account? Did she seem to understand *Redbook* readers well? How would she have changed the essay if she were writing to the readers of *Family Circle* or *Ladies' Home Journal?* How would she have changed it if she were writing to *Cosmopolitan* subscribers?

5. What voice and tone did she adopt? Was she sincere in her advocacy of bodybuilding? Explain.

6. How would you revise this draft?

FOCUS: PERSUASIVE LANGUAGE AND THE APPEAL TO THE EMOTIONS

In an effective argument, the writer's words and phrases play an important part because they form the foundation of the emotional appeal. Whereas the logical and ethical appeals are based on content (presenting facts and conclusions based on valid assumptions and establishing one's credibility through research), the emotional appeal evolves largely from how one phrases that content. Of course, in advertising and in propaganda, the words and even the content may be manipulated to appeal to the emotions of the reader, but in honest persuasion, the writer works out a logical argument and then heightens the reader's response through language. In some situations, the writer's audience might not respond to such language, of course; sometimes the members of the scientific community, for example, will be persuaded only by factual content. But in most arguments, the emotional appeal is a significant component.

The tools of persuasive language are many: connotation, figurative language, allusion, repetition, humor, categorical statements, and logical terms.

The writer's language must also, of course, be appropriate for the audience and reflect his or her tone (see p. 333).

Connotation

Connotative language is the most commonly used appeal to the emotions. *Connotation* refers to the overlays of meaning that our culture or segments of our culture attach to a word regardless of its denotation, or strictly literal meaning. The denotative meaning of a word is usually the first definition in the dictionary; the connotative meanings follow. Often, as words are so mercurial in our society, the writers of dictionaries cannot keep abreast of the current associations that words have for people. On the other hand, many words that once had fresh connotations have been used so frequently that they have become clichéd and have lost their excitement.

The astute writer is aware of the connotations of words and singles out from a group of possible choices the word that most clearly and freshly states her or his meaning. How many among us, for example, would not prefer to be called *slim* rather than *thin* or *skinny?* Although these words have similar denotations (or literal meanings), their connotations (or associated meanings) are quite different. And if *slim* seems to you to have been overworked, perhaps *slender* seems fresher.

Notice the writer's use of connotation in this paragraph from *Time* magazine that introduces an essay on the acquisition of former President Jimmy Carter's briefing papers by Ronald Reagan's campaign staff before the 1980 debate.

> There are moments in American life when events lurch out of context, when the public is hurtled from dim awareness of a seemingly trivial news item into a maelstrom of moral reappraisal. That appears to be happening in the affair that the Washington press corps has predictably dubbed "Debategate."

Words like *lurch, hurtled,* and *maelstrom* create turbulence in us, and when we see them immediately coupled with *American life* and *moral reappraisal,* we may feel fear and insecurity. Although other words and phrases like *moments, seemingly trivial, news item,* and *predictably dubbed* suggest that the cause of the turbulence is trivial, the language of this introduction implies that an apparently unimportant issue may possess real legal or moral significance. In this paragraph, no facts or assumptions are stated directly, but the language has strongly involved the reader's emotions.

The American novelist William Faulkner also made use of connotation in one of the most famous speeches of our time, given when he accepted the Nobel Prize for Literature. Referring to the human fear of being "blown up" in war, he said:

Until he relearns these things, he will write as though he stood among and watched the end of man. I decline to accept the end of man. It is easy enough to say that man is immortal simply because he will endure; that when the last ding-dong of doom has clanged and faded from the last worthless rock hanging tideless in the last red and dying evening, that even then there will still be one more sound: that of his puny inexhaustible voice, still talking. I refuse to accept this. I believe that man will not merely endure; he will prevail. He is immortal, not because he alone among creatures has an inexhaustible voice, but because he has a soul, a spirit capable of compassion and sacrifice and endurance. The poet's, the writer's, duty is to write about these things. It is his privilege to help man endure by lifting his heart, by reminding him of the courage and honor and hope and pride and compassion and pity and sacrifice which have been the glory of his past. The poet's voice need not merely be the record of man; it can be one of the props, the pillars, to help him endure and prevail.

Some of Faulkner's phrases have vividly negative connotations: "ding-dong of doom," "the last worthless rock hanging tideless in the last red and dying evening," "his puny inexhaustible voice." These images are contrasted with words with strong moral, even religious, positive connotations: "man is immortal," "man will not merely endure; he will prevail," "he has a soul, a spirit capable of compassion and sacrifice and endurance," "courage and honor and hope and pride and compassion and pity and sacrifice." Faulkner was not offering a strongly logical argument; rather, through the sheer impact of his words, he hoped to enlist our emotions in affirming that humans will not only endure but prevail.

Figurative Language

Metaphors and similes also aid the writer of persuasion. As we noted in the "Focus" section of Chapter 6, both figures of speech compare one's subject to another that is not really like it in kind but is like it in some other way that the writer has determined. "That car is a monster" is a metaphor in which two unlike things are compared because they both create fear. "The child waddles like (or as) a duck" is a simile because of the injection of the word *like* or *as*. The point of similarity is obvious: both children and ducks waddle. Whereas the comparison in similes is always clearly stated, the comparison may be submerged in metaphor; in "the car growled," the comparison between car and monster is only implied. Figurative language is used in persuasion because it is highly connotative.

These figures of speech abound in the speeches of our presidents and of other leaders. Abraham Lincoln's speeches during the Civil War used and created metaphors that are still famous: he quoted the Bible in asserting that "A house divided against itself cannot stand" and asked that Americans "bind up the nation's wounds." In a speech on the night of Mahatma Gandhi's death, Indian Prime Minister Jawaharlal Nehru said:

The light has gone out, I said, and yet I was wrong. For the light that shone in this country was no ordinary light. The light that has illumined this country for these many years will illumine this country for many more years, and a thousand years later that light will still be seen in this country and the world will see it and it will give solace to innumerable hearts. For that light represented the living truth . . . the eternal truths, reminding us of the right path, drawing us from error, taking this ancient country to freedom.

Allusion

Allusion, especially to cultural heroes and myths, is another effective use of language in presenting arguments. Many writers allude to the Bible, because it has always been a cornerstone of our own national mythology. We have already quoted a figure of speech from the Bible used by Abraham Lincoln. And Adlai Stevenson, in accepting the nomination as Democratic Party candidate for president in 1952, alluded to Jesus's agony in the Garden of Gethsemane: "I have asked the merciful Father, the Father to us all, to let this cup pass from me. But from such dread responsibility one does not shrink in fear, in self-interest, or in false humility. So, 'If this cup may not pass from me, except I drink it, Thy will be done.' "

Repetition

One of the most frequently used language patterns in persuasion is repetition. Although repetition, if not handled well, can be boring, when handled skillfully, it can achieve quite impressive effects. In one of the most famous speeches of World War II, given after the Battle of Dunkirk, Winston Churchill concluded:

Even though large tracts of Europe and many old and famous states have fallen or may fall into the grip of the Gestapo and all the odious apparatus of Nazi rule, we shall not flag or fail. We shall go on to the end, we shall fight in France, we shall fight on the seas and oceans, we shall fight with growing confidence and growing strength in the air, we shall defend our island, whatever the cost may be, we shall fight on the beaches, we shall fight on the landing grounds, we shall fight in the fields and in the streets, we shall fight in the hills; we shall never surrender, and even if, which I do not for a moment believe, this island or a large part of it were subjugated and starving, then our Empire beyond the seas, armed and guarded by the British fleet, would carry on the struggle, until, in God's good time, the New World, with all its power and might, steps forth to the rescue and the liberation of the old.

And Franklin Delano Roosevelt, after the bombing of Pearl Harbor by the Japanese, asked Congress for a declaration of war against Japan. In strikingly effective repetition, he said;

Yesterday the Japanese government also launched an attack against Malaya.
Last night Japanese forces attacked Hong Kong.
Last night Japanese forces attacked Guam.
Last night Japanese forces attacked the Philippine Islands.
Last night the Japanese attacked Wake Island.
And this morning the Japanese attacked Midway Island.

Humor and Satire

Humor can often accomplish for the writer what straight logical argument cannot. Woody Allen, in a speech to the graduating class of 1979, argued that science has failed us:

Put in its simplest form, the problem is: How is it possible to find meaning in a finite world given my waist and shirt size? This is a very difficult question when we realize that science has failed us. True, it has conquered many diseases, broken the genetic code, and even placed human beings on the moon, and yet when a man of 80 is left in a room with two 18-year-old cocktail waitresses nothing happens. Because the real problems never change. After all, can the human soul be glimpsed through a microscope? Maybe—but you'd definitely need one of those very good ones with two eyepieces. We know that the most advanced computer in the world does not have a brain as sophisticated as that of an ant. True, we could say that of many of our relatives but we only have to put up with them at weddings or special occasions. Science is something we depend on all the time. If I develop a pain in the chest I must take an X-ray. But what if the radiation from the X-ray causes me deeper problems? Before I know it, I'm going in for surgery. Naturally, while they're giving me oxygen an intern decides to light up a cigarette. The next thing you know I'm rocketing over the World Trade Center in bed clothes. Is this science? True, science has taught us how to pasteurize cheese. And true, this can be fun in mixed company—but what of the H-bomb? Have you ever seen what happens when one of those things falls off a desk accidentally? And where is science when one ponders the eternal riddles? How did the cosmos originate? How long has it been around? Did matter begin with an explosion or by the word of God? And if by the latter, could He not have begun it just two weeks earlier to take advantage of some of the warmer weather? Exactly what do we mean when we say, man is mortal? Obviously it's not a compliment.

In one of the most famous arguments of all time, Jonathan Swift made "a modest proposal" that the Irish eat their children because they were too poor to feed them: "I have been assured by a very knowing American of my acquaintance in London, that a young healthy child well nursed is at a year old a most delicious, nourishing, and wholesome food, whether stewed, roasted, baked, or broiled; and I make no doubt that it will equally serve in a fricassee or a ragout." Because most of his readers were shocked, Swift was very effective in his use of satire, which is the humorous or critical treatment of a subject in order to expose the subject's or the audience's vices or follies. Swift was, of course, not seriously proposing this remedy for the poverty of the Irish, but he wielded the sword of satire in an effort to move the English to alleviate their misery.

Categorical Statements

The writer of argument may speak in categorical statements that emphasize his or her position by assuring the reader that there are no qualifications to the argument and will be no wavering in his or her position. Thus Abraham Lincoln promised, "We shall not fail—if we stand firm, we shall not fail"; Winston Churchill intoned, "we shall defend our island, whatever the cost may be"; and William Faulkner asserted, "I believe that man not only will endure; he will prevail."

Logical Terms

The writer of argument often, of course, uses the terminology of logic in making her or his presentation. In arguing that the poor have every reason for accommodating to poverty, as their situation is "usually hopeless," John Kenneth Galbraith, the economist, stated that the acceptance by the poor of their fate is "a profoundly rational response" and that "The deeply rational character of accommodation lies back, at least in part, of the central instruction of the principal world religions." Through the use of the word *rational*, he hammered away at the prejudices of the rich against the poor, whom the rich blame for accepting their condition.

Tone and Audience

Two other language considerations that the writer of argument must be aware of are how language conveys his or her tone and what language is appropriate to his or her audience. If the tone is serious, then the language must be serious. If the audience is educated, then the language should be educated. (For other discussions of tone, see Chapter 6, pp. 220–221; Chapter 8, p. 333; and Chapter 9, p. 421.)

SOME PRACTICE WITH THE LANGUAGE OF PERSUASION

1. Read "Letter from a Birmingham Jail" for Martin Luther King's use of language in attempting to persuade his audience—eight white Alabama ministers who had publicly disavowed his method—to accept his nonviolent method of gaining civil rights for American black people.

Letter from a Birmingham Jail
Martin Luther King, Jr.

I must confess that over the past few years I have been gravely disappointed with the white moderate. I have almost reached the regrettable conclusion that the Negro's great stumbling block in his stride toward freedom is not the White Citizen's Counciler or the Ku Klux Klanner, but the white moderate, who is more devoted to "order" than to justice; who prefers a negative peace which is the absence of tension to a positive peace which is the presence of justice; who constantly says: "I agree with you in the goal you seek, but I cannot agree with your methods of direct action"; who paternalistically believes he can set the timetable for another man's freedom; who lives by a mythical concept of time and who constantly advises the Negro to wait for a "more convenient season." Shallow understanding from people of good will is more frustrating than absolute misunderstanding from people of ill will. Lukewarm acceptance is much more bewildering than outright rejection.

I had hoped that the white moderate would understand that law and order exist for the purpose of establishing justice and that when they fail in this purpose they become the dangerously structured dams that block the flow of social progress. I had hoped that the white moderate would understand that the present tension in the South is a necessary phase of the transition from an obnoxious negative peace, in which the Negro passively accepted his unjust plight, to a substantive and positive peace, in which all men will respect the dignity and worth of human personality. Actually, we who engage in nonviolent direct action are not the creators of tension. We merely bring to the surface the hidden tension that is already alive. We bring it out in the open, where it can be seen and dealt with. Like a boil that can never be cured so long as it is covered up but must be opened with all its ugliness to the natural medicines of air and light, injustice must be exposed, with all the tension its exposure creates, to the light of human conscience and the air of national opinion before it can be cured.

In your statement you assert that our actions, even though peaceful, must be condemned because they precipitate violence. But is this a logical assertion? Isn't this like condemning a robbed man because his possession of money precipitated the evil act of robbery? Isn't this like condemning Socrates because his unswerving commitment to truth and his philosophical inquiries precipitated the act by the misguided populace in which they made him drink hemlock? Isn't this like condemning Jesus because his unique God-consciousness and never-ceasing devotion to God's will precipitated the evil act of crucifixion? We must come to see that, as the federal courts have consistently affirmed, it is wrong to urge an individual to cease his efforts to gain his basic constitutional rights because the quest may precipitate violence. Society must protect the robbed and punish the robber.

I had also hoped that the white moderate would reject the myth concerning time in relation to the struggle for freedom. I have just received a letter from a white brother in Texas. He writes: "All Christians know that the colored people will receive equal rights eventually, but it is possible that you are in too great a religious hurry. It has taken Christianity almost two thousand years to accomplish what it has. The teachings of Christ take time to come to earth." Such an attitude stems from a tragic misconception of time, from the strangely irrational notion that there is something in the very flow of time that will inevitably cure all ills. Actually, time itself is neutral; it can be used either destructively or constructively. More and more I feel that the people of ill will have used time much more effectively than have the people of good will. We will have to repent in this generation not merely for the hateful words and actions of the bad people but for the appalling silence of the good people. Human progress never rolls in on wheels of inevitability; it comes through the tireless efforts of men willing to be co-workers with God, and without this hard work, time itself becomes an ally of the forces of social stagnation. We must use time creatively, in the knowledge that the time is always ripe to do right. Now is the time to make real the promise of democracy and transform our pending national elegy into a creative psalm of brotherhood. Now is the time to lift our national policy from the quicksand of racial injustice to the solid rock of human dignity.

You speak of our activity in Birmingham as extreme. At first I was rather disappointed that fellow clergymen would see my nonviolent efforts as those of an extremist. I began thinking about the fact that I stand in the middle of two opposing forces in the Negro community. One is a force of complacency, made up in part of Negroes who, as a result of long years of oppression, are so drained of self-respect and a sense of "somebodiness" that they have adjusted to segregation; and in part of a few middle-class Negroes who, because of a degree of academic and economic security and because in some ways they profit by segregation, have become insensitive to the problems of the masses. The other force is one of bitterness and hatred, and it comes perilously close to advocating violence. It is expressed in the various black nationalist groups that are springing up across the nation, the largest and best-known being Elijah Muhammad's Muslim movement. Nourished by the Negro's frustration over the continued existence of racial discrimination, this movement is made up of people who have lost faith in America, who have absolutely repudiated Christianity, and who have concluded that the white man is an incorrigible "devil."

I have tried to stand between these two forces, saying that we need emulate neither the "do-nothingism" of the complacent nor the hatred and despair of the black nationalist. For there is the more excellent way of love and nonviolent protest. I am grateful to God that, through the influence of the Negro church, the way of nonviolence became an integral part of our struggle.

If this philosophy had not emerged, by now many streets of the South would, I am convinced, be flowing with blood. And I am further convinced that if our white brothers dismiss as "rabble-rousers" and "outside agitators" those of us who employ nonviolent direct action, and if they refuse to support our nonviolent efforts, millions of Negroes will, out of frustration and despair, seek solace and security in black-nationalist ideologies—a development that would inevitably lead to a frightening racial nightmare.

Oppressed people cannot remain oppressed forever. The yearning for freedom eventually manifests itself, and that is what has happened to the American Negro. Something within has reminded him of his birthright of freedom, and something without has reminded him that it can be gained. Consciously or unconsciously, he has been caught up by the *Zeitgeist,* and with his black brothers of Africa and his brown and yellow brothers of Asia, South America and the Caribbean, the United States Negro is moving with a sense of great urgency toward the promised land of racial justice. If one recognizes this vital urge that has engulfed the Negro community, one should readily understand why public demonstrations are taking place. The Negro has many pent-up resentments and latent frustrations and he must release them. So let him march; let him make prayer pilgrimages to the city hall; let him go on freedom rides—and try to understand why he must do so. If his repressed emotions are not released in nonviolent ways, they will seek expression through violence; this is not a threat but a fact of history. So I have not said to my people: "Get rid of your discontent." Rather, I have tried to say that this normal and healthy discontent can be channeled into the creative outlet of nonviolent direct action. And now this approach is being termed extremist.

But though I was initially disappointed at being categorized as an extremist, as I continued to think about the matter I gradually gained a measure of satisfaction from the label. Was not Jesus an extremist for love: "Love your enemies, bless them that curse you, do good to them that hate you, and pray for them which despitefully use you, and persecute you." Was not Amos an extremist for justice: "Let justice roll down like the waters and righteousness like an ever-flowing stream." Was not Paul an extremist for the Christian gospel: "I bear in my body the marks of the Lord Jesus." Was not Martin Luther an extremist: "Here I stand; I cannot do otherwise, so help me God." And John Bunyan: "I will stay in jail to the end of my days before I make a butchery of my conscience." And Abraham Lincoln: "This nation cannot survive half slave and half free." And Thomas Jefferson: "We hold these truths to be self-evident, that all men are created equal . . ." So the question is not whether we will be extremists, but what kind of extremists we will be. Will we be extremists for hate or for love? Will we be extremists for the preservation of injustice or for the extension of justice? In that dramatic scene on Calvary's hill three men were crucified. We must never forget that all three were crucified for the same crime—the crime of extremism. Two were extremists for immorality, and thus fell below their environment. The other, Jesus Christ, was an extremist for love, truth and goodness, and thereby rose above his environment. Perhaps the South, the nation and the world are in dire need of creative extremists.

I had hoped that the white moderate would see this need. Perhaps I was too optimistic; perhaps I expected too much. I suppose I should have realized that few members of the oppressor race can understand the deep groans and passionate yearnings of the oppressor race, and still fewer have the vision to see that injustice must be rooted out by strong, persistent and determined action. I am thankful, however, that some of our white brothers in the South have grasped the meaning of this social revolution and committed themselves to it. They are still all too few in quantity, but they are big in quality. Some—such as Ralph McGill, Lillian Smith, Harry Golden, James McBride Dabbs, Ann Braden and Sarah Patton Boyle—have written about our struggle in eloquent and prophetic terms. Others have marched with us down nameless streets of the South. They have languished in filthy, roach-infested jails, suffering the abuse and brutality of policemen who view them as "dirty nigger-lovers." Unlike so many of their moderate brothers and sisters, they have recognized the urgency of the moment and sensed the need for powerful "action" antidotes to combat the disease of segregation.

a. What are the logical components of King's argument? Are they primarily inductive, deductive, or a combination? Did he appeal to a higher priority in refuting his opposition? If so, what higher priority did he establish?

b. What was his attitude toward his audience? How did this attitude affect his tone? What words and phrases indicate what his tone is?

c. King made extensive use of connotative language. What connotative meanings do phrases like the following have, and how do they make an emotional appeal for his argument: "obnoxious negative peace," "unjust plight," "deep groans and passionate yearnings," "dignity and worth of human personality," "prayer pilgrimages," "creative extremists," and "strong, persistent and determined action"?

d. His letter also abounds in figurative language and allusions. What are some of the many metaphors he used? What are some of the allusions? What effects were these intended to have on his readers? Some of his metaphors are clichés like "the time is always ripe." Why would King use clichés in writing to this audience?

e. Repetition is another key element in King's appeal to his reader's emotions. Point out an instance of this repetition and discuss its usefulness.

f. King also presented his argument in categorical statements. Which do you think are most effective in arousing the reader?

g. Where did King insert logical terms, either to denigrate his opponent's use of reason or to support his own logic? How important a role does this type of emotional appeal play? Explain.

h. How did King's audience's frame of reference affect his choice of words? How would his persuasive language have changed if he had been writing to a group of U.S. Senators?

2. Choose one of the following enthymemes and develop it in a paragraph or two. Once you are satisfied with the logic of your argument, revise your paragraph by using one or more of the methods of persuasive language. Write to an audience of your choosing and convey your tone clearly:

Leisure time affects the quality of life more than does work because that is when we have an opportunity to think.

Everyone should participate in games because games can teach us how to compete gracefully.

Stress must be dealt with because it is a constant in modern life.

3. Discuss the use of persuasive language by the framers of the Declaration of Independence (pp. 344–346). Compare and contrast their use of such language with that of Martin Luther King. How can you account for any substantial differences?

REWRITING

Obtaining Feedback on Your Rough Draft

Because persuasive writing depends more on audience response than does any other type of writing, the feedback that you receive on your rough draft will be crucial to the success of your final product. Therefore you must solicit the most thoughtful response. Whether this response comes from your "other, critical self," a peer group, or your instructor, the respondent should play to the best of his or her ability the role that you have established for your audience.

In playing the role of your audience, your respondent should know your audience's frame of reference and their point of view on your subject. He or she should be willing to defend your audience's position in order to elicit from you the most effective argument possible. He or she may indicate to you, for example, that you have not appealed to the most telling higher priority and will need to reevaluate the basis of your argument.

You will want to analyze also how your audience has responded to your language and tone, to your evidence, and to your refutation. At some point, your reader(s) should also switch sides and tell you how to better defend you own position.

Try answering the questions of the "Audience Response Guide" for the student essay on bodybuilding (see pp. 347–349) before you rewrite your essay.

———— AUDIENCE RESPONSE GUIDE ————

1. What do you think the writer wanted to say in this paper? What is her or his purpose in writing? What does she or he want the paper to mean?

2. How does this paper affect the reader for whom it was intended?

3. How effective has the writer been in conveying her or his purpose and meaning? What are the strengths of the paper? What are the weaknesses?

4. How should the paper be revised to better fulfill its purpose and meaning?

The student who wrote the rough draft on "Bodybuilding: The Shape of the Future" obtained the following comments from her peer evaluation group:

1. They knew that she was arguing that because bodybuilding is a necessity to all who are conscious of their appearance and their health, women should pursue the sport.

2. As readers of Redbook Magazine, her audience felt that the writer had bridged the gap between the images in the media of the bodybuilding woman as an unattractive athlete, on the one hand, and as a sexual athlete, on the other. They felt her concern about both health and appearance was very convincing.

3. Her readers were impressed by her authoritative, yet friendly presentation. They liked the chair analogy, but they felt the paragraphs in the body of the essay were too short and choppy and suggested she rearrange her material on the different elements of the bodybuilder's routine.

4. They were curious about how bodybuilding relates to the women's movement. They also wanted to be reassured that they would not grow "big" muscles.

How do these comments compare with those that you made? Here is the student's revised draft.

BODYBUILDING: THE SHAPE OF THE FUTURE

I am a female bodybuilder who has been actively engaged in body-building for many years. When you hear the word bodybuilding, the first image that probably comes to mind is a man who is clumsy or muscle-bound and a woman who looks manly. Although some people's attitudes have changed, most are still unaware of the benefits of body-building. Bodybuilding has become more than a sport--it has become a way of life. A woman bodybuilder does not lose any of her femininity; she gains sexuality.

In the past, the woman's place was in the home. She was expected to grow up, get married, have babies, clean, cook, and turn into the all-American frumpy housewife. Well, times have changed; more women have their own careers and goals. Along with career changes have come changes in how women feel about themselves and their bodies. More and more women are discovering bodybuilding as a way of staying fit and youthful.

What would you rather have, fat or muscle? A shapely, firm body or a spongy, saggy one? I am sure everyone would choose muscle and a shapely, firm body. That is the best reason to start bodybuilding. Don't sit back and accept saggy, cellulite bodies as part of nature. And you won't gain large, manly muscles. A woman's level of testosterone, the hormone that causes men to grow large muscles, is generally one tenth that of a man's. Though a woman's muscular strength grows from weightlifting, she does not gain the muscle bulk of the man. Yet she does gain a strong, sleek, sexy body.

Because bodybuilding has long been considered a man's sport, one thinks of bodybuilders as clumsy and muscle-bound, but in reality, bodybuilders build their agility along with their muscles. It is important for a bodybuilder to be agile and flexible in order to prevent injuries.

The program for physical fitness can be compared to a chair. One of the legs on the chair is stretching exercises. Stretching exercises increase flexibility and minimize injuries. These exercises help to keep you agile. The second leg is aerobic exercises. Aerobic exercises are running, swimming, and cycling. These exercises strengthen your cardiovascular system, resulting in keeping a strong heart. The third leg is weight training. These exercises increase your strength and power and give you a defined, firm body. The fourth leg is nutrition. Nutrition is essential in keeping your body healthy. You need all four legs to hold up the chair. If one is missing, the chair will fall. And so if one of these components is missing from your routine, then you are not totally fit.

The four legs on the chair of health are part of every bodybuilder's routine; therefore bodybuilders are specimens of perfectly fit human beings. Bodybuilders are fit in all areas, such as strength, agility, flexibility, and muscular and cardiovascular endurance. They are not into just lifting weights. They are totally dedicated to diet and exercise. As men and women develop their physiques, psychological effects also occur, such as self-esteem, confidence, and a new outlook on life.

What changes did the writer make in her rough draft? How can you account for them? What further changes would you recommend that she might make based on the suggestions in the "Revising and Editing Persuasive Writing" section following?

Revising and Editing Persuasive Writing

Revising. When writing persuasively, your aims are to convince the reader of your logic and your credibility. You might apply the following questions to your persuasive essay in order to determine what revisions you might make in strengthening your logic and overall credibility.

1. Have you included weak or extraneous arguments, arguments that you yourself find unconvincing? More important, have you applied the tests for fallacious reasoning to your points? If not, consider whether any of your arguments now appear to be fallacies. Cut all weak, extraneous, or fallacious arguments from your essay.

2. Have you included enough background for your intended reader? Have you included enough examples to prove your argument? Does an analogy now occur to you? Have you refuted all opposing arguments? At this point, you may want to add background, examples, an analogy, a refutation to your essay.

3. How effective is your organization of your arguments? Is your syllogism arranged logically? What pattern of arrangement have you used? Does it correspond to the classical questions that you asked? Is your arrangement of causes, comparisons, classifications, definitions effective? Have you placed your strongest arguments at the end for major effect? If your organization seems illogical or weak, you may want to rearrange your points.

4. If cutting proof that now seems to you unconvincing will leave you with a thin case for your point of view, you might search for a stronger argument as a substitute.

5. Have you neglected to reinforce part of your argument? If so, you might insert mention or proof of this aspect of your case at logical points in your paper. The distributing of an important aspect of your argument reinforces its importance; neglecting it makes the reader wonder why you mentioned it in the first place.

6. Do you want to retain some of your weak arguments but don't know how to make them seem convincing? You might want to consolidate them under an inclusive heading to bolster their significance.

Editing.   As with the prose you wrote for your scientific paper, your writing for a persuasive paper should be clear and concrete in order to assure the reader of your credibility. Terms should be carefully defined, and facts should be clearly stated.

Unlike scientific prose, persuasive writing does employ figurative language in its appeal to the emotions of the reader. The Focus section of this chapter suggests the use of connotative language, wit, humor, irony, and figures of speech in an effort to engage the reader's emotions. You might reexamine the language of your essay to see if you have chosen words for their emotional connotations as well as their literal meanings, included figures of speech that make comparisons the reader will respond to, and perhaps added touches of humor that will engage the reader further.

BECOMING AWARE OF YOURSELF AS A WRITER

1. In presenting your argument, did you convince your audience of your point of view? What methods did you use to convince your audience? How could you have been more convincing? How can you be more convincing in the future?

2. How were you able to use logic in arguing your points? How were you able to achieve sincerity? What effect did your logic and sincerity have on your audience?

3. How were you able to use such elements of language as connotation, metaphor, allusion, and repetition to argue your points effectively?

4. From your work with the techniques of persuasion, can you imagine how such techniques can be misused and abused by those seeking to sell a product or to persuade at any cost? Do you feel more powerful as a writer now that you have begun to develop persuasive skills yourself?

5. What have you learned about responding to the arguments of others by fulfilling this task? How might you argue a particular point differently from how you have argued it in the past?

9

Writing About an Issue

PURPOSE

In the writing task for Chapter 8, you were asked to create an argument and to write persuasively, avoiding certain logical fallacies and reasoning deductively toward a specific goal. If you considered the views of others, it was quite possibly only to refute them or at least to show the superiority of your view to theirs. Your purpose was to lead your audience to the conclusion that your argument, and only your argument, was the best. There is another form of thinking and discourse, however, that you are often asked to engage in. In this writing strategy, you may also write on a topic that carries considerable room for disagreement or controversy. But rather than assume a specific point of view or role, you become a disinterested observer—you assume, in effect, all of the roles. This strategy is called critical thinking.

The reading and writing activities in this chapter begin with the assumption that critical thinking results from two linked activities that we discussed in Chapters 6 and 7: generalizing and exemplifying. As we have seen, from the simplest observations to the most complex operations of thought, human beings unceasingly form concepts and select experiences or observations that act as supports for those concepts. To arrive at general ideas, or generalizations, without adequate examples is to reason ineffectively. To interpret our particular experience and points of view without trying to connect them to some larger idea or pattern of thought is also to limit the worth and effectiveness of our thinking. Thinking, whether it is directed toward the acts of writing or reading, involves an ever extending linkage of generalizations and examples.

Much of the writing that college students are asked to do is in the form of essay examinations, "Compare and contrast . . ." "trace the causes of . . ." "show the relationship between. . . ." These are all recognizable rhetorical formulas of exposition that students acquire from their earliest days as writers. All of them require careful analysis and understanding of the material or issues involved. All of them require the ability to create interlocking chains of generalizations and examples that are clear and reasonable. The writer is expected to show sufficient knowledge of the subject and to be able to arrange this knowledge so that it reveals the relationships announced in the examination question.

In this chapter, you will be presented with the opportunity to sharpen your critical thinking skills and apply them in the writing task. The generating ideas section will suggest how to go about thinking critically, and the audience section will discuss how role playing can help the writer to further examine an issue objectively. In the task section nine professional essays on three issues of vital concern to our society—affirmative action, euthanasia, and pornography—will give you a possible subject and considerable material with which to work in developing the task.

GENERATING IDEAS: CRITICAL THINKING

One conclusion you might make from the kinds of writing tasks and activities you have undertaken in this book is that you have benefitted from the examination of your writing process these tasks and activities call for. You may see that the more you examine this process, the more you realize how closely it is related to how you think. You may see, therefore, how important it is for your development as a writer to submit your methods of thinking to objective examination. Any activity of understanding and explaining how we think, of developing a self-consciousness about our methods of arriving at conclusions, is called critical thinking.

Critical thinking teaches us to be more cautious and less hasty with our judgments and often to suspend our final views on an issue until we are satisfied that we have examined it thoroughly from as many different perspectives as we can. Critical thinking is not very easy to accomplish. The more controversial the issue, the more each side of the issue stakes out a position with which the other side finds it impossible to agree. The result is often inclusive and unsatisfying, as each side is unable to move beyond its own self-made limitation of perception and understanding.

The subject of abortion, for example, is as intensely argued as any single issue in our society. To apply critical thinking here would require the participants to examine the significance and application of at least some of the following contexts of that issue: the status of the fetus with respect to scientific, moral, and legal opinion; freedom of choice; the priority of religious or secular views; the conflict between liberal and conservative attitudes on sexual behavior; the role of majority and minority opinion in a democracy; the function of the media; the conflict between public and private morality; the differences in regional and ethnic opinion; the emergence of women's rights as a major social force.

Critical thinking, therefore, requires us to examine (1) our interaction with the issue itself, (2) viewpoints of the specific parties involved, (3) the larger group of human beings affected by this issue, and (4) other ideas and issues that become implicated as a result of the process of critical thinking. For example, critical thinking might reveal to participants in the abortion discussion that (1) freedom of choice also entails social responsibility, (2) expressions of religious or moral conscience must be weighed against prevailing secular opinion, (3) private sexual behavior also has broad social ramifications, and (4) the word "life" is subject to varying definitions dependent on the different perspectives of the users.

Arriving at a Synthesis

Let's say the issue is whether college students should pursue a general liberal arts curriculum or a specialized vocational program. You have read several essays arguing for or against the values of both kinds of college undergraduate education. In order to generate ideas for your essay, you try to form generalizations about the main idea of each essay. The following questions can help you as you try to generalize about each essay's approach:

1. What is the essay's point of view? How clearly is it stated?
2. How logical is the main idea? How consistent?
3. How does the writer present and organize his or her information?
4. How much authority does the essay convey?
5. What tone of voice does the essay reveal?
6. How sufficient is the evidence provided for by each generalization?
7. What attitude does the essay take toward opposing points of view? What are these opposing points of view?
8. How closely do the essay's conclusions coincide with your point of view?
9. How justified are the writer's conclusions from the supporting information?
10. What kinds of conclusions, whether practical or philosophical, specific or abstract, does the writer make? How appropriate are they for the essay? What effects do they have on the reader?

Let's assume one essay opts for the traditional liberal arts curriculum, recommends a return to the study of accepted classics, and advocates a moral and ethical foundation as the basis for college work. Another essay favors a technical vocational curriculum and an emphasis on practical contemporary concerns. Still a third essay focuses on the increasingly diverse population of American colleges, especially the tailoring of the curriculum to help minority groups. As a reader—and a college student as well—you find many of their ideas and points of view interesting and reasonable. In some ways their positions converge, in other ways they seem far apart. But rather than dispose of the side you find objectionable through the attack of argument, you have the opportunity to try to resolve these various points of view. You can create a new, modified, perhaps even more persuasive point of view that synthesizes, or brings together, elements of all the major generalizations in the essays, thus forming a new generalization of your own.

Applying the four critical thinking skills to the issue, you discover that (1) the issue is what is best for all students; (2) some students want vocational skills, some want a traditional liberal arts education, and some want a diversified education that recognizes their ethnic identities; (3) the decision will affect how America competes in the job market, how individual Americans feel about their ethnic identities, and how future citizens make important decisions; and (4) the questions arise as to whether students know what is best for them, and on the other hand, whether what has been done historically has a bearing on planning for the future. Your synthesis might suggest a new curriculum for the college student that includes both traditional subject matter and ideas that meet the needs of the changing population of today's college students. Notice that this synthesis attempts to resolve conflicting ideas by creating other generalizations that can then be tested by other readers. Rather than closing off discussion by claiming you are right and the others are wrong, you encourage a continuing dialogue with your readers, for you recognize that all generalizations possess a tentativeness that requires them to be submitted to examination.

Using the Journal

Perhaps the best way to begin to work toward a final generalization is to use your journal. You might begin by writing brief summaries of essays representing all points of view on an issue. Writing summaries gives you a clearer picture of the chain of generalizations and examples by reducing the discussion to its essential ideas. Remember that a summary tries to retain the basic form of the original by giving the equivalent space to parts in the original essay (see Chapter 7, pp. 274–275). This will give you a feel for the author's point of view and method of argument as well as allow you to grasp the main ideas and supporting examples of each essay.

The summaries can be used as a starting point for free writing about your own views on the issues of each essay. Write about your past encounters with the issues and what you think has shaped your own attitudes on them. What recent news events have highlighted each issue? Has it caused any recent controversy in your community? If so, how was it resolved?

Another way to "get inside" each issue is to create a dialogue between two persons having contradictory points of view. They don't have to be participants in the issue; they might represent different roles or positions that are somehow affected. Here is an example:

Jack: I just think pornography is out of place in a moral society.

Joan: Perhaps. But aren't you really saying "ideal" society? It's obvious that in many ways our society is quite imperfect, pornography being one of the lesser evils we have to tolerate.

Jack: But why tolerate it if we can pass laws that will make it illegal?

Joan: You're assuming that laws can simply make something disappear. What would happen to the reasons why we have pornography? Would they just go away? I don't think so.

Jack: I agree, but don't we have to do something? Should we just allow it to continue to do damage to our society?

Joan: But I'm not so sure it really does do damage. Explain what you mean. . . .

Creating an imaginary discussion such as the one above allows you to observe how ideas are connected, how arguments are advanced by the expression of contradictory or conflicting ideas. It also gives you an understanding of points of view that differ from your own. It helps you to avoid the creation of a straw-man character, one who takes easily refuted or even ridiculous positions that do little to advance the discussion but make your own point of view look good by comparison.

Collaboration Groups

An issue like euthanasia touches on so many sensitive areas that the individual writer can hardly expect to know and understand all the feelings and thoughts of the many persons affected by it. By learning to listen to the thoughts of others, we also learn more about the issue than we could by ourselves. We learn to see our own beliefs in the context of different life experiences. Thus, we become aware that our own ideas might need to be modified in light of these differences. In this human interaction we find that a series of linked generalizations and examples often leads to a reasoned compromise in which everyone benefits. In collaboration, for example, you might exchange essay summaries with other members of your class to compare how closely you agreed on the main ideas and supporting examples. Or you might create a case in which each member of the group assumes a different role and tries to explain the issue in terms of that role. Through a series of linked explanations, you can then arrive at a larger theory or generalization that will resolve the issue to the satisfaction of your group. This new idea represents the efforts of the entire group and as such emerges only because individuals in the group were able to modify their own views by listening to others.

SOME PRACTICE WITH CRITICAL THINKING

1. Write an imaginary dialogue between a male firefighter and a newly appointed female firefighter in which the former questions the latter's fitness for the job and the latter responds. Then, bring in a third character who attempts to resolve the issue through critical thinking.

2. In order to understand how the media deal with controversy, select from one of the newsmagazines or television news programs like *Nightline* a controversial topic like the Strategic Defense Initiative (Star Wars), child abuse, or illegal immigration. Show how the various media present their arguments. How do the media strive for objectivity? Should they take sides? Why or why not? How could they enable the parties involved to seek compromise in order to resolve their varying points of view?

3. Collaborate with your group on a social or political topic that is currently a subject of controversy in your school or community. To what extent have your individual positions been modified? After further collaboration, compare the results with the ideas that evolved after the first collaboration. What generalizations were developed further? What connections were made between ideas?

4. Make a list of issues that probably cannot be resolved by compromise. What characteristics do these issues have in common?

5. Take an issue you believe to be irresolvable and write a one-paragraph theme in your journal that tries to show how the varying points of view on this issue might be synthesized.

6. Write a brief theme on an issue you have very strong feelings about, but write about it from the opposing point of view. How convincing is your argument? What points did you omit?

AUDIENCE: THE INFORMED READER

In Chapter 3, you wrote for your teacher in order to experiment with the problem of bridging the gap between yourself and someone whose perspective and ideas on your subject might be quite different from your own. Now we would like you to think about writing for someone who, like your teacher, is well informed about a particular field of knowledge. If you are taking an essay exam, for example, you are writing for an audience who knows more about the subject than you do. This is the case with most of the papers that you do in school as well. The problem you thus face is not how to bridge the gap between yourself and someone whose interests might be different from yours; in this case, you share your interest in the subject with the reader. Rather, your problem is how to present your own insights into the subject so that your reader, who has already studied the subject, might be interested in and perhaps even enlightened by your views.

On the one hand, you want to try to find something original to say about your subject; your own honest response may be the one piece of information that you can provide that will be new to your reader. On the other hand, you want to impress your audience with your ability both to write about the subject with a knowledge of the issues and viewpoints involved and to use accurately the vocabulary and concepts employed by those in the field; you want to keep your focus less on your response to the subject per se than on what your response contributes to a better understanding of the subject. You want, in short, to demonstrate that you are thinking intelligently and, perhaps most important, critically about the subject.

Just how can you accomplish this? One answer is simply to employ the methods of critical thinking to which you were introduced in the previous section on generating ideas. Let us look now in more detail at one of those methods, that of playing out the role of each point of view one can take toward an issue, exploring the strengths and the weaknesses of these roles, examining the relationships between them, and so finally evaluating them from a more dispassionate and objective perspective than any one of them represents alone.

Role Playing

In the "Audience" section of Chapter 3, we invited you to experiment with some of the roles each individual plays in life, to explore the difference, for example, between writing about a subject in the voice and from the perspective of a parent and those of a child, or an employer and an employee, or a friend and a stranger. Writing the paper in Chapter 3, you played a role that was an aspect of yourself, speaking in the voice of that role in order to express yourself as honestly as possible.

Now, we invite you to experiment with role play again. This time, though, we would like you to try out roles that you do not fully identify with, that are not typical aspects of yourself. We would like you to act out, in fact, a number of roles that may clash not only with one another but also with your own most private and personal sense of who you are.

For example, you might try the following exercise: Write a paragraph in which you freely express your feelings about violence in sports. Then, examine your personal point of view from the perspective of each of the following roles: the wife of a professional football player whose career was ended by an on-the-field injury, a college football player praised in the newspapers for his aggressive play, a high school football coach. How does such role play broaden your perspective on the subject of violence in sports? How might it help you to think more critically about the subject and thus to write more successfully for an audience who is informed about the subject, for a sociology or a psychology teacher, perhaps, who has been studying and teaching classes on this subject for some time?

Role-Playing the Informed Reader

By employing methods of critical thinking, you demonstrate that you are informed both about your subject and about your audience, that you understand how an informed reader thinks and what will be of interest to such a reader. In a sense, you play the role of such a reader yourself.

This should caution you against doing a number of things. You should probably avoid writing at length about what your reader already knows, except to the degree that you are using such information to illustrate and explain your own knowledge of and ideas about the subject. Also, it is probably a good idea to avoid straying from the subject at hand, especially by dwelling at length on your views of peripheral issues. If you are writing about violence in sports, for example, do not stray too far into an expression of your personal distaste for violence of any kind. Stick to what you know about the viewpoints on the central issue.

Finally, you should find it useful to observe the formal conventions of grammar and organization that will appeal to an educated and informed audience. If you want to sound well informed, at least for such an audience, you probably need to sound reasonably logical, thorough, and articulate as well.

SOME PRACTICE WITH WRITING FOR AN INFORMED AUDIENCE

1. Examine your own views about gun control. What might a member of the National Rifle Association think of your views? What might a member of the local police force think? A liberal Democrat? A conservative Republican? Play the roles of each of these segments of society with viewpoints on gun control. How informed do you imagine each of these potential readers to be about the issue of gun control? How objective? Does being knowledgeable about an issue necessarily lead one to be objective?

2. Pick a controversial topic, such as gun control, abortion, or capital punishment, and canvas your class members for their views and knowledge of it. Use role

play to identify with each point of view. Then put together a composite sketch of a person whose point of view on the topic reflects the point of view of the class as a whole. How well informed might such a person be? How might you write about the topic if your reader were such a person?

3. What role might you assume in writing about each of the following topics if your audience were to be a reader who knew little about the topic?

   a. *The National Enquirer*

   b. Fraternity hazing

   c. Sibling rivalry

   d. The Great Depression

   e. The Equal Rights Amendment

Explain how your approach might change if, instead, your audience were to be a teacher with experience in a subject area associated with the topic: a journalism teacher in the case of Topic a, an anthropology teacher in the case of Topic b, a psychology teacher in the case of Topic c, an American history teacher in the case of Topic d, and a political science teacher in the case of Topic e.

TASK: WRITING ABOUT AN ISSUE

Your task will be to write an essay in which, having read the different viewpoints on a vital social issue, you explain the factors involved—emotional, political, ethical, economic, religious—and attempt to synthesize the various points of view. You will create a new, modified, perhaps even more persuasive point of view that synthesizes, or brings together, elements of all the major generalizations in the essays, thus forming a new generalization of your own.

In attempting to arrive at a synthesis, then, you will be acting as a disinterested observer who will think about the issue critically by analyzing the various positions on it and attempt to arrive at a broader, more objective stance.

Included in the following pages are three essays on each of three social issues: affirmative action, euthanasia, and pornography. (Your instructor or your group may wish to choose three essays on a different or additional social issue.) Select the issue you or your group would like to explore and write about and read the following essays on it. As you read, ask yourself the following questions: How do these essays coincide with or run counter to my own personal experiences with or informed views of the subject? (If none describes a point of view on the subject that you or your group feels is legitimate, you might want to locate and add for consideration an essay that reflects this point of view.) What inferences can be drawn from all these essays about the attitudes of people in my school, community, or culture on this subject? How might these issues have affected these people? How might these issues be resolved? What obstacles would need to be overcome before a resolution could occur?

Your audience for this task will be an informed reader, most likely your instructor. Your reader will understand the factors involved in the issue and can judge how reasonable your synthesis is.

In organizing the essay, you will most likely want to analyze the issue from the various viewpoints and then present your own synthesis, utilizing a syllogistic organizational plan (see p. 409). In addition, you might want to announce your synthesis first and follow it with the varying points of view in a deductive approach to arranging your essay, or you may want to announce your synthesis last in a climactic approach.

Following are nine essays: three on affirmative action, three on euthanasia, and three on pornography. The questions following each set of essays are drawn from those on how to read critically in the generating ideas section and may help you to better understand the writers' points of view.

Affirmative Action Essays

A Defense of Quotas
Charles Krauthammer

As recently as three years ago Nathan Glazer noted with dismay the inability, or unwillingness, of the most conservative American administration in 50 years to do anything about the growing entrenchment, in law and in practice, of racial quotas. It seemed that officially sanctioned race consciousness was becoming irrevocably woven into American life.

Glazer's pessimism was premature. In the last two years a revolution has been brewing on the issue of affirmative action. It is marked not by the pronouncements of Clarence Pendleton, or the change in composition and ideology of the United States Commission on Civil Rights. That is for show. It is marked by a series of court rulings and administration actions that, step by step, will define affirmative action out of existence.

How far this process had gone was dramatized by the leak of a draft executive order that would outlaw in federal government contracting not only quotas and statistical measures but any "preference . . . on the basis of race, color, religion, sex or national origin . . . with respect to any aspect of employment." Although this appeared as a bolt from a blue August sky, it was, in fact, the culmination of a process that has been building over the last several years. It amounts to a counterrevolution in stages on the issue of race-conscious social policy.

The counterrevolution has occurred in what is probably the most crucial domain of affirmative action: employment. Classic affirmative action mandates preference for blacks (and women and other favored groups) at all four steps in the employment process: recruitment, hiring, promotion, and firing. The counterre-volution has attacked such preferences at each step of the way, beginning at the end.

The first major breach in the edifice of affirmative action was the Supreme Court's Memphis fire fighters decision of June 1984. The City of Memphis had been under a court-ordered consent decree to increase the number of blacks in the fire department. When layoffs came in 1981, a U.S. District Court ruled that last-hired blacks could not be the first fired, as the seniority system dictated. Three whites were laid off instead. The Supreme Court reversed that decision. It ruled that in a clash between a bona fide seniority system and affirmative action, sen-iority prevails.

You cannot fire by race. But can you promote? Can you hire? The next, more tentative, step in the counterrevolution occurred this past spring in the District of Columbia. A suit originally filed in the waning days of the Carter administration had resulted in mandated preferential hiring and promotions for minorities in the city's fire departments. In March the D.C. fire chief, according to one of the judge's directives in the case, ordered that five black fire fighters be promoted over whites who had scored higher than they had.

The union immediately filed suit to block the promotions. And the Justice De-partment joined the suit on the union's side. The judge in the case then rendered a Solomonic decision prohibiting race consciousness in promotion, but permitting it in hiring.

The case is under appeal and no one knows how it will come out. The reason is that no one knows how to interpret *Memphis*. Did this ruling apply only to layoffs, as suggested to civil rights groups trying to limit their losses? Or did it apply also to hiring and/or promotion, the other crucial career choke points? You can read *Memphis* either way, and everyone is waiting for the Court to say.

Everyone, that is, except William Bradford Reynolds, head of the Justice De-partment's Civil Rights Division, and leading *contra*. Reynolds is a conservative in a hurry. Invoking *Memphis* as his authority, he ordered 51 jurisdictions from New York to Los Angeles to cleanse existing consent decrees (which mandated goals—quotas—in hiring) of any hint of group or racial preference. Not only would pref-erences be outlawed from now on, but existing decrees would have to be revised to reflect the new dispensation.

Reynold's target is to root out race consciousness in toto, from firing to pro-motion to hiring. Everything, it seems, except recruitment. Last June, at the start of Reynold's confirmation hearings for the number three job at Justice (he was eventually turned down), he sent a letter to Senator Edward Kennedy stating that he favored affirmative action in recruitment. He argued that it is the only permis-sible affirmative action; in fact, it is how you determine its success. Its success could be "measured," he wrote, "in the number of persons who are recruited to apply."

Recruiting, it seems, would be the last refuge for affirmative action. Or so it seemed, until the final step: draft executive order 11246 revising the affirmative action order that since 1968 has mandated race consciousness and statistical norms (quotas) in employment for government contractors. The draft executive order would repeal it all: goals, timetables, statistical norms, and other forms of racial preference.

It appears to do so even for Reynold's cherished exception, recruitment. Hard to tell, though. The first section of the draft order seems to define affirmative action, as Reynolds likes to, as exclusively applicable to recruitment. "Each government contractor . . . shall engage in affirmative recruitment . . . to . . . expand[ing] the number of qualified minorities and women who receive full consideration for hiring and promotion." But the very next section continues: "Nothing in this executive order shall be interpreted to require . . . any preference . . . on the basis of race . . . with respect to any aspect of employment, including . . . recruitment. . . ."

Either the drafters are exceedingly careless, or the internal administration debate over whether to go the very last mile in eradicating race consciousness has yet to be decided. In either case, recruitment poses a logical problem for Reynolds & Company (if race consciousness is in principle unjust, how can it be O.K. for recruitment?). But it is not, in practice, a serious issue. If preferential treatment is outlawed for firing, promotion, and hiring, then recruitment really is the last mile: affirmative action expires long before it is reached. The administration and its civil rights opponents seem to agree that if this program—renegotiating the consent decrees and draft executive order 11246—is enacted, recruitment or not, race-conscious affirmative action is dead.

They disagree about whether that would be a good thing. Is race-conscious affirmative action worth saving?

There are three arguments in favor. The first, marshaled principally against Reynolds's revisionist consent decree, is profoundly conservative. It says that at this late date things are working out well, whatever the merits. Let well enough alone. The Justice Department would "disturb the acquiescence of the community in the new systems established after much travail and effort under the consent decrees," charged the NAACP. It will "threaten social peace for the sake of ideology," said *The Washington Post*. "Don't stick your nose in cases that have already been resolved," said Representative Don Edwards, one of five representatives who wrote to the attorney general asking him to cease and desist.

The irony here, of course, is that the NAACP is relatively new to the cause of "settledness." Not always has it argued that justice should be deferred so as not to "disturb the acquiescence of the community" in existing social arrangements. That was the segregationist case. And in that case, it was argued, correctly, that although settledness and social peace have some claims to make, they cannot prevail over the claims of justice.

It works, argues William H. Hudnut, the Republican mayor of Indianapolis, of his city's consent decree setting aside a quarter of its police and fire fighting slots for minorities. Why fix what ain't broke?

Because justice is not interested in what's broke and what's not; it is interested in justice. Hence the second argument for affirmative action, the familiar argument: that while color blindness may be a value, remedying centuries of discrimination through (temporary) race consciousness is a higher value.

Does the right of the disadvantaged to redress (through preferential treatment) override the right of individuals to equal treatment? *Memphis* and the D.C. fire fighters decision begin to parse the issue. The logic of these decisions is that in layoffs and promotion the aggrieved whites have, by dint of service, acquired *additional* individual claims that outweigh the historical claims of blacks. But what about unadorned individual claims? When hired you bring your citizenship with you and nothing else. Shouldn't that be enough to entitle you to equal, color-blind treatment?

It is not clear how to adjudicate the competing claims, that of a historically oppressed community for redress, and of the blameless individual for equal treatment. One side claims the mantle of—indeed, it defines itself as the side of—civil rights. But that is surely a semantic claim. The movement began, of course, as a civil rights movement. But when, for example, the D.C. Office of Human Rights declares that its primary mission is to ensure that blacks end up in city jobs in proportion "equal to their group representation in the available work force," the issue has ceased to be rights. It is group advancement.

The other side claims the mantle of individual rights and equal treatment. That is not a semantic claim. But it is not an absolute one either. After all, either by design or default, we constantly enact social policies that favor certain groups at the expense of others, the individuals in neither group having done anything to deserve their fate. One routine, and devastating, exercise in social engineering is the government-induced recession, periodically applied to the economy to curb inflation. The inevitable result is suffering, suffering that we know well in advance will be borne disproportionately by the poor and working class.

Is this discrimination by class? Certainly. It is not admitted to be so, and it is certainly not the primary effect. But it is an inevitable and predictable side effect. Yet in the face of an overriding national priority—saving the currency—we adopt policies that disproportionately injure a recognized class of blameless individuals. (Similarly, the draft discriminates by age, the placement of toxic waste dumps by geography, etc. We continually ask one group or another to bear special burdens for the sake of the community as a whole.)

If controlling inflation is a social goal urgent and worthy enough to warrant disproportionate injury to a recognized class of blameless individuals, is not the goal of helping blacks rapidly gain the mainstream of American life? Which suggests a third, and to my mind most convincing, line of defense for affirmative action. It admits that the issue is not decidable on the grounds of justice. It argues instead a more humble question of policy: that the rapid integration of blacks into American life is an overriding national goal, and that affirmative action is the means to that goal.

To be sure, affirmative action has myriad effects. They even include such subtle negative psychological effects on blacks as the "rumors of inferiority" studied by Jeff Howard and Ray Hammond (TNR [The New Republic], September 9). The calculation is complex. But it is hard to credit the argument that on balance affirmative action actually harms blacks. Usually advanced by opponents of affirmative action, this argument is about as ingenuous as Jerry Falwell's support of the Botha regime out of concern for South African blacks. One needs a willing suspension of disbelief to maintain that a policy whose essence is to favor blacks hurts them. Even the Reagan administration admits (in a report sent to Congress in February) that executive order 11246 has helped skilled black men.

The Reagan counterrevolutionaries want to end the breach of justice that is affirmative action. A breach it is, and must be admitted to be. It is not clear, however, that correcting this breach is any more morally compelling than redressing the historic injustice done to blacks. In the absence of a compelling moral case, then, the Reagan counterrevolution would retard a valuable social goal: rapid black advancement and integration. Justice would perhaps score a narrow, ambiguous victory. American society would suffer a wide and deepening loss.

None of This Is Fair

Richard Rodriguez

My plan to become a professor of English—my ambition during long years in college at Stanford, then in graduate school at Columbia and Berkeley—was complicated by feelings of embarrassment and guilt. So many times I would see other Mexican-Americans and know we were alike only in race. And yet, simply because our race was the same, I was, during the last years of my schooling, the beneficiary of their situation. Affirmative Action programs had made it all possible. The disadvantages of others permitted my promotion; the absence of many Mexican-Americans from academic life allowed my designation as a "minority student."

For me opportunities had been extravagant. There were fellowships, summer research grants, and teaching assistantships. After only two years in graduate school, I was offered teaching jobs by several colleges. Invitations to Washington conferences arrived and I had the chance to travel abroad as a "Mexican-American representative." The benefits were often, however, too gaudy to please. In three published essays, in conversations with teachers, in letters to politicians and at conferences, I worried the issue of Affirmative Action. Often I proposed contradictory opinions. Though consistent was the admission that—because of an early, excellent education—I was no longer a principal victim of racism or any other social oppression. I said that but still I continued to indicate on applications for financial aid that I was a Hispanic-American. It didn't really occur to me to say anything else, or to leave the question unanswered.

Thus I complied with and encouraged the odd bureaucratic logic of Affirmative Action. I let government officials treat the disadvantaged condition of many Mexican-Americans with my advancement. Each fall my presence was noted by Health, Education, and Welfare department statisticians. As I pursued advanced literary studies and learned the skill of reading Spenser and Wordsworth and Empson, I would hear myself numbered among the culturally disadvantaged. Still, silent, I didn't object.

But the irony cut deep. And guilt would not be evaded by averting my glance when I confronted a face like my own in a crowd. By late 1975, nearing the completion of my graduate studies at Berkeley, I was so wary of the benefits of Affirmative Action that I feared my inevitable success as an applicant for a teaching position. The months of fall—traditionally that time of academic job-searching—passed without my applying to a single school. When one of my professors chanced to learn this in late November, he was astonished, then furious. He yelled at me: Did I think that because I was a minority student jobs would just come looking for me? What was I thinking? Did I realize that he and several other faculty members had already written letters on my behalf? Was I going to start acting like some other minority students he had known? They struggled for success and then, when it was almost within reach, grew strangely afraid and let it pass. Was that it? Was I determined to fail?

I did not respond to his questions. I didn't want to admit to him, and thus to myself, the reason I delayed.

I merely agreed to write to several schools. (In my letter I wrote: "I cannot claim to represent disadvantaged Mexican-Americans. The very fact that I am in a position to apply for this job should make that clear.") After two or three days, there were telegrams and phone calls, invitations to interviews, then airplane trips. A blur of faces and the murmur of their soft questions. And, over someone's shoulder, the sight of campus buildings shadowing pictures I had seen years before when I leafed through Ivy League catalogues with great expectations. At the end of each visit, interviewers would smile and wonder if I had any questions. A few times I quietly wondered what advantage my race had given me over other applicants. But that was an impossible question for them to answer without embarrassing me. Quickly, several persons insisted that my ethnic identity had given me no more than a "foot inside the door"; at most, I had a "slight edge" over other applicants. "We just looked at your dossier with extra care and we like what we saw. There was never any question of having to alter our standards. You can be certain of that."

In the early part of January, offers arrived on stiffly elegant stationery. Most schools promised terms appropriate for any new assistant professor. A few made matters worse—and almost more tempting—by offering more: the use of university housing; an unusually large starting salary; a reduced teaching schedule. As the stack of letters mounted, my hesitation increased. I started calling department chairmen to ask for another week, then 10 more days—"more time to reach a decision"—to avoid the decision I would need to make.

At school, meantime, some students hadn't received a single job offer. One man, probably the best student in the department, did not even get a request for his dossier. He and I met outside a classroom one day and he asked about my opportunities. He seemed happy for me. Faculty members beamed. They said they had expected it. "After all, not many schools are going to pass up getting a Chicano with a Ph.D. in Renaissance literature," somebody said laughing. Friends wanted to know which of the offers I was going to accept. But I couldn't make up my mind. February came and I was running out of time and excuses. (One chairman guessed my delay was a bargaining ploy and increased his offer with each of my calls.) I had to promise a decision by the 10th; the 12th at the very latest.

On the 18th of February, late in the afternoon, I was in the office I shared with several other teaching assistants. Another graduate student was sitting across the room at his desk. When I got up to leave, he looked over to say in an uneventful voice that he had some big news. He had finally decided to accept a position at a faraway university. It was not a job he especially wanted, he admitted. But he had to take it because there hadn't been any other offers. He felt trapped, and depressed, since his job would separate him from his young daughter.

I tried to encourage him by remarking that he was lucky at least to have found a job. So many others hadn't been able to get anything. But before I finished speaking I realized that I had said the wrong thing. And I anticipated his next question.

"What are your plans?" he wanted to know. "Is it true you've gotten an offer from Yale?"

I said that it was. "Only, I still haven't made up my mind."

He stared at me as I put on my jacket. And smiling, then unsmiling, he asked if I knew that he too had written to Yale. In his case, however, no one had bothered to acknowledge his letter with even a postcard. What did I think of that?

He gave me no time to answer.

"Damn!" he said sharply and his chair rasped the floor as he pushed himself back. Suddenly, it was to *me* that he was complaining. "It's just not right, Richard. None of this is fair. You've done some good work, but so have I. I'll bet our records are just about equal. But when we look for jobs this year, it's a different story. You get all of the breaks."

To evade his criticism, I wanted to side with him. I was about to admit the injustice of Affirmative Action. But he went on, his voice hard with accusation. "It's all *very* simple this year. You're a Chicano. And I am a Jew. That's the only real difference between us."

His words stung me: there was nothing he was telling me that I didn't know. I had admitted everything already. But to hear someone else say these things, and in such an accusing tone, was suddenly hard to take. In a deceptively calm voice, I responded that he had simplified the whole issue. The phrases came like bubbles to the tip of my tongue: "new blood"; "the importance of cultural diversity"; "the goal of racial integration." These were all the arguments I had proposed several years ago—and had long since abandoned. Of course the offers were unjustifiable. I knew that. All I was saying amounted to a frantic self-defense. I tried to find an end to a sentence. My voice faltered to a stop.

"Yeah, sure," he said. "I've heard all that before. Nothing you say really changes the fact that Affirmative Action is unfair. You see that, don't you? There isn't any way for me to compete with you. Once there were quotas to keep my parents out of certain schools; now there are quotas to get you in and the effect on me is the same as it was for them."

I listened to *every* word he spoke. But my mind was really on something else. I knew at that moment that I would reject all of the offers. I stood there silently surprised by what an easy conclusion it was. Having prepared for so many years to teach, having trained myself to do nothing else, I had hesitated out of practical fear. But now that it was made, the decision came with relief. I immediately knew I had made the right choice.

My colleague continued talking and I realized that he was simply right. Affirmative Action programs *are* unfair to white students. But as I listened to him assert his rights, I thought of the seriously disadvantaged. How different they were from white, middle-class students who come armed with the testimony of their grades and aptitude scores and self-confidence to complain about the unequal treatment they now receive. I listen to them. I do not want to be careless about what they say. Their rights are important to protect. But inevitably when I hear them or their lawyers, I think about the most seriously disadvantaged, not simply Mexican-Americans, but of all those who do not ever imagine themselves going to college or becoming doctors: white, black, brown. Always poor. Silent. They are not plaintiffs before the court or against the misdirection of Affirmative Action. They lack the confidence (my confidence!) to assume their right to a good education.

They lack the confidence and skills a good primary and secondary education provides and which are prerequisites for informed public life. They remain silent.

The debate drones on and surrounds them in stillness. They are distant, faraway figures like the boys I have seen peering down from freeway overpasses in some other part of town.

Why Women Are Paid Less Than Men
Lester C. Thurow

In the 40 years from 1939 to 1979 white women who work full time have with monotonous regularity made slightly less than 60 percent as much as white men. Why?

Over the same time period, minorities have made substantial progress in catching up with whites, with minority women making even more progress than minority men.

Black men now earn 72 percent as much as white men (up 16 percentage points since the mid-1950's) but black women earn 92 percent as much as white women. Hispanic men make 71 percent of what their white counterparts do, but Hispanic women make 82 percent as much as white women. As a result of their faster progress, fully employed black women make 75 percent as much as fully employed black men while Hispanic women earn 68 percent as much as Hispanic men.

This faster progress may, however, end when minority women finally catch up with white women. In the bible of the New Right, George Gilder's "Wealth and Poverty," the 60 percent is just one of Mother Nature's constants like the speed of light or the force of gravity.

Men are programmed to provide for their families economically while women are programmed to take care of their families emotionally and physically. As a result men put more effort into their jobs than women. The net result is a difference in work intensity that leads to that 40 percent gap in earnings. But there is no discrimination against women—only the biological facts of life.

The problem with this assertion is just that. It is an assertion with no evidence for it other than the fact that white women have made 60 percent as much as men for a long period of time.

"Discrimination against women" is an easy answer but it also has its problems as an adequate explanation. Why is discrimination against women not declining under the same social forces that are leading to a lessening of discrimination against minorities? In recent years women have made more use of the enforcement provisions of the Equal Employment Opportunities Commission and the courts than minorities. Why do the laws that prohibit discrimination against women and minorities work for minorities but not for women?

When men discriminate against women, they run into a problem. To discriminate against women is to discriminate against your own wife and to lower your own family income. To prevent women from working is to force men to work more.

When whites discriminate against blacks, they can at least think that they are raising their own incomes. When men discriminate against women they have to know that they are lowering their own family income and increasing their own work effort.

While discrimination undoubtedly explains part of the male–female earnings differential, one has to believe that men are monumentally stupid or irrational to explain all of the earnings gap in terms of discrimination. There must be something else going on.

Back in 1939 it was possible to attribute the earnings gap to large differences in educational attainments. But the educational gap between men and women has been eliminated since World War II. It is no longer possible to use education as an explanation for the lower earnings of women.

Some observers have argued that women earn less money since they are less reliable workers who are more apt to leave the labor force. But it is difficult to maintain this position since women are less apt to quit one job to take another and as a result they tend to work as long, or longer, for any one employer. From any employer's perspective they are more reliable, not less reliable, than men.

Part of the answer is visible if you look at the lifetime earnings profile of men. Suppose that you were asked to predict which men in a group of 25-year-olds would become economically successful. At age 25 it is difficult to tell who will be economically successful and your predictions are apt to be highly inaccurate.

But suppose that you were asked to predict which men in a group of 35-year-olds would become economically successful. If you are successful at age 35, you are very likely to remain successful for the rest of your life. If you have not become economically successful by age 35, you are very unlikely to do so later.

The decade between 25 and 35 is when men either succeed or fail. It is the decade when lawyers become partners in the good firms, when business managers make it onto the "fast track," when academics get tenure at good universities, and when blue collar workers find the job opportunities that will lead to training opportunities and the skills that will generate high earnings.

If there is any one decade when it pays to work hard and to be consistently in the labor force, it is the decade between 25 and 35. For those who succeed, earnings will rise rapidly. For those who fail, earnings will remain flat for the rest of their lives.

But the decade between 25 and 35 is precisely the decade when women are most apt to leave the labor force or become part-time workers to have children. When they do, the current system of promotion and skill acquisition will extract an enormous lifetime price.

This leaves essentially two avenues for equalizing male and female earnings.

Families where women who wish to have successful careers, compete with men, and achieve the same earnings should alter their family plans and have their children either before or after 35. Or society can attempt to alter the existing promotion and skill acquisition system so that there is a longer time period in which both men and women can attempt to successfully enter the labor force.

Without some combination of these two factors, a substantial fraction of the male–female earnings differentials are apt to persist for the next 40 years, even if discrimination against women is eliminated.

AFFIRMATIVE ACTION—QUESTIONS ON ESSAYS

1. What generalization does each essay make? What subgeneralizations are made? What concrete examples do the writers include? Which writer do you think supports his point of view most logically (as a writer—whether you agree with his stand on the issue or not)? What are your reasons for thinking so?

2. What point of view does each writer have on the issue? Are their points of view similar or different? Do any two writers agree more with each other than with the third? Which essay most clearly represents your point of view?

3. What points of view other than those held by the writers themselves do they refer to in their essays? How many points of view do there seem to be on this issue? What attitude toward other points of view does each writer take?

4. Which essays intend to persuade the reader of their point of view? Do any have another purpose? Are any primarily expressive, for example, or exploratory, or explanatory, rather than argumentative?

5. Analyze the style, voice, and tone of these essays. Which writer uses the most abstract language? Which uses the most concrete? Lester Thurow is an economist; Richard Rodriguez, a writer; and Charles Krauthammer, a columnist for *The New Republic,* a magazine of political analysis. Does knowing who the writers are affect your analysis of their voice? Based on the style, voice, and tone, who would you say is the audience for which each writer wrote?

6. What segments of society other than those addressed here would be interested in reading about these issues? How would a writer go about persuading any of these groups of her or his point of view on the issue?

Euthanasia Essays

Active and Passive Euthanasia
James Rachels

The distinction between active and passive euthanasia is thought to be crucial for medical ethics. The idea is that it is permissible, at least in some cases, to withhold treatment and allow a patient to die, but it is never permissible to take any direct action designed to kill the patient. This doctrine seems to be accepted by most doctors, and it is endorsed in a statement adopted by the House of Delegates of the American Medical Association on December 4, 1973:

> The intentional termination of the life of one human being by another—mercy killing—is contrary to that for which the medical

profession stands and is contrary to the policy of the American
Medical Association.

The cessation of the employment of extraordinary means to
prolong the life of the body when there is irrefutable evidence
that biological death is imminent is the decision of the patient
and/or his immediate family. The advice and judgment of the
physician should be freely available to the patient and/or his immediate family.

However, a strong case can be made against this doctrine. In what follows I will
set out some of the relevant arguments, and urge doctors to reconsider their views
on this matter.

To begin with a familiar type of situation, a patient who is dying of incurable
cancer of the throat is in terrible pain, which can no longer be satisfactorily alle-
viated. He is certain to die within a few days, even if present treatment is continued, but he does not want to go on living for those days since the pain is un-
bearable. So he asks the doctor for an end to it, and his family joins in the
request.

Suppose the doctor agrees to withhold treatment, as the conventional doctrine
says he may. The justification for his doing so is that the patient is in terrible
agony, and since he is going to die anyway, it would be wrong to prolong his
suffering needlessly. But now notice this. If one simply withholds treatment, it may
take the patient longer to die, and so he may suffer more than he would if more
direct action were taken and a lethal injection given. This fact provides strong
reason for thinking that, once the initial decision not to prolong his agony has
been made, active euthanasia is actually preferable to passive euthanasia, rather
than the reverse. To say otherwise is to endorse the option that leads to more
suffering rather than less, and is contrary to the humanitarian impulse that prompts
the decision not to prolong his life in the first place.

Part of my point is that the process of being "allowed to die" can be relatively
slow and painful, whereas being given a lethal injection is relatively quick and
painless. Let me give a different sort of example. In the United States about one
in 600 babies is born with Down's syndrome. Most of these babies are otherwise
healthy—that is, with only the usual pediatric care, they will proceed to an otherwise normal infancy. Some, however, are born with congenital defects such as
intestinal obstructions that require operations if they are to live. Sometimes, the
parents and the doctor will decide not to operate, and let the infant die. Anthony
Shaw describes what happens then:

> . . . When surgery is denied [the doctor] must try to keep the
> infant from suffering while natural forces sap the baby's life away.
> As a surgeon whose natural inclination is to use the scalpel to fight
> off death, standing by and watching a salvageable baby die is the
> most emotionally exhausting experience I know. It is easy at a
> conference, in a theoretical discussion, to decide that such infants
> should be allowed to die. It is altogether different to stand by in
> the nursery and watch as dehydration and infection wither a tiny
> being over hours and days. This is a terrible ordeal for me and

the hospital staff—much more so than for the parents who never
set foot in the nursery.[1]

I can understand why some people are opposed to all euthanasia, and insist that
such infants must be allowed to live. I think I can also understand why other
people favor destroying these babies quickly and painlessly. But why should anyone favor letting "dehydration and infection wither a tiny being over hours and
days?" The doctrine that says that a baby may be allowed to dehydrate and
wither, but may not be given an injection that would end its life without suffering,
seems so patently cruel as to require no further refutation. The strong language is
not intended to offend, but only to put the point in the clearest possible way.

My second argument is that the conventional doctrine leads to decisions concerning life and death made on irrelevant grounds.

Consider again the case of the infants with Down's syndrome who need operations for congenital defects unrelated to the syndrome to live. Sometimes, there
is no operation, and the baby dies, but when there is no such defect, the baby
lives on. Now, an operation such as that to remove an intestinal obstruction is not
prohibitively difficult. The reason why such operations are not performed in these
cases is, clearly, that the child has Down's syndrome and the parents and doctor
judge that because of that fact it is better for the child to die.

But notice that this situation is absurd, no matter what view one takes of the
lives and potentials of such babies. If the life of such an infant is worth preserving,
what does it matter if it needs a simple operation? Or, if one thinks it better that
such a baby should not live on, what difference does it make that it happens to
have an unobstructed intestinal tract? In either case, the matter of life and death
is being decided on irrelevant grounds. It is the Down's syndrome, and not the
intestines, that is the issue. The matter should be decided, if at all, on that basis,
and not be allowed to depend on the essentially irrelevant question of whether
the intestinal tract is blocked.

What makes this situation possible, of course, is the idea that when there is an
intestinal blockage, one can "let the baby die," but when there is no such defect
there is nothing that can be done, for one must not "kill" it. The fact that this
idea leads to such results as deciding life or death on irrelevant grounds is another
good reason why the doctrine should be rejected.

One reason why so many people think that there is an important moral difference between active and passive euthanasia is that they think killing someone is
morally worse than letting someone die. But is it? Is killing, in itself, worse than
letting die? To investigate this issue, two cases may be considered that are exactly
alike except that one involves killing whereas the other involves letting someone
die. Then, it can be asked whether this difference makes any difference to the
moral assessments. It is important that the cases be exactly alike, except for this
one difference, since otherwise one cannot be confident that it is this difference
and not some other that accounts for any variation in the assessments of the two
cases. So, let us consider this pair of cases:

[1]A. Shaw, "Doctor, Do We Have a Choice?" *The New York Times Magazine*, January 30, 1972,
p. 54.

In the first, Smith stands to gain a large inheritance if anything should happen to his six-year-old cousin. One evening while the child is taking his bath, Smith sneaks into the bathroom and drowns the child, and then arranges things so that it will look like an accident.

In the second, Jones also stands to gain if anything should happen to his six-year-old cousin. Like Smith, Jones sneaks in planning to drown the child in his bath. However, just as he enters the bathroom Jones sees the child slip and hit his head, and fall face down in the water. Jones is delighted; he stands by, ready to push the child's head back under if it is necessary, but it is not necessary. With only a little thrashing about, the child drowns all by himself, "accidentally," as Jones watches and does nothing.

Now Smith killed the child, whereas Jones "merely" let the child die. That is the only difference between them. Did either man behave better, from a moral point of view? If the difference between killing and letting die were in itself a morally important matter, one should say that Jones's behavior was less reprehensible than Smith's. But does one really want to say that? I think not. In the first place, both men acted from the same motive, personal gain, and both had exactly the same end in view when they acted. It may be inferred from Smith's conduct that he is a bad man, although that judgment may be withdrawn or modified if certain further facts are learned about him—for example, that he is mentally deranged. But would not the very same thing be inferred about Jones from his conduct? And would not the same further considerations also be relevant to any modification of this judgment? Moreover, suppose Jones pleaded, in his own defense, "After all, I didn't do anything except just stand there and watch the child drown. I didn't kill him; I only let him die." Again, if letting die were in itself less bad than killing, this defense should have at least some weight. But it does not. Such a "defense" can only be regarded as a grotesque perversion of moral reasoning. Morally speaking, it is no defense at all.

Now, it may be pointed out, quite properly, that the cases of euthanasia with which doctors are concerned are not like this at all. They do not involve personal gain or the destruction of normal healthy children. Doctors are concerned only with cases in which the patient's life is of no further use to him, or in which the patient's life has become or will soon become a terrible burden. However, the point is the same in these cases: the bare difference between killing and letting die does not, in itself, make a moral difference. If a doctor lets a patient die, for humane reasons, he is in the same moral position as if he had given the patient a lethal injection for humane reasons. If his decision was wrong—if, for example, the patient's illness was in fact curable—the decision would be equally regrettable no matter which method was used to carry it out. And if the doctor's decision was the right one, the method used is not in itself important.

The AMA policy statement isolates the crucial issue very well; the crucial issue is "the intentional termination of the life of one human being by another." But after identifying this issue, and forbidding "mercy killing," the statement goes on to deny that the cessation of treatment is the intentional termination of a life. This is where the mistake comes in, for what is the cessation of treatment, in these circumstances, if it is not "the intentional termination of the life of one human being by another"? Of course it is exactly that, and if it were not, there would be no point to it.

Many people will find this judgment hard to accept. One reason, I think, is that it is very easy to conflate the question of whether killing is, in itself, worse than letting die, with the very different question of whether most actual cases of killing are more reprehensible than most actual cases of letting die. Most actual cases of killing are clearly terrible (think, for example, of all the murders reported in the newspapers), and one hears of such cases every day. On the other hand, one hardly ever hears of a case of letting die, except for the actions of doctors who are motivated by humanitarian reasons. So one learns to think of killing in a much worse light than of letting die. But this does not mean that there is something about killing that makes it in itself worse than letting die, for it is not the bare difference between killing and letting die that makes the difference in these cases. Rather, the other factors—the murderer's motive of personal gain, for example, contrasted with the doctor's humanitarian motivation—account for different reactions to the different cases.

I have argued that killing is not in itself any worse than letting die; if my contention is right, it follows that active euthanasia is not any worse than passive euthanasia. What arguments can be given on the other side? The most common, I believe, is the following:

"The important difference between active and passive euthanasia is that, in passive euthanasia, the doctor does not do anything to bring about the patient's death. The doctor does nothing, and the patient dies of whatever ills already afflict him. In active euthanasia, however, the doctor does something to bring about the patient's death: he kills him. The doctor who gives the patient with cancer a lethal injection has himself caused his patient's death; whereas if he merely ceases treatment, the cancer is the cause of the death."

A number of points need to be made here. The first is that it is not exactly correct to say that in passive euthanasia the doctor does nothing, for he does do one thing that is very important: he lets the patient die. "Letting someone die" is certainly different, in some respects, from other types of action—mainly in that it is a kind of action that one may perform by way of not performing certain other actions. For example, one may let a patient die by way of not giving medication, just as one may insult someone by way of not shaking his hand. But for any purpose of moral assessment, it is a type of action nonetheless. The decision to let a patient die is subject to moral appraisal in the same way that a decision to kill him would be subject to moral appraisal: it may be assessed as wise or unwise, compassionate or sadistic, right or wrong. If a doctor deliberately let a patient die who was suffering from a routinely curable illness, the doctor would certainly be to blame for what he had done, just as he would be to blame if he had needlessly killed the patient. Charges against him would then be appropriate. If so, it would be no defense at all for him to insist that he didn't "do anything." He would have done something very serious indeed, for he let his patient die.

Fixing the cause of death may be very important from a legal point of view, for it may determine whether criminal charges are brought against the doctor. But I do not think that this notion can be used to show a moral difference between active and passive euthanasia. The reason why it is considered bad to be the cause of someone's death is that death is regarded as a great evil—and so it is. However, if it has been decided that euthanasia—even passive euthanasia—is desirable in a given case, it has also been decided that in this instance death is no greater an evil than the patient's continued existence. And if this is true, the usual reason for not wanting to be the cause of someone's death simply does not apply.

Finally, doctors may think that all of this is only of academic interest—the sort of thing that philosophers may worry about but that has no practical bearing on their own work. After all, doctors must be concerned about the legal consequences of what they do, and active euthanasia is clearly forbidden by the law. But even so, doctors should also be concerned with the fact that the law is forcing upon them a moral doctrine that may well be indefensible, and has a considerable effect on their practices. Of course, most doctors are not now in the position of being coerced in this matter, for they do not regard themselves as merely going along with what the law requires. Rather, in statements such as the AMA policy statement that I have quoted, they are endorsing this doctrine as a central point of medical ethics. In that statement, active euthanasia is condemned not merely as illegal but as "contrary to that for which the medical profession stands," whereas passive euthanasia is approved. However, the preceding considerations suggest that there is really no moral difference between the two, considered in themselves (there may be important moral differences in some cases in their *consequences,* but, as I pointed out, these differences may make active euthanasia, and not passive euthanasia, the morally preferable option). So, whereas doctors may have to discriminate between active and passive euthanasia to satisfy the law, they should not do any more than that. In particular, they should not give the distinction any added authority and weight by writing it into official statements of medical ethics.

Mercy

Richard Selzer

It is October at the Villa Serbelloni, where I have come for a month to write. On the window ledges the cluster flies are dying. The climate is full of uncertainty. Should it cool down? Or warm up? Each day it overshoots the mark, veering from frost to steam. The flies have no uncertainty. They understand that their time has come.

What a lot of energy it takes to die! The frenzy of it. Long after they have collapsed and stayed motionless, the flies are capable of suddenly spinning so rapidly that they cannot be seen. Or seen only as a blurred glitter. They are like dervishes who whirl, then stop, and lie as quiet as before, only now and then waving a leg or two feebly, in a stuporous reenactment of locomotion. Until the very moment of death, the awful buzzing as though to swarm again.

Every morning I scoop up three dozen or so corpses with a dustpan and brush. Into the wastebasket they go, and I sit to begin the day's writing. All at once, from the wastebasket, the frantic knocking of resurrection. Here, death has not yet secured the premises. No matter the numbers slaughtered, no matter that the windows be kept shut all day, each evening the flies gather on the ledges to die, as they have lived, *ensemble.* It must be companionable to die so, matching spin for spin, knock for knock, and buzz for buzz with one's fellows. We humans have no such fraternity, but each of us must buzz and spin and knock alone.

I think of a man in New Haven! He has been my patient for seven years, ever since the day I explored his abdomen in the operating room and found the surprise lurking there—a cancer of the pancreas. He was forty-two years old then. For this man, these have been seven years of famine. For his wife and his mother as well. Until three days ago his suffering was marked by slowly increasing pain, vomiting and fatigue. Still, it was endurable. With morphine. Three days ago the pain rollicked out of control, and he entered that elect band whose suffering cannot be relieved by any means short of death. In his bed at home he seemed an eighty-pound concentrate of pain from which all other pain must be made by serial dilution. He twisted under the lash of it. An ambulance arrived. At the hospital nothing was to be done to prolong his life. Only the administration of large doses of narcotics.

"Please," he begs me. In his open mouth, upon his teeth, a brown paste of saliva. All night long he has thrashed, as though to hollow out a grave in the bed.

"I won't let you suffer," I tell him. In his struggle the sheet is thrust aside. I see the old abandoned incision, the belly stuffed with tumor. His penis, even, is skinny. One foot with five blue toes is exposed. In my cupped hand, they are cold. I think of the twenty bones of that foot laced together with tendon, each ray accompanied by its own nerve and artery. Now, this foot seems a beautiful dead animal that had once been trained to transmit the command of a man's brain to the earth.

"I'll get rid of the pain," I tell his wife.

But there is no way to kill the pain without killing the man who owns it. Morphine to the lethal dose . . . and still he miaows and bays and makes other sounds like a boat breaking up in a heavy sea. I think his pain will live on long after he dies.

"Please," begs his wife, "we cannot go on like this."

"Do it," says the old woman, his mother. "Do it now."

"To give him any more would kill him," I tell her.

"Then do it," she says. The face of the old woman is hoof-beaten with intersecting curves of loose skin. Her hair is donkey brown, donkey gray.

They wait with him while I go to the nurses' station to prepare the syringes. It is a thing that I cannot ask anyone to do for me. When I return to the room, there are three loaded syringes in my hand, a rubber tourniquet and an alcohol sponge. Alcohol sponge! To prevent infection? The old woman is standing on a small stool and leaning over the side rail of the bed. Her bosom is just above his upturned face, as though she were weaning him with sorrow and gentleness from her still-full breasts. All at once she says severely, the way she must have said it to him years ago:

"Go home, son. Go home now."

I wait just inside the doorway. The only sound is a flapping, a rustling, as in a room to which a small animal, a bat perhaps, has retreated to die. The women turn to leave. There is neither gratitude nor reproach in their gaze. I should be hooded.

At last we are alone. I stand at the bedside.

"Listen," I say, "I can get rid of the pain." The man's eyes regain their focus.

His gaze is like a wound that radiates its pain outward so that all upon whom it fell would know the need of relief.

"With these." I hold up the syringes.

"Yes," he gasps. "Yes." And while the rest of his body stirs in answer to the pain, he holds his left, his acquiescent arm still for the tourniquet. An even dew of sweat covers his body. I wipe the skin with the alcohol sponge, and tap the arm smartly to bring out the veins. There is one that is still patent; the others have long since clotted and broken down. I go to insert the needle, but the tourniquet has come unknotted; the vein has collapsed. Damn! Again I tie the tourniquet. Slowly the vein fills with blood. This time it stays distended.

He reacts not at all to the puncture. In a wild sea what is one tiny wave? I press the barrel and deposit the load, detach the syringe from the needle and replace it with the second syringe. I send this home, and go on to the third. When they are all given, I pull out the needle. A drop of blood blooms on his forearm. I blot it with the alcohol sponge. It is done. In less than a minute, it is done.

"Go home," I say, repeating the words of the old woman. I turn off the light. In the darkness the contents of the bed are theoretical. No! I must watch. I turn the light back on. How reduced he is, a folded parcel, something chipped away until only its shape and a little breath are left. His impatient bones gleam as though to burst through the papery skin. I am impatient, too. I want to get it over with, then step out into the corridor where the women are waiting. His death is like a jewel to them.

My fingers at his pulse. The same rhythm as mine! As though there were one pulse that beat throughout all of nature, and every creature's heart throbbed precisely.

"You can go home now," I say. The familiar emaciated body untenses. The respirations slow down. Eight per minute . . . six . . . It won't be long. The pulse wavers in and out of touch. It won't be long.

"Is that better?" I ask him. His gaze is distant, opaque, preoccupied. Minutes go by. Outside, in the corridor, the murmuring of women's voices.

But this man will not die! The skeleton rouses from its stupor. The snout twitches as if to fend off a fly. What is it that shakes him like a gourd full of beans? The pulse returns, melts away, comes back again, and stays. The respirations are twelve, then fourteen. I have not done it. I did not murder him. I am innocent!

I shall walk out of the room into the corridor. They will look at me, holding their breath, expectant. I lift the sheet to cover him. All at once, there is a sharp sting in my thumb. The same needle with which I meant to kill him has pricked *me*. A drop of blood appears. I press it with the alcohol sponge. My fresh blood deepens the stain of his on the gauze. Never mind. The man in the bed swallows. His Adam's apple bobs slowly. It would be so easy to do it. Three minutes of pressure on the larynx. He is still not conscious, wouldn't feel it, wouldn't know. My thumb and fingertips hover, land on his windpipe. My pulse beating in his neck, his in mine. I look back over my shoulder. No one. Two bare IV poles in a corner, their looped metal eyes witnessing. Do it! Fingers press. Again he swallows. Look back again. How closed the door is. And . . . my hand wilts. I cannot. It is not in me to do it. Not that way. The man's head swivels like an upturned fish. The squadron of ribs battles on.

I back away from the bed, turn and flee toward the doorway. In the mirror, a glimpse of my face. It is the face of someone who has been resuscitated after a long period of cardiac arrest. There is no spot of color in the cheeks, as though this person were in shock at what he had just seen on the yonder side of the grave.

In the corridor the women lean against the wall, against each other. They are like a band of angels dispatched here to take possession of his body. It is the only thing that will satisfy them.

"He didn't die," I say. "He won't . . . or can't." They are silent.

"He isn't ready yet," I say.

"He *is* ready," the old woman says. "*You* ain't."

The Vatican's Declaration on Euthanasia, 1980

Introduction

The rights and values pertaining to the human person occupy an important place among the questions discussed today. In this regard, the Second Vatican Ecumenical Council solemnly reaffirmed the lofty dignity of the human person, and in a special way his or her right to life. The Council therefore condemned crimes against life "such as any type of murder, genocide, abortion, euthanasia, or wilful suicide" (Pastoral Constitution *Gaudium et Spes,* 27).

More recently, the Sacred Congregation for the Doctrine of the Faith has reminded all the faithful of Catholic teaching on procured abortion.[1] The Congregation now considers it opportune to set forth the church's teaching on euthanasia.

It is indeed true that, in this sphere of teaching, the recent Popes have explained the principles, and these retain their full force;[2] but the progress of medical science in recent years has brought to the fore new aspects of the question of euthanasia, and these aspects call for further elucidation on the ethical level.

In modern society, in which even the fundamental values of human life are often called into question, cultural change exercises an influence upon the way of looking at suffering and death; moreover, medicine has increased its capacity to cure and to prolong life in particular circumstances, which sometimes give rise to moral problems. Thus people living in this situation experience no little anxiety about the meaning of advanced old age and death. They also begin to wonder whether they have the right to obtain for themselves or their fellowmen an "easy death," which would shorten suffering and which seems to them more in harmony with human dignity.

A number of Episcopal Conferences have raised questions on this subject with the Sacred Congregation for the Doctrine of the Faith. The Congregation, having sought the opinion of experts on the various aspects of euthanasia, now wishes to respond to the Bishops' questions with the present Declaration, in order to help them to give correct teaching to the faithful entrusted to their care, and to offer them elements for reflection that they can present to the civil authorities with regard to this very serious matter.

The considerations set forth in the present document concern in the first place all those who place their faith and hope in Christ, who, through his life, death and Resurrection, has given a new meaning to existence and especially to the death of the Christian, as Saint Paul says: "If we live, we live to the Lord, and if we die, we die to the Lord" (*Rom* 14:8; cf. *Phil* 1:20).

As for those who profess other religions, many will agree with us that faith in God the Creator, Provider and Lord of life—if they share this belief—confers a lofty dignity upon every human person and guarantees respect for him or her.

It is hoped that this Declaration will meet with the approval of many people of good will, who, philosophical or ideological differences notwithstanding, have nevertheless a lively awareness of the rights of the human person. These rights have often in fact been proclaimed in recent years through declarations issued by International Congresses;[3] and since it is a question here of fundamental rights inherent in every human person, it is obviously wrong to have recourse to arguments from political pluralism or religious freedom in order to deny the universal value of those rights.

I
The Value of Human Life

Human life is the basis of all goods, and is the necessary source and condition of every human activity and of all society. Most people regard life as something sacred and hold that no one may dispose of it at will, but believers see in life something greater, namely a gift of God's love, which they are called upon to preserve and make fruitful. And it is this latter consideration that gives rise to the following consequences:

1. No one can make an attempt on the life of an innocent person without opposing God's love for that person, without violating a fundamental right, and therefore without committing a crime of the utmost gravity.[4]

2. Everyone has the duty to lead his or her life in accordance with God's plan. That life is entrusted to the individual as a good that must bear fruit already here on earth, but that finds its full perfection only in eternal life.

3. Intentionally causing one's own death, or suicide, is therefore equally as wrong as murder; such an action on the part of a person is to be considered as a rejection of God's sovereignty and loving plan. Furthermore, suicide is also often a refusal of love for self, the denial of the natural instinct to live, a flight from the duties of justice and charity owed to one's neighbour, to various communities or to the whole of society—although, as is generally recognized, at times there are psychological factors present that can diminish responsibility or even completely remove it.

However, one must clearly distinguish suicide from that sacrifice of one's life whereby for a higher cause, such as God's glory, the salvation of souls or the service of one's brethren, a person offers his or her own life or puts it in danger (cf. *Jn* 15:14).

II
Euthanasia

In order that the question of euthanasia can be properly dealt with, it is first necessary to define the words used.

Etymologically speaking, in ancient times *euthanasia* meant an *easy death* without severe suffering. Today one no longer thinks of this original meaning of the word, but rather of some intervention of medicine whereby the sufferings of sickness or of the final agony are reduced, sometimes also with the danger of suppressing life prematurely. Ultimately, the word *euthanasia* is used in a more particular sense to mean "mercy killing," for the purpose of putting an end to extreme suffering, or saving abnormal babies, the mentally ill or the incurably sick from the prolongation, perhaps for many years, of a miserable life, which could impose too heavy a burden on their families or on society.

It is therefore necessary to state clearly in what sense the word is used in the present document.

By euthanasia is understood an action or an omission which of itself or by intention causes death, in order that all suffering may in this way be eliminated. Euthanasia's terms of reference, therefore, are to be found in the intention of the will and in the methods used.

It is necessary to state firmly once more that nothing and no one can in any way permit the killing of an innocent human being, whether a foetus or an embryo, an infant or an adult, an old person, or one suffering from an incurable disease, or a person who is dying. Furthermore, no one is permitted to ask for this act of killing, either for himself or herself or for another person entrusted to his or her care, nor can he or she consent to it, either explicitly or implicitly. Nor can any authority legitimately recommend or permit such an action. For it is a question of the violation of the divine law, an offence against the dignity of the human person, a crime against life, and an attack on humanity.

It may happen that, by reason of prolonged and barely tolerable pain, for deeply personal or other reasons, people may be led to believe that they can legitimately ask for death or obtain it for others. Although in these cases the guilt of the individual may be reduced or completely absent, nevertheless the error of judgment into which the conscience falls, perhaps in good faith, does not change the nature of this act of killing, which will always be in itself something to be rejected. The pleas of gravely ill people who sometimes ask for death are not to be understood as implying a true desire for euthanasia; in fact it is almost always a case of an anguished plea for help and love. What a sick person needs, besides medical care, is love, the human and supernatural warmth with which the sick person can and ought to be surrounded by all those close to him or her, parents and children, doctors and nurses.

III
The Meaning of Suffering for Christians and the Use of Painkillers

Death does not always come in dramatic circumstances after barely tolerable sufferings. Nor do we have to think only of extreme cases. Numerous testimonies which confirm one another lead one to the conclusion that nature itself has made provision to render more bearable at the moment of death separations that would be terribly painful to a person in full health. Hence it is that a prolonged illness, advanced old age, or a state of loneliness or neglect can bring about psychological conditions that facilitate the acceptance of death.

Nevertheless the fact remains that death, often preceded or accompanied by severe and prolonged suffering, is something which naturally causes people anguish.

Physical suffering is certainly an unavoidable element of the human condition; on the biological level, it constitutes a warning of which no one denies the usefulness; but, since it affects the human psychological makeup, it often exceeds its own biological usefulness and so can become so severe as to cause the desire to remove it at any cost.

According to Christian teaching, however, suffering, especially suffering during the last moments of life, has a special place in God's saving plan; it is in fact a sharing in Christ's Passion and a union with the redeeming sacrifice which he offered in obedience to the Father's will. Therefore one must not be surprised if some Christians prefer to moderate their use of painkillers, in order to accept voluntarily at least a part of their sufferings and thus associate themselves in a conscious way with the sufferings of Christ crucified (cf. *Mt* 27:34). Nevertheless it would be imprudent to impose a heroic way of acting as a general rule. On the contrary, human and Christian prudence suggest for the majority of sick people the use of medicines capable of alleviating or suppressing pain, even though these may cause as a secondary effect semiconsciousness and reduced lucidity. As for those who are not in a state to express themselves, one can reasonably presume that they wish to take these painkillers, and have them administered according to the doctor's advice.

But the intensive use of painkillers is not without difficulties, because the phenomenon of habituation generally makes it necessary to increase their dosage in order to maintain their efficacy. At this point it is fitting to recall a declaration by Pius XII, which retains its full force; in answer to a group of doctors who had put the question: "Is the suppression of pain and consciousness by the use of narcotics . . . permitted by religion and morality to the doctor and the patient (even at the approach of death and if one foresees that the use of narcotics will shorten life)?" the Pope said: "If no other means exist, and if, in the given circumstances, this does not prevent the carrying out of other religious and moral duties: Yes."[5] In this case, of course, death is in no way intended or sought, even if the risk of it is reasonably taken; the intention is simply to relieve pain effectively, using for this purpose painkillers available to medicine.

However, painkillers that cause unconsciousness need special consideration. For a person not only has to be able to satisfy his or her moral duties and family obligations; he or she also has to prepare himself or herself with full consciousness for meeting Christ. Thus Pius XII warns: "It is not right to deprive the dying person of consciousness without a serious reason."[6]

IV
Due Proportion in the Use of Remedies

Today it is very important to protect, at the moment of death, both the dignity of the human person and the Christian concept of life, against a technological attitude that threatens to become an abuse. Thus, some people speak of a "right to die," which is an expression that does not mean the right to procure death either by one's own hand or by means of someone else, as one pleases, but rather the right to die peacefully with human and Christian dignity. From this point of view, the use of therapeutic means can sometimes pose problems.

In numerous cases, the complexity of the situation can be such as to cause doubts about the way ethical principles should be applied. In the final analysis, it pertains to the conscience either of the sick person, or of those qualified to speak in the sick person's name, or of the doctors, to decide, in the light of moral obligations and of the various aspects of the case.

Everyone has the duty to care for his or her own health or to seek such care from others. Those whose task it is to care for the sick must do so conscientiously and administer the remedies that seem necessary or useful.

However, is it necessary in all circumstances to have recourse to all possible remedies?

In the past, moralists replied that one is never obliged to use "extraordinary" means. This reply, which as a principle still holds good, is perhaps less clear today, by reason of the imprecision of the term and the rapid progress made in the treatment of sickness. Thus some people prefer to speak of "proportionate" and "disproportionate" means. In any case, it will be possible to make a correct judgment as to the means by studying the type of treatment to be used, its degree of complexity or risk, its cost and the possibilities of using it, and comparing these elements with the result that can be expected, taking into account the state of the sick person and his or her physical and moral resources.

In order to facilitate the application of these general principles, the following clarifications can be added:

> If there are no other sufficient remedies, it is permitted, with the patient's consent, to have recourse to the means provided by the most advanced medical techniques, even if these means are still at the experimental stage and are not without a certain risk. By accepting them, the patient can even show generosity in the service of humanity.

> It is also permitted, with the patient's consent, to interrupt these means, where the results fall short of expectations. But for such a decision to be made, account will have to be taken of the reasonable wishes of the patient and the patient's family, as also of the advice of the doctors who are specially competent in the matter. The latter may in particular judge that the investment in instruments and personnel is disproportionate to the results foreseen; they may also judge that the techniques applied impose on the patient strain or suffering out of proportion with the benefits which he or she may gain from such techniques.

> It is also permissible to make do with the normal means that medicine can offer. Therefore one cannot impose on anyone the obligation to have recourse to a technique which is already in use but which carries a risk or is burdensome. Such a refusal is not the equivalent of suicide; on the contrary, it should be considered as an acceptance of the human condition, or a wish to avoid the application of a medical procedure disproportionate to the results that can be expected, or a desire not to impose excessive expense on the family or the community.

> When inevitable death is imminent in spite of the means used, it is permitted in conscience to take the decision to refuse forms of treatment that would only secure a precarious and burdensome prolongation of life, so long as the normal care due to the sick person in similar cases is not interrupted. In

such circumstances the doctor has no reason to reproach himself with failing to help the person in danger.

Conclusion

The norms contained in the present Declaration are inspired by a profound desire to serve people in accordance with the plan of the Creator. Life is a gift of God, and on the other hand death is unavoidable; it is necessary therefore that we, without in any way hastening the hour of death, should be able to accept it with full responsibility and dignity. It is true that death marks the end of our earthly existence, but at the same time it opens the door to immortal life. Therefore all must prepare themselves for this event in the light of human values, and Christians even more so in the light of faith.

As for those who work in the medical profession, they ought to neglect no means of making all their skill available to the sick and the dying; but they should also remember how much more necessary it is to provide them with the comfort of boundless kindness and heartfelt charity. Such service to people is also service to Christ the Lord, who said: "As you did it to one of the least of these my brethren, you did it to me" (*Mt* 25:40).

At the audience granted to the undersigned Prefect, His Holiness Pope John Paul II approved this Declaration, adopted at the ordinary meeting of the Sacred Congregation for the Doctrine of the Faith, and ordered its publication.

Rome, the Sacred Congregation for the Doctrine of the Faith, 5 May 1980.

FRANJO Card. ŠEPER
Prefect

†Jérôme Hamer, O. P.
Tit. Archbishop of Lorium
Secretary

Notes

1. *Declaration on Procured Abortion*, 18 November 1974: AAS 66 (1974), pp. 730–747.
2. PIUS XII, *Address to those attending the Congress of the International Union of Catholic Women's Leagues, 11 September 1947*: AAS 39 (1947), p. 483; *Address to the Italian Catholic Union of Midwives*, 29 October 1951: AAS 43 (1951), pp. 835–854; *Speech to the members of the International Office of military medicine documentation*, 19 October 1953: AAS 45 (1953), pp. 744–754; *Address to those taking part in the IXth Congress of the Italian Anaesthesiological Society*, 24 February 1957: AAS 49 (1957), p. 146; cf. also *Address on "reanimation"* 24 November 1957: AAS 49 (1957), pp. 1027–1033; PAUL VI, *Address to the members of the United Nations Special Committee on Apartheid*, 22 May 1974: AAS 66 (1974), p. 346; JOHN PAUL II: *Address to the Bishops of the United States of America*, 5 October 1979: AAS 71 (1979), p. 1225.
3. One thinks especially of Recommendation 779 (1976) on the rights of the sick and dying, of the Parliamentary Assembly of the Council of Europe at its XXVIIth Ordinary Session; cf. SIPECA, No. 1, March 1977, pp. 14–15.
4. We leave aside completely the problems of the death penalty and of war, which involve specific considerations that do not concern the present subject.
5. PIUS XII, *Address of 24 February 1957*: AAS 49 (1957), p. 147.
6. PIUS XII, *ibid.*, p. 145; cf. *Address of 9 September 1958*: AAS 50 (1958), p. 694.

EUTHANASIA—QUESTIONS ON ESSAYS

1. What generalization does each essay make? What subgeneralizations are made? What concrete examples do the writers include? Which writer do you think supports his point of view most logically (as a writer—whether you agree with his stand on the issue or not). Why do you think so?

2. What point of view does each writer have on the issue? To what extent are their points of view similar? Do any two writers agree more with each other than with the third? Which essay most clearly represents your point of view?

3. What points of view other than those held by the writers themselves do they refer to in their essays? How many points of view do there seem to be on this issue? What attitude toward other points of view does each writer take?

4. Which essays intend to persuade the reader of their point of view? Do any have another purpose? Are any primarily expressive, for example, or exploratory, or explanatory, rather than argumentative?

5. James Rachels is a moral philosopher writing for the *New England Journal of Medicine;* his audience therefore consists of doctors who are members of the American Medical Association. How does his essay reflect his awareness of his audience?

6. Whom do you imagine Richard Selzer's audience to be? What evidence for your decision exists in the essay itself?

7. Who does the intended readership of "The Vatican's Declaration on Euthanasia" appear to be? What internal evidence exists of this audience? How did the writers of the declaration aim for this audience?

8. What segments of society other than those addressed here would be interested in reading about these issues? How would a writer go about persuading any of these groups of his or her point of view on the issue?

Pornography Essays

Partners Against Porn

Alan M. Dershowitz

> *From an essay by Alan M. Dershowitz that appeared as part of "Pornography: Love or Death?" a symposium in the December issue of* Film Comment. *Dershowitz is a professor at Harvard Law School and author of* The Best Defense.

By focusing their wrath on "pornography," feminists who advocate censorship have made their Faustian pact with the devil—the Reverend Jerry Falwell and his gang of fundamentalist censors. Although there is little reliable evidence that non-violent pornography—explicit depictions of couples making love—causes violence against women, these feminists have decided that the only way of putting together an effective censorship coalition is to agree with fundamentalists that pornography is the villain. Falwell has been keeping his end of the bargain: he now condemns pornography not only as immoral and godless but also as "violence against women"—an issue he was never very big on before the dirty deal was struck.

If the feminist censors had limited their attack to violent (or sexist) films, they would have had difficulty joining forces with the fundamentalists, many of whom thrive on violence (and sexism) of all kinds. The shortsightedness of the feminists is evident when you scratch just a bit below the surface of the alliance, for the very next group of people—after pornographers—on the fundamentalists' hit list are feminists, especially those of the Andrea Dworkin variety. Dworkin, who advocates a lesbian life style, freely uses dirty language and obscenities to demonstrate the alleged evils of pornography. In a public debate, I asked a fundamentalist minister who has joined forces with feminist censors in their war against pornography whether he would, if he had the power, ban Dworkin's writings. He answered without hesitation: "We would most certainly ban such ungodly writings."

Brian De Palma is one filmmaker many feminists would really like to censor. His films vividly portray violence against women in a sexist manner. But the trouble is that he doesn't make pornographic films. Sure there is a lot of nudity and some non-explicit sex, but De Palma's films pass the constitutional test of protected free speech. Indeed, if not for the nudity and sex, the Moral Majority would have few complaints. The "morality" of De Palma's films has striking parallels to the morality of many of Falwell's followers: the punishment for promiscuous sex is death or disfigurement.

If the feminist censors were candid, they would come out directly and say that they want to censor sexist films (and other forms of expression) that are demeaning and dangerous to women. But then they would risk their unholy alliance with those fundamentalists who care not a damn about sexism or violence against women, but who oppose depictions of explicit sexuality and deviance on moralistic grounds.

The hard facts of life are that only a small percentage of Americans favor censoring violence and sexism. But a large percentage favor censoring explicit sexuality. So in order to construct a winning poker hand, the censorial feminists are willing to use the wild cards of the Moral Majority to fill in their open straight. The upshot is a brand of moral and political opportunism that would make Machiavelli's Prince proud.

There is simply no justification for governmental censorship of offensive material of any kind. To conclude that a film is sexist or violent is not to conclude that it should be taken out of the marketplace of ideas. Some social science researchers claim they can prove that people who watch violent pornography come away from the experience with a reduced sympathy for the alleged rape victim. So be it! It is the function of free expression to persuade and to change minds. If pornography convinces some viewers to be less sympathetic to alleged rape victims, that is *not* an argument in favor of banning it—any more than one would ban a *speech* advocating skepticism toward the stories of alleged rape victims. Some feminist censors call pornography "sexist propaganda." But all propaganda—sexist as well as feminist—should be protected by the First Amendment.

The answer to "bad" speech is "good" speech. The proper approach to the marketplace of ideas is not to close by governmental fiat those stalls that sell disagreeable merchandise, but to offer competing merchandise and to persuade the public to buy *your* product rather than theirs, or simply not to buy theirs.

There are too few places in the world where real choices are available. Let us not allow Jerry Falwell, Chief Justice Burger, or Andrea Dworkin to make our choices for us.

Erotica vs. Pornography
Gloria Steinem

Look at or imagine images of people making love; really making love. Those images may be very diverse, but there is likely to be a mutual pleasure and touch and warmth, an empathy for each other's bodies and nerve endings, a shared sensuality and a spontaneous sense of two people who are there because they *want* to be.

Now look at or imagine images of sex in which there is force, violence, or symbols of unequal power. They may be very blatant: whips and chains of bondage, even torture and murder presented as sexually titillating, the clear evidence of wounds and bruises, or an adult's power being used sexually over a child. They may be more subtle: the use of class, race, authority, or just body poses to convey conqueror and victim; unequal nudity, with one person's body exposed and vulnerable while the other is armored with clothes; or even a woman by herself, exposed for an unseen but powerful viewer whom she clearly is trying to please. (It's interesting that, even when only the woman is seen, we often know whether she is there for her own pleasure or being displayed for someone else's.) But blatant or subtle, there is no equal power or mutuality. In fact, much of the tension and drama comes from the clear idea that one person is dominating another.

These two sorts of images are as different as love is from rape, as dignity is from humiliation, as partnership is from slavery, as pleasure is from pain. Yet they are confused and lumped together as "pornography" or "obscenity," "erotica" or "explicit sex," because sex and violence are so dangerously intertwined and confused. After all, it takes violence or the threat of it to maintain the unearned dominance of any group of human beings over another. Moreover, the threat must be the most persuasive wherever men and women come together intimately and are most in danger of recognizing each other's humanity.

The confusion of sex with violence is most obvious in any form of sadomasochism. The gender-based barrier to empathy has become so great that a torturer or even murderer may actually believe pain or loss of life to be the natural fate of the victim; and the victim may have been so deprived of self-respect or of empathetic human contact that she expects pain or loss of freedom as the price of any intimacy or attention at all. It's unlikely that even a masochist expects death. Nonetheless, "snuff" movies and much current pornographic literature insist that a slow death from sexual torture is the final orgasm and ultimate pleasure. It's a form of "suicide" reserved for women. Though men in fact are far more likely to kill themselves, male suicide is almost never presented as sexually pleasurable. But sex is also confused with violence and aggression in all forms of popular culture, and in respectable theories of psychology and sexual behavior as well. The idea that aggression is a "normal" part of male sexuality, and that passivity or even the need for male aggression is a "normal" part of female sexuality, are part of the male-dominant culture we live in, the books we learn from, and the air we breathe.

Even the words we are given to express our feelings are suffused with the same assumptions. Sexual phrases are the most common synonyms for conquering and humiliation *(being had, being screwed, getting fucked);* the sexually aggressive woman is a *slut* or a *nymphomaniac,* but the sexually aggressive man is just *normal;* and real or scientific descriptions of sex may perpetuate the same roles; for instance, a woman is always *penetrated* by a man though she might also be said to have *enveloped* him.

Obviously, untangling sex from aggression and violence or the threat of it is going to take a very long time. And the process is going to be greatly resisted as a challenge to the very heart of male dominance and male centrality.

But we do have the common sense of our bodies to guide us. Pain is a warning of damage and danger. If that sensation is not mixed with all the intimacy we know as children, we are unlikely to confuse pain with pleasure and love. As we discover our free will and strength, we are also more likely to discover our own initiative and pleasure in sex. As men no longer can dominate and have to find an identity that doesn't depend on superiority, they also discover that cooperation is more interesting than submission, that empathy with their sex partner increases their own pleasure, and that anxieties about their own ability to "perform" tend to disappear along with stereotyped ideas about masculinity.

But women will be the main fighters of this new sexual revolution. It is our freedom, our safety, our lives, and our pleasure that are mostly at stake.

We began by trying to separate sex and violence in those areas where the physical danger was and is the most immediate: challenging rape as the one crime that was considered biologically irresistible for the criminal and perhaps invited by the victim; refusing to allow male–female beatings to be classified as "domestic violence" and ignored by the law; exposing forced prostitution and sexual slavery as national and international crimes. With the exception of wife beating, those challenges were made somewhat easier by men who wanted to punish other men for taking their female property. Women still rarely have the power to protect each other.

Such instances of real antiwoman warfare led us directly to the propaganda that teaches and legitimizes them—pornography. Just as we had begun to separate rape from sex, we realized that we must find some way of separating pornographic depictions of sex as an antiwoman weapon from those images of freely chosen, mutual sexuality.

Fortunately, there is truth in the origin of words. *Pornography* comes from the Greek root *porné* (harlot, prostitute, or female captive) and *graphos* (writing about or description of). Thus, it means a description of either the purchase of sex, which implies an imbalance of power in itself, or sexual slavery.

This definition includes, and should include, all such degradation, regardless of whether it is females who are the slaves and males who are the captors or vice versa. There is certainly homosexual pornography, for instance, with a man in the "feminine" role of victim. There is also role-reversal pornography, with a woman whipping or punishing a man, though it's significant that this genre is created by men for their own pleasure, not by or for women, and allows men to *pretend* to be victims—but without real danger. There could also be lesbian pornography, with a woman assuming the "masculine" role of victimizing another woman. That women rarely choose this role of victimizer is due to no biological superiority, but a culture that doesn't addict women to violence. But whatever the gender of the participants, all pornography is an imitation of the male–female, conqueror–victim paradigm, and almost all of it actually portrays or implies enslaved woman and master.

Even the 1970 Presidential Commission on Obscenity and Pornography, whose report is often accused of suppressing or ignoring evidence of the causal link between pornography and violence against women, defined the subject of their study as pictorial or verbal descriptions of sexual behavior characterized by "the degrading and demeaning portrayal of the role and status of the human female."

In short, pornography is not about sex. It's about an imbalance of male–female power that allows and even requires sex to be used as a form of aggression.

Erotica may be the word that can differentiate sex from violence and rescue sexual pleasure. It comes from the Greek root *eros* (sexual desire or passionate love, named for Eros, the son of Aphrodite), and so contains the idea of love, positive choice, and the yearning for a particular person. Unlike pornography's reference to a harlot or prostitute, *erotica* leaves entirely open the question of gender. (In fact, we may owe its sense of shared power to the Greek idea that a man's love for another man was more worthy than love for a woman, but at least that bias isn't present in the word.) Though both erotica and pornography refer to verbal or pictorial representations of sexual behavior, they are as different as a room with doors open and one with doors locked. The first might be a home, but the second could only be a prison.

The problem is that there is so little erotica. Women have rarely been free enough to pursue erotic pleasure in our own lives, much less to create it in the worlds of film, magazines, art, books, television, and popular culture—all the areas of communication we rarely control. Very few male authors and filmmakers have been able to escape society's message of what a man should do, much less to imagine their way into the identity of a woman. Some women and men are trying to portray equal and erotic sex, but it is still not a part of popular culture.

And the problem is there is so much pornography. This underground stream of antiwoman propaganda that exists in all male-dominant societies has now become a flood in our streets and theaters and even our homes. Perhaps that's better in the long run. Women can no longer pretend pornography does not exist. We must either face our own humiliation and torture every day on magazine covers and television screens or fight back. There is hardly a newsstand without women's bodies in chains and bondage, in full labial display for the conquering male viewer, bruised or on our knees, screaming in real or pretended pain, pretending to enjoy what we don't enjoy. The same images are in mainstream movie theaters and respectable hotel rooms via closed-circuit TV for the traveling businessman. They are brought into our own homes not only in magazines, but in the new form of video cassettes. Even video games offer such features as a smiling, rope-bound woman and a male figure with an erection, the game's object being to rape the woman as many times as possible. (Like much of pornography, that game is fascist on racial grounds as well as sexual ones. The smiling woman is an Indian maiden, the rapist is General Custer, and the game is called "Custer's Revenge.") Though "snuff" movies in which real women were eviscerated and finally killed have been driven underground (in part because the graves of many murdered women were discovered around the shack of just one filmmaker in California), movies that simulate the torture murders of women are still going strong. *(Snuff* is the porn term for killing a woman for sexual pleasure. There is not even the seriousness of a word like *murder.)* So are the "kiddie porn" or "chicken porn" movies and magazines that show adult men undressing, fondling, and sexually using children; often with the titillating theme that "fathers" are raping "daughters." Some "chicken porn" magazines offer explicit tips on how to use a child sexually without leaving physical evidence of rape, the premise being that children's testimony is even less likely to be believed than that of adult women.

Add this pornography industry up, from magazines like *Playboy* and *Hustler,* to movies like *Love Gestapo Style, Deep Throat,* or *Angels in Pain,* and the total sales come to a staggering eight billion dollars a year—more than all the sales of the conventional film and record industry combined. And that doesn't count the fact that many "conventional" film and music images are also pornographic, from gynocidal record jackets like the famous *I'm "Black and Blue" from the Rolling Stones—and I Love It!* (which showed a seminude black woman bound to a chair) to the hundreds of teenage sex-and-horror movies in which young women die sadistic deaths and rape is presented not as a crime but as sexual excitement. Nor do those industries include the sales of the supposedly "literary" forms of pornography, from *The Story of O* to the works of the Marquis de Sade.

If Nazi propaganda that justified the torture and killing of Jews were the theme of half of our most popular movies and magazines, would we not be outraged? If Ku Klux Klan propaganda that preached and even glamorized the enslavement of blacks were the subject of much-praised "classic" novels, would we not protest? We know that such racist propaganda precedes and justifies the racist acts of pogroms and lynchings. We know that watching a violent film causes test subjects to both condone more violence afterward and to be willing to perpetuate it themselves. Why is the propaganda of sexual aggression against women of all races the one form in which the "conventional wisdom" sees no danger? Why is pornography the only media violence that is supposed to be a "safety valve" to satisfy men's "natural" aggressiveness somewhere short of acting it out?

The first reason is the confusion of *all* nonprocreative sex with pornography. Any description of sexual behavior, or even nudity, may be called pornographic or obscene (a word whose Latin derivative means *dirty* or *containing filth*) by those who insist that the only moral purpose of sex is procreative, or even that any portrayal of sexuality or nudity is against the will of God.

In fact, human beings seem to be the only animals that experience the same sex drive and pleasure at times when we can and cannot conceive. Other animals experience periods of heat or estrus. Humans do not.

Just as we developed uniquely human capacities for language, planning, memory, and invention along our evolutionary path, we also developed sexuality as a form of expression, a way of communicating that is separable from our reproductive need. For human beings, sexuality can be and often is a way of bonding, of giving and receiving pleasure, bridging differentness, discovering sameness, and communicating emotion.

We developed this and other human gifts through our ability to change our environment, adapt to it physically, and so in the very long run to affect our own evolution. But as an emotional result of this spiraling path away from other animals, we seem to alternate between periods of exploring our unique abilities and feelings of loneliness in the unknown that we ourselves have created, a fear that sometimes sends us back to the comfort of the animal world by encouraging us to look for a sameness that is not there.

For instance, the separation of "play" from "work" is a feature of the human world. So is the difference between art and nature, or an intellectual accomplishment and a physical one. As a result, we celebrate play, art, and invention as pleasurable and important leaps into the unknown; yet any temporary trouble can send us back to a nostalgia for our primate past and a conviction that the basics of survival, nature, and physical labor are somehow more worthwhile or even more moral.

In the same way, we have explored our sexuality as separable from conception: a pleasurable, empathetic, important bridge to others of our species. We have even invented contraception, a skill that has probably existed in some form since our ancestors figured out the process of conception and birth, in order to extend and protect this uniquely human gift. Yet we also have times of atavistic suspicion that sex is not complete, or even legal or intended by God, if it does not or could not end in conception.

No wonder the very different concepts of "erotica" and "pornography" can be so confused. Both assume that sex can be separated from conception; that human sexuality has additional uses and goals. This is the major reason why, even in our current culture, both may still be condemned as equally obscene and immoral. Such gross condemnation of all sexuality that isn't harnessed to childbirth (and to patriarchal marriage so that children are properly "owned" by men) has been increased by the current backlash against women's independence. Out of fear that the whole patriarchal structure will be eventually upset if we as women really have the autonomous power to decide our sexual and reproductive futures (that is, if we can control our own bodies, and thus the means of reproduction), anti-equality groups are not only denouncing sex education and family planning as "pornographic," but are trying to use obscenity laws to stop the sending of all contraceptive information through the mails. Any sex or nudity outside the context of patriarchal marriage and forced childbirth is their target. In fact, Phyllis Schlafly[1] has denounced the entire women's movement as "obscene."

Not surprisingly, this religious, visceral backlash has a secular, intellectual counterpart that relies heavily on applying the "natural" behavior of some selected part of the animal world to humans. This is questionable in itself, but such Lionel Tiger-ish[2] studies make their political purpose even more clear by the animals they choose and the habits they emphasize. For example, some male primates

---

[1] Conservative opponent of the women's movement.
[2] The allusion is to anthropologist Lionel Tiger, author of *Men in Groups.*

carry and generally "mother" their infants, male lions care for their young, female elephants often lead the clan, and male penguins literally do everything except give birth, from hatching the eggs to sacrificing their own membranes to feed the new arrivals. Perhaps that's why many male supremacists prefer to discuss chimps and baboons (many of whom are studied in atypical conditions of captivity) whose behavior is suitably male-dominant. The message is that human females should accept their animal "destiny" of being sexually dependent and devote themselves to bearing and rearing their young.

Defending against such repression and reaction leads to the temptation to merely reverse the terms and declare that *all* nonprocreative sex is good. In fact, however, this human activity can be as constructive or destructive, moral or immoral, as any other. Sex as communication can send messages as different as mutual pleasure and dominance, life and death, "erotica" and "pornography."

The second kind of problem comes not from those who oppose women's equality in nonsexual areas, whether on grounds of God or nature, but from men (and some women, too) who present themselves as friends of civil liberties and progress. Their opposition may take the form of a concern about privacy, on the grounds that a challenge to pornography invades private sexual behavior and the philosophy of "whatever turns you on." It may be a concern about class bias, on the premise that pornography is just "workingmen's erotica." Sometimes, it's the simple argument that they themselves like pornography and therefore it must be okay. Most often, however, this resistance attaches itself to or hides behind an expressed concern about censorship, freedom of the press, and the First Amendment.

In each case, such liberal objections are more easily countered than the anti-equality ones because they are less based on fact. It's true, for instance, that women's independence and autonomy would upset the whole patriarchal apple cart: the conservatives are right to be worried. It's not true, however, that pornography is a private concern. If it were just a matter of men making male-supremacist literature in their own basements to assuage their own sexual hang-ups, there would be sorrow and avoidance among women, but not the anger, outrage, and fear produced by being confronted with the preaching of sexual fascism on our newstands, movie screens, television sets, and public streets. It is a multibillion-dollar industry, which involves the making of public policy, if only to decide whether, as is now the case, crimes committed in the manufacture and sale of pornography will continue to go largely unprosecuted. Zoning regulations on the public display of pornography are not enforced, the sexual slavery and exploitation of children goes unpunished, the forcible use of teenage runaways is ignored by police, and even the torture and murder of prostitutes for men's sexual titillation is obscured by some mitigating notion that the women asked for it.

In all other areas of privacy, the limitation is infringement on the rights and lives and safety of others. That must become true for pornography. Right now, it is exempt: almost "below the law."

As for class bias, it's simply not accurate to say that pornography is erotica with less education. From the origins of the words, as well as the careful way that feminists working against pornography are trying to use them, it's clear there is a substantive difference, not an artistic or economic one. Pornography is about dominance. Erotica is about mutuality. (Any man able to empathize with women can easily tell the difference by looking at a photograph or film and putting himself in the woman's skin. There is some evidence that poor or discriminated-against men are better able to do this than rich ones.) Perhaps the most revealing thing is that this argument is generally made *on behalf* of the working class by propornography liberals, but not *by* working-class spokespeople themselves.

Of course, the idea that enjoying pornography makes it okay is an overwhelmingly male one. From Kinsey forward, research has confirmed that men are the purchasers of pornography, and that the majority of men are turned on by it, while the majority of women find it angering, humiliating, and not a turn-on at all. This was true even though women were shown sexually explicit material that may have included erotica, since Kinsey and others did not make that distinction. If such rare examples of equal sex were entirely deleted, pornography itself could probably serve as sex aversion-therapy for most women; yet many men and some psychologists continue to call women prudish, frigid, or generally unhealthy if they are not turned on by their own domination. The same men might be less likely to argue that anti-Semitic and racist literature was equally okay because it gave them pleasure, or that they wanted their children to grow up with the same feelings about people of other races, other classes, that had been inflicted on them. The problem is that the degradation of women of all races is still thought to be normal.

Nonetheless, there are a few well-meaning women who are both turned on by pornography and angered that other women are not. Some of their anger is misunderstanding: objections to pornography are not condemnations of women who have been raised to believe sex and domination are synonymous, but objections to the idea that such domination is the only form that normal sexuality can take. Sometimes, this anger results from an underestimation of themselves: being turned on by a rape fantasy is not the same thing as wanting to be raped. As Robin Morgan[3] has pointed out, the distinguishing feature of a fantasy is that the fantasizer herself is in control. Both men and women have "ravishment" fantasies in which we are passive while others act out our unspoken wishes—but they are still *our* wishes. And some anger, especially when it comes from women who consider themselves feminists, is a refusal to differentiate between what may be true for them now and what might be improved for all women in the future. To use a small but related example, a woman may now be attracted only to men who are taller, heavier, and older than she, but still understand that such superficial restrictions on the men she loves and enjoys going to bed with won't exist in a more free and less-stereotyped future. Similarly, some lesbians may find themselves following the masculine–feminine patterns that were our only model for intimate relationships, heterosexual or not, but still see these old patterns clearly and try to equalize them. It isn't that women attracted to pornography cannot also be feminists, but that pornography itself must be recognized as an adversary of women's safety and equality, and therefore, in the long run, of feminism.

Finally, there is the First Amendment argument against feminist anti-pornography campaigns: the most respectable and public opposition, but also the one with the least basis in fact.

Feminist groups are not arguing for censorship of pornography, or for censor-

---

[3] A feminist writer.

ship of Nazi literature or racist propaganda of the Ku Klux Klan. For one thing, any societal definition of pornography in a male-dominant society (or of racist literature in a racist society) probably would punish the wrong people. Freely chosen homosexual expression might be considered more "pornographic" than snuff movies, or contraceptive courses for teenagers more "obscene" than bondage. Furthermore, censorship in itself, even with the proper definitions, would only drive pornography into more underground activity and, were it to follow the pattern of drug traffic, into even more profitability. Most important, the First Amendment is part of a statement of individual rights against government intervention that feminism seeks to expand, not contract: for instance, a woman's right to decide whether and when to have children. When we protest against pornography and educate others about it, as I am doing now, we are strengthening the First Amendment by exercising it.

The only legal steps suggested by feminists thus far have been the prosecution of those pornography makers who are accused of murder or assault and battery, prosecution of those who use children under the age of consent, enforcement of existing zoning and other codes that are breached because of payoffs to law-enforcement officials and enormous rents paid to pornography's landlords, and use of public-nuisance statutes to require that pornography not be displayed in public places where its sight cannot reasonably be avoided. All of those measures involve enforcement of existing law, and none has been interpreted as a danger to the First Amendment.

Perhaps the reason for this controversy is less substance than smokescreen. Just as earlier feminist campaigns to combat rape were condemned by some civil libertarians as efforts that would end by putting only men of color or poor men in jail, or in perpetuating the death penalty, anti-pornography campaigns are now similarly opposed. In fact, the greater publicity given to rape exposed the fact that white psychiatrists, educators, and other professionals were just as likely to be rapists, and changes in the law reduced penalties to ones that were more appropriate and thus more likely to be administered. Feminist efforts also changed the definition to sexual assault so that men were protected, too.

Though there are no statistics on the purchasers of pornography, clerks, movie-house owners, video-cassette dealers, mail-order houses, and others who serve this clientele usually remark on their respectability, their professional standing, suits, briefcases, white skins, and middle-class zip codes. For instance, the last screening of a snuff movie showing a real murder was traced to the monthly pornographic film showings of a senior partner in a respected law firm; an event regularly held by him for a group of friends including other lawyers and judges. One who was present reported that many were "embarrassed" and "didn't know what to say." But not one man was willing to object, much less offer this evidence of murder to the police. Though some concern about censorship is sincere—the result of false reports that feminist anti-pornography campaigns were really calling for censorship, or of confusion with right-wing groups who both misdefine pornography and want to censor it—much of it seems to be a cover for the preservation of the pornographic status quo.

In fact, the obstacles to taking on pornography seem suspiciously like the virgin–whore divisions that have been women's only choices in the past. The right wing says all that is not virginal or motherly is pornographic, and thus they campaign against sexuality and nudity in general. The left wing says all sex is good as long as it's male-defined, and thus pornography must be protected. Women who feel endangered by being the victim, and men who feel demeaned by being the victimizer, have a long struggle ahead. In fact, pornography will continue as long as boys are raised to believe they must control or conquer women as a measure of manhood, as long as society rewards men who believe that success or even functioning—in sex as in other areas of life—depends on women's subservience.

But we now have words to describe our outrage and separate sex from violence. We now have the courage to demonstrate publicly against pornography, to keep its magazines and films out of our houses, to boycott its purveyors, to treat even friends and family members who support it as seriously as we would treat someone who supported and enjoyed Nazi literature or the teachings of the Klan.

But until we finally untangle sexuality and aggression, there will be more pornography and less erotica. There will be little murders in our beds—and very little love.

Pornographic Minds
George Will

Today's pornographers do not slight the life of the mind. Hugh Hefner of *Playboy* dabbles in metaphysics. And Larry Flynt, publisher of *Hustler,* has a sociological flair. He explains his magazine's success in terms of the American psyche, as revealed in the public's enthusiasm for the film *Jaws:*

"The shark wasn't repressed. The American people don't like repression."

It is impossible to describe *Hustler*—even to report what is printed on the cover—without becoming a collaborator in its assault on sensibility. Suffice it to say that Flynt has been a pathbreaker in the accelerating movement to make human sexuality resemble that of sharks and other unrepressed creatures free from "hangups."

But recently Flynt came a cropper in Cincinnati, a community now being roundly despised by libertarians. Flynt was fined and sentenced to seven to twenty-five years in prison for participating in "organized crime" (the crime of distributing obscenity), and was fined and sentenced to six months for "pandering obscenity."

The Supreme Court has ruled that there is no inherent incompatability between the First Amendment and statutes regulating obscenity. And it has held that juries can judge obscenity by "community" standards which, the Court's language suggests, can be statewide standards. There is little reason to doubt that *Hustler* would be declared obscene by community standards applied by any representative jury in any of the fifty states.

If Flynt and his lawyers did not know that, by Ohio standards, he was manufacturing and distributing obscenity, then he has foolish lawyers and his lawyers have a fool for a client. But, of course, he not only knew but boasted that he was producing obscenity unprecedented in a slick, mass-circulation magazine.

Much criticism of the *Hustler* ruling involves general objections to the "organized crime" charge. Critics also questioned why the distributor of the magazine was not the appropriate target, if there was to be prosecution, and emphasized the fact that Flynt operates out of Columbus, Ohio, not Cincinnati. But these arguments are not the essence of the familiar libertarian complaint, which is that "obscenity is a subjective matter."

The idea is that "obscenity" (unlike, presumably, "unfair labor practices" or "fraudulent advertising") is too subjective a category for other than capricious use in law. So censorship of obscenity is opposed by those who cite the "slippery slope" argument: "Once it starts, how will society know when to stop?"

The "slippery slope" argument also can be made against taxation and police: taxation might become expropriation; police forces might become gestapos. But self-government rests on the confidence that communities can, generally and within a tolerable margin of error, make reasonable distinctions.

The "slippery slope" argument against censoring *Hustler* is that the magazine, although loathsome, must be protected or even James Joyce's *Ulysses* cannot be protected. The logic of this argument is that censorship of anything endangers everything because all standards are equally arbitrary and idiosyncratic.

Former Supreme Court Justice William Douglas, the archetypal libertarian, argued with equal vehemence and thoughtfulness two propositions. One was that, "The idea of a Free Society written into our Constitution . . . is that people are mature enough . . . to recognize trash when they see it." His second proposition was that the distinction between trash and art is merely a matter of taste, no more rationally defensible than a taste for anchovies or ripe olives.

But if there are no critical standards to identify trash, then there are no critical standards to identify art. The authentic voice of this school of thought is the New York Civil Liberties Union, which has argued that tattooing is an "art form" enjoying First Amendment protection.

A few years ago, the Court wisely modified (by broadening) the principle that a community could only regulate material that is "utterly without redeeming social value." There is, alas, no community so far off the beaten path of the march of intellect that some professor cannot be flown there to testify to the cathartic, or otherwise redemptive, value of anything.

Indeed, a professor, Walter Bennett, declares that even laws prohibiting incest are unconstitutionally repressive: "It seems clear that the incest taboo is not instinctive but the product of cultural conditioning, because no aversion to sexual intercourse between relatives exists in animals other than man."

So goes the libertarian argument for ending the "repression" that prevents human sexuality from ascending to the level of shark sexuality—the level of "animals other than man."

PORNOGRAPHY—QUESTIONS ON ESSAYS

1. What generalization does each essay make? What subgeneralizations are made? What concrete examples do the writers include? Which writer do you think supports his or her point of view most logically? What role does the varying lengths of the essays play in your decision?

2. What point of view does each writer have on the issue? Are their points of view similar or different? Do any two writers agree more with each other than with the third? How can you account for any agreement? Which essay most clearly represents your point of view?

3. What points of view other than those held by the writers themselves do they refer to in their essays? Do they refer to each other's arguments? How many points of view do there seem to be on this issue? What attitude toward other points of view does each writer take?

4. These essays intend to persuade the reader of their point of view on the issue. How has each writer organized his or her argument; which are primarily inductive and which are deductive, for example?

5. Analyze the style and tone of these essays. Which writer uses the most abstract language? Which uses the most concrete? How does the writer's voice differ from essay to essay? Based on the style and tone, what type of audience would you say each essay was intended for?

6. What segments of society other than those addressed here would be interested in reading about these issues? How would a writer go about persuading any of these groups of her or his point of view on the issue?

WRITING THE ESSAY

Using Critical Thinking Skills as a Way of Generating Ideas

Once you have chosen the issue you want to write about and have studied the points of view on that issue of the writers included in the task section, as well as the points of view of any other writers you, your group, or your teacher may have added, you are ready to begin the process that will lead you to a synthesis of the varying viewpoints. The four critical thinking approaches presented in the "Generating Ideas" section suggest you look first at the issue itself, then at the points of view of all parties involved including your own, then at the ramifications for sizeable groups within our society or society as a whole, and finally at corollary issues that have a bearing on the issue. These insights can be gathered from simply reading the essays on the subject for the most part, but analyzing them according to this critical thinking procedure may give you an enlarged perspective.

In order to apply critical thinking to your issue, you might use your journal to summarize the various points of view, to explore your own stand on the issue as a way of clarifying your personal attitudes, to examine how the various solutions posed would affect society, and to explore other issues that seem to have a bearing on any synthesis that will be achieved. In order to get "inside" the controversy, you may create in your journal a dialogue or conversation between the parties involved so that, in effect, you are role-playing the points of view.

Having a group role-play the varying points of view can provide a useful insight into the thoughts and emotions of those involved as well. By switching roles frequently, all group members can gain understanding of the issue from the perspective of all parties.

In synthesizing, you will attempt to resolve the conflicting points of view by forming a generalization other than those posed by the parties involved, one that all can subscribe to, or at least one that creates an opportunity for dialogue to begin and continue. A useful process for arriving at a synthesis is that of the syllogism: If it is true that (point of view 1), and if it is true that (point of view 2), and if it is true that (point of view 3), then it must be true that (your synthesizing point of view).

Addressing the Informed Reader

Both you and your reader, whether it is your teacher or some other informed reader, will be playing the same role—that of disinterested observer, one who knows all points of view on the subject and supports no particular one but instead seeks to synthesize all responses into a new point of view, one that embraces all sides or seeks to move the controversy onto common ground so that dialogue can continue.

Your synthesis may be new to your reader, however much he or she may have thought about the subject, and in order to impress your reader with the soundness of your new generalization, you will want to present what you know about the issue and what you have resolved about it thoroughly, clearly, and articulately.

Arranging the Essay

The four aspects of critical thinking will probably find their way into your essay, and this is one possible arrangement pattern for this task. In other words, you may want to explore the issue itself, perhaps presenting some background, proceed to the various points of view, arranging them syllogistically as suggested above, suggest the ramifications of the various solutions for the parties involved as well as society as a whole, and finally bring in related issues that must be considered in any attempt at resolution or synthesis.

Where should you state your synthesis? Quintillian, a Roman rhetorician, said that we have essentially two choices in presenting our major points: We can put some of them first and some of them last with our minor ones in the middle, or we can put our weaker ones first and ascend to the stronger ones.

We cannot, said he, lead off with our strongest point and end with our weakest one. In deciding whether to state your synthesis at the beginning of your essay or at the end, you might take Quintillian's advice into account. What effect will placing your synthesis at the beginning have on your reader? Will the rest of the paper be anticlimactic? Is it in fact better to place it last? Or is there a way in which some aspect of your synthesis can introduce your essay and another aspect of it find its way into your conclusion?

Writing the Rough Draft

Following is the rough draft of a student essay on the issue of pornography. As you read the essay, ask yourself the following questions: How well has the writer stated the issue? How thoroughly and objectively has she presented the various points of view? Has she considered the ramifications of the various solutions for groups within society, for society itself? Has she considered all the major related issues, issues that must be considered if her synthesis is to be useful? What is her synthesis? To what extent does it in fact synthesize the varying points of view?

PORNOGRAPHY AND ME AND YOU

Porn flicks, girlie magazines, smutty paperbacks--I have always felt removed from, insulated against their seaminess here in my clean, comfortable, middle-class existence. Exposure to obscenity in my suburban neighborhood would never be inadvertent but intentionally and diligently sought. There are no x-rated movie houses here, no racks of offensive books or sex-peddling periodicals on display in our local stationery store. My husband does not subscribe to Hustler. None of this unpleasantness (or to some people, pleasantness) touches me. Or does it?

In her essay, "Erotica vs. Pornography," Gloria Steinem made such keen observations about pornography's allure in our society that she compelled me to sit up and take notice of a topic that had previously never concerned or interested me.

First she makes a distinction between pornography (dominance and submission) and erotica (mutuality). She then points out that the seeds of pornography are not sown by the Larry Flynts of our society but by you and me as a result of our own complacency about and tolerance of a societal structure in which males have greater power than females.

Those of us who think it is cute when a young boy struts, postures, or is openly aggressive and a young girl shies away, is coy, or flagrantly flirtatious, are, on the other hand, extremely offended by depictions of aggression and submission in pornographic films and magazines. We never see the obvious relation that exists between the cute and the offensive.

If we were able to clear away the smoke screen emitted by the social mechanisms of sexual role playing and gender identification, we would see this cute behavior of children as equally obscene as the portrayals in so-called "adult" magazines, books, and films. Pornography is not a disease, as many people seem to think, but merely a symptom of the disease of sexism that pervades our society. We should be seeking a cure and not simply masking the disease by treating the symptoms, because then the disease continues to spread unchecked.

I recently came across a perfect example of blind acceptance of the status quo as it pertains to male/female roles. In a letter to The New York Times, Diana Trilling responded to an article by Fred M. Hechinger about the legal dispute touched off by a public school's attempt to discipline a high school student for using sexual innuendo in a campaign speech supporting a fellow student. Ms. Trilling referred to "a student's decent acceptance of male sexuality as an aspect of male strength. . . ."

That is an outrageous statement! Is she saying that male sexual prowess has a legitimate place in a political campaign (albeit a high school election)? Would a frank allusion to the sexual attributes of a female candidate have been equally indicative of an acceptance of female strength?

I doubt it! On the contrary, when a woman emphasizes her sexuality, she is typically viewed as irrational and therefore politically weak.

Ms. Trilling's aim is to oppose censorship, and she offers a valid argument, yet at the same time she unwittingly endorses male sexual prowess as a valid qualification for political office. That student's speech was, in my opinion, obscene even though he made no specific reference to genitalia or sexual acts because it represented the commonly held belief that male power stems solely from physical traits, which perpetuates the oppression of women.

Pornography is just one of many subtle forces that chisel away at our collective subconscious and almost imperceptibly sculpt our ideas about male–female relationships. It is just one more thing that contributes to what I see as an intolerable situation for women, a situation that even sways political decisions and that certainly has an effect on everyone, even me.

FOCUS: STYLE—FIGURATIVE AND LITERAL LANGUAGE

As you no doubt have been aware in responding to the tasks in this book, and as we have pointed out at various times throughout, both your purpose in writing and your intended audience affect your choice of words. The language you used in essays with an expressive purpose differed from that in your scientific paper; and when you wrote for yourself, you wrote differently from when you wrote for your peers or your instructor. (See "Audience" and "Writing the Essay" sections of Chapters 1, 7, and 8 as well as the "Focus" sections in Chapters 6 and 8.)

The ability to change your language to suit your purpose and intended reader is vital to good writing. You must also, of course, know when it is appropriate to do so. By studying the purpose, audience, and language of the essays included in the task section of this chapter, you may arrive at a greater understanding of when to use figurative language and when to use literal language, as well as when to be abstract and when to be concrete, as we saw in Chapter 6.

All nine essays in this chapter, whether on affirmative action, euthanasia, or pornography, whether intended to be primarily expressive, exploratory, explanatory, or persuasive, contain a strong persuasive element. For example, while Richard Rodriguez's essay on affirmative action and Richard Selzer's on euthanasia express personal experiences, both also draw us into a particular point of view on a controversial issue. Their persuasive technique is, of course, a form of induction, as we have learned (see Chapter 8, pp. 315–322).

From our discussion of persuasive writing and our study of some outstanding persuasive essays in Chapter 8, we have come to expect that writing with a persuasive aim will utilize language that has many levels of meaning: connotation, figures of speech, allusion, satire, irony. Analyzing advertisements and political speeches will also indicate the use of multileveled language. In this chapter, Richard Selzer uses such figurative language in "Mercy," his essay on euthanasia. At first glance, therefore, persuasive language does not appear to be literal language such as that used by the scientist (see Chapter 7). And yet, among the nine essays in this chapter, you will find some writing, such as that of the Vatican writer, that is literal; does not use language that suggests other than its literal, denotative meaning; and does not use what we have come to recognize as emotionally persuasive language, even though its aim is to persuade as well as to inform.

The Reader and Figurative Language

Why have some writers chosen figurative language and others literal? Let us analyze further Richard Selzer's essay "Mercy" and "The Vatican's Declaration on Euthanasia." Selzer's purpose, as we indicated above, is primarily expressive, even though it has the effect of persuasion. He wishes to dramatize an agonizing encounter he had with a dying man whose family wanted him, as the man's doctor, to commit a mercy killing. He attempts to do so, but when the patient continues to live, he finds he cannot take further action. His plight persuades us of the difficulty of taking even such a life.

Figures of speech occur in nearly every line of Selzer's work: the flies are "like dervishes who whirl" (allusion/simile), "death has not yet secured the premises" (personification), the patient "twisted under the lash" of his pain (metaphor), "the squadron of ribs battles on" (synedoche—in which a part [the ribs] is taken for the whole [body]), "his death is like a jewel to them" (simile). He also uses language with strong connotations—the patient has upon his teeth "a brown paste of saliva," his belly is "stuffed with tumor." Why does this use of figurative language suit Selzer's purpose? No doubt your reading of his essay has suggested an answer: His comparisons and connotations weave the bright colors of other scenes and other emotions into his tapestry, which enriches both our comprehension and appreciation of his experience.

What does his language suggest about his intended reader? What reader, in other words, responds best to figurative language? Language theorists have suggested that the making of comparisons indicates a greater range of thought than usual on the part of both writer and reader. From this we can conclude that Selzer intended his reader to be mature and to some extent well-read.

Purpose and Language

To consider next "The Vatican's Declaration on Euthanasia," we encounter a piece of writing that contains almost no figurative language, other than random allusions to biblical images such as "life is entrusted to the individual as a good that must bear fruit." The language is almost completely literal in that each word has only one meaning—is denotative and not connotative—and no comparisons invite additional meaning. Because Vatican pronouncements are meant to govern the morality of those belonging to the Roman Catholic faith, the writer must ensure that his language does not encourage possible misinterpretation. Figurative language often is ambiguous language, because various readers may interpret the comparisons and connotations in varying ways; literal language allows no such range of interpretations. The writer's purpose then may require such literal language even when his audience is mature and well-read.

Cliché and Audience

Charles Krauthammer's "A Defense of Quotas" also abounds with figurative language: "officially sanctioned race consciousness was becoming irrevocably woven into American life," "a revolution has been brewing on the issue of affirmative action," "Reynold's target is to root out race consciousness," "recruiting . . . would be the last refuge of affirmative action," "the other side claims the mantle of individual rights and equal treatment." Each of these figures, however, consists of a cliché. A cliché contains a metaphor that has so worked its way into the language that we are scarcely aware of its metaphoric origins, and yet we sense that the language lacks vitality.

What does his use of cliché indicate to us of Krauthammer's purpose and readership? Like Selzer, he intends to use figurative language, but unlike Selzer, he has not sought fresh comparisons. His purpose is clearly not expressive since cliché obscures insight. When would a writer whose purpose is to explore, explain, or persuade use cliché? Certainly Martin Luther King and the framers of the Declaration of Independence (Chapter 8) created new and startling images. Since Krauthammer writes for a weekly magazine, he appears to intend a timely argument in response to current events. Because the reader of a weekly magazine often has little time to dwell on multiple meanings, Krauthammer delivers his facts and interpretations in a style that is easy to read because it relies on clichéd expressions.

What do our analyses of these essays indicate to us about the use of language? As readers, we see that figurative language is engaging, that it requires maturity, experience, and even education to appreciate, that it can often become overused and lose its effectiveness. As readers, we can also see the need on occasion for literal language that eschews levels of meaning and therefore varying interpretations.

Purpose, Audience, and Language

As writers, we need to consider both purpose and audience. Does our purpose require literal language because we wish a precise interpretation of our meaning, or will our purpose be enhanced by the broadening, deepening, and heightening of meaning created by figurative language? What effect will our audience have on our style? Are our readers willing to read for meaning or will (or must) they skim? To what extent does the freedom to create our own audience, as writers of books like Selzer and Rodriguez had, determine our choice of language?

SOME PRACTICE WITH FIGURATIVE AND LITERAL LANGUAGE

1. Rodriguez's purpose in writing, like Selzer's, is expressive, and yet he does not use figurative language. Is his language literal? Compare his use of language with that of the Vatican writer. How does his language differ from both Selzer's and that of those writers who use literal language? What effect does Rodriguez's language achieve? Who does his audience appear to be? Has his sense of audience affected his language?

2. Lester Thurow wrote for *The New York Times*, a newspaper whose educated readership is similar to that of *The New Republic*, for which Charles Krauthammer wrote. Does Thurow use clichés? How similar to Krauthammer's is Thurow's language? How similar therefore do their purposes and audiences seem to be? Is it possible for writers writing in the same publication to use different language? What further light does this shed on the interplay between language and reader, between language and purpose, between writer and reader?

3. George Will and Alan Dershowitz are also writing for newsmagazines. How similar to Charles Krauthammer's is their style? To what extent do these writers project the same voice and tone even though they may be on different ends of the political spectrum? How would you characterize each writer's voice and tone?

4. Gloria Steinem and James Rachels to varying degrees use literal language. Steinem was writing for *Ms.* of which she is editor, and James Rachels, a moral philosopher, was writing for the *New England Journal of Medicine.* How might these audiences have affected both their purpose and style?

5. In Chapter 6 we discussed another language continuum, that between abstract and concrete language. To what extent does this continuum overlap with the figurative–literal continuum? Does a pattern exist? What significance might such a pattern have for the stylistic choices that writers make?

6. Search through your journal or other private writing and also writing you have done for school for examples of figurative language: connotation, figures of speech, irony, allusion, satire. If you locate figurative language (even clichés), analyze why you might have used it in this context: How might purpose and audience have affected your choices? If you cannot find any figurative language, what reasons can you give for its absence? Again, have purpose and audience played a role?

7. Take a piece of writing you have done for which figurative language seems appropriate, altering your original concept of purpose and audience if necessary. Using Richard Selzer's use of vivid figurative language as a model, experiment with enriching your meaning through the insertion of figures of speech. Replace any clichés you may have used with fresh comparisons.

REWRITING

Obtaining Feedback on Your Rough Draft

Before evaluating—or having your group evaluate—your essay and before reading the following peer evaluation of "Pornography and Me and You," the rough draft of the student essay on pages 410–412, you might take time now, if you haven't already done so, to do your own critique of her essay. Because all the professional essays in the chapter are persuasive essays, "Pornography and Me and You" is the single model in fulfillment of the task, which is to synthesize opposing points of view rather than to support one or another of them. As you read, ask yourself in particular, how objective has the writer been, how well has she played the role of disinterested observer?

Using the "Audience Response Guide" to critique both her rough draft and your own might help you and/or your group to evaluate the success of both essays. Then, compare your evaluation with the student critique below of "Pornography and Me and You."

———— AUDIENCE RESPONSE GUIDE ————

1. **What do you think the writer wanted to say in this paper? What is his or her purpose in writing?**
2. **How does the paper affect the reader for whom it was intended?**
3. **How effective has the writer been in conveying his or her purpose and meaning? What are the strengths of the paper? What are the weaknesses?**
4. **How should the paper be revised to better fulfill its purpose and meaning?**

---

1. The group, playing the role of expert reader, agreed that her purpose in writing was to persuade the reader that pornography is just a surface issue, that in fact the real issue is that our society encourages harmful distinctions between male and female roles and relationships.

2. On the one hand, they felt that the paper is thoughtful and intelligently written; on the other, they believed that the writer has not responded to the other positions in the controversy on pornography. She argues her own point rather than developing a synthesis. Some of the group members wanted her to support her comments on the Hechinger–Trilling dialogue with more details.

3. The group felt the essay is effective in touching on important problems and particularly so in analyzing the situation to see that the problem is deeper than most participants realize. However, she considers only one side of the issue and lets her outrage take over.

4. The group wanted the writer to demonstrate more thoroughly how her conclusion derives from a critical analysis of all three points of view and serves to synthesize those points of view. She also needs to supply details about the Hechinger–Trilling dialogue and recognize the conflict between heredity and environment in the paragraph on children's role playing.

Following is the student's revision of her rough draft. How effective do you now think it to be as a model of this chapter's task? What further revisions might she make in response to the suggestions in the "Revising and Editing to Sharpen Critical Thinking" section pp. 420–421?

PORNOGRAPHY AND ME AND YOU

Porn flicks, girlie magazines, smutty paperbacks--I have always felt removed from, insulated against their seaminess here in my clean, comfortable, middle-class existence. Exposure to obscenity in my suburban neighborhood would never be inadvertent but intentionally and diligently sought. There are no x-rated movie houses here, no racks of offensive books or sex-peddling periodicals on display in our local stationery store. My husband does not subscribe to Hustler. None of this unpleasantness (or to some people, pleasantness) touches me. Or does it?

In her essay "Erotica vs. Pornography," Gloria Steinem made such keen observations about pornography's allure in our society that she compelled me to sit up and take notice of a topic that had previously never concerned or interested me.

First, she makes a distinction between pornography, which entails dominance and submission, and erotica, which describes mutuality. She then points out that the seeds of pornography are not sown by the Larry Flynts of our society but by you and me as a result of our own complacency about, and tolerance of, a societal structure in which males have greater power than females.

Those of us who think it is cute when a young boy struts, postures, or is openly aggressive and a young girl shies away, is coy, or flagrantly flirtatious, are, on the other hand, extremely offended by depictions of aggression and submission in pornographic films and magazines. We never see the obvious parallels that exist between the cute and the offensive.

If we are able to clear away the smoke screen emitted by the social mechanisms of sexual role playing and gender identification, we might see this cute behavior of children as equally obscene as the portrayals in so-called "adult" magazines, books, and films. Some would disagree with this train of thought, because although it is undeniable that we are social beings influenced in many ways by societal expectations, whether or not some of this sexual role playing is innate and therefore normal and acceptable behavior is a controversial topic open to debate, and neither theory has yet to be proven.

I recently came across a perfect example of blind acceptance of the status quo as it pertains to male-female roles. In a letter to The New York Times, Diana Trilling responded to an article by Fred M. Hechinger about the legal dispute touched off by a public school's attempt to discipline a high school student for using sexual innuendo in a campaign speech supporting a fellow student. The student, Matthew N. Frazer, described the candidate he supported as "a man who is firm--he's firm in his pants, he's firm in his shirt, his character is firm." Ms. Trilling lauded Mr. Hechinger's support of the student's right to speak, regardless of his age and circumstance, and referred to Matthew Frazer's speech as "a student's decent acceptance of male sexuality as an aspect of male strength. . . ."

Is she saying that male sexual prowess has a legitimate place in a political campaign (albeit a high school election)? Would a frank allusion to the sexual attributes of a female candidate have been equally indicative of an acceptance of female strength?

On the contrary, when a woman emphasizes her sexuality, she is typically viewed as irrational and therefore politically weak. This view is often defended as valid by those who believe that women, and men, are born with a certain emotional makeup as the result of chance chromosomal combination--that women are naturally just less logical, less aggressive, and more emotional than men.

Ms. Trilling's aim is to oppose censorship, defend this young man's right to free speech, yet at the same time she unwittingly endorses male sexual prowess as a valid qualification for political office.

Pornography is just one of many subtle forces that chisel away at our collective subconscious and almost imperceptibly sculpt our ideas about male-female relationships. It is just one more thing that contributes to and aids in perpetuating the oppression of women. Yet, to advocate censorship of pornography would be detrimental to the feminist cause.

As Alan M. Dershowitz points out in his essay "Partners Against Porn," if feminists, banded together with Falwell's fundamentalists, were successful in censoring pornographers, what is to prevent fundamentalists from securing censorship of feminists? By denying the First Amendment protection to some, they may be setting a precedent that would justify denying the same protection to others. In joining with fundamentalists and pressing for censorship of pornographers, feminists may be digging their own grave.

On the other hand, fear of an avalanche effect could be used as justification for the prevention of many other types of legislation and government control. George Will points out in his essay, "Pornographic Minds," that some could argue against having police forces because they "might become gestapos." He contends that by taking a stance, making value judgments, men (meaning humankind) are practicing a form of repression, but by doing so, they are pointing up the difference between humans and all other animals--humans are capable of rationality. It is his opinion that by allowing pornography to flourish behind the skirts of the First Amendment we relinquish our high position among animals.

For those who see pornography as a cancerous blight on society, treating the symptoms with censorship will not check the spread of the disease. Those who are offended should utilize their own freedom of speech to encourage a more critical view of the roles of men and women in our society and instill healthy respect for the individual's thought processes and ability to make changes based on those processes.

Revising and Editing to Sharpen Critical Thinking

Revising.   In applying critical thinking to a subject you are writing about, you assume the role of a disinterested observer. In writing to fulfill the task for this chapter, you are also writing for an informed audience. In revising your essay, you will want to keep both your role and that of your reader in mind. The following questions applied to the six revision strategies may help you in making these revisions.

1. Have you included too many points supporting one point of view on the issue? Have you included too much background for an informed reader, material that he or she already knows? If so, you will want to cut these parts of your essay.

2. Have you supplied adequate support for all points of view? As a disinterested observer, you will want to include persuasive arguments for each side of the controversy. If you have not in fact done so, you will want to add this material in revising your essay.

3. Have you arranged the various arguments and their supporting evidence in a pattern that best prepares the reader for your synthesis? Have you placed your synthesis for maximum effect; i.e., at the end as a climax, rather than at the beginning causing your essay to lose momentum? Consider rearranging your essay if necessary in order to show your thinking at its most effective.

4. Have you supplied the best possible evidence for each point of view? Have you marshalled the most successful reasons for your synthesis? If not, you may want to substitute better evidence or more successful reasons in revising your essay.

5. Have you mentioned the various points of view on your issue only to drop them when presenting your synthesis? If so, you might want to distribute them more systematically throughout the essay in order to assure the reader that you have taken all arguments into account when creating your synthesis.

6. Just as the various strands should be distributed throughout the essay, so should they be consolidated at the point when you are building your synthesis. Have you built your synthesis clearly on all points of view? If not, you will want to consolidate mention of them as you analyze the issue and synthesize all vantage points.

Editing.   In writing critically for an informed audience, you will want to sound as knowledgeable as possible. You will want to demonstrate command of the concepts and vocabulary of the field of thought from which the issue arises. You will want to observe the attributes of expository writing suggested in Chapter 7: clarity, concreteness, economy, appropriateness. In addition, you may want to call on some of the attributes of persuasive writing suggested in Chapter 8, such as figurative language, as in attempting to arrive at a synthesis for a highly controversial issue, you may want to appeal to the audience's emotions. In critical thinking, however, the appeal to the reader's intelligence should be paramount and figurative language used with great care so that you do not appear to undermine your objectivity. Likewise, you will probably want to adopt a serious, reasonable tone, rather than any of the many attitudes toward his or her subject the persuasive writer may choose. (See Chapter 8, p. 333.)

BECOMING AWARE OF YOURSELF AS A WRITER

1. What new insights did the essays in the task section of this chapter provide you on the issue you chose for your task? If you read the essays on either or both of the other issues, what new perspectives did these essays provide?

2. Did you have a strong opinion about the issue you chose before beginning your task? Did thinking critically about the issue alter your opinion in any way? How effective might critical thinking be in thawing out the frozen positions in an old controversy so that dialogue can flow again?

3. By thinking critically about the other two issues represented by the essays in the task section, what synthesis can you now arrive at for each of them?

4. You can argue about a controversial issue or you can think critically about it and attempt to reach a synthesis; both are legitimate approaches used every day. In what situations would argumentation be appropriate? When should critical thinking be applied instead?

5. How effective has role play proven to be as a method of understanding other people and other points of view? What other techniques may have proven to be more valuable to you in identifying with others?

Handbook

Grammar

PARTS OF SPEECH

The Noun

A noun designates a person, a place, an object, a quality, or an idea. It names something.

A common noun refers to a member of a general class of things, such as an *artist*, a *town*, a *car*, *beauty*, *goodness*.

A proper noun names a specific person, place or thing, such as *Pablo Picasso* or *St. Louis, Missouri*. It may name a particular kind of common noun, such as a *Model-T Ford*. Proper nouns are capitalized.

Most nouns are either singular or plural. The plural is formed with *s* (one *car*, two *cars*) or *es* (one *sandwich*, two *sandwiches*). A few nouns form the plural by a change in their spelling (one *child*, many *children*; one *man*, many *men*). Refer to a good dictionary if you are uncertain about the plural form of any noun.

Adding an apostrophe and an *s* to most nouns indicates possession or ownership (the *woman's* car).

The Pronoun

A pronoun substitutes for a noun or a noun phrase. The noun that a pronoun replaces is called the *antecedent* of the pronoun.

Pronouns help a writer to sound less repetitious, as in the sentence

Joe drove his new car home,

where the pronoun *his* has replaced the proper noun *Joe's*.

Pronouns fall into one of the following categories:

425

Personal Pronouns. Personal pronouns take different forms, depending on whether they are used as subjects (subjective form), as objects or indirect objects (objective form), or to indicate ownership (possessive form):

	Subjective		*Objective*		*Possessive*	
	Singular	*Plural*	*Singular*	*Plural*	*Singular*	*Plural*
1st person	I	we	me	us	my, mine	our, ours
2nd person	you	you	you	you	your(s)	your(s)
3rd person	he, she, it	they	him, her, it	them	his, her(s), its	their(s)

Reflexive Pronouns. Reflexive pronouns indicate an action that affects the person who performs it. They are also used for emphasis:

myself	himself
ourselves	herself
yourself	itself
yourselves	themselves

Indefinite Pronouns. Indefinite pronouns refer to unspecified persons or things, and so they have no antecedent:

all	everybody	no one
another	everyone	none
any	everything	one
anybody	few	some
anyone	many	somebody
anything	most	someone
both	nobody	something
each		

Demonstrative Pronouns. Demonstrative pronouns point something or someone out:

this	these
that	those

Relative Pronouns. Relative pronouns introduce noun or adjective clauses:

who (subjective)	which
whom (objective)	that
whose (possessive)	

Interrogative Pronouns. Interrogative pronouns ask questions:

who/whom   which
whose   what

The Verb

A verb expresses an action *(to drive)* or a state of being *(to live)*. The root or plain form of any verb is the infinitive, the form listed in the dictionary and usually combined with *to*. This plain form is altered in a variety of ways, depending on how the verb is being used.

All verbs add *s* or *es* to the plain form in order to indicate third-person singular present (she *drives*, he *lives*); the only exceptions are *to be* (she *is*) and *to have* (he *has*).

What are called *regular verbs* add *d* or *ed* to the plain form in order to indicate the past tense (he *lived*). What are called *irregular verbs* indicate the past tense by more radical alterations of form (she *drove*, he *swam*).

Most verbs form the past participle, which indicates a completed action, by adding *d, ed, n,* or *en* to the plain form *(lived, driven)*, although again there are irregularly formed past participles of verbs such as *to do (done)* or *to keep (kept)*. The present participle, which indicates a continuing action, is formed by the addition of *ing* to the plain form of a verb *(living, driving, doing, keeping)*.

Refer to a dictionary if you are uncertain about the past tense or the past participle of a verb. Any good dictionary lists the past tense if it is irregular, the past participle, and the present participle of a verb.

A verb can be combined with an auxiliary or helping verb to indicate different relationships between the action or state of being that the verb describes and the passage of time (tense), or the actor (voice), or the writer's view of the action (mood). The modal auxiliaries are *can, could, do, does, did, many, might, must, shall, should, will,* and *would.*

Tense.   Verb tense indicates the relationships between an action or state of being and the passage of time. The present tense indicates that something is taking place now (I *live*, you *live*, he or she *lives*, we *live*, you *live*, they *live*). The past tense indicates that something was completed in the past (he *lived*, she *drove*). The future tense indicates that something will take place in the future (she *will drive*).

Each of these three tenses may be formed by use of the past or the present participle. The combination of a past participle with a form of the auxiliary verb *to have* produces what are called the *perfect tenses*, which focus on a completed action: present perfect (I *have driven*, she *has driven*); past perfect (she *had driven*); and future perfect (she *will have driven*). The combination of a present participle with a form of the auxiliary verb *to be* produces what are called the *progressive tenses*, which focus on an ongoing or continuing action: present progressive (I *am living*, you *are living*, he *is living*, we, you, they *are living*); past progressive (I *was driving*, you *were driving*, she *was driving*, we, you, they *were driving*); and future progressive (she *will be driving*).

More complex combinations of verb forms are possible, for example, the present perfect progressive (she *has been driving*), which focuses on an ongoing action in the past.

Voice.   A verb may be either active or passive, depending on whether the subject of the verb is performing the action (she *drives* the car) or is being acted on (the car *was driven* by her; she *was driven* crazy by her car). The passive voice is formed with a past participle and the auxiliary verb *to be*.

Note: The active voice tends to be more direct and concise than the passive. Compare the following:

Joe reeled in the fish. (ACTIVE)

The fish was reeled in by Joe. (PASSIVE)

But the passive voice is useful if you want to focus on a person or thing that has been acted upon

The thief was finally caught by the police.

or if you don't know or don't need to say who or what performed the action.

A week after the hurricane, the electricity was finally restored to our neighborhood.

(For a more complete discussion of active and passive constructions, see the "Focus" section in Chapter 6, p. 243.)

Mood.   A verb may be formed to reflect any one of three different moods or attitudes: the indicative mood states a fact or an opinion (she *drives* carefully), or it asks a question (*does* she *drive* carefully?); the imperative mood gives commands or directions (*drive* carefully); the subjunctive mood expresses doubt or uncertainty (I'm not sure that she *should drive* at all), or it states a condition (if she *were to drive* carefully, she'd make me feel better), or it expresses a suggestion or a wish (I'd like it if she *would drive* carefully), or it states a requirement (it is important that she *be* a careful driver). Note that the subjunctive employs *be* (rather than *am, is,* or *are*) in the present tense and *were* (rather than *was*) in the past tense.

The Adjective

An adjective modifies a noun by describing a particular attribute of it (a *blue* car), by qualifying it (a *good* car), or by specifying it (the *second* car; *my* car). In qualifying a noun, an adjective may limit (*that* car) or broaden (*any* car; *most* cars) the meaning of the noun.

An attributive adjective comes immediately before or after the noun it modifies (it is a *dangerous* car). A predicate adjective is separated from its noun by a linking verb (the car is *dangerous*).

An adjective often can be identified by its suffix: *-able, -ous, -full, -less, -ic, -er, -est.* The last two suffixes indicate the comparative and superlative forms of many adjectives *(happy, happier, happiest).* Other adjectives form the comparative and superlative by combining with *more* and *most (dangerous, more dangerous, most dangerous).*

The Adverb

An adverb modifies a verb (she drives *slowly*), an adjective (the road is *dangerously* steep), another adverb (she drives *more* slowly), or a complete clause or sentence (*evidently*, she is a careful driver).

Many adverbs are formed by adding *ly* to an adjective:

shy, shyly	beautiful, beautifully
nice, nicely	hopeless, hopelessly
terrible, terribly	comical, comically
dangerous, dangerously	

Adverbs often specify when something happened (the storm ended *today*; I got lost *again*); where it happened (it was colder *inside* than *outside*; I tried to call you *there*); the manner in which it happened (she left *quickly*; she spoke *hoarsely*); or the extent or degree to which it happened (she *almost* lost her wallet; he *never* thought about it).

Most adverbs form comparatives and superlatives by combining with *more* and *most,* although a few add *er* and *es (soon, sooner, soonest).*

The Conjunction

A conjunction links one part of a sentence to another part. It joins words, phrases, and clauses to one another, showing the relationships between them; for example, the coordinating conjunction *and* shows equality between two parts of a sentence, whereas the subordinating conjunction *because* indicates a cause-and-effect relationship.

Coordinating conjunctions link words or phrases or clauses of equal grammatical rank. They may link one word to another (dogs *and* cats), one phrase to another (in the house *or* in the car), or one clause to another (I like candy, *but* I am on a diet). The coordinating conjunctions are *and, but, or, nor, for, so,* and *yet.*

Correlative conjunctions work in pairs, such as *both . . . and, not only . . . but also, either . . . or, neither . . . nor* (*either* knock on the door *or* ring the bell).

Subordinating conjunctions link dependent clauses, which cannot stand by themselves as sentences, to independent clauses, which can stand by themselves as sentences (she took the blue car *because* it is faster). Subordinating conjunctions include *after, although, as, because, before, if, in order that, once, since, so, than, unless, until, when, whenever, where, wherever,* and *while.*

The Conjunctive Adverb

Conjunctive adverbs, or sentence connectors, link independent clauses. Like conjunctions, they focus attention on the nature of the relationship between the clauses, although often they do so more emphatically. In the sentence

They could not get their car started; consequently, they walked home,

the conjunctive adverb *consequently* emphasizes the cause-and-effect relationship between the two clauses. In the example

The first time they met, he didn't like her at all. The next time, however, he fell in love.

the conjunctive adverb *however* emphasizes the contrast between the two sentences.

Whereas coordinating conjunctions are usually preceded by a comma, conjunctive adverbs are usually preceded by a semicolon. Also, whereas both coordinating and subordinating conjunctions always stand between the two parts of the sentence that they join, a conjunctive adverb may be moved around within the second clause:

They could not get their car started; they, consequently, walked home.

Conjunctive adverbs include the following:

accordingly	as a result	conversely	for instance
also	besides	earlier	further
afterward	certainly	finally	hence
anyway	consequently	for example	however
in addition	meanwhile	on the other hand	thereafter
indeed	moreover	otherwise	therefore
instead	nevertheless	similarly	thus
in the same way	next	still	undoubtedly
likewise	nonetheless	subsequently	
later	now	then	

The Preposition

A preposition links a noun, a pronoun, or a group of words functioning as a noun to some other word in a sentence. It indicates the relationship in time, space, or logic between the linked words (the car is *in* the garage).

Prepositions include the following:

about	behind	except	onto	toward
above	below	for	out	under
across	beneath	from	outside	underneath
after	beside	in	over	unlike
against	between	inside	past	until
along	beyond	into	regarding	up
among	by	like	round	upon
around	concerning	near	since	with
as	despite	of	through	within
at	down	off	throughout	without
before	during	on	to	

The noun linked to another word by a preposition is called the *object* of the preposition. The combination of the preposition, its object, and any words modifying the object is called a *prepositional phrase*. In the prepositional phrase *in the garage*, the preposition is *in*, the object is *garage*, and the modifier is *the*.

Prepositional phrases usually function as adjectives or adverbs in sentences. The phrase *in the garage* is adverbial, describing where the car is located. In the following sentences, the prepositional phrases function as adjectives:

The house *around the corner* burned down.
The girl *in the green* coat sneezed.
It was John, *with his mother*.

In the next group of sentences, the prepositional phrases are adverbial:

She ran *around the track*.
He left *in a hurry*.
John writes *with clarity and skill*.

The Article

The articles are *a*, *an*, and *the*. They modify nouns. *A* and *an* are indefinite; *a car* could mean any car. *The* is definite; *the car* indicates a specific car.

The article *a* precedes nouns that start with a consonant sound *(a rocket)*. The article *an* precedes nouns that start with a vowel sound *(an astronaut)*.

REVIEW EXERCISE—PARTS OF SPEECH

Identify as a noun, verb, adjective, or adverb each underlined word in the following passage and explain why you identify it that way. For example, the word *boxed* in the sentence *They boxed me in* is a verb, as indicated by the *-ed* ending and by the action the word conveys.

For days, Jackson gazed searchingly at the sky for a break in the weather. But the biting cold persisted. It was the coldest fall on record. The area where he used to garden and the field where he took his walks had turned yellow. Yellow was the dominant color everywhere, a light shade, sulphurous almost, that seemed to infect the light in the sky as well. Growing old was bitter, he told himself. When he had been younger, he never minded these turns in the season. In those days, no matter how much nature trashed the woods, his own vital force never diminished. But now the winds knifed into his soul. And only with a grave distrust, and with a quaking in his innermost being, could he eye that horizon line of trees beyond the window.

PARTS OF SENTENCES

The Subject

A subject is a noun (or a word or a group of words serving as a noun) that tells who or what is doing the action or experiencing the state of being expressed by the verb in a clause. In the main clause

The boy's mother had to drive home slowly,

mother is the simple subject, the noun without any modifiers: *the boy's mother* is the complete subject, the noun with its modifiers.

A pronoun, of course, may act as a subject, but other parts of speech may do so also. For example, in the sentence

Driving home look a long time.

the gerund phrase *driving home* serves as a noun and is the subject.

The Predicate

A predicate is usually said to include all parts of a clause other than the subject and its modifiers. A simple predicate is the verb and its auxiliaries, such as the verb *to drive* and its auxiliary *had* in the sentence

The boy's mother had to drive home slowly.

The complete predicate includes any modifiers of the verb *(slowly)* and any complements *(home)*.

The Complement

A complement is a word or a word group that completes or modifies the subject, the verb, or the object of a clause.

Subject complements are called *predicate adjectives* or *predicate nominatives.* A predicate adjective follows a linking verb (often a form of *to be* or a verb like *to become, to appear,* or *to seem*) and modifies the subject, as does the adjective *cautious* in the sentence

She is cautious.

A predicate nominative is a noun (or a noun substitute) that follows a linking verb and defines the subject more specifically, as does the noun *driver* in the sentence

She is the driver of the car.

Verb complements are called *direct* and *indirect objects.* A direct object is a noun (or a noun substitute) that names who or what is affected by the action of the verb. In the sentence

She gave the keys to him.

the direct object is *keys,* and the indirect object is *him.* An indirect object is a noun (or its substitute) that names to or for whom or what the action is done.

Object complements are adjectives and nouns (or their substitutes) that modify direct objects. In the sentence

She gave the car keys to him.

car is an object complement.

BASE SENTENCES

The most basic sentence structure is a simple subject and predicate:

She drives.

This structure is often expanded by the addition of complements to the predicate:

> She drives the car cautiously.

Such base sentences may be combined with others to form longer, more complicated sentence structures. These longer sentences may be composed of clusters of words (usually phrases) that act as free modifiers, and/or coordinate clauses, and/or subordinate clauses. See the "Focus" section of Chapter 5 (pp. 197–202).

PHRASES AND CLAUSES

The Phrase

A phrase is a group of words that acts as a single part of a speech. Unlike a clause, it has no subject and predicate.

The following are the most common types of phrases:

The Noun Phrase. A noun phrase is a noun *(car)* and its modifiers. The most common modifiers are articles *(the car),* adjectives (the *blue* car), and prepositional phrases (the blue car *in the garage*). A noun phrase functions as a single noun in a sentence. In the sentence

> The blue car in the garage is mine.

the noun phrase functions as the subject.

The Verb Phrase. A verb phrase is a verb *(drive)* and its auxiliaries (*should* drive). It may be expanded by the addition of one or more adverbs (should drive *slowly*), prepositional phrases (should drive slowly *on this road*), or complements (should drive the *car* slowly on this road).

The Prepositional Phrase. A prepositional phrase is a preposition combined with its object and any modifiers. It usually functions as an adjective or an adverb in a clause. In the sentence

> The girl at the beach likes to swim.

the prepositional phrase *at the beach* functions as an adjective; in the sentence

> She likes to swim at the beach.

the same phrase functions as an adverb.

The Infinitive Phrase. An infinitive phrase consists of an infinitive form of a verb along with its subject, and/or object, and/or modifiers. In the sentence

We expected John to tell his mother right away.

John is the subject of the infinitive *to tell, mother* is the object, and *right away* is an adverbial modifier; within the sentence, this infinitive phrase functions as the direct object of the verb *expected* and so is being used as a noun. An infinitive phrase may also be used as an adjective:

John is the person to tell his mother.

or as an adverb:

John left to tell his mother.

The Participial Phrase. A participial phrase consists of a past or present participle along with its object and/or any modifiers. Participial phrases function as adjectives. In the sentence

Soaked to the skin, they came in out of the storm.

the participial phrase *soaked* (past participle) *to the skin* modifies the pronoun *they*. In the sentence

Soaking wet, they came in out of the storm.

the participial phrase *soaking* (present participle) *wet* functions similarly.

The Gerund Phrase. A gerund phrase consists of an *-ing* verb when it serves as a noun, along with its subject, and/or object, and/or any modifiers. Gerund phrases function as nouns. In the sentence

His driving the car recklessly made her nervous.

the gerund phrase consists of the gerund *driving* along with its subject *(his),* its object *(car),* and an adverbial modifier *(recklessly);* the entire phrase serves as the subject of the sentence.

The Absolute Phrase. An absolute phrase consists of a noun or pronoun and a participle, along with any modifiers. It modifies a whole base sentence rather than a single word within the base sentence. In the sentence

The car skidding on the rain slick road, the driver held his breath.

the phrase preceding *the driver* is absolute; it has its own subject *(car)* and modifies the whole base sentence. Compare it to the participial phrase that follows and modifies only *the car* in the following sentence:

The driver held his breath as he felt the car skidding on the rain-slick road.

The Clause

A clause is a group of words that contains a subject and a predicate.
A main or independent clause can stand alone as a sentence:

He drove to the bank.

Two or more main clauses may be linked to form a single sentence with a coordinating conjunction, or a semicolon, or a conjunctive adverb;

He drove to the bank, and he deposited the money.

or

He drove to the bank; and he deposited the money.

or

He drove to the bank; then he deposited the money.

A subordinate or dependent clause cannot stand alone as a sentence because it is introduced by either a relative pronoun, such as *that* or *which,* or a subordinating conjunction, such as *because* or *if* or *when.* Subordinate clauses function as nouns, adjectives, or adverbs in a sentence. Noun clauses and adjective clauses usually begin with a relative pronoun. Adverbial clauses always begin with a subordinating conjunction. In the sentence

That you drive carefully is a comfort to me.

the noun clause *(that you drive carefully)* acts as the subject. In the sentence

The new front tire, which he just bought yesterday, went flat today.

the adjective clause *(which he just bought yesterday)* modifies the noun *tire.* In the sentence

When he hit the brakes, the car swerved to the left.

the adverbial clause *(when he hit the brakes)* modifies the verb *swerved.*

COMBINED OR EXPANDED SENTENCES

Base sentences may be combined or expanded to form compound, complex, or compound-complex sentences. A base sentence, or simple sentence, consists of a single main clause:

The red sportscar in the garage is mine.

A compound sentence consists of two or more main clauses linked by a coordinating conjunction, a semicolon, or a conjunctive adverb:

The red sportscar in the garage is mine; however, I might sell it.

A complex sentence consists of one main clause and one or more subordinate clauses:

Although I will miss driving the car, I will sell it if I can get a good price.

A compound-complex sentence consists of two or more main clauses and one or more subordinate clauses:

The red sportscar in the garage is mine, but I might sell it if I can get a good price.

A simple sentence, then, may be expanded into one with a more complicated structure by the addition of phrases, by the coordination of one or more main clauses, or by a combination of main clauses with subordinate and relative clauses. See the "Focus" sections of Chapters 5 (pp. 197–202) and 6 (242–249) for additional discussion of sentence length and style.

REVIEW EXERCISE—PARTS AND TYPES OF SENTENCES

In the following paragraph, identify the parts of each sentence, the subject, the predicate, and their complements. How many different types of phrases can you identify? How many subordinate clauses? Label each sentence as simple, compound, complex, or compound-complex. Finally, rewrite the paragraph, combining its base sentences into larger sentence units:

Nick sat against the wall of the church where they had dragged him to be clear of machine-gun fire in the street. Both legs stuck out awkwardly. He had been hit in the spine. His face was sweaty and dirty. The sun shone on his face. The day was very hot. Rinaldi, big backed, his equipment sprawling, lay face downward against the wall. Nick looked straight ahead brilliantly. The pink wall of the house opposite had fallen out from the roof, and an iron bedstead hung twisted toward the street. Two Austrian dead lay in the rubble in the shade of the house. Up the street were other dead. Things were getting forward in the town. It was going well. Stretcher bearers would be along any time now. Nick turned his head carefully and looked at Rinaldi. "Senta Rinaldi. Senta. You and me we've made a separate peace." Rinaldi lay still in the sun breathing with difficulty. "Not patriots." Nick turned his head carefully away smiling sweatily. Rinaldi was a disappointing audience.

—**Ernest Hemingway,** *In Our Time*

AWKWARD SENTENCES

Sentences become awkward or confused for many reasons: a writer may employ faulty coordination or subordination, may omit necessary sentence elements, may mix elements that are incompatible, or may make inconsistent shifts in point of view.

Faulty Coordination or Subordination

When the logical connection between two coordinated clauses, phrases, or words is unclear, the writing suffers from faulty coordination: in the sentence

She likes to drive, but her teeth hurt.

the coordinating conjunction *(but)* fails to make clear why the writer has chosen to link the subject's feelings about driving to the subject's problems with her teeth.

When the logical connection between a subordinate clause and a main clause is unclear, the writing suffers from faulty subordination: in the sentence

Because my brakes failed, I hit the tree instead of the pedestrian.

the subordinating conjunction *(because)* fails to explain why the driver hit the tree rather than hitting the pedestrian. Often faulty subordination occurs when a writer subordinates what seems to be the main idea of the sentence: the sentence

When I hit the tree, I had never had an accident before.

might be better revised so that the emphasis falls on the main point:

Although I had never had an accident before, I hit the tree.

Incomplete Sentences

Incomplete sentences are missing necessary words or phrases.

In a compound construction, a word that functions as but differs grammatically from a preceding word should not be omitted. For example, in the sentence

The car was given an oil change, and its flat tire (was) fixed.

the second *was* might be omitted; but if the subject of the second clause were plural, its verb could not be so shortened:

The car was given an oil change, and its wheels (were) aligned.

An incomplete sentence also results when a comparison is made incompletely or illogically. In the sentence

My car is faster.

a reader is not told what the car is faster than. In the sentence

She likes the car better than her brother.

a reader is uncertain if the subject likes the car better than she likes her brother or better than her brother likes the car.

If two things are being compared that are not really comparable, the sentence will be logically incomplete. In the sentence

The engine in his car was more powerful than most of the other cars in the race.

an engine is being compared to other cars rather than to the engines of others cars.

Incomplete sentences also result when a writer omits a needed article or preposition. For example, the sentence

The boy has both a talent and love of fixing engines.

is incomplete because the preposition *for* is needed after the word *talent* and the article *a* is needed before the word *love.*

Mixed Sentences

In a mixed sentence, two parts are presented as compatible either in grammar or in meaning when they actually are incompatible. For example, in the sentence

After driving all night made him feel exhausted.

a prepositional phrase *(after driving all night)* is being treated ungrammatically as a subject and is linked to a predicate *(made him feel exhausted.)*
   In the sentence

Driving all night is when he feels exhausted.

an adverbial clause *(when he feels exhausted)* is being equated, illogically, with a noun substitute *(driving all night)*. When a predicate does not apply logically to a subject in this way, it is called *faulty predication*. A linking verb, like *is,* should connect a noun with another noun that is logically comparable to it, as in the revised sentence

Driving all night is an activity that makes him feel exhausted.

Do not link a subject and a predicate together that are not logically comparable, as in the sentence

The use of seat belts was invented to save lives.

The *seat belts* themselves, not their *use,* were invented to save lives.

Inconsistent Point of View

A sentence or a paragraph can become awkward if there are logical inconsistencies in the verb tense or mood or voice. In the sentence

He drove the car home and parks it in the garage.

the writer has shifted confusingly from past to present tense. In the sentence

I was mad when I failed the driving test because I practiced for so many weeks before taking it.

the point of view with regard to verb tense is awkward because the verb *practiced,* which indicates an action that was completed before the test was taken, should be placed in the past perfect tense *(had practiced)*. In the sentence

If you are caught speeding, you would get a ticket.

the shift from indicative to subjunctive mood is a confusing inconsistency; *would* should be changed to *will.* In the sentence

Ann waxed the car after it had been washed.

the shift from active voice *(Ann waxed the car)* to passive voice *(it had been washed)* creates an ambiguity about who actually washed the car; if Ann washed it, the subordinate clause might be better revised to read *after she had washed it.*

A sentence also may become awkward if there are inconsistencies in person or number with reference to pronouns. In the sentence

If one drives too slowly on the highway, you can cause an accident.

the shift from third person *(one)* to the second person *(you)* is confusing. Similarly, if in this sentence the writer had substituted *they* for *you,* the shift from singular *(one)* to plural *(they)* would have been awkward.

REVIEW EXERCISE—AWKWARD SENTENCES

Recast each of the following sentences so that it is no longer awkward. Make whatever changes or additions that you need in order to clarify the meaning of each sentence.

1. If a person thinks about it, you would understand why it's easy for anyone to make mistakes.

2. Buying a computer is easy; learning to use one is where you run into trouble.

3. The driver of the car said that the reason why he crashed into the fence was because of a cow in the road.

4. The store had only been open a week, and the thief pulled out his gun.

5. Her muscles were twice the size of anyone else in the gym.

6. The little boy was climbing in the apple tree, which blossoms each year in May, when he fell and broke his leg.

7. While the table was being cleared, she broke a dish and two glasses.

8. She took the weather report more seriously than her brother, since living in Wisconsin and never having seen a hurricane before was something that frightened her, and he sees them often, living now in Florida.

COMMON GRAMMATICAL ERRORS

Faulty Agreement

A verb should agree in person and number with its subject. A pronoun should agree in person, number, and gender with its antecedent.

Subject/Verb Agreement.   In the sentence

Her car runs well.

the third-person-singular subject *(car)* and the third-person-singular verb *(runs)* are in agreement. If the subject were to become plural *(cars)*, the verb would have to be altered to a plural form *(run)*. If the subject were plural in form but singular in meaning, however, it would take a singular verb:

The news is good.

When a phrase comes between a subject and its verb, do not make the verb agree with a noun in the phrase rather than with the subject:

The car with new tires and new brakes costs (SINGULAR) more than the other cars.

Phrases beginning with *in addition to* or *as well as* do not change the subject's number:

Her car, as well as the other two, was (SINGULAR) broken into.

A compound subject joined by *and* usually takes a plural verb. One exception occurs when the parts of the subject refer to a single entity:

Ice cream and cake is (SINGULAR) my favorite dessert.

Another exception occurs when a compound subject is preceded by *each* or *every:*

Every car and truck on the lot was (SINGULAR) sold.

The indefinite pronouns tend to be singular:

Each of them is (not *are*) right.
Everyone is (not *are*) doing it.

All, any, none, and *some* may be either singular or plural:

> Some of his time is (SINGULAR) spent at home.
> When they get home at night, some of them watch (PLURAL) television.

Two singular subjects joined by *or* or *nor* take a singular verb:

> Either Ann or Al is going to pick up the pizza.

Two plural subjects joined by *or* or *nor* take a plural verb:

> Either the girls or the boys are going.

If one of the subjects is singular and one is plural, however, the verb agrees with the subject that is closer to it:

> Ann or the boys are going.
> The girls or Al is going.

When a sentence begins with *there,* the subject tends to follow the verb. Special attention should be paid to agreement:

> There was one hole in the muffler; there were two holes in the tire.

When *there* precedes a compound subject, the verb is singular if the first part of the subject is singular:

> There is a hole in the muffler and two flat tires.

When a subject complement follows a linking verb, make sure that the verb agrees with the subject, not with its complement:

> Cars and trucks are my hobby.
> My hobby is cars and trucks.

A collective noun, which names a group of individuals, takes a singular or a plural verb, depending on whether the group is acting as a unit or as separate individuals:

> The team is traveling to the game by bus.
> The team are traveling to the game in their own cars.

A singular verb follows a title, a word that is being defined, and a word denoting some form of measurement (weight, an amount of money, a period of time):

Forty thousand miles is a lot to put on a car in a year.

When a relative pronoun is the subject of a clause, the verb should agree in number with the antecedent of the relative pronoun. In the sentence

She is one of those drivers who never get a ticket.

the antecedent of *who* is *drivers,* and hence the verb *get* is plural.

Pronoun/Antecedent Agreement. In the sentence

Ann washed her car.

the third-person-singular feminine pronoun *(her)* agrees with its third-person-singular feminine antecedent *(Ann)*. If the antecedent were changed in person, number, and/or gender, the pronoun would have to be changed accordingly:

Joe washed his car.
Joe and Ann washed their cars.

(Note that in the last example the word *cars* is pluralized because Joe and Ann washed different cars; if they washed a single car that they owned together, the object *car* would be singular.)

A compound antecedent joined by *and* usually takes a plural pronoun. One exception occurs when the parts of the antecedent refer to a single entity:

The soldier and patriot was given a ticker tape parade by his home-town neighbors.

Another exception occurs when the compound antecedent is preceded by *each* or *every;*

Each car and truck was parked in its proper place.

The indefinite pronouns, when they serve as antecedents, usually require a singular pronoun:

Everybody will have a chance to take his or her turn.

When the gender of the antecedent is not specifically masculine or feminine but both, two singular pronouns *(his or her)* are used. It is acceptable to substitute a plural pronoun *(their)* in such cases. Simply to write either *his* or *her* in reference to an indefinite antecedent is now considered sexist.

Note that sometimes it is awkward to follow an indefinite antecedent with a singular pronoun, as in the sentence

When everybody arrived, I asked him or her to sit down.

Substituting *them* for *him or her* in this sentence does not really clarify matters. The sentence might be better revised to read

When all of them arrived, I asked them to sit down.

or

As each of them arrived, I asked him or her to sit down.

Two singular antecedents joined by *or* or *nor* take a singular pronoun:

Neither Ann nor Sally washed her car.

Two plural antecedents joined by *or* or *nor* take a plural pronoun:

Neither the girls nor the boys washed their cars.

If one of the antecedents is singular and the other is plural, the plural anteced- ent should come second and the pronoun should agree with it:

Neither Ann nor the girls washed their cars.

Note that in this last example, if the word *cars* were made singular *(car)*, it would indicate that Ann and the girls own one car together.

A collective noun, when used as an antecedent, takes a singular or a plural pronoun, depending on whether it refers to a group that is acting as a unit or as separate individuals:

The family is coming in its car.
The family are coming in their cars.

Faulty Reference

A pronoun should refer clearly to its antecedent. (See p. 425.) If there is any ambiguity or confusion about who or what the antecedent of a pronoun is, the pronoun reference is faulty.

If there is more than one possible antecedent, the sentence should be re- vised. The sentence

Sam told Don that he had used his car.

might be revised to read

Sam said to Don, "I used your car."

The sentence

He hit the ball on the roof, and it fell down.

might be revised to read

After he hit it on the roof, the ball fell down.

Ambiguity may result if the pronoun is placed too far away from its ante-cedent in a long sentence. In the sentence

The lake is large and pretty with a cabin on the shore and plenty of fish in it.

does the pronoun *it* refer to the cabin or to the lake?

Ambiguity often results when a pronoun such as *this, that, which,* or *it* refers to an entire clause rather than a specifically defined antecedent. In the sentence

We drove all morning and then stopped for a picnic lunch, which made me sleepy.

the relative pronoun, which, could refer to the drive and/or the lunch. The reference would be clearer if it were less broad:

We drove all morning, which made me sleepy, and then we stopped for a picnic lunch.

Another way to clarify the reference would be to define the antecedent more specifically:

We drove all morning and then stopped for a picnic lunch; the drive com-bined with the lunch made me sleepy.

A similar kind of error involves the use of a pronoun whose antecedent is implied rather than specifically expressed. In the sentence

In George Orwell's novel *1984,* he describes a world where love is a crime.

no specific antecedent for the pronoun *he* is named; if the reference is intended to be to Orwell, the sentence should be revised to make this intention clear:

> In his novel *1984,* George Orwell describes a world where love is a crime.

Often this sort of ambiguity results when a writer employs the pronoun *it* or *they* or *you* without a definite antecedent: in the sentence

> In college, they expect you to type your papers.

no possible antecedent for *they* is mentioned. Note also that when the pronoun *it* is used in more than one way in a sentence, the results are often confusing:

> Because it is hot by the lake, it looks inviting.

Finally, the pronoun *which* should not be used to refer to people. Use *who* to refer to people, *which* to refer to animals or objects or places. *That* may refer both to people and to animals, objects, or places. For example:

> The man *who* went out this morning caught a huge bluefish.
> He caught the fish, *which* weighed over fifteen pounds, just off the point.
> "You think this one's big," he said. "You should've seen the one *that* got away!"

Case Errors

The most common case errors involve the use of a subjective form of a pronoun when an objective form is required or the use of an objective form of a pronoun when a subjective form is required.

Generally, the subjective forms should be used if the pronoun is part of the subject of a clause:

> The truck driver and I (SUBJECTIVE) stopped at the light.
> The light turned green before we (SUBJECTIVE) drove on.

The subjective case is also used for a subject complement after any form of the verb *to be:*

> It is I (SUBJECTIVE).
> It was they (SUBJECTIVE) who went home last.

The objective forms should be used if the pronoun is a direct object in a clause:

Joe invited her (OBJECTIVE) and me (OBJECTIVE).

an indirect object in a clause:

Joe lent him (OBJECTIVE) the car.

or the object of a preposition:

Joe is in love with her (OBJECTIVE).

Note that the objective forms should be used not only when a pronoun is the object of an infinitive:

Joe wanted to give her (OBJECTIVE) the car.

but also when the pronoun is the subject of an infinitive:

Joe wanted him (OBJECTIVE) to return the car.

There are a number of situations in which many writers find the choice of case confusing:
When the first-person-plural pronoun is used with a noun, its case depends on how the noun is being used. If the noun is a subject, the writer should use *we* along with it.

We students love summer vacation.

If the noun is an object, the writer should use *us* along with it, as in the following sentence, in which the noun *students* is the object of the preposition *of*:

All of us students love summer vacation.

When a pronoun is used as an appositive, appearing next to a noun that it helps to identify or explain, its case depends on how the noun is being used. If the noun is a subject, the appositive pronoun should be in the subjective case:

Three boys, Joe, Sam, and I (SUBJECTIVE), went camping.

If the noun is an object, the appositive pronoun should be in the objective case:

Joe went camping with two other boys, Sam and me (OBJECTIVE).

Note: One case is sometimes incorrectly substituted for another in common, everyday expressions. Such expressions as *just between you and I* or *Him and me went home* are faulty. In formal writing, it is best to use the correct forms, *just between you and me* and *He and I went home.*

Who is always used to refer to a subject; *whom* is always used to refer to an object. If you are writing a question, use a personal pronoun to formulate the answer first; the case of the personal pronoun in your answer will indicate whether you should start the question with *who* or *whom:* the answer

She is the judge.

should be rephrased into the question

Who is the judge?

The answer

She sentenced him to a fifty-dollar fine.

should be rephrased into the question

Whom did she sentence to a fifty-dollar fine?

When *who* or *whom* is used in a subordinate clause, the case depends on how the pronoun is being used in the clause. The case depends upon the use of the pronoun in the clause no matter how the clause itself is being used in the sentence. In the sentence

A judge is a person who is honest.

who is the subject of the clause *who is honest;* the clause itself modifies the direct object, *person.* In the sentence

A judge is a person whom most people trust.

whom is the object of the modifying clause *whom most people trust.* If you rewrite the clause as a separate sentence, substituting a personal pronoun for *who* or *whom,* the proper choice of case is often clarified:

She *(who)* is honest. Most people trust her *(whom).*

Finally, the possessive form of a pronoun should be used before a gerund, an *ing* verb that is being used as a noun:

I approved of his (POSSESSIVE) going out with my sister.

Misplaced and Dangling Modifiers

Misplaced Modifiers.   A modifier is misplaced if its position in a sentence causes ambiguity about just what part of the sentence it is modifying. For example, in the sentence

I gave the shirt to my brother with the red pinstripes.

the prepositional phrase *with the red pinstripes* is misplaced: Does it modify *brother* or *shirt?* The sentence should be revised to read

I gave the shirt with the red pinstripes to my brother.

Similarly, a subordinate clause can be misplaced. In the sentence

He parked the car in the garage after he had washed it.

did the subject wash the car or the garage? Again, one can revise the sentence simply by moving the misplaced modifier to another position:

After he had washed it, he parked the car in the garage.

Usually, a modifier should be placed as closely as possible to the word or words that it is meant to modify. This is particularly important when a writer is using what are called *limiting modifiers,* single-word adverbs such as *almost, exactly, hardly, just, nearly, only,* and *simply.* Misplacing one of these modifiers can change the meaning of a sentence radically. Thus you might write

The old Ford is the only car that I will drive.

if you are unwilling to drive any other car, but

The old Ford is the car that only I will drive.

if no one else but you is willing to drive the old Ford.

Sometimes a writer positions a modifier so that a reader cannot determine if it modifies the words that come right before it or the words that come right after it. Such modifiers are called *squinting modifiers.* For example, in the sentence

Joe had told her in May they would go to the beach.

did Joe tell her in *May* that they would go to the beach at some future time, or did Joe tell her that they would go to the beach *in May?* A squinting modifier should be repositioned away from the part of the sentence that it is not meant to modify:

In May, Joe had told her they would go to the beach.

or

Joe had told her they would go to the beach in May.

Dangling Modifiers.   A dangling modifier is a phrase or cause that does not sensibly describe any specific word in its sentence. For example, in the sentence

Arriving after midnight, the house seemed deserted.

the only word that the opening phrase could modify is *house,* but clearly it is not the house that arrived after midnight; the actual word that the phrase modifies is missing, and the sentence must be revised to include it:

Because we arrived after midnight, the house seemed deserted.

A writer most often produces dangling modifiers by starting or ending a sentence with a phrase that lacks a subject itself, such as the participial phrase that starts the sentence

Soaked to the skin, the walk home in the rain was no fun.

or the infinitive phrase that ends the sentence

An umbrella should be taken to walk in the rain.

Also an elliptical clause, a subordinate clause in which the subject is unstated but understood, often becomes a dangling modifier. In the sentence

When I was only a small boy, I often went fishing.

the opening clause might be made elliptical by the omission of *I was;* if this elliptical clause is then used to introduce a main clause in which the subject is no longer *I,* a dangling construction results:

When only a small boy, my father often took me fishing.

To correct a dangling modifier, add the missing word or words to which it refers. You can do this by changing the subject of the main clause:

When only a small boy, I was often taken fishing by my father.

You can also do it by rewriting the dangling modifier as a complete subordinate clause:

When I was only a small boy, my father often took me fishing.

Faulty Parallelism

Faulty parallelism occurs when elements in a sentence or a paragraph that express comparable ideas and that perform similar grammatical functions are expressed in different grammatical form. In the sentence

Walking on the beach relaxes him more than a swim.

the parallelism is faulty because one comparable idea, *walking on the beach,* is expressed as a gerund phrase, whereas the other, *a swim,* is expressed as an unmodified noun. The sentence might be revised to read

Walking on the beach relaxes him more than swimming in the ocean.

or

A walk on the beach relaxes him more than a swim in the ocean.

Elements linked by coordinating or correlative conjunctions should be expressed in parallel form. To correct the faulty parallelism of the sentence

He is an excellent musician, a talented dancer, and puts on an exciting performance.

you might rephrase the last of the coordinated elements:

He is an excellent musician, a talented dancer, and an exciting performer.

As an alternative, you might subordinate the last element:

He is an excellent musician and a talented dancer who puts on an exciting performance.

Note that faulty parallelism often occurs with correlative conjunctions because the writer omits a preposition or an infinitive marker *(to)* after the second conjunction: in the sentence

He was overtired not from working too hard but sleeping too little.

a second *from* should be added after *but;* in the sentence

She told him either to wait for her or leave.

a second *to* should be added after *or,* or perhaps a parallel prepositional phrase should be added after *leave,* such as *without her.*

Run-on Sentences and Comma Splices

A run-on sentence (also called a *fused sentence*) occurs when a writer fails to separate two or more main clauses with any punctuation; for example,

He likes music he likes to dance.

A comma splice occurs when a writer links two or more main clauses with commas; for example,

He likes music, he likes to dance.

A run-on sentence or a comma splice can be corrected simply if each main clause is punctuated as a separate sentence:

He likes music. He likes to dance.

A second option is to link the main clauses with semicolons:

He likes music; he likes to dance.

A third option is to link the main clauses with coordinating conjunctions:

He likes music, and he likes to dance.

A fourth option is to link the clauses with subordinating conjunctions or relative pronouns, leaving only one main clause:

He likes music because he likes to dance.

Run-ons and comma splices often result when a writer links two or more main clauses with conjunctive adverbs. Conjunctive adverbs, like *also, however,* and *then,* should always follow either a semicolon or a period when they are being used to link main clauses.

He likes to dance, therefore he likes music.

is a comma splice; it should be repunctuated to read

He likes to dance; therefore he likes music.

or

He likes to dance. Therefore he likes music.

Note, however, that comma splices are used effectively by writers to emphasize the link or the contrast between ideas, particularly if the main clauses expressing the ideas are short and are phrased in a parallel fashion. The following sentences can make their point more effectively as one long comma splice:

I love the circus, I love the clowns, I love the acrobats, I love the side show, I love the whole spectacle.

"Be sensible," she pleaded, "listen to reason, open your mind."

I have my secrets, you have your secrets, everyone has something to hide.

Similarly, two or more contrasting ideas expressed in parallel phrasing may be punctuated as a comma splice to emphasize the contrast:

She did not hate him, she pitied him.

Act now, tomorrow will be too late.

The first house was destroyed by the storm, the second was damaged but remained standing, the third was untouched.

Sentence Fragments

A fragment is a part of a sentence that is punctuated with an initial capital letter and a final period as if it were a complete sentence. Often fragments give a reader trouble, because they convey the impression that the writer's thoughts are incomplete.

A sentence fragment may lack a subject, as does the verb phrase

Drove home at night

It may lack a verb, as does the noun phrase

The boy on the bicycle.

It may lack both a subject and a verb, as does the prepositional phrase

On the beach.

It may include both a subject and a verb but begin with a subordinating conjunction, as does the subordinate clause

Because I love strawberries.

or with a relative pronoun, as does the relative clause

Which is my favorite.

If a fragment lacks a subject and/or a verb, you can correct it by adding the missing part or parts:

He drove home at night.
The boy on the bicycle left.
She is walking on the beach.

You can also correct it by linking it to a complete sentence:

He stayed for dinner, then drove home at night.

If a fragment is a dependent clause, you can correct it by rewriting the clause as an independent or main clause:

I love strawberries.

You can also correct it by linking it to a complete sentence:

I like vanilla but prefer chocolate, which is my favorite.

A fragment often results when a writer adds on information after completing a sentence. The added information might be the answer to a question:

What kind of day was it? A great day.

The information might be a modifying word or phrase:

My uncle is a conservative man. Old-fashioned.
He is a farmer. Living off the land.

Or the information might be a clause that further explains or qualifies:

She pitied him. Even though he was cruel to her.

Like comma splices, fragments can be used effectively by a writer for emphasis. Instructions are often written as fragments:

Bake in preheated oven (425°). One hour. Remove. Let cool before slicing.

Sometimes a definition is easier to remember if it is written in fragments:

Alcoholism. A disease. Both physiological and psychological.

A description may sometimes be made more vivid if some of the images that compose it are fragments:

The schoolroom was quiet. Empty desks. Rows of them. The board cleaned of chalk. The afternoon light fading outside the closed windows.

In general, because a fragment isolates a piece of information, it focuses a reader's attention on that information. If a writer can make use of fragments for this purpose without confusing the reader, there is no reason not to employ them on occasion.

REVIEW EXERCISE—COMMON GRAMMATICAL ERRORS

Each of the following sentences contains one or more grammatical errors. Rewrite them, correcting each error you identify.

1. Every one of the twenty-five students in the class are required to write five papers this term and type it before handing it in.

2. Either Lois or one of her cousins, Al and Don, who own the restaurant, keep the accounts, paying each of the bills as soon as they come in.

3. Joe called his brother once a week after he went to college, which cost him a lot of money, although he insisted it was worth it.

4. Whom do you think did better on the exam, me, who studied in the library half the night, or my two roommates that were asleep by 10 o'clock?

5. At the stables, they wanted she and I to rub down the horses after taking them for a ride.

6. Sitting up in the bleachers, the game started, and we bought hotdogs for the children with mustard that cost $1.25.

7. The sky had been ominous all day when, suddenly growing dark, we watched out the window as the rain began to fall, and the lightning began to flash, and thunder was booming.

8. "You must be very happy," Uncle George said, "it's a wonderful thing to get married." Which was true, of course. But she wasn't at all sure she was happy, indeed she had half a mind to call it off. Just wedding day jitters? That's what she finally told herself, it was normal for the bride to feel unsure about it. The groom too, with only a few hours left to go before the ceremony.

Punctuation

The conventions of punctuation that follow are more complete than those offered in the "Focus" section on sentence combining in Chapter 5 (p. 203). The basic information about how punctuation marks can help a reader to follow the separations or links that you wish to make between sentences and parts of sentences is the same.

THE PERIOD (.)

A period is one way to end a sentence. It may be used to end any declarative sentence, any statement:

She is at the office.

It may be used to end a mild command:

Think about it.
Let me know.

It may be used to end an indirect question, a report of what someone has asked:

She wondered why they had to leave so early.

Periods are also used with many abbreviations: cities (N.Y.C., L.A.); states (Pa., Ill., Ariz.); names (Franklin D. Roosevelt); titles (Mr., Ms., Dr., Rev.); degrees (B.A., Ph.D., D.D.S.); months (Sept.); addresses (St., Ave., Rte.); Latin abbreviations (ibid., etc., et al.). Note that when an abbreviation is the last element in a sentence, a single period is used both to end the abbreviation and to end the sentence:

He lives in Washington, D.C.

Periods are not used with the capital letter abbreviations of technical terms (FM, IQ); organizations (NFL, AFL-CIO); corporations (CBS, IBM); or government agencies (FBI, TVA). Nor are periods used with acronyms, pronounceable words formed from the initial letters in a multiword title (NATO, VISTA).

Additional information on abbreviations is offered below in the section on abbreviations.

THE QUESTION MARK (?)

A question mark is used to end a direct question:

What do you want to be when you grow up?

Note that if you write a series of questions, each is followed by a question mark:

He asked, "What profession do you think you will enter? Medicine? Law? Business?

Note also that a question mark is never combined with another question mark or with a period or comma or exclamation point. The question

Who asked, "What do you want to be when you grow up?"

does not take a second question mark after the final quotation mark. The statement

He asked her, "What profession do you plan to enter?"

does not take a period after the final quotation mark.

A question mark may also be used within parentheses to indicate uncertainty within a statement:

My grandfather was ninety-two (?) when he remarried.
Someone—my brother Al (?)—borrowed my favorite shirt.

THE EXCLAMATION POINT (!)

An exclamation point is used after a sentence or a phrase or a word that expresses a strong emotion:

> Leave me alone!
>
> What a wonderful day!
>
> Yes! I must go home right now!

Its use should be reserved to indicate unusually strong emphasis.

Note that an exclamation point should not be used in parentheses to express amazement or irony or sarcasm, as in the sentence

> My brother borrowed (!) my favorite shirt.

The context should indicate that a word, in this case *borrowed,* is being used ironically.

THE COMMA (,)

A comma is used, above all else, to prevent misreading, by signaling that the reader should pause slightly before reading on. For example, although a comma is not absolutely required following a short introductory phrase, sometimes inserting one can clarify a sentence: in the sentence

> After tomorrow morning choir practice will begin.

the meaning is different depending on whether a comma is inserted following *tomorrow* or following *morning.* Alternatively, it is sometimes necessary to omit a comma at a point in a sentence where one would ordinarily be inserted: in the line

> The woods are lovely, dark and deep.

from "Stopping by the Woods on a Snowy Evening," the poet Robert Frost left out the comma that ordinarily would be inserted after *dark;* had he inserted the comma, the three adjectives would have seemed equivalent descriptions of the woods; by omitting the comma, Frost suggested that the phrase *dark and deep* modifies *lovely,* that the woods are lovely because they are dark and deep. Commas, then, should be used with common sense as tools that can help a reader see how words, phrases, and clauses in a sentence are meant to be linked together or set apart from one another.

Generally, a comma is used to set off an introductory word, phrase, or clause from the rest of the sentence.

Undoubtedly, the villain will be caught. To catch him, the authorities will set a trap. Once the trap is set, we can sit back and relax.

Certainly, the comma may be omitted after a single introductory word or a short introductory phrase or clause if no confusion will arise as a result. Note that a comma is not needed after an introductory conjunction:

Yet the villain may escape

A comma is inserted before a coordinating conjunction that links two main clauses in a sentence:

The authorities are armed with the most modern investigative tools, but the villain may prove too clever for them.

If the main clauses are short, however, and no confusion will arise, the comma may be omitted:

The authorities have set a trap but the villain may escape.

See the following section on the semicolon for information about when a semicolon should replace a comma that links two main clauses.

Note that a comma should not be inserted between two words or phrases that are joined by a coordinating conjunction. In the sentence

The authorities, and the criminal are clever.

the comma after *authorities* should be omitted.

Commas are used to separate two or more adjectives that precede a noun that they modify equally:

The criminal is a clever, ingenious thief.

If the adjective nearer the noun is more closely related to the noun in meaning, however, no comma should separate it from the preceding adjectives:

The authorities have clever legal minds.

If you can rearrange the adjectives or insert the conjunction *and* between them without changing the meaning, the comma should be used: thus you might write the phrase *an ingenious, clever thief,* or *a clever and ingenious thief,* but you would not write *legal, clever minds,* or *clever and legal minds.*

Commas are used to join three or more words, phrases, or clauses in a series:

> The thief is tall, dark, and handsome. He is suspected of stealing a diamond tiara in New York, a ruby brooch in Paris, and a pearl necklace in Singapore. His manners are charming, his victims are never suspicious of him, and his real name is a mystery.

The final comma in the series, the comma that comes before the conjunction, is regularly omitted by some writers and is regularly inserted by others. It is probably best to use the final comma consistently, except when you wish to emphasize the link between the final two items in a series, to identify the final two items as a single element:

> The thief is handsome, tall and dark.

See the following section on the semicolon for information about when semicolons should replace commas that separate items in a series.

Commas are used to set off a nonrestrictive modifier, a phrase or clause that offers additional (in a sense, parenthetical) information about an element in a sentence. Because the information offered by a nonrestrictive modifier is not essential to the meaning of the sentence, the modifier can be omitted without causing any confusion in the reader's mind. In the sentence

> The left front tire, which had forty thousand miles on it, blew out.

the relative clause *which had forty thousand miles on it* is nonrestrictive; the basic meaning of the sentence is that the left front tire blew out; it is not essential to know that the tire had forty thousand miles on it.

On the other hand, in the sentence

> The tire that had forty thousand miles on it blew out.

the relative clause *that blew out* is restrictive; if it is omitted, the reader has no way of knowing which tire blew out. A restricted phrase or clause is not set off with commas.

Note that although both nonrestrictive and restrictive clauses may begin with *which,* only restrictive clauses begin with *that.*

An appositive, a noun or noun phrase that renames or further identifies the noun immediately before it, also may be nonrestrictive or restrictive. In the sentence

My brother John is a Marine.

John is an appositive that further identifies the writer's brother. Because it is not set off by commas, it is restrictive, essential to the meaning of the sentence; presumably, the writer has other brothers, so he must distinguish his brother John from his brother Michael or his brother Arthur. If the sentence is rewritten

My only brother, John, is a Marine.

the appositive is nonrestrictive; the writer has only one brother, and his brother's name happens to be John.

Commas may be used to set off an absolute phrase:

The day drawing to a close, we headed home.

A phrase of contrast:

Speed, not strength, is a boxer's most important asset.

A conjunctive adverb:

He got home, however, before the rain started.

An additional explanation or example preceded by such expressions as *for example, namely,* and *such as:*

His favorite sports are team sports, such as baseball and soccer.

A noun of address:

John, you must get up now.

Also, a comma follows the salutation in a personal letter.

Conventional usage requires that commas separate the items in a date, an address, or the name of a place. Within a sentence, each date, address, or place is also followed by a comma, unless it appears at the end of the sentence:

On December 7, 1942, the weather was mild in New York.

His old address is 705 Walton Avenue, Mamaroneck, New York.

One final note: never use a comma to separate a subject from its verb or a verb from its object, unless there are words between them that must be set off by commas. Thus you might write

My brother, John, is a Marine.

setting off *John* is a nonrestrictive appositive; but you should not write

My brother John, is a Marine.

Similarly, you might write

She ate, not a dietetic snack, but a hot fudge sundae.

setting off the phrase of contrast; but you should not write

She ate, a hot fudge sundae.

For the use of commas with quotation marks, see the section on quotation marks.

THE SEMICOLON (;)

A semicolon may be used, instead of a period, to separate two main clauses:

She loves to roller-skate; he loves to ice-skate.

A semicolon is used to emphasize that two or more main clauses are closely related in meaning:

Someone had left a window open; it was freezing in the house.

A semicolon is used between two main clauses when the second clause contains a conjunctive adverb:

In the morning he jogs; however, yesterday morning he slept late.

Note that the semicolon in this instance may be replaced by a period, in which case the first letter of the second clause is capitalized. Note also that the semicolon may be used even if the conjunctive adverb does not immediately follow the initial clause:

In the morning he jogs; yesterday morning, however, he slept late.

In this case, a comma is inserted both before and after the adverb.
When two main clauses are linked by a coordinating conjunction, it is help-

ful to use a semicolon, rather than a comma, before the conjunction if the clauses are long and/or contain internal punctuation:

> Driving down the icy mountain road, he downshifted, pumped the brakes, and honked the horn as he rounded each curve; and he breathed a sigh of relief when, rounding the last curve, he saw the road level out before him.

Similarly, it is helpful to separate the items in a series with semicolons when those items are long and/or contain internal punctuation:

> It was a scary drive because the road was icy, steep, and narrow; the night was dark, and one of the headlights was out; and the car, with its worn tires, kept skidding each time he drove around a sharp curve.

> *Note:* a semicolon should not be used between a phrase and a clause, between a main clause and a subordinate clause, or to introduce a list.

> **Incorrect:** To get up early; he sets the alarm.
> **Revised:** To get up early, he sets the alarm.

> **Incorrect:** He always sleeps late; if the alarm fails to ring.
> **Revised:** He always sleeps late if the alarm fails to ring.

> **Incorrect:** You need the following ingredients; eggs, butter, milk, flour, and chocolate chips.
> **Revised:** You need the following ingredients: eggs, butter, milk, flour, and chocolate chips.

THE COLON:

A colon is used to introduce a list or series:

> There are many different writing tools: the pencil, the pen, the typewriter, and now the word processor.

Note, however, that a colon should not be used to introduce a list if the colon interrupts the completion of a main clause by coming between a verb and its object or a preposition and its object.

> **Incorrect:** Some different writing tools are: the pencil, the pen, and the typewriter.
> **Revised:** Some different writing tools are the pencil, the pen, and the typewriter.

Incorrect: A pencil is made of: lead, rubber, and wood.
Revised: A pencil is made of lead, rubber, and wood.

A colon is used to introduce an explanation or summary of the statement that it follows:

She writes only with a pencil or a pen: She hates to type.

Note that if the material following the colon is a complete sentence, it may begin with an initial capital letter.

A colon may be used instead of a comma to introduce a quotation. See the section below on quotation marks.

A colon is also used in the following ways: to separate a subtitle from a title.

In Bluebeard's Castle: Some Notes Toward a Redefinition of Culture

to separate the hour from the minute in a time reference.

2:15 P.M.

to separate chapter from verse in a biblical citation.

Genesis 19:24–28

after the salutation in a formal letter.

Dear Mr. President:

For the use of colons in footnote and bibliographic entries, see the "Focus" section of Chapter 7 (pp. 288–293).

THE DASH (— or - -)

A dash (two hyphens placed without spacing against preceding and following letters when you are typing) indicates a sudden interruption in tone or thought:

She looked sincere—although looks can be deceiving—when she testified in court.

Note: To replace the two dashes in the preceding example with parentheses would suggest that the interrupting clause is less relevant; to replace the two dashes with commas would make the interruption less emphatic.

She looked sincere (although looks can be deceiving) when she testified in court.

She looked sincere, although looks can be deceiving, when she testified in court.

A dash may be used to lend greater emphasis to an appositive:

My mother—a wonderful woman—is coming to visit.

It may be used to set off a word, a phrase, or a clause that summarizes a preceding list:

Men, women, children—people of all ages love the circus.

It may be used to emphasize an important idea at the end of a sentence:

There was nothing wrong with their marriage—but she wanted more from life.

Also, a dash may replace a colon before a list, although it is considered less formal than a colon.

When you go to the store, get everything we need for lunch—bread, peanut butter, jelly, and milk.

Note: Because it lends emphasis to your thoughts, it is a good idea not to overuse the dash.

PARENTHESES AND BRACKETS ( )/[ ]

Parentheses

Parentheses are used to enclose words, phrases, and clauses that are not essential to the meaning of a sentence or paragraph but that clarify or comment on a point made in the sentence or paragraph. Parenthetical expressions may offer—

Factual Information:
On the day that Pearl Harbor was attacked (December 7, 1942), my father was studying in his dormitory room.

Examples:
He likes any kind of pasta (spaghetti, linguine, or ravioli), as long is it is smothered in tomato sauce.

Explanations:

The suicide squeeze (in which the batter bunts and the runner on third races for home) is one of baseball's most exciting plays.

Qualifications:

He said he was so upset (although "angry" may be a better description) that he could not eat or sleep.

When a complete sentence is enclosed in parentheses, it needs no capital letter at the start or period at the end if the parentheses fall within another sentence:

The day that he left home (it was a sad day for all of us), rain fell all morning.

Note that although a comma may follow the closing parenthesis within a sentence, no comma comes before the opening parenthesis.

When a complete sentence is enclosed in parentheses that fall between two sentences, the sentence in the parentheses does begin with a capital letter and end with a period:

The day that he left home, rain fell all morning. (It was a sad day for all of us.) In the afternoon, however, the sky cleared.

Parentheses also are used to enclose cross-references: (see Freud's *Totem and Taboo*, p. 27); and to enclose letters or numbers that label items in a list:

There were a number of reasons that he preferred taking the train to driving: (1) he could sleep on the train; (2) the train got him there faster; and (3) he did not have to worry about parking his car when he arrived.

Brackets

Brackets are used to enclose your own explanations, comments, and corrections within a quotation from another writer. They may be used to add information:

E. B. White believes that "*Walden* [published in 1854] is an oddity in American letters."

They may be used to enclose a substitute word or phrase for a part of a quotation that, without the substitution, would be unclear, as in the following sentence, where the bracketed name has replaced the pronoun *his:*

E. B. White writes that *"Walden* is [Henry David Thoreau's] acknowledgement of the gift of life."

Note that the Latin word *sic* may be placed in brackets after an error in quotation to indicate that the error was made by the author of the quotation. Also, brackets replace parentheses that are inserted within parentheses.

White's essay on Thoreau ("A Slight Sound at Evening," *Essays of E. B. White* [New York: Harper & Row, 1977], 234–242) is both sensitive and insightful.

THE ELLIPSIS (. . .)

An ellipsis is three periods separated from one another by single spaces. It indicates that material has been omitted from a quotation. If a comma, a semicolon, or a colon precedes the ellipsis, it is dropped. If a complete sentence precedes the ellipsis, the period ending the sentence is retained and is followed by the periods of the ellipsis.

Look at the following quotation from an essay by E. B. White on Thoreau's *Walden:*

Thoreau said he required of every writer, first and last, a simple and sincere account of his own life. Having delivered himself of this chesty dictum, he proceeded to ignore it. In his books and even in his enormous journal, he withheld or disguised most of the facts from which an understanding of his life could be drawn.

To omit the phrase "first and last" from the first sentence along with the entire second sentence, two ellipsis marks are necessary:

Thoreau said he required of every writer . . . a simple and sincere account of his own life. . . . In his books and even in his enormous journal, he withheld or disguised most of the facts from which an understanding of his life could be drawn.

Some writers use ellipsis marks to indicate that they have omitted material at the end of a quoted message:

"In his books and even in his enormous journal, he withheld or disguised most of the facts. . . ."

Others feel that the ellipsis is unnecessary in this case.

Note that an ellipsis may be used to indicate a pause or an incomplete statement in dialogue or quoted speech:

"Oh, no . . ." she said; then her words were drowned in tears.

Note also that a line of ellipsis marks across the full width of an indented quotation can be used to indicate that one or more lines of poetry have been omitted.

> Now therefore, while the youthful hue
> Sits on thy skin like morning dew
> And while thy willing soul transpires
> At every pore with instant fires,
> Now let us sport us while we may . . .
>
> Now therefore, while the youthful hue
> Sits on thy skin like morning dew
>
> . . . .
> Now let us sport us while we may . . .
>
> **—Andrew Marvell,**
> *"To His Coy Mistress"*

QUOTATION MARKS (" ")

Quotation marks are used to enclose words, phrases, or sentences that are quoted directly from speech or writing:

The mayor said he was "confident" that he would win reelection. According to the local paper, however, his popularity is "the lowest that it has been since his term began." In yesterday's editorial, the paper threw its support to his opponent. "While the incumbent has done a respectable job," the editorial said, "his opponent is better qualified in every respect."

Note that an indirect quotation, which reports what someone has said or written, but not in the exact words, should not be enclosed in quotation marks.

The mayor voiced his confidence in his ability to win reelection, despite the fact that his popularity is at its lowest and the local paper is supporting his opponent who, the editors feel, is more qualified in every way.

Single quotation marks are used to enclose a quotation within a quotation:

Yesterday's editorial went on to say, "The challenger's promise that she will hire more teachers, 'even if it means raising taxes,' is another reason that she has earned this paper's support."

If you are writing a dialogue, begin a new paragraph each time the speaker changes.

"I don't like the mayor," she said. "He doesn't understand the problems that women face in this town. He's insensitive and chauvinistic."

"Nonsense," I told her. "Mayor Tubbs is all right. He's just a little old-fashioned."

"Old-fashioned! Huh! He's a cave man!"

"Oh, come on, Gloria," I argued. "Aren't you overreacting just a bit?" But I couldn't convince her.

Note that if you are quoting more than a single line of poetry, you should mark the line divisions with slashes:

Frost wrote, "The woods are lovely, dark and deep,/But I have promises to keep."

If you are quoting more than three lines of poetry or more than four lines of prose, you should not use quotation marks; instead, use indentation to indicate where the quotation begins and ends. End the sentence introducing the quotation with a colon, double-space both above and below the quotation, and indent the quotation itself ten spaces from the left-hand margin (and an additional five spaces to start a new paragraph). Note the following example, in which quotations from Thoreau and Frost are each preceded by an introductory sentence:

Thoreau's optimism is apparent in the following passage from *Walden:*

I think that we may safely trust a good deal more than we do. We may waive just so much care of ourselves as we honestly bestow elsewhere. Nature is as well adapted to our weakness as to our strength. The incessant anxiety and strain of some is a well-nigh incurable form of disease.

Frost seemed more careworn when he wrote:

The woods are lovely, dark and deep,
But I have promises to keep,
And miles to go before I sleep,
And miles to go before I sleep.

Quotation marks are used to indicate the title of a part or a chapter of a book ("Economy" is the first chapter of *Walden*); the title of an essay ("The Angry Winter," by Loren Eiseley); the title of a short story ("Rip Van Winkle," by Washington Irving); the title of a short poem ("To His Coy Mistress," by Andrew Marvell); the title of a magazine article ("What Do Babies Know?" in *Time*); the title of a song ("Yesterday," by the Beatles); or the title of an episode of a television or radio series ("The Miracle of Life," on *Nova*). Note that quotation marks are not used around the title on the title page of a paper that you have written.

Quotation marks are used by some writers to indicate that they are raising a question about the way a word is being used:

What he called his "new" car turned out to be a ten-year-old wreck.

Note, however, that when they are defining a word, most writers set it off by italicizing it. See the section on italics below.

When a single word or phrase is placed within quotation marks, no punctuation is needed to introduce it. When one or more sentences are placed within quotation marks, either an introductory comma or an introductory colon is needed. Some writers use a comma before a single sentence, a colon before two or more sentences.

He said, "Let's go home now." She replied: "First I've got to stop at the bank. Then we'll go home."

Other writers use a comma to introduce quoted speech and a colon to introduce quoted writing.

Use a comma at the end of a quoted sentence that is followed by a tag:

"I think that we may safely trust a good deal more than we do," Thoreau tells us.

If the quoted sentence is a question or an exclamation, however, it should end with a question mark or an exclamation point:

"Do you agree with Thoreau?" he asked.

In either case, the tag begins with a lowercase, not a capital, letter.

If a tag interrupts a quoted sentence, it is set off by two commas:

"I think," Thoreau wrote, "that we may safely trust a good deal more than we do."

If a tag is placed between two quoted sentences, the first quoted sentence is followed by a comma, the tag is followed by a semicolon or a period, and the second quoted sentence begins with a capital letter and ends with a period:

"Nature is as well adapted to our weakness as to our strength," Thoreau wrote; "The incessant anxiety and strain of some is a well-nigh incurable form of disease."

Note that at the end of a quotation, a period or a comma is always placed inside the closing quotation mark, and a semicolon or colon is always placed outside the closing quotation mark. A dash, an exclamation point, or a question mark is placed inside the closing quotation mark only if it is part of the quotation:

"Do you understand?" she asked.

If the dash, exclamation point, or question mark applies to the whole sentence, however, it is placed outside the closing quotation mark:

Does anyone understand what Thoreau meant when he wrote that "we may safely trust a good deal more than we do"?

THE APOSTROPHE

An apostrophe followed by *s* is used to form the possessive case of singular and plural nouns that do not end in *s*: the *boy's* dog, the *man's* property, *women's* rights, *children's* toys.

Singular common nouns ending in *s* also take an apostrophe followed by *s* to form the possessive: the *boss's* daughter, the *business's* manager. Singular proper nouns ending in *s* may form the possessive with an apostrophe followed by *s* or with an apostrophe alone: *Doris's* house or *Doris'* house, Mr. *Jones's* apartment or Mr. *Jones'* apartment. There are a few singular nouns ending in an *s* or a *z* sound that form the possessive with an apostrophe alone: for *conscience'* sake, *Moses'* law. Often such forms are rephrased to omit the apostrophe altogether: *for the sake of conscience, the law of Moses.*

An apostrophe alone is used to form the possessive case of plural nouns that end in *s*: *babies'* cribs, the two *boys'* tree house, the *Joneses'* apartment, the *Smiths'* home.

An apostrophe followed by *s* is added to the last word of a compound noun to indicate possession: my *sister-in-law's* car, *somebody else's* truck.

Only the last of two or more nouns takes the apostrophe (and the *s*, if needed) to indicate joint possession: the phrase *the boy and the girl's dog* indicates that the boy and the girl own one dog together; if this phrase is revised to read the *boy's and girl's dogs,* it indicates that the boy and the girl each own one or more dogs individually.

An apostrophe followed by *s* is used to form the possessive of indefinite pronouns: *everybody's* favorite ice cream, *someone's* dirty laundry. Note, however, that the possessive personal pronouns do not require an apostrophe to indicate ownership:

This house, that is *hers.*

I like *their* house, but *its* backyard is so small.

An apostrophe is also used to indicate that letters, words, or numbers have been omitted in contractions: *can't* (cannot), *doesn't* (does not), *don't* (do not), *he's* (he is), *I'll* (I will), *isn't* (is not), *it's* (it is), *I've* (I have), *ma'am* (madam), *o'clock* (of the clock), *she's* (she is), *they're* (they are), *you're* (you are), *we're* (we are), *weren't* (were not), *who's* (who is), *won't* (will not), *'84* (1984). Note that the contraction *would've* means *would have;* do not write *would of* instead of *would've.* Better yet, do not use this contraction; write *would have.*

Note also that the personal pronouns *its, their, your,* and *whose* should not be confused with the contractions *it's, they're, you're,* and *who's.* See the section below on spelling for examples of the proper use of each of these pronouns and contractions.

An apostrophe followed by *s* is used to form the plural of abbreviations with periods, lowercase letters used as nouns, and capital letters that would be confusing if *s* alone were added:

The college graduated 275 B.A.'s.

She is learning her abc's.

Sam Smith has two S's in his name.

At the same time single or multiple letters used as words and numbers (spelled out or in figures) add *s* alone to form the plural, as long as omitting the apostrophe will cause no confusion:

She is studying the three Rs.

He works out at three different YMCAs.

My father was in his early twenties in the 1940s.

Mechanics

CAPITALIZATION

To capitalize a word, make the first letter of the word a capital letter.
Capitalize the first word of a sentence:

She hates to type.

Capitalizing the first word of a sentence that follows a colon is optional:

She writes only with a pencil or a pen: She (*or* she) hates to type.

Capitalizing the first word of a direct quotation is necessary if the original begins with a capital letter:

I said to my sister's teacher, "She hates to type."

Capitalize proper nouns, such as the names of specific persons, places, events, institutions, and organizations:

Aunt Sally	the Renaissance
George Washington	World War I
Fifth Avenue	the New York Public Library
Los Angeles	Mamaroneck High School
the Rocky Mountains	Michigan State University
Lake Michigan	the Internal Revenue Service
the Pacific Ocean	the Boy Scouts of America
France	the Boston Red Sox
Africa	the United Nations
Jupiter	

475

Note that common nouns like *avenue, mountain, lake, ocean, high school,* and *university* are capitalized when they are part of the name of a place or an institution.

> I went to Lakeville High School.
> I was in high school from 1960 to 1964.
>
> He sailed across the Atlantic Ocean.
> We swam in the ocean on our vacation.

The article preceding a proper noun and any preposition that is part of a proper noun are not capitalized.

Capitalize proper adjectives formed from proper nouns:

> a *Shakespearean* play
> an *American* car
> the *Republican* party

Capitalize trade names:

> *Scotch* tape
> *Kleenex* tissues
> a *Xerox* copier

Capitalize the names of the points of the compass when they refer to specific geographical regions:

> the *Midwest*
> the *North Pole*
> *Western civilization*

Do not capitalize the points of the compass when they simply indicate direction:

> a *southerly* wind

Capitalize the days of the week, the months of the year, and holidays.
Capitalize the names of religions, their followers, and their sacred books:

> Protestantism   Muslims
> Judaism   the Bible
> Christians   the Korean

Also capitalize all words used to designate the deity, including pronouns:

He	the *Lord*
His	*Allah*
God	*Buddha*

Capitalize abbreviations of academic degrees (B.A., Ph.D., M.D.); titles (Mr., Jr., Dr.); and all letters of acronyms (NATO, NASA, VISTA).
Capitalize a title that comes before a proper name.

President Reagan is seeking reelection.

If the title refers to only one person and can substitute for his or her name, capitalize it.

The President announced his plans to run for a second term.

But if the title can refer to more than one person, do not capitalize it when it substitutes for a specific person.

Mayor Jones ran for Congress in 1964. It was a close election, but the mayor lost.

Note: In the sentence

The president in our system is limited to two terms in office.

President is used as a general term for the chief executive officer of the government and is not capitalized. Similarly, a word designating a relationship *(father, aunt)* is not capitalized, unless it forms a part of or substitutes for a proper name.

She is my aunt on my mother's side.
My brother went to pick up Uncle George at the station.
"I want to go home now, Grandpa," I said.

Capitalize all words in the title of a book or a chapter of a book, a magazine or newspaper or an article in either, an essay, a short story, a poem, a musical composition, a painting, a play, a film, or a television or radio show. Note, however, that no article, conjunction, or preposition of less than five letters is capitalized unless it is the first word of the title:

For Whom the Bell Tolls
Romeo and Juliet
Gone with the Wind

Always capitalize the first person singular pronoun, *I*.

ITALICS

Italic type slants upward to the right. You can use italics to set off and emphasize words and phrases. In a typed or handwritten paper, you italicize a word of phrase by underlining it.

Italics are used to give emphasis to a word:

I don't want to know what *she* thinks; I want to know what *you* think.

Italics are also used to set off a word that is being treated as a word:

What does the word *love* really mean?

Why must you preface everything you say with *I think?*

Italics are used to identify a foreign word or phrase not yet accepted as a standard English expression: the phrase *carpe diem* is italicized, whereas the phrase per diem is not. Consult a dictionary to check whether a foreign expression is italicized.

Italics are used to indicate the title of a book *(Walden);* a long poem (the *Odyssey*); a play *(Romeo and Juliet);* a magazine *(Time);* a newspaper (the *Philadelphia Inquirer*); a pamphlet *(Common Sense);* a published speech (the *Gettysburg Address*); a long musical work *(Rubber Soul);* a work of visual art (the *Mona Lisa);* a movie *(Star Wars);* and a television or radio show *(60 Minutes).* Note, however, that the Bible and the books within it are neither italicized nor placed in quotation marks, although they are capitalized:

Genesis is the first book of the Bible.

Italics are also used to indicate the name of trains (the *Orient Express*); ships (the *Queen Elizabeth II*); airplanes (the *Spirit of St. Louis*); and spacecraft *(Apollo 8).*

ABBREVIATIONS

The more formal you wish to make your writing, the less you should abbreviate words and phrases. Although special abbreviations may be used regularly in the technical writings of business, law, scholarship, and science, common abbreviations should be used only moderately in most formal writing. If you are uncertain about whether or not a term should be abbreviated, spell it out fully.

Titles that accompany a proper name may be abbreviated:

Ms. Jones   Mary Stuart, D.D.S.
Dr. Smith   John Doe, Jr.
Rev. Wilson

Note that some writers feel that the titles of religious, government, and military leaders should be spelled out in full:

the Reverend Martin Luther King, Jr.
Senator John Glenn
General George Patton

Titles should not be abbreviated when they appear without a proper name:

I called the doctor for an appointment.

Titles of academic degrees are an exception:

I received my B.A. this June.

Well-known abbreviations of organizations, corporations, people, and some countries are acceptable. When they are comprised of the first letters of three or more words, they are usually written without periods:

FBI   FDR
YMCA   JFK
ITT   USA
NBC   USSR

Abbreviations that specify a date or a time of day are acceptable:

621 B.C.   10:30 A.M.
A.D. 1983   1:17 P.M.

Note also that the abbreviations for number *(no.)* and dollars *($)* may be used with specific numbers: *no.* 9, *$5.50*. None of these abbreviations should be used without a specific numerical reference: in the sentence

I feel asleep in the P.M.

P.M. should be changed to *afternoon.*
    Note that if an abbreviation comes at the end of a declarative sentence, the period that marks the end of the abbreviation also marks the end of the sentence.

We left at 3:30 P.M.

If an abbreviation comes at the end of question, the question mark follows the period that marks the end of the abbreviation:

Did you leave before 3:00 P.M.?

In formal writing, the following should not be abbreviated:

Units of measurement, such as *inches (in.)* or *pounds (lbs.).* Long phrases such as *miles per hour (mph)* are an exception.
    Geographical names, such as *Fifth Avenue (Ave.)* or *California (Calif.).* USA and *USSR* are exceptions, as are *Mount (Mt. Washington)* and *Saint (St. Louis).*
    Names of days, months, and holidays, such as *Wednesday (Wed.), September (Sept.),* or *Christmas (Xmas).*
    Names of people, such as *Charles (Chas.)* or *Robert (Robt.).*
    Academic subjects, such as *economics (econ.)* or *English (Eng.).*
    Divisions in books such as *page (p.), chapter (chap.)* or *volume (vol.).* These abbreviations are acceptable, however, in footnote and bibliographic entries, and in cross-references, in a formal research paper.

Note finally that common Latin abbreviations that may be used in parenthetical references in informal writing, such as *e.g., (for example), etc. (and so forth),* and *i.e. (that is),* should be replaced by their equivalent English phrases in formal writing:

In some of the songs in *Blood on the Tracks,* for example, "Idiot Wind," Dylan returns to the biting social criticism of his early career.

NUMBERS

Like abbreviations, numbers written as figures are used only moderately in formal writing, as compared to their regular use in technical and informal writing.

Generally, in formal writing, numbers are spelled out if they can be expressed in one or two words:

He lived to be one hundred years old.

If a number is hyphenated, it is considered one word:

The car has eighty-two thousand miles on it.

If spelling out a number takes more than two words, the number should be written in figures:

The book has 372 pages.

Note, however, that if several numbers appear in a sentence or a paragraph, they should be spelled out or written in figures consistently:

In the crowd of 275 people attending the rehearsal of the circus, there were only 25 grown men and 37 grown women; all the rest, a total of 213, were children.

Use figures to write the following: a date *(September 2, 1947)*; a time of day *(8:45 A.M.)*; an address *(705 Walton Avenue)*; a telephone number *(631-6303)*; an exact sum of money *($12.42)*; a decimal *(a 4.0 grade average)*; a statistic *(37 percent)*; a score *(7 to 3)*; a volume, chapter, and/or page number in a book *(Volume 3, Chapter 10, page 105)*; and an act, scene, and/or line number in a play *(Act II, Scene 3, lines 12–14)*.

Note, however, that if the name of a street when the street is numbered can be spelled out in one or two words, it should be *(42 Fifth Avenue)*, unless a word such as *East, West, North,* or *South* precedes the street name *(42 East 57th Street)*. Also, a figure in round numbers may be written out *(ten cents, two o'clock, a hundred miles)*.

Finally, always spell out numbers that begin a sentence:

Thirteen is my lucky number.

If the number requires more than two words to be spelled out, rearrange the sentence: the sentence

275 people attended the rehearsal.

should be revised to read

The rehearsal was attended by 275 people.

HYPHENATION

A hyphen may be used to divide a word between the end of one line and the beginning of the next line. The hyphen should be placed only at the end of the first line, never at the start of the second. The last word on a page should not be divided with a hyphen.

When dividing a word with a hyphen, break the word only between syllables *(divi-sion, hyphen-ation)*. Consult a dictionary to check the syllable breaks in a word. Words that have a prefix or a suffix should be divided between the prefix and the root *(dis-approve)* or between the root and the suffix *(happi-ness)*. A compound word should be divided between the two words that form the compound *(air-plane)*.

Never divide a word of only one syllable; for example, the word *dropped* cannot be divided between the two *p*'s.

Some writers prefer not to divide a word so that a single letter is left at the end of a line *(a-men)* or so that fewer than three letters appear at the start of a line *(com-ic)*. Also, some writers prefer not to divide a word if the division creates a pronunciation problem *(con-science)*.

A hyphen is also used to form some compound nouns *(a vice-president)* and some compound adjectives when they appear before a noun *(a hard-boiled egg)*. Note that many compound nouns are simply written as one word *(playhouse)* or as two words *(hair stylist)*. Many compound adjectives are written as one word *(childlike)* or as two words when they appear after a noun in a sentence *(he is well liked)*. Consult a dictionary to check whether a compound noun or adjective should be written as a single word, as a hyphenated word, or as two words.

A hyphen is used to join a prefix to a proper noun *(un-American)*. It is not used to join a prefix to a common noun, an adjective, or a verb *(superpatriot, profile, rejoin)*, unless it is needed to avoid a misreading; for example, it is used to distinguish the word *re-creation* (something that has been created over again) from the word *recreation* (relaxation).

A hyphen is used to divide compound numbers written as words between *twenty-one* and *ninety-nine*. Some writers use the hyphen to divide fractions written as words *(three-fourths)*.

Finally, hyphens are used in a series such as the following: *a two-and-one-half-, a three-, or a four-minute egg.*

SPELLING

The most important thing to keep in mind with regard to spelling is that you should consult a dictionary whenever you have any doubt about whether you have spelled a word correctly. If, in addition, you keep a notebook in which you list the words that you misspell frequently, along with their proper spelling, you will have a valuable tool that you can use whenever you are proofreading a paper. Always proofread your papers for spelling.

Beyond these preparations, there are a few basic rules that you can follow to avoid common spelling errors:

Put *i* before *e*, except after *c* or when pronounced like *a*, as in *neighbor* or *weigh*. Thus, write *believe* or *grief*, but *ceiling* or *receive*. Other exceptions to the rule of putting *i* before *e* include *either*, *leisure*, *foreign*, *seize*, and *weird*.

Generally, a final *e* is dropped before a suffix that begins with a vowel:

    love, lovable, loving
    imagine, imagination, imaginary
    grieve, grieving, grievous

Some exceptions are *changeable, courageous, mileage, shoeing.*

Generally, a final *e* is retained before a suffix that begins with a consonant: *lovely, arrangement, fineness.* Some exceptions are *truly* and *judgment.*

Generally, a final *y* is changed to *i* before a suffix is added to a word:

    beauty, beauties, beautiful
    copy, copies, copied

One exception occurs when the suffix is *ing; copying.* Another exception occurs when the final *y* comes after a vowel:

    obeyed, days, journeys

Generally, in a one-syllable word that ends in a consonant preceded by a single vowel, the final consonant is doubled before a suffix that begins with a vowel:

    drop, dropped
    slap, slapping
    win, winner

However, when the final consonant of a one-syllable word is preceded by two vowels or by a vowel and another consonant, the final consonant is not doubled before a suffix that begins with a vowel:

cool, cooler   park, parking
real, realized   strong, strongest

Generally, in a word of two or more syllables that ends in a consonant, the final consonant is doubled before a suffix that begins with a vowel, if the accent falls on the last syllable of the word and if a single vowel precedes the final consonant:

begin, beginning
occur, occurred
regret, regrettable

The final consonant is not doubled if the accent does not fall on the last syllable:

enter, entered

Nor is it doubled if the final consonant is preceded by two vowels or by a vowel and another consonant:

despair, despairing
return, returning

Note: Avoid the common mistake of joining words that should be written separately, such as *a lot* and *all right,* or separating words that should be joined, such as *together* and *throughout.*

Commonly Confused Homonyms

Finally, many times spelling errors arise because a writer confuses two words that sound alike but that differ both in spelling and in meaning. Such words are called *homonyms.* The following is a list of some commonly confused homonyms:

Accept/except.   *Accept* is a verb meaning "receive" or "agree to":

He accepted her terms.

Except is used most often as a preposition meaning "but for" or "other than":

I like every kind of music except rock and roll.

As a verb, *except* means "leave out" or "exclude":

Excepting his accountant, no one knows how rich he is.

Advice/advise. *Advice* is a noun meaning "recommendation" or "guidance":

She gave her son good advice.

Advise is a verb meaning "give advice to":

She advised him to study hard.

Affect/effect. *Affect* is used most often as a verb meaning to "change" or "influence":

The jury's decision was affected by her testimony.

It also can mean "pretend to feel":

He affected amusement, even though he was really quite angry.

Effect is used most often as a noun meaning "result" or "consequence":

The side effects of the medicine are unknown.

As a verb, *effect* means to "bring about" or "perform":

The senator's efforts effected change in the tax laws.

All ready/already. *All ready* means "completely prepared":

She was all ready to leave.

Already means "by this time" or "by that time":

The game was already half over when we got there.

All together/altogether. *All together* means "in a group":

The family was all together at my aunt's house last Thanksgiving.

Altogether means "completely" or "entirely":

He changed his mind partially but not altogether.

An/and.   *An* is an article:

I ate an apple.

And is a coordinating conjunction:

I love apples and oranges.

Buy/by.   *Buy* is a verb meaning "purchase":

We need to buy a new car.

By is most often used as a preposition meaning "near to," "through," or "with":

The house by the station was destroyed by fire.

By is also used as an adverb:

The time went by.

Conscience/conscious.   *Conscience* is a noun meaning "a sense of right and wrong":

She thought about cheating, but her conscience kept her from doing it.

Conscious is an adjective meaning "aware" or "awake";

He was conscious for a few minutes after the accident, but then he passed out.

Every day/everyday.   *Every day* means "daily":

She jogs two miles every day.

Everyday means "common," "ordinary," or "regular":

"Oh," she said, "this old thing is just an everyday dress."

Formally/formerly.   *Formally* means "in a formal or ceremonious way";

He was dressed formally, in a white tuxedo, at his wedding.

Formerly means "previously," or "at an earlier time":

She was formerly a student, but now she works on Wall Street.

Hear/here. *Hear* is a verb meaning to "perceive," to "listen,"or to "learn" by the ear or by being told:

I hear you are leaving town.

Here is an adverb meaning "in or to or at this place or point":

I am not leaving; I am staying right here.

Its/it's. *Its* is a possessive pronoun:

He likes the car but not its price.

It's is a contraction meaning "it is":

Unfortunately, it's too expensive.

Know/no. *Know* is a verb meaning to "understand," "perceive," or "be aware of":

Do you know what I mean?

No is used as an adverb to express denial, dissent, or refusal:

No, I do not understand.

No is also used commonly as an adjective meaning "not any" or "not at all":

I have no idea what you mean.

Later/latter. *Later* refers to time:

I have to finish a paper right now so I'll call you later.

Latter refers to the second of two things previously mentioned:

When David fought Goliath, the former used his brain, the latter used only his brawn.

May be/maybe. *May be* is a verb phrase:

My brother, who is overseas, may be coming home.

Maybe is an adverb meaning "perhaps":

Maybe he will sell it, if he gets a good enough offer.

Peace/piece. *Peace* is a noun meaning "freedom from war or strife," "harmony," or "calm":

Why can't we live in peace with one another?

Piece, used as a noun, means "a limited quantity or part of something" *(a piece of land),* or "a specimen of workmanship" *(a piece of music),* or "an individual article in a set or a collection or a class" *(a piece of furniture).* *Piece* is also used as a verb meaning to "mend" or "join together":

A detective pieces clues together to solve a mystery.

Principal/principle. *Principal,* used as a noun, means "chief administrator":

The school principal ran the assembly.

It also means a "capital sum of money":

He had to pay the interest on the principal of his car loan.

Principal, used as an adjective, means "main" or "most important":

The principal reason that I fear cats is the memory I have of being scratched as a child.

Principle is a noun meaning "rule" or "basic truth" or "law":

He followed the principle of doing unto others as he would have them do unto him.

Right/write. *Right,* used as an adjective, means "proper," "correct," "genuine," or "legitimate":

Apologizing was the right thing to do.

Right, used as a noun, means a "just claim" or a "privilege" *(freedom of speech is a basic right).* Used as an adverb, it means "directly" or "exactly" *(do it right now)* or the opposite of "left." Used as a verb, it means to "set up" or to "set in order":

It took a crane to right the fallen statue.

Write is a verb meaning "trace words on paper" or "communicate" or "compose":

My sister is writing a novel.

Sight/site. *Sight,* used as a verb, means to "observe" or to "perceive with one's eyes":

The sailor on the mast was the first to sight land.

Sight, used as a noun, means "vision" or "spectacle":

After the food fight, the dining room was a sight to behold.

Site is used most often as a noun meaning "location":

This hill is the site we have chosen to build the house on.

Site is also used as a verb meaning to "locate." Note: Do not confuse *sight* or *site* with *cite,* a verb that means to "refer to" or to "mention":

The lawer cited the case of *Jones* v. *Jones* in his argument before the judge.

Some/sum. *Some* is used as an adjective, an adverb, or a pronoun to indicate a certain unspecified number, amount, or degree of something:

We are having dinner with some friends.

Sum, used as a noun, means a "total" or a "quantity":

One million dollars is a large sum of money.

Sum is also used as a verb meaning to "combine into a total" or to "form an overall estimate or view of":

The lawyer summed up her case for the jury.

Than/then. *Than* is a conjunction used in making comparisons:

I like the blue shirt better than the yellow.

Then is an adverb used in referring to the passage of time:

He put the cake in the oven; then he waited an hour before checking to see if it was done.

Their/there/they're.   *Their* is a third-person-plural possessive pronoun:

Their car is in the driveway.

There indicates a place:

The kids will like the park, so let's go there.

There is also used in the expressions "there is" and "there are." *They're* is a contraction meaning "they are":

I always root for the home team, even when they're having a bad year.

Threw/through.   *Threw* is a past-tense form of the verb "to throw":

He threw the ball to her.

Through is used as a preposition, an adverb, and an adjective meaning "in one end and out the other," "between or among," "during the whole period of," "having finished," "by means of," or "by reason of":

She finished the marathon through sheer willpower.

Note: Do not employ the popular shortened form *thru* for *through;* similarly avoid the shortened form *nite* for *night* or *tho* for *though.*

To/too/two.   *To* is a preposition that indicates place, direction, or position:

We have flown to the moon.

To also forms the infinitive with all verbs.

I'd like to get to know you.

Too is an adverb meaning "also" or "excessively":

She is too tired to go out tonight.

Two is a number:

Two plus two equals four.

Were/we're/where.   *Were* is a past-tense form of the verb to "be":

They were not home.

Were is also used to form the subjunctive mood:

If they were home, we would visit them.

We're is a contraction meaning "we are":

We're planning to go on our vacation next month.

Where is used as an adverb or as a conjunction to indicate a place or a position:

Where are the keys? They are where you left them.

Who's/whose.   *Who's* is a contraction meaning "who is":

Who's coming to the party?

Whose is a possessive form of the pronoun who:

Whose party is it?

Your/you're.   *Your* is a possessive form of the pronoun you:

I saw your sister today.

You're is a contraction meaning "you are":

She said that you're leaving for college this week.

REVIEW EXERCISE—PUNCTUATION AND MECHANICS

The following paragraphs, from an essay by E. B. White called "Coon Tree," contain punctuation and mechanical errors. Add proper punctuation and capitalization, wherever you think necessary. Check to see where italics, abbreviations, or numbers might be used. Correct any misspellings that you come across.

Today ive been rereading a cheerful forecast for the comming century prepared by some farsighted professors at the california institute of technology and
published not long ago in the times. man, it would appear is standing at the
gateway to a new era of civilization, technology will be king. Everything man
needs the report says is at hand all we require is air, sea water, ordinary rock and
sunlight. The population of the earth will increase and multiply but that'll be no
problem the granite of the earths crust contains enough uranium and thorium to
supply an abundance of power for everybody. If we just pound rock, were sitting
pretty.

I have made a few private tests of my own and my findings differ somewhat
from those of the california technology men. We have two stoves in our kitchen
hear in maine a big black iron stove that burns wood and a small white electric
stove that draws its strength from the bangor hydro electric company. We use
both. One represents the past the other represents the future. If we had to give
up one in favor of the other and cook on just one stove there isnt the slightest
question in anybodys mind in my household witch is the one we'd keep. It would
be the big black Home crawford Eight Twenty made by walker and pratt, with its
woodbox that has to be filled with wood, its water tank that has to be replenished
with water, its ashpan that has to be emptied of ashes, its flue pipe that has to be
renewed when it gets rusty, its grates that need freeing when they get cloged and
all its other foibles and deficiencies. . . .

My stove witch Im sure would be impracticle in many american homes, is
never the less a symbol of my belief. The technologists with there vision of hap-
pyness at the core of the rock, see only halve the rock halve of mans dream and
his need. Perhaps sucess in the future will depend partly on our ability to generate
cheep power but I think it will depend to a greater extent on our ability to resist
a technological formula that is sterile: peas without pageantry . . . knowledge
without wisdom, kitchens without a warm stove. There is more to these rocks
then uranium there is the lichen on the rock, the smell of the fern who's feet are
upon the rock, the veiw from the rock.

Index

493